NATHANIEL HAWTHORNE

The American Years

NATHANIEL HAWTHORNE

From the photograph of a daguerreotype, made about 1848, formerly in possession of Dr. J. B. Holder, New York City.

Nathaniel Hawthorne:

THE AMERICAN YEARS *title*

by Robert Cantwell

(With an additional essay by the author)

1971

OCTAGON BOOKS

New York

Reprinted 1971
by special arrangement with Holt, Rinehart and Winston, Inc.

OCTAGON BOOKS
A DIVISION OF FARRAR, STRAUS & GIROUX, INC.
19 Union Square West
New York, N. Y. 10003

LIBRARY OF CONGRESS CATALOG CARD NUMBER: 77-159172

ISBN 0-374-91277-7

Printed in U.S.A. by
NOBLE OFFSET PRINTERS, INC.
NEW YORK 3, N. Y.

To my Wife and Our Daughters

Joan McNeice, Betsy Ann and Mary Elizabeth Emmett Cantwell

NOTE: The family name was spelled both Hathorne and Hawthorne. I have used the form that Nathaniel Hawthorne finally employed, to avoid confusion, since the disputes between the different branches of the family have been forgotten, and his work has pretty much settled the matter, and cast its luster over them all.

F O R E W O R D

$\mathcal{T}$he origins of this book go back many years, to the summer of 1939 and the beginning of the war in Europe. I had been, until shortly before that time, working in the book department of *Time* magazine, and through a peculiar series of happenings, vacations, and the trips abroad of the regular staff members, I found myself, at the time of the German-Russian pact, in temporary charge of the department of foreign news. This was not a position I would have chosen for myself, nor one for which I felt myself to be particularly qualified, though as the weeks passed and the meaning of events in Europe grew clearer, I became conscious, in myself and among the people with whom I worked, of an intensity of feeling, a clarification of values, a renewal of purpose, more compelling than I have ever witnessed anywhere, and strong enough to compensate, at least in part, for the deficiencies in education and experience that we brought to the task of interpreting the great events that were then unfolding.

It became my task, more and more, to write of what was happening in England. There seemed to be a kind of hush, deeply moving, over the events on the island, as of conscious preparation for an ordeal that was faced with a quietude neither resigned nor embittered—something for which we have no word, and for which there is no parallel in the American character. On one evening in this period, when my mind was charged with images from the day's work, the moving of the children from London, the preparations for the bombings, the first victims of the submarines, I happened to pick up Hawthorne's *Our Old Home*, his book based on his years in England as consul at Liverpool, and I read it, or rather re-read it, with a sense of wonder at his power of observation and at the close application of his insights to the events of another century.

From that occasion this book has grown. It began originally as an essay on Hawthorne's interpretation of England, then grew to a small book based on his English experiences, after which, such being the way a subject like this takes hold of the imagination, a full-length biography of Hawthorne seemed needed. There are several biographies of Hawthorne in print, perhaps more than of any other American author. Most of them are good, and some of them are excellent; I have not read one which did not throw some light upon his character and his work, and I believe that with one or two exceptions I have read them all. Another one needs some additional reason for existing, beyond the inspiration of the thoughts of Hawthorne in England.

Most of the works on Hawthorne are critical studies drawing their facts from Julian Hawthorne's biography of his father. That work, while it is more candid than most, is still a family biography, with the reticences and family feelings that characterize such books. When it is in error, or partial in its accounts, as it often is, the critical studies based upon it have consequently been distorted, and there has grown up, it seems to me, a narrow and lop-sided portrait of one of the greatest, if not the greatest, American novelist. That critical portrait is of a man who lived in seclusion throughout his youth in his town of Salem, a seclusion certainly grave, if not morbid, obsessed with the Puritan sense of guilt and haunted by a family curse, writing his wonderful stories that no one knew he had written, working at the dull routine of the Custom House to provide for his family, and emerging in his early middle age, with the publication of *The Scarlet Letter*, to take part in a contemporary world he had scarcely known existed. Such a portrait, with its angular shadows, its El Greco distortions, its melancholy, its brooding seclusion, is in itself an interesting product of the American imagination, all the more interesting for being placed against a background of an ancient seaport, where the old ships crumbled to pieces tied to the decaying wharves. Each generation has added something to it, deepening its shadows. It is in itself a work of art, but I found it less and less like Hawthorne the more I learned of him.

This is perhaps as good a moment as any to try to restore to the picture some of its original colors, to illuminate the shadowed areas that time and literary fashions and psychological theories have darkened beyond recognition. If not for Hawthorne's sake, then for ours. For if we attribute to the greatest American literary men such seclusion and despondency, and such a sense of estrangement from the life of their time, we will tend to find something of the same characteristics in their later and lesser followers, an attribution doubly unfortunate if it should

turn out not to have been true of them as, I believe, it was not true of
Hawthorne. He was a great writer and a great man, leading an active
and vigorous life of considerable excitement and some hazard. He was
an active politician in the Democratic party, a circumstance which has
made me, in view of its treatment of him, and insofar as I have any
political opinions on the issues of the time, a Federalist. He was a skillful journalist. The depth and the nature of his political work is mysterious. That is the true mystery of his life. He was forever visiting
scenes where explosions had occurred or where violence of some sort
was threatened or where smugglers were active. Loneliness and seclusion
were his portion, certainly, but they had less to do with his writing and
with his view of the world than with his duties in the customs service.
I cannot characterize his work more clearly than that, for it is, to a
considerable extent, what this book is about.

It is customary in a work of this sort for the author to submit his
qualifications for the task, and such new discoveries as he has made,
together with his acknowledgments for the assistance he has received.
My own qualifications, I am afraid, sound less like those of an authority
on New England literature than those of an applicant for a job. I
approached it with no greater confidence than I felt when I wrote
foreign news. I found as I wrote, however, that I was led into scenes
more wonderful than I had known existed, into the presence of characters possessed of an animation and zest in living as some people possess
a gift for writing or painting, and into the midst of a body of literature
fresh and unfamiliar, and at its best including some of the finest stories
in English.

This biography differs from other studies in its fuller treatment of
people whose lives were linked with his. They were such characters as his
uncle, Simon Forrester, one of the greatest and wealthiest American
privateers; Hawthorne's sister, Elizabeth, a strange, subtle and witty
girl, originally thought of as the genius of the family, partly, no doubt,
because she had learned to walk and to talk at nine months of age;
Hawthorne's roommate at Bowdoin, Alfred Mason, whose father was
generally considered the greatest lawyer who had ever practiced in New
England; Charlotte Story Forrester, the sister of Supreme Court Justice Story, who married Hawthorne's cousin; Caleb Foote, the editor
of the Salem *Gazette*, who first published Hawthorne's stories; Mary
White Foote, his wife, a vivacious and high-spirited woman who was a

girlhood friend of the woman Hawthorne married—these are some of the characters who came into the book, not precisely uninvited, but in such a storm of color and amusement, and with so much to say of themselves, Hawthorne, Salem, New England, literature, politics, commerce, journalism, life, that it would have been uncivil not to have written of them in all the detail possible. This biography contains some heretofore unpublished material on Hawthorne's early teacher, the Reverend Caleb Bradley, of Stroudwater, Maine, and some new material, published before, but not previously included in Hawthorne's biography, on the man who prepared him for Bowdoin, the eccentric scientist and inventor, Dr. Benjamin Lynde Oliver, of Salem. Dr. Oliver was the sort of physician, said Marianne Silsbee, a wonderful little Salem poetess, who believed that a patient should discard more clothing with each rise of the quicksilver in the thermometer. Finding the originals of characters in novels is always a dubious business, but I believe that Dr. Oliver was the original of the daffy old quack pictured in Hawthorne's unfinished *The Dolliver Romance.* I have also included in this biography the details of two events of great importance in Hawthorne's life and in the lives of his friends—the duel in which his friend Jonathan Cilley was killed, and the building of the dam across the Kennebec River that wiped out the fortune of his friend, Horatio Bridge. Insofar as the book possesses any outstanding heretofore unpublished discoveries of historical or biographical importance, they are, I believe, the material on Hawthorne's mother's family, and the material I have drawn from the diary of Hawthorne's wife, in the years before their marriage, written while she lived on a coffee plantation in Cuba.

The first of these, the material on Hawthorne's mother, Betsy Hawthorne, as she was generally known, is fascinating. She was left a widow, with three small children, at a very early age. Her husband, a sea captain, died on a voyage to Surinam. In February, 1946, with the assistance of my wife, I traced the voyages of Captain Hawthorne in the Ship News of the Salem *Gazette,* working in the library of the Essex Institute in Salem, an extremely tedious and difficult task, and one which had not previously been done. Since that time, the Ship News has been carefully analyzed, especially in James Duncan Phillips *Salem and the Indies,* but at that time there had been no work done on it, and there was no way to trace the voyages of Hawthorne's father except to go over the record of sailings each day from about 1790 to 1808.

I have tried, in the notes, to give the sources of the information I have used. I have also included there the names of the librarians and others to whom I am indebted for much assistance generously given. Both lists are, however, incomplete. I should like to take this occasion to thank Henry Luce, John Billings, Thomas Matthews and Roy Larsen, of Time, Incorporated, for making, at the time I resigned from the magazine, a settlement generous enough to give me three years of uninterrupted work on the biography; and Stanley Rinehart and the staff of Rinehart and Company, especially John Lamont, for their unfailing encouragement and editorial assistance. I cannot, however, possibly do justice to the friends, known and unknown, who have aided me in the composition of this work, and I take this opportunity to let them know that if their names are not mentioned it is not from any lack of appreciation of the help they have given me.

PREFACE TO THE OCTAGON EDITION

IN the preceding pages reference is made to an essay on Hawthorne in England, written at the start of the second World War. Originally published in The American Quarterly, the essay, which follows this new preface, was part of an examination of Hawthorne's views on the relations of Great Britain and the United States, and I hoped to make it the opening chapter of a book on that subject. Hawthorne had come to believe in the re-unification of England and America. His belief is evident throughout Our Old Home, and is more explicitly stated in the novels he left unfinished at his death, especially in The Ancestral Footstep.

He was not concerned with a political alliance. What he had in mind was some form of dual citizenship, an interchange of peoples, co-existing with the established governments of both countries. He recognized the difficulties in the way of any such fusion, but he believed that the people of the United States and England had shown enough political genius in the creation of democratic government, and enough ingenuity in forming and adjusting its institutions, to overcome the problems if they had the will to do so. Writing during the Civil War, in the midst of strong nationalist feelings that were intensified by English support of the Confederacy, he could hardly have been more explicit than he was, and his personal feelings were expressed in the very title of Our Old Home.

It is sometimes said that Hawthorne died as a result of the War. Carl Sandburg wrote of him, "There were sensitive spirits so finely spun that the war news, war imaginings, war chaos and its seeming lack of meaning, slowly wore away their life threads." And Van Wyck Brooks described Hawthorne's last days, "Hard as he tried to write, pulling down the blinds and locking the door, he could not bring his mind into focus. The novel became two novels, and the two became four. . . He made four beginnings, constantly changing his perspective, until he could scarcely bear to touch his blurred and meaningless manuscripts." Hawthorne himself wrote that the War, the present, "has proved too potent for me. It takes away not only my scanty faculty, but even my desire for imaginative composition, and leaves me sadly content to scatter a thousand peaceful fantasies upon the hurricane that is sweeping us all along with it."

Sandburg and Brooks were right, and Hawthorne was literally a war casualty, but their comments were conclusions, and the work that Hawthorne did, or that he tried to do, leading to those conclusions, retained its value in a later period of history. His unfinished work, hasty and scattered and even, on occasions, incoherent and cryptic, nevertheless remained a work of genius, testimony not so much to his failing powers as to the difficulty of the problem he faced. He was a sensitive and finely-spun writer, reacting with physical distress to the tragedy of the country, but he was also a practical politician, the closest personal friend of President Franklin Pierce, and perhaps the only disinterested friend that unfortunate politician ever had, an experienced political observer, much of whose adult life had been spent in government work. He did not see how the South, even if conquered, could be truly brought into a free and democratic nation. Visualizing a post-Civil War period, he thought of a distinct Southern society, existing with its own hidden culture and ways of life despite a superficial or official unity with the rest of the nation. He thought that such a state within the state—or outside the state, if the South should be allowed to secede—implied the reunion of New England and Old England. Much of *The Ancestral Footstep* is given over to the discussions on that subject between a young, idealistic American, held captive in an English country house, and an elderly British aristocrat, worldly-wise, civilized and urbane, who holds him captive to try to free him of his democratic illusions. Their discussions focus on a hard question: Why, if the two nations should again come together, was it necessary for them to separate in the first place? If they could rejoin, what had been gained by the long American struggle alone?

Hawthorne could not answer the question. He was only certain that both countries would gain if Englishmen were settled in America and Americans in England. Pending that distant interchange of populations there still remained a common cultural heritage to be explored, strengthened and made meaningful on both sides of the ocean. Two and a half decades after the second World War the course of American statesmanship had become so eccentric that it seemed doubtful that any prudent people would wish to link their fortunes with those of the United States, but in the 1940s the possibility of an American and English reunion did not seem remote, and the program that Clarence Streit advocated in such works as *Union Now with Britain* was at least possible. Hawthorne, it seemed to me, had gone beyond such programs in 1861: any governmental structure would be meaningless unless accompanied by a cultural interchange that reached into all levels of both populations. In the meantime there was sufficient evidence that the differences, disagreements and occasional periods of near-hostility of the two democracies were alone enough to make possible the progress and triumphs of the dictatorial states.

My attention has been called to some mistakes in *Nathaniel Hawthorne: The American Years*. His father was the mate, not the captain, of the *Perseverance* (page 17). The footnote on page 147, quoting a description of Hawthorne as suggesting "a boned pirate" should read "a bored pirate." And on page 274, in which a stranger in North Adams says to Hawthorne, "there is something of the hawk eye about you," the passage should read, "There is something of the Hawkeye about you"—an obvious reference to James Fenimore Cooper's hero.

Robert Cantwell

New York, N.Y.
July, 1971

HAWTHORNE AND DELIA BACON*

by ROBERT CANTWELL

I

EACH morning Nathaniel Hawthorne left his house in Rock Park and boarded the 9:30 steamer that carried him two miles down the muddy river to Liverpool. He was at this time forty-nine, a tall, reticent man, usually carrying an umbrella. The steamer passed the shipyards and tobacco warehouses, and the wharves concealed beneath an intricate forest of masts, beyond which he could see the dense center of the city. Leaving the ferry landing at St. Nicholas Place, he walked along Goree, crossed Water Street or Back Goree, turned into Brunswick Street, climbed the narrow streets of a shabby brick building—Washington Building—and entered the consulate of the United States.

The air vibrated with the rumble of heavy machinery. Across the narrow street, outside Hawthorne's window, stood a tall, smoke-blackened, ugly brick warehouse, with bags of salt constantly raised or lowered on its derricks. Julian Hawthorne, in his autobiography, changed these bags of salt into bales of cotton, but it was salt, the staple cargo of the returning cargo schooners, an essential American import, twelve million bushels a year, on which the English had a virtual monopoly and the lack of which counted heavily against the South in the Civil War. Hawthorne's office was a room about twelve by fifteen feet, with high ceilings. The noise of the derricks so resounded through it that conversation was difficult. In the anteroom there was usually a delegation of sailors, wearing flannel shirts—drunkards, desperados, vagabonds, shanghaied landsmen, invalids, impostors, bruised and bloody wretches—and another group like it in the inner office.

The vice-consul came into Hawthorne's office and placed on his desk the

* "Hawthorne and Delia Bacon," *American Quarterly*, Vol. I, No. 4, pp. 343-60 (1949). Copyright, 1949, Trustees of the University of Pennsylvania. Reprinted by permission.

money, in gold, taken in by the consulate the day before. The amounts ranged from eight to nineteen sovereigns, the equivalent of one hundred to two hundred dollars, approximately, in terms of present-day purchasing power. The routine of the day then began, and it is a remarkable fact that, despite the voluminous record of Hawthorne's notebooks, it is difficult to determine what he actually did. At about one o'clock he walked out into the city and drank a glass of porter. He says that he preferred the darker and dingier streets, with their gin mills every few steps. He seems not to have walked far, perhaps half-a-dozen blocks, to the region around Tithe Barn Road, where the squalor was worse than anything he had ever read of or imagined. At about five o'clock he returned to Rock Park.

The official dinners, the speeches, the laying of cornerstones, the breakfasts on newly launched vessels accounted for little of his time. Seven hundred ships a year departed from Liverpool for American ports, but his office staff (which was entirely English) handled the details, and his desk work consisted primarily of signing invoices. As time went on he interviewed the unfortunate Americans who came to his office for help, investigated deaths on shipboard, attended inquests, received delegations, searched for heirs, buried the dead, visited poorhouses and almshouses, sailors' boarding houses and insane asylums, armament works and shipyards. But these tasks were spaced out over several years. He began work on August 1, 1853. He made the first entry in his notebook three days later. There seems to have been no period of getting acquainted, and no question in his mind about what a consul should do. Perhaps his customhouse duties in Salem and Boston had given him a rough idea of what to expect. His friend, Zachariah Burchmore, was the British consul in Salem, and his former superior in the Salem Custom House, Ephriam Miller, later held the same post.

The incident that prompted his first notebook entry was a visit from a young woman. She told him that she was an American, though she did not speak like one. Her story was that she had come to England to visit an uncle, whom she found dead, and had no way of returning to America. Hawthorne did not believe her. He thought it probable that she was an Englishwoman, married to an American and divorced, probably for infidelity, of no very decided virtue, but not abandoned. He gave no reason for this conjecture. He thought arrangements might be made for an American shipmaster to take her to America as a stewardess, gave her half a crown, and then wrote an account of the interview, beginning the record which is to an amazing extent his expression of his doubts, his suspicions, and his fear of being deceived. Presumably he wrote at times to fill in the blank spaces of the day, or to give his own interpretation of happenings which, like this one, might be misrepresented.

With the main body of Hawthorne's English notebooks—the magnificent evocation of the English countryside, and the sensitive observation of the English character—this present account has nothing to do. But this repeated note of doubt that the people who came before him were what they represented themselves as being is an aspect of his work that seems not to have been examined. He did not believe that one in twenty of those who came to his office was a genuine American. The estimate is astonishing, both for what it reveals of conditions in England that led so many to seek refuge in American citizenship, and for the strain placed on his own common sense by such a parade of impostors. Moreover the strain on his sense of balance or perspective was increased because so many of those who were unquestionably Americans were mildly demented, and the combination of these two elements —the sailors, beaten and mistreated, with tales of horror, and the well-to-do eccentric or unbalanced, with tales of madness—added a note of queerness to his daily life, without which any account of his English years would be inadequate.

The most superficial reading of his notebooks reveals the stories of the sailors—the mate of the *John and Albert* who came to his office to charge that he had been assaulted, beaten, and stabbed by four members of the crew; the captain from New Orleans who announced regretfully that he had shot and killed a member of his crew while the ship was still in the Mississippi; the sailors who came to the office secretly to swear that the shooting had been entirely unprovoked. The famous case of Daniel Smith is enough to give the character of these incidents. Smith owned a small farm near Charleston, South Carolina. He had a wife and two children and sold butter, eggs, and poultry in the city. On one visit to Charleston he helped a man carry a trunk aboard the *George A. Ropley* and the ship sailed for Liverpool, Smith being kept aboard by force. He was beaten by the captain and mate and then left in Liverpool. When he appeared in Hawthorne's office, his face and eyes were bruised, as well as his head and body; he was forlorn, ragged, wretched, and almost witless with suffering and with the cruel senselessness of what had befallen him.

Hawthorne ordered him placed in a hospital, and presently received word that Smith was dying. He hurried to the hospital with a deposition of the evidence that Smith had given against the captain and the mate of the *George A. Ropley*. Smith was too weak to sign it. He lay in a recess formed by a projecting window, breathing in short gasps, tossing restlessly, his eyes closed, clutching a small earthen vessel in which to spit. The doctor asked him loudly: "Do you know that you are dying?" and Smith replied, "Oh, I want you to get me well! I want to get away from here!"

Hawthorne returned to his office and began to write an account of the entire affair, which he had not noted when it came up two weeks before. While he was writing it, a note was handed him telling him that Smith had died. He sent an account to the State Department, which referred the matter to Attorney General Caleb Cushing, who in turn referred it to the attorney general of South Carolina.

Every reader of Hawthorne's notebooks is likewise aware of his American eccentrics—the Connecticut storekeeper who had been swindled out of all his money in a vain attempt to visit Queen Victoria; the visitor who claimed half of Liverpool; the spinsters from Maine who believed they were of royal blood and feared that English lawyers would not press their claim "from a disinclination to admit new members into the royal family"; the gifted American musician, supposedly abandoned by her lover in England, who lived in an almshouse and would only answer to the name of Jenny Lind. For one of these characters, however, the record is so full and can so readily be checked that it affords a clear indication of how Hawthorne dealt with them at the time. Soon after he began his duties, the police of a Liverpool suburb picked up a twenty-five-year-old American, from Providence, Rhode Island, named George Ruggles. He had a ticket on the steamer *Andes*, which had sailed five days before. Rather than leave him in jail, Hawthorne ordered him placed in the lunatic asylum, a rather strange decision, it would seem, but one for which Hawthorne gave no explanation.

Ruggles needed clean clothing, but said his luggage had been seized by the landlord of the American Hotel because he could not pay his bill. Hawthorne went to the hotel, whose landlady told him that Ruggles had taken his luggage when he left without paying. She had followed him to another hotel, where he had spent two nights with a woman. The landlady demanded her money, and Ruggles went with her to a pawnshop, pawned his watch for five pounds, and paid her.

Hawthorne went to the asylum, but was not permitted to see Ruggles. He went directly home to Rock Park. There he found a visitor, who, by a strange coincidence, knew a great deal about Ruggles. The visitor was a Mrs. Blodget, at whose boardinghouse in Duke Street the Hawthornes had stayed when they first arrived in Liverpool—she was a celebrated character and her boarding-house a favorite meeting place for Americans. Her information was that Ruggles' mother was well-to-do, had married a second time, and was living with her husband and children in Italy; Ruggles had his mother's power of attorney to sell some of her property in Europe.

Ruggles claimed to have been a midshipman in the navy. This seems to have been false. On his second visit to the asylum, Hawthorne was told that Ruggles was worse—he now claimed that he was persecuted for political reasons—and Hawthorne was not permitted to visit him. By his own account, Hawthorne made no attempt to investigate Ruggles' case; he simply wrote to Ruggles' mother. She appeared at the consulate with four of her children, who made a somewhat better impression on him than she did, and he escorted her to the asylum, considering how painful a moment it must have been for her when she went through the gates. He met her again that afternoon in the coffee shop of the Waterloo Hotel. There she told him that she was going to take up quarters near the asylum as soon as the children had something to eat. This seems to have ended Hawthorne's interest in the matter. He apparently made no attempt to check on Ruggles' story, but accepted without question the accounts of Mrs. Blodget and the landlady of the American Hotel.

Actually there were obscure elements in Ruggles' life. He was the child of George Ruggles of Newport and Sarah Mason, who were married in 1825. In 1837 his mother married Levi Eaton, and had seven children by this second marriage in the next ten years. George Ruggles apparently died in the Butler Asylum in 1860, but the obscurity of his life continued after his death, his identity being confused because there is also record of another George Ruggles, born the same day, who also went abroad, but who returned, married, and died in Rhode Island in 1878.

II

None of these stories was so poignant and meaningful as that of Delia Bacon. No one would attempt to improve on Hawthorne's account of her in *Recollections of a Gifted Woman*, but the factual background of her career and its relation to similar cases in Hawthorne's consular experience suggest something of the significance her story had for her contemporaries. She was an intimate friend of Hawthorne's sister-in-law, Elizabeth Peabody. Her father, a Connecticut Congregational minister, died in 1817, when she was six years old. Until she was fifteen she was raised by a family in Hartford; then, with an older sister, she opened a series of schools—in Stonington, Connecticut; in Perth Amboy, New Jersey; on Long Island; in Hartford; and at Penn Yan, New York. In 1831, when she was twenty, she published her first book, anonymously, *Tales of the Puritans*. She also wrote a play and became a popular lecturer in New York and Boston.

She was tall, with dark brown hair and gray-black eyes. In her middle thirties she had been heartbroken by the ending of the love affair of her life and had been in ill-health for several years, suffering from neuralgia. She was self-educated, had taught herself Greek and Latin, and had given courses of study, principally in ancient history, at which she lectured each day to groups of women, for two hours at each lecture.

Sometime in these years she began to study the Elizabethans and to question the authorship of Shakespeare's plays. Summarizing her article in *Putnam's Magazine*, it appears that she did not have a fixed belief, but a fixed disbelief—she did not believe that the historically known figure of Shakespeare could have written the great national epic which the plays, considered as a whole, make up. Instead of concluding that therefore more needed to be known of Shakespeare, she reasoned that more than one author must have written them. She doubted on internal evidence that Shakespeare had written them; there was no precedent in literature for such a phenomenon. The plays were a new manifestation of creative energy; they were the great myth of the modern age and were to England what the Homeric poems were to Greece. She also doubted Shakespeare's authorship on scholarly grounds. The Homeric poems were the song of the nation, old, and their origin lost in tradition twenty-five centuries ago; they came out of the whole national life of Greece and could not appear before Greece had become a nation. The Shakespearian plays were comparably the crowning literary achievement of the Elizabethan age. They were even the crowning achievement of many preceding ages of growth and culture, for the age of Elizabeth was the beginning of a new period that summed up the slow ages before it. If the plays were considered the work of an untaught villager, they seemed to be almost a new and mystic manifestation of nature. The slow progression of periods of history was denied if such a belief was accepted. Instead of one age leading to another, moving with the slow accumulation of painfully won knowledge, contributing something and losing something, there seemed to have been a sudden upwelling of occult forces, a flowering without cultivation, laughing at history and telling the laboring ages that their sweat and blood had been unnecessary. The plays of Shakespeare were crowded with the best of a glorious epoch, its subtlest refinement, its costliest wit, its broadest, freshest range of experience, its most varied culture, profoundest insight, boldest comprehension. In view of the learning in them, the theory that they were the work of an actor, the poor poacher of Stratford, was unthinkable.

But how could such a mistake have been made? Columbus discovered America, but the continent is named for someone else, and Delia Bacon believed that we live in a period like that in which Amerigo Vespucci was given credit for Columbus' discovery. "Whose name is it," she asked, "that has drunk into its melody, forever, all the music of hope and promise which the young continent of Columbus still whispers?"

When she thought of the London of Elizabeth's time, she imagined an immortal group of statesmen and heroes, and scholars and wits and poets, with all their varied mental activities in conflict, and each strong individuality impressing itself on the others. In the thick-coming change of that time-bettering age, life grew warm, and in the old the new was stirring and in the many the one. The time had nurtured new freedoms. The wits and philosophers and poets and men of action were learning to veil, in double or triple meanings, their bold expressions of them. They wrote in ciphers and spoke in them, and concealed their freedom in their crowded conceits and unimagined subtleties of form. They were the magnificently endowed men of a wonderful age and left their lives in it, woven in its web throughout.

Bacon with his insight and his will, his science that wrung secrets from physical nature, his covert humor, his driest prose, pressed and bursting with Shakespearian beauty; Raleigh with his worldwide experience, his fiery mind, whose rush and outbreak darted all through his time—was it too much to suppose that such men might not use the theater as a way of reaching and teaching the masses? Or to suppose that having done so they might not ascribe to the plays' producer authorship they dared not claim? Delia was sure that in their works the secret of their strength was to be found, the secret of their lost philosophy, the secret of the Elizabethan age, what it was that then freed the power of the little island kingdom and carried it on to mastery of the world.

There was another side to the attribution of the plays to an untaught villager. Mankind *wanted* to believe that learning and discipline and art could be achieved without labor. England wanted to believe that untaught Shakespeare was better fitted than anyone else to have written the plays, and so a great myth was created, meaningful as the myth of blind Homer, to assert that inspiration was spontaneous and genius the property of the careless, the lawless, the villagers, the masses. Delia did not object to the myth. Indeed, she thought it beautiful—the wonderful origin of the plays was one of the most wonderful things about them. The obscurity of Shakespeare's life was its true Shakespearian element. This was the real enchantment of the Shakespearian legend—that with his miraculous inspiration he needed nothing else. She thought that the English found something wonderfully appealing in the belief that at last a genius had appeared who was not nurtured in the grand old cities where learning was enthroned. Nor had the genius that created the plays come out of the church or the state or English professional life: England had created the myth of the village Shakespeare. "In the boundless sea of negation around his theatre, he had hidden himself in the profoundest depths of the stuff that myths are made of. Who shall dive to the bottom of that sea to pluck his drowned honors from him?"

Whatever might be said of her theory, her vision was truly Elizabethan. In a sense she anticipated Trotsky's bold portrait of Stalin as a commonplace individual elevated to heroic stature by the bureaucracy, but she imagined a bureaucracy gifted, poetic, learned, planning to conquer the world with poetry and philosophy, rather than by revolution and bloodshed.

The vision of an intellectual brotherhood, communicating to each other and the world through the plays, planning to use their knowledge of science and humanity to transform the way people lived, the breath-taking sweep of their ambitions, their careful preparations and concealments as they worked within an old, suspicious, dying, military government—her words—the triumph of their work, and then the punishment for their ambition and their deception as their titanic efforts were hailed the work of one of their agents, and the secret of their strength was lost—such a concept was Shakespearian. In comparison with the substance of the *Idylls of the King*, which also assumed the existence of a brotherhood of genius in England's youth, and which strove to restore, not learning, but chivalry and selflessness, the vision was as meaty and vigorous in its underlying thought as the Elizabethans themselves. The gnarled questions and scornful answers quickened Delia's pages with a restless intellectual play that sometimes, after a few pages, became an intellectual torment. Her writing lacked grace and repose, and she was often tiring and irritating. But she was never banal, never hypocritical, never insipid, never vacantly pious or touched with the vapors and affectations, the false pathos and the stupefying humor, that marked so much of the writing of the age of Victoria.

III

Emerson and Elizabeth Peabody had tried to interest Hawthorne in Delia Bacon. They planned to board her with a family in Concord, trusting in her nearness and their words to win his attention. They failed, however, and she had never met Hawthorne and his wife, though she had once seen their children. She sailed for England three months before them, the money for her research paid by a wealthy New Yorker named Charles Butler. Emerson had arranged for her to visit Carlyle, and she made a good impression on him, though when she told him of her theory he burst into laughter that she thought could be heard a mile. She settled in London, in a room over a grocery at 12 Spring Street, Sussex Gardens, paying 18 shillings a week for her room and her food; and there, with her volumes of Bacon and Raleigh and her copies of the plays, she wrote her book. After a year Butler sent her enough money to pay her debts and return home. She used the money to remain another year. The English publishers rejected her book. She arranged some of it for magazine publication and sent the manuscript to Emerson, who sent it to *Putnam's Magazine*, which published one chapter. Emerson's brother got the manuscript in New York and gave it to Sophy Ripley to take to a Boston publisher, and Miss Ripley lost it in the carriage that was taking her to Staten Island from William Emerson's office.

General Campbell, the American consul general in London, advanced Delia Bacon twenty pounds, and then made life miserable for her trying to collect. Her brother, a clergyman, sent her ten pounds. When it was exhausted, she wrote to Hawthorne, who sent her ten pounds (though she had not asked for money) and made himself responsible for the money that Campbell had loaned her. When he was in London he called on her.

He had expected someone ugly and old and was pleasantly surprised at her dark hair and dark eyes, which shone as she spoke, her expressive features, the color that came into her cheeks, her friendly tone, and the lack of embarrassment in her manner. In her youth she had been uncommonly beautiful and was still striking and vivid. She spoke in a low, quiet voice. They talked for an hour. He found her a very good talker, pleasant, sunny and shadowy, often piquant, suggesting all a woman's various moods and humors, and with an earnestness that produced something like a temporary faith in her belief. He thought her extremely intelligent. Her great idea had thrown her off her balance, and in regard to it she was a monomaniac, but it had wonderfully developed her intellect, and at the same time she was practically wiser than her theory indicated, with a ladylike feeling of propriety, a New England orderliness, and a sturdy common sense to protect her.

He proposed to submit her book to Routledge, and she agreed at once. It impressed Hawthorne that she herself did not like her own theory; she would rather it had never occurred to her and would have been willing to take it to the grave with her if she thought she had a right to. But she had studied Shakespeare's sonnets, whose author had insisted so much, so strongly, and so repetitiously on the wrong done to humanity and the fraud done to nature when the individual fails to do justice to the gifts he is born with. She believed that this thought, as expressed in the sonnets, was not an echo of Plato, but something new, a fragment of the lost philosophy incorporated into the plays, and their author's "fresh and beautiful study of nature's law, and his own new and scientific doctrine of conservation and advancement." Her discovery, she believed, laid a responsibility upon her that she could not evade. Hawthorne's voice in the outer darkness revived her mortal life when it was well-nigh gone, and she took it as an omen that there was more to be done, for she thought that Providence had led him to her in this hour.

His visit was on the afternoon of July 29, 1856. On August 12, he wrote her that he had twice visited Routledges, and discussed the book with one of the partners, without getting much encouragement. On the fourteenth, he wrote to her brother in the United States, from whom she was estranged, and told him that she was well, cheerful, and comfortably lodged with a good family, that she conversed with great power and intelligence, and that her book was remarkable, written with wonderful earnestness and ability and full of very profound criticism. Its merits, he observed acutely, are entirely independent of the truth of her theory about the plays. "I will say to you in confidence, my dear Sir, that I should dread the effect on her mind, of any compulsory measures on the part of her friends, towards a removal"—the question of bringing her home had apparently been raised.

At about this time she became ill. She did not share Hawthorne's opinion of the landlord—she said that the mercy of lodginghouse keepers was small when the difference in price between the nutritious article and the poisonous one goes to them. It had become absolutely necessary, she said, that she make a change. However, she was again in debt. Her doctor told her that she must go to the country, to a farmhouse. She replied that she was very poor. He answered that she could live very cheaply there and have the sort of diet she needed. A sum of money arrived unexpectedly, enough to pay her bill in full and to leave her a small amount over. A friend of hers from Boston, Mrs. Eliza Farrar, who had heard her first lectures, but who had been out of touch with her for a long time, sent some nice things "but I think they came too late. They don't revive or strengthen me at all that I can see." On Monday, August 24, she made her arrangements to go to the country. On Tuesday she was too weak to sit up. Tuesday night, a servant packed her trunks for her. "It nearly killed me. I am dying partly, principally I think, for want of proper food, proper for an invalid."

There had been a death in Mrs. Farrar's house, and she was not receiving visitors. One night in this period a servant told her that there was a lady at the door who wished to speak to her. Mrs. Farrar said that she could see no one. The woman refused to go away or to leave her name. Mrs. Farrar went to the door and found Delia Bacon there, pale and sad, gasping for breath and unable to speak. Mrs. Farrar gave her a glass of port, and when Miss Bacon recovered from her faintness she said that she had given her manuscript to Hawthorne, to dispose of as he thought best, and that she was going to Stratford to verify her theory by opening Shakespeare's tomb. Mrs. Farrar tried to dissuade her and, failing, took her to the station and placed her on the train on August 29. She was so weak that she hardly knew how she left London.

The train carried her into the countryside where Shakespeare was born, through the gentle hills and fields dozing in the dim English sunshine, along hedges and through wooded parks, past hamlets of thatched cottages, ancient farmhouses and old mills, streamlets and pools, the smooth gleam and shadow of the slow rivers and the glimpses of the gray stone castles through the willows. Around her lay country whose very sods had been humanized by mingling so much of man's toil and care among them. The wildest things in

England, said Hawthorne, were more than half tame. The trees were never wild, ivy and mistletoe climbed over their moss-covered trunks, since the winter was not bitter enough to nip them or the summer sun hot enough to burn the life out of them. The deer that rested in their shade seemed to have been taught to make themselves tributory to the scenic effect and were scarcely wilder than sheep—the stags threw their antlers aloft, the does vanished lightly from light into shadow, the fawns at their heels, and sometimes the herd tossed their heads and ran in a kind of mimic terror, or something akin to feminine skittishness, with a dim demembrance of having come from wild stock.

When she got off the train at Stratford she was so deathly ill she could not stay at an ordinary lodginghouse. She went through the nondescript streets of Stratford, with shabby old dwellings, mean-looking modern houses, and a few ancient homes, to the Red Horse Inn. There she asked directions for finding rooms near the church. Someone had heard that Mrs. Terrett had a room. She did not take lodgers, but she had planned to have a friend come live with her; something had gone wrong and it was possible that she would take a lodger for company. Miss Bacon could not walk the short distance from the inn to Mrs. Terrett's house. She took a cab. A little maid opened the door and said that Mrs. Terrett was at church—something about the Jews, she said, which Miss Bacon thought a good omen. She ordered her luggage placed in the hall and sat down in the room she had decided to make her own. She tried to compose her features to get as much life into them as she could to impress Mrs. Terrett. She went into the kitchen. The walls were painted cerulean blue and everything in it shone like gold. She decided to stay. The maid seemed to have some misgivings and asked her anxiously, "Do you know Mrs. Terrett?" She did not, but she said she would take the blame if she had done anything wrong.

Church was over. The maid ran upstairs and, looking out the window, reported that her mistress was coming. Mrs. Terrett was kind and motherly, astonished at finding a stranger in her house, especially since, while she had thought vaguely of having a lodger for company, she did not remember having told anyone of it. For the two large, well-furnished rooms, board, and linen, Mrs. Terrett asked seven shillings a week. Delia Bacon lay down on the sofa and Mrs. Terrett covered her and went off to prepare some food for her. It was twenty-four hours since she had left London. A deathly, deathly weakness again swept over her. From her window she could see the Avon and the spire of Holy Trinity, Shakespeare's church. It stood in the great green shadow of lime trees. The spire rose above the tree tops and the Gothic battlements and buttresses and vast arched windows were visible through the boughs. The tranquil Avon, the mirror of Shakespeare's gorgeous vision, flowed past the churchyard, forget-me-nots growing among its flags and water weeds. She lay as quiet and as helpless as a baby. The church spire and the trees seemed like dreamland to her.

She was in the heart of England. Around her lay a wonderland of rural plenty and old legends, the country of Lady Godiva and King Cymbeline, where reality receded into the distant ocean line of the past. There were roads and paths that were old in the twilight ages a thousand years before the medieval darkness, cities that were founded in the year one, houses that looked like honeycombs, fields of grass and grain, towers with high-windowed walls, hedge-bordered walks and shadowy groves, sleepy rivers with their imperceptible lapse and tranquil gleam, rooks cawing and chattering in the tops of the old trees, and over it all the peace and grace of the summer's end. This England was enchanted. It was the true setting of *The Tempest*. It was a wonderland, full of wisdom and old music; and the strangest of its wonders was that the English did not know it. The air was pure and the quiet soothed her. She fell asleep and slept for eight hours.

The next day she wrote to Sophie Hawthorne. She drew a table beside her bed, wrote for a brief time, rested, and then wrote again. She sent an account of her leaving London, omitting any mention of Mrs. Farrar. For a woman supposedly unbalanced, she certainly wrote with extraordinary clarity. When she grew stronger she began to haunt the church. She studied and measured the flagstone beneath the altar that covered Shakespeare's grave. All day long pilgrims came into the church to stare at the grave and listen to the guide's words. The bust of Shakespeare, with its long upper lip and prominent forehead, was fastened to the northern wall; the east window of the church was brilliant with a new stained glass. A certain hesitancy came into her manner. She believed that the archives of the secret philosophical society were buried somewhere, here in this grave, or perhaps in more places than one, in Lord Bacon's tomb, Spenser's, or Raleigh's.

She was not dismayed by the difficulty. The great secret of the Elizabethan age did not lie where any superficial research could discover it. It had to be hidden deeply if it was to be preserved through the reigns of Elizabeth and James. It was buried in the lowest deeps of the deep Elizabethan art. The puns and charades of its authors, the enigmas and anagrams, the ciphers and puzzles were deadly serious; they had to be solvable only to those who should solve them. These men had lived at a time when all the latent capacities of the English language were put in requisition, and it was flashing and crackling with puns and quips, conceits and jokes and satires, and interlined with philosophic secrets that opened down into the bottom of the tomb—that opened into the Tower—that opened on the scaffold and the block.

She asked permission to examine the tomb when there were no visitors in the church. The clerk gave her a key, let her in at seven o'clock, and promised to call for her at ten. She carried a dark lantern and tools to open the tomb. As she set out she met Mrs. Terrett and asked her to go with her. Mrs. Terrett did so, reluctantly, afraid of the dark church. Miss Bacon groped her way through the chancel and lit the lantern. The clerk appeared. She reassured him about her plans, and he left with Mrs. Terrett.

She was now at liberty to break into the tomb. But she could not do so; she could not violate the trust that the clerk had placed in her; and if she failed, she would have no other opportunity. She sat alone in the church. On her right was the Old Player, looking down on her, but she could not see him. She looked up to the ceiling but it was not visible; there was something that looked like the midnight sky, and the long aisle was in utter darkness. From time to time she heard cautious, creaking footsteps. Then the clerk appeared and confessed that he had been watching her ever since she came into the church.

A strange sort of weariness fell upon her. In James's story, "The Beast in the Jungle," the hero throws himself upon the grave of the woman he loved when he realizes, after her death, that she loved him, why she had behaved as she did during her life, why he had haunted her grave after her death—a moment of awareness whose power James evoked by the image of the leap of the beast in the jungle. So in a sense it was with Delia Bacon as she sat in the darkness by Shakespeare's tomb. The cipher night lay clear before her. All the puzzles were solved. The hidden meanings were revealed through the blurred and dubious words, the charades and anagrams, the riddle wind in the lime trees, the cipher step of the sexton, the silver Avon, the bust of Shakespeare, which she could not see, the midnight sky, and in the center, herself. The ciphers in the plays led to the Tower of London, to the scaffold, to the block, or to where she now sat, holding her lantern, ill, alone, without friends, without money, in a foreign land, considered mad. The enigmas were in the

everyday world—her brother, who wanted her to turn her book into a novel
(he knew how to express himself according to the prescribed rules of Christian kindness when he was most cruel), Hawthorne, publishers, lodginghouse
keepers, and the mayor of Stratford, a surgeon named David Rice, kindly and
thoughtful, who at the Christmas season ordered her committed to the insane
asylum at Henley in the Forest of Arden.

She was in the asylum four months. Her brother's son, a graduate of the
Naval Academy at Annapolis the year before, was homeward bound from
China, where he had been master of the steam frigate *Mississippi* in the East
India squadron. Finding his aunt in the asylum he surrendered his own
passage home and took her with him the following week, and they arrived
in New York on April 13, 1858. Delia Bacon was taken to the Hartford Retreat, an asylum in Hartford, Connecticut, where she died on September
2, 1859.

Hawthorne said: This has been too sad a story. To free his mind of it, he
lingered over his recollections of his walks around Stratford, savoring the
lengthened, loitering, drowsy enjoyment of the stately elms in Charlecote Park,
watching the tame, playful deer. It was something far different to have killed
one of the velvet deer that roamed around these parks than it was to hunt for
deer in the thickets of America. At Shakespeare's birthplace he noted the
basement with its butcher-stall that one of Shakespeare's descendants had
kept, the cleaver cuts on its counter, the floor of gray stone slabs, the kitchen
with its rough fireplace and immense chimney through which Shakespeare
may have seen the blue sky and the stars glimmering down at him by night.
It gave him a depressing idea of the stifled, poor, somber kind of life that
must have been lived there, and a knowledge of how hardy a plant Shakespeare's genius was, how inevitable its development, that it was not blighted
there. The world, including Shakespeare, was not as good as Delia Bacon
believed. He thought of the pitiful picture of the wounded stag in *As You
Like It*, the wretched animal whose groans stretched his leathern coat almost
to bursting—what did it say of the poacher who had killed one of them in his
youth?

And yet in another sense the world and Shakespeare were better. He would
have understood her. She had laid upon his tomb the noblest wreath that had
ever been placed there. She had recognized in his works a depth that scholars
had never imagined in them; and he would surely, with his tenderness of
love and pity, have answered the injustice she sought to do him by seeing the

high justice that she really did. And in his own way Hawthorne came to agree with her. Something of immeasurable value lay hidden, not in the stones of Shakespeare's tomb, but in the cultural inheritance of which Shakespeare was a part, and he respected the impulse that had led his countrywoman, in her blind and pathetic pilgrimage, to throw herself on the tomb as if she would break into the rick with her bare hands. There was a secret hidden there, in the genius, in the quality of the life, in the great perception that had taken the old grim legends and the dark and bloody struggles of the old English kings and transformed and ennobled them in the plays.

No one had done so much for American history, and nowhere was that view of life more needed than at home, where in our politics we tended to impute the basest of motives, to degrade, to force down, to strip of all but the coarsest significance, the conflicts that were leading to civil war. The very characters who came into Hawthorne's office were Shakespearian, each with the vivid flicker of his own personality, though he appeared for only a moment and said only a few lines—George Ruggles and his mother; Daniel Smith of Charleston; the sailors forever shanghaied, beaten, robbed; the captains forever complaining of their mutinous crews. Each had his life, vivid and unpredictable, and the sense of their individuality, and the value of it, was part of what had come to us from England. Hawthorne was an American, and perhaps never so conscious of it, or so proud of it, as at this time, but as he brooded on these matters, and on the unfilled promise of American life— the unfullment that the life of Delia Bacon exemplified—he wrote: "Our philosophers have not taught us what is best, nor have our poets sung what is beautifullest, in the kind of life that we must lead; and therefore we still read the old English wisdom and pluck upon the ancient strings. . . ."

ILLUSTRATIONS

NATHANIEL HAWTHORNE

The American Years

CHAPTER ONE

I

*N*athaniel Hawthorne was born July 4, 1804, in a small room over the parlor of an old house on Union Street in Salem, Massachusetts. The Hawthorne house stood midway in the block, on the eastern side of the street, its front door opening at the street level. The house was wooden, solidly and squarely built, two stories in height, with a huge central chimney. The roof line was broken to protect the upper rooms from the summer heat or the full force of the winter wind that swept from the bay two blocks away. The house was remarkable for a complete absence of decoration, sturdy and somewhat blunt, yet too businesslike and too darksome to be snug.

The location was good, but without distinction. The house overlooked no important sites, and the view of the wharves was cut off by the adjoining houses. Union Street was not, in Hawthorne's lifetime, a desirable address. It was a very short street, connecting Essex and Derby. Near the intersection with Essex there was the Manning blacksmith shop, livery stable, and stagecoach office. At the intersection of Union and Derby there stood Newport's restaurant, open at night and patronized by criminals. Number 27 Union Street—though the houses were not numbered then—stood at the very boundary line of a dangerous and disreputable area of Salem life.[1]

Only a hundred paces or so in the direction away from the wharves was Essex Street, one of the finest thoroughfares in America, curving slightly, with a few dwellings intermixed with its shops and offices. There were the Sun and Ship taverns, the Essex Coffee House, Samuel Archer's hardware store, Henry Pratt's drugstore, Walter Bartlett's auction room, Joseph Hiller's silversmith shop, Charles Cleveland's brokerage shop, and the stores—Savage's, Hawthorne's, and a dozen others.[2] The ships arriving almost daily gave them an extraordinary variety of merchandise—wineglasses and easy chairs, kid gloves, silk

3

from China, tea from Ceylon, opium, almonds, figs, raisins, bear and
buffalo skins, English novels, tea trays, anchors, ship's bread, chintzes,
muslin, song books, cotton yarn, woolen goods, flannels, broadcloth,
olive oil, cheese, Amsterdam gin, logwood, varnish, spice, and baconed
hams. Prices were low on Essex Street, despite its elegance. Rum was
$1.08 a gallon, sugar, fifteen cents a pound, anchors, ten dollars apiece,
butter, twenty cents a pound, coffee thirty-two cents a pound.[3]

Beyond Essex Street was the common. At the time Hawthorne was
born it had just been fenced in, leveled, drained, and planted with oats
and six hundred trees. It was a beautiful park, all the more pleasing to
the eye because it emerged green and cool from the close-packed, unpainted houses and narrow streets, with the Lombardy poplars flashing
in the sun and shimmering in the breeze.[4]

A considerable amount of Salem history and an immense amount
of Salem wealth were concentrated in the inconspicuous house where
Hawthorne was born. On June 20, 1767, Captain Daniel Hawthorne,
the novelist's grandfather, left Salem in command of the *Salisbury*,
bound for the Azores. Hawthorne's grandfather was a round-faced,
double-chinned, clear-eyed, rather phlegmatic-appearing man, then
thirty-five years old, a capable, though not a notably successful mariner. His destination was Fayal, but he stopped in Liverpool. There the
Salisbury was boarded by a nineteen-year-old Irish youth, with incalculable effects upon the history of the Hawthorne family and upon the
town of Salem.

The stranger said that his name was Simon Forrester and that he
was born in Ireland, near Cork, on May 10, 1748. He was a dark, handsome, reckless, and adventurous youth whose origins were obscured by
his own candid accounts of them. They had the eerie consistency of
literal truth. His story was that he had run away from home and that
he was the son of an Irish family of Scottish descent who lived on a
200-acre farm. His family was descended from Baron Forrester of
Carstorphine, Scotland. They claimed kinship with the philosopher,
Francis Bacon. His mother's mother was the daughter of Oliver Hely,
and her uncle was the grandfather of the Earl of Donoughmore in Ireland—a line of descent so complicated it seemed to involve both a
knowledge of Irish history and a genealogical sense of humor. The
young Irishman said that he had gone to Cloyne College. He was put
to work reaping the grain on his father's farm. When the harvest was

in he threw down his reaping hook, saying, "This is the last time I will reap grain in old Ireland." The next day he drove a wagon into Cork, took passage to Liverpool, and shipped on the *Salisbury* as a hand before the mast.[5]

Such a story could either be the romancing of an imaginative runaway or the truth. It was the truth, in its essentials at least. Simon Forrester's older brother had died, so Captain Hawthorne was returning to Salem with the young heir of a family of noble blood serving as a seaman on his ship. The *Salisbury* reached Salem on September 8, 1767. At that time Captain Hawthorne was still living on the old Hawthorne farm on the South River in Salem, with his wife, whom he had married eleven years before, and his three daughters, Rachel, ten, Sarah, four, and Eunice, who was one year old. His only son, Daniel, had died four years before, at the age of four.[6]

Salem was then a town of about five thousand people, with a busy port from which around 350 vessels cleared each year, for the West Indies, Portugal, Spain—trade with the East Indies had not yet begun, but there had been wealthy merchants in Salem for a century. Now, upon returning from the Azores, Simon Forrester entered Captain Hawthorne's home, at first, apparently, as an apprentice, and was then virtually adopted by him, and raised as his son.

A month after their arrival, the new tax on tea was announced, one of the bitterest apples of discord the British crown ever threw among its American subjects.

Simon Forrester and Captain Daniel Hawthorne had come to Salem at a moment when the first premonitory tremors of the Revolution were unmistakable. Captain Hawthorne did not prosper under such conditions, but they seemed to be made for Simon Forrester. His status as an apprentice was quickly forgotten. He was soon on intimate terms with the family. He was too independent and aggressive to remain in a subordinate position, and was soon a captain in his own right. By the time he was thirty he was one of the wealthiest men in America.[7]

On July 25, 1768, another son was born to Captain Hawthorne. He also was named Daniel. Two years later another daughter, Judith, was born. In 1772, Captain Hawthorne, whose affairs were apparently in difficulty, exchanged the old family land in Salem for the land on Union Street. There, on May 19, 1775, Nathaniel, the father of the novelist, was born.[8]

Captain Daniel Hawthorne's wife was Ruth Phelps, and her parents transferred the Union Street house to him. It was not the property that Captain Daniel acquired, however, that was of interest, but the land he left. The original Hawthorne homestead in Salem could fairly claim to be called historic, if not haunted, for three generations of the same family had lived and died there, gone forth to war or sailed across the ocean, always to return to the same pleasant rolling ground beside the South River. It had been in the family since 1636, granted to the first Hawthorne in America on condition that he settle there, it being considered a benefit to the town that he should become an inhabitant. There was no finer land in Salem, and since so many of the land grants were fraudulently acquired, or the titles confused, its record was as good as any in New England.[9]

There, William Hawthorne, the first of the line in America, lived while he led the career that made him an eminent man in the colonies: he fought Indians, was a member of the legislature and speaker of the house, an assistant to the royal governors, and the judge who ordered the persecution of the Quakers in Salem. When William Hawthorne died in 1681 he left the farm to his son John, who also led a life of great distinction: a soldier, a judge, and a counselor for twenty-three years. This John Hawthorne was the witchcraft judge. In the summer of 1692 he left his farm to serve in one of the most difficult and confused trials in American legal history, the witchcraft trials of Salem, in which more than a hundred persons were accused of witchcraft, fifty were found guilty, nineteen hanged, and one tortured to death. Colonel Hawthorne had but little responsibility for the trials, merely sending the accused to the special courts set up to try them. He was a soldier, not a judge, and the French and English were engaged in that long war of religious persecution and terror known as the War of the Protestant Succession; but the horror of the proceedings lingered and some of it was attached to his name, all the more so because one of the dying women laid a curse upon him and his descendants.[10]

Colonel John Hawthorne left the farm to his son Joseph, who married a daughter of the Bowditch family, the great navigators of Salem, and thus began the seafaring tradition of the family. Thus it was natural that Daniel Hawthorne, at fourteen, after the tradition of the Bowditches, should go to sea, and work his way to command; and equally natural that he should have less feeling for the ancestral farmlands than his father, his grandfather, or his great-grandfather before him. When Daniel Hawthorne acquired the Union Street house in 1772, the old farm had been in the Hawthorne family for a hundred and thirty-two years, and Nathaniel Hawthorne, who had a poor opinion of his grandfather and called him an old man of the sea, never forgave him for parting with it.[11]

But Hawthorne was mistaken about Captain Daniel Hawthorne. He thought that Captain Daniel had exchanged the old farm for land near the wharves, "convenient to his business," and had then built the house himself. It would indeed have been a wretched bargain to have traded a fine and flourishing farm for the crowded property that brought the family to the very edge of a neighborhood of vice, and such, it seems, was Hawthorne's impression of what his grandfather had done. But Hawthorne was mistaken; Captain Daniel's parents-in-law had transferred the Union Street property to him, and the house had been standing a hundred years when he acquired it.[12]

Hawthorne's father was the first Hawthorne to be born on Union Street, and, like his famous son, bore the name of that disciple in whom there was no guile.[13] The Revolution had already begun when he was born, and both his father, Captain Daniel Hawthorne, and young Simon Forrester commanded privateers. Theirs were two of the 626 Massachusetts ships authorized to prey on enemy shipping.[14] On October 28, 1776, Daniel Hawthorne fought a two-hour battle with an armed packet, which he captured, with a loss of three killed and ten wounded. In January, 1777, he was in command of the *True American*, of twelve guns.[15]

Young Forrester, however, was vastly more successful. He was in command of the sloop *Rover*, carrying sixty men and mounting six guns. He was an astonishingly bold and able privateer. On October 16, 1775, he captured four prizes, two of them very valuable. Six days later he attacked a Bristol ship bound for British Guiana. It blew up, and only three of the twenty-eight men aboard were saved. In October, 1776, Simon Forrester took five prizes, one reportedly carrying $175,000 in English gold. Their value was estimated at $500,000. The next month, Forrester sold four prizes—the *Mary and James*, the *Good Intent*, the *Mary Ann*, and the *James*—for $11,200 and their cargoes of sea coal, earthenware, beef, pepper, compasses, anchors and cordage for $14,500 more.[16]

On December 7, 1776, he married Rachel Hawthorne, the oldest child of his benefactor, in the First Church in Salem. The date—the first year of the Revolution—is most significant. Rachel was then nineteen, a dark-haired girl with attractive and expressive features; Forrester was twenty-eight, dark, attractive, dangerous, swarthy and dashing, with a mildly sardonic expression on his long narrow features, and black hair that fell loosely over his forehead.[17]

He sailed his most successful privateer, the *Break of Day*, into the English Channel. Once he captured a ship laden with an almost priceless cargo of indigo, and released it because its owner had known his father in Cork. The misfortunes that dogged other privateers, such as capture as they were homeward bound with their booty—an occurrence so frequent it sometimes seemed that both American privateers and the British Navy were preying on the merchants of both countries—never seemed to touch Simon Forrester.[18] At the end of the war he had laid the foundations of a fortune that amounted to a million and a half dollars. At his death in 1817, despite tremendous losses, Simon Forrester still had $162,264.74 in gold stored away in banks in England.[19]

II

The lives of Captain Daniel Hawthorne's other children followed the ordinary course of Salem society. His last child, Ruth, was born on January 20, 1778—twenty-one years separated his youngest daughter from his oldest. The two sons, Daniel and Nathaniel, grew up in the house on Union Street, and in the course of time went to sea, shipping before the mast, and working their way to the quarter-deck—Daniel making his first voyage about 1782 and Nathaniel shipping out some seven years later. Of the daughters, Sarah married John Crowninshield, on March 2, 1792. He was a merchant and one of the most engaging characters in Salem history. On the same day, her sister Judith married George Archer, a merchant and adventurer. There were thus three different branches of the family all engaged in Salem commerce, all prospering, all flourishing, and all political and commercial rivals, and Hawthorne's father sailed first for one and then for another, always for his sisters' husbands, and though he was a great sailor, highly respected and never without a command, he never sailed a ship that he himself owned.[20]

The Revolution ended, and Forrester continued to prosper. In 1792 he bought a large and elegant house on Derby Street, at the opposite end of town from Captain Daniel Hawthorne's home. He commanded the privateers *Centurion*, the *Jason*, the *Patty* and the *Exchange*, during the war, and volunteered for an expedition into Rhode Island. After the war, he owned the *Black Snake*, the *Washington*, the *Good Hope*, the *Good Intent*, the *Perseverance*, the *Sukey*, the *Eliza*, the *Bonetta*, the *Endeavor*, the *Vigilant*, the *Little James*, the *Restitution* and the *Messenger*. The cargo of the *Perseverance*, 180,000 pounds of tea, on one voyage from Canton, sold for $140,000 in Salem.[21]

Fourteen children—ten daughters and four sons—were born to Simon Forrester and Rachel Hawthorne, and in these early years it seemed that they were launching one of the great families, like the Derbys and the Crowninshields, that dominated Salem commerce. In his early middle age—indeed, by the time he was forty—Forrester was one of the half dozen merchants, of whom the greatest was Elias Hasket Derby, who pioneered in the Eastern trade and made Salem famous throughout the world. He was the only newcomer who could be mentioned with Derby, with William Gray, George Crowninshield, and Israel Thorndike, though his accomplishment was greater than theirs, for he had no family behind him, and no long-established connection in the New World. The recklessness of his privateering exploits disappeared: he was a careful merchant, never going beyond his means, free from rash speculation, generous with his employees, and conducting his business with honor and ease.[22] He was a man of good taste; his home on Derby Street was beautifully proportioned, simple and unpretentious. The large wooden mantel was painted with a picture representing young Simon setting out from Ireland, a pack on his back, an eerily suggestive painting of small figures and an indistinct background of trees and fields that genuinely calls to mind the haunted countryside of Cork.

His sons were carefully educated, three of them graduates of Harvard, a considerable distinction, for there had been only about a hundred Harvard graduates in Salem since its founding.[23] Forrester's friends were Nathaniel Bowditch and John Pickering. This was an indication of his character, for Bowditch was Salem's native genius, a self-taught astronomer and mathematician whose *Practical Navigator* saved the lives of countless seamen; and John Pickering was the son of Colonel Timothy Pickering, the founder of West Point and Washington's secretary of state.[24] John Pickering was the first Greek scholar in New England, a master of twenty languages, including Arabic, Chinese, Egyptian, Cochin-Chinese, and the dialects of the South Seas and the American Indians.[25]

Salem was prospering, in these years, almost beyond belief. All over the world there were savages who thought, from the number of vessels that they saw, that there was a great kingdom somewhere beyond the sea, of vast population and fabulous wealth, called Salem.[26] Nor were they altogether wrong. The city had grown until its population was about twelve thousand, but there were more than a hundred vessels registered in the port, giving each citizen, so to speak, the prominence and power of a hundred landlocked townsmen of less enterprising places. There were four or five ships a day clearing or entering from the distant harbors—Demerera, Oporto, Havana (then called "the Havannah"), Sumatra, Bilbao, Santo Domingo, Isle of France, Martinico, Nantes, Amsterdam, Canton, Calcutta, Point Petre, Cayenne, Batavia, Jacquemel, Port-au-Prince, Port Republican, Malaga—and in their passage blazoning the name of the town until it appeared on the map of the world as prominently as that of a small country. A schooner cost as much as a well-equipped farm. A fairly new ship of about two hundred tons could be purchased for six thousand dollars, which was almost exactly the price of the land, buildings and livestock of a farm of around a hundred acres. The huge clipper ships, requiring great capital and large crews, had not yet been built, and the small schooners were within the means of almost any group willing to face the risks that sailing then involved. An investor could buy a share in the profits of a voyage—significantly called an adventure—and if it succeeded buy a ship with the proceeds.[27]

This was the generation of seamen to which Hawthorne's father belonged. His first command was Simon Forrester's *Perseverance*, a beautiful new ship. He was her captain on a wonderful voyage to Batavia when he was only twenty-one. Prior to this, however, he sailed for the Crowninshields. It will be remembered that his sister Sarah Hawthorne married John Crowninshield. The first voyage of Hawthorne's father of which there is a record was with Jacob Crowninshield, his brother-in-law John's most famous brother.

Elias Derby had bought, in France, a ship which he named *America*

and sold to Jacob and Benjamin Crowninshield. There were at least
six vessels named *America* under Salem registry. (There were also
45 *Betseys*, 33 *Sallys*, 26 *Pollys*.) The Crowninshields already owned
one ship named *America*. They had bought it in Bordeaux during the
French Revolution. It was formerly a French frigate, called the *Blonde*,
654 tons, the largest vessel in the American merchant marine.[28] It sometimes seems that all these ships were given the same names for the sole
purpose of mystifying posterity; but the merchants were shrewd, the
ships changed hands, and perhaps names, very frequently; very often
they had been taken as prizes, their rig altered to make them unrecognizable, and their papers prepared to mislead the French and British
warships that stopped and searched them at sea.

A friend of young Hawthorne's had given him a logbook as he set
sail on the *America*. He kept a daily record of the weather, the distance
covered each day, and any noteworthy events on the voyage. For much
of the voyage he recorded only day after day of pleasant mornings, with
moderate breezes, broken in the afternoons with sudden squalls and
thunderstorms, and ending at night with hazy weather of a squally
appearance. The *America* cleared Calcutta on December 3, 1795, in fine
weather and with a moderate breeze.[29] The hot and rainy season was
beginning in southern India, and the southwest trade winds, which blow
from April to October, had ceased. In the cargo, besides sugar, was
an elephant, the first ever brought to America, a female, six feet four
inches high, that sold in New York for $10,000.[30]

Very little transpired that young Hawthorne thought worthy of
record. The *America* loitered rather mysteriously outside the Isle of
France, then ran into harbor, remained there a week, and departed suddenly, half an hour before midnight, Hawthorne himself steering the
vessel out of the harbor. The *America* met a vessel near the Cape of
Good Hope, and lay by for two hours, raced with the *Fame* from the Isle
of France to Ascension Island, and won, stopped at St. Helena to take
on water and greens for the elephant, and picked up a stowaway who
was found the next day. Somewhere off the African coast "We found the
place where the ship leaked aft, and plugged it with a bag of sugar."
The *America* ran into a British squadron blockading the French West
Indies, but Captain Crowninshield's papers were in order, and he was
allowed to proceed. They were stopped again by a British warship off
Long Island, though whether the British were suspicious of them or

merely wanted to see the elephant is a matter of conjecture. Hawthorne's youthfulness shows through the brief entries in his log in a thousand ways, in his stiffness and consciousness of his position, his cheerful unawareness of the dangers he ran, his sanguine conviction that his voyage would end well, his pride in the ship, though it leaked and rolled, his concern about the speed of the *America* in comparison with other anonymous vessels on the horizon, his satisfaction with his seamanship, the crew, the elephant and the time of the passage. He seemed never to know how severe a trial he was undergoing: gales were squalls to him, storms gales, and the fierce tempests that shook the *America* and cracked her seams, storms.[31]

The *America* reached New York Sunday, April 10, 1796. Eight days later Captain Daniel Hawthorne died in Salem. Captain Daniel left little property. His widow and his two unmarried sisters lived in the house on Union Street, where Nathaniel also lived while he was in port. The *America* did not reach Salem until October, and Hawthorne was apparently there only two months.[32]

III

There lived in the house behind the Hawthorne house the family of Richard Manning, with four sons and four daughters. Richard Manning came to Salem in 1776. His house was Number 12 Herbert Street. He was a blacksmith, and his blacksmith shop and stable stood near the corner of Union and Essex. He also made stagecoaches. He was born in Ispwich, Massachusetts, a few miles from Salem, on May 29, 1755. His ancestors had been gunsmiths and blacksmiths in New England for five generations.[33]

The third of his children was Elizabeth Clarke Manning, usually called Betsey. She was born September 6, 1780, and was thus five years younger than Captain Nathaniel. She was a slight, attractive girl with extraordinary gray luminous eyes, quiet and reserved, with deep resources of intelligence and a tenderness and sensitivity so profound they lived in her children as dominant qualities in their lives. On August 2, 1801, she married Captain Nathaniel Hawthorne; on March 2, 1802, seven months later, their first child, Elizabeth, was born, and two years later, on July 4, 1804, their second, Nathaniel Hawthorne, the subject of this biography.[34]

In 1796, however, at the time young Hawthorne returned from
India, Betsey Manning was sixteen. The youngest Manning child was
four years old, the oldest nineteen. Her father Richard Manning had
done very well in the twenty years he had lived in Salem. He was a
Federalist, a member of the Essex Lodge of Freemasons, a representative, and the owner of an enormous grant of land in Maine.[35] At this
time he was investing heavily in land at Danvers, near Salem, in Salem
itself, and in the Maine wilderness.

The land grants were usually gifts of the colonial government to
veterans for services in the Indian wars. The land titles were so confused, and frauds in connection with them were so common, that ownership was questionable, the boundaries of the grants indistinct, and the
right to sell often in doubt. The land grant in which Richard Manning
was buying in 1796 had been first given to Captain William Raymond
and sixty others, for their services in the French and Indian War of
1690. They were the members of a company of militia recruited at
Beverly, Massachusetts, a Federalist stronghold lying across the North
River from Salem. The grant was made in 1735, but the land was found
to be in New Hampshire, property which, of course, the Massachusetts
government had no right to give away, and a new grant was made to
the heirs in 1765 and confirmed by the Massachusetts legislature two
years later.

The land stretched along one of the most strategic areas in the
northeast border country. Diagonally across lower Maine, from the
White Mountains, which close off New Hampshire and Canada, to a
point near Portland, there lies a chain of lakes, ponds and small rivers,
constituting both a natural barrier to invasion and a waterway to the
interior. The largest of the lakes, and the one closest to the sea, is
Sebago Lake, fourteen miles long and eight miles across, only twenty-
five miles from Portland.

The land grant that Richard Manning bought lay along the southern end of Lake Sebago. Its original area was 37,750 acres. Of this
428 acres were taken out for Rattlesnake Mountain, which rose beside
the lake and was so named because it was so infested with rattlesnakes
that they were caught for their oil. Another 5,945 acres were taken
out for ponds. A township named Raymond, after the captain of the
militia company, was located at the outlet of the lake.

Raymond was a primitive community, deep in the wilderness, destined to prosper, in a few years, when lumbering and shipbuilding began on a grand scale in Maine; but now isolated and remote, with a store and a grist mill in the village and the houses of the settlers located in ragged clearings in the woods. Richard Manning was the secretary of the company made up of the heirs of the original grantees, and was purchasing the titles of the other owners; his investments often made it necessary for him to travel from Salem to Raymond, a long and dangerous journey.[36]

Betsey Manning was not an heiress, but she was one of the heirs to land which promised to be worth a fortune; Nathaniel Hawthorne was not wealthy, but he stood at the threshold of a career which, under ordinary circumstances, should carry him in a few years to moderate wealth, to ownership of one of the fine, simple homes of the sea captains in Salem, and to a position of respectability and influence in the town, if not in the state and nation. Such was the course of his contemporaries no better endowed—Jacob Crowninshield, Nathaniel Bowditch, Richard Jeffery Cleveland, Nathaniel Silsbee, and a dozen others.

Captain Nathaniel Hawthorne remained in Salem until after the election of 1796. The two parties at that time were called Federalist and Anti-Federalist. As the feeling for and against the extremists in the French Revolution, the Jacobins, increased, the followers of Jefferson were called Jacobins. They then called themselves Republican and Democrat-Republicans. Since they were the predecessors of the Democratic party, it has seemed desirable, in the interests of simplicity and accuracy, to refer to them as Democrats throughout, a liberty justified by the fact that the ablest theoreticians of the New England Federalists— Jeremiah Mason and Nathan Dane—were in their economic thought and opinions on slavery forerunners of the Republican party. Captain Hawthorne was a Democrat. So were the Crowninshields. His former captain, Jacob Crowninshield, indeed, was appointed secretary of the navy by Jefferson, but refused the appointment because of ill-health, though the official records still listed him as secretary two years after his death.

Salem was almost evenly divided between the Federalists and the Democrats. The Federalists had about 600 out of 1,100 votes, and the Democrats were reducing the margin at each election. Marblehead, around the Cape from Salem, was solidly Democratic—something like

270 to 32. Beverly had almost the exact opposite—200 Federalist votes to 40 Democratic.

The difference gave no indication of the greater extent of Federalist influence. Every judge and every lawyer in the county was a Federalist, as were the merchants and most of the clergymen. The Salem *Gazette*, a wonderful newspaper, expertly edited and crowded with the world news the captains brought home, was Federalist. Its tone was gloomily brilliant; Elizabethan poetry and masterpieces of conservative reasoning covered its front pages, supporting and giving emphasis to the news of disorder it carried elsewhere: the awful uprisings of the Negroes in the West Indies, the savagery of the torture on pirate ships, the cost and waste of the ships embargoed—every line of which made law and order the minimum necessities of a dangerous and not very happy world.[37]

The Federalists organized the parades, conducted the meetings, built and sailed the ships, built the houses whose fine lines still make them outstanding among the houses of America—in short, ran the town and put the stamp of their thought permanently upon it. Federalist thought had not yet become bitter, and a friendly simplicity characterized its works, not at all the acrid aloofness tradition ascribes to it. The voyages to China and the public square were equally products of the Federalist imagination. Washington Square in Salem was in particular evidence of their work. It had been the common, covered with stagnant ponds, unenclosed, and a range for horses, cattle, ducks, geese, hens, and stray pigs, until Elias Hasket Derby raised by subscription the $2,600 necessary to level it, fill in the ponds, put an oak railing around it and poplar-lined gravel walks through it—a fund to which most Salem people of consequence contributed, and many who had but little means.[38] A few workmen gave their labor.

The Federalists loved oratory, at which they excelled—they were incensed that Jefferson and Monroe, who could not compete with their masters in that field, submitted their messages in writing. Their literary productions, beautifully finished, tended to a somberness and that the condition of the times warranted, but their gravity had none of the affected melancholy of the period that followed and arose from their close linkage with the world of affairs, and their concern for its inhabitants, rather than from a romantic rejection of it. Moreover, they were losing, and knew it, and a stoic acceptance of fate, noble in its best expression, gave their work a quiet dignity. The question was what defeat would mean. They believed that every measure of the Democrats was designed to further a cause which "if it succeeded, must deluge the country in blood, as it has in France." They were condemned as Tories, aristocrats, monarchists, and with some reason feared the fate of the aristocrats of France while innocent, all of them, of the practices the French aristocrats had been guilty of. They went into the elections inspired by Shakespeare, with this motto on their leaflets:

> *Be just and fear not.*
> *Let all the ends thou aim'st at be thy country's,*
> *Thy God's, and truth's.*[39]

When they lost elections, and the threatened revolution did not break out, they were, momentarily, in an awkward position. The mob did not storm through the streets, the guillotine was not set up, and atheism was not ordered by the state. Yet they were not wrong. Their leaders seemed to be cut down as surely as if a revolutionary tribunal had ordered it, one after another; the embargo and the War of 1812 changed their city as much as a revolution would have; disbelief could hardly have been more widespread if a dictator had decreed it, and prosperity vanished. They faced the future, nevertheless, with calm certainty.

"To permit an evil, in its nature unavoidable, to depress all our fortitude, argues a want of confidence in the Providence of God and betrays a criminal pusillanimity of intellect . . ." Thus the Salem *Gazette* editorialized. "Allowances may be made for the first convulsive struggles of irritable nature, but beyond that we impeach the justice of Omnipotence. Our own conduct in the natural world inculcates practical lessons for improvement in the moral. When clouds blacken the horizon, and the thunder roars destruction, we relieve ourselves from the horrors around us by reflecting that the sun will soon return with a lovelier lustre.

"In the moral government of the world, when the heart is sore under the pressure of present evils, let us look for the same benevolence in chastisement. The world has so many attractions, and eternity so many terrors, that unless pain and misery blunted the force of the one, and reconciled us more to the other, death, when it did come, would be doubly tremendous. Sharp must be the thorn to the foot inured only to the pressure of roses. Affliction thus calls forth latent virtues from the heart, which would otherwise have lain dormant and unnoticed. It is a severe school undoubtedly, but such severity is the nurse of vigorous virtue. Nothing great was ever achieved without difficulty in the struggle. When the talents are thus put to the test, and abide the rigor of the scrutiny, the pleasure that the mind derives from contemplation of the conquest, is greater than all the toils and dangers of the battle. Weak and pusillanimous souls shrink at the first appearance of danger, and as it approaches resign the victory without a blow. The words of Hector, when he beheld Ulysses and death approaching, forcibly apply to the condition of every one who is doomed to encounter the calamities of life:

> *War is our business, but to whom is giv'n*
> *To die or triumph, that determines Heav'n.*

"But the Christian has a consolation which the dying Hector had not. Revelation assures us that we are exercised by one who is 'touched with our infirmities,' and who will not afflict us beyond what our fortitude can bear. The victory we may be assured will be ours, if we will but exert the talents which the Deity has given us to obtain it, and a garland, more glorious than earth can boast of, will be our exceedingly great reward." [40]

IV

On December 13, 1796, Captain Hawthorne cleared Salem for Batavia, in command of the *Perseverance*. She was a new ship, of 245 tons, built in Haverhill for Simon Forrester only two years before.

The *Perseverance* was slower than the *America*. It needed repair; the carpenter figured in the log as he never had aboard the *America* —the tiller was lost in a gale, the rails swept away, the deck needed calking. The *Perseverance* reached Batavia on May 1. She sailed from Batavia to Manila in 31 days, and from Manila to Canton in two weeks. She lay in Canton until November 30, 1797, perhaps four months, having then been absent from Salem for almost a year, and returned to Salem in the spring of 1798. Captain Hawthorne's career was brief and he had few commands. He sailed the *Mary and Eliza* to the Orient, the *Neptune* to the West Indies and to Europe, and the *Nabby* to the West Indies and to Surinam.[41] His life was hard, without a relief since he had gone to sea at fourteen. His marriage to Betsey Manning in the summer of 1801 brought happiness to a life singularly devoid of anything but years of lonely effort at sea, and how happy their marriage was her grief at his death, and the profound impression of him that she implanted in the minds of their children, lived on to bear witness.

They lived in his mother's house. Elizabeth, their first child, was beautiful, with raven hair and the extraordinary gray luminous eyes of her mother, with long tapering hands and a vivid precocious intelligence which made her, all her life, a character of subtlety and strangeness.[42] Nathaniel was a healthy robust child who in these years rolled in the grass under the famous apple tree in the back yard, and picked a plenitude of currants from the bushes that grew along the fence.[43] Salem was a wonderfully healthy town in those days. With a population of 12,000 there were only about 215 deaths a year. Death in childbed was very rare. In the year Nathaniel was born there was an epidemic of cholera infantum that carried off thirty-two babies, but the infant mortality was usually around fifty or sixty a year. Shipwreck took a heavy toll of life, but few in view of the number and length of the voyages. There were years when as many as forty-eight sailors were lost, and as few as twelve. The annual average was twenty-eight.[44]

Betsey Manning was the first of her family to marry and for many years hers were the only Manning grandchildren. The Mannings were flourishing. They were growing into a picturesque and amiable family of independent and strongly marked characters—great horsemen, restless investors and inventors, forever building new houses and clearing new homesites, living in them briefly and moving on and perhaps leaving behind some large, not-quite-completed mansion which soon became known as Manning's Folly. They were outdoor people, blacksmiths and stagecoach drivers, vigorous, ambitious, and willing to take chances in a new company, a privateer's cruise, or a share in a voyage to the East, but a curious gentle quality characterized them also, a love of books, solitude, flowers and fruit trees.

Richard Manning, Betsey's father, was one of Salem's leading citizens. He contributed a thousand dollars to the building of the *Essex* in 1800 when that vessel, a large part of the navy of the United States, was built by popular subscription in Salem. He was a good Federalist, though not active in politics. Richard Manning, Jr., Betsey's younger brother, was a stagecoach driver, and in those days it was said that the stagecoach driver was the next best man to the minister, out of jail.[45]

Young Richard Manning was also a member of the First Ward Committee of the Federalist party, along with a score of others— Derbys, Forresters, Pickmans—a list of solid citizens that could hardly be equaled in any other section of the country.[46] Salem people were not deeply interested in politics, though politics occupied more and more of their lives. The Federalist appeals to the voters revealed their weariness in the admission that if they would just bring out the vote for this election they would have a ten months' respite from electioneering and the polls. Politics now threatened their very livelihood; but political conflicts had grown uglier, and like most contented and industrious people they shrank from the raucousness and rawness of campaigns in which, moreover, the language grew increasingly violent. In 1802 the Federalists had a margin of 121 votes over the Democrats. In the town election of 1804, however, Colonel John Hawthorne recived 533 Democratic votes for head selectman, to 456 Federalists votes for William Gray. "The talents of Colonel Hawthorne," said the *Gazette*, "were never suspected of being of that peculiar kind, that would lead this last best hope of man to seek a refuge in them . . ."

Colonel John Hawthorne's term of office was stormy. The selectmen barred Henry Gardiner from voting. Gardiner was a Federalist. He left Salem in 1775, became a British subject, and his estate was confiscated. He returned before the end of the war, served on some of the privateers, but was never naturalized. He was refused a vote on the ground that he was an alien. Gardiner brought suit against the selectmen. The decision of the court was in favor of Gardiner. Colonel Hawthorne was fined for having debarred him from voting. Colonel Hawthorne still refused to permit Gardiner to vote, however. A town meeting was held to select the Salem representative to the legislature. Colonel Hawthorne was a candidate. He was also presiding over the meeting and threw out Gardiner's vote, which would unquestionably have been cast against him.

The Federalists set up a committee to examine the town's finances. John Pickering was a member. The committee found that Colonel Hawthorne and the selectmen had charged the town more than $300 for counsel fees, witnesses, carriage hire and tavern bills, in the Gardiner lawsuit. The selectmen had bought timber for a cistern at $3.50 a hundred when the market price was $2.50 a hundred. They had ordered the town clerk to direct the town treasurer to pay the cistern's builder $353 without accounting for the money. Salem's expenses had increased from $18,955.28 to $25,655.66 in three years of Colonel Hawthorne's government, and the town was $7,000 in debt. At the next election Colonel Hawthorne ran on the Democratic ticket against Samuel Ropes on the Federalist. He lost by one vote—500 for Ropes to 499 for Hawthorne.[47]

V

At the time of Nathaniel Hawthorne's birth the town was evenly divided between the Federalists and the Democrats, as the nation had been evenly divided between Adams and Jefferson. Whether the country was to follow Virginia or New England, to be a partisan of Napoleon or of England, whether it was to expand in small freeholdings, as in the Northwest Territory, or in enormous plantations, as in the Louisiana Purchase, whether its wealth was to be based on trade and commerce and a free intermingling with people all over the globe, or whether it was to depend on agriculture and a self-supporting economy, closed against the rest of the world, whether the cast of its thought was to be English, rooted in English laws and traditions and culture, or European, skeptical, doctrinaire, and authoritarian—all these issues were in the balance, and the life of the country was poised between its two great alternatives.[48]

The Fourth of July, Hawthorne's birthday, began in Salem with cannon fire as the Salem Artillery saluted the dawn. At Orne's Wharf a boy, helping some mechanics fire a cannon, had two fingers blown off. At noon the Federal parade formed on Court Street, the Salem Artillery, with a band, providing an escort. The committee of arrangements and distinguished visitors marched ahead. Behind them came the clergy, the magistrates and public officers, the merchants and tradesmen, making it clear that the most respectable citizens were arrayed on the side of Federalism. As the procession began to move a salute of seventeen guns was fired from Castle Hill.

St. Peter's Episcopal Church had been open since eleven o'clock, but only ladies were admitted before the procession arrived. It was crowded. The Reverend Mr. Fisher opened the meeting with a prayer. An ode, written for the occasion, was sung by Mrs. Jones, and the oration, a review of American political history, "calculated at once to cherish our hopes, alarm our apprehensions and awaken our vigilance" was delivered by John Pickering. The appeal to the emotion of the audience with which it closed was beautiful. Stirred and sobered, the procession formed again, and marched to Concert Hall to dinner. An announcement was made of the injury of the boy at Orne's Wharf. Four hundred and thirty-eight dollars was collected for his relief. Two visiting clergymen bore the prayers and gratitude of the company to the throne of heaven.

Then, after dinner, the toasts were drunk, while the band played appropriate music and the artillery company discharged salutes. The first was to The Day! May it ever be justly considered as the most fortunate, as well as the most glorious, in the annals of American history! The artillery fired a salute. The band played "Yankee Doodle." The second toast was to the memory of Washington. The band played "The Dead March." Then there were toasts to John Adams, and then to "The President of the United States *("May he imitate, as well as praise, the virtues of Washington"),* to the Governor, to Our Foreign Minister, to Charles Pickering *("Above all fear, flattery or corruption! He never crouched to the despotism of Republican France, nor committed the honor of his country"),* to Independence, to Louisiana, the Union, the commerce of the United States, an independent judiciary, aliens, Massachusetts, the rights of the minority, economy, the Salem artillery, the ship *Constitution,* and various prominent Federalists who were present. As they mounted up they became perceptibly unsteadier and more enthusiastic. When glasses were raised to Our Fellow Citizens in Slavery at Tripoli, the band struck up "The Galley Slave." William Gray proposed: "Reformation of those who bow to the shadow of the Constitution while they despoil it of its substance!" Some one else called for "No illegal proceedings under pretense of their being constitutional, ⅗ of a slave and ⅖ of a freeman ought not to make a legal voter!" The enthusiasm at this time was at its height; the volleys of salutes were almost constant.

Meanwhile the Salem Cadets, having dined generously at Osgood's, were bringing the day's exercises to an end with maneuvers, marches and firings, performed with spirit and accuracy. General Elias Hasket Derby, toward the end of the day, proposed a quiet toast to a part of Salem the others had overlooked, and raised his glass to Our Industrious Northern Seamen. His kinsman Ezekial Hersey Derby called for another, to Agriculture and Commerce, may they ever be treated as twin sisters. Another toast was drunk to the standard of the Salem Artillery—may it never be struck. The band played "Knox's March." Another toast, the last, was drunk to the Salem Cadets, and the band played "Greene's March." More than thirty toasts were drunk. A clear line was apparent in them, a clear division in the Federalists between those who, like Pickering and Gray, tried to make the meeting provocative, and fan its anti-Jefferson feeling into flame, and those who, like the Derbys and Samuel Putman, tried to avoid provocation, at which they could not compete with the Democrats, and keep attention concentrated on local achievements and men. The Salem Artillery fired its sunset salutes, and the day closed with a great ball at General Derby's mansion, attended by forty ladies in a brilliant display of beautiful gowns.[49]

The men of Salem were scattered over the seven seas. Captain Searl was bringing the *Good Intent* into port. Captain Silver was on his way from Cuba to New York. Captain Daniel Hawthorne was leaving plague-stricken Havana. The *Good Hope,* the *Ocean,* the *Concord,* the *Two Friends,* the *Active,* and the *Increase* were on the Atlantic, bound for Ireland, Sumatra and Bilbao; the *Hannah* was two weeks out of Gibraltar, homeward bound for Salem; the *Andromeda* and the *Vulcan* were sailing from Ireland, and the *Fish-Hawk* was home from Jacquemel and the *Reboreus* from Martinique. Captain Nathaniel Hawthorne's old ship, the *America,* was sailing for Calcutta, under Hawthorne's brother-in-law Crowninshield, one day out of port; the *John* and the *Telemachus* had cleared for the West Indies, and the schooner *Snake-in-the-Grass* for Santo Domingo.[50]

Captain Nathaniel Hawthorne was homeward bound from Batavia. He had had a difficult and wearisome trip. Squalls and storms attended his outward passage. He sailed through a storm in the Indian Ocean, hail, rain and seas so high he could not keep the *Mary and Eliza* on her course.[51] Forty-five neutral ships, principally American, had loaded at Batavia between September and June. The coffee crop was exhausted, and there was no more to be had for the season. Six or seven American ships had had to sail for Bengal and other ports without securing any. Captain Nathaniel Hawthorne got his cargo and sailed for home on June 22. He made the passage in 113 days, and reached Salem on

October 16.[52] His brother Daniel had just cleared for Malaga on the *Morning Star*.

Hawthorne's father remained in Salem until November 27, 1804. He saw his son very rarely, and for only brief periods; it is possible that these few weeks in Hawthorne's infancy were the longest time that the father and son were together. The captain's standing in the town had been enhanced. There were few voyages reported in such detail as his. No doubt his successful voyage was principally responsible, for the *Gazette*, though it kept politics out of the Ship News for the most part, did not waste its space on Democrats. And Captain Hawthorne was a Democrat—at least he had been opposed to Adams—but the restrictions that Jefferson placed on commerce were driving the New England mariners of all beliefs into the Federalist party. The astute men around the *Gazette* could be counted upon to make welcome a voter whose vote was undecided in a contest as close as the one approaching.

A greater likelihood is that Captain Hawthorne had been viewed, until this voyage or until about this time, as a minor figure in the host of Crowninshields and Forresters to whom he was related by marriage, and had now suddenly emerged in the sight of the town as a man of equal stature with his famous and wealthy kinsmen. The possibility is strengthened because the personal popularity of the Crowninshields was evaporating in the heat of their political battles; and the Forresters were entering the period of crisis which, in another few years, ended their fortune and the family name. In two generations the male line of the family was extinct.

Fearful misfortunes overcame Simon Forrester as the century drew to a close and the new century began. Only six of his children outlived him. His ships were robbed and wrecked, and fires broke out in his warehouses. In 1807 his son Simon, only twenty-two years old, was lost at sea, on a ship returning from the East Indies. During the War of 1812 Forrester's daughter Rachel died. In 1816 his 21-year-old son Charles died. He had graduated from Harvard at eighteen. Reverend Bentley, author of a famous Salem diary who had not been in Forrester's home for thirty years, wrote of Forrester: "Upon his prosperity he became intemperate, and severe in his family and irregular. But his wealth gained him suitors for his daughters, first a young merchant, then a young doctor, then a young clergyman. [An Episcopalian; Bentley was a Congregationalist.] One of his sons leaped from the

windows of a cabin into the sea. Another has died this day in fits after
a few hours illness. He has two sons left, one at sea, the whole [family]
eccentric."

Forrester's son Thomas Healy Forrester, after successfully beginning as a merchant, dealing in nankeen, sugar and tea, began to
drink heavily, and became so deeply involved with swindlers and black-
mailers that attendants were placed with him constantly to guard him
from indiscretions. The attendants then became involved with him in
turn, one of them suing him for $1,500, which he claimed Thomas For-
rester had promised to give his twelve-year-old son—a claim the court
denied. Simon Forrester's remaining children married, prospered moder-
ately, struggled somewhat over the remainder of their father's estate,
and in a few years the wealth had vanished. As the tragedies in the lives
of his children multiplied, the ruin of Simon Forrester's family seemed
to be enacted in broad daylight, with all Salem as spectators, and there
was a ring of truth in his Democratic enemies' description of Simon
Forrester as a fierce, determined, industrious, passionate and willful
man, with "a mind full of superstition, with a temper as boisterous as
a Tempest, and with habits of occasional intemperance like a ship without a helm . . ." [53]

The misfortunes of the Forresters coincided with the defeats of the
Federalists. In 1804 the Democrats carried the state by a heavy majority, 420 towns reporting 25,452 Federal votes to 29,424 for the Democrats. Soon after the election, Captain Nathaniel Hawthorne sailed for
the West Indies on the schooner *Neptune*. The log of this vessel has been
lost, and a certain mystery attends his voyages in it. He returned to
Salem from Martinique on April 9, 1805, after a 38-day trip on which
he spoke nothing. He sailed almost at once—April 23—for Bordeaux.
His brother Daniel was lost that year at sea, on the *Morning Star*.

Captain Nathaniel Hawthorne sailed after his brother's tragic
voyage, but before word of his death reached Salem. On October 1,
1805, when the English and French fleets were preparing for the Battle
of Trafalger, the *Neptune*, still under his command, was left at Nantes,
with her cargo unsold. She returned to Salem on December 4, but under
the command of Robert Brookhouse.[54]

Salem shipping by this time was in a fearful condition, and it did
not improve. By the end of 1805 there were sixty-six vessels lying in
Salem harbor—22 ships, 4 barks, 27 brigs and 14 schooners. The dis-

tress of the smaller ports was so great that the Federalists won the election of 1806, though many of the ablest Federalists had had enough of politics and refused to stand for office—Elias Derby refused to run for senator, and Fisher Ames declined the presidency of Harvard.[55] The year 1807, in which the embargo passed, saw a deepening of the tension. William Gray, who had become a Democrat, moved his headquarters to Boston, beginning the flight of capital from Salem. There were 700 applications for assistance at the soup kitchen in Salem in one week at the end of 1808, and 1,200 the week following.[56] It was estimated that 20 per cent of the entire population depended on charity in some form for existence. The value of exports dropped from $110,000,000 to $20,000,000 a year. The embargo cost New England $50,000,000 a year, which was a large share of the national income.[57]

Captain Nathaniel Hawthorne sailed for the West Indies in command of the *Nabby*. The *Nabby* was a 154-ton brig, built in Falmouth four years before, bought by Benjamin Babbidge, Samuel Archer 3rd and John Andrew, and registered on June 26, 1807. (John Andrew was the husband of Simon Forrester's oldest daughter, Catherine.) Captain Hawthorne sailed first for Cayenne. He left there with a cargo of cotton and cocoa for the firm of Archer and Andrew, on September 15. He reached Salem on Sunday, October 14, 1807. There were a few other New England vessels in Cayenne, the *Sally* of Newport, the *Experiment* of Philadelphia, and "some others not recollected." [58] He soon sailed again, this time for Surinam, Dutch Guiana. Surinam was a tough port, famed for its slave traders.[59]

On January 9, 1808, his third child, Maria Louisa, was born in the house on Union Street. Elizabeth was now nearly six, Nathaniel four, and their mother twenty-eight—Captain Nathaniel was thirty-three. The children slept in the rooms adjoining their mother's over the little parlor of the house. The time was one of deepening crisis: the beginning of the embargo, the ending of the slave trade. On April 19, 1808, word was received in Salem of Captain Hawthorne's death in Surinam of yellow fever. To the end of her life Elizabeth Hawthorne could remember her mother coming into their room and telling her and Nathaniel that their father was dead.[60]

CHAPTER TWO

I

*H*awthorne was an ordinary child. His sister Elizabeth could walk and talk at nine months of age, but his development was average. The pale spring sunlight of New England, filtering through the leaves of the apple tree, played over an ordinary childhood of pets and games, uncles, aunts and grandparents, equally over him and his sisters as over a hundred children of their age and time in the town. He was sturdy and in good health. His appetite was good; his recollections and those of his sisters abounded in memories of currants, apples, pears, chocolate and hard candy, which the boys of Salem called Gibraltars. He teased his sisters, who retaliated when they were young women. He had a childhood playmate named William. When Hawthorne tossed a pet kitten over the fence, and Elizabeth told him the cat would never play with him again, he said airily, "Oh, she'll think it was William." [1]

Behind Salem there lay a long ridge, rising out of the level country like a whale's back out of a calm sea. At the base of the hill there was a lonely road, overshadowed with chestnut trees, and bordered with barberry bushes, running parallel with the towering ridge. A third of a mile along the road there was a desolate old farmhouse. A brook ran near the house. There lived Hawthorne's country cousins, with whom he often played, Mary Ann Foster and her older brother. She was two years younger than Hawthorne's baby sister Louisa, and tagged along behind the boys when they climbed the high ridge behind the house. Beside the old farmhouse there was a deep well, and Hawthorne used to peer over the curb to see his reflection in its echoing depth.

He liked his country cousin Foster. He liked to leave the crowded Manning household and, turning off on the lonely road at the base of the hill, suddenly leave the busy town behind, and find himself in a seclusion as deep and as mysterious as when his ancestor first settled in Salem. Across the brook he and his cousin built a dam, piling stones

26

and packing the crevices between them with debris, with the concentrated and purposeful labor of boyhood, until the water backed up behind it and almost overflowed the road. From time to time Amstis Foster would call out in her high, strained, sad voice. Hawthorne did not like her. She was a tall, meager, brown-faced, shriveled, elderly dame, abused and wronged by her husband without remorse or opposition. Still less did he like Benjamin Foster—an old hunk of a farmer, he called him—tough and ugly, who went barefoot and dressed in homespun. Perhaps to get away from them, the boys climbed the steep ridge of Browne's Hill. There the wind blew strongly over the remote, deserted hilltop, scarred with the ruins of some ancient excavation. The faint outlines of two connected cellars could be traced on the overgrown ground. Earth had filled them, and clusters of barberry bushes grew in them, but they were still deep enough to shelter a person from the wind. There they played, Hawthorne and his cousin, who was older than he was, and Mary Ann, until the crumbling outlines of the ruin fastened itself in his memory so vividly that thirty years later he could visualize the rooms of the house that had once stood there from the size of the cellars that remained.

He did not know why the place exercised its powerful hold on his growing imagination. The windswept hill, the antiquity of the crumbling brick foundations, the grim and isolated stone house at the base of the hill, the boy and the little girl outlined against the sea-gray sky, their voices fading faintly in the immensity of earth and air, formed an image that repeated itself again and again in his mind. No doubt he knew, in a vague, indifferent way, that Benjamin Foster deserted his lawful wife in his declining years and took himself a mistress. Around them there was an atmosphere of vice, narrowness and hardness, without grace or beauty of any kind to cover its traits with even the scantiest of foliage. The knowledge was without significance to him, except, perhaps, to add a faint glimpse of the meaning of social exclusion to the picture of the desolate farmhouse and the ruins on the hill, something to ponder, momentarily, as he looked into the deep open well at his reflection framed in the water.

No doubt he knew dimly that Benjamin Foster was a miser, who built himself a stone house solid as a strongbox. He was a usurer, lending money at exorbitant rates; and no doubt Hawthorne had a sense of the fierceness of his business in a time when half the people in jail were in jail for debt. Little Mary Ann had tuberculosis. Each year the disease gnawed deeper and deeper. Miraculously, she lived to womanhood, although he did not know it; nor did he know that the ruins on the hilltop were all that remained of a great mansion, Browne's Folly, built in 1740, famous for the balls in the great ballroom. There had always been a dream in England that the hard-working New World could become a pleasure resort. A balcony had been built around the ballroom, under the ceiling, from which the dancers could be watched, and the house, visible for miles at sea, looked out over Salem and Beverly on one side and out over the level farmlands of the interior on the other.[2]

He liked the stagecoach office and the livery stables. Stagecoaches in Salem were far more glamorous than clipper ships. During the embargo they were far more prosperous. The Boston and Salem stages, built in his grandfather's Union Street shop, were large, shiny, varnished, brightly painted and equipped with newly invented springs that made them ride better on the road and lessened the danger of upsets. One stage a day left for Boston. It went over the Essex Turnpike, through the Great Pastures, Breeds Island, the Lynn Marshes, across the Mystic River to a point near the Navy Yard. Service was constantly speeded until the Manning Stages made four round trips each day.

In his childhood, Hawthorne sat on the stoop at the stagecoach office and watched the stages arrive and depart. Even when he was sick he was bundled up and carried to the office. The art of wheeling those great vehicles, with six-foot wheels and room inside for nine passengers, always fascinated him, though curiously enough, with so much of his life spent among horses, he never drove himself. The Manning shop also built fine custom-built phaetons. The air was savory with the smell of varnish and paint, harness oil and shavings.

The Boston stage swung away from the entrance of the office, his tall, handsome uncle Richard Manning on the driver's seat, directing the four horses. There were conventions and courtesies connected with the stagecoach business that made the task of driving, impressive enough in itself, doubly impressive. Each driver was an honored figure. In Salem, where sea captains were everywhere, the names of such stagecoach families as the Potters, the Anabels, the Ackermans, Carneys, Conants, Drakes, Knights, Marshalls, Mays, Mannings, Patches, Robinsons, Shaws, Tenneys, Tozzers and Winchesters were proud ones.

The skill of the drivers in guiding the horses over the unlighted roads at night, of driving for years without overturning—the huge Eastern Stage Lines never lost a passenger—and their responsibility for their horses, the mail, and their passengers gave them a curious distinction.

They were required to be men of discretion, since they transacted business in outlying towns for the local merchants, and business in Salem for the merchants of the interior. They had to possess physical strength, courage, agility; and they had to know how to handle the horses stretching out ahead in so long a span that the very task of making the turn on to the turnpike was momentous. The horses were spirited and well kept, the equipment good, competition keen. The biggest stage line was chartered by the state, but it was a singular fact that nothing in its charter said what business it was to engage in. Profits were fabulous. Because of the curious nature of the business, the fact that originally individual owners had made short hauls from town to town, its profits were a closely guarded secret, and only a handful of men in New England participated in them. The companies were being consolidated into large organizations covering the entire area. In a few years Eastern Stage Lines owned 500 horses, turnpike, bridge and bank stocks, hotels and livery stables, and employed 150 drivers. It paid $8,000 to $9,000 a year in tolls, was free of debt and paid a semi-annual dividend of 8 per cent on stock valued at $150 a share. The Manning Lines were smaller, but no less important, and when Samuel Manning extended his line to Gloucester and Marblehead, and stages were arriving and departing from eight in the morning until eleven at night, the business was large, and an important link in New England transportation.[3]

After her husband's death, the time of the move not altogether clear, Betsey Hawthorne moved with her three children across the back yard to her father's house. His grandfather Manning, with his books, his recollections, and his humor, was Hawthorne's teacher and friend in these early years, a good, kindly man, with a vague resemblance to Samuel Johnson.[4] He had been a blacksmith and a gunsmith, as had his father, his grandfather, and his great-grandfather, back to the dim, mysterious days in 1662 when Nicholas Manning, in the *Hannah and Elizabeth*, brought a shipload of immigrants from England to Salem.[5]

Hawthorne's grandfather had a shelf of books, and from them Hawthorne learned to read. He seldom went to school. He pulled down the books from shelves that were not very high, stretching on tiptoe to reach them. Then he lay on the floor and absorbed through the pores of his mind books that were beyond his years. His favorite was Boswell's *Life of Johnson.* He did not understand it, and it was perhaps not the best reading for him—Johnson's awful fear of death was too close to the fear of death that haunted him—but the picture that he formed of Samuel Johnson in his childish imagination amused and absorbed him because it reminded him of Grandfather Manning. "I laughed at him, sometimes, standing beside his knee." [6]

Hawthorne had an ordinary childhood, except, perhaps, that after his first years so much of his life was spent among women. His early stories deal often with the rather mortifying masculine experience of encountering women whose sexual experience is greater than his own. The theme comes again and again into his work, sometimes in a comic, or at least an ironic sense, and more often with its tragic implications, setting in motion the doubts, the self-distrust and the doubts of others that may lead to tragedy. Yet coupled with this wry acknowledgment of his perennial innocence, there was a perception of feminine tenderness deeper and more poignant than that expressed by any other American writer. The sisters in *The Wives of the Dead,* Hester in *The Scarlet Letter,* the Quaker's wife in *The Gentle Boy,* the farmer's wife in *The Canterbury Pilgrims,* and the hundreds of simple women who appear in his works, working, sacrificing themselves, and making their simple statements that reveal the unconscious heroism of their lives, are a people of such purity and innocence that worldly wisdom and malicious humor are the last qualities that could be attributed to them.

At every turn in the story of Hawthorne's life one comes upon the poignant figure of his mother. In his manhood, the thought of the tragic emptiness of her life was unbearable to her son. She did nothing, nothing at all. She spent her girlhood in her father's house, married a sea captain who lived next door, and then, after his death, vanished from the world as completely as if she too had taken one of those mysterious voyages to Surinam. Except for the few years in Raymond, she lived in an upstairs room and seldom left it. Her meals were served to her there, or left outside her door on a tray. She bought no new clothes, but continued to wear the old-fashioned dresses, the costumes of before the War of 1812, that she had worn when her husband was alive. Thus she lived for forty years.[7]

Around her the household changed, her sisters and brothers grew older, her children grew older, the town of Salem changed, the ships disappeared, the stagecoaches no longer ran, and one after another of the great families that had dominated the town left it forever. From time to time her brothers sought her out, for her signature was needed on the deeds when they sold another tract of land in Maine. She left proof of her continued existence in the office of the land records of Cumberland County in Portland. There were two volumes of them. Otherwise the world might well question whether she ever had a real being, and was not an imagined figure to fulfill the requirements of the romantic story of the time.

She was twenty-eight when her husband died, though her seclusion had probably begun before. At sixty-seven she took her first meal with the family—and not with her family, but with Hawthorne, his wife and his children. Through the countless Salem mornings, cold and bitter in winter, wind-swept in the spring and warm and quiet in midsummer, she busied herself in her room, in which the even temperature of her life remained the same. It remained the same when the War of 1812 set the men of the town digging trenches in the streets.

Hawthorne spoke of her as a woman of strong will. He must have meant in the resolution of her voluntary inprisonment, for otherwise her life seems will-less. For many years she was the only member of her family to marry, as if her tragic experience had darkened the lives of all of them. She was like Hester in *The Scarlet Letter.* Her family and the community had driven her into seclusion, just as, in Hawthorne's story, Boston had forced Hester to wear the scarlet A as a badge of infamy. But as the years passed the letter ceased to be a novelty and became a familiar sight in the town, and finally it conferred a kind of distinction upon its wearer. So it was with Hawthorne's mother, and her seclusion, from being an outward sign of disgrace, became, from its unchanging quietness in the turbulent and disorderly town, a triumph.

It was the custom for the men of Salem to stand outside the insurance company offices on Essex Street and make comments on the women and the girls who passed by. The young women faced this ordeal with half-fascinated dread; if they survived the walk, all was well with them for another day.[8] Then, perhaps, the time came when they preferred to stay at home. But Betsey Hawthorne never left her room. There had no doubt been a time when she too had tried to make her way from Buffum's Corner down the narrow street, a passage more dangerous than rounding Cape Horn. When she then retired to her room, to reappear no more in the light of day, it was an end, not of her life, but of the meaning of those comments from the sidewalk. She said nothing of the men who made the remarks, or of the town.

Salem was one of the greatest ports on earth, and one of the largest cities in the country, at the time her seclusion began. Before it ended, the town was a small, seldom-used harbor, filled with odd old characters and antiquated ships crumbling into ruin at the docks. Still she remained in her upstairs room. Sometimes people caught a glimpse of her clipping roses in the garden, a sweet-faced woman wearing a sunbonnet. But they did not know whether it wasn't one of her sisters. At one time she taught Sunday School.[9] Once, it seems, she made an effort to escape Salem. Soon after her father's death, and probably with her share of the first division of his estate, she bought a farm in Bridgton, Maine, with one of her sisters. Bridgton was at the end of the earth from Salem—Raymond was remote, but Bridgton was far in the wilderness, at the opposite end of the chain of lakes. Her sister died, however, soon after the purchase, and the farm was never occupied by them.[10]

Betsey Hawthorne's sister-in-law, Rachel Forrester, still lived in her mansion on Derby Street. About the time of Hawthorne's father's death, there came into the Forrester family a character as remarkable as Simon Forrester had been when he first arrived in Salem with Captain Daniel Hawthorne. This was Charlotte Story.

Charlotte was one of the eighteen children of Dr. Elisha Story of Marblehead. She was a vivid, attractive woman who led the migration of her family from the little fishing village to the metropolis of Salem.[11] "Mrs. Forrester," said Elizabeth Hawthorne, "was a Story."[12] Charlotte Story certainly was, in more senses than one. She married John Forrester, the soberest and steadiest of Forrester's children, a lawyer and a Harvard graduate.

Soon after their marriage, her brother Joseph Story moved to Salem and opened his law office, beginning the career that led him to the Supreme Court. Story had recently graduated from Harvard, second in the class in which William Ellery Channing was first. Story was a poet, a Democrat—every other lawyer in the county was a Federalist —a scholar, and the master of a prose style that made him the greatest

writer on the law since Blackstone. He followed Jacob Crowninshield
to Congress. The Salem *Gazette* grudgingly conceded that Story was a
man of genius, and hoped that he would also be a man of independence.
He was. He began as a follower of Jefferson, but broke with Jefferson
over the embargo, finally coming to believe that Jefferson was determined to drive the country to revolution. Jefferson, in turn, detested
him, called him a pseudo Republican, and declared that he had delivered a wound to the party's interest that could never be healed.
Meanwhile Story began his lifelong work of digesting, from the confused
mass of colonial and federal and English records, the laws that were
relevant to the new nation. By the time Hawthorne was nine, Story was
one of Salem's most famous citizens. John Forrester was Hawthorne's
cousin, and he and his wife made Hawthorne welcome in their home.
Old Simon Forrester always noticed Hawthorne kindly when they met.
Hawthorne did not notice his uncle in the same spirit. Once the aging
merchant met Nathaniel and Elizabeth, stopped to talk to them, and
offered Nathaniel a five-dollar bill. Nathaniel refused it. Elizabeth
thought it was uncivil of him, and said so.

The femininity of Hawthorne's world was increased when, at the
age of nine, he injured his foot. He had been playing ball. The circumstances of the injury are vague. It was said that one foot ceased
to grow, and he was threatened with lameness. At any rate, it was
plain that he could not go to school. He was delighted, and made the
most of his mysterious ailment to stay home. Hannah Lord, the hired
girl, bundled him up and carried him out into the street. He hopped
down to the stagecoach office. One remedy attempted was to pour cold
water on his foot from an upper window.[13] The War of 1812 began,
with so close a vote in favor of the declaration of war that its very
beginning was an admission that much of the country—especially New
England—was opposed to fighting it. Hawthorne continued to stay
home from school while his stubborn ailment responded feebly to treatment. His kinspeople were Federalists, and the Federalists almost to
a man believed that "the war between us and Great Britain was undertaken to serve the interests and gratify the passions of his Imperial
and Royal Majesty of France."[14] Shipping was ruined, Salem was all
but ruined, and the country was filled with sullen and vengeful men,
as the ghastly record of American defeats, culminating in the burning
of Washington, rolled in.[15]

The British man-of-war *Shannon* lay outside Salem Harbor, capturing the ships as they tried to reach port. The captain of the *Shannon* insolently sent away his escorting warships and challenged the American frigate *Chesapeake*, lying in Boston Harbor with a semimutinous crew, to a duel; and Captain James Lawrence, who had tried to avoid being placed in command of the *Chesapeake*, refused. The *Shannon* sailed up and down the coast, capturing prizes at will. When at last Lawrence ordered the *Chesapeake* down the bay, all of coastal New England knew the duel was to be fought. When the *Chesapeake* passed the Lighthouse at 1:30 P.M. on June 1, 1813, the *Shannon* bore east southeast, six leagues distant, standing on a wind to the southward.

All of Boston that could move poured down the Essex Turnpike to see the battle—carriages, horses, and 120 stagecoaches. Crowds were swarming up the hills above Salem Harbor, until a hundred thousand people had assembled. At 3:30 the *Shannon* bore up before the wind and stood for sea. At four o'clock the *Chesapeake* hauled up and fired a gun, the ships about seven miles apart. The enemy immediately bore to, reefed his topsails, and lay by on the starboard tack, the *Chesapeake* in close. At 4:30 the wind changed to a fresh breeze, south southwest. The *Chesapeake* took in topgallant sails and royals, and hoisted the American flag at the main topgallant masthead. At 5:30 the *Shannon* hoisted jib and filled the main topsail and steered close by the wind. The *Chesapeake* was on the enemy's weather quarter, standing toward him, about three miles distant. At 5:45 the *Chesapeake* hauled her foresails, closing fast with the enemy.

At five minutes before six, the enemy commenced the action. The *Shannon* fired her aftergun on the starboard side. The shot was returned by the *Chesapeake*. The action became general. At five minutes after six, the *Chesapeake*, being on the starboard bow of the enemy, bore down across his hawse and appeared to board him. Both ships kept away before the wind. The firing ceased from the great guns. At ten minutes past six there appeared to be a great explosion from the quarter-deck of the *Chesapeake*. At fifteen minutes past six the ships separated, the *Chesapeake* on the starboard tack. The English flag was hoisted aboard her, over the American.

The crowds climbed silently down the hill in the summer twilight as the British ship and the defeated American sailed out of harbor to Halifax. The carriages and coaches again covered the turnpike to

Boston, fleeing a visible manifestation of British power and British dramatic genius. Probably no more effective scene in psychological warfare was ever staged. There had never been a possibility of American victory. Half the crew of the *Chesapeake*, when the *Shannon*'s men boarded her, remained below decks and refused to fight, though the ships drifted apart in the fighting and their resistance could have overwhelmed the small British boarding party that was cut off as the ships separated and endangered by the musket fire from the *Shannon*. Lawrence's tragic cry—"Don't give up the ship! Blow her up!"—lived in history with the second phrase forgotten. He died of his wounds on the way to Halifax, and his body was returned to Salem under a flag of truce, and buried with honors, Story delivering the oration, though much of the frightened town refused to attend the service.[16]

Henry Wadsworth Longfellow in Portland, whose family also was Federalist, had a similar mysterious foot ailment at the same time, and was left indoors. Hawthorne had another reason to remain secluded. On April 17, 1813, his grandfather, Richard Manning, set out for Raymond, Maine. He was fifty-nine years old and in perfect health when he left his family. He reached Newbury, twenty-odd miles away, and remained there over Sunday, the following day. A famous chain bridge crossed the Merrimack River at Deer Island, connecting Newbury with Salisbury on the opposite side. Stone piers were built at the edge of the river and upon them wooden towers carried the chain, with links twelve inches long and three or four inches wide, high in the air. There was a lodging at Deer Island in midstream. Hawthorne's grandfather spent the night of April 18, 1813, there. He was found dead in his bed in the morning.

The same day, in Salem, Hawthorne's grandmother Hawthorne died.[17]

II

Richard Manning's estate was not divided at his death. His widow, Miriam, was administratrix. The sons managed the property. Robert Manning went to Raymond and began building a large, square, high-roofed farmhouse beside Dingley Brook.

In the fall of 1813, Dr. Gideon Barstow became Hawthorne's physician.[18] Dr. Barstow was a young, affable doctor, who had married, in 1812, Nancy Forrester. She was one of Simon's younger daughters, only nineteen at the time of her marriage. Gideon Barstow did not practice for very long. Simon Forrester made handsome property settlements on his daughters, usually giving them a house when they married, and Barstow, who was a merchant, eventually dropped medicine entirely and became a shipowner, entered politics, and became a congressman.[19]

It was probably at this time that Hawthorne's habits of reading were formed and his taste for a solitary life—or a life, at any rate, in the semiseclusion of his grandmother's home. In those days it was unusual for anyone whose family had any means at all to attend a public school, except in the country. There were four public schools in Salem, with 465 boys and 295 girls, the girls attending an hour at noon and another in the afternoon, but education for children of the position of the Hawthornes was almost always private.[20] The public schools were sometimes rough, and the private schools varied according to the ability and experience of the teacher. It was not unusual that Hawthorne was educated at home.

He had, however, a teacher of remarkable qualities. Young Joseph Worcester had recently graduated from Yale and opened a school in Salem. Tall and thin, absent-minded and preoccupied, he was an innate conservative to whom the innovations in education that were sweeping the country were fundamentally wrong. Just as Joseph Story, in his alarm at Jefferson's disregard for the great inheritance of English common law, set himself to winnowing the records, so Worcester set himself to write a dictionary which would preserve the richness and succulence of the English language for American scholars. It became his lifework.[21] Webster's spare, terse, rigorous dictionary was popular with the mass of the population, but Worcester's became the book on which New England's men of letters depended. It was symbolic that Hawthorne studied under a man to whom English words were like precious heirlooms of inestimable value, each to be polished and weighed, treasured as long as it had meaning, tested and applied, savored and perhaps slightly changed, and discarded reluctantly, only when it no longer had any usefulness or use. The upholders of such convictions were not popular. They were considered aligned with treasonable activities. Sometimes they were. Traitors, however, were not usually men of such character; and the hatred of England threw a shadow over their work, whatever its quality and however self-sacrificing. It may have been significant that Worcester came to the Manning house after dark to hear Hawthorne's lessons.

Dr. Barstow ceased to treat Hawthorne's ailment, and Dr. Kitteredge became his physician. Kitteredge's politics may be inferred from the fact that he was the Reverend Mr. Bentley's physician. Reverend Bentley was a dogmatic and spiteful politician, and a source, it seems, of much of the distrust that was felt in Washington about Salem. Bentley was an anonymous contributor to the Democratic *Essex Register*. When the *Register* called the venerable Timothy Pickering a traitor, Pickering sued for libel in an attempt to discover who had written the article. Bentley was summoned as a witness. He refused to appear. He wrote to Washington, asking for the help of the Attorney General, who, however, advised him to attend the trial. Reverend Bentley then got a certificate of inability from Dr. Kitteredge and did not testify. The medical certificate was challenged. "Bentley's defense was pretty thin," but he never testified, and the printer of the paper went to jail and the authorship of the libelous article was never revealed.[22]

Hawthorne was still kept out of school. He now had no inclination to go to school at all, and would never have been educated had his mother not persevered, behind an apparent indifference and helplessness, in a determination that he should be educated. Her first plan to move to Bridgton ended when, on May 20, 1814, a year and a month after Richard Manning's death, her sister Maria died.[23] She was buried in Richard Manning's tomb in the Howard Street cemetery, the second body to be placed there.[24] It was impossible for Hawthorne's mother to go to Bridgton alone, and the farm was sold. Robert Manning was now completing the Manning house in Raymond. It was the largest in the village, and was called Manning's Folly by the townspeople. It was Before it was completed, Robert Manning began another house across Dingley Brook for Mrs. Hawthorne and her children. Work was started about 1814, but the house was still unfinished four years later, a huge, plain, grim-looking farmhouse.

In Salem, Hawthorne was still under the doctor's care. A new family had moved into Union Street in 1812. It was that of Dr. Nathaniel Peabody, a doctor and dentist. He was a Federalist, and a new member

of the Essex Lodge of Freemasons.[25] He was reportedly a graduate of
Dartmouth, though Joseph Barlow, who graduated from Dartmouth
in 1813 and started a school in Salem, did not list him as such.[26] Dr.
Peabody then had five children, three daughters and two sons. His oldest
daughter, Elizabeth, was the same age as Hawthorne. She was a playmate of Elizabeth Hawthorne, and often noticed the young brother
who became her father's patient. The third Peabody daughter, Sophia,
was then five years old, and was destined to become, when she grew up,
Hawthorne's wife.

Dr. Peabody failed to help Hawthorne; it was, observed Elizabeth
Hawthorne, Dr. Time who finally cured him. When Nathaniel was twelve
or thirteen years old he again started school. During the play hour he
went into the schoolroom to declaim. He got on the platform to speak
one of the high-flown exercises in rhetoric that were then a part of the
education of youth. The older boys ridiculed him and pulled him down,
and so enraged and mortified him that he refused thereafter to speak
even when the rules of the school required him to do so.[27]

It was soon after this that Mrs. Hawthorne moved with her family
to Raymond, with every intention, it seemed, of never again returning
to Salem. The house she was to live in was unfurnished, and she stayed
with Elizabeth, Nathaniel and Maria Louisa in the home of a tenant
farmer on the property. The period that they were now entering was
the happiest that the children had ever known. They had no schooling
and apparently no friends, but no duties either, and Mrs. Hawthorne
let them run, as free as the birds of the air.

All their lives the children treasured the memory of their days in
Maine. Dingley Brook flowed beside the house, a swift and powerful,
noisy stream, flowing a rocky mile from Thomas Pond back in the hills
to Sebago Lake, and turning Jacob Dingley's grist mill in its descent
over a fifteen-foot falls. At their very door the smooth expanse of
Sebago Lake spread out, lying at the base of the mountains. The woods
were full of game, deer, wildfowl, and even bear, one of which Nathaniel
followed one time on a solitary walk in the woods. Nathaniel had a gun,
as was fitting for the grandson of a gunsmith, perhaps a gift from his
uncle Richard, who collected guns. It was an old fowling piece, and he
learned to shoot. He went for endless rambles with Elizabeth into the
forest. She loved to walk; all her life she was outdoors whenever she

could be, and she walked rapidly, her eyes eager and alert for the sights along the way. There was something moving in the picture of the children's vanishing into the wilderness that reached in an almost unbroken expanse of green for three thousand miles to the west. They would never have returned to civilization if the choice had been left to them.

Hawthorne would never have written a line. And yet the life that he treasured was not easy. The country was raw and rough, with the emptiness and desolation of land that is being logged over. Their house was not very comfortable; food was not plentiful; the farm was still being cleared; the winters were intensely cold and fearfully dangerous. Their neighbors, the Tarboxes, froze to death that first winter in Raymond. They ran out of provisions during a blizzard and the father of the family, struggling toward town, was caught in the drifting snow and died. His wife, trying to rescue him, died beside his body. Hawthorne's uncle Richard and his wife adopted their child, little Betsey Tarbox.

The cold descended on the frontier country with the force of a storm on the coast. The long chain of lakes reaching into the interior grew motionless and glassy as the ice formed over them, a broad, level deserted highway that reached into the heart of the forest. Hawthorne skated over the lakes, mile after mile through the enchanted forest, with the shadow of the great hills on either hand. When he grew tired he would take refuge in one of the rough cabins, set in a ragged clearing, beside the lake.[28]

The fact that he did so was in itself an admission that he was now in friendly country. The Mannings still owned much of this land. They were selling it piecemeal, the whole 12,000 acres, in 100-acre lots. The cabins were the homes of the purchasers. They were roughly constructed. Beyond Raymond, with its store and grist mill and cluster of houses, there were miles without a dwelling, or even a fence, and the whole face of nature was as uncultivated as when none but the Indian ranged through its wilds. In places the land was burned over, and the bare and barkless trees, rising a hundred feet above the ground, presented an aspect of inconceivable desolation. Where the fire had not reached, and logging had not begun, the forest of majestic pines rose upon the view, lifting their evergreen heads to the skies, and within them, at intervals of a few miles, were the log cabins of the settlers.

In the towns, even in the wilderness, the houses were neat, painted, and with Venetian blinds in their windows; but these forest cabins, thirty feet square, of unhewn logs dovetailed at the ends, and a huge fireplace making one wall, were as primitive as the first houses that Governor Endicott and his men built when they landed in Salem. It was indicative of the depths of the forest gloom that the clearing around such a cabin was known as an opening.[29] It was a revelation of the loneliness of the life in them that Nathaniel knew, as he took off his skates and approached the cabin, that he would be sure of a welcome. A great fire roared in the fireplace, and he rested beside it, watching the sparks ascending the open chimney, through which he could see the stars in the darkening sky.

He read a great deal in those solitary days, especially *Pilgrim's Progress* and Shakespeare and any poetry or light books that he could find. Elizabeth Hawthorne, with her precocious skill, wrote before her brother did, and published her works in the Maine newspapers, not quite then, but within a few years, and probably wrote with Nathaniel in this first winter of freedom in Maine. Richard Manning probably gave Hawthorne a notebook in which to keep a diary.[30] He was operating the village store in Raymond. He married Susan Dingley, the daughter of the first settler in the town, but their marriage was childless, and her young brother Jacob lived with them, and, after the death of her parents, Betsey Tarbox. Richard Manning operated the stage line between Raymond and the coast. He became justice of the peace, a post of honor; and the village storekeeper in those days was ordinarily the best informed man in the town, his opinion sought by the state and even the national politicians on the issues that faced the country. Richard Manning was a keen businessman, very dignified, and at the height of his prosperity kept servants and lived in considerable luxury. Now he still drove the stage up the long hill outside Raymond.[31]

The weather cleared; the ice broke up on Sebago Lake; the snow disappeared from Lymington Mountain. By the middle of May the garden was planted, the grass and trees green, and the roads good. For Nathaniel the fresh air and the exultant life riveted him to the countryside, and filled his memory with its images: the rough bark rubbing off the logs as they jammed together in the log rafts on the lake; the wildfowl breaking the smooth surface of the water as they ascended into the air; the miry roads where the wagons passed and the teamsters stopped to talk. In the summer he hunted and fished. He swam in Crooked River until one of the neighbor boys was drowned there, and his mother forbade him to swim its swift current. The passive and rather shrinking quality of his days in Salem vanished; he learned to skate, to fish and swim, to shoot partridges and hen hawks, to work in the garden for his mother, making up in a year for the years of insulated life among his kinspeople in the port.[32]

By and by his mother began to think that something else was necessary for her boy. Had the choice been left to Hawthorne, he would no doubt have lived happily the rest of his days in Raymond, or at least until Raymond grew more civilized, when he would have moved again into the western wilderness, perfectly content to fish and hunt, read and observe, and indolently let the days go by—"that sweet, bewitching, enervating indolence which is better, after all, than most of the enjoyments within mortal grasp,"[33] and whose delights he always tended to rate highly, if not to exaggerate.

He was now fourteen, and if he had followed the tradition of his father and grandfather he would have gone to sea at this age. The year in Raymond had given him good health that never left him until his old age. He was tall and rather slender, with the dark hair and gray eyes that were so remarkable in his mother and sister. His forehead was high and his nose straight, his lips firm and his features memorable for their clear symmetry. His complexion was fair. A boyish evasiveness was his outstanding characteristic, a tendency to find his own amusements and keep his own counsel, select his own reading and choose his own companions—or, more often, no companion at all—and to resist those disciplines which ran counter to his choices not so much by outright opposition as by warily gliding into the thickets of reserve like an Indian hiding in the underbrush until Braddock's columns of redcoats had passed. The evasiveness was in part laziness, a knowledge that he was loved and indulged in; and in part a deeper wisdom, a husbanding of resources, and an instinctive rejection of the careers and the way of life that his kinspeople were planning for him. The hopes and aspirations that were placed on him were more than he wanted to carry; yet he absorbed the conviction of his kinspeople that some great future was prepared for him, and he rejected their plans, not because he felt unequal to the task of fulfilling them but because he sensed that their standards of achievement and their local prides and ambitions were those of a world that had ceased to exist.

The first school selected for him was the Reverend Caleb Bradley's at Stroudwater. His house stood at a crossroads on the main road between Portland and Boston, a few miles from where the road to Raymond and the west branched off. In the winter, caravans of sleighs from beyond the Notch of the White Mountains in New Hampshire, hundreds of them, passed on that road, laden with produce for Portland.[34] Bradley's house was a large, square, two-storied white house, one of the best in the village, hip-roofed, with six windows across the upper floor in front and four along the sides. There was a picket fence before it, and three elms in the yard. The front door was in the middle of the house, and the stairs were directly inside the door. There was a step down into the kitchen, which was lower than the rest of the house. A large barn stood behind the house, for Parson Bradley's land enclosed a considerable farm. The land lay in gently rising ground near the Fore and Stroudwater rivers. By common usage the crossroads was known as Bradley's Corner.[35]

Hawthorne's room was directly above the parlor. The schoolroom was a separate building, a single room about eighteen by twenty-five feet, attached to the eastern wall of the house.[36] Hawthorne's room was cold and drafty. His mother had returned to Salem; home was a hundred miles away. Parson Bradley was a strange and eccentric character, with a perpetual scowl and an expression of sour distaste on his heavily jowled features.[37] He was born in Dracut, near the New Hampshire state line, on March 12, 1772. His father was a farmer. Dracut was remarkable for its Democratic majority, one of the highest, if not the highest, in the state—13 Federalists to 145 Democrats.[38] Caleb Bradley attended Dartmouth, left, entered Harvard, and was found after examination to be deficient in Latin. He was enrolled and graduated from Harvard in 1795.[39] He was ordained in Stroudwater in 1799, the previous minister, Brown, having died the year before. Bradley preached there for thirty years, marrying 550 couples and conducting the services at 1,400 funerals. He married three times, his first wife, Sally Crocker, bearing him ten children, four of whom died in infancy, and one, his son Edward, who grew to manhood and died at sea. Parson Bradley kept a diary. At the time that Hawthorne studied in his school he was forty-six, irascible, contentious, filling his notebooks with lamentations on the triumphs of the Democrats and grim notations on his small congregations ("preached to thirteen hearers") and the low state of morals in the community.[40]

It was said that a hogshead of rum a day was consumed at Stroudwater. The town had passed through its greatest prosperity, when there were nineteen ships on the ways, and through its deepest depression, during the years of the embargo, when ships rotted at the wharves. It was now flourishing and settled, with its sawmills, its grist mill, and the tanneries near the parsonage. A mill for grinding gypsum from Nova Scotia stood at the water's edge, the gypsum lifted to the upper floor by tidewater power. There was a considerable business in collecting black grass, a mosslike grass which grew on the tideflat and was valued by the farmers as winter feed for their cattle. The streets in the better part of town were paved with tanbark. It was bark of hickory, used in tanning hides, and ground to a powdery consistency. The wicked part of town was called the Holy Land. It stood below Pork Hill, on the opposite side from Saccarappa Village, covered over with a thick layer of "the mildew of depravity."

On the opposite side of the road from Bradley's house, and about half a mile east, stood Broad's Tavern. The stagecoaches from Boston to Portland had been speeded constantly until the run was now made in one day; but it became the custom for travelers to stop at Broad's Tavern overnight, rest and enter Portland refreshed on the next morning.

The townsmen—the Means, Smiths, Jordons, Knights, Ilseys, Starbirds, Winslows, Prebles, Tukys, Frosts, Haskells, Hunts, Brewers, Dales, Conants, Riggses, Titcombs, Porterfields, Seals—were well-to-do, deliberate, deeply rooted in their own community, and yet somehow seeming, through family ties or close connections with people in politics, to exercise some influence in state and national affairs far beyond their personal fame or the importance of their town. Reverend Bradley's diary noted their services to him: how they shoveled the snow from his door after a snowstorm, and how they hauled nine loads of slabs from the sawmill for his winter firewood—"gratis except for Mark Haskell." Once he recorded that forty men and sixty oxen worked through the afternoon getting in his hay; and on another day "Some person broke into my house this afternoon and took away a decanter partly filled with rum. A villain." Parson Bradley was very fond of rum and pretty young women. There was a considerable change in opinion of him in

Stroudwater as the years went by, from the time, in 1801, when his parishioners hauled his firewood, to the day, twenty years later, when the church tax was repealed and a large part of the congregation immediately withdrew from the church. His diary for the year when Hawthorne was his student is lost, if he ever kept it, and the only surviving story of him and Hawthorne is that he told Hawthorne that he would never amount to anything in any genteel calling, and had better go back to Raymond and raise potatoes.[41]

But Hawthorne was again under discipline, and he rebelled. Richard Manning was responsible for his studying at Bradley's, for his wife's brother, young Jacob Dingley, was a student there with Hawthorne. On his part Hawthorne never mentioned the old pastor in his occasional recollections of his early life, or his study in Stroudwater in his account of his education. He did write two stories based on his winter there, or, more exactly, one story and a biographical article about one of Parson Bradley's ancestors. Both he published anonymously. Bradley's great-grandmother was Hannah Duston, of whom every New Englander had heard in childhood, who was captured by Indians when her youngest child was only a week old. Her baby was killed before her eyes, but her husband and seven of the children escaped. Hannah Duston was a woman of tremendous courage and of a cunning greater than that of the redskins. She endured her captivity passively, while the Indians led her a hundred miles into the forest toward Canada. One night she stole a tomahawk while the Indians slept. She killed them all. With foresight, even in such a moment of tension, so great that Hawthorne thought of her as an awful woman, she scalped ten of them, and returned to civilization, where she collected bounties on their scalps.[42]

III

In January Hawthorne returned to Raymond. He had not written once since he went to school. Robert Manning was now living in the Raymond farm, and from this time on took an active part in planning where and when Nathaniel should be educated. He first enrolled in the school at Raymond. On March 9, 1819, Robert Manning wrote to Betsey Hawthorne: "In three weeks more his term will be out—doleful complaints no mama to take care of him, what shall I do with him when he comes. I think of sending him to Salem."

Robert Manning, however, returned to Salem, and Nathaniel remained in Raymond, where, presently, Mrs. Hawthorne and Maria Louisa joined him. At the end of April Richard reported to his brother: "I have no chance to send Nathaniel, nor is he willing to come to Salem. Mrs. Hawthorne and Maria have been unwell, but have got better." Hawthorne was busy with his mother's farm. By the middle of May, he wrote, the garden was planted. He was sorry that Robert Manning had decided to send him to school, and wrote that his mother needed him to help her.[43]

If he hoped by this appeal, and a pleasant account of Raymond life, to be allowed to remain there he was disappointed: Robert Manning went to Raymond, and Hawthorne, in the middle of June, was sent to Salem. On July 5, 1819, one day after his fifteenth birthday, he was enrolled as a student in Samuel Archer's school on Marlborough Street. Archer was a distant relative of Hawthorne's. His aunt Judith, who married Captain George Archer, had three children, about the age of the Hawthorne children. The Samuel Archer who taught school was their third cousin.[44]

Summer life in Salem was so different from winter it might almost have been, not another season, but another country. A winter day began at seven-thirty; a summer day began at six. On a winter morning the bedrooms were at the freezing point, ice in the water pitchers, unmelted frost on the windows. A roaring fire, with backlog, backstick and forestick, split wood and cut stick, chips for kindling, and big bellows to blow the flame; breakfast at eight, hot bread cakes, rye griddle cakes, Indian-meal johnnycakes, smoking from its board, or drop cakes baked on the floor of the oven; coffee; spread or dip toast; milk and honey for the children. Coffee was a licensed drink, as dyspepsia was an unacknowledged sin. Breakfast over, the children's next duty was to fit themselves for the outside world: wadded hoods, long tippets, knit mittens, carpet moccasins, woolen overcoats, for the girls; greased boots, ugly beaver hats, or knit caps shaped like a pudding bag, for the boys. Then came the fun of sliding in the wide gutter all the way to school, or plodding through deep snowbanks which buried them up to their heads. "Only boys were permitted by public opinion to drag sleds, and the sole girl who dared to do so was called Tom-boy by way of showing the superior good manners of the numerous critics." Dinner was at one o'clock. The Federalists served the pudding first, then the meat. The

Democrats began with the meat. Since the children had to be back in school at one, there was no dessert, and fruit was disposed of at odd seasons. Tea was at six, and after the "second girl" cleared the table, the children surrounded it, with books, work, games, slates, pencils, and a dish of rosy apples—the light did not shine on distant corners—and at ten the winter's day was ended.

But in summer—"happy were the little feet that walked in Salem, free to wander up and down the shady streets, out in the green lanes and through the trim gardens." Early in May the andirons, shovels and tongs were relegated to the garret, the woolen clothes given away or shut up in spare closet drawers, and the daughters made happy in new calicoes for school and white cambrics for Sunday, or wretched in last summer's dresses with a tuck let down. The hen-tailor, Martha Stevens, came to fit new clothes on the boys, and the sight of her pressboard and the smell of her hot iron were an abomination to the girls. Their dressmaker was Sally Floyd, with a quaint little figure, neat as a Quakeress, with smooth gray hair and a turban; she did not know that her admirable, simple, well-fitted little dresses were fifty years in advance of the styles. There were gardens to play in, full of sweet william, pinks, bluebells, larkspur, hyacinth, and periwinkles. Marianne Silsbee ran home one afternoon to tell her family breathlessly that she had seen a pretty lady dressed in a green silk gown, and that she looked just like a rose in its green leaves.[45]

As Hawthorne started school, a struggle, lasting almost twenty years, began between him and Robert Manning. It raged and subsided irregularly, with long periods of armistice followed by renewed quarrels as Hawthorne fought against some plan Robert Manning had made for him. There was always something weary about Hawthorne's attempts to frustrate Uncle Robert, a gloomy foreknowledge that, even if he won, Uncle Robert would immediately reappear with some plan equally forbidding. Besides, he seldom won. They slept together. Hawthorne dreamed he was walking beside Lake Sebago, and was so angry when he awakened and found it a delusion that he gave Uncle Robert a horrible kick— an accident that seemed to cause him some satisfaction. If recurring phrases and metaphors are a useful revelation of a great writer's character, the most frequent line in Hawthorne's early writing was "Don't show this to Uncle Robert."[46]

Elizabeth Hawthorne, with her gift for precision, summed up the difficulty concisely when she wrote, in her old age, that they were much happier in Raymond but that "by some fatality we all seemed to be brought back to Salem, in spite of our intentions and even resolutions." The will that was stronger than theirs was the will of Robert Manning, and yet not so much his alone as the will of the other sisters in the Manning family exercised through him. He had great influence with Betsey Hawthorne, yet he seems not to have used it unless his sisters Mary and Priscilla Miriam persuaded him to do so. He was perhaps a vain man, beneath a quiet and retiring exterior. He had a profound conviction of his rightness, and a low opinion of Hawthorne's character and ability, which he did not conceal from him or from others. Yet he was also extremely sensitive, intellectually resourceful, and moved by a genuine affection for his sister and her children, and perhaps by a deeper perception of what was best for them than Hawthorne ever credited him with.

Robert Manning started, in Salem, the first pomological gardens in America for the identification of fruits. He began modestly, without special equipment and with no facilities for research, but in time had set out two thousand varieties of fruit trees in Salem. He was deeply interested in the Raymond farm. Butternut trees and an orchard were planted beside the house. Louisa Hawthorne had goats, which were kept on an island in Sebago Lake after one of them tried to kill her. There was a flower garden, a vegetable garden, sheep, pigs, chickens, and a cow. Robert Manning had begun to plant pear trees there. Eventually his orchard contained a thousand varieties of pear trees. He planted five hundred apple trees, cherry trees, peach trees, and plum trees. While Samuel Manning ran the stagecoach business, which had now grown extensive, and Richard Manning ran the Raymond store, Robert Manning experimented with cherry trees, developing a new type of cherry which bore his name. He began to exchange seeds and cuttings with European growers, who sent him species unknown to America, to study the horticultural journals, and to work in his orchard until it became the largest in the country and larger than all but a few in Europe.[47]

The arrangement of the lives of the Hawthorne children, however, for which he must be considered at least partially responsible, was always a little wrong. They were sent to Raymond in the winter, and the winters there were deadly cold, and returned to Salem in the summer, though the summers at Raymond were delightful and the town became, eventually, a summer resort. Their lives were choppy and disorganized; Nathaniel was in Raymond while the family was in Salem, and in Salem while his mother and sisters were in Maine. The children had almost no opportunity to form lasting connections with boys and girls their own age. They adjusted themselves to Salem only to be sent to Raymond; when they were comfortably established in Raymond they were moved back to Salem. Meanwhile the years passed and the girls grew older; when Nathaniel saw his sister Elizabeth, after this long separation, he did not recognize her.[48]

Time has rubbed smooth the rough discomforts of that age, a process aided by the fact that the truth had a poignancy too keen for the imagination to linger over it. It was true, as Hawthorne's closest friend observed, that in the long run the world owed a debt to Robert Manning, though perhaps it was not so much the world as Bowdoin and New England, and of them, only a part. But the day-by-day life of the children has in retrospect an unforgettable sadness. They survived, and within limits they developed their powers, but no one can read the fragmentary writings of the girls without a conviction that they could have done much more; or study the devotion they lavished on their brother without regretting that they did not have families of their own to fulfill the gift they were endowed with. All that they had was a close-knit family life, and it was this which was being shattered in the constant moves they were compelled to make.

When Hawthorne was older it seemed to him that nothing was more touching and beautiful than the care of poor children for children still younger—"the superintendence which some of these small people (too small, one would think, to be sent into the street alone, had there been any other nursery for them) exercised over still smaller ones. Whence they derived such a sense of duty, unless immediately from God, I cannot tell; but it was wonderful to observe the expression of responsibility in their deportment, the anxious fidelity with which they discharged their unfit office, the tender patience with which they linked their less pliant impulses to the wayward footsteps of an infant, and let it guide them withersoever it liked.

"In the hollow-cheeked, large-eyed girl of ten, whom I saw giving such cheerless oversight to her baby brother, I did not so much marvel at it. She had merely come a little earlier than usual to the perception of what was to be her business in life. But I admired the sickly-looking little boy, who did violence to his boyish nature by making himself the servant of his little sister—she too small to walk and he too small to take her in his arms—and therefore working a kind of miracle to transport her from one dirt heap to another. Beholding such works of love and duty, I took heart again, and deemed it not so impossible, after all, for these neglected children to find a path through the squalor and evil of their circumstances up to the gate of heaven . . . Yet sometimes again I saw, with surprise and a sense as if I had been asleep and dreaming, the bright, intelligent, merry face of a child whose dark eyes gleamed with vivacious expression through the dirt that encrusted its skin, like sunshine struggling through a very dusty window-pane." [49]

Hawthorne made these observations of children he saw in the streets of London, but they might have been applied to him and his sisters in their own childhood. The large-eyed, hollow-cheeked girl of ten who had come earlier than usual to what was to be her business in life might have been Elizabeth; the sickly looking little boy might have been himself in his care for Maria Louisa. She was herself a child whose bright, intelligent, merry face gleams with a vivacious expression through the dull records of the years. Between her and Robert Manning there was an affection as deep as the hostility between Hawthorne and his uncle. She wrote to him of the trees and bushes at the farm, of the cow who had got a pretty calf, and of her flower garden: "The first of the month we had pretty flowers and the trees are most leaved out. I should like to have a dark gown fit to wear every day. Elizabeth wishes hers light . . ." [50]

Through the winter of 1819-1820, Nathaniel remained in Salem, attending school. The separation at least compelled him to write letters, some of which have been preserved. He was full of scraps of poetry; he could not keep it out of his brain:

> *Oh earthly pomp is but a dream*
> *And like a meteor's short-lived gleam . . .*

He complained that he was now going to a five-dollar school, when he had once been to a ten-dollar one.

> *And all the sons of glory soon*
> *Will rest beneath the mouldering stone.*

He read constantly, the Waverley Novels, the *Mysteries of Udolpho*, the *Arabian Nights*, and wrote love songs:

> *Oh do not bid me part from thee,*
> *For I will leave thee never,*
> *Although thou throwest thy scorn on me*
> *Yet I will love forever* . . . [51]

Hawthorne wrote verse with remarkable facility, and ridiculed it. In Raymond his mother and sister were sick with colds. Wild animals crossed the ice to the islands in Sebago Lake and killed Louisa's goats. In the spring Robert Manning and Mary Manning visited Raymond, and stayed two months. Hawthorne was left behind in Salem.

This was perhaps the turning point in his relationship with his Manning relatives. After two months, when Robert and Mary Manning returned to Salem, they brought his sister Maria Louisa with them. The trip took three days. They got to Saco the first night, Greenland the second, and Salem the third day about two o'clock. Rain drenched their clothes before they got to Portland, and Louisa "was a little stuffed for two or three nights and that was all." Hawthorne was overjoyed to see his sister. She wrote gravely to her mother: "Nathaniel has not laughed at me or pestered me more than once or twice since I came here." Simultaneously, the Forrester sisters—Mrs. Carlisle and Mrs. Barstow and Mrs. Charlotte Story Forrester—became interested in Maria Louisa.

She was astonishingly acute. She had the gift, more common to innocence than to maturity, of relating all essential information in the midst of apparent irrelevancies, and the freedom and grace in expression, and the unconcern with formal rules, that is the mark of a born writer: she wrote the way children dance. "*How does the kitten do are the chickens well has my hen hatched out yet do my flowers grow well have any more of them come up,*" she wrote breathlessly. "Hannah had a tooth out this morning and a piece of the jawbone came out with it it hurt very much. I am going to Mr. Dike's store today with Mary to be weighed." [52]

Several times a week she went to Mr. Tucker's dancing school, which Nathaniel also attended; dancing was an indispensable accomplishment in Salem. Dancers danced in those days, said Marianne Silsbee, and it would not be easy for even an active imagination to picture

NATHANIEL HAWTHORNE
Born July 4, 1804; died May 18, 1864. *(Essex Institute)*

HAWTHORNE'S BIRTHPLACE

"A considerable amount of Salem history, and an immense amount of Salem wealth, was concentrated in this inconspicuous dwelling." *(Essex Institute)*

CAPTAIN DANIEL HAWTHORNE
Born 1732; died April 19, 1796.
(Essex Institute)

SIMON FORRESTER
Born May 10, 1748; died July 5,
1817.

"Fierce, determined, industrious,
passionate and wilful."—Reverend
Bentley

"His career was honorable and his
liberality conspicuous."—Marianne
Silsbee *(Essex Institute)*

the agility and dexterity with which feet and legs were used. Young gentlemen occasionally bounded into the chairs, and the pirouettes, flicflacs, and pigeonwings introduced into the perpetual motion of an old-fashioned contradance made a sight worth seeing. A dance was a contradance when it was not a reel; a voluntary was one for which the gentlemen were at liberty to draw their partners; a draw-dance was a sort of lottery—the ladies and gentlemen each had numbers, and might or might not be especially pleased with their luck. Dances all voluntary was not a very judicious arrangement for Salem. Usually there were draw-dances to begin the evening: the manager called, "Number one, a lady," and number one took her place at the head of the room, a little anxious about "number one, a gentleman," who on being summoned took his stand opposite the lady, and soon the lines were filled. At a stamp of that trimly dressed foot the music struck up, and away went the head couple.[53]

When school was over, Louisa visited her cousin Nancy, Dr. Barstow's wife. Nancy Forrester Barstow had three young sons. Or she went to Mrs. Carlisle's, whose third child, and first son, Thomas, was born July 6, 1819. Or she called on Aunt Ruth Hawthorne, her father's sister, with her school friend Abigail Moriarty for a companion. Saturday nights she bathed in Abigail's bathing tub—"it is a very large one." She took her dancing lessons seriously, and seemed to Nathaniel to be constantly putting on stately airs and making curtsies. Robert Manning wrote to her mother that it was "much time and money lost to no good purpose I fear—however I always find fault."

It was almost two years since Hawthorne had seen his mother. His repeated warnings in his letters home, that what he wrote should not be shown to the Mannings, at last seemed to have influence with her, for she wrote to Louisa, rather sadly, addressing the letter to him, "Dear Maria, I am glad you find time to write to us, I think with your two schools and visiting your time must be very much taken up. Aunt Mary says you are a pretty good girl. I hope you will endeavor to assist her with all your power, make as little trouble as possible with your clothes, you must visit upon Grandmamma whenever you are at home, and be kind and obliging to all your friends do not exert yourself too much with dancing. If you do not belong entirely to Aunt Mary you must obey her as you would a mother . . ."[54]

Through the summer Nathaniel printed out by hand, neatly, a

little family newspaper, the *Spectator*, full of essays and poems, family jokes, news of the arrival of kittens, and letters of appreciation to the editor. It was probably written for Louisa. When he was twelve he had spent his afternoons teaching her to read. The *Spectator* was written with a Chineselike patience and craftsmanship, the letters neatly formed, the margins even, and the make-up a professional imitation of the *Gazette*. Hawthorne caught the tone of the *Gazette*'s essay to perfection. "I remember when I was a School boy," he wrote, in a wise, sixteen-year-old's observations *On Courage*, "being somewhat disconcerted by the horrours of a battle of snow-balls, I blundered into the Enemy's ranks. No sooner did I discover my mistake than I rectified it with the greatest possible speed, and on my return to my own party, was greeted with ill-deserved praise, for daring to venture into the very middle of the dreaded Foe . . ."

Or he discoursed *On Wealth:* "When I was a boy I one day made an inroad into a closet, the secret recesses of which I had often wished to penetrate. I there discovered a quantity of very fine apples. At first I determined to take only one, which I put in my pocket. But those which remained were so very inviting, that it was against my conscience to leave them, and I filled all my pockets and departed, wishing that they would hold more. But alas! An apple which was unable to find space among its companions, bounced down upon the floor, before all the family. I was immediately searched, and forced, very unwillingly, to deliver up all my Booty." [55]

Both Nathaniel and Louisa were going to summer school. There was no school on Wednesday and Saturday afternoons. The boys ran through town and watched the sailors leaning on the old spiked cannon on Derby Street. Their favorite haunt was the Neck. It was just one country mile—a country mile was a mile that seemed longer than an ordinary mile—from Buffum's corner in town to the Neck Gate. The gate was closed in the morning when the cattle were led out to pasture in the fields beside the bay. Beyond the Neck lay Winter Island, connected by a causeway. Fort Pickering stood on Winter Island, crumbling to ruins, and on the Neck was the poorhouse, with its red brick walls. A hermit had dug a cave, with several rooms in it, into the cliff near by.

Colonel John Hawthorne lived in his mansion far out on the Neck, beside the cool, fresh, spray-wet shore. Currants grew in profusion around the dooryard, and he let the boys eat all they wanted, only insisting they visit him for a while first, while he sat in his dooryard and smoked his pipe. The water off Hawthorne's Point was said to be the deepest in the harbor.

Buttonhole was the district on the lower part of St. Peter's Street, near the jail, and the boys from that part of town were called the Buttonholers. Knockers Hole was the region around High Street and Creek Street, so named because, when vessels were built there, the sound of hammering was incessant. There were also Down-towners, the Up-in-towners, the Bridge Streeters, the Beverly Beaners, Danvers Hawkers and Salem Shags. There was a cry:

> *Danvers hawkers put up your wrappers*
> *And down to Salem run.*
> *Salem Chaps, put on your hats*
> *And chase them away like fun.*

The Salem Cadets wore red coats, and were called lobster-backs, and the Light Infantry wore gray; sometimes they fought for the right to drill on Central Street. The Willows, where the smallpox hospital was located, and the banks of the Juniper south of the Willows were the holiday haunts of boyhood. So were South Fields and Castle Hill, Cold Spring and Jeggle's Island, and Stage Point where ships were hauled up to be coppered and repaired and where stood Caleb Smith's sperm-oil and candle factory. Salem boys bought their gibraltars—rock candy— at Aunt Hannah's circulating library and variety shop on Old Paved Street, and their liquorice at Dr. Long's apothecary at the corner of Essex and Liberty. They found acorns beside Cold Spring and flagroot beneath Legge's Hill. They knew the important people of the town: Blind Dolliver, the organist at First Church with an eye in every finger; Squire Savage, who was always frowning; Mullet, the blind town crier; the two Trues, Abraham, the grocer, and his brother Tom, the wood carver, and Jo Monarch, the stately Portuguese who lived far down on Essex Street. There was a large colony of Negroes in Salem. They lived in the district called Nigger Huts, near the entrance of the Salem Turnpike.[56]

Nathaniel's school closed late in the summer. He delivered an oration at the closing exercises, the last one he delivered for thirty-four years, and went to the dancing school ball on October 24. Louisa's life was taken up through the autumn with preparations for the ball. It was a splendid affair with the girls wearing short-sleeved white gowns, long white kid gloves, pink sashes, and black spangled kid shoes. Her father's sister, Aunt Ruth Hawthorne, gave her a gown of plain Indian muslin. All week Nathaniel and Louisa prepared for the ball with dancing classes "Monday forenoon, Tuesday all day, Wednesday all day and Thursday from nine in the forenoon till three in the afternoon and then Thursday night the ball . . ." At six or a little after the children marched into the ballroom with the grand march. There was a big crowd; Louisa was thrilled and had a beautiful time. She did not get home until after one o'clock, and slept the next day until two.[57]

IV

In February, 1820, Robert Manning wrote to Louisa that he had nothing for Hawthorne to do, and was thinking of apprenticing him to turn a cutler's wheel. He said finally that money was the reason.[58] A month later he began preparing him for college.

Hawthorne was placed in charge of Benjamin Lynde Oliver, who was to train him in the entrance requirements for Bowdoin. Oliver lived on Essex Street, across from the Sun Tavern. He was a sixty-year-old physician who had a sort of "respectable decayed look" and who seemed "a kind, unselfish man who had lost his ambition as regards appearances."[59] Dr. Oliver was "a doser of the old school; the row of vials displayed during an illness was appalling. He had many excellences, but did not attach enough importance to the text, 'Cleanliness next to Godliness.' He was a skillful physician, an adept of elegant literature, a scientific musician, and a true gentleman."[60]

The name Oliver was a famous one in Salem. The Oliver mansion, now crumbling in ruins, built in 1700, was full of the heirlooms of its great days. Books and papers littered the floor of the house, brocades of the Oliver heiresses and the tarnished family silver were strewn in confusion through the unused rooms. The family portraits, including some by Copley, which were worth a fortune, were appraised in the inventory of the doctor's estate at two dollars apiece.

Dr. Benjamin Lynde Oliver was an inventor. He was a lens grinder, built reflecting telescopes, and spent his leisure time grinding and polishing mirrors. When Hawthorne became his student he was working on an antifriction crank, on which he soon took out a patent. His house contained fine mirrors, telescopes, microscopes, apparatus for grinding and polishing, mathematical instruments and an electrical machine. He was a musician, a composer, and imported from England one of the first organs brought to America. Deeply learned, unmarried, profoundly skilled in the study of optics, interested in philosophy, a student of Italian, Benjamin Lynde Oliver had a local reputation as a philosopher. He collaborated with John Pickering on the *Greek Lexicon*, published in 1826.[61]

Entrance requirements of Bowdoin consisted of an ability to write Latin correctly, an understanding of the fundamental rules of arithmetic, an acquaintance with Cumming's *Geography*, Cicero's *Select Orations*, Virgil's *Bucolics*, *Georgics* and *Aeneid*, Sallust, the Greek Testament, and the *Collectanea Graeco Minora*.[62] Hawthorne was fifteen. He had had very little schooling, not more than a few months in his entire life. He arose early every morning and at seven, before the day's work began, hurried from the Manning house on Herbert Street to Dr. Oliver's. He went half a block, turned left on Essex and passed the Manning stables on Union Street where the eight-o'clock stage for Boston was being made ready. The mail stage south had left at four in the morning, and the stage from Marblehead was due at eight. Essex Street was paved with cobblestones, rough and uneven. The streets were muddy and slippery; the hardhearted east wind swept up what is now Hawthorne Boulevard almost strong enough to sweep him off his feet. He had a curious whimsical imagination: he thought how pleasant it would be if people could walk about six inches above the ground instead of having to step directly on the earth and sidewalk. How many falls and tumbles would be averted! How many gowns would be unspattered!

He shivered on the corner where the Hawthorne Hotel now stands. Diagonally across the street, most imposing in the morning light, rose the magnificent mansion of his cousin Catherine Forrester Andrew, the four beautiful columns, set in from the corner facing the street, and fronting the light garden, with its delicate tracery of thin trees and bushes, giving it lines of grace to counteract its massive square bulk. A block away stood John and Charlotte Story Forrester's home. When old Simon Forrester died on July 4, 1817, he left each of his children $132,655.95, with which they began trying to outdo each other in

Salem society, John and Charlotte building their magnificent brick mansion on Washington Square, John Andrew * another, even more imposing, and Eleanor, who married the rector of St. Peter's Episcopal Church, living in considerable style in a house that had once been owned by General Derby.[63]

Hawthorne passed the home of his wealthy kinspeople, passed the mansion of the old merchant Joseph White, passed the wooden Indian before Mickleweed's tobacco shop, and came to the old Sun Tavern. It was once the residence of the merchant William Gray. It was of rough plastered finish, three stories high, with a gambrel roof, and looked more like an English tavern than most of the taverns of England. A sign "Coffee House" swung before it. Directly across the street was the old Oliver house, which he entered to recite his lessons to the doctor.

If there was ever a house in Salem that justified the legends of witchcraft and family curses, it was the Oliver mansion. Probably no one thought of it, for no one knew much early colonial history in those days. The house was black with age, the stairs and floors were rickety. A large cellar was dug out beneath it.[64] The doctor's electrical machine and his telescopes and his grinding and polishing materials were scattered in disorder everywhere. His brother, Peter, who was deranged, lived with him in the house, which the two surviving Oliver brothers had inhabited alone since the death of their mother in 1807.[65]

Hawthorne left two unfinished novels, *The Dolliver Romance* and *Dr. Grimshaw's Secret,* for which Benjamin Lynde Oliver appears to have been the inspiration. Both have as the central characters an old Salem doctor, a portly, rumbling, gruff old man, whose professional reputation has vanished and who drinks pretty heavily, reviving and taking an interest in life through the arrival of children into his bachelor household. Dr. Grimshaw is a genuine old toper who is making some infernal brew of great potency from spiderwebs, a manufacturing process which forces him to keep great numbers of spiders busily spinning their webs all over his house.

Dr. Grimshaw is overdrawn, and Hawthorne laid the book aside after a time and began *The Dolliver Romance,* a much happier conception, with a portrait of Dr. Dolliver which seems to fit Dr. Oliver to perfection. Probably Dr. Oliver opened the door for him as he described

* John Andrew was the uncle of John Albion Andrew, governor of Massachusetts during the Civil War.

Dr. Dolliver in the morning, pulling aside the faded moreen curtains of his ancient bed, and thrusting his head into a beam of sunshine that caused him to wink and withdraw it again. He wore a flannel nightcap, fringed round with stray locks of silvery white hair, and surmounting a meager and duskily yellow visage, crossed and crisscrossed with a record of his long life in wrinkles. He had rheumatism, and moved cautiously, with an occasional groan and a frequent ahem. His patchwork dressing gown, rose color, crimson, violet, green, gray and black, had an Eastern fragrance from the smell of drugs, herbs and spicy gums that had been spilled over it. "Many an old acquaintance had gone to sleep with the flavor of Dr. Dolliver's tinctures and powders upon his tongue; it was the patient's final bitter taste of this world." No longer regarded as a doctor, interesting to the public as the oldest citizen, who could remember the Great Fire and the Great Snow, the old doctor could not get it through his head that he was old and it seemed to him that his stiffening shoulders, his quailing knees, his cloudiness of sight and brain, his confused forgetfulness of men and affairs, were troublesome accidents that did not really belong to him.[66]

All of Dr. Oliver's family were royalists. All except his father, who was a scientist, fled during the Revolution. All were graduates and benefactors of Harvard. Dr. Oliver was born in Boston in 1760, studied medicine under Dr. Edward Holyoke, who lived to be a hundred years old, and began practice at Williamsburg, Virginia, when he was twenty. He practiced there six years, becoming acquainted with the professors at William and Mary College, and returned to Salem where he lived with his widowed mother and his brother Peter. He was a friend of Benjamin Crowninshield, who had attended William and Mary College.

When Hawthorne was his student, Dr. Oliver was not quite so decrepit as the doctor pictured in *The Dolliver Romance*, though his career was nearly over. He had received an honorary degree from Harvard in 1808 and was a fellow of the Massachusetts Medical Society, librarian of the local medical society, was in full possession of his faculties, and became editor of a Salem newspaper three years later. He was much impressed with Hawthorne's intelligence and aptitude, and was, perhaps, the first person to recognize the quality of his mind.[67]

After his recitations at Dr. Oliver's, Hawthorne hurried back to the stagecoach office to work on the books of the company and write William Manning's letters. He had a fine handwriting, even in the day when penmanship was an art. He received a dollar a week in wages, and the promise of a suit of clothes.[68] From four in the morning until eleven at night stages arrived and departed; the Manning stagecoach office was a busy place.[69] With all his work and with his limited preparation, Hawthorne was ready by fall, in Oliver's opinion, to enter college.

The ease with which Hawthorne had mastered the entrance requirements was disconcerting. Robert Manning postponed his college for a year, on the grounds that he would be compelled to study too hard if he entered at this time—a reason which proved to be ill founded, as Hawthorne never studied at Bowdoin as hard as he studied in Salem preparing to go there.

Hawthorne was not tractable. More than anything else he wanted to be free of Robert Manning's control over his destiny. He doubted Robert Manning's word, and he was now beginning to question his good will. The effort that he had made preparing for college, which must have been intense, was wasted by the year's delay in starting; he could have taken another full year to prepare. He did not believe he would ever go to college. Nor did he greatly care, for aside from the fact that he did not want to be a lawyer, or a minister, or a doctor, which is what college would have prepared him for, he did not want to live on Robert Manning's charity for the four years—four of the best years—that college would take out of his life.[70] He no longer confided in Robert Manning. He made no secret of his dislike for his uncle William Manning, in whose office he worked. His letters to his mother and sisters in Raymond became filled with warnings against communicating what he said to the Mannings. He corresponded in codes and in invisible ink in writing letters which could carry their essential messages and still be read by Robert Manning without his suspecting what they were about. These letters involved a double deception. It was necessary for them to be answered without giving any indication that they had been received.[71]

His aunt Mary Manning continually scolded him. His grandmother Manning hardly ever spoke a pleasant word to him. If he spoke in his own defense they accused him of impudence. Their eternal fault-finding wore upon his nerves; their own strained affairs wore upon theirs. The land in Maine was not selling as profitably as they hoped; Hawthorne informed Robert Manning that a letter he had written about the land had been shown to John Andrew, with the result that

"I am afraid you will not sell much of the land." The members of the family were quarreling among themselves. Robert Manning resigned as secretary of the stage company. In this turbulent, prospering and ill-natured household, Hawthorne studied Greek in the forenoons with Dr. Oliver and in the afternoons wrote letters for William Manning. It was an occasion in his life when he visited the theater in Boston. He had a new suit of dark-blue broadcloth, with yellow buttons. On March 5, 1820, he went to Boston to see Edmund Kean in *King Lear*, the greatest of actors in his best role, at the height of his career—a performance that Coleridge described as reading Shakespeare by lightning flashes. Hawthorne said that it would have made him cry if he had been in a place where he could cry. "It was enough to have drawn tears from a millstone," he wrote to his mother. But there were few such occasions in his life.[72]

What did Hawthorne find it necessary to conceal from the Mannings? He bought a book—Scott's *Lord of the Isles*—for his sister Louisa. He was insistent that Robert Manning should not hear of it. He concealed the amount and character of his readings, which is not strange, since his taste ran to the rowdy and bawdy early English novels, *Tom Jones* and *Roderick Random*, which the Mannings might well have considered not proper for him and his sisters. He concealed his plans and hopes for his own career, plans and hopes that were extraordinarily clearheaded for a youth of seventeen in any age, and were bold, almost heroic, in the early days of the administration of Monroe.[73] He wanted to be a writer, and he was emphatic that the Mannings should not know of it. He outlined his prospects and the difficulties with lawyerlike arguments and presented his qualifications, or his lack of them, with cool honesty. He could not be a minister because he could not vegetate forever in one spot, nor a lawyer because there were already too many lawyers, nor a doctor because he could not live upon the sickness and infirmities of his fellow men. A writer was the remaining alternative, and this required an income he did not have. Such were the thoughts, at seventeen, he was insistent the Mannings should not share. He enforced on his mother and sisters absolute obedience and concealment—concealment and obedience which his sister Elizabeth, at least, came to feel were wrong.[74]

It was at this time that the Hawthornes began to develop their semiprivate language, their use of the names of people as verbs, and their refinement of puns into a semicode. Hawthorne also seems to have broken words into syllables and transposed the syllables. The titles of books were certainly used to say more than he wanted to write out in detail. "I have read Hogg's Tales," he wrote in one eerie cryptogrammatic note to his sister Louisa, in which a faint gleam of sense shows through the double meaning of its nonsense. Similarly, his sister Elizabeth wrote: "Mrs. Forrester was a Story" . . . perhaps the most arresting sentence in all the biographical writing about Hawthorne. (She liked to discuss her kinship with the Hawthornes, added Elizabeth.)

Hawthorne continued to use such codes. Many years later, when he wanted to pay a tribute to a living English writer, Henry Bright, who had befriended him, he wrote: "It would justify my cherished remembrance of this dear friend, if I could manage, without offending him, to introduce his name upon my page. Bright was the illumination of my dusky little apartment, as often as he made his appearance there!" [75] The mental and verbal exercises these tricks involved were probably not seriously intended with him all the time; they were the products of a mind and an imagination of greater power than they had material to work upon. "I have almost given up writing poetry," he went on in the previously quoted letter to Louisa. "No man can be a Poet and a bookkeeper at the same time. I do find this place most 'dismal' and have taken to chewing tobacco with all my might, which, I think, raises my spirits. Say nothing of it in your letters. You may cut off this part of the letter and show the other to Uncle Richard. Do write me some letters in skimmed milk . . ."

In April, 1821, Robert Manning went to Raymond, leaving both Nathaniel and Louisa in Salem. The summer passed quietly, except for the execution of seventeen-year-old Stephen Clark for arson, an event which Hawthorne tersely communicated to his mother.[76] On June 12 Nathaniel came home one day to see a tall, handsome young woman of twenty, a stranger, in the house. She was well and expensively dressed; her white Leghorn hat had cost fifteen dollars.[77] Hawthorne did not know her. He then saw Robert Manning, and recognized his sister Elizabeth. The hat was a present from her uncle William Manning. She had been seventeen when they separated, the companion of his walks in the woods; she was now a village belle at Raymond, where she had too many beaux to want to leave.[78] She believed, and so did Nathaniel, that she was soon going back there.

The subsequent maneuvers of the Mannings in persuading Mrs. Hawthorne to leave Raymond and return to Salem had the skill and precision that indicated long mastery of domestic intrigue. How much of it was conscious and deliberate, and how much the mere working out of unguided wants, cannot be determined now; in either case the result was the opposite of what Nathaniel, Elizabeth, Mrs. Hawthorne, and Grandmother Manning desired. Hawthorne was reconciled to going to Bowdoin on the promise that he could spend his vacations with his mother in Raymond. He had not seen her since he left there. Raymond was close enough to Bowdoin to make this possible. It was too far from Salem, and the stagecoach fare was too high, to enable him to get there from college even during the long vacations.

Elizabeth had evidently intended to return to Raymond after a brief Salem visit. When Robert Manning returned in July, however, he took Maria Louisa with him instead. The subtlest move in what Hawthorne considered the Manning strategy was now made. Elizabeth left the Manning household to visit Mrs. Archer (Judith Hawthorne). Her desire to return to Raymond consequently lessened. "I believe she is much pleased with her situation," Hawthorne wrote to his mother, though he feared she was "too deeply immersed in the waters of dissipation" to want to go home.

His aunts Mary Manning and Priscilla Miriam Manning Dike now began to try to persuade Mrs. Hawthorne to return to Salem to live, using the argument that Elizabeth Hawthorne was in Salem. Nathaniel did not believe that Aunts Mary and Priscilla alone could influence his mother. They could, however, persuade Robert Manning, whose word carried weight with Mrs. Hawthorne. Hawthorne wrote to her on June 19, 1821, a characteristic letter in its diplomatic avoidance of direct statements. A short time before he had complained in letters about the bickering among the Mannings; he now quoted poetry:

> *Lo, what an entertaining sight*
> *Are kindred who agree!*

"I hope, my dear mother," he wrote, "that you will not be tempted by their entreaties to return to Salem to live. You can never have so much comfort here as you now enjoy. You are now undisputed mistress of your own house. . . . Elizabeth is as anxious for you to stay as myself. She says she is contented to remain here for a short time, but greatly prefers Raymond as a permanent place of residence. The reason for my saying so much on this subject is that Mrs. Dike and Miss Manning are very earnest for you to return to Salem, and I am afraid they will commission Uncle Robert to persuade you to it. But, mother, if you wish to live in peace, I conjure you not to consent to it. Grandmother, I think, is rather in favor of your staying." [79]

His fear was justified; soon after he went to Bowdoin, Mrs. Hawthorne and Louisa joined Elizabeth in Salem. As he anticipated, it was impossible for him to return there during his vacations. He had passed almost three years apart from his mother and sister, and the peculiar situation he found himself in at Bowdoin lengthened the separation to seven years. The Hawthornes never again lived in the little Maine town where they had been happiest. In view of what happened, it was extraordinary that Hawthorne's affection for his family survived, and still more remarkable that he himself lived to rejoin them and rejoin the family life where it had been broken off.

V

On September 30, Hawthorne and Robert Manning left Salem for Raymond on their way to Bowdoin.[80] The stage picked up its passengers at the Ship Tavern. The road followed the coast. One mile out of town it crossed the North River into Beverly, over the toll bridge. Hawthorne used to walk there to visit with his old friend, the tollgatherer. It was an admirable place from which to study Salem, this old bridge over which produce, strangers, and the stages must pass. Five miles farther the stage stopped at the Fishes at Wenham.

Hawthorne and Manning were riding over the main line of their richest competitor, the Boston-Portsmouth run of the Eastern Stage Lines. Six miles beyond Wenham brought the stage to Crompton's at Ipswich, and three and a half miles to the Half Way House at Rowley, equidistant from Boston and Portsmouth. It was eight miles to Newbury by Thorell's Bridge. The stage passed at the base of a hill on which stood the long unbroken line of mansions built by the sea captains, and entered the old town, much like Salem in its narrow streets and its vanished prosperity. Two and a half miles on, it crossed the

Merrimack to Salisbury, the home town of Daniel Webster. Half an hour after leaving Salisbury it stopped at Norton's in Hampton. Another hour or so carried it to Johnson's Tavern in Greenland, about five miles from Portsmouth.[81]

Nathaniel and his uncle did not go directly to Bowdoin, but turned off on the road to Raymond, where they remained overnight with Mrs. Hawthorne. The following day they set out for the college.[82] It must have been at Portland that they changed stages, and in so doing found themselves with three other students bound for college—Franklin Pierce, Jonathan Cilley, and Alfred Mason. Each was destined to have a profound influence on Hawthorne's life.[83]

Pierce was a sophomore. He was seventeen, of middle height, with a fair complexion, light hair, and a military bearing. His father was the leader of the Democratic party in New Hampshire.[84] Jonathan Cilley was a tall, thin, nineteen-year-old country boy, with an ingratiating twisted smile, a forceful manner, and a strong rustic self-possession. His father was dead. His was a military family, his grandfather having been a famous Revolutionary officer, and his brother Joseph a terrific soldier, one of the heroes in an outstanding action in the War of 1812. He was a natural fighter, quick-witted, energetic, with a love of argument in which he excelled. One saw boys like him all over New England, boys who looked like him, thought as he did, had the same shrewdness and resolution and often the same background of early loss, and responsibility.[85]

The third passenger was Alfred Mason. He was Hawthorne's age, a dark-haired, quiet, reserved youth, the third son of Jeremiah Mason. His father was generally considered to be the greatest lawyer in New England. Jeremiah Mason was perhaps the foremost theoretician of the Federalist party after Hamilton, a gigantic man, six feet six and one half inches tall, born in Lebanon, Connecticut, graduated from Yale, and the leading lawyer of Portsmouth, where his practice was greater than that of all the other lawyers combined. He was a brother-in-law of the saintly Jesse Appleton, the second president of Bowdoin, who had recently died. He was an opponent, year after year, of Franklin Pierce's father, and of Pierce's father's friends. He was a close friend of Daniel Webster, who considered him a greater lawyer than John Marshall. Jeremiah Mason had drafted the arguments in the celebrated Dartmouth College Case, which has been called the most important law case in the history of the world. Mason believed that the legislature had no more right to take the assets of the college, and transfer them to a different group of trustees, than it would have to take his home and give it to another man. It was his argument (Webster did the actual pleading) that resulted in the dissolution of Dartmouth University, and the restoration of the charter to Dartmouth College. The Supreme Court decision that accomplished this removed from office William Allen, who then became president of Bowdoin upon Jesse Appleton's death.

Mason was a giant, but he was also a singularly gentle and considerate man. Every young lawyer in New England knew at least two things about him—that he was a very great lawyer and that he was a very tall man. A Quaker stopped him one day and remarked, "From thy size and by thy language, I perceive that thou art Jeremiah Mason." Such was the nature of his fame. He should have had a distinguished political career. His schooling, however, had started very late, and he spoke with a dry New England drawl, entirely unable to orate, or to make eloquent appeals to the emotions of his audience. When he argued with the jury he conversed, twirling his gold-rimmed glasses. He excelled at cross-examination, never browbeating witnesses, finding contradictions in their stories where none was apparent, drawing them out quietly until the fatal lie was crystal clear, the courtroom still as death, the witness pale and silent, whereupon, gravely and without triumph, Mason would say, "You may step down, sir." It would be too much to expect that at this moment of Democratic triumph and Federalist disgrace, the young Democrats would not lord it over the son of the biggest Federalist in the world. Entirely surrounded by Democrats, riding in a stage operated by his father's enemies (Benjamin Hale of the Eastern Stage Lines had been a trustee of the short-lived university and had tried to hire a lawyer to oppose Webster at the Supreme Court), going to a college run by the man his father had put out of office, Alfred Mason seemed not so much a freshman entering school as the victim of a gang who was being taken for a ride.[86]

These were Hawthorne's new companions. He had moved at once from the quiet family circles in Salem and Raymond into relationships as intricate and dramatic and conflicting as any that ever figured in his fiction. A volume would be required to trace the ramifications of the struggles in which the families of these boys were involved. Essentially, however, it was this: the New Hampshire Federalists, with Jeremiah Mason at their head, after controlling the state for many years, had now lost to the Democrats in whose councils the Pierces were most prominent. The Federalists were at this time fighting defensively. The struggle was not only political: it involved the presidencies of the colleges, the Bank of the United States, the ministers of the churches, and, a most frequent cause of conflict, the choice of the professorships of theology in the schools. Within both the Democratic and Federalist parties, however, there were divisions almost as great as those between the two parties. Within both parties there were conflicting cultural movements: the Federalists, conservative in politics, were often most liberal in religion, frequently Unitarians, and followers of Channing; the Democrats, often radical, often supporters of the French Revolution and of Napoleon, were often, like President Allen of Bowdoin, relentlessly orthodox in their preaching. Robert Manning was orthodox; Mary Manning was a Unitarian.

At Dartmouth, for example, where the trustees were predominately Federalist and the president a Democrat, the conflict began when the president arbitrarily discharged the professor of theology. When the trustees discharged the president, both sides took their case to the people, and it became a leading political issue. The Democratic legislature dissolved the college and established Dartmouth University in its place, only to have the university in turn dissolved by the famous Supreme Court decision. The Pierces and the Woodburys, another prominent family among the New Hampshire Democrats, had been supporters of the short-lived university. Yet young Pierce was a bitter enemy of the Reverend William Allen, who had been its president and was now president of Bowdoin. Likewise, the Federalists had bitterly fought Levi Woodbury (Jackson's secretary of the navy and, later, of the treasury) but they united with the conservative Democrats to elect him governor of New Hampshire in place of a more radical Democrat.

Emerson considered Hawthorne's friendship with Pierce a disaster to American literature. There always remained in Hawthorne's career an element of mystery, centering principally on his friendship with the men of Bowdoin who were not esentially men of letters and who seemed to have no appreciation of his genius beyond a vague well-wishing for him, and a desire to use his writing for their own ends. Hawthorne's sister-in-law, Elizabeth Peabody, contributed to the confusion, after

Hawthorne's death, by a fanciful description of him in college as a youth of great personal beauty, who signed his letters with the pseudonym Oberon.

The result of this was to make Hawthorne seem a very sissified young man, if not homosexual, an impression which his secluded way of life in Salem after leaving college intensified. The main outlines of his story so presented were very meager. He supposedly spent his early years among his family in Salem, went to Bowdoin, where he began his lifelong friendship with Pierce, Cilley, and Horatio Bridge, then returned to Salem, where he spent ten years in melancholy seclusion, until *Twice-told Tales* brought him to the attention of New England's literary men. This legend was unusual on the face of it. Moreover, it left unexplained a great deal more than it explained. Yet it persisted as the basic story of the greatest American novelist.

One missing element in it is the intensity of the conflicts in which his friends were involved. The families of Pierce, Mason, Bridge, and to a lesser extent, Cilley, were mixed up in political adventures as desperate as the boldest exploits of the merchants of Salem. The college life of the boys was a reflection in miniature of the struggle of their parents —a distorted reflection, for they were too strong-willed and independent to follow their parents blindly. They were already powerful characters. They had even then shrewdness and calculation, a determination to win, and the cool self-seeking of their personal ambitions within the clannish determination to advance their family within its political party, and their political party in the life of the nation. They were ambitious. They meant to run the country. For a time they virtually did so. It was a remarkable fact that a dozen men in a single class of thirty-eight students in a new and remote provincial college had national and even international reputations by the time they reached middle age.[87] In many cases their fame was brief. The tragedy of their lives was that they lacked youth, and Hawthorne, who returned only once to Bowdoin after his graduation, felt when he grew older that college students should be daydreamers, every one of them. There had been too little daydreaming in his own fierce college days.

They were the first generation whose lives had been wholly lived since the country had become independent. They were all children of the nineteenth century, born soon after 1800—Democrats had been in office all their lives. Life was hard, and had hardened them. Cold winters and grim needs, hard work, poor clothes, cold schoolrooms, poverty, work that was as dangerous as warfare and sicknesses that were like death sentences, hurried their youth. The country they had inherited was magnificent. It lay around them in half wilderness, the lives of its ten million citizens scarcely changing the vast forest that remained as it had been after two hundred years of white men's settlement and clearing. Indians still ruled most of it. The eyes that Hawthorne turned to the roadside were quick and alive, rewarded at every turn by some unsuspected scene that no painter had ever pictured or any poet brought to life. He loved these long stagecoach rides, the stops in the villages, the horn of the driver echoing through the hills, the narrow road with the forest crowding so near it seemed that one step beyond its dim verge and one would be lost forever. He loved the early fall, when the sunshine made the American autumn seem all that the poets claimed for it, and when there seemed to be something in the atmosphere that made laughter and joyous voices seem infinitely more elastic and gladsome than at any other season. He loved the clear evenings, with their autumnal chill, the hills and hollows shaded with oaks and walnuts, with the rich sun brightening in the midst of the open spaces and mellowing and fading into the shade. The ridges and the trees gave few distant landscapes, perhaps a vista across a river, showing houses or a church and a surrounding village, or sunny pastures, walled in by oak shade, or a meetinghouse in the distance with the sun shining through the windows of its belfry. Along the coast, where the fresh breeze blew from land seaward, the roughness of the sea took the gleam off the water and gave it the appearance of iron after cooling. In Maine the country swelled back from the rivers in the hills and ridges, without an interval of level ground, the woods filling the valleys or crowding the summits. The land was good, the farms neat, the barns large, the houses small, one-storied, and comfortable. The autumnal landscape was rich, the oaks a deep brown, red, the walnuts a bright sunny yellow, the elms with golden branches intermingled with the green. There were yellow rustling bundles of Indian-corn stalks in the fields beside the road, rows of white cabbages, sometimes a farmhouse with pumpkins piled against the corner as high as the window sill. There were men hoeing potatoes, boys gathering walnuts, men gathering apples, their coats flung over a fence beside the road. Sometimes beside a dark lake, shadowed by the pines on its opposite shore, wild ducks rose, shimmering the surface of the glassy stream, breaking its dark water with a bright streak, and sweeping round, gradually rising high enough to fly away. As the evening drew on, the travelers were wrapped in topcoats, the country shops beside the road were closed, and he could see the gleam of fires on the ceilings of the houses as he passed. He loved these bright glimpses of his native land; he reveled in its freshness and youth, and, silent and watchful though he was, he loved in the same way and with the same spirit the company of these young men who were, like himself, a most important part of it.[88]

VI

He arrived at Brunswick on October 2, 1821. In all probability he and Robert Manning stayed at Ward's Tavern. The tavern stood between the college and the village, on a corner of the college grounds. Its owner had committed suicide the year before, in September 1820. His daughter now ran the tavern. She was an affable, good-looking woman of thirty who was "always ready to give moderate credit for the little suppers and other comforts that students might desire."[89]

Passing the tavern to take their entrance examinations, the students went through the gate in the fence that lined the college grounds. The wooden, unpainted chapel, with its domed steeple, stood before them. On one side stood Maine Hall, a four-story building of brick and wood, a long, rectangular barracklike affair, containing dormitories and study rooms; and on the other side was Massachusetts Hall, similar to it in shape, but newer, and with a white wooden belfry over it.

The examination was at 8:30, Tuesday morning. Hawthorne went to the lecture room and found about thirty others standing around the door, waiting for the professors and tutors to come. There were Mason and Cilley, Longfellow and Edward Preble, John Appleton, William Hale, Horatio Bridge—some of the best that New England had. They were not the sons of wealth, or the most brilliant scholars, but the children of farmers, lawyers, naval officers, preachers, storekeepers—people of moderate means, independent, enterprising, and newly prospering. The candidates were pale and nervous. Some of them were walking up and down, endeavoring to appear as careless and lighthearted as possible, making a manifest effort to appear at ease.[90] Hawthorne passed his entrance examination without difficulty. He was assigned to Maine Hall, his roommate Alfred Mason.[91] The choice was wonderful. Whatever might have been said of Bowdoin under Allen's administration it was plain that someone in the college administration was fully aware of the situation that both boys were in. Mason's ties with Bowdoin were many, and he was familiar with its history. His older brother, George, was a recent graduate, his uncle, the late Jesse Appleton, a former president, his cousin, William Appleton, a student, and another cousin, Jane Appleton, was the girl who became the wife of Franklin Pierce.[92]

Manning left Hawthorne after he passed his examination, telling him that he would leave some money for him at the office.[93] Hawthorne and Mason's room was on the ground floor of Maine Hall. It had a desk, chair, beds and a fireplace. There was no curtain over the window that looked over the yard, and no rug on the rough wooden floor. The autumn air was already chill. They moved uncertainly in a new and vaguely hostile environment, unpacked their few clothes—Hawthorne never had enough clothes—and went to their boarding house for their evening meal. They boarded at Professor Samuel Newman's. He was the language professor, newly installed.[94]

They were a long way from home. The wind from Maquoit Bay blew through the pines in the yard. Their room was lighted with oil lamps, set on the desk where, in theory, they studied through the evening study period. Firelight brightened the room wonderfully, and across the yard, after the evening prayers, the lights in the windows of Massachusetts Hall gave a dusky cheerfulness to the scene. One of Hawthorne's classmates wrote his recollections of the first days at school that probably answered for most of the class: "I was very much afraid I should not awake in time to attend prayers. This fear gave me a night of troubled dreams. I awoke two or three times before day, and looked at my watch by the bright rays of the moon, and felt so lonely that I longed to be at home again.

"At last I got up and dressed me an hour before the prayer bell rung. I lighted my candle and sat down to look over my morning lesson, but I could not study, for the tears filled my eyes as I thought of home and the friends I had left. I felt ashamed of my weakness, but I thought I was out in the great world all alone.

"At last the prayer bell rung. It was just before sunrise. The students began to pour out of the college doors, and flock into the chapel. My room-mate and I mingled in the crowd, and in the excitement of this new scene I forgot, in a considerable degree, my home-sickness . . ."[95] There were about a hundred and forty students at Bowdoin. The freshman did not know it, but it would have been hard to find anywhere better company, or men whose careers were of such interest, in his generation. Somewhere in the group crowding into the chapel, among the faces of the strangers, was Nathaniel Hawthorne, as lonely and as frightened as himself; and young Horatio Bridge, who was to be his friend; and a brilliant child, about ready to graduate, William Pitt Fessenden, born out of wedlock, who was to become Lincoln's secretary of the treasury.

Longfellow, Hawthorne, Pierce, Edward Preble, John and Gorham Abbott, Alpheus Felch, William Pitt Fessenden, George and Henry Cheever, John and William Appleton, James Bell, Luther Bell, John Hale, James Hall, John Russwurm, Calvin Stowe, William Hale, Seargent Prentiss, Jonathan Cilley, George Washington Pierce, David Shepley, Josiah Hook, Cullen Sawtelle, Jeremiah Dummer, Gorham Deane, Josiah Little, Zenas Caldwell, Horatio Bridge, William Browne, Hiram Hobbs, Barrett, Bowman, Bartlett, Odell, Smith—their names were woven in and out of the history of New England, exerting an influence, and an influence for good, far greater than the size or the wealth of the school promised.

Henry Wadsworth Longfellow was enrolled in college, but because of his extreme youth—he was only fourteen—lived at home in Portland and studied the freshman class lessons under a local teacher. Edward Preble was the son of Commodore Preble, the hero of the war with Tripoli, one of the first five lieutenants commissioned when the United States Navy was organized in 1798. Young Preble was the son of one of Maine's greatest heroes, a neighbor of Longfellow's, gifted, universally popular, wealthy, indolent, a boy with a quaint humor and a fondness for strange literature, of whom great things were expected.

They were remarkable, all the more so in that they came from a remote college in a new state, with inadequate facilities, a small staff, and a long history of conflict with the trustees, the president, and the legislature. The senior tutor at Bowdoin was the former cashier of a Portland bank, served as acting treasurer when the regular treasurer failed in business, and was for a long period the professor of ancient languages, though some doubt always persisted as to whether he knew any Latin or Greek.[96] The professor of chemistry and geology was also secretary of the college and lectured on anatomy in the newly established medical school, though he had never studied medicine, never traveled, would never cross a river except by a bridge and never cross a bridge without first carefully testing its strength.[97] He was a wonderful professor, and the whole staff, though it was constantly at war with the president, who in turn had the utmost difficulty in restraining the students from breaking the windows in the tutors' rooms, somehow contrived to produce a group of graduates whose names became household words.

The morning service lasted fifteen minutes. It was conducted by Allen, who was punctual and very strict, and only Professor Parker Cleveland, the professor of geology, shy, big-boned and awkward, was allowed to be late, because of his long years on the faculty. Reverend Allen was only thirty-seven. He was short, round-faced, with a slow, methodical walk and speech. His gait never varied, whether the campus was drowsing in the summer heat or was swept by the winter storms. His speech seems to have been particularly irritating to the students.[98] He was strictly orthodox in his preaching, even aggressively so, at a time when the Unitarians were sweeping over New England and the old severity in preaching hell-fire and damnation was slackening. He was considered one of the most learned men of his time. His reputation rested upon his massive Biographical Dictionary, which he had written after graduating from Harvard, a collection of the names, places of birth, education and careers of the leaders of the country, the first such directory that had appeared. The freshmen no doubt had heard of Allen's father, Thomas Allen. He was a doughty Revolutionary hero of Pittsfield, Massachusetts.

After prayers the students went to their first class. In his first term, Hawthorne studied Xenophon, Livy, and arithmetic.[99] Classes had about forty students apiece, and the tutor called upon one and then another without warning, taking any part of the lesson to ensure they had mastered it all. Immediately after recitation Hawthorne went to his room. In a few minutes the bell rang for breakfast. It was then about eight o'clock. As he walked through the college yard with Mason, the students were dispersing in every direction to their boardinghouses, scattered throughout the village. After breakfast he and Mason returned to Maine Hall. The students for a few minutes clustered around the doors, talking with one another. A few were playing ball in the yard, and one was carrying around a subscription paper to raise money to purchase a couple of footballs. At nine o'clock the bell rang again, and they hurried to their rooms, since the rules required that they remain in them through the study period.

The study period lasted from nine until eleven, when the bell rang again for the next class. When it was finished the students were free until dinner at one o'clock.[100] In one of these free periods in his day, Hawthorne called at the office to get the money Robert Manning claimed to have left for him. There was none there.

Hawthorne waited until October 9 before writing to Manning to ask for the money. On October 17 he wrote home, rather desperately, saying he had received no money and no letters. On October 30 he wrote again that he had received no letters.[101]

His board bill was a $1.75 a week—eight and a third cents a meal. This was what most of the students paid. Most of them, however, had enough spending money to patronize the village store between meals. Firewood cost a dollar a cord, and the rooms were cold without a fire, and pleasant and cheerful when one blazed in the open hearth. The chambermaids received $1.11 each term from each student. Library fees were fifty cents and room rent eight dollars a term—this last extremely expensive by the standards of the time, and more than was paid at Harvard.[102] Then there were the constant fines—ten cents for tardiness, ten cents for being unprepared in class, ten cents for refusing to recite, fifty cents for gaming, twenty-five cents for sneaking out during study periods—petty, annoying, inflexible, and amounting to a considerable portion of the college expenses. In a day when ten cents would buy a meal, and a dollar a week was Hawthorne's stagecoach office earnings, a fine of fifty cents was considerable.

He had no money at all. His clothes were poor. Mason's father was a rich man, as well as a famous one, and Hawthorne was impressed by how much money he had. Most of his classmates had money in their own right. In this month when Hawthorne did not hear from home, Mason came to his rescue and advanced him money enough to pay his incidental expenses. November passed, and Hawthorne received a bundle of clothes from home, but no letters. On December 4 he received ten dollars. He paid his debt to Alfred Mason.[103]

The mornings passed swiftly, but in the afternoons the students were left very much to themselves. At two o'clock the bell rang again for a study period. This lasted until four-thirty. It was at this time that the real work of the college was to be accomplished, for there were, actually, very few recitations, and the long periods of study, alone and without supervision, were a strengthening of the powers of concentration and a training of the will. The late fall afternoons had a singular beauty whose savor Hawthorne always loved. It was the best time of the year for him, as in a sense it is for New England, and all his life he delighted in trying to picture it. When the college drowsed through the fall afternoons he slipped out of his room and vanished into the shadow of those tall academic pines. He had brought his gun with him to college. A little river flowed through the college grounds, ran parallel with the main street of town, crossed the road to Bath near Professor Cleveland's house, and emptied into the Androscoggin River below the falls. He fished along its banks and hunted in the woods beside it, only managing to return to his room before four-thirty, when the bell rang for the last recitation of the day. At half past five he assembled with the others for evening prayers. After four years of college, Hawthorne rarely went to church.[104]

When evening prayers were over he went to Professor Newman's for supper. Evening, after supper, and until seven-thirty, was free time, spent in walks and in games, and after the seven-thirty bell they remained in their rooms, studying, until bedtime at nine.

Or there they remained if they obeyed the college rules. The students of Bowdoin were fined for gambling, fighting, neglecting their duties, hazing, turning livestock loose, drunkenness, unchastity, and the improper use of pistols.[105] They were much like students a century later —not college students, perhaps, but those in some intermediate position between boarding school and the later years of college. When they were depressed they said they had the blues.[106] They called a drunk a blow. They smoked cigars and pipes. Their humor was characteristic college humor—when Ned Preble started a newspaper, he called it *The Old Dominion Zeitung*.[107] They sneaked out at night to drink in Ward's Tavern, and smuggled wine into their rooms. The usual method was to buy a new lamp. Under the pretext of filling it with oil, the students carried it across the campus in broad daylight, to the grocery store, and filled the base with wine.[108] Several trips, or several lampfuls, were enough for a blow. Cider mixed with brandy made a powerful, inexpensive drink.

Except for a curious fondness for blackening their faces with

burnt cork, their pranks were generally pretty good. They seemed to
have an inordinate liking for starting bonfires, though this is partially
explained by the fact that fires were a fearful danger, and arson
punishable by death. They would take a barrel of tar, carry it to the
yard of the college at night, stumbling and falling, and risk breaking
their necks, getting expelled, or burning down Maine Hall, as they set it
afire. This they called a scrape. At night, tired of studying, one student
would turn to his roommate, and say, "Chum, let us have a scrape
tonight."

"Agreed; but what shall we do?"

"A bonfire would look nobly this dark night."

"Very well, light the dark lantern, and—here, turn your coat
inside out, so that no one will know you. And where is that piece of
burnt cork? We had better black our faces a little."

When they carried the empty tar barrel to the college, stumbling
through the mud, they talked like this:

"Is this what you call fun?"

"To be sure, I can conceive of a more agreeable situation for a man
to be in." [109]

The adventures of both Hawthorne and Mason were a little more
purposeful. Mason was fortunate. He was taken in charge by Parker
Cleveland, whose most brilliant student he became. Cleveland was the
professor who would never cross a bridge without testing its strength.
He virtually adopted Alfred Mason during his years at Bowdoin. He
was then a man of forty, with eight children. The best professor in the
college, his voice was never raised in disciplining the students, except
to ask for leniency. He was offered professorships both at William and
Mary and at Harvard, at critical moments in Bowdoin's history, and
refused them; they would have taken from the college the last professor
from its old days under Appleton.

Cleveland became interested in minerology and geology in the way
that Audubon became interested in American birds. In 1807 a millrace
was being built for a sawmill at Brunswick, and a blast revealed a ledge
of strange rock. Cleveland was called to identify it, and from his study
began a collection of native stones. James Bowdoin had left seven hundred specimens to the college; Cleveland added to these and in 1816
published his work on American geology. It became a standard text-
book. Cleveland lectured and gave courses in chemistry in Portsmouth

and Portland in which the first families of the town humbly enrolled to gain a little of the strange new science their sons were learning in school. Cleveland was fearfully overworked at Bowdoin. He served as its secretary. He lectured in the newly established medical school. The college never bought any materials for his laboratory. He taught mathematics, natural philosophy, and chemistry, with six hours a day of classroom work and sixteen hours out of the twenty-four given to the school. He wandered about the rocky coasts and the stony fields of Maine, whose boulders farmers and sailors had dreaded for so many years, chipping off fragments and returning to the college laden with rocks whose value no one else could determine in the slightest. Mason accompanied him. Slowly the collection grew until it became the largest in the country. In all his years at Bowdoin Cleveland taught about two thousand students, but few of them, perhaps Alfred Mason alone, received his personal attention so generously given. Mason was honored by it, and responded with an industry and an aptitude for learning that justified Cleveland's effort.[110]

At Exeter, Mason had been a schoolmate of a Portsmouth boy named William Hale. Hale's roommate at Bowdoin was a fifteen-year-old boy from Augusta, Horatio Bridge, the son of a banker and lawyer. Through Hale, Bridge met Alfred Mason, liked him, and stopped at his room one night early in his first year at school, and in so doing met Hawthorne. This friendship began at once.[111] Bridge was a likable, easygoing youth. He had a high domed forehead, thin features, high cheekbones, and a good-humored, cheerful expression. He was two years younger than Hawthorne, but in many respects—knowledge of the involved political conflicts of the college, for example, or the family background of the students—seemed older and wiser, at least in the worldly sense of understanding why some things were working out as they were. His older brother Edmund had graduated from Bowdoin with honors in English, in 1818, and had settled in Augusta, where he was beginning the career that made him a prominent Democrat, editor of the *Maine Patriot*.[112] From the first, Horatio Bridge was insistent that some great future was in store for Hawthorne, and throughout their college years he insisted, almost as if he had some information he could not disclose, that success would be his if he would write.[113]

Bowdoin was an admirable site for the underground railroad, which soon had a station in Professor Smyth's home.[114] The college grounds were wild and interesting, with paths winding under the pines and along the shadowy little stream that wandered riverward through the forest. Bridge and Hawthorne explored it together. They could walk for miles without meeting anyone, or hearing a sound except the occasional chatter of a squirrel, or the sighing of the wind from the bay through the branches overhead. By crossing the road that led to Bath they came to another division of the pine woods, where the sandy soil was not so level, and where the stream flowed after passing the hill near Professor Cleveland's house. They loitered along its banks, listening to its murmur, saying little. Sometimes they walked to the bridge that crossed the Androscoggin River below the falls. Sometimes they walked the three miles to Maquoit Bay, where a dilapidated wharf reached out into the water, with two or three melancholy sloops, loaded with firewood and lumber for Portland, tied beside it. During the study hour they wandered away from the college, to shoot pigeons or gray squirrels in the autumn woods. Hawthorne was a tireless walker. He walked with a square, firm stride, and looked down as he walked, his head slightly bent to one side. He had an uncanny facility for imprinting upon his memory the exact details of apparently undistinguished scenes—a stretch of nondescript riverbank, an overgrown woodland path, a ruined dam across a brook, a hidden valley or a cavelike opening in a cliff—except that, with him, the stretch of riverbank might be one over which a flood would wash, and the path one by which a fugitive could escape, the height one an army could fortify, and the cave one where supplies could be stored. He seldom spoke, though he did not discourage his companions from talking.

Bridge and Hawthorne stood on the point of land watching the battered sloops loaded with firewood set out for Portland from Maquoit Bay. President Allen had written a poem:

> *All you who would be seamen*
> *Must bear a valiant heart,*
> *And when you come upon the sea*
> *You must not think to start;*
> *Nor once to be faint-hearted*
> *In hail, rain, wind or snow;*
> *Nor to think for to shrink*
> *When the stormy winds do blow.*

Bridge said it must have been inspired by the loads of firewood making sail for Portland. Hawthorne said nothing. He had other things on his mind, perhaps, nonsense and serious problems intermingled, perceptions which had not graduated into knowledge, and the learning of youth, which, not quite crystallizing into understanding, always escaped into the haze of partial insights, momentary clarifications. They walked under the tall and thick-standing trees, drank from the stream, using the bark of a birch tree for a cup, or climbed the hill from which they could look down at the cluster of buildings of the college and hear the chapel bell calling the students to evening prayers. A bend in the stream, where it emptied into a deep pool, and where the current had worn a hollow under the roots of a leafless oak; a cliff, with trees and bushes clinging to the rock, and fragments of stone half buried in the shrubbery at its base—such scenes fastened themselves on Hawthorne's memory without his knowing why.[115]

They came to know each other's history. Horatio was the fourth of seven children of James Bridge and Hannah North. His father was a Harvard classmate of John Quincy Adams. He studied law with Judge Theophilus Parsons, and became judge of probate at Augusta. He was a dignified, serious man, who suffered from indigestion too severely to follow a political career. He was tall, able, logical, and possessed of discriminating literary taste, had great industry and wore his austerity of manner "like a leathern doublet." His dyspeptic habits, in the language of the times, led him to retire early, to read much, and to have little social life. His favorite authors were Johnson and Scott. In 1802 he became a law partner of Reuel Williams, afterward chairman of the Senate Committee of Naval Affairs. In 1812 he retired from practice because of ill-health. His wife was a woman of great personal beauty, of medium size, graceful and affectionate. Their children were tall, handsome, high-spirited, rather reckless—the girls sociable, informal, with easy manners, the boys with a disposition to take chances for large stakes where their father had been cautious and conservative. They lived in a cheerfully hospitable household, in a twenty-room mansion on the bank of the Kennebec outside Augusta.[116]

Horatio Bridge's powers of observation were almost as acute as those of Hawthorne. They were, however, of a different order: his judgment of people was shrewd and exact, and his ability to visualize a social situation was highly developed. He had a deep love of literature, and his mind was stocked with poetry he could quote at length. He had a natural gift of phrase, a wide interest in people, and superb critical judgment; he was the first person to insist upon Hawthorne's genius. He never thought of himself as a man of letters; he was a lawyer, a businessman, and eventually, in his middle age, a naval officer, yet he had perceived at the start the quality of Hawthorne's ability, and his confidence in it never wavered, though for years there was scarcely another person, aside from Hawthorne's family, who believed as he did. A hundred writers who have been forgotten flourished at the same time, became celebrated, or even, briefly, world famous, but Bridge stubbornly clung to his faith that Hawthorne would someday surpass them. More than that. Among their own classmates there were men of really remarkable abilities, in literature and in law and in finance, whose writings began while they were still in school or soon after they graduated —Longfellow, Cheever, and the Abbott brothers, to name only three of them, or Fessenden and Seargent Prentiss—and their fame grew while Hawthorne, for sixteen years after his meeting with Bridge, remained totally unknown.

Time has vindicated, not so much Hawthorne, as Bridge, for Hawthorne had none of Bridge's faith in his own ability. There is no other instance in American literary history of a friendship so constant and enduring, or of one so honest and manly, so solidly based on a foundation of mutual respect and affection, or so rewarding—American fiction, in one sense, may be said to have begun when the door opened one night and Horatio Bridge walked into Hawthorne's room in Maine Hall. From whence came Bridge's faith? Not, certainly, from his older brother's literary interests, though that may have helped, or from the comments of the literary men of the college, for Bridge was not on friendly terms with them. There was something within himself that wanted expression, beyond his powers of expressing it—a love of the life of his time and his native country, a depth of hope, and a tenderness he could not communicate, a desire to find a voice that could articulate what was wonderful and new in the world around them, and of which no word ever appeared in the writing of the time, and of which he called upon Hawthorne to speak.

There are periods of inward as well as outward revolution, said the greatest of the preachers of New England, when new depths are broken up in the soul, and new wants are felt by the multitude, and a new and undefined good is thirsted for, when in truth to dare is the highest wisdom.[117] Bridge and Hawthorne were children of that age. For Hawthorne there was always the solace, when his work seemed to break like soap bubbles against the world's actuality, of his own silent craftsmanship, the chamber music of his words. But for Bridge, when the years passed and that which he wanted said seemed to remain unspoken, a kind of sickness of the spirit seemed to be the only fruit of his labor. He had no cloistered vision of Hawthorne's tough ability— he wanted him to write of plain things, of a dam that the Bridge family built across the Kennebec, for example, or a naval cruise into the South Seas—and doubtless he would have valued an article on the dam that helped sell stock in it, and a report on the cruise that furthered his own and Hawthorne's careers in the navy. But his profit was incidental to his main purpose of getting Hawthorne to write, and he never thought of these apparently routine tasks as lowering the quality of Hawthorne's work—he wanted that mind, with its wonderful facility for stripping away irrelevancies, and its quick and generous perception of goods which others did not see, to devote itself to the daily business of this world.

One of their walks was to a sparsely settled street in Brunswick, along the riverbank. An old fortuneteller lived in an unpainted cottage at the end of the street. From a soiled pack of cards and for a small coin she foretold their fortunes, always giving them brilliant futures in which the most attractive of the promised gifts were abundance of of gold and great wealth of wives. "Lovely beings, these wives of destiny were sure to be," Bridge mused, "some dark-complected and some light-complected, but all surprisingly beautiful." It was odd, he thought, that the prophecy did come true, except the part about the gold, and they did marry happily, without a dangerous procession of blondes and brunettes; and each had the highest appreciation of the excellent qualities of his friend's wife.

They walked to the bank of the river, above the bridge over the Androscoggin. The huge pine logs floated past by the hundreds, balanced on the brink of the falls for a moment, and plunged into the foamy pool below. Another long walk was to the house of a carpenter just beyond the limits of Brunswick. The first Negro student of Bowdoin, except in the medical school, lived there. His name was John Russwurm. He was dignified, easy in his manners, and too sensitive because of his color to return visits. In the evening, when the laws of the school required that they be studying in their rooms, Bridge and Hawthorne made their way to the carpenter's house and sat down to talk with the young Negro whose knowledge reached a side of the local life they could not penetrate.[118]

Russwurm was then twenty-two years old. He was born at Port Antonio, on the island of Jamaica, in 1799, and at the age of eight was sent to school in Quebec. His father moved to the United States, settled in the District of Maine, and married. His wife insisted that the young Negro should be sent for and raised as one of the family. The father died soon afterward, but his widow proved "a faithful mother to the tawny youth," sending him to school, procuring funds for him and, when she married again, stipulating that he should not lose his home.

The first Negro to graduate from Bowdoin's medical school was Dr. James Hall. He was an Episcopalian, a man of erect and more than ordinary stature, with a good head and features and large keen eyes. He was always gentlemanly in his deportment, a great reader, especially in history and politics, with a sound intellect, "sagacious in men and things." He was somewhat indolent, but was a man of strict integrity, "a good husband, father, master, friend." [119]

With his friendship for Bridge, it was strange that Bridge was not a member of the Pot-8-0 Club that Hawthorne organized. Bowdoin was full of these secret societies. They seem to have been stimulated by hunger. Hawthorne and Mason soon stopped boarding with Professor Newman, and took their meals at Mrs. Adams's on Federal Street, directly across the street from President Allen's house. She was the widow of a Brunswick physician who had left her with only moderate means, and she rented two or three rooms in her large house to students. She had two charming daughters, and Mason and Hawthorne found the food much better than at Professor Newman's.[120]

The maximum that Bowdoin students paid for board was $2.50 a week. Obviously, this left their appetites unsatisfied. The boys could roast potatoes in their fireplace, but the trouble of preparing them prompted the thought that they might be eaten in company. Hawthorne drew up the constitution with the care he had given to the *Spectator*. The club was characteristic of his games with words, the hidden puns and ciphers that so often suggest depths in stories clear and transparent as a spring. Article Five of the constitution provided that at the club meetings an entertainment shall be provided, "consisting of roasted Potatoes, Butter, Salt, Cider, or some other mild drink, but ardent spirits shall never be introduced."

The club met once a week. The proceedings were secret. The potatoes were to be delivered to the steward's room at least four hours before the meeting. There was a master of ceremonies, secretary and treasurer. One member was required to read an original dissertation or poem at each meeting. Dues consisted of an initial payment of twenty-five cents. "Being convinced," the preamble of the constitution began, "that it is beneficial both to the health and understanding of Man, to use a vegetable diet, and considering that the Potato is nutritious, easy of digestion, and procured with less difficulty and expense than most other vegetables, do hereby agree to form ourselves into an association under the name of the Pot-8-0 Club."

Mason and Hawthorne signed. Two other members were roommates, George Washington Pierce and David Shepley. George Washington Pierce was no relation to Franklin Pierce, though they studied law together in Amherst after graduating. He was an eighteen-year-old Maine boy, who later became a prominent Democratic political writer for Maine newspapers. Jeremiah Dummer was a medical student. He was sixteen, probably Cilley's roommate. None of the group with whom Hawthorne gambled was a member.[121]

Hawthorne's games always had an underlying purpose: his jokes were serious; his social evenings were as watchful as his walks through the woods at Bowdoin. Jonathan Cilley was the member of the club who gave its activities importance. Cilley was becoming the most influential student in the school. He was a born politician. With his long face and pleasant manners, his natural friendliness, his quick intelligence, his real kindness and sympathy, he was bound to take a leading part in the school's doings as he did upon graduating in the affairs of the state. In the political rallies for Jackson, in the meetings of the Athenaeans, of which he was president, in mock trials, when judge, jury, lawyers, prisoner and witnesses were impersonated by the students, Cilley was a fervid and successful advocate, powerful, with a free and natural eloquence and a flow of pertinent ideas in language of unstudied appropriateness. He seemed to be able to make his compelling speeches accomplish precisely the result he intended for them. Hawthorne perhaps exaggerated his skill, because of his own inability to speak, but he admired him, took from him an edged bantering he would not have taken from anyone else, and regarded him almost as an elder brother. Only Cilley's sinewy tact, his ability to seize on each man's weak point and mold him to serve his own plans, gave Hawthorne a caution and reservation with Cilley that never left him.[122]

On March 4, 1822, the afternoon study period was suspended, and the students went to a lecture. At three o'clock it was discovered that Maine Hall was afire. The fire had begun in the garret. The flames swept through the upper floors before the students could get there from the lecture, and was soon out of control, gutting the building. Hawthorne and Mason managed to get into their ground-floor room and save their possessions, Hawthorne suffering no damage except in having his coat torn, and it was his old one. But the other students stood by and watched their belongings burn, about $1,500 worth. The building was uninhabitable.[123] The students scattered to different quarters, and Hawthorne and Mason moved into a room at Mrs. Adams's.

Hawthorne and Bridge had begun to gamble. One of the upper-classmen was a distant relative of Hawthorne's. His name was William Pitt Fessenden. He was only fifteen years old, and in his third year at school—his birthday was October 6, 1821. He was tall, rather thin, with symmetrical features, and keen, intelligent eyes. He was warm in his friendships, ardent, hot-tempered, combative, with a sharpness of speech and an independence of manner that made him the terror of the school.

Pitt Fessenden's mind was so quick that the ordinary rules of college scarcely applied to him. He had an absolute indifference to titles, prestige, position, or any of the attributes of authority, viewing the president of the college—or of the United States—with the same unsparing candor he gave to his college friends. He mastered his subjects too easily to study and was too confident of his knowledge to be impressed by his professors. Fessenden had been prepared to enter college at eleven. He could have graduated at fifteen as easily as at seventeen. His terrible record in conduct held him back. He wrote brilliantly, was an excellent debater, and a financial genius.[124]

But he was principally interested in playing cards. A group of students met in each other's rooms to gamble. Besides Fessenden, Bridge and Hawthorne, there were two juniors, Josiah Hook and Hiram

MRS. RACHEL HAWTHORNE
FORRESTER

"Mrs. Forrester must have been possessed of great attraction, if the lovely picture of her old age is a faithful reminder of her youth."
—Marianne Silsbee *(Essex Institute)*

CAPTAIN NATHANIEL HAWTHORNE

Born May 19, 1775; died in Surinam, death recorded in Salem April 19, 1808. *(Essex Institute)*

The home of Richard Manning (1757-1813), Hawthorne's grandfather.
The Manning house stood directly behind the Hawthorne house, facing
Herbert Street.

Ship *Perseverance*

Owned by Simon Forrester; master, Captain Nathaniel Hawthorne
(Hawthorne's father).

"The cargo of the *Perseverance,* 180,000 pounds of tea, on one voyage
from Canton sold for $140,000 in Salem." *(Essex Institute)*

Hobbs, the principal organizers of the games, and five others, Barrett, Bartlett, Bowman, Odell, and Smith.[125]

Their game was lanterloo. It was fast and exciting, even if it had not had the threat of punishment, of suspension, expulsion, or fines, if they were found out. Three cards were dealt each player. A dummy hand, called the "miss," was dealt face down. The top card of the remaining pack was turned up, to determine trumps. After anteing up the players looked at their hands and decided whether they would play or pass. A player had the right to discard his hand and pick up the miss, but if he did so, had to play it out. High card won each trick, unless a player unable to follow suit played a trump. The first player had to play the ace of trumps if he held it, or the king if the ace had been played, or one trump if he held two in his hand. The winner of the first trick had to lead a trump if he could. When the hand was played, the winners of the three tricks divided the pool, and everyone anted up for a new hand.

Stakes were high. The bets on each hand might be small, but the hands were quickly played out. Unlike poker, losses were never heavy enough on a single hand to discourage a player, yet they could be considerable in an evening because of the rapidity of the play. Unlike poker, the players who passed did not necessarily lose their ante if everyone passed except one player. In that case the dealer played the miss, and whatever trick he won with it remained to swell the pot for the next hand. When three were playing, and each won one trick, their bets remained for the next hand. When four were playing, and three won one trick apiece, the fourth was "looed" and alone anted up for the next hand.[126] With half a dozen students playing, at Ward's, or in a student's room, at night, in secrecy, with wine smuggled from the village grocery, or with a drink of cider and brandy mixed, it was tense and dangerous.

On the winter nights, when the rain descended in an almost continuous sheet, with occasional powerful gusts of wind driving it against the windows, they slipped out of their rooms, into the tavern or into a dormitory room picked for the night's game. Each student entered stealthily, the rain dripping from his cloak. A fire burned brightly on the hearth. The wine and glasses stood on the table before it.

Hawthorne played quietly. He needed to win. He drank heavily, but did not get drunk—or, if he did, never seemed to lose his self-possession, or to grow less reserved or noisier.[127] The card players were a strangely assorted group. Fessenden was a hard-driven, embattled spirit. He was defiant, haughty, bitter and uncompromising in his hatreds. He hated Allen; his violations of the rules were flagrant. He was a spoiled child and an infant prodigy, but he had none of the ill-temper of a spoiled child or the oddity of a boyish genius; it was rather that he strove desperately to be an ordinary man, and was debarred forever from being one by the misfortune of his extraordinary good looks no less than by his genius as a financier.

The secret underlying his character may not have been known to his companions around the table. The silent and attentive Hawthorne, the lighthearted Horatio Bridge, the taciturn Hiram Hobbs, had no such background as Pitt Fessenden. He was the son of a prominent Portland attorney, Samuel Fessenden, one of the earliest abolitionists and Ruth Green. Born out of wedlock, Pitt Fessenden was taken in his infancy to his grandfather's home in Freyburg.[128] Freyburg stood on the winding Saco River near the Maine-New Hampshire border, at the base of the White Mountains. A short distance across the New Hampshire line was the mysterious Notch in the White Mountains, the narrow, hidden pass that for generations had been known only to the Indians, who mystified the settlers of western Maine by suddenly sweeping down upon them, apparently from nowhere. The main trade route between Maine and Canada passed through Freyburg and the Notch. It was over this road that caravans of sleighs passed in the winter, the caravans Hawthorne had watched from Parson Bradley's house.[129]

When Pitt was six years old, his father married. Pitt was taken into his home and raised as his son. When he was a child in Freyburg, Daniel Webster was teaching school there. When he was christened, Webster was his godfather, making the trip to Freyburg to attend the ceremony. Pitt was always precocious—he had completed Gorham Academy at eleven—and always so outstandingly and unhappily handsome that he was a marked man. His father, becoming an abolitionist, became increasingly radical. Pitt Fessenden became increasingly conservative. It seemed impossible that with his pronounced individuality and his freedom from control he could escape ruin in these wild years of his youth. But he had, like so many of the New Englanders, a native caution and a shrewd hardheadedness beneath his independence. His escapades were never so reckless or purposeless as they seemed to be.

They were, like his sharp tongue, a part of his protective coloration in which he concealed the honesty that made Abraham Lincoln trust him, and the aptitude that made him a great financier, the finest lawyer in Maine, and secretary of the treasury during the Civil War.[130]

As the night advanced, and the wine took effect, a strange, wild glee spread from one of the players to another. All of them were conscious that they were on forbidden ground and that the wine they drank was an unlawful draught. The secret of their mirth was in the troubled state of their spirits, which, like the vexed ocean at midnight, tossed forth a mysterious brightness. Undefined apprehensions distracted them, mixed with an indescribable joy. The inspiration spread, until each was wittier than he had ever been suspected of being. They quarreled, or nearly quarreled. Sometimes the nights ended in a riot. Once they wrecked the tavern—or so Hawthorne pictured it, one of the students drinking huge stupefying draughts, one after another, and breaking chairs, windows and mirrors, while outside the storm raged. The sky grew Egyptian, and the rain fell in a torrent.

Hawthorne awakened in the morning with the immemorial sensations of a hangover—a heavy weight upon his mind, the cause of which he was unable to recollect; a belief that he was in hell; a raging thirst that seemed to have absorbed all the moisture of his throat and stomach; a desire for a drink of cold water; a throbbing head, a whirling brain, dizziness, and a degradation of mind. In the depth of his misery he resolved to stop drinking. But with characteristic prudence, he did not resolve to stop drinking entirely; he merely resolved to refrain in the future from drinking too much.[131]

Early in April he was nearly caught. One of the students was suspended. He wrote to his sister that two in his class were fined. One of them may have been himself; he was fined one dollar that month. The money that Robert Manning sent him did not arrive. He was advanced some by the college treasurer. He stopped gambling. He was afraid that if word of his misdeeds reached Richard Manning in Raymond, he would be taken out of school.[132]

Twelve thousand acres of the Manning lands around Sebago Lake were sold. The sales were over a period of years, the income from them was intermittent, and Hawthorne's fear of Richard Manning revealed more of the situation in the family than his long battle with Robert Manning. In January, 1822, he visited Raymond. The visit was apparently not pleasant. He went only once more. On the second visit he found Richard Manning far from pleased to see him, and Mrs. Manning cold and freezing. He resolved never to go again:[133]

Richard Manning had grown lame. It was said he had injured his leg leaping from a stagecoach. He made the house that Mrs. Hawthorne had occupied a stagecoach tavern. He had begun to collect guns. Soon his big house was filled with them. Confined to his wheel chair, he still had them always within reach—on racks on the walls, in all the rooms, even in his bedroom, within reach of his bed.[134]

Hawthorne's fear that news of his dissipations would become known was soon justified. Late in May one of the card games was raided. Bridge, who had been present, escaped. Josiah Hook was caught. He was suspended. The next day—May 28—Hiram Hobbs was disciplined. He refused to give evidence, and was suspended until the next term.[135] Someone had told the authorities, however, and Hawthorne was called before Allen.

Allen was round-faced, short, precise in his dress, industrious and conscientious. His hair started far back on his forehead. He tried to appear dignified, and succeeded in seeming precise and formal. His eyes were rather narrow, and as the administration of his office grew more and more harassed, and the students less tractable, a vague and troubled look of pain settled upon his features. Allen had the mind of a lawyer—in the sense not of comprehending the meaning of the law but of being engrossed in its complexities and exactitudes. He was vigilant in securing the legal rights of the college. But in striving for them constantly, and keeping them in the foreground of discussion, he actually succeeded in making the college subservient to the legislature.[136]

When Hawthorne entered the president's office, Allen asked him if he had played cards for money on a specific date in the first term of the school year. Hawthorne was instantly relieved. Was that all! He had gambled throughout the term. He knew the occasion Allen referred to; it was a night they had played for a jug of wine.

He admitted that he had. Allen asked him what the stakes had been. Hawthorne replied, "Fifty cents." Since a jug of wine cost fifty cents, he felt he had come near enough to the truth. Fessenden, Bartlett, Bowman, Smith, Odell, Barrett, and Cullen Sawtelle were called in, and fined. Hawthorne got off lightly. Bridge was not caught at all. Fessenden was intractable. His diploma, which he would have received at sixteen, was withheld for a year because of his insubordination.

Allen wrote to Hawthorne's mother, asking her cooperation in persuading Nathaniel "faithfully to observe the laws of this institution," adding that he might not have gamed "had it not been for the influence of a student we have dismissed from college." Hawthorne wrote in answer: "I was fully as willing to play as the person he suspects of having enticed me, and would have been influenced by no one. I have a great mind to commence playing again, merely to show him that I scorn to be seduced by another into anything wrong." His fine created a sensation among the Mannings. It had the effect of inducing his sister Elizabeth to write to him sternly, the first letter she had written since he had been in school. It infuriated him. He wrote back with a younger brother's complete lack of gallantry, saying that moral advice from her, of all people, was strange—a reference to Elizabeth that figured in many of his letters, and a state of mind, between brother and sister, that frequently figured in his stories.[137]

VII

There was then no system of grading in school. Another fifty years passed before grades indicated the quality of a student's work. There was then only the distribution of honors at Commencement to indicate the relative position of each student in the class.

Hawthorne's college career, under this system, was without distinction. He was a mediocre student, wretched in mathematics, tolerable, though lazy, in English, a good Latin scholar, whose exercises were highly praised without, apparently, stimulating him to any greater efforts. In declamation, a compulsory course, he was, Bridge said, literally nowhere. This was fatal to any hope he may have had of making a success of his college years. President Allen was devoted to the subject. It was necessary for the involved and long-drawn-out ceremonies at Commencement that the best students in other subjects should also excel at declamation. Public speaking was an indispensable accomplishment for college graduates, whether they intended to be preachers, lawyers, politicians, and to accustom them to it they declaimed throughout their college years. In their freshman year they declaimed privately in the chapel, on Wednesday afternoons, and in the later years, before the class, once or twice a week, in addition to the debates that were a regular feature of school life.

At graduation, Hawthorne stood nineteenth in a class of thirty-eight. There was something almost mysterious in this locating him right in the center of the class, where he belonged neither with the good students nor the bad, and where he was, in a sense, plainly inconspicuous. For many years he had the protective coloring of mediocrity. There was nothing in his past, in his family, his appearance, his apparent capabilities, to justify any particular faith in his ever doing more than standing midway in whatever group he found himself. He had, thus far, done nothing exceptional, unless his snubbing of Simon Forrester in his boyhood be taken as an indication of independence, and his quick mastery of his lessons under Dr. Oliver be taken as proof of latent abilities.

His first two years at Bowdoin are fairly well documented. His letters home, with his nervous appeals for money, Bridge's recollections, the Pot-8-0 Club, and the trials of the gamblers, provide a clear indication of his attitude toward the school. The records of his junior and senior years are meager. They consist of a few lazy and drawling letters to his sister, the fines paid for not attending classes, the course of study, and the many and varied accounts—since the class of 1825 contained so many men who became famous—of the graduation exercises. In them Hawthorne appears as the quiet figure on the edge of the picture, barely visible in the beaming figures around him. Meager as the glimpses are, it is nevertheless plain that during them Hawthorne changed so much as to be almost unrecognizable as the boy who had started school four years before. The driving anxiety that had dominated him disappeared. He no longer splashed through the mud to get to his morning lessons, as he had hurried to Dr. Oliver's, or worried about his mother's plans, or Uncle Robert's. He seems to have gone to class pretty much when he felt like it, and paid his fines for being absent. In his junior year his fines amounted to $11.63, sufficient to pay for 116 classes that he did not attend.

He slept a great deal. He stayed in his room on Sunday morning, instead of going to church, and rolled over and faced the wall when visitors tried to arouse him. There seems to be no other case on record of a poor boy who did so little to make his way in the world. In all this there appears to have been no willful flouting of the authorities of the school, or the conventions of the time—too much trouble—but rather a quiet recognition that, when he dispensed with the driving concerns of his school mates, and when he disregarded the instructions of his professors, there remained an unequaled opportunity to sleep, read, loaf, visit, or, as he recollected to Bridge, to enjoy college by gathering blueberries, in study hours, under those tall academic pines; or watching the great logs, as they tumbled along the current of the Androscoggin; or shooting pigeons and gray squirrels in the woods; or batfowling in the summer twilight; "or catching trout in the shadowy little stream which, I suppose, is still wandering riverward through the forest—though you and I will never cast a line in it again—two idle lads, in short (as we need not fear to acknowledge now), doing a hundred things that the faculty never heard of, or else it had been the worse for us . . ." [138]

A wonderful life. And a wonderful education. It was even more wonderful then than it would have been later. For Hawthorne lived at a time when New England education was still dominated by the teachings of Calvin, and resistance to authority such as he exercised required sustained courage. Since mankind was innately depraved, the misdeeds of youth were not errors to be corrected, but the outward expressions of their innately sinful natures. And so their preachers and teachers expounded to them, as one expounded to Horace Mann, "all the doctrines of total depravity, election, and reprobation, and not only the eternity, but the extremity, of hell-torments, unflinchingly and in their most terrible significance; while he rarely if ever descanted upon the joys of heaven, and never, to my recollection, upon the essential and necessary happiness of a virtuous life . . . It might be that I accepted the doctrines too literally, or did not temper them with the proper qualifications; but, in the way in which they came to my youthful mind, a certain number of souls were to be forever lost, and nothing—not powers, nor principalities, nor man, nor angel, nor Christ, nor the Holy Spirit, nay, not God Himself—could save them; for he had sworn, before time was, to get eternal glory out of their eternal torment. But perhaps I might not be one of the lost! But my little sister might be, my mother might be, or others whom I loved; and I felt that, if they were in hell, it would make a hell of whatever other part of the universe I might inhabit; for I could never get a glimpse of consolation from the idea that my own nature could be so transformed, and become so like what God's was said to be, that I could rejoice in their sufferings. Like all children, I believed what I was taught. To my vivid imagination, a physical hell was a living reality, as much so as though I could have heard the shrieks of the tormented, or stretched out my hand to grasp their burning souls, in a vain endeavor for this rescue. Such a faith spread a pall of blackness over the whole heavens, shutting out every beautiful and glorious thing; while beyond that curtain of darkness I could see the bottomless and seething lake filled with torments, and hear the wailing and agony of its victims." [139]

Hawthorne's rebellion against this grim view of the hereafter was not violent, nor was it, in a sense, ever expressly stated. He did not praise nature, but went for a walk; he did not condemn the preachings of Allen, or take much part in the students' protests (they rioted, hanged the preacher in effigy, boycotted the Fast Day services, started bonfires, and shot off fireworks), but wandered down the riverbank or visited the old fortuneteller on the other side of town. He did not join the abolitionists, but visited John Russwurm. He took no part in the fierce struggle of the Unitarians and the orthodox—Longfellow tried to start a Unitarian society on the campus—doctrinal disputes were foreign to his habits of thought. But his life exemplified the release that teachings of Channing gave to New England. "All Christian morals," Channing said, "may be reduced to one word, love. God is love. Christ is love. The gospel is an exhibition of love, and its end is to transform men into love. The blood of Christ was shed to make this plant of heaven flourish on earth." [140] Hawthorne inclined toward the Unitarians; the finality of his choice is shown in that he married the daughter of one of New England's prominent Unitarian families. He had too keen a sense of the evil in men to accept Unitarianism as his generation came to interpret it; it was characteristic of him, in thinking of Christ, not to dwell, as they did, on His perfect goodness, but to think of what men had done to Him. [141]

So he glided through the thickets of controversy like a stream descending a hillside. There were turns and pauses in his progress, pauses where he lingered over what interested him, and avoidance of what he could neither correct nor consider without growing involved in the fruitless agitations that warped the nerves of his schoolmates. He did not study much but he settled in a corner of the college library and read what he wanted to. One day he came across a tattered volume of the poems of the old Federalist poet, Thomas Green Fessenden, who was to become an important figure in his adult life. He thought they were wonderful, the most original expressions of the native Yankee genius that he had ever read. This Thomas Green Fessenden was a farm boy who entered Dartmouth College at twenty-one. One day, when the students were reading their English compositions, stale imitations of classic models, characterized by the lack of native thought and feeling, cold pedantry, customary verbiage and threadbare sentiment, Fessenden electrified the college by reading his *Jonathan's Courtship*, an excellent ballad, with a strange, dog-trot rhythm, that caught the very spirit of the society as it existed around him, with every line imbued with a peculiar yet perfectly natural and homely humor.[142]

There, probably, was Hawthorne. He loafed in a corner of the library (it was open only two hours a day) enjoying Fessenden's humor while the fierce wrangles of the students and the rigorous discipline of the classes passed before him. He would not declaim. He refused to do so in his first year at college and continued to pay his fines throughout his four years. There was a profound significance in his inability to stand before a group of his classmates and declaim. It was partly his indifference to the motives, in the desire for honors, or pre-eminence in school, of his classmates, and partly his natural shyness. But it was also his recognition of the essential falseness and foolishness of these high-flown exercises in eloquence, and most deeply his instinctive recognition that the part of the country's intellectual life which they represented was finished. The old sonorous orations, the quotations, the studied gestures, had no meaning in relation to the life of the stagecoach office, the land sales of Raymond, the miser of Browne's Hill, or the cold winters in Parson Bradley's home. Something had taken the life out of these classical exercises, so that the students who trained for them, with their enthusiasm and earnestness, their intense concentration that so often left them broken in health, suddenly seemed, when they came to recite, to be vacantly posturing through a rite as remote and tradition-encrusted as a scene from Chinese drama. This side of the intellectual life, with all its interrelations with education and politics and religion, was finished; but the new and freer speech and writing, employing the common language of the time, had not yet appeared. Something of the same condition existed in literature. Hawthorne had the ability to see through the falseness of contemporary forms and the genius to create a new literature out of the life around him without losing the best of the

old; but he did not have the energy or the means or the will to stand
before his contemporaries and declaim according to the involved and
ceremonious rules that then prevailed.

It would be wrong, however, to give the impression that his way
of life was irresponsible. It was in resistance to a part of education,
not to all; or it was responsible to a view of society, perhaps only dimly
seen, that made much of the life of the college without meaning to him.
Some experience, perhaps his studies with Dr. Oliver, had given him a
respectable-citizen view of his duties, even while he rejected the duties
of declaiming, going to classes that did not interest him, or going to
church. At the end of his sophomore year, when one of the students in
the medical school graduated, Hawthorne wrote to Elizabeth in Salem:
"There is in the medical class a certain Dr. Ward, of Salem, where he
intends to settle, after taking his degree of M.D., which will be given
him this term, I shall give him a letter of introduction to you when he
returns to Salem, which he intends in about a fortnight. He is the best
scholar among the medicals, and I hope you will use your influence to
get him into practice."[143]

Another action, not quite so pleasant, threw its light on his habits
of thought. Late in his college life he wrote, anonymously, an account,
entirely fiction, of a deadly and mysterious blight that was sweeping
through the orchards of the region. He managed to get it published in
a Boston paper that he knew his uncle Robert Manning would read.[144]
Robert Manning, now thirty-eight, had begun to cultivate pear trees
on a large scale. The *New England Farmer* (which old Thomas Green
Fessenden, long since forgotten as a poet, had started) declared that
Robert Manning had proved and tested a greater number of trees
than any other individual in the United States or Europe. The purpose
of the hoax, presumably, was to call to Uncle Robert's attention, in
language he could understand, some of the menaces the Hawthornes,
as children, had been exposed to. Robert Manning might be obtuse
about the cold winters in Raymond, or the illness of the Fosters, or the
grim parson's fireside in Stroudwater; but he could be expected to understand a blight sweeping his orchards. Perhaps the joke was meaningless. Perhaps it was prompted by the singular fatality that swept down
so many of the most promising students of Bowdoin. The class of 1825
was celebrated for the number of famous men it produced. But in
Hawthorne's time it was remarkable also for the number of brilliant

students whose careers ended in disaster. Seven of the thirty-eight, and seven of the most promising, died, either in college or soon after graduating, almost before their careers began.

Sometimes Hawthorne seems older than his classmates, wiser, more reserved, cautious in his friendships, wary lest he overvalue his own and his friends' abilities, temperate in his enthusiasms, and sensible in getting out of college what he needed without wasting his strength on its unessentials. Sometimes the impression is one of loneliness and frailty. Then it seems that he walked around because he had nothing else to do, and slept through the holidays because he could not go home, refused to declaim because his clothes were not so good as the other students', and listened to Bridge's talk about his great future as a writer because he had nothing else to look forward to. Yet even when this impression is strongest there is still with him an underlying firmness and resolution that gives a queer kind of half-conscious purpose to even the wasted days of his boyhood.

These were the years when the teachings of Channing broke the hold that long years of doctrinal disputes had laid on the New England imagination. Hawthorne seems to have escaped both the rigorous teachings of the classic theologians and the robust practicability of the men who came after them. The seasons of thought intermingled; there was still the frosty brilliance and vivid logic of the Puritans persisting in the warm diffuse sunlight of Channing and his followers. Over Bowdoin, now busy and growing, quarrelsome, overworked, with a new medical school and the largest classes in history, the spirit of the old days still hovered, when Appleton had individually tutored each student in theology, and the graduates were distinguished by their maturity of vision and the all-pervading thoroughness of their religious training. Then college had no connotations of pleasure. There was no school spirit, no grades, no athletics, no cheers, no games, no organized sports, songs, colors, teams, baseball, football, dances, fraternities—there was scarcely more notion of sentimental attachment to a college than there would be to a reform school, a factory, or a bunkhouse in a logging camp. No one had written anything about college life; the notion of a Frank Merriwell, performing prodigies for his school, would have been bewildering to the students of that day. A great deal of New England's secret history lay hidden in the square unfurnished rooms in these bleak dormitories scattered through the forest. Lifelong enmities that later

reached into the country's political life, deep friendships, groups within
political parties, the semiblackmail of reference to college misdoings,
rivalries inexplicable except to those in school at the same time, had
their origin in them. It is impossible to read their history without a
sense that there was more involved in the struggle for their control than
ever appeared in the records; and it is impossible to reconcile their
rigid discipline, their grimness and unfriendliness, with the recollections
of graduates who always, unfortunately, seemed to have attended college at a time when licentiousness, disruption, gaming, godlessness,
drinking and vice (stimulated by the French Revolution) had never
been more widespread. A sense of betrayal was quite as common as any
feeling of attachment: consider the fierceness of Emerson's denunciation
of the Harvard Divinity School as "a garnished sepulchre, where may
be found some relics of the body of Jesus"—and which he thought was
doomed to be buried and forgotten forever unless such master spirits
as Appleton and Channing rescued it.[145]

If Hawthorne had gone to college five years earlier he would have
trained under Jesse Appleton, the tall, consecrated genius, with his angular El Greco features, his high domed head—he was completely bald
at thirty-five—and his selfless air of complete sincerity and devotion.
The son of a farmer, he had intended to become a mechanic. His interest
in education was too deep, however, and one of his brothers gave up his
own opportunity to be educated in order that Jesse Appleton might go
to college—a common occurrence in the biographies of the time, and a
theme for drama that American intellectuals, perhaps from a guilty
conscience, have never developed. Appleton attended Dartmouth. He
settled at Hampton on the New Hampshire coast, where his salary was
$450 a year, and married a sister-in-law of Jeremiah Mason, who bore
him three children. There was an astronomical gleam in his writing, like
stars seen in daylight, and he composed and worked over his sermons
as if they were poems. The immensity of God, the ages preceding creation, the time when the space now occupied by this earth, by the heavens,
and by the universe itself was a mighty void, the miracle of creation,
the mystery of this material system rising instantaneously into life—
such were the thoughts, clothed in images of great beauty, that Appleton gave his congregation in the little New England town.

"That creation, of which we can entertain any tolerable conception,
is nothing more than the change of one thing into another," he said.

"When a tree, or a plant is produced, certain particles from the earth, and air, are differently arranged, placed in a new relation to each other, and then assume a new appearance. Yet strictly speaking, there is in all this no new creation; matter only assumes a different form;—all the material was provided before. But there was a time when there were no materials in the universe; and when all the matter, which is now in existence, was created from nothing. This surpasses our comprehension, and the thought confounds us. Our astonishment still increases when we are told that all this took place, without anything like that which is called labor. God spoke and it was done."

Appleton's coming to Bowdoin came about in the following way: a man without personal ambition, he had nevertheless, from his obscure parish, become a leader of the conservatives in the church, and was their candidate when the Hollis professorship of divinity at Harvard, the most influential clerical position in America, became vacant in 1807. He was rejected for this post and then accepted the presidency of Bowdoin, which had then been in existence only five years. He gave himself unsparingly to the work of the school. His death in 1821 removed one of the most powerful and best ordered minds in New England, and coming when it did, in the midst of the chaos that the Dartmouth College Case had created in educational circles, it left the school vulnerable to political agitation and restless strivings.[146]

Hawthorne was thus educated in an interim period, when the old ascetic training was disappearing, and with it the purity and elevation of thought of Appleton's administration, and the newer teachings, pertaining far less to matters of the spirit, had not yet become organized. In addition to Latin and Greek, he studied algebra and geometry, Euclid, logic, surveying, the measurement of solids, heights and distances, navigation, English composition, Horace, mechanics, conic sections, hydrostatics, pneumatics, magnetism, electricity, optics, chemistry, theology, philosophy, astronomy, geometry, trigonometry, and law. He also studied medicine for one term, a special course that cost $15. Tuition was eight dollars a term—$24 a year. Room rent was $3.74 a term, and board $1.75 a week. Library fees were 50 cents, the chambermaids received $1.11 a term, and other fees amounted to about a dollar. An average bill for a term was $14.50—$43.00 a year. With no expenses for clothing or recreation, a student's expenses were at least $106 and probably $150 a year.[147]

Hawthorne appears to have been worried about money throughout his first two years at school. Thereafter he affected a lordly indifference to the subject. He left off rooming with Mason, after two years, and took a room alone at Mrs. Dunning's outside the college grounds, where he took his meals. In his last year at school he neglected to pay his college bills. He now dressed with care, bought a new watch chain, a cane, and a pair of white gloves. He attended classes irregularly. He joined the Athenaeans, in his sophomore year. It was one of the two literary societies on the campus, and the one which was, roughly, the newer and more radical. Pierce, Bridge, Cilley, and Fessenden were prominent Athenaeans. Longfellow, Calvin Stowe, Seargent Prentiss, and Alfred Mason were representative Peucinians—Mason and Longfellow were initiated together the year after Hawthorne joined the rival club. The social life of the upperclassmen had none of the noisy brawling exuberance of their early days. They now dined quietly once a week at Ward's Tavern, visited in Portland, or Augusta, where Hawthorne seems to have spent a vacation with Bridge, played cards in the Androscoggin Loo Club, which they organized, went driving, and lived, if not exactly fashionably, with a gentlemanly air that marked their new station in life.[148]

Hawthorne and Longfellow were not intimate friends in college. Hawthorne was, however, on friendly terms with Longfellow's older brother Stephen, a rough-and-tumble character who was constantly in trouble with the college authorities. Henry Longfellow, in addition to being younger than Hawthorne and his companions, entered school a year after them. He was constantly ill and nervous, with vague apprehensions and "an unpleasant feeling in my head—a continual swimming and aching in my head—a fullness and heaviness." This at fifteen. His first poems, published when he was twelve, included *An Elegy on the Death of the Reverend Jesse Appleton, the Late President of Bowdoin College.*

At eighteen, in his senior year, Longfellow was already known as a poet. He was a correspondent to literary magazines, an essayist, and published sixteen poems, principally in the Portland newspapers, in his last year at school. His clear youthful verses, with their modesty and their exquisite finish, their simple descriptive charm, stand out in the journalism of the time still alive and enduring in the ruins of the news around them.[149]

Hawthorne had no desire to follow his example. His seclusion may have been accidental in his first years at school, but by the time he graduated it was deliberate. Late in 1825 his aunt Priscilla's husband, John Dike, visited him in Brunswick. Dike was a merchant. He had a number of small ships, principally sailing to Ireland. Dr. Gideon Barstow was his partner in many of his ventures.[150] Returning to Salem, Dike spoke of Hawthorne in the highest terms, and seems particularly to have praised Hawthorne to his mother. Hawthorne was displeased, and on July 14, 1825, he wrote: "The family had before conceived much too high an opinion of my talents, and had probably formed expectations which I shall never realize. I have thought much upon the subject, and have finally come to the conclusion that I shall never make a distinguished figure in the world, and all I hope or wish is to plod along with the multitude. I do not say this for the purpose of drawing any flattery from you, but merely to set mother right upon a point where your partiality has led you astray. I did hope that Uncle Robert's opinion of me was nearer the truth, as his deportment toward me never expressed a very high estimation of my abilities.[151]

This would seem to be definite enough, in view of the low appraisals of his character and ability that Robert Manning had expressed. After all the years of bitterness, in which Manning had insisted so stubbornly that Hawthorne was no good and the money spent on him wasted, Hawthorne now, on the eve of graduation, agreed with him. Robert Manning was right. There are two other incidents illustrating Hawthorne's attitude toward his kinspeople, and his constancy of purpose. One Sunday he went to Portland, and as he entered a tavern he saw a familiar figure, extremely drunk, surrounded by tavern loungers. He was trying to amuse them by reading. As Hawthorne approached he recognized the features of his cousin Thomas Forrester. There was a wealth of meaning in the picture of Simon Forrester's son sitting in a tavern, trying drunkenly to read aloud, a commentary on education as well as on himself, as the tavern loungers listened, not even amused, to words he could not get straight. Hawthorne came face to face with him. He started back as if he had come upon his own image in some unfamiliar place. Forrester did not recognize him, and Hawthorne, who was glad of it, turned and walked away.[152]

On December 20, 1824, Robert Manning married Rebecca Dodge Burnham in Salem.[153] Shortly before Robert Manning's marriage, Hawthorne and Jonathan Cilley fell into an argument over marriage in general and over Hawthorne's own plans in particular. It was probably the only time Hawthorne revealed his purpose, and it was characteristic of Cilley's power that he ferreted out what Hawthorne was determined to keep secret. They made a solemn wager, signed and sealed it, and left it with Horatio Bridge. It was dated Bowdoin, November 14, 1824. It read: *"If Nathaniel Hawthorne is neither a married man nor a widower on the fourteenth day of November, One Thousand Eight Hundred and Thirty-six, I bind myself upon my honor to pay the said Hawthorne a barrel of the best old Madeira wine. Witness my hand and seal. Jonathan Cilley."*

Hawthorne wrote a similar note: *"If I am a married man or a widower on the fourteenth day of November, One Thousand Eight Hundred and Thirty-six, I bind myself, upon my honor, to pay Jonathan Cilley a barrel of the best old Madeira wine."* The bet was to be paid within a month after the expiration of the time. The letters were sealed in a package and Hawthorne wrote across it. "Mr. Horatio Bridge is requested to take charge of this paper, and not to open it until the fifteenth day of November, 1836, unless at the joint request of Cilley and Hawthorne.[154]

Hawthorne had already begun to write; he conceived of a dozen years of solitary effort as essential to his purpose. Meanwhile, until he was ready, there was to be no exaggeration of his abilities to create greater expectations than he could satisfy, or to hurry him into work before he was ready to undertake it. The trouble with this rigorous program, of course, was that it made no provision for the unforeseeable accidents and conflicting purposes of the intervening years. Although he did not then see it—he did later on—the plan he had adopted necessarily placed its limits on experience: so much was to be admitted, and no more; life was to be lived within the boundaries of a fixed purpose, and whatever threatened that purpose was excluded. He thought he could imagine all passions, all feelings, and states of the heart and mind —"How little," he said, a dozen years later, "did I know!" [155]

What did he mean to exclude from his life as endangering his purpose? Politics, scholarship, the attraction of contrary impulses, the early successes of Longfellow, the dissipations of Thomas Forrester, the recklessness of Cilley, the flattery of his family, passion, the vanity of local triumphs, the wastefulness of personal competition—whatever disturbed and distorted the vision of his own work; whatever threatened, by being more intrinsically appealing, to drag him away from it. The lives of two of his college friends seemed to symbolize what he meant to avoid.

One was Franklin Pierce. Pierce was, Hawthorne said, a youth "with the boy and man in him, vivacious, mirthful, slender, of a fair complexion, with light hair that had a curl in it; his bright and cheerful aspect had a kind of sunshine, both as regarded its radiance and its warmth; inasmuch that no shyness of disposition, in his associates, could well resist its influence."

Pierce was an officer in the Bowdoin Cadets, in which Hawthorne was a buck private. To the end of his life Hawthorne could remember Pierce's intense earnestness in drilling his lazy company, the contrast between his youthful appearance and his veteran's airs as he barked out the orders he had learned from his father.[156] On one occasion, President Allen ordered him to move his company from the ground beside the president's house, where he had been drilling. Pierce refused, apparently in anger at Allen's highhanded manner. He was in grave scholastic difficulty. He had entered school a year before Hawthorne and Bridge and Cilley, when the influence of Appleton was still strong in the college, and his classmates were of the older type of Bowdoin students, "not boys," Hawthorne said, "but for the most part, well advanced toward maturity; and, having wrought out their own means of education, were little inclined to neglect the opportunities they had won at so much cost. They knew the value of time, and had a sense of the responsibilities of their position."

Pierce did not. Pierce's roommate was Zenas Caldwell, a brother of Professor Merritt Caldwell of Dickinson College. He was a Methodist, several years older than Pierce, pure minded, studious, and devoutly religious. Pierce's close friend was Josiah Little, independently wealthy, and one of the best scholars in the college, Pierce was impulsive, generous, courteous, manly, and warmhearted. He was also as popular as any student in Bowdoin. A kind of willful recklessness, however, underlay his ease and his friendliness; he was armored against everything except unpopularity. He had lived so long in an atmosphere of affection, and was so confident of being welcomed, of having his own native good cheer responded to, and his misdoings forgiven, that when his position grew serious he could only make it worse, as if subjecting his standing to its final test in seeing how far he could go.[157] He was deep; that was what people seeing only his charm and his gaiety missed in him—"Deep, deep, deep," Hawthorne said, and willing to play a terrible game for a tremendous stake.[158]

In his junior year the relative positions of the members of his class was determined, and Pierce's name was placed at the bottom of the list. He resolved never to attend another recitation. For several days he remained away from his classes, setting out on a course of conduct which he thought would get him expelled. The faculty took no notice of his behavior. When he had grown cool, Little and Zenas Caldwell took him in hand and tried to persuade him to settle down. Pierce at length agreed to try once more, saying, "If I do so, you will see a change."

His mind had run wild for so long a period that concentration was almost impossible. For three months he arose at four every morning, worked over his books all day, and often did not get to bed until midnight. After that length of time, he did not need to apply himself so intensely, and from that time until he graduated he was never censured, never unprepared for his classes, was only twice absent, both times unavoidably, and graduated as the third scholar in his class.[159]

At the time that Pierce was recovering his place in the college, the tragedy of Gorham Deane made a profound impression on the students. Deane was one of the most brilliant students in school. He had tuberculosis. He was excessively studious, brilliant, in poor health, which his hard study, little exercise and little sleep steadily worsened. As he moved through his tragic last days, the pathos and the meaning of his fate powerfully affected the students: a kind of hush of intensity settled on the school as Commencement and his last days approached together. It led to the question of Hawthorne's first novel: "Where is the happiness of superior knowledge?" Deane's uncomplaining devotion to the study he knew he could never live to apply, his resolute attention to knowledge which seemed every day more meaningless in comparison with the awful considerations of eternity that faced him every hour— these were the aspects of his tragedy that moved Hawthorne profoundly.[160] College students should be daydreamers, he thought, all of them—"when cloud land is one and the same thing with the substantial earth." [161]

Deane died on August 11, 1825, on the eve of Commencement. He was given second place when honors were awarded for his class. At about this same time, Zenas Caldwell, who had graduated with Franklin Pierce the year before, also died unexpectedly, the first of the two brilliant Bowdoin students whose careers ended before they actually began. Others came to grief within a few years. There was nothing to relate these tragedies to Bowdoin, except the fact that they had all gone to school there, nor any reason, except their number, for finding in them more than the normal accidents of the time. This is what intensified the impression they made, all the stronger for being indefinite, a vague sense of evil abroad, not a recognizable danger to be avoided, a fatality which seemed to strike down the most promising youth capriciously and senselessly, like a plague whose symptoms are dimly recognizable but for which no name has been found.

Hawthorne said his farewells to the graduating class without much regret. Allen called him into the office, and told him that, while his work in general was satisfactory, he was not given a place on the Commencement exercises because of his refusal to declaim. Except for Bridge and Pierce, Hawthorne did not keep in touch with his college friends. Even Bridge seemed never to know exactly where Hawthorne was, or what he was doing, though they wrote regularly and Bridge visited him in Salem. The Navy Club, whose membership was made up of all those left off the Commencement exercises, and the Androscoggin Loo Club, which met weekly, disbanded, and with them ended Hawthorne's social life.[162]

Booths were erected along the fences of the yard, where hucksters sold pies, gingerbread, root beer and liquor. A platform was built in the open region near the pine grove. Families drove in from the farms for miles around and, mingling with the parents and families of the graduates, formed a summer assemblage like the crowd at a country fair. The fly-troubled horses were tied to the railing of a fence, and the crowd listened to young Henry Longfellow read a brilliant paper on the need for a native American literature. Almost every line of it might have been addressed to Hawthorne.[163] They met again in Cullen Sawtelle's room, where Longfellow read a poem to the graduating class. Then they separated. Hawthorne gave Bridge a watch seal that had belonged to his father, gold, with a carnelian stone, made in 1802. Half the class remained away from President Allen's reception for the graduates.

Longfellow went home to Portland, back to Bowdoin as a teacher, and to Europe. Ned Preble went to his luxurious home in Portland, and presently sailed to Germany, where he lived in a street called Jew Alley in Göttingen and wrote parodies ridiculing President Allen. He returned at length to Portland, where he died, still a young man, without fulfilling the promise of his youth. Josiah Little also died in early manhood. Pitt Fessenden settled to the study of law in Portland, and began courting Ellen Longfellow, who died on the eve of their marriage. Jonathan Cilley moved to Thomaston, Maine, entered politics and almost at once came into conflict with the regular Democratic organization, was expelled from the party caucus, branded as a traitor, organized his own opposition, and soon held the balance of power in the state. Pierce was elected to the legislature, became speaker of the House, went to Congress, was elected senator, and married Jane Appleton, Jesse Appleton's daughter. Alfred Mason studied medicine in Portsmouth and Philadelphia.

Hawthorne differed fundamentally from them. Behind Jonathan Cilley there was always the sense of desperate effort, of struggle whose outcome always meant the difference between triumph and catastrophe. Behind Franklin Pierce there were years of a happy childhood and the sense of belonging to a great and prospering family: victory was pleasant, but failure, for him, was not ruin. Behind Alfred Mason lay quiet years that had given him some of the characteristics, in his reserved courtesy, of the station in life his family occupied. Hawthorne was alone among them in the unsteadiness and loneliness of his early years, living in the conditions of poverty without being poor, moving from place to place without being homeless, and having no roots in his home town although, since his family had helped found it and his ancestors had made its history, he could never be a stranger there.

Behind him lay years, too, of extraordinary complexity—the death of his father, the suffering of his mother; the business of his relatives, whose operations went on, noisily and yet secretively, just beyond the boundary of his knowledge, a part of his life and yet without significance to him; his strange schooling, with brief periods of severe study and long years of half-dreamy, half-purposeful browsing; his wonderful imagination, which seized upon the trifles of Salem life and polished them until they brightened the rooms of the mind, but which when faced with the ordinary roughnesses of life, or its accidents and illnesses, magnified them into horrors, dreadful in their reasonableness and in the lack of an accompanying indignation or fear, terrifying as a child's words which unknowingly reveal the plot of a murder.

VIII

Hawthorne went at once to Salem and began to write. He finished his first book, *Seven Tales of My Native Land,* before the end of the summer. He was driven by stronger external motives, and a more passionate impulse within, than he felt for many years. He wrote all night, until his visions were a bright reality and the voices of his family, and the rattling of the wheels of the Manning stagecoaches, as they started on the morning road to Boston, seemed like faint sounds in a dream. His characters became more real than life to him. The gray dawn found him wide awake and feverish, victim of his own enchantment. He was inspired; walking in the starlit evenings, in the pure and bracing air, he became all soul and felt as if he could climb the sky and run a race along the Milky Way. He had the sense of certainty that comes with inspiration, the clear images, the vivid scenes that follow one another inexhaustibly, the flow of language, when ideas and phrases, each seeming perfectly apt and each generating new metaphors and new interlocking images, race through the mind faster than the pen can record them. He wanted to throw over his readers a ghostly glimmer, so that his imagination would take from Salem its everyday aspect and make it a proper theater for such wild scenes as he visualized.[164]

Only one of the stories of his first book has been preserved. Hawthorne destroyed the others, but *Alice Doane's Appeal* he rewrote in later years, adding to it an account of his original intentions with the story. It opened darkly with the discovery of a murder.

One December day in 1692—so, it seems, was the original beginning —three miles outside Salem on the road to Boston, a traveler found the body of a murdered man. It lay some distance back from the road, beside a small, ice-covered lake. A thick growth of dwarf pines separated the lake from the road. The surface of the ice had been hacked, perhaps with the same instrument used in the murder, as if the murderer had intended to hide his victim in the ice, and had been frightened away.

The murdered man was young, fashionably dressed, and had the appearance of one of good birth who had fallen upon evil times. His features were lined with marks of dissipation. The traveler who discovered his body—his dog led him to it—cleared away the snow that had fallen on the body, and was frightened at the expression of evil and scornful triumph that had hardened on them, so lifelike and terrible that it seemed the corpse might rise up and follow him.

The body was identified as that of Walter Brome. He was a stranger in Salem, who had arrived a few months before from England. His murder caused intense excitement. The search for the murderer was unavailing, and he was buried in the old graveyard where all of the dead of the town, since its foundation in 1628, were laid away.

Two of the mourners at the funeral were his only friends in Salem. They were a brother and sister, Alice and Leonard Doane. They were the only surviving members of their family; all the others had been killed in an Indian massacre in their childhood. Or so they believed, though what had happened on the night of the Indian raid was obscured in the dim depths of the memories of childhood. A sense of horror and loss, a broken and confused memory that caused a deep and troubling pain when it returned, were all that remained—though there was a deep taint in Leonard's nature; his feelings were morbid and his imagination diseased. He was gifted, but his gifts seemed to bear no fruit. Their loneliness brought brother and sister together. Alice was beautiful and virtuous, and only her excellence calmed the wild heart of her brother.

They had both been attracted to Walter Brome. Alice felt a powerful and undefined attraction for him, and he openly sought her love. As they met more frequently, Leonard Doane became conscious of a strange impression that the youth from overseas was like someone he knew; his features seemed the same as those of someone somehow buried deep in his memory, at whose recollection a sense of dread and horror swept over him. He and Walter were much alike. Sometimes the same thoughts would express themselves at the same time from their lips. He shrank in loathing from the image of himself written large in Walter's scornful features. But the talents that had not yet flowered in Leonard had already withered in Walter Brome. The wickedness that Leonard knew only in imagination, and the passions of which he was dimly aware, the stranger knew in actuality. Yet there was a resemblance between them from which Leonard Doane shrank with sickness, and horror, as if his own features had come and stared at him in some solitary place.

Outside the town, beneath a range of rocks, there stood a hut where lived an old wizard—a small, gray, withered man who was somehow responsible for bringing Walter to Salem, and who worked to bring him and Leonard and Alice together. Living, most of the time, with a vacant and lifeless expression on his face, feeble and half senseless, he nevertheless had a grisly power and a fiendish skill in playing upon the suspicions and fears that were growing in Leonard's mind. Leonard discovered, or thought that he discovered, a secret sympathy between Alice and Walter. A distempered jealousy maddened him, and he perceived that Alice loved the newcomer because he was so much like himself. The thought brought a savage one in its train. Here was a man whom Alice might love with all the strength of sisterly affection, added to that impure passion which alone engrosses all the heart. So he brooded in his deepening agony: the stranger would have more than the love that had gathered to him from the many graves of their household. Leonard would be left desolate. With some mysterious knowledge of his process of thought, and of his life, and of the life of the stranger, the old wizard encouraged him. Thus when Walter and Leonard met on the road outside town, and Walter tormented Leonard with proof of Alice's guilt, Leonard killed him.

As he bent over his fallen enemy a confused and broken memory, long haunting and troubling his consciousness, swept over him with its first distinctness. The years since childhood rolled back. It seemed to him that he was standing beside the hearth of the cabin where his father lay dead. He was weeping. He heard Alice cry. His own cry rose with hers as they beheld the features of their father, fierce with strife, and distorted by the pain in which his spirit had passed away.

The vision vanished. He stood again in the lonesome road, weeping as he had wept after the night of horror when the Indians had killed his father. The face of the dead man seemed to him like the features of his father. He shrank from the fixed glare of its eyes. He tried to recapture his first triumphant sense of release and could not. He carried the body through the pines to the shore of the lake, and began to chop feverishly on the ice, thinking to hide the body beneath it. Then he heard two travelers approaching, and fled. Snow began to fall. A little drifted heap partially covered the body and lay deepest over the pale dead face. The next day Walter Brome's body was found and the tragic story of Leonard and Alice approached its end.

Tortured by the idea of his sister's guilt, and yet sometimes yielding to a conviction of her purity; stung with remorse for the death of

Walter Brome, and shuddering with a deeper sense of some unutterable crime, perpetrated, as he imagined, in madness or a dream; moved also by dark impulses, as if a fiend were whispering him to meditate violence against the life of Alice, Leonard left his sister on the night after the funeral and went out into the storm. He reached the hut of the wizard. The old man sat beside a smoldering fire, the water beating against the low roof overhead. There was a flash of expression across his vacant features as Leonard came into the room. Driven by an obscure impulse —for under certain conditions the wizard had no power to withhold his aid in helping him unravel the mystery—Leonard poured out his confession of the murder. He spoke of the closeness of the tie that united him and Alice. He told of the consecrated fervor of their affection from childhood upward, their sense of lonely sufficiency to each other, because they only of their family had escaped death in the Indian massacre. A grisly smile flitted across the features of the wizard. He sat listening to what he already knew. Sometimes, when Leonard paused, he spoke a word or two, mysteriously filling up some void in the narrative. He nodded with pleasurable interest when Leonard's confused description of the resemblance between himself and Walter threw a glimmering light into the mystery. When the young man told how Walter Brome had taunted him with indubitable proofs of Alice's shame, and how he died by her brother's hand before the triumphant sneer could vanish from his face, the wizard laughed aloud. Leonard started. A gust of wind came down the chimney. It sounded like the old man's slow unvaried laughter. "I was deceived," Leonard thought. He went on with his fearful story. "I trod out his accursed soul," he said, "and knew that he was dead; for my spirit bounded as if a chain had fallen from it and left me free. But the burst of exalting certainty soon fled, and was succeeded by a torpor over my brain and a dimness before my eyes, with the sensation of one who struggles through a dream. So I bent down over the body of Walter Brome, gazing into his face, and striving to make my soul glad with the thought that he, in very truth, lay dead before me. I know not what space of time I had thus stood, nor how the vision came. But it seemed to me that the irrevocable years since childhood had rolled back, and a scene, that had long been confused and broken in my memory, arrayed itself with all its first distinctness. Methought I stood a weeping infant by my father's hearth —by the cold and blood-stained hearth where he lay dead. I heard the childish wail of Alice, and my own cry arose with hers. . . . As I gazed, a cold wind whistled by and waved my father's hair. Immediately I stood again in the lonesome road, no more a sinless child, but a man of blood, whose tears were fast falling over the face of his dead enemy."

Still tortured by the idea of Alice's guilt, Leonard returned to her, and the wretched brother and sister made their way, on the following night, to the graveyard. The funeral of Walter Brome had taken place three days before. As they walked at midnight they seemed to see the wizard gliding by their side or walking dimly on the path before them. The storm had ended. The moon was bright; the blue firmament appeared to glow with an inherent brightness; the greater stars were burning in their spheres; the northern lights threw their mysterious glare far over the horizon; the few small clouds aloft were burdened with radiance; but the sky, with all its variety of light, was scarcely so brilliant as the earth. The rain had frozen as it fell. The trees were hung with diamonds and many-colored gems; the houses were overlaid with silver, and the streets paved with slippery brightness; a frigid glory was flung over all familiar things, from the cottage chimney to the steeple of the meetinghouse that gleamed upward to the sky. The world seemed the creation of a wizard power, with so much of resemblance to known objects that a man might shudder at the ghostly shape of his old beloved dwelling, and the shadow of a ghostly tree before his door. One looked to behold inhabitants suited to such a town, glittering in icy garments, with motionless features, cold sparkling eyes, and just sensation enough in their frozen hearts to shiver at each other's presence. For a few moments, in the bright and silent midnight, Leonard and Alice stood alone beside the new-made grave.

But suddenly there was a multitude of people among the graves. Each family tomb had given up its inhabitants. The specters of the early settlers, soldiers and pastors, housewives and maidens, reappeared where the mourners had left them. Yet only accursed souls were there. Moonbeams on the ice glittered through the breastplate on the ghost of a warrior. The letters of the tombstones could be read through the forms that stood before them. A breeze swept the old men's hoary beards, the women's fearful beauty, into one indistinguishable cloud. Their countenances were contorted by intolerable pain or unearthly and derisive merriment. This company of devils had come to revel in the discovery of as foul a crime as was ever imagined in their dreadful abode. For the wizard possessed a secret that the others did not. He knew that the Brome family had not been wiped out in the Indian raid of their childhood. Another survived besides Leonard and Alice—Leonard's twin brother, rescued, taken to England, and raised there. The old wizard, feeble as a child and senseless as an idiot in all good purposes, nevertheless had a superhuman power in executing evil: he had contrived that Walter Brome should tempt Alice to sin and shame, and himself perish by the hand of Leonard. The revelry of fiends continued until Alice appealed to the specter of Walter Brome; he absolved her of every stain; the apparitions vanished, and Leonard and Alice stood alone beside the grave of their brother.

IX

Hawthorne said of these early years that he had blindly believed he could imagine all passions and feelings and all states of the mind and heart. For a youth of twenty-one it seems he came remarkably close to picturing passions and feelings beyond the range of his experience, an Elizabethan world of jealousy and madness, revenge, incest, horror— which, probably, is what he meant when he added, "How little did I know!" Of passion in the elemental sense, *Alice Doane's Appeal* [165] had aplenty; what he did not know (in imagination) was not these darker aspects of existence, but the full flow of common experience against which its excesses are measured. Like all youth, he thought of knowledge of the world as meaning a knowledge of its wickedness or of its tragedies, into which he bored deeper and deeper in a search for understanding; what he did not know, in these first fustian days, was its happiness, its ordinariness, its unculminated tragedies, its neglected revenges, its fiendish plots that remain locked in the mind of the plottor, its forgotten purposes and forgivenesses—and then, too, the winter days too cold for tragedy, the hard-working summers too busy for brooding, the mornings that banish the nightmares of doubt, and the simple enjoyment of life that makes such terrifying visions of evil no more than exercises of the imagination, compelling because of their remoteness from the plain life around us.

Even so, the story is Elizabethan; no other word is adequate. It has the violence and passion of Elizabethan tragedy, and its unevenness, the grimly literal descriptions alternating with unearthly imaginative flights. *Alice Doane's Appeal* was the synopsis of an opera, or a story for a ballet; it was not so much a work of fiction as it was a gifted child's story of a Shakespearean play he had seen. But the play had never been produced and no one else had seen it; and Hawthorne seemed to be always appealing to the reader to wait a moment and he, too, would see this wonderful drama that had been played over the footlights of his mind. All the ingredients of his story, except the final climax of the dance of the fiends—which is, indeed, its weakest part—had come right out of Salem. The brother and sister were real enough. The year, 1692, had its local meaning: that was the year of the witches. The wiping out of a family in an Indian raid was common; and the separation of the survivors, with a brother in England and a brother and sister in America, growing up unknown to each other was plausible. The old man addling the minds of the children was not overdrawn for the time, and the strangest feature of the story is that its most unearthly scene, the rain freezing as it falls and encasing the trees in ice that glitters with a frigid glory in the moonlight, is photographic, a characteristic of Salem winter. There is a deeper meaning to *Alice Doane's Appeal*. The struggle of Old and New England was embodied in Hawthorne's first ardent and reckless story. It was summed up in the relation of Leonard and Walter, the sense of injury that the early colonists had, of having been abandoned in a wild and savage country or of having been driven to it, and then left unprotected against the attacks of the Indians; their resentment at the ease of life in the old country, and their hidden jealousy of its greater talents, or even of its vice, their dim recognition of a lost kinship and a broken brotherhood, and the hateful recognition of their own sins or their own lost innocence written plainly in the lives of each other.

CHAPTER THREE

I

$\mathcal{E}$lizabeth Hawthorne was then twenty-three years old. She was tall, with black hair, gray eyes, thin features, a good-humored mouth, and a knowledge of life almost frightening. There was a judicial quality in her mind, and if Hawthorne always seemed a prosecuting attorney of the imagination, she was like a judge who has grown too familiar with the crimes of mankind to have many illusions about it. The strangeness of her personality was that her sagacious air was combined with the appearance and manner of a pretty, sprightly, graceful young woman of twenty-three.

Hawthorne called her Ebie. She should have been dressed in dark soft silks, with a large, half-idle fan before her lips. It would have fitted her exotic appearance and personality. But the Hawthornes had no money for either such costumes or a painter to paint her portrait in them. She dressed in a quaint round dress of lightish brown mohair. She was as hardheaded as a shrewd Yankee farmer or one of her seafaring ancestors trading coffee in Batavia. She was deeply interested in politics, and appeared to have considerable political influence through her friendship with men of office, though her position as an unmarried young woman, surrounded by censorious aunts and uncles, forced her to conduct herself with great circumspection, and the exact nature of her relationship to the affairs of her time is unknown. It is, however, known that her influence, or even her power, existed; she was almost a legendary figure in Salem, and a visit from her was esteemed an honor. She was never away from the sound of the sea if she could help it. She liked the companionship of old people, and loved to walk—she was lithe and quick, with an ardent, darting glance for sights along the way. Her long eyelashes and broadly sweeping eyebrows were distinct against the pallor of her skin, which had the delicately clear, vigorous gleam of

110

moonlight. When she walked, even in her old age, her cheeks colored like a young girl's.[1]

Hawthorne always respected her judgment. When they collaborated it was impossible to say where her writing left off and his began. The difference was that she had a quick and pleasant wit, not the humor of Hawthorne, with his occasional broad comedy, and his really skillful parodies of his own writing, but a light and glancing comic view of life. It was characteristic of her that she should set herself to translating Cervantes.[2] She thought that Salem was funny, and she thought Hawthorne was funny, at least part of the time, and usually when he did not intend to be. The spooks and goblins did not frighten her, nor the gloomy legends of a family curse. The superior young collegians were another matter. When Bridge came to Salem to visit Hawthorne, she was not at home.[3]

She was able to laugh at Hawthorne's extravagances; but she did not think that *Alice Doane's Appeal* was funny. She liked it. She thought it had Hawthorne's peculiar genius in it, and she was right.[4] Hawthorne had been working on his book of stories in college; he finished them in the summer, and set about at once to have them published. While they were in the hands of the printer he began another book, which he intended to bring out before *Seven Tales of My Native Land* appeared.

Hawthorne was then living in the Manning house on Herbert Street. It is probable that he crossed the back yards, when he went to work, and locked himself up in his old chamber under the eaves in the Hawthorne house on Union Street. He took his meals with the Mannings. The living arrangements were highly informal, however, and the members of the household lived pretty much as they pleased. His mother still ate her meals in her own room; his sister Elizabeth usually slept until noon. Robert Manning had built a house on Dearborn Street for his bride, and now began building another beside it for Mrs. Hawthorne.

Hawthorne slept late. He borrowed his aunt Mary Manning's library card and walked downtown to the Salem Athenaeum and borrowed a book. The library was open only an hour a day, so his visits were at midday. The librarians, who earned $25 a year, were young college graduates; they remained very briefly at the post. But the Athenaeum was an excellent private library. It was built around a shipment of books captured by a privateer during the Revolution.[5]

He worked through the afternoons. Each evening, after tea, he left the house and walked for an hour. He walked to Cold Spring, or along the beach to the Neck, and out past the almshouse to Winter Island.[6] A causeway now connected it with the Neck, and the Orient Powder Company, which made a fortune selling gunpowder in Africa, had a powder magazine there. Or he walked along the beaches to the Juniper, treading through the seaweed driven ashore by the winds, and past the old ten-gun battery, overgrown with whiteweed and clover, and on past the smallpox hospital, with the yellow flag of warning flying around it, through thick grass trodden by no one but himself.[7]

Often he walked in the evening to Gallows Hill. Every fifth of November, Guy Fawkes Day, the young men of Salem lighted bonfires on the haunted height, without knowing what event they commemorated. He went through the town, passed the street of tanners and curriers at its outskirts, crossed the pasture and climbed the hill that from the road looked like the wall of a fort. No grass grew on Gallows Hill. It was covered with woodwax, dark and glossy green, except for the short periods in the summer when it put forth yellow blossoms and covered the hill with gold.[8]

From the height he could see out over the bay to its distant islands. North and south the two arms of the bay curved inland: southeast was the point around which lay Marblehead, and northeast the coast was deserted. Bakers Island and Great Misery Island were almost due east, and in the harbor were Little Haste and Great Haste, Coney, Eagle, Cutthroat Ledge, South Gooseberry, and Amber Rock.[9] At the foot of the hill, covering the flatland to the water's edge, lay the town, level as a chessboard, filling the whole peninsula with wooden roofs, church spires, trees whose branches rose above the housetops. The witches of Salem had been hanged on Gallows Hill. The grave of the wizard whose story he had told in *Alice Doane's Appeal* was somewhere near by.

From the hill he could watch the ships setting sail for the distant ports of the world. He had no love of the sea—to that extent he was a kindred spirit of Silsbee and Cleveland—but how the sea worked on his imagination! He paced along the tide-worked sand as lonely as Robinson Crusoe; he could scarcely have been more secluded had he been cast away on an island.[10] At night, when he could not sleep, and wished to summon up pleasant thoughts to calm his mind, he dreamed

of the merry bounding of a ship before the breeze. It was as happy a
thought as he knew, on the same level with the pictures of children playing round the door of a schoolhouse, or the radiance round the hearth
of a young man and his bride, or the last dance of rosy girls in a splendid ballroom, or the brilliant circle in a crowded theater as the curtain
fell on a light and airy scene.[11] Yet the sea was not romantic to him.
He had no illusions about the mariners of Salem. He said they were
smugglers—not all of them, or perhaps many of them, but enough.
He said that the Custom House officials connived with them. He said
that nothing could exceed the vigilance and alacrity with which they
locked up a delinquent vessel after a wagonload of valuable merchandise
had been smuggled ashore, at noonday, directly under their unsuspicious noses.[12]

Sometimes Hawthorne walked along the beach all day, vowing to
say nothing to anyone until sunset. He carried a few biscuits for his
lunch and an apple for dessert. His footprints marked the broad space
of sand, brown and sparkling, between the sea and the cliffs. He walked
near the water's edge, where the wet margin glistened brightly in the
sunshine and reflected objects like a mirror. A dry spot flashed around
his footsteps and grew moist again as he lifted his foot. Beach birds
preceded him along the strand, chasing each wave as it swept back,
and running up swiftly before the impending wave. Sometimes the waves
caught them and they floated lightly on the breaking crest. He passed
a lobster, an immense seaweed, a dead seal in a heap of sea grass, a
shark, a large gray bird that resembled a loon, the jawbone of a whale,
bejeweled with barnacles and shellfish. He skipped rocks acróss the
water, watched the fishing boats anchored offshore. Where Cold Spring
emptied into the cove he ate his lunch, making a feast of bread and
water. Then he lay in the sand in the sunshine, letting his mind rove
where it would. He dreamed of his stories—a story of two lovers, of
sunken ships and where they lie, of islands afar and undiscovered, whose
tawny children are unconscious of other islands and continents, and
deemed the stars of heaven their nearest neighbors. He sailed little ships
of driftwood across the cove, with the feather of a sea gull for a sail.
How the merchants of Salem would sneer at him![13]

Ships in the harbor, with the sunlight on their sails; yellow-flower-
ing shrubs and rosebushes, with their reddened leaves and glassy seed
berries; small fish darting to and fro and hiding themselves in the sea-

weeds; three little girls paddling their bare feet in the water; waves breaking through a passage in the cliff, filling it with tumultuous foam, and leaving its floor of black pebbles bare and glistening; the grass fields bestrewn with whiteweed; a gray mare feeding in a sunny pasture, walled irregularly in oakshade, and a small colt rubbing his head, alternately, with each hind leg; the setting sun kindling up the windows of the jail, as if there were a bright, comfortable light within its darksome stone wall; the town of Salem mirrored in the water of North River at evening, with the shadow of the moon dancing in it—hour after hour he sharpened his perceptions on the familiar sights of home, as if half consciously strengthening his observation for its greater tasks. He bathed in the cove, overhung with maples, the water cool and thrilling. At a distance it sparkled bright and blue in the breeze and sun. There were jellyfish swimming about, and several left to melt away on the shore. Sprouting on the shore, among the sand and gravel, he found samphire growing somewhat like asparagus—"an excellent salad at this season, salt, yet with an herb-like vivacity, and very tender." [14]

When he returned he ate a bowl of chocolate with bread crumbled in it. In the evenings he read. Maria Louisa sewed. Elizabeth tried to interest him in political arguments. She usually failed. His political interests were vague and intermittent, and only her contentious spirit kept the subject alive. There were a good many novels in that day, largely forgotten fifty years later, but very good reading then—they came in large shipments from England—and presently Elizabeth gave up trying to presuade Hawthorne to talk and settled down to read.[15] Once a week Horace Connolly and David Roberts called to play whist. Roberts was a young lawyer, afterward mayor of Salem, a writer on admiralty law, a state assemblyman, a man with a wide jaw, a straight mouth, a beard, deep-set eyes, and a high forehead. Horace Connolly was a cousin of the Hawthornes'—not a cousin by birth, but by adoption. He was a Yale graduate, a man of distinguished appearance, thin features, narrow eyes, a thin, arched nose—a typical New England face, yet with a curious quizzical and childlike expression instead of the characteristic New England shrewdness—a lawyer who later became an Episcopalian rector. He was adopted by Susan Hawthorne Ingersoll (Captain Daniel's sister), a widow, and changed his name to Ingersoll. Old Aunt Susie, as the Hawthornes called her, lived in the queer old house with its many gables at the opposite end of town from the Hawthornes—that house of small rooms and cubistic architecture which Hawthorne wrote about in *The House of the Seven Gables.* Horace Connolly figures in a poor light in Hawthorne's biography. Many years after this time, when Hawthorne was in grave difficulties, Connolly appeared among the ranks of his enemies who drove him out of his post in the Custom House. Yet individually he seems a pleasant enough character and the group of four—Elizabeth did not play—congenial companions.[16]

Sometimes Hawthorne worked all day while the raindrops pattered on his windowpane. When evening had fairly set in he sallied forth, tightly buttoning his shaggy overcoat, and hoisting his umbrella, the silken dome of which immediately resounded with the heavy drumming of invisible raindrops. The lamps threw their circles of red light around him, and twinkling from corner to corner other beacons marshaled his way to a brighter spot. The blinds of the windows in the tall buildings were closed. The collected rain tinkled down the tin spouts of their gutters. In the center of Salem the lights in the shop windows cast a glow from side to side, and the sidewalks gleamed with a wet sheen of red light. A retired sea captain passed him, on his way to the Marine Insurance Office, to spin yarns with a crew of old sea dogs like himself. A young man and a girl, on their way to a party, huddled under their umbrella. Through a window he caught a glimpse of a family circle—grandmother, parents, and children—all flickering, shadowlike, in the glow of a wood fire. He went on to the utmost limits of the town, where the last lamp struggled feebly with the darkness, like the farthest star that stands sentinel on the borders of uncreated space. The mail coach, outward bound, rolled heavily off the pavement and splashed through the mud and water of the road, the passengers tossing to and fro between drowsy watch and troubled sleep.[17]

It was probably six o'clock then, at which time, at least in the old days, the last Manning stage of the day set out for Boston. Perhaps it was later, for at eleven o'clock the stage of a connecting company, coming from Newburyport, passed through Salem on its way to the city. On other days he was up before dawn. In the dim, gray, dewy summer's morning he made his way to the old drawbridge over the North River, between Salem and Beverly. The incoming tide rushed with a murmuring sound among the massive beams of the bridge. Beside the tollgates there stood the small, square tollhouse, with its half-extinguished lantern gleaming dimly in the uncertain light—the tollhouse, with the tollgatherer asleep inside. A load of hay passed, the farmer stalking beside the oxen; the wheels creaked, and the haymow vanished in the morning mist. As the sun rose, there was a rattling thunder of wheels, a confused clatter of hoofs, and the mail stage, which had been traveling all night at the same headlong, restless rate, raced up on the bridge. He glanced inside at the sleepy passengers, stirring their torpid limbs and sniffing a cordial in briny air. That must have been the Eastern Stage Company's stage from Newbury, Portsmouth, and Portland.

Sometimes he loafed all day on the bridge. Strollers came from town to quaff the freshening breeze. Some of them dropped long lines into the water, and hauled up flounders, or cunners, or small cod, or perhaps an eel. The traffic grew heavy—a family of vacationers in a chaise, a half dozen pretty girls in a carryall, bound for a picnic, a country preacher on horseback, a butcher with his cart, two old ladies peddling huckleberries, a milk cart, a man packing a wheelbarrow load of lobsters, a pair of honeymooners in a new barouche, a tin peddler, flocks of sheep to market, a group of ladies on horseback in green riding habits, with gentlemen attendant, a Swiss jeweler, two sailors in a gig, smoking cigars and swearing all manner of forecastle oaths.[18]

And then on other days he read. In nine years he borrowed about seven hundred books from the library. He read everything—bound volumes of old newspapers, sermons, almanacs, histories, memoirs, travel books, English magazines, orations, diaries, geographies, encyclopedias, books on fruit trees and botany, works in French and Latin (Juvenal), zoology and lives of the admirals, Elizabethan dramatics (Massinger), and the work of a celebrated English police commissioner, Colquhoun, *On the Police.*

He read medical jurisprudence and the *United States Service Journal.* Whenever he went to see Horatio Bridge, he read the bound volumes of the *Service Journal* for the preceding years before setting out. He read Ben Franklin's works, Samuel Johnson, Burns, Dryden, Macchiavelli, Increase and Cotton Mather, Montaigne, Rousseau, Voltaire, Richelieu, Boswell, Pascal, Swift, Alexander Hamilton, and the work of his old president at Bowdoin, William Allen. He read the poetry of John Gay, Pope, Coleridge, Shelley, Keats, Matthew Prior, Wordsworth, and Byron. He read the collection of the Massachusetts Historical Society and a rare series of books, the British State Trails. This

was a work of many volumes, covering the trials for treason from remote antiquity to modern times. From it he learned a great deal about
pirates. He read much religious history—the history of the Shakers,
the Remarkables of Cotton Mather, the Laws and Charter of Massachusetts Bay, histories of the Quakers, and so on. And then the books
of travel. There was scarcely a country he left unvisited on these evenings. He read *Adventures on the Columbia River*, Tournefort's *Voyage*,
Maundrell's *Travels*, Bartram's *Travels*, Codell's *Journey Through
Italy and Carniola*, Cobbett's *Ride in France*, Cochran's *Tour in Siberia*,
Cherdin's *Travels*, Pocock's *Travels*, Pinchard's *Notes on the West Indies*, Chishull's *Travels in Turkey*, Savage's *New Zealand*, Poinsett's
Notes on Mexico, Bruce's *Travels*, Lister's *Journey*, Mackenzie's *Year
in Spain*, Heber's *Travels in India*, Madden's *Travels*, and an anony-
mous *Travels in Brazil and Buenos Aires*, Reynolds's *Voyages*, Terry's
Travels in South America, and Temple's *Travels in Peru*.

He deepened his knowledge of New England, already vast, by reading the local histories—the *History of Boston*, *History of Haverhill*, Lewis's *History of Plymouth*, Deane's *History of Scituate*,
History of Nantucket. He read a great deal of English botany and
zoology. He read works like Dunlap's *History of American Design* and
Jared Sparks' *Library of American Biography* as they appeared. He
read diaries and journals and the bound volumes of old magazines;
economics and philosophy and Baines's *History of Cotton Manufacture*. At one time Hawthorne considered writing or editing a series of
lives of the great merchants. It is unfortunate that he did not do so.
Their achievements were already being forgotten, and soon would be as
hard to recapture as the times of the Puritans.

Much of his reading was topical. During the nullification crisis
he read a history of South Carolina, for example. In his early days
in Salem, after his return from college, he read a good deal of law and
many works in French. The deepening of his interest in history is clear
as the years passed.

The books provide an almost weekly record of his whereabouts for
nine years. The legendary mystery of these years is in itself dissipated
by them. There is hardly another literary figure about whom so much
is known; indeed, there are few individuals in the history of the time
whose whereabouts can be placed so exactly. Only the keepers of diaries
have left so complete a record, and in their case the records are some-

times suspect, for they at times consciously wrote to give a favorable
impression of their activities. He read books of a high quality, though
by no means with a sense of "improving his mind"; his taste was naturally good, and writing was his work. He said that in these years he did
a great deal of good and good-for-nothing reading, and since Elizabeth
mentioned that he read a great many novels, and made an artistic study
of them, it is probable that the books he took from the library were
books he used in his work, and his reading for relaxation the popular
fiction of the time. He was no scholar, by his own account. He idly
turned the pages of a light magazine—probably *Gentleman's Magazine,*
the complete file of which he borrowed—and found at the end of the day
the peculiar weariness and depression that came from wasted effort.

In August, 1828, he began reading the bound volumes of the Boston newspapers of almost a century before. He read those of the entire
period covered by the Revolution. In September he studied the bound
volumes of the Salem *Gazette* of 1801 and 1802. The *Gazette* was never
better than it was in those years, and the paper no doubt had a deeper
interest for him because of the records of the lives of his kinspeople
it contained.[19]

There was no evidence in them, he observed, that morality was
higher then than now. There seemed to be quite as many frauds and
robberies; there were murders, in hot blood and malice, and "some of
our fathers appear to have been yoked to unfaithful wives." The winters
seemed to have rushed upon our ancestors with fiercer snows than now,
the cold was more piercing and lingered longer in the spring; lightning
was called the thunder stone, and struck more often. In the Boston
papers of 1736 and 1739 he read of slaves for sale, both black and
white. Samuel Waldo had a shipload of Irish girls for sale, Captain
Bulfinch a likely Negro wench. There was a great trade in them, and
they were more frequently advertised than any other commodity—
Negro wenches of many desirable qualities, Negro women, honest,
healthy and capable, Negro men, fit for almost any household work,
and one Negro man "very fit for a tailor." Sometimes Negro children
were given away. Negroes were not excluded from domestic affections.
The fire in the evening glowed on their dark, shining faces, intermixed
familiarly with their master's children. Their lot was not so painful
then, Hawthorne reflected, for there were white slaves along with them,

sold, though only for a term of years, but as actual slaves, to the highest bidder.[20]

II

Hawthorne had used his knowledge of New England history in *Seven Tales;* he used more of it in the stories that followed: *Fanshawe,* which he wrote immediately after finishing *Seven Tales,* and which he intended to publish first; *Roger Malvin's Burial, My Kinsman, Major Molineaux,* and *The Gentle Boy.* Since these last four stories were in the hands of a publisher in 1829, it seems clear that within four years of leaving college he had written the equivalent of at least two books of stories and a novel. He had probably written much more. None of this, however, had as yet appeared under his own name. Only *Fanshawe* had been printed, at his own expense. He paid a Boston firm, Marsh and Capen, $100 to bring out the book.[21]

He was dissatisfied with the chaotic formlessness of his early stories. His first novel he made a cool, balanced production, as if rigorously setting himself to answer some charge of incoherence or excess brought out against *Alice Doane's Appeal. Fanshawe* is a singular book. It is one of the first stories of college life in American literature, if not the first. Tradition ascribes its setting as Bowdoin. I am inclined to believe that Hawthorne had Dartmouth in mind when he wrote the book, at least in the external features of the school. Dartmouth was, like the college in the novel, situated in a spot as remote as the Happy Valley of Abyssinia. *Fanshawe* is laid in 1745, long before the founding of Bowdoin, and at a time appropriate in the history of Dartmouth. Then, too, in the college described in *Fanshawe* there are among the students a number of Indians "to whom an impractical philanthropy was endeavoring to impart the benefits of civilization." Dartmouth was originally an Indian school. Indeed, at the time of the Dartmouth College Case, it was charged that the original charter had been violated because the school no longer educated Indians; and the story circulated that Webster hurriedly smuggled a few bewildered redskins to the campus before the case came to trail. During Hawthorne's early years the Dartmouth College Case was a leading political issue throughout New England, and its history was told and retold. Moreover, Hawthorne had connections with people who were involved in the case—Alfred

Mason's father, as has been said, was one of its leading figures, and so was President Allen.

The point is one of interest, but not of primary importance. Hawthorne borrowed freely in his writing—the names of places and people, many of which he culled from the early issues of the Salem *Gazette*. The innkeeper in *Fanshawe*, for example, is a retired pirate named Hugh Crombie. There was a Crombie Inn in Salem at the time of the Revolution. The story of the novel is simple. Its motivations, compared to the obscurities of *Alice Doane*, are crystal clear.

Fanshawe is generally considered the weakest of Hawthorne's works. He was principally responsible for its reputation. Soon after it was published, he secured all the copies that he could locate, and burned them. He had given copies to his sister Elizabeth and Bridge. Elizabeth did not like the book; she thought it had less of Hawthorne's peculiar genius in it than *Seven Tales*. He asked that they return them, and included their copies in his bonfire. All traces of the novel disappeared. Bridge once tried to talk to Hawthorne about it. The subject was so painful that he never attempted it again. Hawthorne published the book anonymously and insisted his family and friends keep the secret: "and of course we did," said Elizabeth, "with one or two exceptions, for we were in those days absolutely obedient to him. I do not quite approve of either obedience or concealment." [22]

And yet the book was not a failure. It was read, reviewed, and remembered; Hawthorne's publisher, Goodrich, later told him that it would have been a success had its printer had any way of selling the copies. For fifty years it remained buried. In 1876—twelve years after Hawthorne's death—his family discovered a copy, and it was reissued. [23] Appearing then, when Hawthorne's fame was greatest, and when his biographies were being published, his collected works and journals edited, it was generally pronounced as without distinction compared to his best work.

Yet it would be difficult to find another first novel, written by anyone of his age—twenty-two or twenty-three—as well done. Had the book been reissued under a pseudonym it is doubtful that authorship would ever have been attributed to Hawthorne. If it were not for the fact that two people who read the novel when it first appeared—Bridge and Elizabeth Hawthorne—were still alive, it might well have been considered an excellent forgery, written by someone with a profound knowledge of Hawthorne's life and style, and with all of his quality except his intensity. Only in occasional lines and scenes—the grief of Fanshawe in facing his futile study, the remorse of the pirate at his mother's death—and a few rare and haunting descriptions—the little stream by the college, the bell of the chapel calling the students to evening prayer—does Hawthorne's quality emerge. He had imposed a rigorous discipline on himself, checking at every point the flights of his imagination, though under the smooth surface of the story the power of genius shows like the muscles of a race horse held in check.

Fanshawe is more like the stories of Robert Louis Stevenson than it was like the ponderous romances that were being written in the 1820's. It is readable, full of pirates and runaways, escapes and remarkable coincidences. Its story is, indeed, the opening of *Treasure Island*, without the voyage, the island, or the treasure. *Fanshawe* is a story of the vice around a college town. Consider its situation: the proprietor of the tavern beside the college is a pirate who fled inland to escape the noose, married the tavernkeeper's widow, and became respectable. (The tavern in *Fanshawe*, incidentally, is plainly modeled on Ward's Tavern in Brunswick.) While he is enjoying his new station in life, an old shipmate from the *Black Andrew* appears, and blackmails him into helping him kidnap the ward of the college president.

Pirates were still fairly common at the time Hawthorne wrote his novel, and were much commoner at the time in which the story is laid. They had the same connotations of terror as gangsters a century later. John Forrester's *New Endeavor* had been boarded by pirates in 1825 and robbed of $4,500 in gold. The last reported case of piracy in the West Indies took place a few years later, when the *Mexican* of Salem was boarded. The pirates in this case were captured, tried, and seven of them hanged in Salem. At the time Hawthorne's novel was published, the *New Priscilla* of Salem was found deserted in the West Indies, her stern-boat tackles hanging in the water. It was believed that pirates had murdered all of the crew. The body of a boy was found spiked to the deck.[24]

To continue with Hawthorne's novel: the ward of the president is an heiress. Her father is a wealthy American merchant, living in England, who had entrusted his daughter to the president in his absence. The plan of the kidnaper (who had been in the merchant's employ before he turned to crime) is to seize the girl on the pretext of taking her to her father, and compel her to marry him. He deceives her guardian with a story planted in the newspapers, falsely reporting her father's death in a shipwreck. He deceives her with a report that her father is ruined in business and needs her at once, swearing her to secrecy to prevent news of the failure from becoming known. He is checked by the girl's two admirers, rivals for her hand, among the college students. One is Edward Wolcott, a headstrong, reckless youth, who seems plainly modeled on Franklin Pierce. The other is Fanshawe, ill, melancholy, brilliant, a typical romantic portrait of the student and scholar, obviously inspired by Gorham Deane.

Ellen, the heroine of the novel, cannot be identified so positively. She may have been modeled on Jane Appleton, whose marriage to Franklin Pierce took place not long after *Fanshawe* was published. Jane Appleton had a certain oblique resemblance to Ellen. As Jesse Appleton's daughter and Jeremiah Mason's niece, she was a member of a prominent Federalist family; as Franklin Pierce's bride, she joined the circles of the most enlightened and statesman-like of the New England Democrats. There was a Romeo-and-Juliet conflict of houses ended by her marriage. Frail, beautiful, with a pensive, ethereal charm, she was loved and admired; the hostility directed toward Franklin Pierce never included her.*

At about the time *Fanshawe* was published, her cousin Alfred Mason, Hawthorne's old Bowdoin roommate, died in New York. He had begun his medical training in Portsmouth, where his first patients were the elderly ladies in the almshouse. He studied in Philadelphia, then took a competitive examination for the post of assistant surgeon at Bellevue, won, and served under an old friend of his father's. He had barely begun his duties when an epidemic of yellow fever swept the wards; he exhausted himself caring for the victims, contracted the disease, and died on April 12, 1828.[25] Whether his death, coming so soon after the death of Deane and Caldwell, had anything to do with Hawthorne's withdrawing *Fanshawe* from publication is doubtful; though there does seem to be a connection between them and Hawthorne's attitude toward his school and his classmates.

If he had tried to correct the excesses of his first stories, he had

---

* The wife of General Robert E. Lee, who knew her well, and who had known many of the wives of the presidents in her lifetime, considered her the most truly excellent of them all.

perhaps succeeded too well. The flaw in *Fanshawe* is not that it is youthful and awkward, but that it is too skillfully done. Unlike his short stories, which were always somehow a little lopsided, it is perfectly symmetrical, its formal excellence unsurpassed by anything he later wrote. Its plot is worked out with absolute precision. Its humor is engaging and easy. It is lucid and rational, with none of the imaginative flights that linked the early stories to Elizabethan tragedy. And so it slips away from memory, a work too polished and supple to be remembered.

Even in so carefully balanced a work, however, the unexpected strength and momentary inspirations intervene to destroy the precise design, as they do in life. The minor figure of the pirate is, in the end, the only really strong character in the book. Fanshawe is almost a stock character. The reason for his melancholy is unclear, and as a result both his renunciation of Ellen and his absorption in study are without the meaning and emotion attributed to them. Gorham Deane made a profound impression on Hawthorne in college because he spent his last days in the pursuit of knowledge he would never live to apply; but in *Fanshawe* the reader never learns what it is that has given the hero his premonition of an early death. He remains indistinct, and the sunburned, sea-flushed pirate, home after a life of crime, bold, forceful, and yet with a subtle uneasiness undermining his courage, is a more powerful creation. It is Fanshawe who conquers him, just as, in New England history, the wild privateers were tamed by the academies, and as, in his own family, the exploits of Captain Daniel and Simon Forrester gave way to the quiet study and labor of his life.

III

The days lengthened into years. His work remained unpublished and his name remained unknown. He sat each day in the chamber in the old house and wrote. If I should ever have a biographer, he said— he has had more than any other American writer—if I should ever have a biographer, he ought to make great mention of this chamber in my memoirs. It was haunted, he said, and it still seems haunted. Visions came to him there, thousands and thousands of them. His youth was spent there; there his mind and character were formed. It seemed to him, as the years passed, that he was already in his grave, with only

life enough to be chilled and benumbed. Yet he was happy, as happy
as he knew how to be—happy enough, with a perplexing restless resignation, not to want to escape, happy enough, indeed, to voluntarily
lock himself up in his prison each morning and remain there all day.
And as is always the case—one reason why critics are discouraged
in writing of him—he made the best characterization of the years in the
haunted chamber when he spoke of the viewless bolts and bars that
kept him in.[26]

Now, of what nature were the visions that came to him, and of
which a few, he said, have become known to the world? Taking a group
of representative stories written before he was twenty-six or twenty-
seven—*Roger Malvin's Burial, My Kinsman, Major Molineaux, The
Hollow of the Three Hills, The Gentle Boy*—and a few others written
when he was about thirty—*Young Goodman Brown, The Canterbury
Pilgrims, The Haunted Mind, Wakefield*—the dominant impression that
they convey is of the mastery with which Hawthorne's historical knowledge is grained into the texts. The first of these, except *The Gentle Boy*,
are formally almost flawless. *Roger Malvin's Burial* is the story of a
young soldier who leaves a companion to die in the forest. Both are
wounded; he does not desert the dying man, who, on the contrary, forces
him to go on to save himself, since if he remains both are certain to
perish. Yet a lingering sense of guilt haunts him all his life. His townsmen, and his companion's daughter—who becomes his wife—believe
that he remained with the dying man, and buried him; the young soldier's only sin is that he lets the story grow rather than confess, not
cowardice but what he fears will be considered cowardice. And thus
his life is twisted and his strength dissipated; eventually he loses his
farm, and sets out with his wife and son into the wilderness to clear land
for another one, stopping, by a fatal mischance, at the point where his
companion had died many years before, and where, in a ghastly rework-
ing of the old tragedy, he kills his own son in an accident while hunting.

There are in these stories the archaic usages that weaken their
effect on modern readers. All these shrieks and cries of anguish, all these
precise retributions, are so carefully worked out that it sometimes seems
Nemesis was a kind of New England storekeeper, doling out so much
poetic justice, in exactly the same terms and in exactly the same currency at the precise place where the previous crime was committed, or
the previous indebtedness incurred. They are the natural result of

Hawthorne's desire to achieve a formal perfection in a very narrow and rigid framework, while at the same time making the stories carry the burden of historical fact he was steadily accumulating. When allowances are made for them—and they are, after all, a trivial flaw of his work—their original contribution becomes clearer and his purpose plain. The New England character was his subject, of which these tales were facets. Only in this particular part of the globe, he seems to say, was there the moral fortitude that made the dying man drive his young companion from him, and the scruples that made the young soldier fear to confess an action so blameless. The story is not really a story, despite its cunning plot—that, it may be, is why Hawthorne worked over the plots of his stories with such care—but an essay surrounded by incidents from history. So he remarks in passing, in explaining the young soldier's ruin, that the New Englanders had a tendency to turn to lawsuits to settle their disputes, an observation which, coming in the midst of the fine-spun observations on the moral problem of his guiltless guilt, throws a light on the wan and trembling hopes and aspirations of the little communities of those early days.

The depth of his historical research is clearer in *My Kinsman, Major Molineux*. It should perhaps be said at the outset that Hawthorne appears to have had little enthusiasm for the Revolution. Washington he profoundly admired, and the New England farmers who left their plows and became brigadier generals, after which they took up their interrupted farming, seemed to him what military men should be. He thought Timothy Pickering's homespun manual for training the militia a classic. He thought that if Pickering had known more military science it would not be so good. Yet the Revolution as such, as the schoolboys learned of it, did not make much appeal to his imagination. His knowledge of the pre-Revolutionary years was too great. He perhaps thought it unnecessary. What other meaning can be read into the opening sentences of *The Gray Champion*: "There was once a time when New England groaned under the actual pressure of heavier wrongs than those threatened ones which brought on the Revolution?"

My Kinsman, Major Molineux is the story of young Robin, who makes his way from the country to Boston to live with his famous and wealthy kinsman, the Major, just as the Major is tarred and feathered and driven out of the colonies. It is a genuinely high-spirited, comic story, the bewilderment of the boy who wanders onto the stage just as the plot is coming to a climax, his baffled attempt to find out what is happening, and his encounters with desperadoes, rebels, prostitutes, and friends in disguise. Its high moment is perhaps the incident when Robin stops a passer-by to ask his way to the Major's house, and finds that one side of his face is painted red and the other black, as he rushes off to join the mob—"strange things we travelers see!" says Robin. In this story the historical details are fused with the action in an almost flawless pattern. The clothing of a country boy of that period, the value of the depreciated currency of the colony, the interior of a barbershop, the advertisements on the tavern walls, the mechanics of the conspiracy, the girls beckoning from the dark doorways, and the awful humiliation of the Major, give it a photographic reality. Its light and jaunty mood is almost essential, with any other tone it would be unbearable in its grim account of a cold-blooded, excited, and yet rigidly controlled mob in action: "There, in tar-and-feathery dignity, sat his kinsman, Major Molineux! He was an elderly man, of large and majestic person, and strong, square features, bespeaking steady soul; but steady as it was, his enemies had found means to shake it. His face was pale as death, and far more ghastly; the broad forehead was contracted in agony, so that his eyebrows formed one grizzled line; his eyes were red and wild, and the foam hung white upon his quivering lip. His whole frame was agitated by a quick and continual tremor, which his pride strove to quell, even in these circumstances of overwhelming humiliation. . . ."

How vivid those visions were! In this same period Hawthorne wrote his early masterpiece, *The Gentle Boy*, a tale of the persecution of the Quakers. Its mood was dark as a pine forest. Wind moved in the trees beyond the ragged clearings of the early settlers, people were summoned to church by a drum rather than the ringing of a bell, snow drifted against the windows and around the crevices of the doors, and to be driven out of the towns, and abandoned in the forest, as the Quakers were, was virtually a sentence of death. The story was good history and good fiction, and though laid in 1659 it had a plain application to New England of 1830. The preaching of the Unitarians had raised an old question, the old problem of uniformity and freedom. Those who followed Channing—not so much Channing himself—the students of Carlyle and German philosophy, who formed the Transcendental Club, carried their faith in the value of intuition to the point where it was almost a denial of reason: "truths which pertain to the soul," said a South Marshfield mechanic, in the best definition of the new philosophy, "cannot be proved by any external evidence whatever." [27] When was the inner call a genuine prompting of the spirit and when was it a cloak for self-deception? The merciless uniformity and discipline that the Puritans imposed on themselves and demanded of everyone was plainly withering, but the extravagance of their opponents, their spiritual license, their wild irresponsibility, and their romantic faith in the value of personal inspiration, was equally unbalanced. The story of *The Gentle Boy* is of these two forces contending for "the empire of the young heart." The young heart is symbolized by a child, the son of a Quaker hanged for heresy. He seems to represent the native spiritual growth of America, its indigenous religious and creative spirit, entangled in the ancient conflicts brought hither from other lands. He is neither strong enough to overcome them nor yet vital enough to flourish independently of them. His imagination is vivid, his perceptions quick and generous, and he possesses a faculty for finding happiness as a witch hazel seeks out hidden streams of water—but his mind, like a forest vine, lacks stamina; it can twine itself beautifully around something stronger than itself, but if left unsupported can only wither on the ground.

On November 12, 1830, the Salem *Gazette* published Hawthorne's *The Hollow of the Three Hills*. It was a very short story, no more than a sketch. If Hawthorne had not included it in *Twice-Told Tales* it is doubtful if authorship would have ever been attributed to him, or that any student, thumbing through the files of the paper, would have said positively that it was Hawthorne's work, though its quality is unmistakable.[28] *The Hollow of the Three Hills* was a story of absolute evil. It was an account of an unfaithful wife's confession to an old crone, in return for learning what had happened to the home she had fled. It was laid in early colonial times. A woman newly arrived from England, graceful in form and feature, though pale and troubled, met an ancient and meanly dressed woman, ill favored, withered, shrunken and decrepit, in a gloomy hollow in the hills where tradition said the witches reveled. For an hour they held their secret meeting. The old crone conjured up visions to the woman of the consequences of her sin—her parents dishonored, her daughter dead, her husband driven mad—until the woman died from their power, whereupon—"Here has been a sweet hour's sport," said the withered crone, chuckling to herself.

There was the other side of this story, told in *Young Goodman Brown*, published a few years later. In it the devil appears to a young man, misleading and deceiving him as the old wizard deceived Leonard in *Alice Doane's Appeal*. When the young man remonstrates that his parents and grandparents never took this path through the forest, the devil tells him what they did to the Quakers and the Indians' children. The parents and grandparents of Young Goodman Brown have a strong resemblance to Colonel John and Colonel William Hawthorne— both good friends of mine, the devil tells Young Goodman Brown reassuringly. When Young Goodman Brown opens his eyes he finds the minister and the deacon of the church, the kind old lady who taught him his prayers and, at last, his own wife, Faith, in the same unholy conclave of revelers. Then the devil tells them that it shall be given to them to know their secret deeds—"how hoary-bearded elders of the church whispered wanton words to the young maids of their households; how many a woman, eager for widow's weeds, has given her husband a drink at bed time, and let him sleep his last sleep in her bosom; how beardless youths have made haste to inherit their father's wealth; and how fair damsels . . . have dug little graves in the garden and bidden me, the sole guest, to an infant's funeral . . ." "Faith, Faith!" cries young Goodman Brown, "look up to Heaven and resist the wicked one!" whereupon the visions vanish and Young Goodman Brown finds himself alone in the forest.

It made no difference that the visions vanished in the clear morning air. It had all been a bad dream—his wife hurried joyously forth to kiss him good morning; the old minister passed by, bestowing a blessing on him—and all that cloudy revelry in the secret glade had been the torment of his imagination, wherein the ordinary and the everyday were transformed into the strange and evil. It made no difference whether the minister had appeared there, or whether Young Goodman Brown only dreamed that he had, for whenever they met afterward Young Goodman Brown shrank away. In either case the devil had laid hands on his imagination, and he was a gloomy man ever afterward.

And so when Hawthorne stepped out of the haunted chamber into the daylight of Salem the visions remained with him. "How much he did for Salem!" exclaimed Oliver Wendell Holmes, many years later. "Ah, how suddenly and easily genius renders the spot rare and full of great and new virtue, when *it* has looked and dwelt! A light falls upon the place not of land or sea! How much he did for Salem! Oh, the purple light, the soft haze, that now rests upon our glaring New England! He has *done* it, and it will never be harsh country again." [29] But for the moment the accomplishment went unnoticed. Thousands and thousands of visions came to him in that haunted chamber—old Colonel William Hawthorne ordering the Quakers whipped through the streets; the mob threatening and the soldiers ready to fire in *The Gray Champion;* the home of the minister and the hidden spring in the woods, in *The Vision of the Fountain;* the crowds passing beside the town pump at the end of Essex and Washington streets in Salem—sights from the steeple, visions from the top of Gallows Hill, scenes from under an umbrella—rainy days, Indian raids, stagecoaches, travelers, royal governors and provincial assemblies.—"But oftener I was happy," Hawthorne thought, as he looked back in those years, "at least as happy as I then knew how to be, or was aware of the possibility of being." [30]

His stories, when they did reach out, touched a generation of readers with a peculiarly poignant appeal. No one knew who had written them. Elizabeth Peabody, living almost next door, read *The Gentle Boy* and thought some elderly enlightened Quaker had written it.[31] In Hampton, New Hampshire, a few years later, a young fellow named Frank Sanborn read and reread them with a sort of intellectual prickling of the scalp.[32] Everyone who loved them thought they could never be popular. They have a kind of second sight, mused John Pickering, revealing, beyond the outward forms of life and being, a sort of spirit world.[33] The mystery of their appeal was perhaps best expressed by Frank Sanborn many years later, after he had lived in the house that Hawthorne had lived in, taught his children, and looked back to the days of his first reading:

> *Thy doomsday pencil Justice doth expose,*
> *Hearing and judging at thy dread assize;*
> *New England's guilt blazoning before all eyes,*
> *No other chronicler than thee she chose.*

IV

In these early years, however, Hawthorne's stories, except for *Fanshawe*, remained unpublished. They accumulated on his desk, until he felt a sense of physical sickness whenever he glanced at them.

The story of his publishing difficulties is extremely involved. When he completed *Seven Tales*, in 1825, he took the book to a Salem printer named Ferdinand Andrews. Andrews was twenty-four years old, an admirable printer, a vigorous writer, hot tempered, gifted, impatient, but too restless to remain very long at one task. Just prior to this time, Andrews had married one of the daughters of the Derby family, and had recently joined the Essex Lodge of Freemasons.

Ferdinand Andrews was a nephew of the wife of Isaac Cushing, the owner and publisher of the Salem *Gazette*.

The *Gazette* had passed its greatest days by 1821, though it was still a powerful newspaper. Under Cushing it had had a bold and independent editorial policy, a high standard of reporting, and a selectivity that made it an important historical source. It earned about $700 a year, and most of Cushing's income came from the printing business.

In addition to the newspaper, Isaac Cushing set up a book-printing office on the corner of Washington and Essex streets, operated by his oldest son, John, and a bookstore on the first floor of the building where the *Gazette* was printed. He ordinarily spent most of his time in the bookstore, which also served as the newspaper office, and which was then, and later, a stopping place for the men of letters and the politicians of the town. The literary interests of all New Englanders at the time have been exaggerated, but they were real. One winter morning John Pickering and Cushing were talking about the beauty of the thaw and rain and freeze, which had left every bud and twig in a diamond casing. Pickering said there was a beautiful poem by one of the minor English poets describing such a phenomenon, and both wished they could find it. The office boy overheard them, and said that it was the Epistle from Phillips to the Earl of Dorset, dated at Copenhagen, in 1709.

This office boy was a remarkable individual, whose life was closely interwoven with Hawthorne's. His name was Caleb Foote. He was born in 1803, a year before Hawthorne, and was left an orphan at an early age. His schooling ended at ten. He worked in his uncle's grocery store, then in Henry Whipple's bookstore, and, when he was fourteen, in the *Gazette*'s office. He started as a printer's devil. His boyhood was real New England poverty, rye and Indian bread, and rye or pea coffee for breakfast, and for his sport, homemade skates built of beef rib bones and tied to his feet. He helped dig trenches in Salem during the War of 1812. He learned arithmetic by making change in the store, and added to his pocket money by whittling snuffboxes in the shape of boots and wooden shoes, and making puzzles and lead cannon and torpedoes, which he sold in the store for a penny apiece. He learned a little Latin from an old Latin grammar, and studied French and Spanish so he could read the newspapers the captains brought back to Salem. He earned six dollars a week at the *Gazette*, paid $3.50 a week for board, and had saved $500. Everybody knew of Caleb's lack of early advantages, and he had the good will of the town. When the literary societies were organized, he was the only member who was not a college graduate. At the same time the young men who had not been to college put him forward on all occasions as their representative.

In 1823, when he was sixty years old, Isaac Cushing's health failed. He turned over the business to his three sons and to Ferdinand Andrews.

Andrews had little taste for books. He soon quarreled with Caleb Cushing, the weak and dreamy son of Isaac. He took over the business himself—"he got rid of Cushing somehow," as Caleb Foote remembered it. He then offered a half interest in the business to Caleb Foote for $1,500.

Foote, as has been said, had saved $500. He borrowed $1,000 from the Exchange Bank of Salem. The notes were endorsed by a group of men of property.

Hawthorne and Foote were friends, though it is impossible to say when their friendship began. Foote always had the highest regard for Hawthorne's writing. Hawthorne took the manuscript to Andrews at about the time that Foote purchased his share in the business. Hawthorne intended to publish *Fanshawe* before *Seven Tales* appeared, probably because he was uneasy about some charge that his narratives were considered too grotesque and extravagant. He need not have worried, however, for Andrews kept the stories a long time, constantly putting off publishing. Then, in October, 1826, Andrews sold the remaining half of his interest in the *Gazette* and left Salem. He moved to Boston, where he engaged in one enterprise after another, but failed to prosper. His interest was purchased by the *Gazette*'s head printer. He had recently come over to the *Gazette* from the *Essex Register*.[34]

Probably all this was the subject of much talk around the table when David Roberts and Horace Ingersoll came to play whist with Hawthorne and Maria Louisa. Why, otherwise, would Hawthorne have imposed such strict secrecy on his family about his authorship of *Fanshawe?* Bearing in mind that Hawthorne, when he rewrote *Alice Doane's Appeal,* described how he had read the story to two pretty girls, who laughed at its extravagances, it seems likely that *Seven Tales* had become a source of embarrassment to Hawthorne long before Andrews returned the manuscript. He followed a different course with *Fanshawe,* with no greater success.

At about this time a young native of Ridgefield, Connecticut, started a publishing house in Boston. His name was Samuel Griswold Goodrich, and he was the son of a minister, a member of a family renowned in Connecticut for its strong Federalist convictions. His uncle, Chauncey Goodrich, had been a leader in the Hartford Convention. Young Samuel might almost have been the original of Robin Molineux in Hawthorne's story. His career began when he left Ridgefield to work in his brother-in-law's store in Danbury. There he found himself involved at once in the politics of the veterans of the Revolution. His brother-in-law's father was the famous Colonel Cooke, a hero of the burning of Danbury.

Goodrich's brother-in-law died, and Sam moved to Hartford, where his uncle found another job for him in another store. The owner of this store, however, had begun to gamble in the craze for merino sheep that was then sweeping the country. He lost his business, and Sam, after serving in the militia in the War of 1812, started a pocketbook factory in Hartford. He then became a publisher, at a time when there were only four or five publishers in the country. He married a daughter of Stephen Rowe Bradley, the comrade-in-arms of Colonel Cooke at the battle of Danbury, the man in whose office Jeremiah Mason studied law. In 1822 his wife and infant daughter died, and he traveled abroad for a period.

He returned with the material for *Peter Parley's Travels in Europe.* This was the first of 116 volumes written under the name of Peter Parley. They were simple, popular, descriptive, informative books of travel, far better than most of the works then available for children. Goodrich had originated a character. His fictitious Peter Parley knew everything—history, geography, astronomy, all manners and customs, which he related in a pontifical way, with occasional rather forced humor, understandable after 116 volumes. Peter Parley became one of the greatest educational forces in the country. Three hundred thousand copies of the books were sold each year, a total of seven million of them. Goodrich could not possibly keep up with the demand for them. He hired other writers to turn them out for him. He sent them the books of history and travel that they needed for research, paid them $300 a book—and the books were long, encyclopedic, eight hundred pages or so—and published them, as he said, "in old Parley's name," taking all the royalties himself.

Goodrich also started *The Token*. It was a literary annual, a large, handsome volume, the work of many authors bound together, appearing each fall and making a handsome Christmas present. Late in 1829 Hawthorne sent Goodrich four of his stories. Goodrich was much impressed with them. He thought the name, N. Hawthorne, on the letter accompanying the stories, was a pseudonym, investigated, and discovered that Hawthorne was "a very substantial personage."

He sent the stories to John Pickering and asked Pickering's opinion of them. A quarter of a century had passed since John Pickering had delivered the Fourth of July oration in Salem on the day that Hawthorne was born. He had moved to Boston and had become city solicitor, a 53-year-old lawyer and scholar, who was six times elected to the legislature.

No one of Pickering's intelligence could miss the power of Hawthorne's early works. Pickering wrote to Goodrich that they displayed a wonderful beauty of style, with a kind of second sight, which revealed, beyond the outward forms of life and being, a sort of spirit world, somewhat as a lake reflects the earth around it and the sky above it—yet he deemed them too mystical to be popular. Goodrich had probably not asked Hawthorne's permission in sending the stories to Pickering. He certainly did not tell Hawthorne of Pickering's opinion of them. He kept the stories almost two years before publishing them.

He believed that he was the first publisher of Hawthorne's works. He had an established reputation before he met Hawthorne; he had published the novels of Charles Brockden Brown, with a biography by Brown's widow, and Nat Willis's *Sketches*. Before Hawthorne's works appeared, Goodrich published George Cheever's *Commonplace Book*. Cheever was Hawthorne's Bowdoin classmate. He was probably a member, with Bridge, of the Navy Club at Bowdoin. Its membership was restricted to those who had been left out of the Commencement exercises, and in it all honors were reversed—the worst student got the most honored post, and so on. In February, 1833, Cheever became minister of the Howard Street Church in Salem.

From Goodrich's point of view, Hawthorne was a minor figure in his gallery of authors. He believed that he was befriending Hawthorne when he offered him $35 for *The Gentle Boy*. He also believed that he was helping Hawthorne when he gave him assignments of the Peter Parley books. Hawthorne in turn farmed the books out to Elizabeth. She wrote *Peter Parley's Universal History*, or most of it, a 754-page work, attractive, readable, a thirty-year favorite that sold a million copies.

Hawthorne and Goodrich had corresponded for some time before they met. The publisher was shocked one day when the door of his School Street office opened and there stood before him a rather sturdy form, his hair dark and bushy, his eyes steel-gray, his brow thick, his mouth sarcastic, his complexion stony, his whole aspect cold, moody, distrustful. Goodrich was Hawthorne's publisher for almost eight years, yet their first meeting summed up their relationship—both Hawthorne's accusatory manner and Goodrich's rather indignant air of innocence.[35]

Goodrich was not Hawthorne's first publisher. The Salem *Gazette* carried the first story whose authorship Hawthorne admitted, on November 12, 1830. It was unsigned. This was unquestionably Caleb Foote's doing. There is a strong likelihood that Hawthorne wrote other stories and articles for the *Gazette* that he did not include in his books. Much of the reading that he did was of the sort a writer of editorial paragraphs would need.

In these eight years, Goodrich published some twenty-eight of Hawthorne's stories in *The Token*—perhaps only twenty-five. Thirteen of these were published in 1837 and 1838, when Hawthorne already had another publishing outlet. In the critical years between 1830 and 1836, Goodrich published only fifteen of Hawthorne's stories, unless there are others buried in *The Token* whose authorship Hawthorne did not care to acknowledge, or which were so changed in editing that he no longer considered them his. In his autobiography, written after Hawthorne had become famous, Goodrich gave the impression that he had rescued Hawthorne from oblivion. Hawthorne said rather ruefully that it had been the other way around. However, he did not feel the point to be worth disputing, and he forbade his sister-in-law, who also abounded in misunderstanding of his early years, to enter a public denial of Goodrich's story.

Goodrich published relatively little of Hawthorne's work, but it included some of the loveliest stories in the English language. Nor did he, until after Hawthorne was independent of him, publish any of Hawthorne's weaker stories. *The Token* in 1831 contained *Sights from a Steeple*, and two lesser-known works, not included in his books, *The Haunted Quack* and *The New England Village*, attributed to him. The following year it included both *The Gentle Boy* and *The Wives of the Dead*; and though there were very few the next two years, in 1835, it contained the two masterpieces, *The Haunted Mind* and *The Village Uncle*, prose that no other American could equal. Goodrich went to remarkable lengths to keep the identity of the author secret. He still wanted to profit by the popularity of the early stories, however. So *My Kinsman, Major Molineux*, was listed as by the author of *Sights from a Steeple*, and *The Man of Adamant* by the author of *The Gentle Boy; The Gray Champion* by the author of *The Gentle Boy* and *Wakefield* by the author of *The Gray Champion*. Very confusing, and yet not altogether without design—an attentive reader could probably have followed the trail from one to another, though Hawthorne's name had not yet appeared in print.

In the summer of 1834 he was thirty years old, and had been writing for nine years, and had published about ten stories in *The Token*. He had no high opinion of his own work. He said of his own stories that they had the pale tint of flowers that have bloomed in too retired a shade. There was not another man writing who could have characterized them in so felicitous a phrase. "Instead of passion there is sentiment," he wrote, "and, even in what purports to be pictures of actual life, we have allegory, not always so warmly dressed in its habiliments of flesh and blood as to be taken into the reader's mind without a shiver. Whether from lack of power, or an unconquerable reserve, the Author's touches have often the effect of tameness; the merriest man can hardly contrive to laugh at his broadest humor; the tenderest woman, one would suppose, will hardly shed warm tears at his deepest pathos. The book, if you would see anything in it, requires to be read in the clear, brown, twilight atmosphere in which it was written; if opened in the sunshine, it is apt to look exceedingly like a volume of blank pages." [36]

The very accuracy of Hawthorne's own criticism of his work stopped other critics. But he judged them harshly. He said that they seemed tame, with a humor that would make no one laugh—though there are many humorists of whom it could be said more truly—with sentiment instead of passion and with allegory, often cold, even in what purported to be scenes of real life. But they had much more, which Hawthorne never credited them with, a tenderness that was never weak or sentimental, a high, unwavering purpose, a clearsighted sanity—the most important thing, he thought, was to keep the imagination sane—and above all a style, a grace in gliding from the particular to the general, weaving a line of thought like a swallow skimming through the evening air.

The stories made him famous, but only among the handful of literary men around the *New England Magazine* and *The Token*, who knew who had written them. In the fall of 1834, Joseph Buckingham, the editor of the Boston *Courier*, transferred the *New England Magazine* to John Sargent and Samuel Howe.[37] Buckingham was a really violent Whig, constantly sitting at the speaker's table with Webster and thundering against Bronson Alcott's schools and books—much as the Salem *Gazette* and the old Federalist papers had railed at Jefferson —but there was now something waspish and disagreeable in conservative writing, which he seemed to exemplify. The group that had taken over the magazine was as interesting as any in New England. Here are a few thumbnail sketches of them:

John Sargent. He was the son of a Gloucester sea captain who graduated from Harvard in 1830. He was a devoted Latin scholar, and an admirer of Horace, whose works he spent a lifetime translating. In January, 1834, he wrote an angry letter on politics to the editor of the Boston *Atlas*, who then hired him to write the editorials for the paper.

Epes Sargent. He was the brother of the above, only twenty-two in 1834, a dapper, elegant little man, neatly attired, swinging a black bamboo cane, the embodiment of cheer. After graduating from Boston Latin School in 1829, he went to Russia with his father. When he returned he joined the staff of the Boston *Advertiser*, then moved to the *Atlas*, and eventually became famous as editor of the *Transcript*. He wrote plays—*Velasco* and *The Bride of Genoa* ("Transcends all dramas written in English in the past fifty years."—Salem *Gazette*) ; and novels

(What's to be Done? and *Peculiar); and poems. Everyone knew his song:

> *A life on the ocean wave*
> *A home on the rolling deep . . .*

Samuel Gridley Howe. He was a slight, quiet man who enlisted in the Greek war of independence; became a surgeon with the rebel forces, and a teacher and historian of some ability, whose *Historical Sketch of the Greek Revolution* was published in 1828. When he returned to the United States he became, in addition to a teacher of the blind, an authority on the various movements for independence in the European countries, and a contact man between the rebellious Poles and Austrians and their American sympathizers.

Park Benjamin. He was a British subject, twenty-six in 1835, born in Demerara, British Guiana. He was an enthusiastic, ardent critic, a poet of distinction, and a wholehearted admirer of Hawthorne's work.[38]

These editors published everything that Hawthorne wrote. In November and December, 1834, the *New England Magazine* published Hawthorne's *Passages from a Relinquished Work* and *Mr. Higginbotham's Catastrophe*. They were originally written as a single story, of almost novel length, and cut and rearranged by Park Benjamin before publication.

In January the magazine published *The Gray Champion*, a story of the overthrow of Governor Andros. In February it carried *Old News*, Hawthorne's analysis of the colonial newspapers. In March it published his essay, *The Old French War*, based on the same source. In the May issue there were two stories by Hawthorne, *Wakefield* and *Young Goodman Brown*. In June it carried his *Graves and Goblins*, *The Ambitious Guest*, a story of the Notch of the White Hills of New Hampshire, and *A Rill from the Town Pump*, an exercise in pure prose. In July Hawthorne published *The White Old Maid* and *The Old Tory*, and in August, *The Vision in the Fountain;* in November, *The Devil in Manuscript*, and *Sketches from Memory. Youth's Keepsake* published *Little Annie's Ramble*, a story of Hawthorne and Anne Marion Forrester, the child of Charlotte Story and John Forrester.

Meanwhile, Hawthorne's stories were appearing frequently in *The Token. The Wedding Knell, The Minister's Black Veil, The Maypole of Merry Mount* were inferior to his best work. The bridegroom going to his wedding in a shroud while the bell tolled a funeral knell is so unhappy an image that only Hawthorne's genius saved it from being burlesque; *The Minister's Black Veil* is less successful than *Wakefield,* whose theme it repeats, and *The Maypole of Merry Mount* is a weaker version of *Young Goodman Brown.* The stories, nevertheless, pleased the critics more. Park Benjamin reviewed them in the *New England Magazine* and declared that the author was "the most pleasing writer of fanciful prose, except Irving, in the country," and an English critic recommended them and quoted from them in the London *Athanaeum,* Hawthorne's name, however, had not yet appeared as the author of them.

In the fall of 1835 the *New England Magazine* was merged with the *American Monthly Magazine* of New York. Park Benjamin, who had had a violent quarrel with Goodrich, left for New York to edit it, carrying some of Hawthorne's manuscripts with him.[39] Hawthorne was again without a regular publishing outlet. He still had *The Token,* which had paid him as much as $35 for a single story. The New England Magazine paid only a dollar a page, but might have paid more to a valued contributor. Hawthorne perhaps made $100 a year from his contributions to *The Token,* and $400 or $500 from the *New England Magazine,* though he may not have been able to collect it all. It is quite possible that he made more, as much as $1,000 in this successful year —a good living. Moreover, his writings were making him a name, and at the end of 1835 he was offered a job as editor of the *American Magazine of Useful and Entertaining Knowledge,* at a salary of $500 a year.

V

Salem had not greatly changed in those years. Ships still arrived and cleared in the same number as before. Boston and New York had grown so rapidly that Salem was a less important port, and its commerce of a different nature. Trade with China had almost ceased. Russia had become the destination of many Salem vessels. One merchant, Joseph Peabody, with an income of $300,000 a year, lived on $3,000 a year, built and sailed eighty-three ships, all freighted with his own cargoes, raised thirty-five boys to the rank of master, paid customhouse duties of $2,000,000 in five years, and sent his ships on forty-seven voyages to St. Petersburg.[40]

Hawthorne never wrote of the ships. He never wrote of the famous men of Salem, Story and Pickering and Bowditch, so close to him in family ties or in their neighborhood homes. His life was not greatly changed. He walked to the library, climbed Gallows Hill or walked through Dark Lane to Danvers. In the evening he read. The household remained much as it had been. His mother rarely ventured from her room.

In these years he began to be haunted by a recurring dream. It seemed to him that he was still in college, or even in school, and he had a sense of having been there a long time, while all his friends had gone beyond him and made their way in the world. He met them, suffering a sense of shame and humiliation so acute that it remained with him after he awakened.[41] To free his mind of its gloomy burden, to shake off a mood of depression—how often those phrases figured in his work!—he closed the door on his books and walked down to the beach or back to the hills. All day, perhaps, he had been absorbed in some ancient tragedy, a trial for treason, or an incident from colonial history, and now at evening its mood lingered over the scene that lay before him. The dark and weather-beaten ships at the wharves, with their slow creaking and murmuring with the movement of the water and the wind, the splintery planks on the docks, the barnacles on the pilings, the briny tonic in the air, bracing and yet melancholy at the same time, the iron-gray water, marked a boundary he was somehow forbidden to cross. His father's old ship, the *America,* lay at Downer's Wharf. Bit by bit it crumbled to atoms, never ceding to the the new era. So it was with Salem. Where else were the little dooryards that held the glint of sunlight so tenaciously, like the still light of wine in a glass? The wharves were not greatly changed from what they had been in his father's day, the streets were the same, and the people were unchanged—witness his mother in her upstairs room. Or he turned away from the harbor and climbed the hill. But where he usually walked was not actually a hill, with a steep climb and ragged boulders, but a rolling eminence, a vast mound, treeless and wind-swept, across which his solitary figure, moving in the darkening air, must have seemed ghostly and startling if anyone glimpsed him from the road. He had then no name for being a man of thought, and with his solitary walks, and his acute observation, he seemed far less a philosophical dreamer than a first-class criminal investigator, or perhaps, to a considerable portion of the town, a criminal.

Those viewless bolts and bars were stronger than he thought. Was there really any difference between his mother's lifelong seclusion, and his own? Was it not possible that he was deceiving himself, not only about the quality, but even about the value, of his work? There appeared to have always been a family tendency toward seclusion, perhaps coming from the paternal side . . . He felt like a man under an enchantment, who sat down by the wayside of life, and a shrubbery sprang up around him, and the bushes grew to be saplings, and the saplings became trees, until no exit appeared possible through the entangling depths of his obscurity. Occasionally he went to Boston, spending an idle Sunday loitering in the Mechanics or the Maverick Bar, or rode to Nahant and studied the summer visitors. He was a silent, slow-spoken man, his habitual expression one of quietly listening. He dressed carefully and well. He kept a notebook, in which he jotted down brief descriptions of scenes on his walks, exactly as a painter might make a sketch of a scene he intended to paint.[42]

His friends had all gone beyond him. They were talking of matters of which he knew nothing, and bristling and crackling with a keen lively humor he could not emulate, joking at their own pretensions with a swift awareness that made his sober earnestness seem, in his own eyes at least, dully simple. Fortunately, or unfortunately, nothing ages so swiftly as this brisk and brittle prattle, and he was just as far behind them now as he had been in his college days, or as far ahead of them. The thing to do at the moment was to take those sonorous rolling phrases of Webster and Harrison Gray Otis and, with just a little flick of irony, or a lamentable weak conclusion after a thundering start, leave them limp and anticlimactic—a sport Hawthorne did not engage in, though he used such mild parodies in his stories. That is not quite an exact description of their wit. It was a sort of toreador verbal dexterity, with little barbs of inappropriate oratory, or misplaced solemnity, planted in the thick hide of fixed New English beliefs. Recall that in those days there was not only Webster, but that every village had its Webster, and every occasion a speech, and it will be clear what a powerful aggregation of clichés they were ridiculing. They were awfully good at it—too good for Hawthorne and, unfortunately, too good for posterity, upon which their brightest efforts were as completely wasted as the dullest of what they ridiculed.

They had all gone beyond him in another sense. There was hardly a member of the survivors of that class of 1825 who had not been elected to the legislature, written a book, made a fortune, married an heiress, or otherwise made himself famous. He was the least successful of the graduates. His life was the least exciting, his work the least impressive. Consider some of his classmates and schoolmates. Pierce was already a congressman, and had been a successful member of the legislature (speaker of the House), and was happily married and the father of a son. John and Gorham Abbot were writers, teachers and clergymen. Jacob Abbott's book, *New England and Her Institutions* was a fine performance, based on a great deal of travel, and characterized by an owlish honest humor—he had traveled into Virginia at the time of Nat Turner's revolt, investigating the state of public opinion, and he wrote about taverns, churches, farmers, stagecoaches, Catholics—he was sternly anti-Catholic—and the new English temperament with a cool positive assurance that made Hawthorne's tentative characterizations seem timid and pale. Jacob wrote two hundred volumes, including the Rollo books. Gorham wrote books about the South Seas. All three brothers were successful teachers, and founded Springer's Institute in New York, one of the best women's colleges in the country, which earned them a fortune.

The others were as successful. John Appleton became chief justice of Maine. James Bell became United States senator from New Hampshire. Alpheus Felch became governor of Michigan. John Hale became a senator, and William Hale (Bridge's roommate), a wealthy merchant. Seargent Prentiss drifted south, and reached Natchez with five borrowed dollars, accumulated $100,000 in five years, and became representative from Mississippi and one of the greatest of southern orators. Calvin Stowe became a Hebrew scholar, and married the woman who wrote *Uncle Tom's Cabin*. The two Negro students, Dr. James Hall and John Russwurm, had careers as vivid. Hall married the daughter of the lieutenant governor of Monrovia, Liberia, and became governor of Cape Palmas, African Maryland Colony. John Russwurm started an abolitionist paper in New York. He became interested in the African recolonization movement, sailed to Africa, became superintendent of schools in Liberia, editor of the *Liberia Herald*, a merchant, colonial secretary, and succeeded Hall as governor of Cape Palmas.[43]

Pitt Fessenden married and established his law office in Portland, opposing his father in many cases, until it became an open question as to which was the best lawyer in the state. Horatio Bridge practiced law in Skowhegan, Maine, moved to Augusta, and, after the death of his father in 1834, lived alone in the twenty-room house beside the Kennebec. He kept his bargain to write regularly to Hawthorne. He went to Cuba, drank some, gambled a little—enough to cause Hawthorne to write him about it. He was nettled at Hawthorne's advice, but accepted it, complaining, however: "a little wickedness will not hurt one, especially if the sinner be of a retiring disposition. It stirs one up," he said, in what was perhaps as clear a statement of his hatred of torpor as could be made. "It stirs one up, and makes him like the rest of the world." [44]

He said he sometimes thought of getting married for as long as ten minutes at a time. Then he decided that he would never marry. He wanted to be like the rest of the world, or he wanted to like the rest of the world, and he hated his own indolence; the worst charge he could bring against himself (aside from the fact that he was vain and proud) was that at thirty he had no settled program for his life. Hawthorne must have written to him very sternly on one occasion, for Bridge jumped as if he had been shot. Hawthorne had a tendency to do this, without quite realizing how hard he hit, or how terrible it was to be on the receiving end of one of his lectures. Bridge reformed; he went into business, speculated in real estate (a terrific land boom was under way), and then joined with his brothers in projecting a mighty dam across the Kennebec River.

Acquiring the water-power rights on the Merrimack River, one of the greatest New England industrialists, Nathan Appleton (Jesse Appleton's cousin) had started with an investment of $5,000 and created a network of factories worth $10,000,000. This was what Bridge proposed to do with the power of the Kennebec. Near Augusta, through Coon's Rapids, Bacon's Rips, Six Mile Falls, Carter's Rapids and Petty's Rips, the Kennebec dropped thirty-six feet in ten miles. Bridge's project was to build a 15-foot dam, with locks 100 by 28 feet, and a 60-foot sluiceway for lumber, and a fishway. It would make Augusta one of the greatest manufacturing centers in the country.

The legislature approved the project, and the company was organized on March 20, 1834, with Horatio Bridge as secretary. The company had a capital stock of $300,000. The stock was offered for sale at $100 a share until June 1, or until two-thirds of all the stock was sold. The next meeting was held on June 3. It was an eloquent commentary on what people thought of the project, since it adjourned, no business.

Colonel Baldwin, an engineer, was hired by the company. Baldwin had once been associated with John Pickering in a water-power project in Salem. Baldwin advised against the erection of the dam. He was fired. In January, 1835, new officers were elected. Edmund Bridge was made president; Edmund, James, and Horatio Bridge were directors; Daniel Williams, their brother-in-law, was secretary and treasurer. James and Horatio were auditors, and Edmund was stock salesman. The dam was now exclusively a Bridge family affair, though Senator Reuel Williams presently replaced Edmund Bridge, and Colonel William Boardman of Nashua, New Hampshire, was hired to replace Baldwin. Boardman was a plain, country-squire looking man, with a rough complexion, a ponderous brow, and the general rigidity of manners of a schoolmaster. Colonel Boardman was a self-taught man. He was a farm boy who had taught himself engineering and worked at his profession for twenty-five years. Testing the river bed below the Bridge estate and Cushmore Island, he found, at the foot of the island, a ledge of rock that reached almost across the river. He estimated that a suitable dam, 13 feet high, with a base 100 feet across, and with suitable locks, could be built for $350,000. Later he widened the base by 25 feet. His plans and drawings were completed by the end of May, at which time forty shares of the stock of the company sold for $42 a share in Augusta, an increase of $17 a share in two months.

Reuel Williams, Daniel Williams, Edmund Bridge, and James and Horatio Bridge each held about one-eighth of the stock. Together they owned a controlling five-eighths. The dam that Colonel Boardman proposed to build was a gigantic causeway across the river. It would create a lake 16 miles long with an average depth of 16 feet, covering 1,200 acres. It was to be made of cribs of timber, bolted and filled with ballast. The upper slope was covered with 5-inch pine planking and the lower slope with 5-inch and 3-inch hemlock planks. The top was covered with stones 8 feet long and secured with iron straps and bolts. The central portion, for 60 feet across, was depressed 20 inches for a sluiceway.

The building of the locks was another enterprise, and the building of the millrace for the power mills still another. The locks walls were granite. The chambers were 101 feet by 28⅓ feet. The lock gates were

built of Chesapeake white oak, with wickets of cast iron. They were
supported by stone piers, 30 feet square at the base, 25 feet square at
the top, and 34 feet high, clamped and strapped with iron. The canals,
50 feet wide, had a 10-foot depth. The dams and the locks required
25,000 bars of iron, 75,000 tons of ballast, 2,500,000 feet of timber,
and 800,000 cubic feet of granite on locks, piers, canal, and bank walls.

The weather along the Kennebec near its mouth was changeable
and dangerous. After the heavy rains the river rose rapidly, and when
the river froze work was impossible. The heavy floods in the spring would
endanger the construction that had been completed up till the time the
river froze. Horatio Bridge had calculated that he might invest
$20,000, perhaps half of his fortune, in the dam. It was a fearful gam-
ble, with a very good likelihood of his losing all he invested, and perhaps
a great deal more. Work had barely begun when it became plain that the
cost would be at least twice the original estimate.[45]

Bridge had gone far beyond Hawthorne in another sense. He was
mixed up in politics in various ways. His brothers were Democratic
politicians, one an Augusta editor. He had a younger brother and sister,
twins. They married a son and daughter of Senator Reuel Williams.
Bridge was at home in naval circles, and in Washington, where he occasionally visited. He was a Jackson Democrat, though apparently opposed to Van Buren. Moreover, he was now in affairs of terrific
consequence, dealing with contractors and workmen, raising money,
negotiating with the legislature, and the work matured and sobered
him.[46]

Jonathan Cilley had had an even more adventurous life. Tall, lean
and rangy, shrewd, ingratiating, warmhearted and yet always conscious
of his own interests, ambitious, terrifyingly ambitious, energetic, a
plain Yankee farmer and yet a politician and a lawyer, quick, bold as a
tiger when necessary, bluffing his way, and yet backing up his bluffs,
a superb stump speaker, in the common language of his time and place,
he was a new figure in American politics, a rural demagogue, and yet
with a conscious honesty that lifted him above a demagogue's artifice.
He was a dangerous man. The Jacksonian revolution, with its idealization of the common man, might have been made for him.

When he graduated, Cilley went to Thomaston, Maine, and studied
law in the office of John Ruggles. In 1828 he opened his own office.
April 12, 1829, he married Deborah Prince, the daughter of a Thomas-

ton lawyer. Their first child, Greenleaf Cilley, was born October 27, 1829. In 1831 Ruggles was appointed a judge of the Court of Common Pleas, and Cilley was elected to the legislature in his place. That same year his daughter Jane was born. Meanwhile, during his first term as legislator, his lifelong quarrel with John Ruggles began.

Ruggles believed that Cilley was not giving the help he could in furthering Ruggles's political career. Cilley had everything to lose in this struggle and nothing to win. He was only thirty, a young lawyer with two children and a practice which had barely begun, in a community where he was a newcomer. He had no powerful family behind him; only one of his three brothers was still alive. His legal training was incomplete; the intensity of Ruggles's political struggles had interrupted it. When Ruggles attacked him Cilley struck back with a ferocity that outraged the older man. Ruggles could not endure the sight of him. The politicians associated with Ruggles walked away whenever Cilley appeared. He was ostracized. The struggle hardened him, and gave him a kind of controlled desperation. He was courteous and good-natured with people who made no secret of their destestation of him, not from weakness but from a certainty of his own strength. But the smile that had been engaging became sly. The native shrewdness became crafty. The wonderful tact that had once made Hawthorne regard him as his brother became an artful skill in manipulating men, seizing on each man's manageable point and using him for his own purposes without the man's suspecting that he was being made a tool of. With both Ruggles's faction and the regular Democratic organization against him, he ran for the legislature again.

He was re-elected. His fight with Ruggles grew more bitter. His third child, Bowdoin, was born in September, 1833, during his second term in the legislature. The family lived on a farm near Thomaston, and Cilley milked his own cows and kept his own bees. In his loneliness the work helped him; he had been a farm boy in his youth. It soothed him to sit by the hour listening to the hum of the bees in the hives. He was re-elected to the legislature in 1834, but the triumph was costly. He was expelled from the Democratic caucuses, and branded as a traitor to the party. He organized his own opposition, which soon held the balance of power. The struggle of Ruggles and Cilley became a part of the struggle for control of Maine, and the fight for the control of Maine became part of the fight for the control of the nation.

The campaign for the governship in 1834 was intense. Cilley maintained that the candidate of the regular Democrats had been unfairly chosen, in order to clear the way for Ruggles to be elected Senator, and supported his opponent. During the summer of that year Cilley's youngest child, Bowdoin, died. In May, 1836, when Cilley was preparing to run for Congress, his daughter Jane, who was five years old, died. This loss broke his heart. He could not believe that she would die, when she was dying, and when he spoke of her afterwards, tears filled his eyes. He had become, in a quiet way, a man of absolutely inflexible purpose, fierce as the man of adamant in Hawthorne's story—although, curiously enough, he seemed rather gentle in his manner, and more sagacious and subtle, as a politician, and more resourceful, as the opposition to him increased, only the final tragedy in his life revealing the depth of his courage.[47]

Longfellow had gone beyond them all. The quiet poet in his youth and young manhood had none of the sweetness of temper that marked his old age and pervaded the words that made him beloved. He sailed to Europe after graduating, to prepare himself for the professorship of modern languages at Bowdoin.

From his querulous letters home it appears doubtful that anybody ever had so little pleasure in Paris as Henry Longfellow at twenty. Spain was more congenial. Germany, when he settled at Göttingen with Ned Preble, was still more so. He returned to Bowdoin and taught for four years, restless, lonely, at odds with President Allen, constantly trying for a diplomatic appointment or a school, or an editorial post, that would take him away. (Bowdoin was still fermenting and bubbling with political fights. Allen had grown so unpopular that the legislature passed an act specifically designed to remove him from office. He appealed, and Supreme Court Justice Story, in an ironic sequel to the Dartmouth College Case, declared the law unconstitutional.)

In 1831 Longfellow married and in 1834, accepting a Harvard professorship, sailed to Europe for eighteen months' study. The party consisted of Longfellow, his wife, a Miss Goddard, and Clara Crowninshield. They visited England, Germany, then traveled overland, by carriage, to Copenhagen, from whence they sailed to Stockholm. There Longfellow studied Swedish and Finnish. Miss Goddard's father died, and she left the party and returned to America. The others sailed to

CHARLOTTE STORY FORRESTER
(Portrait by Stuart)

"Mrs. Forrester was a Story . . ."—Elizabeth Hawthorne *(Essex Institute)*

HAWTHORNE'S MOTHER'S HOUSE IN RAYMOND, MAINE

"Here I ran quite wild . . . fishing all day long, or shooting with an old fowling piece."—Hawthorne *(Essex Institute)*

REVEREND CALEB BRADLEY
Hawthorne's teacher: a strange and eccentric man, fond of rum and pretty young women, preacher at Stroudwater for thirty years, marrying 550 couples and conducting the services at 1400 funerals. *(New York Public Library)*

REVEREND WILLIAM ALLEN
President of the short-lived Dartmouth University, leading figure in the famous Dartmouth College Case, and president of Bowdoin during the time Hawthorne was a student there. *(New York Public Library)*

Rotterdam. There Mary Longfellow's child was prematurely born, and on November 27, 1835, she died.

The following summer Nathan Appleton and his family visiting Europe, met Longfellow and Miss Crowninshield. Appleton's wife was Maria Theresa Gold, of Pittsfield. They had five children. One of these was Frances Appleton, seventeen years old in 1836, dark haired, dark eyed, beautiful, and high-spirited. She had an almost Spanish sultriness of expression, and was a vivid, courageous girl, sensitive and proud, with rather timid literary interests—her brother Tom was a poet— which she exercised cautiously and tentatively, as though fearing ridicule. She was very small, graceful, restless, and quick.

The Reverend Jesse Appleton and Nathan Appleton were alike in their sense of responsibility and gravity—Nathan Appleton was quite sincere in regarding his enormous fortune as a burden. He was like the Yankee King Midas Hawthorne later imagined, at whose touch everything, including his daughter, turned to gold. But unlike Midas he had not asked for the gift.

The Appletons were serious people, but there was a romantic and willful strain in their children, perhaps coming from the Golds and the Meanses. Thomas Gold Appleton, Frances Appleton's brother, was a generous, easy-mannered youth, an habitual diner-out, a Boston wit, but a genial one, sympathetic and generous.* Frances Appleton herself had enough literary interest to be attracted to Longfellow, who was already known as a poet. They studied German together and set about translating German poetry in collaboration. When they left Germany their relationship was a romance, rather scandalous to Boston. The following year, when Frances Appleton was eighteen, Longfellow formally proposed to her and was rebuffed. He was in a frightful situation, a 32-year-old widower publicly rejected by the richest heiress in the country—a curious combination of romantic poet and hardheaded man of affairs, with a considerable share of man-about-town in his make-up, beginning his career as a Harvard professor. With his wonderful facility he turned from poems to prose romances and succeeded in both. He was lively, busy, surrounded by pleasant friends—George Hillard, Richard Cleveland, Charles Sumner—who pursued actresses, advised each other on their courtship of heiresses, and were scholars of distinc-

---

* He called Hawthorne "a boned pirate."

tion. He leaned over the Charles River Bridge at midnight, thinking of jumping in. At last he wrote *Hyperion*, a romance based on his summer with Frances Appleton in Switzerland. This time the scandal was terrific. One spring day Longfellow was walking across the Charles River Bridge when he saw Frances Appleton, also alone, approaching him. They met in midstream, and she walked past with no sign of recognition and no expression on her exquisite features.[48]

In comparison with the lives of his school friends, Hawthorne's early years were dull. Longfellow visited him in Salem, to discuss a new magazine—Hawthorne highly approved—and on another occasion to discuss collaborating on a book of children's stories. This Hawthorne considered, but at last decided not to do. He did, however, give Longfellow, out of his reading in early New England history, the story of the Acadians that Longfellow retold in *Evangeline*. Franklin Pierce and Samuel Dinsmore also visited him in Salem. Pierce was already famed; Dinsmore was the son of a prominent New Hampshire Democratic family. Hawthorne took his visitors to the East India Marine Society Museum. His father had been a member, and Hawthorne, as one of the orphans the society had been set up to aid, had the privileges of membership. The museum was a wonderful place. It was founded in the early days of the Far Eastern trade, and membership was restricted to captains who had sailed around the Cape and back. They returned with rare birds and plants and objects of art from the Orient, which were kept in the museum—they had grown irritated because even educated landsmen thought they were lying when they told of the wonders they had seen. There, among the rare stuffed birds and fishes, Hawthorne talked with the two young politicians. They were his trophies, perhaps, for in Salem respectable Democrats were almost as rare as the rarest objects in the room.[49]

By this time Hawthorne's lack of success had become as noticeable, in its own way, as Pierce's rapid progress. It was his own special distinction. Everything about him was mysterious, his habits, his family, his tastes, his income, his profession, his education, his friends, his aspirations, and his travels. Indeed, his life was too mysterious. It was too obscure to be altogether credible, just as the lives of some men seem too open and aboveboard to be believable. And as we feel in the case of such men that there must be something concealed, so in the life of Hawthorne it seems there must have been something open and aboveboard somewhere; it could not have been all seclusion and mystery, shadows and pseudonyms. If he was bad—if his income was illegal, or his habits disreputable, or if he lay hidden because of vice or some scandal in his past—his story becomes terribly sinister, and there seems nothing, viewing the outward circumstances of his life, that he might not have been guilty of. A formidable argument could be made to establish some such dark area in his background. He was on the scene of too many violent events, and he knew too many people whose lives were involved in plots and intrigues; he knew too much of vice and crime. Two of his friends were ruined, one was murdered, soon after their lives became involved with his, and in each case he prophesied the nature of the tragedies that came to pass. He wrote publicly in terms of the highest praise of people he privately viewed with hostility and fear. He lived with radicals and reformers and worked for causes he did not believe in. Such circumstances, persisting through his life, could be interpreted darkly to explain the mystery with which he surrounded himself.

If he lived as he did because he could not afford to live otherwise, or if his life was in danger through some hostility to him or his family, his story becomes extraordinary because of the network of intrigue in which he was innocently involved. Whatever the reason, the fact was that since leaving college he had lived in a manner which almost inevitably cast suspicion upon him, and made him vulnerable to whatever aspersions his enemies might bring against him.

He was probably a government agent. When he left Salem, a few years later, he entered the customs service, and from that time on was usually in the employ of the government in some investigating capacity, either in the Treasury or in the State Department. The records of the Boston Custom House, at the time he first worked there, were destroyed by fire in 1894, and fragments later discovered revealed only that he had received a higher salary and had a more responsible position at the beginning of his work than his first biographers had believed.[50] It may be that his work was only semiofficial in these early years. Levi Woodbury was secretary of the treasury. Woodbury was Franklin Pierce's political mentor. Pierce had lived with the Woodburys while attending preparatory school. Pierce's father had been responsible for Levi Woodbury's appointment to the New Hampshire Supreme Court. Woodbury was sagacious and even-tempered, head and shoulders above the demagogues who abounded among the New England followers of

Jackson. He had strengthened the Navy during his brief period as secretary, and his administration of the Treasury was excellent. He had tried to prevent the deadly struggle over the Bank of the United States from becoming as costly and bitter as it became; his proposals, while admittedly temporary, were constructive and healing. It was not so much Woodbury's actual work that made him memorable as it was a kind of simple, slow, honest, almost tender approach to the problems that partisans were ready to settle with gunfire. The dread of disunion haunted him in the way that the old Federalists had feared the rule of the mob. What he wanted, in those decades before the Civil War, was the return of a spirit, the true fraternal and compromising spirit in which the union was founded by our fathers. Forms and strict right will avail little without it, he said, "as well one might expect the most holy union of the sexes in private life to flourish long with harmony and usefulness, under daily taunts, and daily reproaches, and daily invasions of domestic calm." He wanted his countrymen not only to do right, but to do it in a friendly and conciliatory spirit. It was planned by the New England Democrats to run him for president in 1852, and it was his death before the convention that forced their last-minute selection of Franklin Pierce.[51]

The point of this is: not only is it likely that Woodbury knew of Hawthorne through Pierce; Woodbury was the type of individual who would have approved of Hawthorne. In so far as Hawthorne's political views were formulated, he was (though there was no such group organized) a Woodbury Democrat. They were the moderates within the Jacksonian democracy, their greatest accomplishment being that they prevented the radicals from having even greater influence over him.

There were other points of contact between Hawthorne and the Administration. The Manning Stage Lines held the contract for carrying the mails. In this period Samuel Manning made at least one trip to Washington, and each summer Hawthorne accompanied Sam on a horse-buying trip throughout New England. There need be no particular meaning attached to these trips, or to their connections with the government, except that when so examined they throw light into areas of Hawthorne's life that otherwise are open to the charge of being morbid or affected.

In the winter of 1830, the social life of Salem was shaken by a series of events so ghastly that the community never recovered its previous reputation. An 83-year-old merchant named Captain Joseph White was murdered in his bed in his house on Essex Street. His mansion stood about two blocks from the Manning house and around the corner from the home of the Andrews' on Washington Square. The old merchant's skull had been fractured, and there were thirteen knife wounds in his body. After the Revolution, Joseph White had been a slave trader. Like most of the former slave traders, he was a Jeffersonian Democrat.[52]

Captain White and his kinsman, Stephen White, had their counting room in the Union Marine Insurance Company Building on Essex Street, a large brick building, with a piazza and recess in front, and four brick pillars sanded to resemble stone.[53] Stephen White was Charlotte Story Forrester's brother-in-law. He had married her sister. The marriage thus united him with the family of Judge Joseph Story, and his seventeen brothers, sisters and brothers-in-law. Several of them (William Fettyplace, Franklin Story, William Story) became Salem shipmasters, sailing Stephen White's ships. The flag of his house, three vertical bars, blue, white and red, flew over some twenty-two vessels registered in Salem. Stephen White had the loveliest garden and grounds in Salem, tended by a Chinaman "that would not suffer a weed to sprout in the wrong place." [54]

The day preceding the murder, a merchant, Joseph Knapp, went bankrupt. He was the owner, or one of the owners, of the *Dolphin*, the *Argus*, the *Fame*, the *Romp*, the *Rover*, the *Success*, and a number of other vessels. The flag of his house was a red and white pennant. He had three sons, Frank, Joseph, and Phippen. Phippen was a Harvard graduate of 1826. On February 6, Captain Joseph Knapp sat up late in his office, signing over the papers of his failure, seeming silent and embittered.[55]

The night was cloudy, though no rain fell. The young men of Salem were out, sauntering through the streets. Charles Page met young John Forrester, Zachariah Burchmore, and another young fellow on Essex Street near Barton's Hotel. They came upon Frank Knapp in his frock coat and his glazed cap, walking alone. Frank Knapp always wore a frock coat with a velvet collar. He asked them to come into the bar and have a drink. John Forrester, Jr., had never met Frank Knapp. They stayed in the hotel about five minutes. Knapp then left, and young Forrester walked with him to Derby Square to Remmon's oyster bar.[56]

The discovery of Captain White's body the following morning created a nation-wide sensation. His murder was the first in the country's history to become a leading topic of newspaper articles from Boston to New Orleans.[57] The authorities made no progress in solving the murder. A Committee of Vigilance was formed. By a curious reversion of history, an atmosphere of panic and suspicion settled on the city. It was very much like the days of the witchcraft trials. Strangers were arrested and questioned, not only by the authorities, but by the committee, to which accusations and rumors poured in abundance.

The horror of the murder was not only in the brutality of the killing, but in the dreadful picture of Salem that unfolded as it progressed: the bankruptcy of the merchants, the vice in connection with emerging industry, the depravity that reached into the families of men whose fleets, a generation before, had circled the earth. The story of the murder unfolded in an atmosphere of dingy hotel-room meetings, nights in brothels, the dissipation of convicts just out of jail, talks along the roads after dark, and in livery stables and oyster shops, moonlit scenes in which someone heard a few words relating to the murder, or a chance meeting in the street in which someone was recognized in a shadowy, muffled instant that destroyed an alibi. Three or four thousand five-franc pieces that one of Captain Knapp's ships had brought to Salem from Guadeloupe, Frank Knapp's frock coat, Richard Crowninshield's dagger, the fact that Captain White's housekeeper's daughter was Joseph Knapp's wife—of such was the evidence compounded. Witnesses appeared with stories that the Knapps had said that if Captain Joseph White died intestate, the housekeeper would inherit $200,000. All sorts of shadowy characters emerged from the underworld—ex-convicts, gamblers, innkeepers, livery-stable men, each with some new item of information which, if it did not throw much light on the murder, revealed a network of vice stupefying in its extent and in the degree to which it enmeshed the children of the town. Meetings in Remmond's Refectory, gambling in Pendergass's Reading Room, talks in Newport's Restaurant and the Salem Hotel, parties in Dustin's Hotel and the Half-way House at Lynn, and murder plots discussed in Richard Crowninshield's broadcloth manufacturing plant in Danvers—such was the nature of the testimony that shocked Salem. At length there appeared an ex-convict from Thomaston, Maine, with a story implicating George and Richard Crowninshield and Joseph and Francis Knapp. They were arrested. Richard Crowninshield was found dead in his cell, hanging by two handkerchiefs, leaving a confession in which he asked that his life serve as a model to keep youth on its path of virtue. His death was listed as suicide. Frank Knapp confessed that he and Joseph Knapp had hired Crowninshield, for $1,000, to murder the old merchant. He then repudiated his confession. The legislature ordered the Supreme Court to hold a special session in Salem to try the case. Public feeling was so intense that newspapers were forbidden to print the testimony. As the trial opened, the Chief Justice of Massachusetts, who was presiding, died.

The standing of the defendants may be judged from the fact that Nathaniel Silsbee was excused from serving on the jury because of his family relationship to them. (He married Mary Crowninshield.) Also, Benjamin Crowninshield, the former Secretary of the Navy, who had moved to Boston, was running for Congress at this time. Samuel Putnam was appointed judge. Daniel Webster was hired as a special prosecutor. Eighty witnesses were called. They were the leading citizens of Salem—men of the standing of Dr. Gideon Barstow and Stephen Phillips. Then there were such younger men as Hawthorne's cousin John Forrester, Jr.,* and his friend Zachariah Burchmore. Webster was at the height of his oratorical powers. Under Massachusetts law he had to prove that the Knapps were actually in the street, aiding and abetting Crowninshield, at the time the fatal blows were struck. The defendants refused to testify in their own defense, though Judge Putnam almost begged them to do so. They remained silent, Frank appearing indifferent and Joseph sanguine, as the evidence against them accumulated, as if they had some secret conviction that, no matter what happened or what was said, they would be released. The courtroom was crowded. Spectators remained in their seats for eleven hours, throughout the recesses, in order to hear it. The crowd thronged Court Street from side to side, silent and motionless in the hot July days, striving to catch the words that came through the open windows. This was the occasion of Webster's famous speech on the guilt of the criminal—"He thinks the whole world sees it in his face, reads it in his eyes, and almost hears its whispers in the very silence of his thoughts." The defendants were

* Thomas Healy Forrester died in May, 1830, before the trial opened.

found guilty. Judge Putnam, a man whose integrity and wisdom grows more and more impressive as one learns more of Salem history, wept as he pronounced the sentence of death. Might it not have been that Judge Hawthorne, a hundred and forty years before, wept as he sentenced the women accused of witchcraft? Frank and Joseph Knapp were hanged, still silent, late in the year, Joseph still appearing sanguine, and Frank still seeming indifferent, still wearing his frock coat with the velvet collar, as he went to the gallows.[58]

VI

Hawthorne had left Salem. By mid-September, shortly before Frank Knapp was executed, he was in southwestern Maine, loitering toward the heart of the White Mountains—those old crystal hills whose mysterious brilliance gleamed upon his distant wanderings. Height after height rose and towered above one another till the clouds began to hang down their peaks. He went through Conway, Intervale, and spent the night at Bartlett.

He was following the old trade route of Canada and New England commerce, connecting Maine, the Green Mountains, and the shores of the St. Lawrence. It led to the bleakest spot in all New England, a country of primitive taverns and hospitable people, where the wind was sharp all the year. It was cold in mid-September, with frost on the grass in the mornings. The dry pine cones made cheerful fires in the mountain cabins. Between the last house in the valley and the first house in the mountains there was a difference almost as great as that from one country to another. He was in a region of wind and cloud and naked rocks and desolate sunshine, of superstitious old people and of lonely mountain girls who were willing to exchange a good night kiss with a loitering teamster. Wagons rattled over the rough roads and the songs of the wagoners echoed among the rocks. There were the red pathways of slides, avalanches of earth, stone, and trees. The mountain people held their breath when a stone rumbled down the slopes, and said, "The old mountain has thrown a stone at us." There were high mountains behind and mightier ones ahead, the timber line a mile above him, dense and dark mists, mountain lakes, deep, bright, clear, and calmly beautiful, summer lightning visible behind him in the valley of the Saco, clouds creeping up the sides of the mountains, concealing its lovely peaks.

The Notch itself might have been carved by hand in the granite. It was a narrow passage, with high and precipitous cliffs on each side. The road followed the Saco. Handsome stagecoaches, with smartly dressed coachmen, rumbled through the pass, carrying tourists and traders. There were good substantial farmhouses in the wild country. The taverns had fires in the parlor and the barroom, and deer antlers and fox tails were nailed to the walls outside.* They were crowded with Green Mountain squires, tall mountaineers, woodcutters, honeymooners, minerologists who, like Alfred Mason, tapped at the rocks with small pickaxes and studied under magnifying glasses the specimens they broke off. It was now a day's journey from Conway on the eastern slope through the Notch to the Connecticut River. Fifty years before, the same journey had taken eighteen days.

Hawthorne went on to Burlington on Lake Champlain. The highlands stretched north and south in a double line of bold blue peaks. The unruffled silvery surface of Lake Champlain impressed him unfavorably; the fresh water had an unpleasant and sickly smell that one breeze of balmy Atlantic fragrance would sweep away. Burlington was a port of entry from Canada. Its buildings had tin roofs like those of Montreal. Irish immigrants, filling the Canadian provinces to the brim, overflowed into Vermont, and built huts and mean dwellings on the shores of the lake—men with lazy strength and careless movements, women with plump waists and brawny limbs. Canadian bank notes circulated freely. The town was full of merchants from Montreal, British officers, French Canadians, Scotsmen, wandering Irishmen, visiting southern gentlemen, country squires, Green Mountain boys.

Hawthorne traveled on southwest, and thirty miles from Utica, somewhere near Little Falls, boarded a packet boat on the Erie Canal. He vowed to travel its length twice that summer. The Erie Canal was an interminable mud puddle. It was dark and turbid, with an imperceptible current, flowing its drowsy way through dismal swamps. Occasionally black and rusty-looking vessels passed, laden with lumber, salt, and flour. They were shaped like a square-toed boot, as if they had two sterns. Sometimes a boat floated by with a family living in a hut on the deck. Once a boatload of Indians passed, staring at the passengers on

* Hawthorne stopped at Ethan Crawford's Tavern in the mountains, a favorite stopping place: Ralph Waldo Emerson had slept there the month before.

the packet with a singular fixedness of eye. Another boat passed bearing a group of Swiss colonists bound for Michigan. Their appearance, their strange costumes, with gay colors, scarlet, yellow and bright blue, pleased Hawthorne more than anything he had seen on his journey. A pretty girl with a pair of naked white arms shouted a joke to him in her native tongue; he replied in English, to their mutual merriment, though neither could understand a word the other said.

Sometimes the scene was a forest, dark, dense and impervious, breaking away occasionally and receding from a lonely tract, covered with dismal black stumps where, on the verge of the canal, might be seen a log cabin with a sallow-faced woman, like poverty personified, half clothed, half fed, and dwelling in a desert, while a tide of wealth was sweeping by her door. Two or three miles farther brought them to a lock. There was a small grocery store there, its goods enumerated in yellow letters on the window shutters in front. Then there were thriving villages, with two taverns and a church spire rising in the midst of the wood and gray-stone dwellings. The canalboat glided into the heart of Utica, among crowded docks and quays, rich warehouses and busy people, then floated between lofty rows of buildings and under arched bridges of hewn stone. The hum and bustle of the town died away and the packet threaded an avenue of the ancient woods again.

The packet boats were decked all over, with a row of curtained windows from stem to stern. They were drawn by three horses plodding along the bank. Nothing interrupted the monotony of the trip but the stop at the docks, or to change horses, or to untangle the towline snarled in a tree trunk. The meals, served on a long table set up in the cabin, were excellent. The canal being only waist deep, the only hazards were the low bridges. The helmsman shouted "Bridge! bridge!" as they approached; the passengers prostrated themselves like a pagan before his idol as they passed underneath. Sometimes the passengers failed to hear the warning and were knocked flat on deck. They boarded and left the packet anywhere along the line, without waiting for it to stop, jumping aboard as it passed under a bridge, or leaping aboard from the bank, sometimes missing their footing and sprawling on the deck or splashing in the water. It was, perhaps, as dangerous in its own way as a voyage to the Indies.

An English traveler paraded the deck, with a rifle in his walking stick, shooting at squirrels and woodpeckers, and sending an occasional bullet among the flocks of tame ducks and geese that abounded in the dirty waters of the canal. Rain began to fall, and drove them indoors. At the close of the evening meal it had become dusky enough for lamplight. The rain pattered unceasingly on the deck, and sometimes came with a sullen rush against the windows, driven by the wind as it stirred through an opening in the forest. They were on "the long level," seventy miles between Utica and Syracuse, so flat that no locks were needed. The English traveler sat in the cabin making notes. Hawthorne considered his fellow travelers, a Yankee schoolmaster home from Virginia, a farmer, a merchant from Detroit, a western lady. The Englishman stared so intently at the lady from the West that she reddened and retired into the women's section of the cabin. Hawthorne wondered what the Englishman made of them all. He could imagine the Englishman's scornful comments on the Yankee schoolmaster, and on the Massachusetts farmer who was talking about the iniquity of the Sunday mails: "Here is the far-famed yeoman of New England," Hawthorne could imagine the Englishman writing, "his religion is gloom on the Sabbath, long prayers every morning and eventide, and illiberality at all times."

What would he make of the merchant? "In this sharp-eyed man, this lean man of wrinkled brow, we see daring enterprise and close-fisted avarice combined. Here is the worshipper of Mammon at noonday; here is the three times bankrupt, richer after every ruin; here, in one word, here is the American." Hawthorne could imagine the Englishman writing of the western lady: "Here is the pure, modest, sensitive and shrinking woman of America—shrinking when no evil is intended, and sensitive like diseased flesh, that thrills if you but point at it; and strangely modest, without confidence in the modesty of other people; and admirably pure, with such a quick apprehension of all impurity." So Hawthorne imagined the Englishman commenting about them all in his forthcoming book of travels. But when he looked up the Englishman was staring intently at him.

He went to bed. A crimson curtain was lowered, dividing the cabin into two rooms, one for the men and one for the women. He could not sleep. His head was close to the curtain, behind which he continually heard whispers and stealthy footsteps—the noise of a comb laid on the table or of a slipper dropped on the floor; the twang, like a broken harp string, caused by loosening a tight belt; the rustling of a gown in its descent; and the unloosing of a pair of stays. "My ear seemed to have the properties of an eye—a visible image pestered by fancy in the darkness; the curtain was withdrawn between me and the western lady, who yet disrobed herself without a flush. Finally all was quiet in that quarter. Still I was more awake than through the whole preceding day, and felt a feverish impulse to toss my limbs miles apart and appease the unquietness of mind by that of matter."

He turned once suddenly and fell out of his narrow berth. He blessed the event and went on deck. A lantern was burning at each end of the boat: A crew member was stationed at the bow, keeping watch as mariners do on the ocean. The rain had ceased. The sky was all one cloud. The darkness was so intense that there seemed to be no world except the little space on which the lantern glimmered. It was an impressive scene. The long level was dismal, a forest of white cedar and black ash, decaying and death-struck by the partial draining of the swamp into the great ditch of the canal. Sometimes the lights were reflected from pools of stagnant water stretching far in among the trunks of the trees, beneath dense masses of dark foliage. But generally the tall stems and intermingled branches were naked. The whiteness of their decay brought them into strong relief against the surrounding gloom. Sometimes he could see the fallen trunk of a giant that had crushed down smaller trees under its immense ruin. Sometimes the lanterns showed a hundred trunks—erect, half overthrown, extended along the ground, resting on their shattered limbs or tossing them desperately into the darkness, all of one ashy white, all naked together, in desolate confusion. "Thus growing out of the night as we glided on, based on obscurity, and overhung and bounded by it, the scene was ghostlike— the very land of unsubstantial things, wither dreams might betake themselves when they quit the slumberer's brain."

The boatman blew a horn, sending a long and melancholy note through the forest avenue, as a signal for some watchers in the wilderness to be ready with a change of horses. Musing on the deck, Hawthorne reflected that the wild nature of America had been driven to this desolate place by the encroachments of civilized man. In other lands Decay sits among fallen palaces; but here her home is in the forests. When the towline became entangled, he jumped ashore and took advantage of the delay to examine the phosphoric light of an old tree in the forest. It lay on the ground, completely rotted, its diseased splendor throwing a ghostliness around it. He considered it—a frigid fire, a funeral light, illumining decay and death. Such ghostlike torches were just fit to light up this dead forest or to blaze coldly in tombs. As he pondered its meaning—an emblem of fame that gleams around a dead man without warming him, or of genius when it owes its brilliancy to moral rottenness—the canalboat went on without him. He shouted after it in vain and then watched it vanish with relief.

At Rochester he visited the falls of the Genesee. It was twilight; the spires, dwellings, and warehouses of the city were indistinctly cheerful, with the twinkling of many lights. It was a favorite vacation spot in the days before Niagara became famous—Judge Story had visited there. So much of the river went to the canals and milldams that the falls were now diminished. Yet they were an impressive sight. From a platform, raised on a naked island on the cliff, in the middle of the cataract, Sam Patch took his last leap, and alighted in the other world. People said he was still alive, hiding in a cave under the falls. Hawthorne thought it unlikely; poor Sam had prized the shouts of the multitude too much not to claim them, if he had survived. Was he any crazier than other men who throw away life in pursuit of empty fame? Thus Hawthorne mused beside the riverbank, "wise in theory, but practically as great a fool as Sam."

The most ancient town in Massachusetts seemed young compared to Rochester. It had grown like a mushroom, but its dusky brick and stone buildings would not seem grayer in a hundred years than they did then. It was youthful, active and eager, crowded with pedestrians, horsemen, stagecoaches, gigs, light wagons, ox teams, farmers bartering their produce, country wives buying supplies, advertisements for lotteries, judges and lawyers, woodsmen with rifles on their shoulders and powder horns across their hearts, drunken Scotch and Irish recruits for the western army posts—a city of many taverns, cheap, homely and comfortable for the farmers, and of magnificent hotels, with Negro waiters, for the wealthier travelers.

He went on to Niagara. A Frenchman, apparently from the French Embassy in Washington, rode in the coach with him. Had Hawthorne never heard of Niagara he would have considered it wonderful. As it was, his mind was too dazed with other people's descriptions to apprehend its majesty. Only at night, lying sleepless in his hotel room, he awakened to its wonder, the rushing sound of the rapids, with the dull muffled thunder of the falls, as though a great tempest was roaring outside, though the leaves of the trees were motionless and the stars were bright overhead.[59]

VII

He was a fugitive. Whether or not his journey had any direct connection with the White murder, it was a psychological record of flight. The early biographers of Hawthorne set the time of this western journey, over which there has always hung an air of mystery, as 1830, apparently without noting that it must then have occurred during the trial of John Francis Knapp for murder.[60] There are two biographical fragments casting doubt on this year—two letters by Hawthorne about the White murder, which came to light many years after his death. They are of such nature, however, that they do not essentially contradict the possibility of his absence from Salem at the time; they are stiff and wooden, unlike his ordinary correspondence, and are overly explanatory in dealing with a situation that everyone was discussing. They may have been written by Hawthorne for the purpose of establishing a complete lack of inside knowledge of the White murder.

The other evidence that establishes Hawthorne's presence in Salem in the summer of 1830 is the list of books taken from the Salem Athenaeum. According to the library records, he borrowed the *History of Geneva* on the day the murder of White was discovered and thereafter, almost every week until the end of the year, he used the library, returning almost every other day. The books taken out were principally, in the early part of the year, the *Massachusetts Historical Collections;* and during the summer, the bound volumes of *Gentleman's Magazine.* The list at this time is perhaps too full and too good to be altogether credible. It is not difficult to imagine Hawthorne, in a time of such universal suspicion, walking to the library and borrowing the works that he did not intend to read, for the purpose of exemplifying plainly in the eyes of the town his harmless and solitary industry. When it is recollected that the agents of the Committee of Vigilance were everywhere and that suspicion fell upon people far better known and more securely established than Hawthorne, the possibility becomes stronger. No doubt his membership was used by the members of his family in his absence. It is likely that *Hitt on Fruit Trees*, borrowed on August 30 and returned September 2, was for Robert Manning. One other detail sets the time of Hawthorne's western trip as 1830: Hawthorne speaks of a farmer on the canalboat condemning the Sunday mails. The agitation against the Sunday mails reached a climax in 1829. It would be unlikely that anyone would have complained against them later than 1830.[61]

The scattered records of Hawthorne's western journey are a record of flight, and yet of a guiltless fugitive. There is an air of watchfulness over them, not of fear. There is even a kind of exhilaration in them; a zest for adventure, something like a child's game of hare and hounds. In the first part of the journey, into the White Mountains, Hawthorne speaks of someone with him. Later on, by the time he reaches Lake Champlain, he is alone. On his return journey, there is a possibility of historical verification of his account. He visited Fort Ticonderoga, and went over the ruins of the fort with a recent graduate of West Point, a young lieutenant of engineers who had gained credit for great military genius.* In all his journey, whether alone or with a companion, he was vigilant, quick, guarded, but unafraid. Some of the details may have been fictionalized. He may have merely imagined what it would have been like to be left behind as the canalboat went on without him. Yet such things happened in those days—his schoolmate Seargent Prentiss was once left on the banks of the Mississippi, and Mary White, stepping out of a carriage to pick up a cloak that had been dropped, watched her hostess drive on without her, and walked all the way to Cambridge.[62]

But if his journey was the record of a flight, from what was he fleeing? Certainly not crime, for he would then have left no record; furthermore, there is no sense of strain or guilt in his narrative. But he might have been fleeing the hostile and suspicious city to avoid being called on the witness stand along with his cousins and his kinspeople among the Forresters. In such an event his solitary and mysterious habits of life would have perhaps looked very strange. He was, moreover, relentlessly honest, the victim of his "inexorable candor,"[63] and had he been called on the stand he would have told all that he knew. Still another possibility is that, as the trial of Frank Knapp began, a deliberate attempt to delay the proceedings was made, and he fled with ostentatious stealth to raise a doubt about the trial by directing

* Identification of this officer should set the time of Hawthorne's journey without further question. The Library of the United States Military Academy at West Point, however, has been unable to do so, and the problem must remain unsolved until undertaken by someone with access to the records of the orders given the graduates at that time.

suspicion elsewhere. It would certainly have seemed the height of madness to have remained in Salem, as Frank and Joseph Knapp did, when there were, as Hawthorne's flight so abundantly proved, so many avenues of escape.

VIII

The year after the Committee of Vigilance swept over Salem, the Reverend Charles Upham began his lectures on the history of witchcraft. These eventually grew into his two-volume authoritative work on the subject. It is probable that his intention was to illustrate the need for caution and tolerance by reminding his listeners of the hysteria of an earlier day.

Upham was of Tory ancestry. His father fled to Canada during the Revolution and became justice of the Supreme Court of New Brunswick. Charles Wentworth Upham was born there, May 2, 1802. He came to the United States, worked as a merchant's clerk, and graduated from Harvard in 1821. When he was chosen minister of Salem's First Church, the Unitarians had the first church in New England established by the Puritan fathers.[64]

Upham's ordination in Salem was a brilliant affair. The church had split over his selection—or over the choice of a Unitarian—and the dissenters withdrew to organize another church.[65] The Unitarians by this time were too well established to face the hostility of an earlier generation; and the men were of a different order. Upham's classmate, George Ripley, who also was to be a powerful influence in Hawthorne's life, attended Upham's ordination. Ripley was a pale, intense young man with brown eyes, spectacles, and brown curly hair, who was already leading a movement of the Unitarians toward social reform.[66]

The First Church embraced only sixty or seventy families. They were, however, families of wealth, and Upham received a salary of $1,000 a year to start, to be increased to $1,500 when his elder colleague died.[67] Upham was a brilliant historian. He delighted in melodramatic scenes, and he interrupted his histories with broad pageantry, treason trials, the conflicts of parents and children, whose ramifications he embellished vividly. He made himself an authority on witchcraft. It may be that this explained his interest in the Hawthornes. Hawthorne's aunt, Mary Manning, was a great admirer of Upham. When he was ordained, Elizabeth wrote to Nathaniel, who was still at

Bowdoin, that Aunt Mary was deeply in love with the young and brilliant preacher. Hawthorne wrote to his aunt to express his congratulations, asked to be invited to the wedding, and inquired, "Is the passion reciprocal?"[68] Time revealed that it was not.

Upham's congregation was intellectual, learned, liberal in its politics, and with a rather lively social life. Hawthorne seldom went to church; he was, however, on friendly terms with Upham in those early days. Upon his return to Salem, in the fall of 1830, he published the first of his stories of witchcraft, *The Hollow of the Three Hills*, of which mention has already been made.

At the same time, *The Token* published a curious story called *The Haunted Quack*, authorship of which has been attributed to Hawthorne, though he never claimed it. He probably wrote it. At the time the story appeared, New England was still thrilled by Webster's terrific closing speech at the trial of Frank Knapp. In actual fact, Webster probably had no business being at the trial. The state did not hire him to prosecute the case. (Stephen White, whose daughter married Webster's son, gave him a yacht.) Webster spoke for three hours, ending with a Shakespearean account of the assassin creeping up the dark stairway and striking the fatal blows, and his awful remorse as the secret preys upon him—"He thinks the whole world sees it in his face," Webster said, "reads it in his eyes, and almost hears its whispers in the very silence of his thoughts. It has become his master. It betrays his discretion, it breaks down his courage, it conquers his prudence. When suspicions from without begin to embrace him and the net of circumstance to entangle him, the fatal secret struggles with even greater violence to break forth. It must be confessed, it will be confessed; there is no refuge from confession but suicide, and suicide is confession."[69]

Hawthorne's story of *The Haunted Quack*—if it is his, as I believe it is—begins: "In the summer of 18—, I made an excursion to Niagara. At Schenectedy, finding the roads nearly impassable, I took passage in a canal boat to Utica."

While on this journey he met a young fellow sleeping on a bench in the cabin of the canalboat, and muttering "murder" and "poison" in his sleep. When Hawthorne awakened him, he said: "I see, sir, that you suspect me of some horrid crime. You are right. My conscience convicts me, and an awful nightly visitation, worse than the waking pangs of remorse, compels me to confess it. Yes. I am a murderer. I have been the unhappy cause of blotting out the life of a fellow being from the page of human existence. In these pallid features, you may read enstamped, in the same characters which the first murderer bore upon his brow, Guilt—guilt—guilt!"

Well, the young man was mistaken. He thought he had killed an elderly patient with a magic elixir; she had recovered, however, and the whole town was searching for him to reward him. There is a lot of slapstick in this story—the young doctor taking over his dead teacher's practice, and concocting brews of brick dust, rosin, treacle, vinegar, rosewater, and alum.

The following summer—in August, 1831—Hawthorne and Sam Manning drove from Salem to Concord, New Hampshire. They reached Concord at noon of the second day—"and before evening," Hawthorne wrote to Louisa, "we both got into the State's Prison and had the iron door of a cell barred upon us. However, you need say nothing about it, as we made our escape very speedily . . . Uncle Sam has already sent home two black mares and bought a gray one to drive tandem, and I should not wonder if we were to gallop into town, he at the head and I at the tail of a whole drove."

The people of New Hampshire in the county villages were as different as possible from the "sulky ruffians of Maine." Hawthorne made innumerable acquaintances, sitting on the doorsteps of county taverns, in the midst of squires, judges, generals, and all the potentates of the land, talking about the price of hay, the value of horseflesh, Captain White's murder in Salem, and "the cowskinning of Isaac Hill." [70] Isaac Hill was the editor of the Concord *Patriot*. He was "a short, small, man, lame, thin and cadaverous, humble in dress, with eyes sharp as needles and an intentness of expression his opponents found fanatical." [71] For twenty years Isaac Hill had fought Jeremiah Mason and the New Hampshire Federalists. He is sometimes credited with having started the attacks of Andrew Jackson on the Bank of the United States, by misrepresenting to Jackson the situation in Portsmouth, Mason's conduct in managing the Portsmouth branch, and Biddle's course in sustaining Mason. Hill posed as a fervent Jackson man, but when the tumult had died away he emerged as a supporter of Calhoun, a fact which gives substance to the charge that he provoked Jackson's attack on the bank. The "cowskinning" to which the

New Hampshire villagers referred was the Senate's rejection of Hill after Jackson had appointed him to the Treasury.

After a day in Concord, Hawthorne and Samuel Manning drove fourteen miles to Canterbury. They passed the Shaker Village on the way. Hawthorne wanted to stop; the Shakers would have given them supper and lodging and kept them over Sunday. Uncle Sam kept straight ahead, looking to neither right nor left, no more than if he had worn the horse's blinders, until they reached Hill's Tavern in Canterbury two miles farther on.[72]

Hill's Tavern stood at a crossroads at the northeast corner of the town. The stages from Boston and from Concord and Freyburg stopped there for a change of horses and for the entertainment of man and beast. It was a large, two-story building, with a porch running the length of the house. The dining room had originally been a tannery. The stables were large, housing as many as thirty horses a night.

The town of Canterbury, spreading over the hills beside the Merrimack, was quiet, prosperous and uneventful, famous principally as the home of the Shakers.[73] The Shakers were members of the United Society of True Believers in Christ's Second Appearing. Their name orginated in the violent and irregular motions—leaping and shouting—that were part of their worship. They believed that God is king, that the sin of Adam is atoned, that man is free of all errors except his own, that earth is heaven, now soiled and stained but ready to be brightened by love and labor. They believed in the immediate revelations of the Holy Ghost, and regarded angels and other spirits as maintaining communication and other intercourse with those who have been exalted by the gift of grace. There was no marriage among them. The sexes occupied separate rooms in the houses. When married couples joined the society, they regarded each other as brother and sister only. They were vegetarians. Liquor was used only as a medicine. Tobacco was outlawed. The men wore broad-brimmed gray hats, square-shirted coats, and old-fashioned waistcoats. Their hair grew long and was brushed back, hanging down their back like women's hair. The women wore long, white gowns and prim little bonnets. The men did farm work and ran the factories. They had dug a three-mile canal into Shaker Village at Canterbury, and operated a power loom, a grist mill, and a lumber mill. They made washing machines, and later manufactured brass clocks, skimmers, ladles, copper teakettles, brass sieves, hats, wheels, wagons, shovels, whips, hoes, scythes, rugs, mats, and fancywork. The women did tailoring and mending, prepared seeds and medicines for market, and made butter and cheese. The colonies prospered, until they had 4,869 members.[74]

Hawthorne and Uncle Sam had barely arrived at Hills Tavern when Uncle Sam became homesick. A large bunch formed on the horse's back, causing him as much pain as if it were on his own. The landlady nursed Uncle Sam and fed them both till they were ready to burst. A horse dealer appeared and sold Uncle Sam a gray mare. Friends of Louisa Hawthorne were visiting in Canterbury, Jacob Stone and his wife and daughter Lois of Newburyport. Hawthorne saw them as they entered Canterbury, and bowed, but they did not recognize him.

The next day—Sunday, August 14—Hawthorne and Dudley Hill, the landlord of the tavern, and the landlord's daughter, rode back two miles to the Shaker Village. It was immensely rich. The land of the Shakers extended two or three miles along the road. There were streets of great houses, painted yellow and topped with red. The Shakers were then building a brick building for their public business, to cost seven or eight thousand dollars.

Hawthorne went to the Shaker meeting. There were about two hundred spectators present. He took a back seat. A grave old Shaker soon came and marched him to a place of honor in the very front row, so that he had a perfect view of the whole business. "There were thirty or forty shaker ladies, some of them quite pretty, all dressed in very light gowns with a muslin handkerchief crossed over the bosom and stiff muslin cap, so that they looked pretty much as if they had just stept out of their coffins. There was nothing remarkable about the men except their stupidity, and it did look queer to see these great boobies cutting all sorts of ridiculous capers with the gravest countenance imaginable. I was most tickled to see a man in a common frock coat and pantaloons between two little boys, and a very fat old lady in a black silk gown, rolling along in a stream of sweat between two young girls, and making ten thousand mistakes in the ceremonies. There were an Englishwoman and her son, recent proselytes, and not admitted to full communion. Every man and woman (except a few who sang) passed within a few inches of me in the course of the dance. Most of the females were about thirty, and the white muslin was very trying on their complexions."

After the service Hawthorne shook hands with Jacob Stone, was introduced to his wife, who was a remarkably plain woman apparently older than her husband, and spoke to Louisa's friend Lois Stone. They were returning to Concord that afternoon, and to Newburyport in due season. Hawthorne returned to the tavern. Sam could hardly tear himself away after dinner. The whole Hill family gathered at the door to bid them good-bye, as if they were the oldest friends in the world. Sam and Hawthorne rode on to Guilford that night. "The next morning the news of your Uncle Sam's arrival spread all over the country, and every man that had a horse mounted him and came galloping to the tavern door, hoping to make a trade or swap, so that they fairly hunted us out of town and we took refuge in the same tavern we had left the day before. Your Uncle Sam complains that his lungs are seriously injured by the immense deal of talking he was forced to do."

The following day, Hawthorne walked to the Shaker Village. He was shown over the establishment. As soon as he explained his business —which was presumably to write about the community—a jolly old Shaker gave him a tumblerful of superb cider, poured from an immense decanter. "It was as much as a common head could cleverly carry." He ate dinner in a well-furnished dining room, his companions two more of "the world's people"—a doctor and a squire. The dinner was excellent. The waitress was a middle-aged Shaker lady, good-looking and cheerful, and not to be distinguished in either appearance or manner from other well-educated women in the country. The Shakers Hawthorne spoke to were intelligent, and appeared happy. "They had a good and comfortable life, and if it were not for their ridiculous ceremonies, a man might not do a wiser thing than join them." [75]

This was the sort of thing Hawthorne enjoyed, and in comparison with it the careers of his friends and kinspeople appeared dull. He could not see himself writing lyrics on *Farewell to the Harp*, for Isaac Hill's Concord *Patriot*, nor becoming a merchant so wealthy that at his bankruptcy even London would be impressed. The summer tours with Samuel Manning had set him on the track of something, though he was still unclear as to its meaning. Those villagers sitting on the porch were more interesting than the writers and poets, the editors and politicians, the fashionable young men of Salem, or the congregation of the Reverend Mr. Upham. They were the people, and when Hawthorne wrote a story based on his trip to the Shaker Village, they were the heroes of it. His story was very simple—two young lovers leaving the Shaker Village for

the world, and meeting a group of dejected pilgrims on their way to
join the colony. They had but stepped across the threshold of their
home when a dark array of cares and sorrows rose up to warn them
back. The defeated in the world went on to the Shaker Village, "seeking
a home where all former ties of nature or society would be severed, and
all old distinctions levelled, and a cold and passionless security be substituted for mortal hope and fear. The lovers, with chastened hopes,
but more confiding affections, went on to mingle in an untried life."

So, in his own way, did Hawthorne. The village of Swampscott,
adjoining Salem, looked as if it had been washed ashore in a storm. It
was a small collection of dwellings ranged in disorder on both sides of a
sandy street. There were little old hovels, built of driftwood, a row of
boathouses, a weather-beaten two-story house, one or two snug white
cottages, pigsties, a shoemaker's shop, and two general stores. There,
in 1833, Hawthorne settled for the summer, a few miles from home,
leaving no address and telling no one where he was going.[76]

There was a store in the center of Swampscott, selling gingerbread
men, fishhooks, pins, needles, sugar plums, and brass thimbles. Working
behind the counter was a slim girl with brown hair, a pale complexion
with a few freckles, a piquant nose, and depth and luster in her eyes.
Her light, quick body, elastic in motion, danced through her daily work,
cooking and cleaning and working in the store, and in the evening walking on the beach. Her name was Susan, and the fishermen of Swampscott
—it was a fishing village—patronized the store out of pure gallantry.[77]

There were such stores in every New England village. When a ship
was lost at sea, and the widows of the mariners were without resources,
relatives came forward with enough money to buy a small stock, a room
in the dwelling was made over, and the goods for sale were displayed in
the window. "In this republican country of ours, amid the fluctuating
waves of our social life, somebody is always at the drowning point.[78]
There were such stores as Hawthorne described in *The House of Seven
Gables*, run by an improverished gentlewoman to keep from starving,
and selling flour and apples, molasses candy, soap and tallow candles,
brown sugar, white beans and split peas, toy soldiers, lucifer matches,
gingerbread and marbles, pearl buttons, jew's-harps, yeast, root beer,
ginger and snuff.

The fishermen loafed around the Swampscott store in their idle
hours, wearing their green baize shirts, oilcloth trousers, and hip-length

browrr leather boots. In good weather they rowed their dories to Paint
Ledge, the Middle Ledge or beyond Egg Rock, and fished for rock cod,
haddock, halibut, and that lovely fish, the mackerel. When the wind was
high the whaleboats anchored off the Point, nodding their slender masts
at each other. The spray broke a hundred feet in the air over the base
of Egg Rock. The brimful and boisterous sea threatened to tumble over
the street of the village. On such days Hawthorne sat in the store,
listening to the fishermen. They were a likely set of men. One sitting on
the counter, another on an oil barrel, while another had planted the
tarry seat of his trousers on a pile of salt, they told stories that might
have startled Sindbad the Sailor.

One evening Hawthorne walked out toward the brook that ran
across King's Beach to the sea. It was twilight. Back of the town the
crimson clouds were fading over the steep hill with its waste of juniper
bushes and wild growth of broken pasture. On the beach the waves were
rolling in. The silver moon was brightening above the hill. A girl was
standing on the little bridge over the brook, fluttering in the breeze
like a sea bird that might skim away. She seemed to Hawthorne a daughter of the viewless wind, a creature of the ocean foam and the crimson
light, and as she struggled with the rude behavior of the wind about her
petticoats she formed an image that fastened itself imperishably in his
memory. She was slender, with the slimmest of all waists, brown hair
curling on her neck, and a pale complexion except where the sea breeze
flushed it. She was Susan, who worked in the store in the center of the
village. She had a delightful roguishness that made her a frank, simple,
kindhearted, sensible, and mirthful girl. She was a child of nature, and,
obeying nature, she was free without indelicacy, innocent as naked Eve.

He fell in love with her. The happiest of his dreams was of marrying her, becoming a fisherman himself, and living out his life with her.
Susan was enchanting. Romance with her had no connotations of im-
practicability: she threw sheer romance over the tasks of her everyday
life, making root beer for the store, cleaning and polishing, working
and living, and in the evening wandering with him on the beach. He
taught her to love the moonlight hour, when the expanse of the encircled
bay was smooth as a great mirror and slept in a transparent shadow.
Beyond Nahant the wind rippled the dim ocean into a dreamy brightness which grew faint afar off without becoming gloomier. He held her
hand and pointed to the long surf wave, as it rolled calmly on the beach,

in an unbroken line of silver; they were silent together till its deep and peaceful murmur had swept by them. She had kindled a domestic fire in his heart, and under the influence of his mind she had grown contemplative. He showed her how the rocks, her native sea, and her own slender beauty all combined into a strain of poetry. One Sunday evening her mother went to bed early and her sister smiled and left them. They sat by the quiet hearth, and she made him feel that here was a deeper poetry and this the dearest hour of them all. Thus went on their wooing, until the daughter of the sea was his.[79]

Swampscott was within walking distance of Salem. It is possible that Hawthorne was never as far from home and the observation of his kinspeople as he thought. There is some evidence that Elizabeth Hawthorne knew Susan. She said that Hawthorne had fancies like this whenever he went from home. "After a sojourn of two or three weeks in Swampscott," she wrote dryly, "he came home captivated in his fanciful way, with a mermaid, as he called her. He would not tell us her name, but said she was the aristocracy of the village, the keeper of a little shop. She gave him a sugar heart, a pink one, which he kept a great while, and then (how boyish, but how like him!) he ate it . . . He said she had a great deal of what the French call *espièglerie*." [80]

The town of Salem was beginning to look at him a little questioningly. Nothing but bad could be expected of a young man who was not a merchant, or a lawyer, or a minister, or a doctor, and Hawthorne's solitary habits made him exceptional. Who was he, and what was he doing? He had begun to write of people who stepped from their homes and disappeared, of people who found they had somehow been carried apart from the main current of life and found it impossible to get back again, of ministers who wore black veils to symbolize the secrecy of the human heart—visions of a solitary existence which were not precisely wistful, though they had an overtone of sadness, slightly puzzled and mildly self-reproachful. These Rip van Winkles of his imagination often expressed a vague wonder at the outlandish situations they found themselves in. What had Wakefield really intended to do when he stepped aside from life and, in a near-by house, watched the grief in the household he had left? How had it come about that the solitary man awakened to find himself parading down Broadway in his shroud? There was often a note of honest indignant surprise in Hawthorne's stories, as if his characters were constantly asking, What am I doing in this dungeon?

Or on this scaffold? There was always a sense of tremendous stakes at issue in their fates. Why had the Puritan Fathers, with their integrity and uprightness, banished Anne Hutchinson from Massachusetts? Why had they turned so fiercely upon the gentle Quakers? He perceived that the Puritans did not dare let Mrs. Hutchinson continue to preach. She struck at the most sensitive point in their social organization. She cited Scripture to prove that the colonial leaders were uncommissioned and unregenerated men. She made the early colonists feel like the children in a fairy tale, who have been enticed far from home, and see the features of their guides change all at once to fiendish shapes.

The more Hawthorne pondered on the New England character the more clearly his own sense of estrangement from it was revealed. He was like an undercover agent appalled at his own knowledge of the crimes of his neighbors. He had virtually finished his historical studies and his portraits of the governors and merchants, the Major Molineux, and Sir William Pepperells, Edward Walcott and Dr. Melmoth; he was now turning toward the fishermen of Swampscott, the sailors, the teamsters and farmers, blacksmiths and mechanics, as if in the hope of finding among them some quality which the intellectual and governing class lacked. His own solitary habits and the strangeness of his life and background separated him from them. He could walk the five miles from Salem to Swampscott, listen to their talk, perhaps row his dory to Egg Rock and fish as they did, and imagine himself one of them, awed at the learning of the schoolmaster and happy with his village bride—but the trip was a vacation at whose end he walked back to Salem and borrowed the poems of Keats and Shelley, and Massinger's plays, from the Salem Athenaeum.

The New Englanders were a hard people to define. They were a hard people to see clearly—harder then than later, for no one had studied them and written about them, no one, that is, except the English travelers whose scornful comments Hawthorne resented even though they remained unuttered. Pierce and Jeremiah Mason, William Allen and Jesse Appleton, Pitt Fessenden, Thomas Green Fessenden, Elizabeth Hawthorne, Jane Appleton, Jonathan Cilley, Joseph Knapp, Daniel Webster, Simon Forrester, Joseph Story and John Pickering, Alice Doane and Robin Molineux, Elias Derby and Richard Jeffery Cleveland—they were characters whose features had not yet crystallized into the combination of qualities indentified as New Englanders.

The term "Yankee," with its connotations of shrewdness and thrift, hardly applied to them. Nor did it leave room for the mysticism of Channing or Emerson, or the Shakers of Canterbury.

Why was it so difficult to characterize them? Sometimes Hawthorne wrote little items in his notebook that seemed to define some one of their attributes—people who made wills in each other's favor, and then waited eagerly for each other's death, or who made curious vows and bargains which destroyed them or made them odd and eccentric. "A fellow without any money," he wrote, "having a hundred and seventy miles to go, fastened a chain and padlock to his legs, and lay down to sleep in a field. He was apprehended, and carried gratis to jail in the town whither he desired to go." [81] That seemed to sum up one side of the Yankee character, but it was not quite what Hawthorne meant. They were shy; even the children were afraid of people making fun of them. They often calmly let their lives pass, planning to marry and then never marrying. Or a day passed, with a peculiar weariness and depression of spirits, reading a light magazine. Or they fought bitter and ruinous feuds, and discovered after the damage was done that their quarrel was based on a mistake. He could imagine a New Englander so cold and hardhearted, so resolutely refusing to acknowledge his brotherhood with mankind, that the earth would not receive his body when he died. He could imagine another with so grand an opinion of himself that he thought he was the prime mover of all sorts of remarkable happenings, to which he had not contributed in the least. Some of them seemed to choose their wives as if they were dissatisfied with all of nature's ready-made works and wanted one particularly manufactured to their order. He could imagine New England women tempted to be unfaithful to their husbands on a whim, or a young New Englander committing a murder with no motive, perhaps only from having read about a murder in the newspapers.

Probably he went back to Swampscott. Susan was too pretty to be left in a town only five miles away. All those walks in the evening, those solitary tramps along the beach, the rainy nights when he walked forth alone, were too much a part of his life not to have their origin in his heart.

Where was he going? Hawthorne was a follower of Jackson and a believer, with reservations, in Jacksonian democracy. But the people in whose name Jackson spoke were a long way from the fishermen and

teamsters. Did they really have anything more in common with newspaper editors like Isaac Hill, or demagogues like Benton of Missouri,
than they had with Webster and the old aristocracy? They were surely
strange representatives of the people, those dueling slaveowners, and
the embittered bankers who had hoped for a share of the deposits of
the Bank of the United States, those drunken politicians and women in
evening dress creating pandemonium in the night sessions of the Senate.

Yet there was a sense in which the people had the qualities the
politicians attributed to them, though of them the politicians never
spoke. The New England girls like Susan of Swampscott, were beautiful. On each of his summer excursions Hawthorne fell in love with her
again, in some other town, bearing another name. They were simple
and intelligent, industrious and lovely, poetic without knowing that they
were in the frank and artless expressions of their youth. Their words
—"I never cared much about moonlight before"—the wonderful self-
respect that gave dignity and grace to their movements as they worked
at the simplest household tasks, gave them a quality to which no romance did justice. A new spirit had swept through the country, and the
Jacksonian revolution, with all its demagoguery and falseness, its vul-
garity and rowdiness, had still in them been wholly beneficent; it had
brought them, as representatives of the sovereign people, to the surface
of life, deepening a knowledge of their own worth that the old stern
aristocracy had denied them. They grew confident without becoming
coarse; they took the good side of Jacksonian democracy, its independence and vitality, and rejected its bitterness, its vendettas and mob
spirit; the new plebeianism meant for them only a wider and freer scope
for their native resourcefulness. The politicians who spoke in their name
were unworthy representatives, dishonest with them and with each
other; the men of letters still lived with and wrote for the old gentility;
but in all the issues of his life Hawthorne was on their side.

CHAPTER FOUR

I

There lived in Boston an obscure poet, editor and legislator who had once been the most famous American author. No one seemed to know very much about him. He had been an ardent Federalist, which was in itself enough to ensure a certain amount of neglect, not to mention suspicion and misrepresentation, being his lot. His name was Thomas Green Fessenden, and he was then sixty-five years old.

One day in January, 1836, Hawthorne, who did not know Fessenden from Adam, knocked at the old poet's door and asked if he could stay there. Now, consider the circumstances of this encounter which, if anybody but Hawthorne had told it, would certainly have been considered fiction. Hawthorne had been hired to edit the *American Magazine*. He borrowed five dollars from Uncle Robert Manning and took the stage for Boston. He brought a cigar for three cents and paid six cents for a glass of wine.[1] After darkness had fallen he made his way to the home of Thomas Green Fessenden and knocked on the door.

Fessenden approached the door slowly, a lamp in his hand, his hair gray, his face solemn and pale, his tall and portly figure bent with a heavier infirmity than befitted his years. His dress was marked by a truly scholastic negligence. He greeted Hawthorne kindly, and with plain, old-fashioned courtesy, though Hawthorne fancied that he somewhat regretted the interruption of his evening's work. After a few moments' conversation at the doorway, Fessenden invited him into his study.[2]

Hawthorne probably knew of Fessenden's magazine work through Robert Manning. The *New England Farmer*, which Fessenden had started, had paid attention to Robert Manning's orchards. Hawthorne also knew Pitt Fessenden, who was becoming celebrated; indeed, he was distantly related to the Fessendens. And then, he remembered *Jonathan's Courtship*. It is likely that the young Democrats who counted

174

Hawthorne as one of them considered Thomas Green Fessenden a suspicious character. His *New England Farmer* had been launched with the help of those archreactionaries, Timothy Pickering and Daniel Webster.[3] He looked odd, he talked strangely, he had spent a great deal of time in England in his youth, and he was what radicals have always most feared, a popular conservative theoretician.

Fessenden was editing three magazines and serving in the legislature. His study was littered with books and pamphlets, manuscripts, newspapers, and stanzas of his new poems. His bass viol stood in one corner of the room, and for relaxation the old man would occasionally drop whatever he was doing and play himself a tune of soothing potency. A cheerful singing sound, like that of an enormous teakettle, filled the room. It came from Fessenden's stove. He had taken out a patent on it. It was a hot-water heater, and buzzed and steamed away noisily while it warmed the room. Various members of Fessenden's family—he was childless—entered and left the room, carried on their conversations and settled themselves wherever they chose, without, apparently, disturbing him in the slightest.

Fessenden settled down with Hawthorne and asked his opinion of some new stanza he had written. He was preparing a new edition of his poem, *Terrible Tractoration*, for the press. While he read, Hawthorne had leisure to glance around the study. There was such a litter, he reflected, as always gathers around a literary man. From the members of Fessenden's family, sitting in the room and talking away without disturbing the old poet, Hawthorne deduced that he had an amiable temper and abstracted habits. "It appeared to me, that, having no children of flesh and blood, Mr. Fessenden had contracted a fatherly fondness for this stove, as being his mental progeny; and it must be owned that the stove well deserved his affection, and repaid him with more warmth."

The evening ended with Hawthorne's becoming a boarder in Fessenden's home.[4] His household consisted of his wife and his niece, a pretty, vivacious girl named Catherine Ainsworth, and apparently other relatives from time to time.[5] Whatever his opinion of Hawthorne's politics, the old man took an instant liking to him. He also hoped, with what must have seemed to his guileless soul deep cunning, that he had found a husband for Catherine.

Hawthorne went to the office of the *American Magazine* the next morning and found his job in such a state of chaos that romance was out of the question. The editor, Alden Bradford, had left, with the next issue unprepared. The *American Magazine* was a picture magazine. A group of engravers had started it in September, 1834.[6] Bradford was a skillful editor, the author of a history of Massachusetts, and the master of a prose style of genuine distinction—vigorous, knotty, gnarled, muscular, the exact opposite of Hawthorne's graceful and smooth-flowing prose.

But Bradford was a reformer. He had campaigned vigorously against slavery. He also opposed capital punishment and tobacco and was an earnest advocate of temperance. Thus Hawthorne's purchase of a glass of wine and a cigar when he came to town was significant.

Alonzo Hartwell, one of the organizers of the Bewick Company, had made a large, handsome engraving of George Washington, for the cover of the March issue, which was to come off the presses by February 5. The engraving was of a bust of Washington on a pedestal, amid battle smoke and lowering clouds, but with a radiance brightening about his head. Around him were the stars and stripes, the liberty cap, cannon, muskets, bayonets, drum, and pyramid of cannon balls. On the right were a group of officers, Washington on horseback among them. Troops and artillery were pictured moving down to the bank of the river, in the Crossing of the Delaware; on the left the troops were pictured embarking, some in the river and some just pushing from the strand.

There were also on hand for the March issue a small woodcut of Major General Benjamin Lincoln, a large half-page illustration of the Walls of Jerusalem, a full-page engraving of the City of New York, and two engravings of the camp of the explorer, Sir John Franklin. They were interesting pictures based on Franklin's sketches. The dogs were unharnessed, the fire kindled, sending its smoke among the wintry pines; a kettle hung over the fire, and Hawthorne stared at the picture with envy, imagining the adventurers eating a rich stew of birds, rabbits, and other delectable ingredients. There was also on hand a quarter-page woodcut of a Hindu temple on the Ganges, and seven illustrations of French soldiers. These were part of a rather unfortunate publishing project. There were originally fourteen of them, showing the uniform and weapons of French grenadiers, lancers, and cavalrymen. Seven of them had been run in the previous issue of the magazine and seven remained to be run, with appropriate comment, in the March issue. They had no doubt been prepared when the war with France seemed certain, together with a good deal of semiconfidential material on the condition of the French Army. The war with France, however, was now a dead issue; it had been avoided by English mediation, and the whole scare looked rather foolish. Hawthorne had this leftover material to work on, twenty-odd pictures.

He set at once to work, writing the entire magazine. He lived meanwhile in Fessenden's home. But he had no money. He had expected to receive a part of the five hundred dollars he had been promised. He seems to have believed that the Bewick Company had actually paid the money to Goodrich, who was to pay him (although he may have merely written this home in order to explain his lack of funds without going into too humiliating detail), and that Goodrich had simply pocketed the money.[7] It may be assumed that his board bill would not have been pressing so long as the Fessendens considered him a potential nephew-in-law, though meals at the Fessendens were not very hearty.

The old man always brightened up at mealtime. His wife Lydia was a woman whose affectionate good sense was a substitute for the worldly sagacity the old poet did not possess and could not learn. They had been married twenty-three years. Old Fessenden could not praise her highly enough. He besought Hawthorne to take himself a similar treasure.[8] Hawthorne apparently had his doubts; and in addition he was so extremely busy that courtship would have been accompanied by the gravest difficulties.

His stock of clean clothes was running out. He sent his laundry to Salem to be done, and wrote frantically to Louisa to have it sent back. He was not allowed to borrow books from the Boston Athenaeum, although he could read in the library. "The Bewick Company are a damned sneaking set," he said, "or they would have a share in the Athenaeum for the use of the Editor *ex officio.*" Thomas Green Fessenden, absorbed in the composition of his new poems, would sometimes pass him in the street without noticing him or nodding to him. He explained that when he was composing he was totally oblivious to his surroundings.[9]

II

What had first interested Hawthorne in Fessenden? Well, for one thing, he had been browsing around the Bowdoin library one afternoon twelve years before and he came upon an illustrated copy of an old book called *Terrible Tractoration*, by one Thomas Green Fessenden. It was a poem with the funniest, most unusual, and grotesque origin in literary history; and it was characteristic of Hawthorne that he could appreciate its humor and its genuine literary merit and not be blinded to them by what dated it. But of this, more later. Hawthorne would not have settled down to learn the author's history only because Fessenden had written a popular poem, long since forgotten, in his early years. Something more was involved.

For one thing, Fessenden could hardly be persuaded to talk about his past. He was too full of plans for the future. His numerous inventions filled his mind so completely that he regretted that he had no time to work on them. He said he should have remained an engineer. He had thoroughly investigated calorics, and desired to look further into the subject. From time to time, wearied with work or upset by his recollections, he would get up and play a soothing tune on his bass viol. Meanwhile he edited the *New England Farmer*. Hawthorne's awkward beginning with his own magazine made him regard the *New England Farmer* with awe. It was the best of agricultural papers, and fertilized the soil like rain from heaven. Fessenden took the problems of his readers to heart. He was their familiar companion; he sat at their firesides, discussing, counseling, devising ways to better their crops and ease their labor, to protect them from error and inform them of dangers.

The spark with which Fessenden first fired Hawthorne's imagination was probably his account of his days at Dartmouth. Fessenden had been a Dartmouth student in the days when its founder, Eleazar Wheelock, was president. He had, moreover, entered at twenty-one, so his recollections were those of an adult. What he had to say was of peculiar importance to Hawthorne, for Fessenden, he believed, had caught the rare art of sketching familiar manners, and of throwing into verse the very spirit of the society as it existed around him. When he left school, Fessenden studied law, in which he was ill qualified to succeed, "by his simplicity of character and his utter inability to acquire an ordinary share of shrewdness and worldly wisdom." He was practicing in Rutland,

REVEREND JESSE APPLETON

President of Bowdoin College before Hawthorne became a student there, a master-spirit in Emerson's words, father of the beautiful Jane Appleton, who became the wife of Hawthorne's friend Franklin Pierce. *(New York Public Library)*

DR. BENJAMIN LYNDE OLIVER

Hawthorne's teacher: an inventor, lens-grinder, and musician; a friend of Benjamin Crowninshield, Secretary of the Navy. He seemed "A kind, unselfish man who had lost his ambition as regards appearances." *(Essex Institute)*

WILLIAM PITT FESSENDEN
Hawthorne's classmate. *(New York Public Library)*

THOMAS HEALY FORRESTER
(Essex Institute)

DARK LANE

"October 25—A walk through Dark Lane and home through the village of Danvers."—Hawthorne *(Essex Institute)*

Vermont, and writing verse under the name of Simon Spunkey, when a Mr. Langdon came forward with a newly invented hydraulic machine, which was supposed to possess the power of raising water to a greater height than had hitherto been considered possible. Fessenden became a member of the company interested in the machine, and was appointed their agent in London to obtain a patent on it.

What followed was the plot of comic melodrama. Certain persons were reported to have acquired the secret of the invention. Fessenden hurried to London to forestall them, arrived on July 4, 1801, consulted Rufus King, the American minister, who introduced him to an eminent English scientist, who gave his opinion that the machine was useless. A letter came from Vermont telling Fessenden that the pump was a failure. He had been lured from his profession by a device as spurious as a perpetual motion machine.

Hawthorne gradually pieced together Fessenden's biography. With characteristic ingenuity, Fessenden had gone to work on the pump and improved it. He built a model of a machine for raising water from coal mines by means of what he called "the renovated pressure of the atmosphere." It cost too much to patent. It seemed to be Fessenden's fatality to fall in with swindlers of every sort. A man claiming to be an American interested him in an ingenuous contrivance for grinding corn. The Lord Mayor of London was the head of a company organized to build mills according to the new design, and Fessenden bought a share in the patent. The results were disastrous. The Lord Mayor withdrew from the company. Presently it appeared that Fessenden was the only member who had actually invested any money. He found four new partners, and set about building one of the patent mills on the Thames, but his plans were thwarted, and after much toil of body and distress of mind he found himself utterly ruined, friendless and penniless, in the midst of London.

Still a third inventor discovered him. He was Benjamin Douglas Perkins. Perkins had invented a device for curing rheumatism by "removing the superfluous electricity." These devices were extremely popular, but were violently opposed by orthodox physicians and surgeons. They were called metallic tractors. Fassenden, as might be expected, believed in the tractors, and at Perkins's request wrote a poem of four cantos in their defense, surely the strangest subject ever to inspire a poet. *Terrible Tractoration* professed to be the work of a Dr. Christopher Caustic who has been ruined because of the success of the metallic tractors, and applies to the Royal College of Physicians for relief and redress. The wits of poor Dr. Caustic have been somewhat shattered by his misfortunes, and with crazy ingenuity he contrives to heap ridicule on the medical profession under pretense of railing against Perkinism and the metallic tractors.

Fessenden shaped out the poem one day during a solitary ramble in the outskirts of London; and the character of Dr. Caustic so strongly impressed itself on his mind that, as he walked homeward through the crowded streets, he burst into frequent fits of laughter. He had modeled Dr. Christopher Caustic on himself.

Terrible Tractoration was a success. Thomas Green Fessenden became what so few of his countrymen ever were, a popular author in London. His early poems were reprinted. They, too, were popular. He returned to America, not exactly in triumph, but a celebrity. Dr. Caustic now reappeared, an American citizen and a Federalist, in *Democracy Unveiled*, satirizing Jefferson and the Democrats, sometimes in satire unpardonably coarse, but in apt and singular rhymes, which even the Democratic papers copied—still another success for its author, who had given expression to the feelings of the Federalists. The poem consisted of six cantos of vituperative verse poured on Jefferson and his supporters. It filled the country from border to border with bitter laughter. Its strange, dog-trot stanzas were familiar to everyone. Fessenden was threatened with physical violence for having written it.

The wits of the New Yorkers in the Salmagundi Club now turned the full power of their ridicule upon Fessenden. Personally kindly, Fessenden never felt a moment's ill will toward the men he satirized. His prose essays, reflecting his deep anxiety for the welfare of the country, attacked principles and measure rather than men, and bore an impressive dignity of thought and style. The dread of the domination of revolutionary France haunted him like a nightmare. He edited the *Weekly Inspector* in New York, in 1806 and 1807. It was too conscientious, and too sparingly spiced with the red pepper of personal abuse, to succeed in those outrageous times. When it failed, the Democrats taunted him with his poverty. He replied that he could have prostituted his principles to party purposes, and become the hireling assassin of the dominant faction. There is no doubt but that the Democrats would have been glad to hire him.

He returned to the law, and practiced at Bellows Falls, on the Connecticut. In 1822 he established the *New England Farmer* in Boston. He also edited the *Horticultural Register* and the *Silk Manual*, made numerous inventions, and wrote occasional treatises on agriculture, while the poetic laurel withered with his gray hairs, and dropped away leaf by leaf. His name, once the most familiar, was forgotten in the list of American bards. He was peculiarly sensitive to the trials of authorship; a little censure did him more harm than much praise did him good, and he never hated the political enemies he satirized, unless they criticized his poetry.

What impressed Hawthorne was that his satire was never really venomous. He had none of the bloodhound ferocity of Swift, for example, who fastened himself on the throat of his victim as if he would drink his lifeblood. Indeed, there was no genuine American political satire. The country was too young and too good-natured; a recognition of one's own oddities always cut into an impassioned attack on another and a belated forgiveness, which was not so much mercy as it was the result of having too many other things to do, prevented the continuance of the relentless, undying, unsparing political antagonisms, which, concentrated in venom, made satire. In Fessenden's work Hawthorne found the clue to the origins of two strains of thought in American literature. American rural poetry, as Longfellow was beginning to practice it and as Whittier later wrote it, was distant, nostalgic, pretty, compared to the honest, funny, jolting, rustic verse that Fessenden had begun and had laid aside for politics and inventions. American political satire, as James Russell Lowell later wrote it, was broad and joking compared to the plunging, impetuous satire that Fessenden had begun and laid aside for the editorship of a practical agricultural journal.

So much for Fessenden's literary contribution. But what of his character? What were his loyalties? One of the clearest indications, in Hawthorne's early years, that he had an investigating position of some sort or other, is in his experience with Fessenden. When he came to write of Fessenden he said that he could find nothing in him but integrity and purity and simple faith in his fellow man and good will toward all the world.[10]

III

His own work with the *American Magazine* grew more harrowing. He had been left with the entire magazine to write, with no money, and with the source of his material—the library—cut off. On January 25 he wrote frantically to Elizabeth to help him with some copy for the next issue, begging for "concoctions, prose and poetical." "Concoct, concoct, concoct," he said. "I make nothing of writing a history or biography before dinner. Do you the same." Since he could not get books from the Boston Athenaeum he borrowed them on his card from the Salem Athenaeum and had them sent to Boston. They were delayed in the mail.

Hawthorne wrote a thousand-word essay on Washington to accompany Hartwell's drawing. Washington was the only American Northerners and Southerners, Democrats and Whigs, could agree on. In the bitterest periods of the fights of the Democrats and Federalists, they had jointly celebrated Washington's birthday. "Other great generals have been idolized by their armies, because victory was sure to follow where they led; their fame has been won by triumphant marches, and conquest on every field. Fortune has been the better half of all their deeds. But his defeats never snatched one laurel from the brow of Washington . . . In our pride of country, let it be the proudest thought, that America, in the very struggle that brought her into existence as a nation, gave to history the purest and loftiest name that ever shone among its pages."

In one sense Hawthorne never wrote better than when he was turning out these biographies before dinner in the hurried winter of 1836. Everything was grist for his mill. At night Thomas Green Fessenden, who was setting him a terrific example of labor as well as of the rewards of literary effort, would set aside his manuscripts from time to time, talk over the old days, play an old-fashioned tune to soothe his nerves, and lament that he had not remained an engineer.

Hawthorne struggled with his biographies of Major General Benjamin Lincoln, Commodore Barry, and Thomas Jefferson—he had decided to run a series of lives of the presidents. He wrote about twenty thousand words for the March issue, in a few days— a paragraph on noses, a descriptive article on Jerusalem, recollections of travel on an Ontario steamboat, perhaps adopted from someone else's contribution, or revised from his own travel sketches in the West, a brief essay on pirates, an essay on New York, a note on the bells of Moscow, an account of Sir John Franklin's explorations in Canada, a note on wigs, a description of human sacrifice in Mexico and Hindu burial on the Ganges, an essay on longevity, a long essay on French soldiers, a review of *The Puritan*, newly published, which he had not read (Elizabeth had, however), and an editorial note explaining Bradford's leaving and his own acceptance of the post. That Hawthorne kept the quality of his writing—or even improved it, for he dropped some rather annoying mannerisms, self-conscious references to himself as the author—make his career in journalism wonderful.

He developed a clear, dry style, unexcelled for communicating the kind of information he had to record. "General Lincoln was a Massachusetts man, and born of respectable parentage, in the year 1733, at Hingham, a town long famous for wooden ware . . ."

Hawthorne had set himself to tell his readers who the patriots were and what they had done, revivifying men who were only dim names to the Sunday loiterers in the Maverick House or the Mechanics Bar. Lincoln was not a great soldier. He served under Gates and Schuyler, contributed to the victory at Saratoga, was wounded, transferred to South Carolina, and defended Charleston from March 30 to May 11, 1780. "Then, the principal inhabitants and county militia having petitioned for a surrender, and the militia of the town having thrown down their arms; the troops being worn down with fatigue, and nothing to eat but rice, nor half enough of that; there being nine thousand men of the flower of the British army, within twenty yards of the American lines, besides their naval force and a great number of blacks; his own troops amounting to but two thousand five hundred, part of whom had refused to act; the cannon being dismounted, or silenced for want of ammunition; the citizens discontented; and affairs generally in a hopeless state; Lincoln found it necessary to ask terms of capitulation."

This essay was followed by one on the science of noses. "Turning over an old book, the other day, we lighted upon a set of rules for discovering people's characters by the length and formation of their noses." This ancient and forgotten science seemed to Hawthorne to be preferable to phrenology. He followed it with a brief history of Jerusalem—"No other city in the world presents such a dismal history of siege, storm, intensive commotion, captivity, famine, pestilence, and every sort of ruin, continued and repeated through a course of ages, as Jerusalem." After the essay on Jerusalem came the mysterious travel sketch, *An Ontario Steamboat*. This was perhaps a tenth of the contents of the March issue of the magazine. He had ten times as much to write in the next few days.

To Elizabeth Hawthorne in Salem these days must have been almost as difficult as they were to Hawthorne. She was then thirty-four. She answered Hawthorne's frantic request for copy by sending him three long quotations from Leonard Withington's *The Puritan,* which Hawthorne printed intact. She drew from the Salem Athenaeum *Debates in Parliament,* the *Edinburgh Review,* Temple's *Works, Curiosities of Literature,* Combe, *On the Constitution of Man,* Babbage, *On the Economy of Machinery,* in the first month of Hawthorne's editorship. She was apparently working on the *Universal History* Hawthorne was writing for Goodrich, and probably wrote the history of Jerusalem for the first number of his magazine.

She could hardly have known the extent of Hawthorne's emergency. She was his only contributor. She worked very slowly, and with great care, concerned to include all relevant facts in the brief space she had.

With her slow and exact methods of composition, like fine needlework, Elizabeth could not turn out a biography before dinner. Hawthorne urged her to take an old magazine and make an abstract—"you can't think how easy it is." She was too much a craftsman. He assigned her to write a life of Hamilton. She borrowed a biography on January 4, and was still working on her sketch in March. It was, however, excellent.[11]

The Manning household where she lived had grown smaller. The death of Samuel Manning in 1833 ended the family connection with the stagecoach business. The financial panic that became acute in the fall was growing severe. The stock of the Eastern Stage Lines dropped to par, then to $60, then to $50. The company sold fifty horses, and then fifty more.[12] The election of 1836 was at hand, and the choice of Hamilton for the cover was in itself a sufficient indication of the political allegiance of the *American Magazine.*

IV

When Hawthorne finished his first issue of the *American Magazine*, he sent a copy to Louisa, with a note: "Read this infernal magazine and send your criticisms. To me it appears very dull and respectable—almost worthy of Mr. Bradford himself."

He did not have enough money to pay the postage on the letter. "For the Devil's sake," he wrote to Louisa on February 15, "if you have any money, send me a little. It is now a month since I left Salem, and not a damned cent have I had, except five dollars that I borrowed of Uncle Robert—and out of that I paid my stage fare and other expenses . . .

"I don't want but two or three dollars. Till I receive some of my own, I shall continue to live as I have done. It is well that I have enough to do; or I should have the blues most damnably here; for of course I have no amusement. My present stock is precisely 34 Cts."

Elizabeth was still working on the biography of Hamilton. He thought he might "get the infernal people to take his head off for the next number. Their pen-and-ink sketch can't possibly be worse than their wood scratching. I am ashamed of the whole concern." A few days later he asked her to do a biography of Jefferson, adding, "If you don't, I must; and it is not a subject that suits me." He told her to extract everything good that she came across—"provided always it be not too good; and even if it should be, perhaps it will not quite ruin the Magazine; my own selections being bad enough to satisfy anybody. I can't help it."

Bridge wrote to him from Havana: "Nothing has given me so much pleasure for many a day as the intelligence concerning your late engagement in active and responsible business. I have always known that whenever you should exert yourself in earnest, that you could command respectability and independence and fame." To Hawthorne, struggling with his second issue, this must have been hard to hear. "Besides, it is no small point gained to get you out of Salem," Bridge went on. "Independently of the fact about 'the prophet,' etc. there is a peculiar dullness about Salem—a heavy atmosphere which no literary man can breathe. You are now fairly embarked with other literary men, and if you can't sail with any other, I'll be damned . . . I am writing with my coat and hat off, doors and windows open, and mosquitoes biting my feet. My letter is neither long nor neat; such as it is, though, it is probably worth the postage . . ." [13]

A few days later Franklin Pierce wrote. He had been trying to get Hawthorne a job in Washington. Pierce's attempts to help Hawthorne were curiously unsuccessful—he always seemed to be applying to the wrong people, for the wrong position, for his friend. Was this a foretaste of his administration? He seemed to have a faculty for disappointing people without their quite knowing it. He had tried to get Hawthorne a job on the Washington *Globe*. This was the Administration's paper. It was, however, Francis Blair's paper, and the organ of the radicals of the party. Hawthorne would have been completely out of place there. Pierce gladly dropped his effort to get Hawthorne on the *Globe*, doubting whether it would have been either agreeable or advantageous. It would have killed him.

"And I congratulate you sincerely upon your installation in the editorial chair of the *American Magazine*," he wrote. "I hope you will find your situation both pleasant and profitable. I wish you to enter my name as a subscriber to the magazine." Pierce then asked two questions that proved Hawthorne was right in saying he was deep. "Where do you board, and where is your office?" Fessenden's household was no place for an applicant for a job on Francis Blair's *Globe*. "I may be in Boston in three or four weeks," Pierce wrote, "and I shall have no time to search out locations. If you do not write to me soon, Hath, I will never write a puff of the *American Magazine*, or say a clever thing of its editor." [14]

Though he complained and fretted, and with reason, Hawthorne must have been extremely happy with his work. He had a natural gift for clear, firm, direct prose. His notebooks, his essays, his biographies of Pierce, Fessenden and Cilley, belong with his best work, and his novels, especially *The House of the Seven Gables* and *The Blithedale Romance*, are strongest when they have simple observation of his journalism. In the following five months he wrote the equivalent of three or four books. Elizabeth helped him, probably more than she has ever been given credit for, but even if all doubtful works are ascribed to her, Hawthorne still wrote an enormous amount. He told Louisa: "I have written all but about half a page with my own pen; except what Ebie wrote. Let her send more; for I have worked my brain hard enough for this month."

In these five months he wrote a biographical essay on Commodore

Richard Dale, an article on the Preservation of the Dead, and a long historical essay on the Boston Tea Party; a long travel sketch of Martha's Vineyard, of the Coffee House Slip, and the old Shot Tower in New York; articles on ancient warriors, snakes, St. John's grave, ancient pilgrims, Fidelity, April Fools, Viscount Exmouth, coinage, the tower of Babel, Wolfe on the Plains of Abraham, Hannah Duston (Parson Caleb Bradley's great-grandmother), John Calhoun, Pennsylvania Hospital, the Nature of Sleep, the Effect of Color on Heat, Bells, Precious Metals, Rainbows, Salt, Dogs, Moors, the Village of Economy, Wild Horsemen, houses, Chinese Pyramids, New York University, the poems of Thomas Green Fessenden, John Bunyan's works, lightning rods, the effect of music on animals, the effect of color on odors, the life of John Adams, cathedrals, the Suffolk Bank in Boston, the Longevity of Animals, Species of Men, the Church of St. Sophia, the weight of the globe, incurable diseases, hats, feminine characteristics, Lapland customs, sugar, Hoboken, papyrus, apes, rice, the temperature of the earth, the Flathead Indians, Norwegian peasants, crossbows (there was a shop in Boston manufacturing them), turtles, gold, locusts, corn planting on the prairies, diamond cutting, suicides in Canton, parrots, roads, tunnels, aqueducts, the Schenectady Lyceum, and the Frazier River Indians.

Hawthorne's Democratic politics certainly did not influence his choice of material to the point of excluding the works of his opponents. He gave his highest praise to Thomas Green Fessenden and wrote with genuine admiration of Timothy Pickering's homespun classic on training soldiers.

His selections from other writers indicated excellent editorial judgment. He reprinted poems by Wordsworth, Hood, and Percival's *Seneca Lake*. He also reprinted passages from Mrs. Trollope, Trelawny, Dunlap, Coomb, *The Life of Newton*, the *North American Review*, *The History of the Inquisition*, Charles Lamb, Nat Willis's *Trenton Falls*, Audubon and Paulding. The back cover of each issue of the *American Magazine* was a piece of music, composed especially for the magazine —"The Castilian Quadrille," "The Prussian Quadrille," and "The Hungarian Quadrille." [15]

He received no money until May 12. He was then paid twenty dollars. He succeeded in postponing the article on Hamilton for a month (until after the Democratic convention that nominated Van

Buren), then hurriedly completed Elizabeth's unfinished sketch. (The New England Democrats had hoped for somebody other than Van Buren.) The owners exercised a firm control over the magazine by scheduling the illustrations. He seldom had more than a day or two to prepare his copy. He was often in disagreement with them. "My mind is pretty much made up about this Goodrich," he wrote owlishly. "He is a good-natured sort of man enough; but rather an unscrupulous one in money matters, and not particularly trustworthy in anything. I don't feel at all obliged to him about this Editorship; for he is a stockholder and director in the Bewick Company; and of course it was his interest to get the best man he could; and I defy them to get another to do for a thousand dollars what I do for $500; and furthermore I have no doubt that Goodrich was authorized to give me $500. He made the best bargain with me he could, and a hard bargain, too. This world is as full of rogues as Beelzebub is of fleas.[16]

Beelzebub was the Hawthornes' cat. In May, the Bewick Company went bankrupt. On June 3, Hawthorne received a note from George Curtis: "In answer to your wish that the company would pay you some money soon, I would say it is impossible to do so just now, as the Company have made an assignment of their property to Mr. Samuel Blake, Esq., for the benefit of their creditors. They were compelled to this course by the tightness of the money market, and losses which they had sustained. We would like to have you, when in the city, sign the assignment. We shall continue the magazine to the end of the volume. Your bills from the 27th May will be settled by the assigne promptly . . ." [17]

In August Hawthorne went back to Salem. He saw old Thomas Green Fessenden briefly before he left. The old poet was ill. His new edition of *Terrible Tractoration* was a failure. He thought it was because the booksellers were in league against him, and revenged himself with a poem, *Wooden Booksellers*. Hawthorne found him in bed, suffering from a dizziness of the brain. There was a purple flush across his brow. He roused himself and grew very cheerful, talking, with a youthful glow of fancy, about emigrating to Illinois and picturing a new life for both of them in that western region.[18]

In September the *American Magazine*'s property was destroyed by fire: the September number never appeared. In October Alden Bradford returned to the editorship. He explained in an editorial note that he had been away writing a book. He had not read the issues Hawthorne had edited, he wrote loftily, but in glancing over the issues it seemed Hawthorne had "desired to preserve the work, according to its original design." [19]

Hawthorne had probably had the most spectacular failure in the history of journalism. He arrived in Boston on January 15, received his first pay on May 12—$20—after which the company went bankrupt, and was out of a job by August. His attitude toward Goodrich was ludicrous. Yet more was unquestionably involved in his editing than the record of his tragicomic letters home would imply. He was working through the first complete collapse (except during the War of 1812) of the American economy. Neither his failure nor his fight with Goodrich injured his standing: *The Token*, published in the fall, carried eight of his stories—*Monsieur du Mirror, Mrs. Bullfrog, Sunday at Home, The Man of Adamant, David Swan, a Fantasy, Fancy's Show Box, The Prophetic Pictures*, and *The Great Carbuncle*. These made up a third of the contents of *The Token*. He received $108 for them—an indication of the fall in prices since *The Gentle Boy* was published. On September 23 Goodrich received the manuscript of *Peter Parley's Universal History* from Hawthorne. It was of two volumes, a total of 754 printed pages. It was unquestionably Elizabeth Hawthorne's work—informative, attractive, readable, and a favorite for thirty years. It sold a million copies, and made a fortune for its publishers. In December Goodrich wrote again to Hawthorne: "If you are disposed to write a volume of six hundred small 12 mo. pages on the manner, customs, and civilities of all countries—for $300—I could probably arrange it with you. I should want a mere compilation of books that I would furnish. It might be commenced immediately. Let me know your views. I would go in old Parley's name.[20]

V

In the middle of September Horatio Bridge stopped at Fessenden's home. He was puzzled and alarmed to learn that Hawthorne was again in Salem, and that someone else was editing the *American Magazine*. Mrs. Fessenden told Bridge that Hawthorne had not been there since the previous winter. Hawthorne had, in fact, edited his last issues from Salem. Disturbed by her apparent hostility and by his own ignorance of Hawthorne's activities and whereabouts, Bridge now began to make

up for his previous neglect and tried, almost feverishly, to get Hawthorne's work in print.[21]

Bridge is one of the pleasantest characters in Hawthorne's biography, a fact which does not in the least detract from a wish, very
frequently, that someone had taken him out and locked him up. He was
good-natured, lazy, wealthy, agreeable, sanguine, and without meaning
to he had patronized Hawthorne for fifteen years. The truth is that
Hawthorne had always been older, graver and more mature than his
friends who, from time to time, with unconscious arrogance, dropped
him a friendly note or stopped in Salem to see him. His experience in
Boston had accelerated his development, and he was now no longer in
their intellectual and cultural world. He was not a Federalist, but he
certainly was not a Democrat in the sense that they were. Moreover,
Jackson's choice of Van Buren to succeed him had thrown the New
England Democrats into obscurity. On political grounds Hawthorne
had every reason to pay no attention to his friends who had been enjoying the benefits of the Democratic control of the country, without
offering him any assistance whatsoever, and who now, after eight
years, sought him out when their faction was whipped. They were a
liability. On personal grounds he owed them nothing except the friendship of their college days, which now appeared in a very different light.
If it would be wrong to say that he now perceived he had helped them,
rather than that they had helped him, it would not be too much to say
he could hardly have escaped the knowledge that he would have bene-
fited more from his college days if he had never met them. It had always
been the Federalists who helped him, Mason and Robert Manning,
Elizabeth and Caleb Foote—they were the people who had always been
at hand when he was in need, though not one of them had the means of
Bridge or Pierce or any of their prominent and powerful political
allies.

So Hawthorne was through with them. He bore them no ill will;
he simply did not want to see them. But for some reason lost to posterity, they could not let him go. They acted as people always do in
such a situation: they became worried at the change in him, wondered
at his lowness of spirits, and found him depressed. He was melancholy,
and it was their duty to cheer him up. Bridge barely succeeded in again
getting on friendly terms with Hawthorne, just before Hawthorne's
fame became assured. Hawthorne's stories in the current *Token* were

alone enough to make his reputation. All of his work assembled would establish him as the master of the finest prose in America and one of the greatest stylists in the English language/ No one except Edgar Allan Poe had ever written such short stories, and Poe's effects were often gained at the expense of the clearheadedness and sanity that distinguished Hawthorne's work. No living critic could equal Hawthorne's concise characterizations, the honesty of his views, or relate literature to life with such unforced and simple perceptions. When, a few years later, he wrote novels, they at once ranked with the best, even in a day when Balzac and Dickens were at the height of their power. In view of this, the achievement of Bridge in restoring his connection with Hawthorne becomes almost heroic. Another few months—perhaps another summer—would have been too late.

If Hawthorne was, for the time being, fed up with his Democratic political friends, he was even less congenial with the literary men. And at heart he loved Pierce and Bridge, though there was a kind of pity mixed up with his affection. He did nothing. He simply sat back and waited to see what Bridge would do.

Bridge returned to Augusta without having seen him. He wrote to Hawthorne, telling him that he had read *The Token*, and planned to write a review of it, naming Hawthorne as the author of several articles, unless Hawthorne objected. He supposed Hawthorne was getting a book ready for publication. "What is the plan of operation? who are the publishers and when the time that you will be known by name as well as your writings are? I hope to God that you will put your name upon the title page, and come before the world at once and on your own responsibility. You could not fail to make a noise and an honorable name, and something besides . . . Write to me soon if it will not interfere with your book that is to come out. Don't flinch, nor delay to publish. Should there be any trouble in a pecuniary way with the publishers, let me know, and I can and will raise the needful with great pleasure." [22]

Hawthorne could not be roused from his depression and lowness of spirits. Franklin Pierce visited him again. Pierce was running for the Senate. They met at Fresh Pond and had a cheerful reunion, part of which was spent discussing their mutual respect and affection for Horatio Bridge. Hawthorne returned to Salem, and sent Horatio word of Pierce's cordial feelings toward him. He did not answer Bridge's questions about his plans, and his careful letter was courteous and friendly, but formal beyond what was customary between such old friends.

Bridge was convinced that Hawthorne needed only to be known as the author of his own works. Pierce thought it essential that Hawthorne should get out of Salem. Both of them were gravely concerned and both had to exercise the utmost caution, for Hawthorne's independence and touchiness had grown; he might take offense at either prying into his personal affairs or an attempt to help him that further wounded his pride. He seemed to feel guilty that he had not quarreled with Goodrich when he first went to Boston, and taken a stand that would have made him independent of Goodrich. And yet he was not sure, and in his indecision thought perhaps he had done right—the whole experience was painful for him, and had humiliated him.

What made Hawthorne's conduct rather mean at this time was that Bridge was in trouble. Work had begun on the Kennebec dam some time before. A horde of Irishmen and French Canadians moved to the site of the construction. They lived in rude huts built along the river, as many as twenty people in a shack twenty feet square, children, old people, whole families and combinations of families. A nest of prostitutes and Negro pimps accompanied them. Back in the woods there were little huddled shacks where old Irishwomen, fierce and wild, sold liquor. Fights broke out between one Irish family and another, and between individuals. They were like small pitched battles, with brick bats tossed across the battlefields. The Irishwomen, immoral but industrious, ranged along the river, washing their clothes where the Bridge children had played in their youth, and where Horatio fished for salmon. Their children crawled along the riverbank beside them. The French Canadians were generally soberer, steady workmen who saved their money and then vanished into Canada with their earnings. They had trouble with the bosses, for they could not understand English, trouble about the pay they were to receive, and with the law. Because Horatio understood French he won their confidence. They appealed to him to serve as their interpreter. He became their protector and adviser, a swarm of them crowding around him whenever he appeared on the scene, with stories of their difficulties and appeals that he help them. The Irish were less tractable. They stole the fences from the grounds that had been the Bridge farm, and defied him when he ordered them off his property.

He lived alone in the house by the riverbank. He prepared his own meals, bread, butter, cheese, crackers, herrings, cold ham or mutton, boiled eggs and milk. A bottle of claret stood on the table. He ate his dinners occasionally at the inn in town. Dealing with the workmen had changed and matured him. He was firm and resolute, fair in his dealings with the men, with whom he was extremely popular.

Inwardly he was deeply concerned at the progress of the dam and the deepening involvement of his own and his brothers' inheritance. A few rooms in the mansion were occupied by a Captain Harriman and his wife. Harriman had been a steamboat captain. His wife was a plump, soft-fleshed, fair-complexioned, comely woman, sociable and laughter-loving, not young, but not middle-aged. She walked with the roll or waddle of a fat woman, though she was not fat. Their servant girl, Nancy, did the little housekeeping that Bridge required. She was a black-eyed, intelligent girl, shy and friendly, who dressed in silks in the afternoon and strolled about the house, looking not only lady-like but pretty, or stared thoughtfully through the window at Bridge crossing the yard, or walked out herself, as if conscious of being watched from behind the green blinds of the house.[23]

The ice broke in 1836 without damaging the piers and erections, and that summer the work was begun in earnest. By the end of June a cofferdam was built and a steam engine erected. The ends of the dam, projecting out into the river from both sides, were finished up as well as possible when the increasing cold forced suspension of the work. Piers were built upstream to protect them from the direct action of the water. But the danger of the water cutting underneath remained, and to guard against it a huge platform of logs was prepared to protect the bottom and buttress the ends. It was to be weighed with stones and sunk in the gap between the ends of the dam. The platform was built in sections. Some sections were prepared for sinking. The work went slowly.[24]

It was at this time, when his own affairs were so hazardous, that Bridge took Hawthorne's problems to heart. He wrote to him positively: "It is lucky you didn't quarrel with Goodrich, he being a practical man who can serve you." This was on October 16. "Dear Hath," Bridge began, using Hawthorne's old spelling of his name. "I have a thousand things to say to you, but can't say more than a hundreth part of them.

You have the blues again. Don't give up to them, for God's sake and your own and mine and everybody's. Brighter days will come, and within six months. . . ."

He had written a notice of Hawthorne for the Boston *Post*. "It is a singular fact that of the few American writers by profession, one of the very best is a gentleman whose name has never yet been made public, though his writings are extremely and favorably known. We refer to Nathaniel Hawthorne, Esq., of Salem, the author of *The Gentle Boy*, *The Gray Champion*, etc., etc. all productions of high merit, which have appeared in the annuals and magazines of the last three or four years. Liberally educated, but bred to no profession, he has devoted himself exclusively to literary pursuits, with an ardor and success which will ere-long give him a high place among the scholars of this country. His style is classical and pure; his imagination exceedingly delicate and fanciful, and through all his writings there runs a vein of sweetest poetry. Perhaps we have no writer so deeply imbued with the early literature of America, or who can so well portray the times and manners of the Puritans. Hitherto, Mr. Hawthorne has published no work of magnitude; but it is to be hoped that one who has shown such unequivocal evidence of talent will soon give to the world some production which shall place him in a higher rank than can be attained by one whose efforts are confined to the sphere of magazines and annuals."

Bridge was beginning to move in on Goodrich in his own territory. He was convinced that Goodrich had no intention of publishing Hawthorne's book. He wrote to him, and asked if there was any pecuniary obstacle in the way. If money was the cause of the delay, Bridge offered to obviate it by guaranteeing the publishers against loss. He was a stranger to Goodrich—a revelation of how completely Hawthorne separated his literary and personal life—and offered Goodrich Boston references.[25]

Actually, Bridge was almost ruined. Cold weather stopped work on the milldam and forced the building of the log platforms to protect the exposed unfinished ends of the structure. The capital of the company was exhausted, and the financial panic made the prospect of raising more extremely doubtful.[26] Bridge was living alone in his house at Augusta. He promptly received a warm reply from Goodrich, on October 20. "I have received your letter in regard to our friend Hawthorne," Goodrich wrote. "It will cost about $450 to print 1000 volumes in good style. I have seen a publisher, and he agrees to publish it if he can be guaranteed $250 as an ultimate resort against loss. If you will find that guaranty, the thing shall be put immediately in hand.

"I am not now a publisher, but I shall take great interest in this work; and I do not think there is any probability that you will ever be called upon for a farthing. The generous spirit of your letter is a reference. I only wish to know if you will take the above risk. The publication will be solely for the benefit of Hawthorne; he receiving ten per cent on the retail prices—the usual terms."

Bridge gave the guarantee at once. He stipulated that his part in the affair should be concealed from Hawthorne. He was sure Hawthorne would refuse to have the book published if he knew of the arrangement.

He had barely sent his answer to Goodrich when he received another note from Hawthorne. He wrote at once, in haste: "Oct. 22, 1836. Dear Hath—I have just received your last, and do not like its tone at all. There is a kind of desperate coolness in it that seems dangerous. I fear that you are too good a subject for suicide, and that some day you will end your mortal woes on your own responsibility. However, I wish you to refrain till next Thursday, when I shall be in Boston. *Deo Volente.* I am not in very good mood myself just now, and am certainly unfit to write or think. Be sure to come and meet me in Boston." [27]

The election of 1836 intervened. There was still only one party in the United States; the election was the choice of one or another of its factions. Jackson had chosen Van Buren to succeed him, and Van Buren was elected. The crash came as he was inaugurated. Banks failed and prices doubled. The newspapers carried long lists of banks whose notes were not accepted in payment, another list of closed banks and still a third list of banks whose notes were doubtful. The Salem *Gazette*'s lists included eight banks whose notes were doubtful, and thirty-six which had been closed.[28]

Bridge was a Democrat, but no supporter of Van Buren. Immediately after the election a serious disappointment befell him. The log platforms that were to be sunk to protect the bottom from the action of the water were floated before the dam preparatory to sinking. About the middle of November, soon after the election, a sudden freshet swept them away. The ballast was emptied into the gap, and injured the western end of the dam.[29]

Hawthorne set about preparing *Twice-Told Tales* for publication. A group of Boston literary men and lawyers had organized the American Stationers Company, to print the works of American authors. One of its first works was Prescott's *Ferdinand and Isabella*—Prescott had been unable to find a publisher. Goodrich took Hawthorne's book to Dr. Samuel Howe, who took it to the American Stationers Company, who agreed to publish it.[30] Grateful for Goodrich's assistance, or perhaps suspecting Bridge's wirepulling behind the scenes, Hawthorne now proposed to dedicate the book to Goodrich. At least, he wrote Bridge that he intended to do so. Bridge replied warily, "I fear you will hurt yourself by puffing Goodrich *undeservedly*—for there is no doubt in my mind of his selfishness in regard to your work and yourself. I am perfectly aware that he has taken a great deal of interest in you, but when did he ever do anything for you without a *quid pro quo* . . . unless you are already committed, do not mar the prospects of your first book by hoisting Goodrich into favor."

Jonathan Cilley was a candidate for Congress. On the eve of his election, Horatio Bridge, in accordance with the orders given him twelve years before, broke the seal on the letter Hawthorne and Cilley had given him when they were in college together. Its contents, with Hawthorne's promise to pay Cilley a barrel of wine if he married before 1836, confounded him. Bridge wrote to Hawthorne, told him that he had won his bet, and insisted that he collect, saying that Cilley would have demanded payment had he won.

Cilley wrote to Hawthorne acknowledging that he had lost. A month's grace was allowed the loser. He congratulated Hawthorne on his forthcoming book—"it would have pleased me more to have heard that you were about to become the author and father of a legitimate and well-begotten boy . . . What! suffer twelve years to pass away, and no wife, no children, to soothe your care, make you happy, and call you blessed? Why in that time I have begotten sons and daughters to the numbers of half a dozen, more or less, though I mourn that some of them are not. Peace be with them! . . .

"Damn that barrel of old Madeira; who cares if I have lost it! If only you and Frank Pierce and Joe Dummer and Sam Boyd and Bridge and Bill Hale were with me, we could have a regular drunk. . . .

What sort of a book have you written, Hath? I hope it is nothing like the damned ranting stuff of John Neal, which you, while at Brunswick, relished so highly. Send me a copy, and I'll review it for you. If I can't make a book, my partisan friends call me good at a political harangue or stump speech. Don't turn up your aristocratic nose, for it is a pathway to fame and honor, as well as the course you have marked out, and attended with more stimulating noise and clatter if not *eclat*, than that of a book author and writer for immortality, who hides himself from his own generation in a study or garret, and neglects in the springtime of life to plant and maintain that posterity to which he looks for praise and commendation." [31]

The Kennebec had frozen solid, with six or eight inches of ice. On December 17 the first snow fell and continued steadily until Wednesday, December 21. It was followed the next day by a violent southeast rain. The river rose eight feet. The ice broke. The swollen waters poured through the gap with fearful power.[32]

From the house, through the storm, Bridge could see the dark water racing past, bearing along great masses of ice, logs, and driftwood. A screen of trees blotted his view of the dam itself. If he felt any agitation he did not show it. Yet living alone in the empty house through the long winter must have been difficult. The household was stranger than ever. Mrs. Harriman, at rather an advanced age, was pregnant. Her child was born in the spring. If Bridge left the room he lived in, his cold ham and claret, and walked to the dam through the storm, he must have had misgivings. The water rose to within two feet of the top of the dam. The exposed ends, since the platform no longer protected them, were undermined. They settled five or six feet.

Three days after the freshet, and while the fate of the dam was still in doubt, he wrote to his friend:

Augusta, December 25, 1836

Dear Hawthorne,—On this Christmas day and Sunday I am writing up my letters. Yours comes first. I am sorry that you didn't get the magazine; because you wanted it, not that I think it very important to you. You will have the more time for your book. I rejoice that you have determined to leave Goodrich to his fate. I do not like him. Whether your book will sell extensively may be doubtful, but that is of small importance in the first book you publish. At all events, keep up your spirits till the result is ascertained; and my word for it, there is more honor and emolument in store for you from your writings than you imagine.

I have been trying to think what you are so miserable for. Although you have not much property, you have good health and powers of writing, which have made and can still make you independent. Suppose you get but $300 per annum for your writings. You can with economy live upon that, though it would be a damned tight squeeze. You have no family dependent on you, and why should you "borrow trouble?" This is taking the worst view of your case that it can possibly have. It seems to me you never look at the bright side with any hope or confidence. It is not the philosophy to make one happy. I expect next summer to be full of money, a part of which shall be heartily at your service if it comes.

And so Frank Pierce is elected Senator. There is an instance of what a man can do for himself by trying. With no very remarkable talents, he, at the age of thirty-four, fills one of the highest stations in the nation. He is a good fellow, and I rejoice at his success. He can do something for you perhaps. The inclination he certainly has. Have you heard from him lately?

H. Bridge.[33]

No, Hawthorne had not heard from Pierce lately. Bridge settled down to endure stoically the testing of the dam. It held. The water subsided and the river froze again. Through the winter the financial crisis grew steadily worse. By spring it was plain that the company could not survive without more capital. By an act of the legislature, on March 17, 1837, the name of the corporation was changed to the Kennebec Lock and Canal Company, and it was authorized to increase its capital stock to $600,000. The ice went out. The water rose over the top of the dam. It had suffered no further damage. The water rushed feather-white over it, and in renewed optimism the directors voted to increase the capital stock sale to the largest limit.

Their optimism was short-lived. There were no purchasers for the stock at any price. Work could not be started on the dam, and the

few weeks of good weather passed, increasing the hazard of the enterprise, since it was doubtful that the dam could be completed by winter
unless work was begun at once.[34]

Goodrich had made his agreement with Bridge, concerning Hawthorne's book, in October. In February he wrote that the book should
be ready for the printers in about ten days. In March, 1837, the Salem
Gazette published one of Hawthorne's stories, *Fancy's Show Box*, on
its front page, with his signature.[35] The truth of Hawthorne's work
was now out. By March 17 *Twice-Told Tales* was published. Bridge read
his copy in Augusta. It made him cry. He wrote to Hawthorne a letter
full of hope, puns, and expressions of confidence. His dam was looking
well. "Though I have forty or fifty thousand at stake, I do not sleep
the worse for it. If I lose, I shall try for the appointment of Purser
in the Navy, and with a good chance of success. This is a profound
secret at present. Good times for both of us are coming. You have
broken the ice; the ice can't break me . . ."[36]

He was mistaken; the ice did break him. Of all the strange motives
entangled in the publication of *Twice-Told Tales*, the strangest were
perhaps those implied by Bridge's admission that he placed it upon an
even footing with the labor of damming the Kennebec. Hawthorne himself appears not to have been eager to have the book published. His
introduction might have been deliberately intended to suppress any
enthusiasm for it. The little book of eighteen stories—for it was only
half the length of the later editions—beginning with *The Gray Champion* and ending with *Dr. Heidegger's Experiment*, had an almost terrifying history. So many people were involved in the effort to see that
it appeared, and so much seemed to depend upon its publication, that
the burden placed upon it might have crushed it at the start. Why was
so much labor and planning required to bring it before the world as
Hawthorne's work? He had published five times as much anonymously
without such travail. Two 'or three issues of *The Token*, or a year of
the *New England Magazine*, contained as much of his work as *Twice-
Told Tales*. The frail little volume that finally appeared, written, as he
said, for his known or unknown friends, simple, unpretending, the stories, which at first glance seemed to be inconsequential happenings of
ancient times, told in a quiet monotone, nevertheless had a quality that
endured beyond the mighty enterprise which was, at least partially,
responsible for their being published at all.[37]

It was a strange coincidence that soon after *Twice-Told Tales* appeared another link was formed between Hawthorne and the friends of his schooldays. Charles Mason, the brother of his Bowdoin roommate, became rector of St. Peter's Episcopal Church in Salem, on May 1, 1837. In June he married Susanna Lawrence, the daughter of the fabulously wealthy Amos Lawrence. Mason remained in Salem ten years. He had many of the qualities of his father. He was a scholar, a student of English literature, especially the Elizabethans, and a master of the old English theologians.[38]

Bridge had wanted Hawthorne's book published for many reasons. Franklin Pierce wanted it to appear so that Hawthorne could be a stronger candidate for the appointment of historian to the South Seas expedition. The appointment would have paid $1,500 a year. The Reynolds Expedition was the first authorized by Congress. As originally planned, it was to be commanded by Commander Thomas Ap Catesby Jones, and to consist of the frigate *Macedonian*, with three brigs and a store ship. It was to cruise the South Pacific and the Antarctic for five years.

It was a brilliant suggestion of Pierce's that Hawthorne should be appointed to the post—one of the happiest thoughts in the whole unhappy history of the relations of American writers and politicians. A cruise to the South Seas was exactly what Hawthorne needed, and the Navy needed nothing quite so badly as it needed an interpreter and recorder of Hawthorne's ability.

Van Buren had reappointed Mahlon Dickerson as secretary of the navy. Dickerson and Reynolds, the sponsor of the expedition, were at odds about it. There was also a factional fight within the Navy to complicate the issue and make the process of getting Hawthorne appointed a delicate one. Pierce certainly worked energetically and skillfully in Hawthorne's behalf.

He saw Reynolds, and described Hawthorne to him: extremely modest, perhaps diffident, but a diffidence having its origin in a high and lofty pride; a man of decided genius, with none of the whims and caprices of genius to impair his efficiency; the author of *Twice-Told Tales*, which had been most favorably reviewed, the successful editor of the *American Magazine*. The quality that Pierce wanted particularly to impress on Reynolds was Hawthorne's steadiness, his freedom from the whims and eccentricities that are supposed to characterize men of genius, and which disqualify them for solid and steady business. "I know Hawthorne's worth," he wrote to Reynolds, "and am sure you would admire him as a man of genius and love him as a companion and friend."

Pierce thought that Reynolds would see Churchill Camberling, the Tammany politician from New York and Van Buren's intimate friend, and persuade Camberling to write a letter to Van Buren, enclosing the material on Hawthorne that Pierce sent to him. This should be enough to secure the appointment. Bridge wrote to George Bancroft asking Bancroft to write to Dickerson in Hawthorne's behalf. Bridge could pledge the entire Maine delegation to speak in Hawthorne's favor. His sister's father-in-law, Reuel Williams, chairman of the Naval Affairs Committee, worked in Hawthorne's interest, as did Cilley. By the middle of April, however, Bridge doubted that Hawthorne would get the post, and by the middle of May he thought it just as well if he did not.

The expedition was attacked in Congress on the grounds of economy. It emerged from the struggle reorganized. Instead of Commander Thomas Ap Catesby Jones and the *Macedonian*, it was now to consist of a squadron of four ships, the *Vincennes*, the *Peacock*, the *Porpoise* and the *Relief*, commanded by Commander Charles Wilkes, who had been, until then, superintendent of the department of charts and instruments in the Navy Department. The voyage was to last four years and to circumnavigate the globe. A British expedition was likewise sailing into the same waters that Wilkes planned to explore.[39]

On May 10, 1837, all the banks in New York City closed their doors. They could no longer redeem their notes in gold or silver. The banks in other cities followed them. The financial crisis was complete.[40] In May Edmund Bridge reported that there was no reasonable prospect of selling the increased stock issue in the present embarrassed state of money affairs. James Bridge was directed to mortgage the personal property of the backers. Enough money was raised to permit work to start again. But not until June was it under way, and there was still a gap in the middle of the river, more than a hundred feet across, to be closed, and in this part of the work the dam was built at the rate of only about ten feet a week.[41] Personal troubles increased the difficulties of the Bridges and the Williams. One of Horatio's sisters became severely ill with dysentery. The doctor said it was because she had assisted in dressing a dead man in his robe. He told her that such was the general effect of contact with a person recently dead.[42] At the end of May, though he still wrote cheerfully and professed to believe that the dam was proceeding famously, Horatio wrote to Hawthorne and asked him to come to Augusta to spend the summer with him.[43]

VI

Hawthorne reached Augusta, Maine, on July 3, 1837, the night before his birthday. He went at once to Bridge's house half a mile from town, on its rising swell of ground beside the Kennebec. The house stood fifty yards back from the road, with a grassy tract and a gravel walk before it. It was large, secluded, and half empty, Captain Harriman's family occupying only half of the house. Mrs. Harriman's baby, a daughter, had been born early in the spring.

Bridge had another visitor living with him, a young Frenchman of German descent named Schaeffer, whom he had taken in to teach him French. Schaeffer was a French teacher in Augusta—one of his students, a Miss Appleton, had translated Hawthorne's *Minister's Black Veil* into French. He was an infidel, a philosopher and, by his own account, a man who had never sinned with a woman, meaning, apparently, that he had never had sexual intercourse with a woman. Hawthorne believed him. Schaeffer was cheerful, odd, picturesque and good-natured, except on the subject of the Yankees who made fun of him. He came in at night and if he found Bridge awake stood at his bedside, talking French, saying, "Je hais—Je hais les Yankees!" He excepted Hawthorne and Bridge from his hatred of Yankees. Bridge he called Monsieur du Pont, and Hawthorne, Monsieur de l' Aubepine; he wanted Hawthorne to go on a walking trip with him to Niagara Falls and Quebec, far away from these damnable Yankees. He was surprisingly well informed, and quaint appearing; he was small, cockeyed, and ill dressed, with a coarse blue coat, thin cotton pants, and unpolished shoes. Yet he was so vivacious and good-natured, and found such a hearty and childlike enjoyment in trifles—sometimes talking Spanish, sometimes chanting Latin in imitation of Catholic priests, sometimes breaking out in a light French song and acting out the words—that he brought a constant gaiety into their bachelor life, and they lived together, said Hawthorne gravely, in great harmony and brotherhood.

The mornings in Maine were beautiful. The sunshine on the wet grass, on the sloping and swelling land across the river, diffused a dim brilliance over the whole surface of the field. The mists slowly rising, part resting on the earth and part ascending, seemed both fog and cloud, too indistinct to be defined as either. Nancy, the servant girl who lived with the family in the other half of the house, left to milk the cows. She was pretty, dark-haired and intelligent, with a bosom Hawthorne found pleasure in studying as she washed the clothes with her bare arms in the water. She came into Bridge's side of the house in the morning to make the beds. She glanced at Hawthorne, smiled, and said, "Good morning," in a pleasant voice—somewhat shy, but willing to converse.

The Frenchman was up at sunrise or before, humming to himself, scuffling about the chamber in his thick boots, and at last taking his departure for a solitary ramble before breakfast. Then he came in, cheerful and vivacious enough, and ate heartily. The little Frenchman impressed Hawthorne strongly—lonely as he was, struggling against the world, with bitter feelings in his breast, and yet talking with the gaiety and vivacity of his nation—making Bridge's house his home from darkness to daylight, and enjoying what little domestic comfort and confidence there was for him, and then going about all the livelong day, teaching French to blockheads who sneered at him.

When breakfast was over, Schaeffer set off down the gravel walk, singing a French song as he walked. Bridge and Hawthorne spent the day together. Hawthorne was impressed at the change in Bridge. He combined more high and admirable qualities than any other Hawthorne had ever met with. He was polished, natural, frank, open and straightforward, yet with a delicate feeling for the sensitiveness of his companions. He had an excellent temper and warm heart; he was well acquainted with the world, and had a keen faculty of observation. He had a code of honor and principle, rigid and nice in its way, from which he never varied. He had strong affections, and was fond of women and children. It was remarkable to Hawthorne that he had never married— he seemed to have made up his mind never to marry. A philosophy was developing in him; Hawthorne thought it likely that Bridge would settle down to this, or to some equally singular mode of life. As for himself, he liked it, and thought that he would easily become attached to this way of life, so independent and so untroubled by the forms and restrictions of society. But he planned to spend only a week or two with Bridge; certainly not two or three months. It would probably be the longest time they would ever spend together; fate seemed to be preparing changes for both of them. "My circumstances, at least, cannot long continue as they are and have been; and Bridge, too, stands betwixt high prosperity and utter ruin."

While they talked, the quiet was broken, two or three times a day, by a sudden thunder from the quarry, where workmen were blasting rocks for the dam. The peals of thunder sounded strange in such a green, sunny and quiet landscape, with the blue sky brightening the river.

On the morning of the Fourth of July—it was curious that Hawthorne never wrote of it as his birthday—Bridge and Hawthorne walked into Augusta. A carpenter was cutting out great letters from an old play bill, in order to print "Van Buren Forever" on a flag. As a fellow Democrat, the carpenter asked Bridge's assistance. "Let every man skin his own skunks," Horatio said.

They walked on. Two printers' apprentices, half-grown lads, dressed in jackets and very tight checked pantaloons so that they looked like harlequins or circus clowns, strolled by, seeming to think themselves in perfect propriety, and sure of the admiration of the town. In the tavern, Hawthorne witnessed a scuffle between the tavernkeeper and a drunken guest. The tavernkeeper was a nervous, passionate man, quick as a flash of gunpowder. After they were separated the innkeeper raved like a madman. His voice had a queerly pathetic or lamentable sound mingled with its rage, as if he were lifting up his voice to weep. Then he jumped into a chaise which was standing near by, whipped up the horse and drove off rapidly, as if in so doing he gave vent to his rage.

The dam impressed Hawthorne unfavorably. It seemed to him only half finished, and with the appearance of a dam that has been ruined by the spring freshets, rather than the foundations of one that is to be. Actually, the work had suddenly begun to go well. After the years of delays, and in spite of the panic, it appeared that work would be completed that fall. The gap between the two sides of the dam was less than a hundred feet across, and if there were no further delays should be closed by the first of September. If it could be completed, Bridge's fortune was made. The lease of the power to the mills that would line the shore of the Kennebec was a tremendous potential income. Ten mills had already signed up for the power. This was using the millrace on only one side of the dam. A similar race on the opposite side of the river meant an equal return.

Hawthorne had no comprehension of what Bridge had at stake, or of the complexity of the legal and financial and engineering problems of the dam. Yet he lighted by his own direct, childlike observation upon its weakest point. It did not require an engineer's training to see that the riverbank directly behind Bridge's home was a singular formation in the earth. The travelers on the road to Augusta stopped at the dam, got out of their wagons, walked to the structure, studied it carefully, and departed, shaking their heads. Hawthorne seemed scarcely to have studied the huge wood-and-stone structure of the dam. He spent hours loafing on the riverbank far above it. He studied the eddying current, and noted how driftwood jammed against the shore, forming little temporary barriers; and how in places the banks had fallen in, exposing the clay beneath the foliage. He seemed to have no clearly formed idea in so doing, but rather to be led by instinct, puzzling at the configuration of the ground and yet coming directly to the spot that was to cause Bridge's ruin. It was natural that the one weak place in the bank should escape Bridge's attention precisely because he knew it so well and had played there so many hours in his boyhood.

They dined in the evening of the Fourth on a cold shoulder of mutton, with ham, smoked beef, and claret and brown sherry to drink. Then they settled down to a long literary and philosophical conversation with Schaeffer. "We philosophers," he would say. It seemed queer to Hawthorne to hear philosophy from such a boyish figure. He thought Schaeffer had just notions on ethics—"though damnably perverted as to religion."

The next day Bridge went to Augusta on business. Hawthorne meant to join him at the hotel for dinner, but found himself unwilling to move when the dinner hour approached. He dined very comfortably on bread, cheese, and eggs. Nancy often stood at the window in the other half of the house, often thoughtful, soon smiling and laughing again. Then she would walk out for a pail of water.[44]

A threatening revolution in Canada increased the tension of the financial crisis in the United States. In 1837 William Lyon Mackenzie began an armed revolution in Canada. He was a journalist and reformer, born in Scotland, who was elected mayor of Toronto. In 1836 he began publishing the *Constitution,* and in 1837 published a virtual declaration of independence from the provincial government, and the revolt began, though it did not reach the stage of actual warfare until December 7, 1838. Meanwhile the "Aroostook War" had broken out between Canada and Maine. The boundary had been in dispute since 1783. The original line had been drawn in good faith, but knowledge of the geography of the territory was imperfect, and the landmarks, the St. Croix River, the Highlands, and Mars Hill, were in dispute. About 12,000 square miles of territory was involved. At the same time the British claim of a right to search American vessels, to suppress the slave trade, was a recurrence of an old dispute.

A week after Hawthorne arrived in Maine an American citizen, entering the disputed territory to take the census, was arrested by the Canadians. The Governor of Maine ordered the militia held in readiness on the grounds that Maine soil had been invaded by British authorities.[45] Hawthorne considered it a curious sort of war that was raging on the Canadian border. The rebellion professed to be a genuine struggle for freedom, real as the War of Independence of the American colonies from England. Hawthorne did not know. He rather doubted it. It depressed him to see energies wasted, and human life and happiness thrown away, for ends that were unwise, and the holy names of liberty and patriotism evoked when they had no right to be.[46] Whatever the rights and wrongs of both the Canadian rebellion and the border dispute, the Maine people—the Maniacs—were excited, truculent, and bold. They were ready to fight. Indeed, all through New England there was a bitter exasperation after eight years of Jackson; men talked of getting out their rifles to demand the repeal of the liquor laws. Hawthorne and Bridge walked to the Mansion House. The Governor and the Council were meeting to consider the affair of the census taker. On their way they passed a Yankee and a Canadian quarreling. The Yankee accused the Canadian of striking his oxen. The Canadian denied it. They were at the point of blows. Bridge separated them.

There was a large crowd around the Mansion House. It was excited; the people wanted the militia called out and the border territory seized. The tavern was crowded. There were lawyers sitting about on the benches of the barroom or on the stoop along the front of the house, the Adjutant General of the state, some Canadians. The stage drivers drank with the aristocracy, and the decanters and wine bottles were constantly on the move, and the beer and soda constantly fizzing from the spigots and siphons. Occasionally a champagne cork popped. The Governor walked through the bar, stared after by the patrons. There was a captain of the British Army staying at the Mansion House. The idea was thrown out that he should be seized as a hostage—retaliation for the arrest of the census taker. Hawthorne rather wished that, for the joke's sake, it had been done.

Hawthorne and Bridge went back to Bridge's home. The Canadian and the Yankee who had been quarreling earlier in the day had, it seemed, begun to fight. The Canadian had whipped the Yankee, though he was but a little fellow, and had been arrested and fined twelve dollars.

On Sunday, July 23, the constable routed out the colony of whores who had been living on the earnings of the millworkers. The constable was a homely, good-natured, business-looking man who enforced the law with a rough, personal justice—Hawthorne observed him arrest an Irishwoman who had thrown a brickbat at a man, and then give her husband good advice on the best way to settle the affair. The whores, however, were cleared out efficiently. Two days later Hawthorne was sitting on the stoop of Barker's Tavern with Bridge when a depressed, neglected, simple-looking individual approached and asked where he could find Mary Ann Russell. She was one of the whores who had been driven from the community. The tavern loungers broke into laughter. A Negro sitting near by, who had acted as their pimp, asked lazily, "Do you want to use her?" Someone else asked, "Is she your daughter?" The stranger was too obtuse to be made very miserable by their jokes: "Why, a little nearer than that, I calkilate," he said. Mary Ann Russell was his wife. She had behaved well until jailed for striking a child, he said; he was away from home at the time, and had not seen her since, and was in search of her intending to get her out of her troubles. He seemed rather hurt by the jokes, yet bore them patiently, and sometimes almost joined in the laughs, and touched Hawthorne when he said, "A man generally places some little dependence on his wife, whether she's good or bad."

From the house Hawthorne could hear the calm, full voice of the river. He could hear the Irishmen hammering on the dam, the sound of their voices, and at frequent intervals, a thunder rolling and reverberating along the banks as stone was blasted. Sometimes rafts of sawed lumber floated by from the sawmill at Waterville, skillfully guided through the rapids formed by the dam. As he loafed by the riverbank a raft floated past, laden with shingles and round bundles of clapboard. "Friend," one of the men called to him, "how is the tide now?" The rivermen tied the raft to a tree, to wait until the tide rose higher before passing the dam. A solitary canoeman passed, the light lonely touch of his paddle in the water making the silence seem deeper. Every few minutes a huge sturgeon, six feet long and thick in proportion, glistening yellowish brown, its fins spread, leaped out of the water, darting straight on end until his tail was clear of the surface, before he fell on his side and disappeared. An Irishwoman was washing clothes on the riverbank, surrounded by her children, whose babbling sounded pleasant along the edge of the water, as did her voice as she answered them cheerfully and sweetly. An Irishman was angling on the shore, with an alder pole and a clothesline.

There was something ugly and ominous going on around them. The line between Hawthorne's purposeful observations, those which related to his central mission, and his casual notations of people and incidents was never clearly defined; they merged into each other, the significant and the inconsequential, with the items of important information often enough hidden in the close, exact descriptions of nature, like the faint tracks of an animal in the woods. He began to explore the country around Bridge's house. It was surprisingly wild. He sat at the river's edge, studying, as if under a microscope, the condition of the bank that would be called upon to hold back the flood when the dam was finished. Its soil was of sand and clay, with a few large stones, and where there was a high bank it had caved away, so that the earth looked fresh and yellow. He began to walk up a small brook that flowed into the Kennebec, examining the ground so carefully he might have been searching for a trail through the woods or a place where blasting powder stolen from the dam might be hidden. But he was only searching for a secluded place to swim, and Bridge for a place to fish. The brook flowed through a wild valley whose walls grew steeper as they ascended. The sun in the west threw a pleasant gloom and brightness in the forest. The brook, its current broken by moss-covered stones, could not be said to brawl—the word did not express its good-natured voice, and the word "murmur" was too quiet—it sang along, sometimes rushing dark and swift, eddying and whitening past some rock or underneath the bank. The valley grew wilder. One bank was at the edge of a cliff; the opposite bank was covered with pines and hemlocks. Farther on it

flowed through a grove of maple and beech, with alder bushes fringing
the brookside. A ruined road, once used for hauling logs, now overgrown
and its timbers rotted, followed the course of the stream. Deep in the
woods there were the ruins of a dam. They lay hidden, overgrown, in
forest almost as primitive as it had been a hundred years before. There
was scarcely a trace of all the work that had gone on around it in all
the intervening years. There Bridge and Hawthorne stopped. Hawthorne swam in the pool that the ruined dam had made. Bridge cast for
trout at the base of it. The setting sun cast a pleasant gloom over the
stream, the valley grew darker, the pool shadowy. Again and again
Hawthorne returned to this symbol of vanished effort, and returned to
the house to study Bridge, the river, the dam, and the people of Maine.
Bridge went to bed early. Hawthorne and Schaeffer sat outside in the
twilight or the early dark, talking philosophy, marriage, or this world
and the next.[47]

VII

The trail led him to Thomaston to see John Cilley. Bridge and
Cilley were political friends, but there was no mistaking Bridge's distrust of him, almost apologetic, as if Bridge, with his fairness, admitted
to himself he could find no reason for it. He believed that Cilley could
help Hawthorne get the post as historian on the exploring expedition.
He was angry at the bet Cilley had made with Hawthorne, as if, when
he opened the package, he had found some explanation for Hawthorne's
depression or some revelation of Cilley's character that he had not
known of before. He had sent Cilley a copy of *Twice-Told Tales*, and
Cilley had spoken of Hawthorne to John O'Sullivan, editor of the newly
established *Democratic Review*.[48]

On his part, Hawthorne rather liked Cilley at their meeting. Cilley
was thirty-five. He was a singular man, shrewd, insinuating, open and
friendly, a crafty man who concealed like a murder secret anything
that it was not good for him to have known. How could Cilley be friendly
and open and crafty? That was his distinctive nature. He was thin, with
thin, sharp, sallow features, a projecting brow and deep-set eyes, and
an insinuating smile and look as he spoke. There was nothing affected
in his frankness or false in the friendliness that he professed; it was this
that made him fascinating. There was so much truth and kindliness and
warm affection in him, Hawthorne thought, that a man's heart opened

to him in spite of himself: he deceived by truth. Hawthorne believed that Cilley had thought out for himself a higher system of morality than any natural integrity would have prompted him to adopt; he had seen the thorough advantage of morality and honesty. He was bold, daring and fierce as a tiger when necessary. Failure might have soured him, but his triumphant warfare had expanded his powers and his sympathies. He had an iron resolution, indomitable perseverance, and an almost terrible energy.

Hawthorne never admitted to being puzzled by people. His reactions were sharp and distinct, and when he revised them, as he often did, it was usually to soften his first judgments. But Cilley puzzled him. Moreover, there was something about John Cilley that made him uneasy —not only with Cilley, but with himself. He drew of Cilley one of the most remarkable brief sketches in American journalism, bettered, perhaps, only by his own sketch of Thomas Green Fessenden; but every line of it trembled with suppressed disquiet that the country had produced this man. For Cilley was not false. He was genuinely proud of his brotherhood with those who had voted for him. At home he was a plain farmer, and proud of being one.[49]

The Jacksonian revolution had set in motion forces that were incalculable. Hawthorne still lived in a world of gentlemen and commoners. He was a Jackson Democrat, but with reservations; he had no liking for the rule of the mob, the vague diffuse democracy of the French Revolution. Cilley was at ease with the professional political commoners and their political language in a way that Hawthorne and Bridge never were. Hawthorne was a democrat in principle; he feared the concentration of power in Washington at the expense of the states; he was opposed to the Federalist program of internal improvements, not because he did not want the improvements made, but because he did not want the spending of enormous sums of public money to be in the hands of appointed federal officials, over whose disbursement the people had no control. The rough political equalitarianism of Jackson that was so often substituted for a genuine democratic friendliness—that was, indeed, opposed to the old relationship of mutual respect between equals —the affected heartiness, the sardonic catchwords, the latent envy, the false toughness that claimed descent from the frontier and was actually spawned in political clubrooms—all this was foreign to him as it never was to Cilley. Cilley accused him of looking down his aristocratic nose at politicians—indeed, he warned Hawthorne not to look down his aristocratic nose at *him*—and though the banter was good-natured, it had enough substance to it, and was so quick and dangerous a distortion of the truth, that it hurt.

Hawthorne stayed in Thomaston at a quiet boardinghouse where there was no bar, and there immediately sprang up a flirtation between him and Mary Trott, the landlady's daughter.[50] She was a frank, free, mirthful young woman, about twenty-four years old and capable, Hawthorne discovered, of entertaining deeper emotions. There were five young women at the boardinghouse, three teachers from Boston and a pretty, fantastic little devil of a brunette, about eighteen years old, newly married. Her walk fascinated Hawthorne; she quivered as if she were made of calf's-foot jelly. Hawthorne enjoyed himself, and found when he parted from the landlady's daughter that they were both rather solemn.

On August 24, soon after returning home, he met Cilley in Boston, and they went to the Navy Yard for lunch. Hawthorne's qualities could not be expected to make much impression on Captain Percival, master commandant of the Charleston Navy Yard. When Hawthorne and Cilley went aboard the cutter *Hamilton,* old Captain Percival sat on the deck of a vessel near by, smoking a cigar, a white-haired, thin-visaged, weather-worn old gentleman in a blue Quaker-style coat, with tarnished lace and brass buttons, a pair of drab trousers, and a brown waistcoat. Cilley and Hawthorne had lunch with Colonel Barnes, the naval officer of Boston, and Captain Scott. They dined aboard the cutter, in the pretty cabin that was finished in bird's-eye maple and mahogany and decorated with two mirrors. Out in the harbor the vessels flitted past, great ships with their intricate rigging and sails, schooners and sloops with one or two broad sheets of canvas, going on different tacks, so that it seemed there was a different wind for each vessel, or that they scudded spontaneously through the water, wherever their own will led them.

Dinner consisted of chowder, fried fish and corned beef, with claret during the meal and champagne after dinner. Captain Scott sent a glass of champagne to Captain Percival. When the waiter returned Captain Scott asked him what Percival had said. "He said, Sir, 'What does he send me this damned stuff for?' " Nevertheless, he drank it.

Presently the steward came into the cabin and spoke to Captain Scott: "Captain Percival is coming aboard of you, Sir."

"Well, ask him to come down into the cabin."

Captain Percival entered, sat down and, taking a glass of champagne in his hand, began a lecture on economy. He was rough, good-hearted and outspoken; he had not risen to his present rank through the Navy, but had been a sailing master before he entered the service. Alluding to the wine bottles on the table, the expensive woodwork of the cabin, he said that it was well that Uncle Sam had a broad back, since it was compelled to bear so many burdens laid upon it. Captain Percival was a Whig. He talked politics with Cilley, arguing with much pertinacity. He was full of antique prejudices, against the mustaches of the young officers, the brooch on Captain Scott's bosom, the fripperies in the modern uniforms, and prophesied little more than disgrace in the event of another war.[51]

Percival was one of the great characters of the Navy. His pistol is still proudly on display in the East India Marine Society Museum in Salem, along with the ship models, the Oriental art, and the portraits of the captains. He was born at West Barnstable on April 5, 1779, went to sea at thirteen and at twenty commanded vessels in the West Indies and transatlantic trade. He was impressed into the British Navy at Lisbon on February 24, 1797, served on the *Victory* and escaped after two years. He served in the American Navy during the naval war with France, was discharged in 1801, and re-entered the merchant marine. He was soon imprisoned for several months and robbed of his ship at Teneriffe in the Canary Islands.

Meanwhile his fame grew. It was said he once navigated his ship from the African coast to Pernambuco with the entire crew sick or dead of fever. He became celebrated as Roaring Jack—or Mad Jack—and a few years later he was the model for the stories of *Tales of the Marines* by Harry Gringo. In 1809 he re-entered the Navy as a sailing master. During the War of 1812, he loaded the fishing smack *Yankee* with vegetables and livestock, hid thirty-two volunteers under hatches, and surprised and captured the British tender *Eagle*, overpowering her crew of thirteen and bringing her into New York Harbor "amidst the plaudits of thousands." He was sailing master of the *Peacock* in her victory over the *Epervier*, and after the war cruised in the *Porpoise* against West Indian pirates. He sailed in the Pacific on the *United States* and pursued the mutineers on the whaler *Globe* in command of the *Dolphin*. In Hawaii he fell foul of the missionaries over the antiprostitution ordinances, against which the sailors had rioted, was court-martialed, and cleared.[52] He consequently spoke with authority.

Scott was called captain only by courtesy; he was actually a first lieutenant, and was not stationed on the *Hamilton*, which was a revenue cutter, until the following month. Hawthorne either misunderstood him, or Scott lied to Hawthorne outrageously, for Hawthorne reported that Scott had said he was a powder monkey on the *Constitution* in its battle with the *Macedonian*. Not only was there no engagement between those ships, but Scott was not given a commission until 1833. Well, Scott said, a cannon shot came through the ship's side, and a man's head was struck off, clean as by a razor. The man was walking pretty briskly at the time of the accident, and Scott said he kept on walking at the same pace, till, after going about twenty paces without a head, he sank down, his legs under him.[53]

Captain Percival said the young officers were no good, and began to talk of the quality of the great commanders of the past. Percival believed that the boys would fight and die for their country, but that there were no longer any officers of the stature of Hull and Stewart of the *Constitution*. Bainbridge, he said, was a sot and a poltroon. Elliot, commanding the *Niagara* in the battle of Lake Erie, was, he said, a liar. All through the afternoon of the battle Elliot had kept the *Niagara* out of range, while the fire of the British ships was concentrated on the *Lawrence,* and only Perry's obstinacy after the *Lawrence* was lost had turned defeat into victory. But Captain Percival spoke in the highest terms of Commodore John Downes.

In the afternoon Hawthorne, Cilley, Captain Percival, and Scott walked through the Navy Yard, and met Commodore John Downes. Downes was fifty-three. He entered the Navy as a waiter to his father, who served as purser's steward on the *Constitution*. Downes, a midshipman at sixteen, was commended for gallantry in the war with Tripoli, and in 1813, in the *Essex*, captured two British vessels. One was outfitted as a cruiser, and he was given command of it. He captured the *Hector*, a privateer, and two other ships, while Admiral Porter captured the *Atlantic* and transferred it to Downes to serve as his flagship. In 1815 Downes sailed with Decatur's squadron for Algiers, in command of the *Epervier*, and maneuvered his ship so skillfully in his fight with an Algerine frigate that he was placed in command of the flagship of the squadron. He cruised in the Pacific and the Mediterranean, and

in 1832, commanding the *Potomac* in the Pacific Station, was ordered
to Quallah Battoo, Sumatra. The Malay pirates there had attacked the
Friendship of Salem (William Story, master), killing several members
of the crew. In February, 1832, Downes reached Quallah Battoo,
stormed the town, and in a 2½-hour battle killed 150 natives, destroyed
half of Quallah Battoo, with casualties of two killed and eleven
wounded.[54]

The respect that Percival and Downes revealed for Hawthorne was
in itself sufficient evidence that his work had not been disregarded, and
that his seclusion was not so deep as he professed. They were two of the
most notable figures in the Navy. As they walked through the Yard
Percival told him of how much the business of the Yard absorbed him,
especially the building of the 74-gun *Columbus*. He seemed to Hawthorne to be the very model of the old integrity, guarding Uncle Sam's
interest as if the money was to come out of his own pocket. He seemed
to have no ambition beyond his present duties, passing his life with a
gruff contentedness, grumbling and growling, yet in good humor enough.
When Hawthorne asked him if it would be well to make a naval officer
secretary of the navy, Captain Percival said, "God forbid." An old
sailor, he said, was always full of prejudices and stubborn whimwhams,
like himself. Hawthorne agreed. Commodore Downes joined them in
their walk around the Yard. He was courteous, frank and good-natured,
and when they watched the men laughing and sporting in the rigging
lofts and on the ships the Commodore told Hawthorne that their good
nature was always much increased when they were at sea.[55]

VIII

That same day in Augusta, Bridge's fortune seemed to be made.
The space between the two ends of the dam was reduced to fourteen
feet. The dam held against the tremendous weight of the water backing
up in the river bed. By September 10 the last opening was closed, and
on Wednesday evening, September 27, the spillways were closed and
the flow of water stopped to fill the pond behind the dam. The enormous structure, with its millions of feet of timber and hundreds of
cubic feet of stones, stood firm. The river bed below the dam was dry;
the flow of the Kennebec stopped. People walked on foot where the river
had poured. A smart rain began to fall, lasting several hours, and

hastening the filling of the pond. For five days the water backed up. The lake reached back sixteen miles. On October 2 the pond was filled, and water flowed over the top of the dam. Ten days later the locks were completed. The townspeople of Augusta, who had been skeptical and dubious, greeted its completion with shouts of joy, the firing of cannon, and a dinner at the Mansion House in honor of Colonel Boardman.

Bridge was wealthy. The great enterprise had succeeded. Victory left him unchanged. In the spring of 1838 he joined the Navy, as he had planned, and was commissioned purser on the *Cyane*. Pursers had charge of all money transactions aboard ship. They lived well; southern pursers ordinarily took their personal slaves along with them on their voyages.

The dam withstood a severe freshet in the spring. Heavy logs tumbled in wild confusion over the dam, battering against the walls that formed the western bank of the river. When the flood had subsided there seemed no further danger of damage. Work was begun on the mill-race and pond, and wheels were installed for ten sawmills.

The Bridge family mansion stood five hundred feet from the river, and on a slope a hundred feet above the waterline. Farther downstream was the home of Horatio's brother Edmund. The storage basin for the mills was so located that it would flood the grounds where Edmund Bridge's house stood, and when it was excavated the house was moved from the east to the west side of the road. By the first of January, 1839, all this work had been completed. The ten wheels were being mounted. There was a sudden thaw. After severe cold weather, wind from the south, blowing a gale and accompanied by a heavy rain, carried off the snow. It melted rapidly. The river rose fast, breaking the ice. Huge chunks raced down the river, tearing at the banks, piling up, forming temporary obstructions that gave way with a roar. The water flooded the streets of the towns along the river. The bells were rung from two o'clock in the morning until daylight to call out the towns-people. Chimneys were blown down by the force of the wind. The dam again stood the fearful test of the river's power. On the west bank, above the dam, a section of the stone wall confining the riverbank was thrown down, but the dam itself was uninjured.

But the river remained unusually high through spring. By May 30 the wheels for the ten sawmills, spaced regularly along the mill race, were nearly mounted. Horatio Bridge had long since sailed on the *Cyane* on a cruise of the Mediterranean, all danger to the dam apparently long since ended. On Friday, May 30, at four o'clock in the morning, during a heavy rain, water began to pour over the guard gates of the canal on the western side of the river.

The canal was of course higher than the level of the water below the dam. The water trickled through the earth from the canal. At first a slight rivulet, it cut a small stream to the river, pouring through a breach in the wall that lined the riverbank. It grew in volume. The huge masonry walls of the canal leaned from the pressure of the water within. One of the guard gates of the canal was forced open. The full force of the river poured down the canal.

The water wheels, mounted but not yet completed, could not withstand the terrific pressure of the water. Preparations were hurriedly made to blow them up, to prevent their smashing the Kennebec Bridge when they collapsed and raced downstream. But before they could be blown up land between the canal and the river began to be gnawed away. The bank, as far downstream as the mills, stood until Friday night. The mills were undermined. During the night they began to fall, one after another, each reverberating like the sound of an explosion in the night. Saturday afternoon the storm continued. The last section of the bank between the river and the canal fell with a tremendous crash.

The river was now flowing around the western end of the dam, which stood like a giant jetty projecting into midstream. The full force of the current swept directly over the ground where the mills were to have stood. It cut through the storage basin of the mills, and passing beyond, undermined the road that passed before Bridge's house. There was nothing in the bank to check its steady progress. Edmund Bridge's house was undermined, fell, and was swept away.

The high crest of ground on which the Bridge mansion stood began to be eaten away. Huge sections of the hillside fell. The clay riverbank that Hawthorne had studied so intently melted down, crumbling as the river swept in a curve around the dam. A crew of men worked feverishly to save the outbuildings. One wing of the house was detached from the main building and pulled to safety on higher ground. Work was begun in dismantling the house. The grounds began to slide more and more rapidly, in larger sections, as the riverbank grew higher. Trees and sections of lawn plunged into the water. The riverbank was now a cliff below which the current roared, steadily undermining the hill, until at last the whole slope, the house, the grounds, the trees, and the last of the Bridge family fortune, poised for an instant at the edge of the flood, and dropped a hundred feet into the discolored water.[56]

IX

All this was somewhat in the future; for the moment the prospects of Hawthorne and his friends seemed brighter than they had ever been. He parted from Cilley in Boston, after their visit to the Navy Yard, and returned to Salem. On November 11 his friend Thomas Green Fessenden died, and Hawthorne attended his funeral.[57]

Cilley meanwhile went on to Washington. He lived there at Mrs. Birth's boardinghouse on Third Street. Mrs. Birth's was one of fifty or so Washington lodging houses taken over by groups of political and personal friends. Senator Franklin Pierce and Jane Pierce lived at Mrs. Birth's. So did Senator and Mrs. Reuel Williams, and Senator and Mrs. Garrett Wall of New Jersey. Wall was an extreme Jackson radical, a political ally of Judge Ruggles, who also was in the Senate.[58]

The House was almost evenly divided. It had been, in fact, tied over the election of Seargent Prentiss, Cilley's old college friend, by a vote of 117 to 117. A question had come up in Mississippi as to whether two congressmen elected for a special session of Congress were elected for the special session only or for the entire term. The Governor had believed, in calling for the election, that it was for the special session only. Prentiss then ran at the regular November election (after the special session had been held) and won by a vote of 7,000, one of the first conservative victories in a decade, and the beginning of the movement that, the following year, swept Georgia, Louisiana, Virginia, and North Carolina. Prentiss's right to his seat was challenged, and after a three-day debate that made him nationally famous, the House was deadlocked over seating him, Speaker Polk finally voting for his opponent.[59]

The next act in the tragedy of Cilley began with the publication, in the New York *Courier and Inquirer*, of a charge of corruption in Congress. The bill to establish a subtreasury, to replace the Bank of the United States, was being debated. A Washington correspondent named Matthew Davis, an intimate friend and biographer of Aaron

Burr, wrote in his column, "The Spy in Washington," that he had proof of the corruption of a member of Congress. Davis had been excluded from the ladies' galley of the House on a charge of gross immorality.[60] The *Courier and Inquirer* was of doubtful authority. Colonel J. Watson Webb, its owner, had been irregularly appointed to the regular Army by John Calhoun, when Calhoun was Monroe's secretary of war. Webb served in Wisconsin in the Indian campaigns, and on one occasion carried across Illinois, in the dead of winter, warning of an impending attack on Fort Snelling, Minnesota. He was trailed by hostile Indians on the way. Impetuous, brave, perhaps quarrelsome by nature, he fought two duels in the Army, resigning in consequence of one of them. He seems not to have been popular in military circles. He was known as "Calhoun's scrub lieutenant." His title of colonel came from his rank in New York State, where he was in command of the engineers. His *Courier and Inquirer* had inaugurated a daily horse express between New York and Washington, with relays of horses every six miles of the way, at a cost of $7,500 a month, getting the Washington news a day earlier than its rivals.[61] The *Courier and Inquirer* was a Whig paper, and had recently hired John Osborne Sargent, (Hawthorne's old editor on the *New England Magazine*) away from the Boston *Atlas*.[62]

Webb had begun the attacks on the Bank of the United States early in Jackson's administration, carrying on a systematic campaign for sixteen months. He had then reversed his stand and begun to support the bank. This in itself was not unusual nor could exception be taken to it. The bank had been unpopular and had been severely criticized before Jackson took up the attack. When the full extent of Jackson's program became clear, many of the bank's critics came to its defense —they had wanted the bank's malpractices stopped, not a complete destruction of the bank or the ruin of the economy of the country. But in Webb's case there was no such question. He dropped his attacks on the bank after accepting three loans from it, for a total of $52,975. The sudden change of his policy outraged the sincere Democrats, such men as William Cullen Bryant, of the New York *Post*. Webb was detested, vilified, even spat on in the street.[63]

Davis's statement in the *Courier and Inquirer* read: "The more brief my statement is the better it will be understood. It is in my power, if brought before the bar of either house, or before a committee, and processes allowed me to compel the attendance of witnesses, to prove by the oath of a respectable and unimpeachable citizen, as well as by written, documentary evidence, that there is at least one member of Congress who has offered to barter his services and his influence with a department or departments for a compensation."

Henry Wise in the House, on February 12, asked for an inquiry of Davis's charge. Davis was called before the House and declared that the person to whom he referred was not in the House of Representatives. Cilley opposed Wise's motion for a committee of inquiry. He asked that the House not depart from its rules, saying of Davis: "If he has charges to make, let him make them distinctly and not vaguely, let him make them under the solemnity of an oath, and then it will be quite time enough to act." He said that he knew nothing of the editor of the *Courier and Inquirer,* but that if he was the same individual who had changed the policy of his paper for $52,000, he did not believe his charges were entitled to much credit by an American Congress.

John Ruggles, in the Washington *Globe,* the Administration paper, wrote that the charges were aimed at him. Cilley's old enemy explained that they were the result of a misunderstanding: he had offered his professional services as a lawyer in connection with a patent for a trunk lock, for a Mr. Jones of New York, receiving in return one-fourth of the patent. The papers had been drawn up and assented to, but nothing had been done about them.[64]

Nine days passed after Cilley's comment. On February 21, Jonathan Cilley received the following note from James Watson Webb, who was staying at Gadsby's Hotel:

> Sir: In the Washington *Globe* of the 12th instant, you are reported to have said, in the course of the debate which took place in the House of Representatives on that day, growing out of a publication made in the New York Courier and Enquirer—"He (you) knew nothing of this editor; but if it was the same editor who once made grave charges against an institution of this country and was afterwards said to have received facilities to the amount of some $52,000, from the same institution, and gave it his hearty support, he did not think his charges were entitled to much credit in an American Congress."
>
> I deem it my duty to apprize you, sir, that I am the edi-

tor of the paper in which the letter from "The Spy in Washington," charging a member of Congress with corruption, was
first published; and the object of this communication is to
enquire of you whether I am the editor to whom you alluded,
and, if so, to ask the explanation which the character of your
remarks renders necessary.

Representative William Graves, a 33-year-old Kentuckian who
lived with Henry Clay, Thomas Crittenden, Richard Menefee, and Tom
Corwin, in Mrs. Hill's boardinghouse, handed the note to Cilley in the
hall of the House of Representatives, while the House was in session.
Graves had read the note and fully understood it.

Cilley refused to receive it. This was correct. As a member of Congress, he could not be called to account for words spoken on the floor
of the House. It was a breach of the highest constitutional privileges of
the House and of the most sacred rights of the people. It was a violation of the constitutional rights of the people to demand of their representative, in a hostile manner, an explanation of words spoken in debate,
to be the bearer of such a demand, to demand a reason for refusing
to receive it, or to demand, under any circumstances, any reason at all.
No member of Congress could be so challenged without impairing his
usefulness as a member. It was the highest offense that could be committed against Congress, against freedom of speech, and against the
spirit and substance of the article of the Constitution that members
shall not be questioned in any other place for any speech or debate in
either house. It violated essentially the right of perfect immunity *elsewhere* for words spoken in Congress, which is essential to the independence of Congress, and of constitutional liberty. Cilley knew this
and so did Graves. Since the conflict soon became a matter involving
the leaders of both Democratic and Whig parties, so did the politicians
on both sides.

Graves wrote a note to Cilley—dating it incorrectly February 20
—about their interview. His note was amazing. He said: "In the interview which I had with you this morning, when you declined receiving
from me the note of Colonel J. W. Webb, asking whether you were
correctly reported in the *Globe* in what you are there represented to
have said of him, in this House, on the 12th instant, you will please
say whether you did not remark, in substance, that in declining to

receive the note, you hoped I would not consider it, in any respect, disrespectful to me; and that the ground on which you rested your declining to receive the note was distinctly this: That you could not consent to get yourself into personal difficulties with the conductors of public journals, for what you might think proper to say in debate upon this floor, in discharge of your duties as a representative of the people; and that you did not rest your objection, in our interview, upon any personal objections to Colonel Webb as a gentlemen."

It appeared that Cilley had uncovered the meaning of Webb's letter more quickly than its author or authors had believed he would. It was also apparent that whoever was behind the plot had underestimated Cilley's intelligence and his courage—something that happened throughout his political life. For Grave's letter marked a complete reversal of the stand on which an explanation was demanded of Cilley. Webb asked satisfaction because Cilley's remarks accused him of dishonorable conduct. Webb had no right to make this demand, not only because Cilley spoke as a member of Congress but because the charge was not original with Cilley: it was a part of the public record, contained in the report of a committee of Congress. Had Webb genuinely demanded satisfaction he would have attacked the members of the committee who first charged him with reversing the policy of his paper in return for loans from the bank. Now Graves's note described Webb's letter to Cilley as merely asking whether Cilley was correctly reported in the *Globe*. But it will be perceived that Webb's note, though Graves always described it so, *does not contain that inquiry*.

Cilley replied to Graves as follows:

"The note which you just placed in my hands has been received. In reply, I have to state that in your interview with me this morning, when you proposed to deliver a communication from Colonel Webb, of the New York *Courier and Inquirer*, I declined to receive it, because I chose to be drawn into no controversy with him. I neither affirmed or denied anything in regard to his character; but when you remarked that this course on my part might place you in an unpleasant situation, I stated to you, and I now repeat, that I intended, by the refusal, no disrespect to you." [65]

The conflict had reached a point where both men consulted the leaders of their parties before taking the next step.[66] On Thursday, February 22, Graves sent his second note to Cilley. It was delivered to him in his seat, during the session of the House, by Representative Menefee of Kentucky. Menefee said that he hoped Cilley would see the propriety of relieving Graves from a situation that was painful to him. Cilley replied that the note should be attended to. Graves wrote:

House of Representatives
February 22, 1838

Sir: Your note of yesterday, in reply to mine of that date, is inexplicit, unsatisfactory, and insufficient. Among other things is this, that, in declining to receive Colonel Webb's communication, it does not *disclaim*, any exception to him as a gentleman. I have, therefore, to inquire *whether you declined to receive his communication on the ground of personal exception to him as a gentleman or a man of honor?* A categorical answer is expected.

Cilley's reply was delivered to Graves by Representative Alexander Duncan, of Ohio. Cilley wrote:

"Your note of this date has just been placed in my hands. I regret that mine of yesterday was unsatisfactory to you; but I cannot admit the right on your part to propound the question to which you ask a categorical answer, and therefore decline any further response to it."

The attempt to change the question to one of Webb's position as a gentleman was stupefying. The entire discussion was out of order, but even had it not been, this particular argument was far more dubious than the original one of the integrity of the *Courier and Inquirer*. Colonel Webb was determined to kill Cilley himself, and to do so secured two assistants, named Daniel Jackson and Major William Morrell, to help him force Cilley to fight. Major Morrell appears to have had no respect for Webb; he simply agreed to go with him, and freely told of Webb's threats and plans.

A few minutes before twelve o'clock, on February 23, 1838, Representative Henry Wise of Virginia called at Mrs. Birth's boardinghouse on Third Street and presented Cilley with Graves's challenge. It read:

Washington City, February 23, 1838

As you have declined accepting a communication which I bore to you from Colonel Webb, and as by your note of yesterday, you have refused to decline on grounds which would exonerate me from all responsibility growing out of the affair, I am left no other alternative but to ask that satisfaction which is recognized among gentlemen. My friend, Hon. Henry A. Wise, is authorized by me to make the arrangements suitable to the occasion. Your obedient servant,

Wm. J. Graves.

In carrying the challenge to Cilley, Wise was guilty of a breach of privilege of the House. It was Wise who insisted that Cilley make some disclaimer which would relieve Graves of his position—i.e., declare that he considered Webb a gentleman and a man of honor.

At about five o'clock on that same day General George Jones, the delegate to Congress from Wisconsin Territory, delivered Cilley's reply to Graves.[67] It is interesting to note that Cilley was the only New Englander in the entire group, on either side. His second was George Wallace Jones, a classmate at Transylvania and a lifelong friend of Jefferson Davis. Jones was born in Vincennes, Indiana, in 1804, the son of a Welshman who had been educated in England. Jones grew up in Missouri, studied law, and became a miner and storekeeper in the Fever River lead mines for ten years, and secured the organization of both Wisconsin and Iowa territories. General Jones saw service in the Black Hawk War. He was a Catholic, a man of courtly manners, a successful diplomat, and a shrewd lobbyist; but he was indiscreet and outspoken and was arrested, in 1861, for treason. (Lincoln released him.)[68]

Jones took Cilley's note to Mrs. Queen's boardinghouse on Pennsylvania Avenue, where Graves lived. It read:

Washington City, Feb. 23, 1838
Your note of this morning has been received. My friend, Gen. Jones, will "make the arrangements suitable to the occasion."

Your obedient servant,
Jona. Cilley

Hon. W. J. Graves [69]

In these last hours of Cilley's life he conducted himself with a gravity and steadiness of purpose wonderful in its luminous clarity. He had somehow taken the fight out of its squalid atmosphere of hotel-room conspiracies and furtive boardinghouse meetings and given it a tragic dignity. He was himself, suddenly, a strange and significant character, thirty-five years old, self-made, and independent, with more to live for and with far greater promise than any of the exact and pompous little scoundrels who made the preparations for the duel. His friends believed that his enemies were driving him to the wall because they dared not let so potentially powerful a figure take his rightful place in the life of the nation. Yet it was Cilley himself who had at each step, with a surgical accuracy, cut through the affectations, the stupidities, the hysteria and corruption, and revealed the base truth of their motives. He had become a hero, not with the consciousness of becoming one but with a deep and awful devotion to intelligence. The duels and the challenges, the demands, the points of honor, the titles and formalities, were crazy; but not until he had given his life was their madness clear and the purposes they served apparent.

The Southerners who thought to trick or to discipline a freshman congressman found they had caught a monster. He was by their standards dreadful, a fierce and humorless and almost selfless fighter who seemed to have intervened in a fight in which he had no stake, and who rejected coldly and contemptuously the conventional compromise they offered him. His oldest boy, Greenleaf, who later commanded the iron-clad *Catskill* in the Civil War, was then eight. His second son, Jonathan Prince, who later refused an appointment to West Point but who served throughout the Civil War, was twice wounded, and won a commission of lieutenant colonel, was then three years old. His youngest daughter, Julia, was born December 20, 1837, after Cilley had gone to Washington; he had never seen her.[70] His marriage was happy. It seemed to Hawthorne that the death of Cilley's two children had left on him "a more abiding impression of tenderness and regret than the death of infants usually makes on the masculine mind." It was in view of the happiness that he left that his resolution became terrible. It was in view of his peaceful and happy home, with its simple occupations and pure enjoyments—the flower garden that he loved to cultivate, the beehives where he sat for hours "watching the labors of the insects and soothed by the hum with which they filled the air" [71]—that the attacks on him, by men who prided themselves upon their code of honor, became unspeakable. He was the challenged party, and had the choice of weapons. He could have fought one of the conventional duels of the time, with pistols lightly charged, which usually ended with one party superficially wounded or with both uninjured. Instead he proposed to fight with rifles under conditions that made the death of one or another or both of the duelists almost certain.

Graves had no rifle. The conditions that Cilley laid down for the duel seem to have made the Southerners sick. They were powerfully explicit:

> Mr. Cilley proposes to meet Mr. Graves, at such place as may be agreed upon between us, tomorrow, at 12 o'clock M. The weapons to be used on the occasion shall be rifles; the parties placed side to side at 80 yards distant from each other; to hold the rifles horizontally at arm's length, downwards; the rifles to be cocked, and triggers set; the words to be, "Gentlemen, are you ready?" After which, neither answering "No," the words shall be, in regular succession, "Fire —one, two, three, four." Neither party shall fire before the word "fire" nor after the word "four." The positions of the parties at the ends of the line to be determined by lot. The second of the party losing the position shall have the giving of the word. The dress to be ordinary winter clothing, and subject to the examination of both parties. Each party may have on the ground, besides his second, a surgeon and two other friends. The seconds, for execution of their respective trusts, are allowed to have a pair of pistols each on the ground, but no other person shall have any weapon. The rifles to be loaded in the presence of the seconds. Should Mr. Graves not be able to procure a rifle by the time prescribed, time shall be allowed for that purpose.
>
> Your obedient servant,
Geo. W. Jones

It was nine o'clock at night before Wise answered.

> Sir: the terms arranging the meeting between Mr. Graves and Mr. Cilley, which you presented to me this evening, though unusual and objectionable, are accepted; with the understanding that the rifles are to be loaded with a single ball, and that neither party is to raise his weapon from the downward horizontal position until the word "fire."

I will inform you, sir, by the hour of 11 o'clock, a.m. tomorrow, whether Mr. Graves has been able to procure a rifle, and, consequently, whether he will require a postponement of the time of meeting.

> Your very obedient servant,
> Henry A. Wise

Meanwhile James Watson Webb was brutally busy. Early on the morning of February 24 he met with Daniel Jackson and William H. Morrell. Jackson was a New Yorker, pliant and shifty, and of little consequence in what transpired. Webb told them of his plan to kill Cilley. It was that they arm themselves, go to Cilley's room, and force him to fight a duel with Webb before he met Graves. If he refused to do either, Webb said, he would shatter his right arm. There could be no escape for Cilley in such an encounter. He would have been murdered, and under circumstances, with Webb's control of the news, that would make his death seem the result of an effort to avoid fighting Graves.

Cilley was not in his room. Neither was Graves at home. In the morning Mrs. Graves's housemaid inadvertently disclosed that Graves was to fight a duel that day, and Mrs. Graves was frantic with fear.* Webb, Jackson, and Morrell, well armed, set out in search of the duelists. They had heard they were at Bladensburg, and hurried there. On the way they revised their plan: Webb was to approach Cilley, claim the quarrel, insist on fighting him and assure him that if he aimed his rifle at Graves, Webb would shoot him on the spot. They considered that Graves or Wise or one of their party would draw a gun on Webb, in which case Webb would instantly shoot Cilley, after which they would defend themselves in the best way they could.

Cilley and Graves were not at Bladensburg. The conspirators followed in pursuit to the old powder magazine, then to the shores of the Potomac, near the arsenal, and then to Greenleaf's Point. Their search

---

* How Mrs. Graves's housemaid knew of it is an aspect of the mystery that seems not to have been investigated, and suggests the presence of an informant in the Graves household. It is unlikely that the informant, if any, was placed there by Cilley's partisans. Mrs. Graves swore out a warrant for the arrest of all parties connected with the duel, and accompanied the marshall in his search for them, despite her feeble health, but was misdirected and abandoned the search.

had taken most of the day. They had, in fact, been misdirected until almost the exact moment the duel ended. They returned to Washington. Not knowing whether Cilley or Graves had won, they made a new plan. Its details are not known, except that, from what they confessed, it was darkly shadowed forth that if Cilley had survived the duel he would have encountered an assassin.

About eight o'clock in the morning Cilley's second left a note in Wise's room:

> Washington City, D. C.
> February 24, 1838
> Sir: I will receive, at Doctor Reilley's, on F Street, any communication you may see proper to make me, until 11 o'clock, a.m. today.
> Respectfully, your obedient servant
> Geo. W. Jones

Graves had been unable to find a rifle, and said that he could not be ready by twelve o'clock. Wise therefore left a note with Jones, saying that Graves was anxious to have the meeting that day, if possible, and that by 12:30 p.m. Wise would inform Jones "what time to procure and prepare a weapon he will require." This somewhat incoherent statement was dated February 24, 1838, 10:00 a.m. While Graves's seconds were apparently searching for a rifle, Webb and Jackson and Morrell were searching for Cilley. Jones replied to Wise at 10:30, saying that he had an excellent rifle, in good order, which "is at the service of Mr. Graves." There was no reply to this note. At 11:00 a.m. Jones sent a rifle, a powder flask, and balls, to Wise's room, with a note that he did so through the politeness of his friend Dr. Duncan of Ohio. At this Wise called on Jones, told him that Graves had procured another rifle, and would be ready for the meeting at 3:00 p.m.

The day was bright, with a strong wind. At two in the afternoon the parties left Washington by hack. With the seconds, doctors and witnesses, there were ten men in the party. They met on the road to Marlborough, in Maryland. Two Kentucky representatives stood by as spectators. The hack drivers were present, and two strangers watched without the consent of either party. Including Graves, there were four representatives from Kentucky on the scene, as well as Senator John Crittenden of Kentucky. Cilley was the only New Englander present.

Jones and Wise paced off the ground. The line of fire was at right angles with the rays of the sun. They drew lots for the position, and Wise won, choosing the northeasterly end of the line. The distance was about ninety-two yards. The wind grew stronger. It fell on the line of fire, at an angle of about 45° against Cilley. The sun was in his favor, the wind against him. He stood in an open field on a slight rise in the ground, outlined against the sky. Graves stood near a woods, and was partly sheltered by it. There was a rail fence behind him. The rifle that Graves had secured was almost twice the caliber of Cilley's. The balls for Cilley's rifle weighed about one-tenth of an ounce. The balls for Graves's rifle weighed about one-fifth of an ounce. Shortly after three o'clock the first shots were exchanged. Cilley fired first. His shot struck the rail of the fence behind Graves. Graves fired a second or two later. The shots came so close together that Graves could not have held his fire, had he been disposed to do so.

Graves missed. Their friends assembled at the request of Wise. Jones asked Wise if Graves was satisfied.

Wise said: "Mr. Jones, these gentlemen have come here without animosity towards each other; they are fighting merely upon a point of honor; cannot Mr. Cilley assign some reason for not receiving at Mr. Graves' hands Colonel Webb's communication, or make some disclaimer which will relieve Mr. Graves from his position?"

Mr. Jones replied: "While the challenge is impending, Mr. Cilley can make no explanations."

Wise said: "The exchange of shots suspends the challenge, and the challenge is suspended for explanation."

Jones walked to where Cilley was standing. The two men conferred. Returning, Jones talked with Wise of putting in writing what had been said. Jones said: "I am authorized by my friend, Mr. Cilley, to say, that in declining to receive the note from Mr. Graves, purporting to be from Colonel Webb, he meant no disrespect to Mr. Graves, because he entertained for him then, as he now does, the highest respects and most kind feelings; but that he declined to receive the note, because he chose not to be drawn into any controversy with Colonel Webb."

Wise said: "This leaves Mr. Graves precisely in the position in which he stood when the challenge was sent."

The challenge was renewed. Cilley and Graves took their places and fired again. Graves fired first, before he had fully elevated his rifle. He missed. Cilley fired about two seconds afterward. His shot splintered one of the chestnut fence rails, directly behind Graves. It passed so close to Graves's breast that it seemed impossible he had not been hit. From his motions, the witnesses thought Graves had been hit. He said at once, "I must have another shot."

Jones said: "Mr. Wise, my friend, in coming to the ground and exchanging shots with Mr. Graves, has shown to the world that, in declining to receive the note of Colonel Webb, he did not do so because he dreaded a controversy. He has shown himself a brave man, and disposed to render satisfaction to Mr. Graves. I think that he has done so, and that the matter should end here."

This was the last attempt at an agreement. It ended quickly. Wise said: "If this matter is not terminated with this shot, and is not settled, I will propose to shorten the distance."

Jones replied: "After this shot, without effect, I will entertain the proposition." [72]

This was the last conference. Cilley said, "They thirst for my blood." [73]

The rifles were loaded. Cilley and Graves resumed their stations. They fired at almost the same time. Cilley was shot through the body. No trace of his third shot was found. He dropped the rifle, beckoned to one of the men near him, and said, "I am shot." He put both hands on his wound, fell, and died in two or three minutes. [74]

His death horrified the country.

X

Hawthorne always considered himself responsible for Cilley's death. It was for many years held to be proof of his morbid sensitivity that he did so; his biographers spoke of his seeing the ghost of Cilley shaking his gory locks at him.

Hawthorne was hardheaded, however, and not given to troubling himself with distressing thoughts that had no basis in reality. The first explanation was that given by his son, Julian Hawthorne, in his biography. He declared that Hawthorne was himself at the point of fighting a duel at that time. He had become involved with a Salem girl identified only as Mary, who told him she had been betrayed by a friend of Hawthorne's identified only as Louis. Hawthorne, so the story ran, challenged Louis, who, however, refused to fight him, but told him facts which proved Mary's accusations to be false. Hawthorne's willingness to fight a duel was offered as an explanation for Cilley's willingness to fight one.

There is no other account of Hawthorne's duel, and most of his biographers have dismissed the story. I think it possible the story may have been a family matter on which Julian Hawthorne desired to throw no more light, but to which he felt some reference should be made. The names Mary and Louis suggest that perhaps Hawthorne's sister Maria Louisa might have been the woman involved. Hawthorne would have been willing to fight a duel if he felt that she had been betrayed, and might have exaggerated a quarrel of hers with her lover into so bitter a dispute.

This still leaves the question of his feeling of responsibility for Cilley's death unsolved. It is possible that Cilley asked him to come to Washington to serve as his second (or to assist him, since the outcome of the quarrel could not then have been foreseen). On February 8 Hawthorne wrote to Bridge that he intended to make a short visit to Washington in about a fortnight. He asked Bridge to meet him in Boston or Salem, swearing him to secrecy, and telling him he might regret it if they failed to meet.[75] If he asked Bridge's advice about such a matter, Bridge would almost certainly have advised him not to go. There is another story to the effect that Cilley had started out to buy his barrel of wine, to pay his bet, when he became involved in the fight that led to the duel.

Whatever the reason, Hawthorne was plunged into even deeper misery at the outcome. Gorham Deane, Alfred Mason, William Appleton, Zenas Caldwell, George Pierce, Jonathan Cilley—the list of Hawthorne's Bowdoin schoolmates whose careers ended in tragedy was rapidly lengthening. He found himself unable to think of it steadily. His features were drawn and he was plainly suffering.[76] The full enormity of the legal murder grew slowly over the North, and the first recognition, which was the true one, was that Cilley had been assassinated. The ghastly shooting gallery beside the road was too much for the country to endure: ex-President John Quincy Adams once turned upon Wise and said, "There came to the House a man with hands and face dripping with the blood of a murder, the blotches of which were yet hanging upon him." [77]

Soon after he arrived in Washington, Cilley had given John Louis O'Sullivan, the editor of the *Democratic Review*, an account of Hawthorne's work, and a request that he help Hawthorne. O'Sullivan accordingly wrote to Hawthorne and asked him to contribute to the magazine, offering him five dollars a page. The first issue of the *Democratic Review* was to appear in July. O'Sullivan was slight, with black hair, weak eyes, green spectacles, and was, in Longfellow's opinion, a humbug.[78] Poe considered him an ass. They were mistaken. He was a dangerous man, one of the most dangerous Hawthorne ever encountered. He was born on shipboard, near Gibraltar, in 1813, of Irish parents, educated in France and England, and graduated from Columbia in 1831, when he was only eighteen. The backers of the *Democratic Review* were a group of New York politicians around Van Buren. Andrew Jackson was their first subscriber. The *Democratic Review* was widely read abroad and was the favorite publication of the Russian Minister of Public Instruction. He praised it because it was not an American imitation of English journals.[79] In that period of deepening Russian and English antagonism, soon to climax in the Crimean War, such praise was significant. The Czar, Sophia Peabody reported a few years later, was spreading over the world a net of jewels, buying influence with prominent men by his gifts of precious stones to their wives.[80]

O'Sullivan did not send his letter direct to Hawthorne. He sent it, oddly enough for a man of his political views, to Elizabeth Peabody, asking her to deliver it.[81]

Elizabeth Peabody was the oldest daughter of Dr. Nathaniel Peabody, who had, years before, treated Hawthorne's foot. She was born at Billerica, on the Concord River, on May 16, 1804. A strong-minded, enthusiastic woman, she was born into a family of high-minded, impractical people whose intellectual interests grew more ardent as their worldly fortunes declined. While the family lived in Boston, she attended the school that William Emerson conducted in his mother's house in Federal Street. Ralph Waldo Emerson was his assistant, and Elizabeth became his private pupil. They were both so shy that they used to sit on opposite sides of the study table, neither daring to look up from the books. At sixteen, when the family was living at Lancaster, Elizabeth started a school of her own.

Elizabeth was a great teacher. Her resolution, in that day, impressed her critics as aggressiveness, and her initiative seemed to be

bold; but she was actually shy and timid and it required all her courage
to drive herself along the lines she was determined to follow. When the
warfare of the Unitarians and the Calvinists became severe, she applied
one day at Reverend Channing's house for a post as his secretary. He
tested her with a quotation from Plato. She translated it, and was hired.
Thenceforth she became almost a member of Channing's household. She
copied his sermons and arranged his press releases and dined with the
family each night.[82] In her later years she developed characteristics
which Boston found picturesque, and which must have been often trying; but in her young womanhood she must have been charming—independent, keen and resourceful, and with an honesty that made her,
among the tedious hypocrisies of the time, constantly refreshing. She
wrote very well, but in a sort of spiraling manner, one thought leading
to another in such a roundabout way that a careful reader was apt,
not so much to follow her argument as get dizzy. Once rearranged to
simple sentences, her writing made good common sense.

When Hawthorne's stories appeared, they made a powerful impression on Elizabeth, though she had no idea who had written them.
When *Twice-Told Tales* was published, and the author identified, Elizabeth Peabody still refused to believe that Hawthorne had written them;
she thought they must be the work of Elizabeth Hawthorne. I do not
know when Elizabeth Peabody and O'Sullivan met, or what was the basis
of their friendship. It seems extraordinary. Carrying O'Sullivan's letter, she called at the Hawthorne house.

She opened her conversation with Louisa by telling her of what
genius her sister possessed.

Louisa said, "My brother, you mean."

"It is your brother, then," Elizabeth said. "If your brother can
write like that he has no right to be idle."

"My brother is never idle," Louisa said truthfully, and on this cool
note the relationship of the Peabody and Hawthorne families began.[83]

Hawthorne never answered O'Sullivan's letter. After a few weeks
O'Sullivan sent a roundabout inquiry by way of a Boston friend, asking whether Hawthorne had ever received it.[84] Meanwhile, however,
Twice-Told Tales had appeared, Hawthorne had gone to Augusta, and
the Cilley duel was impending. The period between the first visit of
Elizabeth Peabody and the Cilley duel was the time when Hawthorne
and Sophia first met—that is, between March of 1837 and February,

1838. Between these two dates, Elizabeth Peabody had become so familiar with the Hawthorne household as to call after Cilley's death.

Cilley was buried on February 27, 1838. The following Thursday evening Elizabeth spent with Ebie and Nathaniel Hawthorne. She found Hawthorne obviously suffering and in great distress; she became greatly agitated, and apparently a quarrel broke out when she made some aspersions against Cilley's character. It should be borne in mind that the first news of Cilley's death had perhaps been too shocking: the papers bluntly called it murder. Within a few days the emphasis changed to a vigorous condemnation of dueling. The *Democratic Review* in a hypocritical passage in Hawthorne's essay on Cilley, almost certainly not his writing, deplored that Cilley had given his life for a trifling argument.

Ministers throughout the North, the preceding Sunday, had used Cilley's death in their sermons, again placing all emphasis on the evil of dueling. The scandal grew throughout the month, until its very magnitude obscured the meaning of the tragedy. It was not only that Cilley's death broke the tie in the House. The Constitution promised perfect immunity elsewhere for words spoken in debate. This was the constitutional provision whose violation was a well-nigh fatal weakness of democracy. Free speech as the founding fathers conceived it meant the right of elected representatives to discuss without fear of retaliation, to themselves or their families, issues of public concern. Free speech among the people at large is an attribute of civilization. The degree of freedom of speech may vary from time to time, or from community to community; it may be suspended during war, or in times of commotion, and the country yet remain a democracy, so long as the representatives of the people in Congress are free to speak their considered words on the issues before them. But freedom of speech came more and more to mean the right of anyone to express his views on any subject, while the congressmen, whose opinions alone were consequential, became increasingly open to retaliation for the views they expressed. It is impossible to read the chronicles of the time without a sense of horror at the repetitions, in a less violent form, of Cilley's tragedy. Again and again the wives or the children of the members grew sick as an important debate began or an issue came to a vote. If ninety per cent of all such occurrences were accidental, the remaining ten per cent were a revelation of a tragic weakness of democracy.

Elizabeth Peabody did not view Cilley's death as tragic. There was too little for hope and memory to dwell on in such a case. The duel to her mind merely made notorious the true character of Hawthorne's friends.

It was probably this that led to quarrel, for even if Hawthorne had agreed with her—and he may have—he would not have admitted it at such a time. Elizabeth told him to get out of politics. What she meant as advice may have been interpreted by him as a threat. She told him to get out of politics, to study German, and to write children's books.* She then became frightened that she had said too much.

Hawthorne and his sister probably walked home with her, to Charter Street, to the square, yellow house beside the old burying ground. The Peabody house was an ordinary wooden dwelling, neither rich nor poor, closely crowded between the house on the left and the old burying ground. A short block away was Derby Street, and the wharves. Hawthorne could not understand why anyone would build a dwelling beside a graveyard. The burying ground was extremely close to the house, and a very ancient one, the first in Salem, with the small flat gravestones tipping unevenly over the graves.

Elizabeth Peabody said good night at her door and went inside. Still troubled by her fear that she had said too much, she sat down and wrote a long, carefully phrased letter to Ebie Hawthorne to make herself clear. At first glance her letter seemed incoherent. More carefully studied, it seemed extremely subtle. She frankly admitted her dislike of Hawthorne's Democratic friends—they were thoughtless, she believed, and they lived in too selfish a world to appreciate him, and, moreover, every social being tended to fall to the level of his associates.

Yet this did not mean that she wanted Hawthorne to retire from any political action. She, too, would have him help govern this great people, but she would have him do so by going to the fountains of greatness and power, the unsoiled souls, and weaving for them his golden web. In every country one man had saved it, as Homer made Greece—so high was her estimate of Hawthorne's genius. She knew that Hawthorne and Ebie considered her enthusiastic, but she knew that her own tendency was to underrate rather than otherwise, and she be-

* On March 21, 1838, Hawthorne wrote to Longfellow and asked his advice on which German grammar to buy to begin a study of the language.

lieved Hawthorne had been gifted and kept apart by nature in order that he might do great things for his country. She feared his loss of ambition. For people as gifted as he was the perilous time was not youth, when the dreams of youth are their own sustenance, but middle age, when a false wisdom made them doubt their own high aspirations and the world came to them, not with the song of the siren, which they had learned to fear, but as a wise old man counseling acquiescence in what is below them.

Elizabeth Hawthorne and her brother walked home to Herbert Street, silenced at the enormity of the conflict growing around them. The household they had just left was tragic. George Peabody, Elizabeth's brother, was ill with consumption of the spinal marrow. Sophia Peabody, her younger sister, was a semi-invalid, living most of the time in her room upstairs, which she had converted into a studio—she was an artist of great natural gifts. Elizabeth Peabody herself was seldom in Salem. She spent most of her time in Boston, where she taught.

Elizabeth Hawthorne did not reply to Elizabeth Peabody's letter. She said she had forgotten how to write letters. She stopped by the Peabody house a short time later and left a book for George Peabody. She frequently came by, bringing him books and flowers.

One evening Elizabeth Peabody was alone in the drawing room when Hawthorne called with Elizabeth and Louisa. Her brother George was in his room, and Sophia, whose health had begun to fail again, was in her chamber. As soon as she could, Elizabeth Peabody ran upstairs and said, "O Sophia, you must get up and dress and come down! The Hawthornes are here, and you never saw anything so splendid as he is— he is handsomer than Lord Byron!"

Sophia laughed, but refused to come, remarking that since he had called once he would call again.

Now, Elizabeth Peabody was already acquainted with Hawthorne. It was nonsense for her to speak of him as if she had never seen him before. But it was characteristic of her to stage a scene such as this one. The Peabodys did not take Sophia into their affairs. She was not told about finances, or illnesses, lest they upset her nerves. This would have been insulting to her intelligence if it were not for the fact that she had a pretty shrewd idea of the truth anyway. She recognized the situation for what it was, and stayed in her room.

Hawthorne probably felt very foolish. He was nicely dressed, and

he looked almost fierce, a natural reaction if he had dressed to impress
her. But Elizabeth Peabody found the evening pleasant. So apparently
did Elizabeth Hawthorne, who with her black hair in beautiful natural
curls, her bright, rather shy eyes, and her frequent low laugh, seemed
experienced in the world. Her frequent low laugh must have been a trial
to her brother, though as the evening wore on his nervousness passed
away and he became interested in the conversation.

He did call again, not long afterward, and this time Sophia came
down, in her simple, white wrapper, and sat on the sofa. As Elizabeth
said, "My sister, Sophia," he rose and looked at her intently—he did
not realize how intently. As they went on talking, Sophia would frequently interpose a remark, in her low, sweet voice. Every time she did
so, Hawthorne would look at her again, with the same piercing indraw-
ing gaze.

Elizabeth was struck with it, and thought, "What if he should fall
in love with her!" The thought troubled her, for Sophia had often told
her that nothing would ever tempt her to marry and inflict on a husband
the care of an invalid.

When Hawthorne got up to go, he told Elizabeth he would come
for her in the evening to call on his sisters. He added, "Miss Sophia,
won't you come too?"

She replied, "I never go out in the evening, Mr. Hawthorne."

"I wish you would," he said, in a low, urgent tone.

She smiled, and shook her head, and he went away.[85]

XI

Brilliant and frail, gifted, nervous, often ill, delighting in companionship, Sophia Peabody was a slight, graceful girl, with small features and a small, turned-up nose—"My poor pug," she called it—
beautiful on occasion, but more often roguish, cute, and with a wit like
a kitten playing with a string. Her hair was light golden brown and her
eyes grayish blue. She was impulsive and spontaneous, affectionate,
cheerful, vivid. Except for the headache that visited her every afternoon, she was radiant. She said that she really began to live in September or October. Then she felt the way an autumn leaf looks. The rest
of the year she was homebound, and much of the time she had been
bound to her room as well.

What made her ill-health tragic was that she lived upon friendship as flowers live upon sunlight. She was forever sending people little gifts, flowers or notes, usually containing some pleasant word that someone had spoken about them. Since she was often confined to her room, it became a meeting place where the girls of Salem stopped on their round of visits to tell her what was happening in the world she wanted to know. Sometimes her whole day passed in a kind of unreal pageant of affection. She awakened in the morning pleased with the elm tree that grew outside her window, and the robin that sang in its branches, the clematis that climbed in her window, and the flowers that people brought her. Ellen Barstow, Hawthorne's cousin Nancy's child, brought her a crimson rose. Her sister Mary brought her a handful of flowers in the morning and she crowed over them awhile before she arose. Mary Channing brought her a Scotch rose. Sally Gardiner brought her an armload of roses. She listened to George Hillard talk agreeable nonsense—he said the postmaster of Cambridge was an old man, a hundred and forty years old, who reminded him of nothing sharpened to a point. Sometimes Ralph Waldo Emerson stopped by. He made her feel like a gem. Mary White's sister, Eliza Dwight, appeared, seeming to Sophia so beautiful that her beauty filled the room and made all of them beautiful.[86]

She had a remarkable life, not so much in the sense of outward adventure as in what she made of the limited circle that weakness confined her to. Her father, as has been said, was a physician and dentist. Her mother was a descendant of the Palmers and Cranches—the Palmers were industrialists (glassmaking) and with one Revolutionary general among them; the Cranches were judges, lawyers, real estate dealers, preachers and poets—distinguished lines, both of them, of the sort Hawthorne fled to Swampscott to escape.[87] Mrs. Peabody was an intellectual, a Unitarian, a translator from the German, a strong-minded woman who impressed upon her children her iron characterizations of their abilities, like clothes which did not quite fit them. Her family had long been associated with Salem, one of the early Cranches having been a watchmaker there.[88]

The Peabodys were poor. The poorer they grew the more resolutely high-minded and impractical they became. With a lordly disregard of realities, they named their son, born just after the War of 1812, Wellington. The first child of Nathaniel and Amelia Peabody was Elizabeth, the most famous of the family, who pioneered in starting kindergartens in the United States. The second was Mary Tyler Peabody, who married the great educator, Horace Mann. The third was Sophia, who became Mrs. Nathaniel Hawthorne.

Elizabeth Peabody was born, said Mrs. Peabody, who believed in prenatal influence, at the happiest time of her life, and consequently was sturdy and resolute, with the strongest constitution of any of the children. The family moved to Cambridge, where, on November 16, 1806, the second daughter, Mary, was born, and to Salem, where Sophia was born on September 21, 1809.* Three sons were then born to Dr. and Mrs. Peabody—Nathaniel, born December 11, 1811; George, born October 10, 1813; and Wellington, born December 16, 1815. The seventh child, Catherine, born April 26, 1819, lived only six weeks.

Mrs. Peabody joined the struggle of the Unitarians with all the fervor that might have been expected of her, and one of the first results of Channing's preaching was a violent quarrel among the various branches of her family. The lines of division are no longer clear, but it is plain that she lost—lost, that is, in terms of finances and social standing, though with the enthusiasm of her faith she never recognized defeat. And, indeed, in the long run, her cause triumphed, and her children flourished; her apparent impracticality was really a long-range hardheadedness. But meanwhile the trials of the children, growing up in the shadow of wealthy and mocking kinspeople, was severe. They seemed always to be moving from town to town, always to some residence not so good as the one they lived in the last time they were there, and to be forever starting school, only to give it up because the teachers were hostile, and remain at home.[89] Presently the time came when they rarely ventured outdoors.

What force was persecuting them? Perhaps they were only a little more sensitive, and the ordinary roughnesses of life struck them more fiercely. Around the professional career of Dr. Peabody there is an undefined dubious atmosphere, whose effects the children may have felt. With a sudden resolution, Elizabeth turned on the aimless passivity of her family and started a school of her own.

The Peabodys knew the Channings in Boston, the Emersons and

* Her birthday is given as September 21, 1811, in Julian Hawthorne's *Hawthorne and His Wife,* and as September 21, 1809, in the Records of Salem.

Hoars in Concord, the Clevelands in Lancaster, the Sturgises and Shaws, the Gardiners in Augusta, Maine, whose home was said to be the finest and most cultivated in the country—and then the rebels, Bronson Alcott, George Ripley, Margaret Fuller, and the Transcendentalists —and then painters like Washington Allston and Thomas Doughty, preachers like Reverend Upham. The Peabodys had been Federalists when there was a Federalist party. The people Sophia knew were Federalists. They varied from the wise and perceptive Federalism of Channing to the narrowness of the old Salem die-hards, arrogant and unchanging and bitter as gall. There were no innkeepers and stagecoach drivers among them, no fishermen or storekeepers, but many ministers, doctors, lawyers, judges, schoolteachers, who might imagine secrets where none existed, but from whose shrewd cold eyes secrets were kept with difficulty.

Sophia's earliest memories were of a fear of violence away from the protection of home. She was a sickly child. When she was four or five, in the period of the War of 1812, she was sent to the house of her grandmother. Her early memory was of playing in a tiny courtyard with two puppies belonging to her aunt Alice. The sunlight flooded the grass and shrubbery; every object was clear and fresh, as if it had been washed and then arrayed in gold. There were great trees overhead, with leaves glistening and fluttering in the wind. She accidentally hurt one of the puppies, and her aunt reached out and shook her violently by the arm.

Sophia was put to bed each day at six o'clock, in an upper room, alone in the dark. She lay in terror, listening to the street noises. She was made to eat the food placed before her, whether she liked it or not, and because a saucer of chocolate was forced on her against her will, she could not tolerate chocolate for the rest of her life. She was taken to church dressed in very tight frocks and made to sit very still during the infinite weariness of the long church services. Her aunts set her in the yard and laughed at her terror when the turkeys, gobbling like fiends, started after her. They made her read the Bible aloud and laughed at her mispronunciations. They asked her if she would like to see the most beautiful garden in the world, and when she said "Yes," they took her to a closed door, opened it, and pushed her inside, down a flight of steps into utter darkness.[90]

From the time she was nine, she was a semi-invalid, suffering from

constant headaches. There was really nothing for her to do, and nothing to be done for her. Her brother Nathaniel became a homeopathic
druggist. There was a conflict in medical circles about that time between
the homeopathic and the allopathic physicians. The homeopathic physicians believed in giving drugs in minute amounts, very frequently; the
others favored large and strenuous dosages of whatever medicine they
prescribed. One after another the doctors tried their hands at curing
Sophia, but without success. Her illness, indeed, like Hawthorne's foot
injury in childhood, came and went with remarkable speed. She loved
horseback riding, for example, and spent hours riding along the Salem
beaches, perhaps on horses hired from the Manning stables. But at
other times she was almost helpless.

She had developed an invalid's temperament. Her thoughts re-
volved around her family, overflowing with gratitude for the simplest
attention, magnifying the outdoor achievements of her brothers and
sisters, and responding to nature, when she did step outside, with the
feverish intensity of a convalescent or an habitual user of drugs. Colors
were abnormally bright, the songs of the birds unbelievably clear, the
moonlight powerful. Her dreams were nightmares: she dreamed of
massive clouds arising to obscure the sunset, or that the Duke of Buckingham had stabbed her in the bosom, and woke up trembling for an
hour.[91]

She was given narcotics. They failed to help her headaches. She
was first given opium. She was then given hyocamus, and this drug,
producing twilight sleep, used upon criminals and others from whom
confessions are desired, seemed to be less harmful to her than others.
When the family was living in Boston, it occurred to Elizabeth that
Sophia might be able to paint. The painter Thomas Doughty had
opened a school in Boston at 220 Washington Street. A landscape
artist, self-taught, famed for his "Scenes on the Susquehanna,"
Doughty had begun to paint in 1820, when he was twenty-seven, and his
small, picturesque, effectively colored scenery had a cool vivid tone,
a true execution, and especially an American character that set them
apart. Doughty simply set up his canvas and had his students watch
while he painted. He was a bitter man; his artistic sensibilities and
financial ill-success made him morbidly despondent. Elizabeth arranged
that he should teach Sophia, setting up his easel in her room, while she
watched him from the bed. When he had gone she copied what he had

done. Elizabeth then got one of Washington Allston's paintings. Sophia copied it also, so exactly that when they were placed together even the critics could not tell which was her work and which was Allston's.[92]

She was gifted, but her undefined capacities could only twine themselves beautifully around something stronger than themselves, and if left unsupported could only wither on the ground. The American mind excelled at imitation, of which her skill at copying was only one example. There was quite as much a racket in the imitation of old masters then as at a later date; and though no one, apparently, commented upon it, it must have been disconcerting to the purchasers of Washington Allston's paintings that an unknown beginner could copy his works so exactly. The puzzle was made deeper by the fact that Allston was New England's greatest painter.

In those years before 1833 Sophia enjoyed a brief but genuine social success. Her health, in its mysterious cycles, had improved. She was under the care of Dr. Walter Channing, the brother of the famous minister. He was the opposite of Reverend Channing—hearty, sociable, exuberant, a brilliant conversationalist. His first wife, Barbara Higginson Perkins, had died after bearing him a son, the redoubtable Ellery, and Ellery was a problem child on whom Sophia alone, for some unexplained reason, had any influence. Ellery had been raised by an aunt in his childhood, and then sent to George Bancroft's Round Hill School in Northhampton. He returned a complete rebel, and his lawlessness increased as he grew older.[93] Sophia alone could tame him. She was a few years older. She was on terms of personal friendship with the doctor's family, as Elizabeth was with the family of Reverend Channing, and Dr. Walter Channing, Boston's foremost obstetrician, at this time was becoming famed as the first dean of Harvard's Medical School, a position he held for many years.[94]

When Sophia was seventeen her mother began tactfully to warn her that she might never marry. Something ere long, she wrote, must be planned out for your future livelihood. To be independent of everyone, as far as money is concerned, is very desirable, "of love and kind offices you may give and receive as liberally as you please." Sophia's sensitive nature, shattered nerves, and precarious health made Mrs. Peabody long to arm her against disappointments; and the girls, ardent and enthusiastic, could not learn not to wear their hearts on their sleeves. "Since you have no physical strength," said her mother, "gird

up the loins of your mind—be strong in faith—be candid—anchor your
soul on domestic love, at the same time that you open your warm affectionate heart to receive the kindness and love of the excellent of the
earth, to whom your kindred nature attaches you. . . ." [95] These were
words of hard honesty and Sophia could not accept them. Without
hope, she said, she would die, and by hope she meant the hope of marrying.[96]

Whatever happened, the period of Sophia's Boston success ended
suddenly. She had been petted, courted, and made over; she was now
whisked from place to place, shushed and guarded, hidden away,
watched over, as if she were the central figure in some terrific scandal
that would become public if she said a single word. She seems to have
been the only person who did not know what everyone else was talking
about. Whatever it was, it was not her responsibility; she was innocent
of the turmoil that was sending her friends flying in all directions, and
the secret still unrevealed. But plainly there was something that had
stirred up the artistic and literary circles of Boston and separated its
members into their molecules.

She greatly admired Washington Allston, Reverend Channing's lifelong friend and brother-in-law—Allston had married Ann Channing, who
died in England many years before. She had tried to borrow one of
Allston's paintings from a Mr. Clarke, to copy it. He refused to lend
it to her, saying Allston had exacted a promise from the purchasers
of his paintings not to permit them to be copied. Whether anything
more lay back of this rebuff is a matter of speculation; plainly, however, it was a rebuff. Sophia fled Boston, first to visit Mr. and Mrs. Sam
Haven at Lowell.[97] Haven was a lawyer, an historian, secretary of the
American Antiquarian Society.[98] The Havens behaved very strangely.
They visited her in the room where she boarded, to see if she was comfortable, and then left her for a day without calling. She sewed, and
read, and wrote in her diary. She had frightful nightmares, and the
headaches grew worse than they had ever been. She got up at night and
watched the autumn moon. There was a snowy wreath of mist where
Wiggam Pond wound itself among the meadows. The moon rose, conquered the clouds, became enveloped in them, while around her a bright
halo of pale crimson formed, softening gradually into white.

No lover appeared beneath her window, and the next morning the
world was full of wind. She read the Lesser Prophets, whom she could

HENRY LONGFELLOW
(New York Public Library)

SUPREME COURT JUSTICE
JOSEPH STORY

"He has delivered a wound to our party interests that can never be healed."—President Thomas Jefferson *(Essex Institute)*

JUDGE DANIEL APPLETON WHITE

(Essex Institute)

JOSEPH WHITE

Wealthy Salem merchant, who was found murdered in his bed on April 7, 1830, with his skull fractured and thirteen stab wounds in his body, a crime for which Richard Crowninshield and Frank and Joseph Knapp died, with Daniel Webster a special prosecutor, in the first American murder trial to make a nation-wide sensation. (Essex Institute)

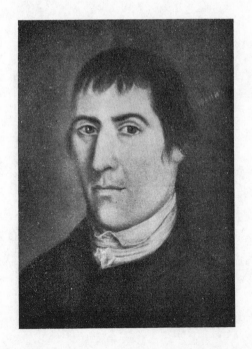

not understand. Rain fell the next day, and the Havens did not call. She read more of the French Minister of the Interior's works, of Fénelon, the *Spectator*, St. Luke, Isaiah, *The Comedy of Errors*, *Taming of the Shrew*, *All's Well that Ends Well*, and *Love's Labours Lost*. She sewed, and lived through a day of clouds and ever-during dark. At midnight she was awakened by a tremendous crack of thunder, and though she went to sleep again, she dreamt of all kinds of horrors.

When the weather was good she fed upon air. A day without a cloud! She awakened in the dewy freshness of sunrise, slept again, and dreamed that she was watching a sunrise in a sky filled with coffin-shaped clouds. When she awoke she could not help shouting. The sky in the east was gold and amethyst, fretted, quivering, gorgeous, a wreck of precious stones. Deep orange and tender green melted into each other, and high above soft fleecy clouds floated in the pale azure. When the sun's first rays struck the dewdrops it seemed as if myriads of diamonds had been flung at that moment upon the earth.

Her Yankee landlady asked her questions about her family. She fell asleep, and dreamed that the Duke of Buckingham had stabbed her in the bosom, and woke up trembling for an hour. She read to herself, and walked by herself, laughed to herself, and even talked to herself a little. Mrs. Haven said she looked perfectly crazy. She felt crazy. When she walked with her friends to see Dedham Court House by moonlight, she started to mention "some little circumstances about Dr. Boyle," apparently in a loud voice, when Sam Haven said the doctor was right behind them. Tears of humiliation filled Sophia's eyes. She felt all at once her want of delicacy and consideration, and thought, "I must never forget this warning." Her diary hesitated at the verge of a horror story. Dr. Boyle was not behind them. Sophia thought that Judge Ware was. Why she was willing to mention something about Dr. Boyle that she wanted Judge Ware to hear she did not say.[99]

She left the Havens and visited Mrs. Rice. Washington Allston visited her there. He said she should go to Europe and study art. She replied that she was an invalid. Sophia was a hero worshiper. It was her custom to write of the people she admired with unblushing candor, and to regard them almost with awe at their many excellences. On occasions, however, when she was really stung, she struck back with ferocious wit, all the more deadly for being accompanied by her quiet and submissive manner. When Allston told her that she should copy

only masterpieces, nothing second rate, she told him that she had tried
to copy his "Spanish Maiden."

He flushed. He said that he would be glad to have her copy anything he had painted. Gentlemen, he said, had no right to make him a
party to their meanness; he had never exacted a promise not to have
his pictures copied.[100] Soon after this, Allston married for the second
time. A short time later, Dr. Walter Channing married his second wife,
Eliza Wainwright of Boston. Sophia returned to Salem, where her
breakdown was complete. She lay in her darkened room, while her mother
guarded the doors of the house to see that none of them was slammed.

At last, on December 6, 1833, she and her sister Mary sailed to
Cuba, to search for health on a plantation in the interior. There was
at that time a close connection between New England and the West
Indies. Many of the merchant families owned plantations in Cuba;
many of the refugees from the Negro uprisings in Santa Domingo and
Guadeloupe had settled in New England. It was fairly common for
girls in the situation of Sophia and Mary to visit there—not exactly
an ordinary procedure, but not so exceptional as to cause speculation.
In Sophia's case the trip was plainly for the sake of her nerves. She
never forgot Dr. Channing's last words to her as she sailed. "Don't
think," he said.[101]

In his household a dreadful situation developed. Ellery Channing,
who refused to address his father's second wife as "mother," one day
left his Harvard class, walked across the Yard, and disappeared. He
was found months later living alone in a cabin on the Merrimack River.
In his absence, Dr. Channing's second wife also died.[102]

XII

For almost two years Sophia and Mary Peabody lived on a sugar
plantation called La Recompensa in the province of Pinar del Rio in
western Cuba. That strange cloudland of Sophia's imagination, flowers
and vivid dreams, ceaseless courtesies and rapturous attentions, seemed
now to have become reality. It was as if, having imagined the world to
be like this, she had been transported to the only place on earth where
such a scene, like a great stage setting, had ever existed.[103]

This was one of the richest sections of the New World. It was a
quadrangle, set aside by the Spanish government for the refugees from

the Negro uprisings in Haiti and Santo Domingo. The northeast boundary lay west of Mariel, running from the River Quiebro Hacha eastward to the mouth of the San Marcos River, at the port of Las Mulatas. Its southern boundary was the coast lying northwest of the Isle of Pines.

Sophia and Mary Peabody lived on one of the plantations of the Morrell family. Their name lingers on in Cuba; it is the name of a town where they once built a hacienda and probably a mill or factory. The family was of Spanish origin, distinguished, and well known in Cuba. The royal road from Havana passed directly before the entrance of the plantation. In wet weather it was impassable. The region was one of enclosed valleys of exquisite charm. The mountains were as high as the Berkshires, and covered with lovely and luxuriant foliage. Two miles from Recompensa there was La Providencia, the coffee plantation of the de Zayas. The family of Don Juan de Zayas was one of the richest and most cultured in Cuba. The remembrance of it remains only in the name of a place. Between the Bacunagua and Los Palacios rivers, where their ancient hacienda was located, there is now the community called Don Juan de Zayas. Contemporary Cubans know of it as the center of a region once called Francia, from the number of distinguished French exiles from Haiti who lived there, and from its associations with a past of splendor and wealth, of gracious living and cultured society, ease and harmony, beautiful estates, lovely landscapes, free and enlightened habits of conduct, and an ancient hidalgo society of great charm and kindliness.[104]

The girls remained a month in Havana, staying with the American consul, Richard Jeffery Cleveland. They had known his three sons in Lancaster. Toward the end of January they set out over the royal road to Recompensa. The coffee trees, a deep, shining green, extended in immense squares in every direction. A wide avenue ran from one side of the house to the front gate of the plantation. On the other side ran the orange allée, a wide avenue of palm, mango, and orange trees. Another great avenue of palms transversed the plantation north and south. There were thus two crossroads where the avenues intersected. The northwest square was covered with coffee trees. A line of coco palms separated it from a square, the same size, of coffee trees and bananas. The central section was filled on one side with a square enclosing the plantation house, the vast lawn before it, the flower gardens, the slave quarters, the coach house, the Negro ballroom, and the out-buildings, and a hedge of limes. The wide sloping lawn ended at the avenue of palms that transversed the plantation. Beyond it there were the limestone driers where the coffee was dried. Across the avenue lead-ing to the outer gate, on the southeast and southwest corners of the plantation, were two more immense squares of coffee. There were fine views of the San Salvador Mountains from Recompensa, their outline graceful on the horizon, their color pale or deep blue.

The thatched cottages of the slaves stood within sight of the plantation. There were hundreds of them. They were kindly treated, and seemed happy. Dozens of naked little ebony imps played all day on the wide lawn before the house. The household consisted of Dr. Mor-rell and his wife, their sixteen-year-old daughter Louisa, two younger sons, Eduardo and Carlito, and the housekeeper, Mrs. Batson, from Philadelphia, and the household slaves—Gepherina, Francesca, Urbano, Antonio, Antonico, Zabrellina, Alesio, Felicina, Sirraco, and Thekla, who called Sophia her *alma,* her *vida,* her *corazón.*

Thus there began two years of enchantment. Daily at dawn Sophia made her way in the semidarkness to the gallery. The plantation bell, hanging on a cedar tree on one side of the laguna, rang before dawn. Her horse had been saddled and a slave stood holding him silently in the shadows. The plantation still slept. Her horse was named Guajamón. She rode for a silent hour of praise and thanksgiving. Every leaf and flower was brilliant with dew, making the long leaves of the coco and palms look like thousands of glittering scimitars, and bringing out the delicious fragrance of orange and lime blossoms. Incense rose as the sun drew up the dew. Opposite the northern side of the estate there was a row of palms three-quarters of a mile in length, and as at sunrise she feasted her eyes on their tapering white trunks she had a dreamlike sensation of being among Grecian columns, or in Palestine or Egypt. She saw herself as part of the picture, on horseback under the brighten-ing sky, riding alone through vast colonnades, almost with a sense of intruding upon the worship of nature.

After breakfast she sat on the gallery, reading the Salem *Gazette,* bundles of which arrived every fortnight, or the *Christian Examiner,* or Reverend Channing's sermons, *Bracebridge Hall,* or *El Renegado.* Her sister Mary taught the Morrell children. Dons and donas filled the house, a few of them interesting and some of them pretty. She made

sketches of them. Often she looked up from her reading to find Don
Fernando, the Marquis de Zayas, on horseback, nodding and smiling at
her. His father, the most influential man on the island, had recently
died. He had dined at the Morrell's, ridden away, contracted cholera,
and died in twenty-four hours. His sons, Fernando, Pepé and Manuel,
haunted Recompensa; it was a second home to them.

After their siestas, she and Louisa joined Don Fernando for a
ride beyond the plantation grounds. They returned at nightfall. The
plantation bell sounded—eighteen strokes—for evening prayers. In
the evening they visited on the gallery, or walked in the moonlight,
while Mrs. Morrell read to the doctor in the house. The strange songs of
the Negroes floated up from the slave quarters. When they held their
dances the air throbbed with the pounding of their drums. Louisa said
they danced wildly, the sedate house servants the most abandoned of
them all. The plantation bell sounded silencio, curfew for the Negroes.
At nine-thirty, at the plantation, they assembled again for tea. Then
Don Fernando and his brothers rode home through the darkness, and
Sophia and Mary and Louisa went to bed.

By April the coffee was in full flower. Miles of blossoms, white as
snowballs, sent up an odor sweeter than frankincense and similar to that
of lilies of the valley. Sophia was enchanted. She rode through the dawn
exulting in its freshness, in rapture at the fragrant breathings of the
winds. The spring weather was varied, changeable, with sudden little
storms, almost playful in their quickness, darting and darkening the air
momentarily and vanishing in brilliant sunshine. She sat on the gallery
writing joyful letters home while the wind tumbled her hair. Bright
sunlight lay around her, but all around the horizon there were moun-
tainous clouds with conelike summits through which the thunder rolled
like the distant chariot wheels of a god. Large tropical birds were
wheeling through the air.

She had grown "round and a little rosy" but strength eluded her.
Her headaches were still bad; she still spent days in bed in her darkened
room. Her hope was like the banyan tree. It found new roots whenever it
fell to the ground. However people spoke of feeling utter despair, she
was convinced that it was impossible to have no hope and live—"I am
pretty sure it is as indestructible as the soul itself." Out on the lawn
before the house a round plot of ground was being made into a flower
garden. It was to be hedged around with roses in perpetual bloom.

The rarest flowers from the gardens of the neighboring plantations were being planted in it. Sophia took a keen interest in the garden. She admired the shell palm, growing in a whirl of green leaves from the bottom to the top like a winding flight of stairs; and the young ceiba she saw on a visit to the Marquis de Arcos's estate. She had never seen its long slender leaves before, and felt as she examined them that she had no right to take advantage of its youth to penetrate into its mysteries. The work went on in the garden, the tropical birds wheeled in time with the distant rolling of the thunder.

Sophia laid aside her letter writing and went to dress for dinner. The rain began to fall gently, good for man, beast, and the garden. A month passed before she wrote on it again. So swiftly and dreamily the time passed.

The dons rode when the sun shone and slept when it rained. The donas made dresses for the Christmas balls. "Much the larger proportion of young men—or rather all young men and women with few exceptions —are entirely without real cultivation and never touch a book." Don Fernando and Pepé were up at dawn every day, hunting. Then they rode to Recompensa, and remained all day.

On other days the storms came rushing from the east with inconceivable rapidity. The rain fell with a roar, plowing the ground. The trees seemed articulate after these outpourings. They lifted their heads when the deluge was over as if to say, with a meaning smile, "Oh, how delightfully I feel!" Then again the storm clouds swept overhead without a drop of rain descending. Sophia sat at her window watching a cloud as black as night. The brilliant sunshine of noon made its darkness darker still. The tall plantation trees waved their long branches. The roses outside her window looked absolutely frightened. Long penetrating rolls of thunder called to each other as deep calls unto deep. A large tropical bird wheeled through the air like a sinister herald of the storm. It sailed in vast circles in the mid-region of the atmosphere, with a slow and majestic movement, as if following the measure of the thunder tones pealing overhead.

She felt lonely and frightened. There were tremors of uneasiness in her letters, though she always wrote cheerfully. She spoke of the plantation as "our lovely prison." When Horace Cleveland unexpectedly arrived, she was glad to see him. They visited, talked Castilian, rode horseback, and she sketched their profiles. Horace told them that in the mountains, where he had been working on a coffee plantation, they made profiles by projecting them against a wall in the moonlight. They went outside and she sketched Fernando's profile. She was thrilled with a sense of the strangeness of the scene, the moonlight casting its shadow, the pale-blue night, the young Marquis fixed and motionless to keep his shadow steady enough for her to outline it, the rustling laughter of Louisa Morrell, looking over his shoulder, and her sister Mary saying, "Quick, quick, Soph!" She felt as if a pack of hounds were at her fingers.

On other days she visited with Mrs. Morrell, riding in the carriage while the children and Louisa and Don Fernando rode horseback. The rain had glorified every created thing. Every leaf was polished like a mirror. The trees and flowers along the border of the Countess de Zanbotti's plantation, scarlet and pale pink and bright golden bells, looked like things that were fit to dream of, not to see. The sea of air, each fresh wave bearing a new fragrance, inspired exultant life within her— Huge plantation houses of glistening marble, with stately cleared forests, of a deep-green foliage, on both sides, oleanders in full bloom, contrasting with the mangoes that were planted alternately with them; cloudless skies, caged nightingales on the staircases, Spanish women with "gray eyes like a June twilight in Cuba"; children sensitive and responsive; little ebony slave children, perfectly formed, tumbling and playing on the wide level lawn; vast palm-covered plains, visible from the mountains, with palm trees growing in columns; Spanish cavaliers of doubtful reputation, very gay and sparkling, riding past and making a twinkle of the hands at her; the crooked moon, and the matchless nights, *white* with stars. Don Fernando sat at the piano and played "La Musica del Niño Fernando," a song of his own composition. Or he played songs the Negroes had taught him and which had never been written down. She transcribed them and sent them to her friends in Salem.

The hurricane swept by, the *mango de viente*, the sleeve of wind, a dark quivering body, resembling the flickering of flames. It did no damage at Recompensa, but at a neighbor's plantation nine people were killed. The lime hedges were twisted and dried and brown. Nothing was left of the forest of coffee trees but pounded stumps and shafts, blackened or browned as if by fire. Not a leaf or a spot of green was visible. The vines and tendrils that had once wound together the coffee

plants, and the palm and ceiba trees in the path of the sirocco, were
seared as if the Destroying Angel had poured one of the vials of his
burning wrath upon the earth.

The rainy season began. The house was soon like an island in a
sea of red mud. Louisa Morrell, sulky and beautiful, took to dressing
elaborately in the evenings and promenading alone along the gallery,
in the drenched evening air, her mantilla over her hair, her features
stormy. In pauses in the rain they rode in an oxcart to the coffee drier
and waltzed in the moonlight on the limestone squares. In the dull afternoons Fernando sat at the piano, playing idly, while Louisa and Sophia
put flowers in each other's hair. They rode again at night in the carreta,
lying on the skins spread over the floor. Sophia pillowed her head on a
heap of leaves. She was suddenly overwhelmingly happy, relaxed with
the gentle motion of the cart, the slow dignified oxen, the tall black
Negro driver calling out the names of the oxen—Abrevido! Arrogant!
Mariposa!—the enchantment of the whole strange expedition through
the Caribbean night. There was not an accident, not a jolt. She snug-
gled contentedly among the leaves, savoring the velvet breeze, the cool
fresh pillow, the voice of the niño, and Louisa's dark expressive eyes.
The moon was disobliging. It appeared and disappeared, hiding among
the thin clouds and lost under the branches of the trees.

Her eyes brightened in the silver light and were veiled in the heat
of the day; the bright colors of Cuba, the flowering reds and the shining
green, were too bold for her twilight spirit. Dawn and evening were
her best hours, and their light was in the frail tenuous lines of her drawings, the pale colors in which she painted, the gentle descriptions she
wrote. The scenes that lived in her memory were slight and elusive—
Louisa walking alone in the gathering darkness, her mantilla over her
hair; the young cavalier of San Marcos riding by and making a twinkle
of the hands for her; the carriage approaching with the mail as she
promenaded with Eduardo in the moonlight; the dreamlike mornings,
when she made her way in the tawny light to the gallery and found
her horse saddled and waiting and—sometimes—Dr. Morrell standing
by in the shadows to wish her a gruff and admiring good morning.

In all her memories the lean smiling features of Fernando emerged
clearer and more lifelike against the dim background. Sometimes he
seemed diabolical to her. Leaning over her as she sat in her chair in the
drawing room, smiling sardonically, he frightened her with the sudden

transformation of his features, ⹁nd she thought of him as the embodiment of all the fallen angels. But usually her thoughts of him were of his exquisite grace, his responsiveness, the infinite ways he found of showing attention, his gallantry, and the web of interest he wove around the life in which they were all imprisoned. On days when he did not call they found themselves trying to read, listening to the ticking of the clock, and starting up at the sound of hoofbeats in the drive. The three señoritas ran to welcome him without a moment's coquetry. He was at the beginning, the middle, and the end of all her accounts of Cuba, because he was at the beginning, the middle, and the end of all their doings. He taught her to dance, to ride, and to play; he taught her Castilian and now he was beginning to teach her to paint. They covenanted with each other: he was to teach her Spanish and she was to teach him English. She learned Spanish but he could not endure the aspera duros of the English language and insisted that she should never say *yes* to him when she meant *sí*. He seemed to her the embodiment of Cuba, though he was of Spanish descent, his family was from Santo Domingo, and much of his life had been spent in France, where he was educated. How different he was from the New Englanders, with their scruples and their caution and their shrewd self-seeking! How different from the intellectuals like Ellery Channing, with their willful eccentricities, their rudeness and moodiness; or from the sons of the merchants, with their preparations for good marriages and prosperous careers! And how different was life from the years in Salem and Boston, the greetings that were coldly acknowledged, the friends who reminded her that her words might be overheard, the patrons of art who refused to let her copy their paintings!

Louisa's seventeenth birthday came on September 12. By the light of the new moon they walked to the palms and the driers. They crossed the wide lawn bathed in the still light, and crossed the roadway leading to the plantation gate. They looked at the long colonnades of palm trees motionless in the dry and windless air. Their voices rose musically as they scattered over the grass, the rising keys and kays of Spanish, its playful diminutives, the whispering rushes of words like the sound of wind in the trees, or the murmur of water sliding past a ship. They left the palms, recrossed the roadway, and walked to the immense squares of limestone at the driers. Louisa sang "Buenas Noches." They played puss in the corner. Its name in Spanish was **La Candelito,** the

Little Candle, "because the one in the middle goes to one of those in the corner and asks where he can get his candle lighted, and while he goes to the person designated, the change of places is made behind his back." They played in the moonlight, with four palm trees for their corners.

The days vanished; the de Zayas went to Havana; presently there was nothing to record but the sameness of this quiet life. She wrote her letters in the form of a journal. Her family bound them, and they circulated among her friends in Salem as a manuscript volume. They had a dreamlike quality, unreal and yet authentic, less like the record of a visit to Cuba than like notations for a piece of music, or fragments of unfinished portraits. Reality forever crowded through the pageantry and the settings—the problems of slavery, the de Zayas' lawsuit, the cholera epidemic, the mud, the loneliness and monotony of plantation life—only to vanish in the clear morning air as if they had never existed. And so it was with the whole record of her Cuban life. It seemed impossible that there could ever have been such a plantation, or people such as she described, days such as she lived, or pictures such as she painted.

For two years she rode almost every day through endless avenues of oranges and past square miles of coffee blossoms. Her escorts were the young Cuban aristocrats whose lives were filled with their half-playful and half-serious courtships. They were wonderfully at ease in their own country, like the trees and the horses, with the lithe, innocent, sun-tanned paganism of Donatello in *The Marble Faun,* direct and affectionate, simple and unstudied, unlearned and yet intelligent, responsive, and yet always with a menacing undercurrent of invitation in their speech and action reminding her that her home was two thousand miles away.

For two years she lived as a blonde young Northerner in the tropics, savoring its drowsy well-being and sensuous enjoyment, the long twilights, the night airs, the soft odors, the ease, the greenery, the sudden weather, the music, the pauses in the talk, the grace, the inertia within which questions and perceptions rippled like trout in a stream. Slowly a tropical strain was woven into the plain fabric of her New England experience and never left it, something vivid and exotic, a Latin-American duskiness and humor, a zest for life, and a frankness and freedom in enjoying it. Its warmth still gleams through her letters and her diaries, more magical and haunting because the society from which it came has vanished from the earth, and even the names of its places have disappeared from the maps of the islands.

XIII

She gave Hawthorne her Cuban diaries to read. He promised to write a story for her based upon them. Then he found that he could not do so—he could not finish it.

The story became an embarrassment to him. He had studied her diary very carefully. He had found in it a passage he interpreted with an uncanny prophetic insight. He thought her wonderful, and yet he thought that her view of life was wrong, and the problem he set for himself was that of making credible to her the unreality of that visionary island world she had lived in. There have not been many imaginations such as his, and we cannot see what he saw in those fleeting glimpses of her life; but the girl in her long white dress, living in the old house beside the old burying ground of Salem, gliding down the stairs, sketching her haunting, shadowless drawings, was somehow for him the answer to a cipher he had tried in vain to solve.

The story that he wrote was suggested by a passage in her diary in which she had described her attempt to sketch Don Fernando. This is what she wrote: "August 2nd. Ay de mi! These divine mornings! Don Fernando came in his most brilliant mood. He was very anxious to know whether I had el ánimo dispensa for my proposed act and when he was satisfied on this point he established himself in the right attitude and lights and I drew him while he was in an animated conversation with Louisa. I caught the inspired look in his eye so well that I wanted to shout—but before I finished it I came to take a siesta, as he was exceedingly concerned that I should not get tired.

Poor Sophy has spoilt Fernando's beautiful portrait and has gone to bed in the agony of her vexation though it is not ten o'clock in the morning, Love to all the folks, Mary.

It was the most beautiful, soul-beaming face I have ever produced —But a touch of the pencil is omnipotent and a false one banished the living soul from the features and changed a high noble look into an expression of utter stupidity and ordinariness." [105]

This passage was significant enough in itself. Hawthorne plainly meant to imply that her mistake was the reality—the expression of utter stupidity and ordinariness was the truth, and the romance she wove around Fernando was her own mistaken idealization of him. These unconscious revelations in her writing made it of value, not the long descriptions and adulations on which she labored and exhausted herself. She could not reconcile this ceaseless striving for nobility with the truth before her. The beliefs she held led her to seek constantly for a higher type of being and a better kind of life than she could find; to find people better and more beautiful than they were; to transform the blunt everyday world into a masquelike pageant on an enchanted island. And yet she knew—not exactly, but with a half-sense of awareness, and an occasional mockery—and when reality broke her vision of the world, she went to bed in an agony of vexation, or lay in her darkened room in the old house in Salem, her spirit fluttering like an injured bird against the transparent barrier of her vision.

When fiction is true it squares with the history of its time and place, regardless of the author's knowledge of history. There are few stories which exemplify it so powerfully as the one Hawthorne wrote for Sophia. It is almost impossible that he should have known so much Cuban history as to have been able to forecast the fate of her Cuban friends, or to perceive so truly the situations they were in. Yet, if the story that he wrote for her is *Edward Randolph's Portrait*, it seems that he did so. He not only imagined, on the basis of Sophia's unguarded words, the political situation in the island and the predicament of the de Zayas. He also imagined their future, and, in twenty years or so, what he visualized came to pass. This was not a mysterious gift of second sight or anything of the sort; it was simply that with a knowledge of history and a sense of character he could reconstruct an environment from the fragments in his possession.

The Cubans he imagined as New Englanders before the Revolution. They had the divided loyalties of the New Englanders, their love of the old country and their sense of resentment at being exploited by it. At the time Sophia was in Cuba there was much unrest there. A new governor, Tacón, had been appointed, and was ruling with an iron hand. Passports were required to travel within the country, and watchmen patroled the streets of Havana.[106] In Spain itself a long-smoldering revolt reached the stage of crisis in the summer of 1835; the Madrid militia revolted. It was therefore appropriate that Hawthorne should lay his story in a comparable period in New England history. He called it *Edward Randolph's Portrait*—Randolph was the most tyrannical of New England's colonial governors.[107]

Sophia he made Alice Vane, the niece of the colonial Governor Hutchinson. Reverend Upham's recently published life of Sir Henry Vane had made that particular colonial period vivid and the characters real. Alice was an ethereal girl, always dressed in white, as Sophia was, a girl with artistic gifts, educated abroad, with something wayward and childlike about her. The situation that he imagined was this: the colony was restless and three regiments of British soldiers had arrived on a fleet from Halifax to overawe the insubordination of the people. Hutchinson faced the responsibility of giving them permission to land and occupy the fort. He hesitated. If blood were shed it would be on his head, and if it were not he would still be guilty of having surrendered New England's liberty.

A portrait hung in the governor's chamber. The canvas was so dark with age, damp and smoke that the features could not be seen. There were all sorts of stories about it—that it was a portrait of the devil, that it could be clearly seen only on the eve of some public calamity, that it was so hideous a face that for years it had been covered with a black cloth: "Some of these legends are really awful," Alice said. Hutchinson told her the stories were nonsense; it was only a faded picture of Edward Randolph. But Randolph was the royal governor who had repealed the provincial charter that gave New England democratic rights. He was of all New England's governors the one whose memory was the most detested. The thought made Hutchinson pause. A hot-blooded young New England soldier urged resistance. A venerable selectman said, "We will strive against the oppressor with prayer and fasting . . . we will submit to whatever lot a wise Providence may send us —always, after our best exertions to amend it." This was a veiled warning Hutchinson understood. Alice interrupted her uncle's deliberations. She indicated Randolph's portrait, and reminded him of the awful weight of a people's curse. Hutchinson started; he knew that Alice, despite her foreign education, was a New England girl—"Peace, silly child," he said, more harshly than he had ever spoken to her. When he left the room with the issue still undecided, she took the portrait from the wall and in cleaning it restored its original colors.

In the evening Hutchinson sat at his table, under the light of half a dozen candles, and prepared to sign the order. The plain, somber selectmen of Boston were present, the council members in their wigs and rich clothing, a British major, the colonial captain of the fort and the British officer who was to support him. As Hutchinson picked up his pen his attention was called to Alice. He called to her and she stepped forward, drawing the curtain from the portrait. It was the portrait of a man in agony. His expression was of one detected in some hideous guilt, and exposed to the withering scorn of a vast multitude, his struggling defiance beaten down and overwhelmed by the crushing weight of ignominy, and the torture of his soul revealed on his features. Through all the years when it had been obscured the portrait had acquired an intenser depth and darkness of expression, until it now gloomed forth and threw its evil omen over the present hour. Hutchinson was momentarily arrested, then furious with Alice for her painter's art, her spirit of intrigue, her tricks of stage effects—"Do you think to influence the councils of rulers and the affairs of nations by such shallow contrivances?" he cried. He signed the order for the landing of the troops. These were the British soldiers whose shots made the Boston Massacre; and it was said that years afterward, when Hutchinson was dying in London and crying out that he was choking on the blood of its victims, his features took on the expression of the portrait on the wall.[108]

XIV

The gravitational pull of the earth on the imagination is always powerful, and never more so than when it plays upon the life of someone we love. The intellectualization of Sophia's Cuban years is one of the clearest revelations of his process of thought. It was as if he had said to himself that none of the simple harmonies that he delighted in would do for the problem that was set before him. The velvet romance of Sophia's writing, the dusky tropical scenes, the obvious invitations to the imagination in the color and warmth and strangeness of the setting and characters—all these he set aside for the sake of the intellectual adventure that her Cuban years involved. The story that he wrote for her, launched from her own experiences rather than woven from them, had none of the surface tenderness of his simpler love stories, none of the quiet serenity of the lovely idyll that he wrote for Susan, or the grace and charm of *A Vision of the Fountain.* It is all brains.

As a piece of writing it is inferior to his average work, the texture of its prose rough and jagged, as if hastily written or purposely left unpolished, yet the flight of his imagination, the clear purity of his political thought, the distillation of the crowded inconsequential episodes of Sophia's diary into a concentrated dramatic scene, not directly drawn from it and yet inseparable from it, make it one of the most remarkable stories that Hawthorne ever wrote. Superficially, its tone is cold and detached, and it seems almost without emotion compared to the gentle, caressing prose of his other work, but it has a diamondlike brilliance, the internal gleam that no color can ever quite reproduce, emerging more plainly when it is held up to the light of the source that inspired it.

He had freed his imagination of the humdrum jealousies that Sophia's unguarded words might be expected to evoke; and the feat of transposing Cuba to New England is so brilliant that one can only wonder at it. It was even more brilliant to conceive of the young Cuban aristocrats as colonists at a moment of fateful decision in their country's history. One of the sons of Juan de Zayas was Manuel. He visited the plantation late in the period of Sophia and Mary's stay there. He was aloof, grave, somewhat sedate, a serious young man wearing a monocle and trying with little success to learn English. He was attentive to Mary as Fernando was to Sophia.[109] He became a character of considerable importance in Cuban history. He became a leading figure in the expeditions of Narciso Lopez. On Lopez's third expedition he acted as harbor pilot. Lopez's forces were divided. Colonel Crittenden and the Americans were captured while Lopez escaped to Las Pozas Bay, and fled to the hills where Sophia and Mary had lived. It was presumably at this time that Manuel de Zayas acted as Lopez's second-in-command. In the fighting, the plantation country of Pinar del Rio was devastated. It never recovered its former wealth. The houses were burned, the population fled, the records were destroyed—a century later the population was half what it had been at the time of Sophia's visit. Lopez was killed and Manuel de Zayas disappeared. He reappeared later as second-in-command of the revolution of Manuel de Cespedes. It, too, met disaster, and Manuel de Zayas was imprisoned and, at the end of seven years, shot.[110]

In the story that Hawthorne wrote for Sophia, granting that it was *Edward Randolph's Portrait*, all that she did was restore to its original color a portrait that time had faded. She was a symbol of warning, a good spirit at the council, vainly and almost wordlessly calling upon the strong and the thoughtless to pause. She was innocent of the fierce projects being debated in her absence, yet not wholly ignorant of their meaning; thrust from the council chamber when the hard-visaged men of the world planned crime or war, and yet called back to them in happier moments when the candles were lit and they needed the solace of her charm. It was not only that she had preserved her identity, that she had remained herself, that she had kept her joyous innocence in the midst of their schemes and calculations, wonderful though that was; the greater wonder was that *they* had kept her, they had preserved her, as some living embodiment of what they knew to be good in life. She was the flaw in their granite exterior, their admission of tenderness, hidden away in an upstairs room, exiled to Cuba, but still a part of their life, contradicting its hardness by her very presence.

The women in Hawthorne's stories were often the innocent who seemed to be guilty because of their kinship or their involvement with the guilty, like Alice in *Alice Doane's Appeal*, or Ellen in *Fanshawe*, or Faith in *Young Goodman Brown*. Coming down the stairs of the old house on Charter Street, Sophia had somehow brought Hawthorne's imagination from the past to the present, as if Mrs. Philip English had suddenly walked into the room, vibrant and good-natured on the eve of her trial for witchcraft, and told him that the dramas of the past were daily re-enacted before his eyes.

XV

A strange, hesitant friendship, far more delicate and tenuous than the relationships of plantation life, grew up among the four women, Ebie and Louisa Hawthorne and Sophia and Mary Peabody. It seemed at times that Mary and Sophia were trying to encourage the friendship of Hawthorne for their older sister; and that Ebie and Louisa in turn, while welcoming the growing friendship of Hawthorne for either Mary or Sophia, or for both of them, and being cordial toward them both, were cool nevertheless toward Elizabeth, not in their personal feeling toward her, but in so far as her intimacy with Hawthorne grew. In this intricate tangle of feminine feelings, which threatened to become so hopelessly snarled that only a complete separation could remedy them, Ebie Hawthorne was the key. Mary sent her notes:

Dear Elizabeth:

Shall we go to the beach? If so, I propose that we set off instantly. I think a sea breeze would be most refreshing this afternoon.

Truly yours,

M. T. P.

Don't forget to ask your brother.[111]

Sophia could not often walk with them. She came to know Ebie Hawthorne later than the others. She walked one afternoon to the Hawthornes' house in Herbert Street. Louisa came to the door and took her upstairs. She did not expect to see Ebie, who did not know that she was coming. "I asked for her immediately, and Louisa said that she would be there in a few minutes! . . . She received me very affectionately, and seemed very glad to see me; and I all at once fell in love with her. I think her eyes are very beautiful and I liked the expression of her taper hands. I stayed in the house an hour! I could not get away; she urged me to stay so much, as if she wanted me . . . She spoke of Wordsworth and Coleridge, and surprised me by saying that she admired Pope. We talked about the sea, and the winds, and various things. . . . I think I should love her very much. I believe it is extreme sensibility which makes her a hermitress. It was difficult to meet her eyes; and I wanted to, because they are uncommonly beautiful. She said tulips were her favorite flower, and she did not wonder that a thousand pounds had formerly been given for a bulb! So I determined that she should have a gorgeous bunch of them as soon as I could procure any."

Elizabeth Peabody from West Newton sent Hawthorne a gift and a bouquet of flowers. Sophia added a bunch of tulips for Ebie and carried them to the Hawthorne house. Sophia had touched Ebie in a vulnerable spot; the tulips hurt her, and opened some secret passage to her heart that she had thought hidden. Days passed before she answered or acknowledged them. Meanwhile she kept the flowers that Elizabeth had sent her brother. Hawthorne professed to believe the love of flowers was not a masculine trait and so, Ebie said, "I permitted him to look at them, and consider them as a gift to myself, and beg you to thank her, in my name, when you write." Ebie wrote with the effortless cadence of her brother. She had the same characteristic rhythm in her phrases, a pause, a long gliding stroke, and a modulated, subdued ending, not quite a dying fall: the tulips, she said, she kept " as long as possible and looked at them almost continually, till, in defiance of my efforts to preserve them, they faded." But it had been so long since she had written to anyone that she had forgotten how to write. She did not know if Sophia could read the scrawl she sent her. The thermometer stood at 98° in the shade after four in the afternoon; it was too hot for her to walk, which, except for reading, was almost her only pleasure.[112]

Hawthorne loved her. She was closer to him than anyone, and more like him, and though his relationship with Louisa was lighter and more bantering, he respected Ebie's intelligence and deferred to her opinions of people. In these weeks of early summer she moved among the Peabody girls in a way that left no doubt as to which of them she favored. When she called at their house, to go walking with Mary, she stopped first at Sophia's chamber. She seemed well pleased with it "but especially admired the elm tree outside." [113]

With Mrs. Peabody Ebie walked to the Cold Spring. This was one of Hawthorne's favorite walks. Mrs. Peabody had many of the characteristics of her daughter, Elizabeth. Like Elizabeth, she concealed from Sophia the problems of the family, only to overwhelm her suddenly with their tragic urgency. Like Elizabeth, too, she was domineering in a feminine, maternal way, implanting her own rigid appraisals on her children.

With Ebie Hawthorne she searched for wild flowers at Cold Spring, finding violets and anemones and a few columbines. They met Mr. John King and his daughter there, also looking for wild flowers. Mrs. Peabody introduced them: Miss Hawthorne hung her head and scarcely answered, and did not open her lips again. Miss Augusta King was a typical converser among many who talked well. There was a charm in her conversation, it glowed, it sparkled, it rolled in a deep channel, or rippled like a brook when sunshine lies lovingly on it.[114] Mr. King walked home with them. He gave Mrs. Peabody some columbines. He put some of them in Miss Hawthorne's hand, saying, "I must make your bunch like Mrs. Peabody's, my dear." These visits and walks Sophia described to her sister in long, impulsive letters. It was a journal of the family life comparable to the one she had kept in Cuba.

It was also a record of dull pain whose interruption was the occasional visit of Hawthorne. Always, she said, she tried to penetrate the mystery of pain. Sometimes in the evenings her headaches ceased, and she seemed to be let down from a great height into a quiet green valley, worn out, as if she had fought a fight all day and had got through.

On one such evening, as she lay down after tea, Hawthorne appeared. He arrived in the way Fernando had appeared at the plantation —unexpectedly, though he walked where Fernando always rode and his manner was direct, even a little brusque, where the Spaniard had been all gallantry and exaggeration. Sophia had made a tiny painting of a forget-me-not. He took it to Boston, and had it set in gold under black crystal and made into a brooch. She wore it constantly. One evening he stopped by and asked for it. She brought it to him. He studied it, and remarked that if he did not like it so much he could wear it better.[115]

It seems to be literally true that at this period all the girls in Salem were beautiful. There was one famous wedding at which every woman present was beautiful; and to be handsome was almost a birthright. They would not grow old, they would not grow ugly, and time seemed only to change lovely girls into lovely ladies. There were at least twenty of remarkable beauty, and twenty more so charming they would have been conspicuous anywhere else. "Their style of conversation was rather ambitious," said Marianne Silsbee, "and I really think—but perhaps it would be better not to say what I think." [116]

They mastered Latin and Greek, or studied Hebrew, as Sophia did for a time, for recreation. They wrote of nature with genuine ardor: "The dear blessed green Mother Earth, and the budding trees waiting to be so bountiful to us, and the millions of flowers all ready to burst forth—and then the June sunshine, and moonlight, and roses, and sweet south wind!" They respected their ancestors' hardihood, but "I am fit for nothing but to be a descendant," said Mary Foote. They did not much approve of causes and crusades—they thought abolitionists should be married to southern girls. Winters they often traveled south, and in the summers went over a route that was becoming fashionable, to Quebec, up the St. Lawrence and over the Great Lakes, and home after a stop at Saratoga. There were as many as forty balls a season in Salem—Mrs. Crowninshield's, Mrs. Barstow's, Mrs. Forrester's, and all through the mansions of the town.[117]

There was the Salem Quintette and the Mozart Club. Mrs. Nathaniel Silsbee gave a tea each week, which ten ladies who lived permanently in the town regularly attended. Ten visitors in town, a different group each week, also attended. They wrote witty letters to each other, trying to characterize their friends. They really were brilliant. Mary White, who learned the alphabet at the age of two (from a cotton handkerchief on which the letters were stamped) and who, after she married Caleb Foote, reviewed books for the Salem *Gazette* while she raised his children and canned tomatoes, seemed to exemplify them. Marianne Silsbee was wittier. They had a kind of adoration for Elizabeth Hoar, and consciously modeled themselves on her. She had been engaged to Charles Emerson, who died on the eve of their marriage—Elizabeth the Wise, Emerson called her, with an extraordinary fineness of perception, and her unswerving balance of mind joined with entire openness to ideas. "She has the clearest head, the soundest common sense, with the most exquisite fancy, the most charming way of saying things; the most lovely manners, full of dignity and grace, and she never says anything that is not worth hearing."

They met in Sophia's studio, where Sophia was working on a medallion of Charles Emerson. The medallion was an exquisitely beautiful thing. By some strange oversight, they did not notice the developing romance of Sophia and Hawthorne. Mrs. Caleb Foote was one of Sophia's close friends, and her husband was a friend of Hawthorne's; both had the greatest admiration for his work. Yet neither knew that Hawthorne and Sophia were interested in each other. Among people who prided themselves on their perceptions and who knew everything, the secretiveness of Hawthorne and Sophia was an accomplishment that would have done credit to a pair of secret agents. Sometimes, it is true, Mary Foote noticed that Sophia grew silent in company, and seemed preoccupied and withdrawn and pale. She wondered about it, but did not dare ask her, fearing she had said something that distressed her.[118]

Sophia had begun to recover, magically, like a character in one of Hawthorne's stories released from a dungeon by love. Small and graceful, with blue eyes with rather large pupils, she had an invalid's strength, a fragile tirelessness; she abounded in exertions in search of health and happiness that stronger people could never have undertaken. Her chestnut-brown hair was fine and abundant, and glinted like sunlight on a pool. She brushed it for an hour every morning, letting the world and her household wait until she finished her rite of peace and recollection. She seldom laughed aloud. She often smiled and she often half-laughed, just as she was sometimes half angry, half vehement, half impulsive, half prudent, and in her quick, vivid, feminine insights almost a genius. Thought with her flowed at once into action, spontaneous and right, a letter, a gift, a flower, and her feminine freedom from analysis left the joyous manners of her girlhood intact. Her half-laugh, unforced and unexpected, would not have startled a bird. Delighted, she threw her head back sideways, raising her hand with its back to her lips for a moment in a frisky, childlike gesture.

In her growing happiness her days brightened. She awakened in the morning and saw a gardener appear to work in the shrubbery around the house. He was dressed in broadcloth and wearing a cambric cravat. He disappeared into the barn, and returned after several minutes transformed into a very dirty workman, though with a distinguished air and manner, and continued to talk about the shrubs growing around the gravestones in very courtly phrases. Ellen Barstow appeared bringing a crimson rose. Ellen was about eleven. Hawthorne did not quite like his cousin Nancy's child as she grew older—he told Sophia that he thought Ellen was not natural. Sophia was lying down, so Ellen left, to return with another child at teatime. They entered with their hands concealed and gleaming faces, and when they were within reach thrust their hands toward her face, each adorned with a crimson rose.[119]

The girls of Salem had overlooked Sophia and Hawthorne. They had probably never really liked his works. "It is a pity," Marianne Silsbee said, "that Hawthorne did not love the town about which he wrote such beautiful stories. The shy, heroic spinister and little Annie, in the charming freedom of childhood, walking by his side through the old Main Street, with look and word ask us to forget his lack of appreciation, and so with our whole hearts we forgive him, in consideration of what he has done for us." [120]

His stories were not for them. They liked Reverend Upham, Catherine Sedgwick, Emerson (with reservations), Channing, Carlyle, the English romantic poets, and the brilliant young ministers of New England. They enjoyed books like William Peabody's wonderful little biography of Alexander Wilson, the first American ornithologist. Wilson was a Scottish weaver, one of the first proletarian poets, tall, red-headed and awkward, who settled in Pennsylvania, intending to teach school, but became fascinated with the songs and colors of the birds of the woods, and began tramping after them, from Vermont to South Carolina. Forever climbing trees and plunging into swamps, Wilson mystified the people, who thought he must be an English spy.[121] That was the sort of book Salem enjoyed. When the going became rougher, when Thoreau turned his microscopic attention to the woods closer home, they did not enjoy it so much. They could see the humor of Thoreau's setting out for a week on the Concord River as soberly and as self-importantly as if setting out in search of the North Pole—but after all, it was a week in a rowboat on a quiet stream, and their fathers had sailed around the world.

CHAPTER FIVE

I

$\mathcal{A}$t 11:30 p.m., July 12, 1838, the public powder magazine at Pittsfield, Massachusetts, exploded. It was demolished. Two dwellings were wrecked. The town hall was badly damaged. The medical school was damaged, as was the Baptist church. The windows of twenty houses were shattered. No one was killed.

It is impossible to say positively that Hawthorne had any direct interest in the explosion. He probably investigated it. In Pittsfield the authorities made no progress in solving the crime. A public meeting was called on July 19; and there was great excitement and indignation in the little mountain town.[1] On July 21, Hawthorne set out for Pittsfield. He stopped by the Peabodys' to say good-bye to Sophia. He told her that he would be away for three months. He said that he was not going to write or be written to; his destination was secret. Since he would not travel under his own name, if he should die on the journey it would be impossible to locate his grave. Mary Peabody came into the room. She asked Hawthorne to keep a journal of his trip. After some thought he said that he believed he would.[2]

He took the stage to Boston and caught the afternoon train to Worcester. He stayed overnight at the Temperance House. An old gentleman from Boston tried to make his acquaintance, questioning him about his age, his name, and his married status. Hawthorne answered him with civility but without giving him any information. At 9:30 the following morning Hawthorne caught the stage to Northampton. He studied the driver and other passengers—two good-looking women, a grocer and his son, a patent medicine peddler, the dark irascible driver.

Between one and two in the morning the stage left Northampton. There were now three other passengers with Hawthorne. In the darkness their features were invisible and they rode on for some hours, saying nothing. Glancing outside the coach, Hawthorne could see the gleam

of the lanterns on wayside objects. Beyond the road lay the forest, so
desolate in the darkness that it seemed one step within its wild, tangled,
many-stemmed and dark-shadowed verge and one would be lost forever.
Sometimes the coach passed a lonely house. Sometimes it rumbled
through a village where the drowsy postmaster appeared, in shirts and
pantaloons, to receive the mail.

The morning air grew cooler. The faces of the passengers grew
partially visible as dawn came on to cloudy day. The road wound
through mountain country, with a stream flowing on one side, bordered
by a bank so steep that the pines growing on it had slipped into the
chasm. The carriage rattled along at ten miles an hour, approaching
within two or three feet of the edge of the precipice. At Windsor, the
highest point on the road, Hawthorne could see for miles over the mountains—a terrible bare bleak spot, with no woods to shelter it, fit only
for sheep. The air grew warmer as they descended the mountain, and he
could see the sunlight shining on the landscape ahead while the stage
was still in chillness and gloom.

He reached Pittsfield in the forenoon. His room at the Berkshire
Hotel was a narrow crib overlooking a back courtyard.* Through the
window he could watch a young man and a boy drawing water for the
maid servants and could listen to their jokes. The town was crowded,
the hotel busy, the bar well patronized. Guests and idlers lounged on the
hotel gallery, watching the stages arrive and depart. Hawthorne noted
the luggage, huge trunks and bandboxes, the courtesy shown the ladies,
the dull looks of the passengers who had ridden all night.[3]

The happenings at Pittsfield were extraordinary. This was the
home town of his old college president, William Allen. It was a town
of four thousand inhabitants. It stood at the headwaters of the Housatonic, on the rim of the Berkshires, near the border of New York State,
thirty miles from Albany and twenty-five miles from Vermont. It was
a manufacturing center, by the standards of the time, with cotton and
woolen mills built at the inlet of Pontoosuc Lake and on the falls on the
east and west branches of the Housatonic. It was the largest private
arms manufacturing center in the United States.

* There is no evidence that he was not traveling alone. The Berkshire
Athenaeum, at Pittsfield, at my request, examined the registers of the
Berkshire Hotel, and reported that it was unable to locate Hawthorne's
registration, although other material of historical interest turned up in the
process of the search.

The public powder magazine was located on the northeast corner of the public square, adjoining the old burial ground. Pittsfield was a crossroads. Mountain walls hemmed it in, generally extending like a rampart on all sides, with isolated great hills rising here and there in the outline. The roads to Boston, Albany, Williamstown, and Stockbridge intersected at the village square, in the center of which stood the Old Elm, its stem rising a hundred feet into the air without a leaf or branch upon it. Two years before the square had been improved, and lindens and slippery elm planted around the old and famous tree. Along the four roads radiating out of town were the houses of the old settlers, whose ancient rivalries reached back to the Revolution, to Shays' Rebellion, to the War of 1812, and now flared again in the strange premonitory outbreaks that foreshadowed the Civil War.

The road to central Massachusetts and Boston rose steeply eastward, its highest point only three miles away. South over the high widening plain were Lenox and Stockbridge. North at the end of the narrow valley that funneled into the mountains lay North Adams, where the new factories were built in small clearings in the forest. A few miles on was Williamstown, where Williams College had been a conservative stronghold for a generation. The hills that surrounded them made each of these towns a natural fortress. An army holding them could cut off New England from the rest of the country.

Stores and hotels ringed the public square in Pittsfield. The Berkshire Hotel, where the stages stopped, was a famous inn, its history going back to the bitter period, not many years before, when there had been one hotel for Federalists and one for Democrats, different stores for each party, different factories, and even different roads. The residences of the old settlers, principally Connecticut men and almost all strict Congregationlists, were simple, well built, distinguished for their fine lines and superb carpenter work, white wooden dwellings, as a rule, with big yards shaded by Lombardy poplars and buttonwood trees.

At the time of the explosion there was a dilapitated old mill in the adjacent town of Coltsville, and not far away a 40-foot factory building in which rooms and power were leased. Carpenter planes were made in one room, buttons in another, wheel hubs in one, and lead pipe in a fourth. There was a tinware shop near the square. On Onota Brook there was a small plant manufacturing carpenter tools. There was an old grist mill on Shaker Brook, and at the foot of Mount Osceola, on the southwest branch of the Housatonic, there was a small wooden mill built for grinding plaster of Paris brought from Nova Scotia.

There were six large mills in Pittsfield, but one of them, a four-story brick factory on the west branch of the Housatonic, was closed.

The outstanding man among Pittsfield's manufacturers was Lemuel Pomeroy. It was his gunshop that made Pittsfield an armament center. He was a commanding figure, cool and courageous, with firm, determined features, imperious and self-asserting, but farsighted and clearheaded, resolute to have the controlling voice in such enterprises as he entered, which were many. His ancestors were blacksmiths and gunsmiths; for seven generations there had always been a Pomeroy at the anvil. In 1799, when he was twenty-one, Lemuel Pomeroy built his blacksmith shop in Pittsfield. He carried over the mountains from Southampton the same anvil that his ancestor had carried up the Connecticut River from Windsor to Southampton. He did general blacksmithing and built wagons, sleighs and plows, until his shop burned in 1805. Thereafter he manufactured muskets exclusively, and for thirty years had a contract with the government, renewed every five years, for two thousand muskets a year.

Pomeroy was just and resolute, unbending, admired and respected rather than liked. His fellow townsmen said that there would have been no living with Lemuel Pomeroy if it had not been that he was almost always right. No one ever did more for the village. He invested his growing fortune in the companies that were organized, carrying them over the periods of depression before their earnings began; and though in return he exacted the decisive influence in their councils, his advice was sound enough to justify his claim to leadership. Meanwhile, though he was Pittsfield's one man of considerable wealth, his intellectual and social influence was negligible. When he had been a Federalist, the minister of his Congregationalist church, Thomas Allen, William Allen's father, a zealous Jeffersonian Democrat, preached vehement political sermons from the pulpit. When the Federalists attempted to start a new church and secure a minister who would not outrage their political convictions, they were excommunicated. The conflict divided Pittsfield for years. When Lemuel Pomeroy read the local paper, the Pittsfield *Sun,* he found vigorous Democratic pronouncements on every page. The worst period of this bitter quarrel was over, but its animosities remained, smoldering like the fires that burned in the limestone kilns in the mountains near to⸱n.

In 1826 Pomeroy bought the United States Cantonment grounds in Pittsfield for $760, removed the barracks, and erected three brick buildings which were used by his son-in-law for a seminary for young men. Ten years later the school was converted into the Maplewood Young Ladies' Institute. It was fashionable and successful, and its young ladies highly popular; it was said of the institute that many more desired to enter its dormitories than were able to get in. There were few affairs in Pittsfield that Lemuel Pomeroy was not interested in— the bank, the turnpikes, the agitation for a railroad—and few happenings that did not immediately affect him and his properties.

In the summer of 1838 a group of nocturnal prowlers, unindentified, but believed to include the sons of prominent families, tore down fences, removed gates, and were guilty of other annoyances. They had somehow secured keys to the powder magazine and stolen an unknown amount of powder. Musket fire and small-arms fire began to sound occasionally in the darkness. It continued until it became incessant, night after night. The authorities appeared to be unable to prevent it. Some time before July 4, 1838, the malefactors had stolen and hidden one of the pieces of artillery belonging to the state—the famous Pittsfield regiment, the Berkshire Grays, had been disbanded two years before. On the night of July 7, one of the cannon was planted opposite Lemuel Pomeroy's home, loaded to the muzzle, and discharged.

Pomeroy lived on East Street. Walking from the square toward his home, one passed the meetinghouse, the town house, the print shop of the Pittsfield *Sun*, a private dwelling, and the home that had been built by the Reverend Thomas Allen, Pittsfield's first minister. Allen was the Democrat whose zealous Jeffersonian sermons and writings had split his congregation a generation before. Pomeroy's house was directly across the street from Allen's. It was a beautiful rectangular building, three stories high, with windows across the front and interior fireplaces, set back behind a picket fence upon landscaped and shaded grounds. Two houses beyond was the large square house of Thomas Gold, whose daughter married Nathan Appleton, and whose granddaughter, Frances Appleton, was soon to marry Henry Wadsworth Longfellow.

The cannon that was discharged on the night of July 7 had been overloaded. Instead of blowing up Pomeroy's house, the cannon itself blew up. It was ruined. Pomeroy's house and that of his neighbor were considerably damaged. Pomeroy appealed to the Adjutant General of Massachusetts, General Henry A. S. Dearborn, of Salem, asking that the remaining pieces of artillery be removed, and at his request they were ordered to Boston.* The atmosphere in Pittsfield grew increasingly tense.

When word spread that Pomeroy had asked that the artillery be moved, a threat was mysteriously circulated through town. It was that the public powder magazine would be blown up if the cannon were taken away. The magazine had contained seven hundred pounds of gunpowder, though the explosion may have prevented an accounting that would have revealed how much had been stolen. Four hundred of the seven hundred pounds were government property, used in testing the muskets manufactured in Pomeroy's armory. No guards were placed at the powder magazine, despite the warning, and at half an hour before midnight, in the hot July midsummer, the slow fuse attached to the gunpowder burned down.[4]

II

What had this to do with Hawthorne? If it had nothing to do with him, his conduct was certainly odd. On the other hand, he behaved strangely if he was actually investigating the explosion or the events in connection with it; he asked no questions, and made no direct attempt, apparently, to find out what had happened. Yet the secrecy of his journey, the strange way he traveled, and his close observation of strangers in the countryside indicate that he had a conscious purpose he could not reveal and which he feared would be discovered.

He saw Horatio Bridge shortly before leaving Boston, having lunch with him on board the sloop of war *Cyane,* which had just returned from the Mediterranean. (He read the bound files of the *United States Service Journal* before seeing Bridge.) His memorial essay on Jonathan Cilley was in the hands of the editors of the *American Monthly Magazine.* There is no evidence, however, to indicate that there was any connection between his article on Cilley and his flight. It was

* This correspondence has disappeared from the files of the Adjutant General's office.

a courageous piece of writing, but not such as would have been likely to get him assassinated. He might have been trapped into a duel because of it, though it is doubtful, after the intense feeling about Cilley's death, that the only people who would have fought about it—Graves, Wise, and their partisans—would risk another right then. Hawthorne went further than anyone else in his denunciation of Wise and Graves ; he also differed from others in putting Cilley's second in the same category with them.

The rebellion in Canada may be considered as a possible influence in the case. The Canadian rebels were at that time storing arms and munitions in preparation for a major uprising in December. If information of it had reached the authorities, the powder stored at Pittsfield and the output of Pomeroy's factory would of course be considered a potential source of supply. Pomeroy may have refused to supply the rebels—something like that. He did not believe in the private manufacture of arms, and later testified in favor of the government arsenal at Springfield at Congressional hearings. When it was established, he abandoned his own gun factory. It is doubtful if Hawthorne would have left any trace of his mission, if he had one. Yet if he had already begun his duties with the customs service, and if arms were then being smuggled over the border—as they were—he might have followed precisely this course, establishing himself at a crossroads on the road to Canada and studying the people who passed by. There is now no way to determine the point except to consider what he did.

He ate lunch at the hotel in Pittsfield, on the day of his arrival, and rested in his room. About sunset a heavy thunderstorm came up. Rain fell and the thunder rumbled round and round the mountain wall. The clouds stretched from rampart to rampart. When the rain abated the clouds all over the heavens were tinted with the light from the setting sun, the lower clouds purple and gold, the higher ones gray. The slender curve of the new moon was visible, heightening the fading brightness of the sunny part of the sky.

The explosion had blown down the door of a tomb across the square. When the rain stopped, Hawthorne left the hotel and went to the burying ground. It was now quite dark. He stopped at a tomb opening into the side of a grassy mound. On its crest stood a marble obelisk. The door of the tomb, broken down by the force of the explosion, was incompletely repaired. He peeped in at the crevices. There were three

coffins within, all with white mold on top. One, a small child's, rested
on top of another. The other coffin was on the opposite side of the tomb.
The lid was considerably displaced. It was too dark for Hawthorne to
see either a corpse or a skeleton. The tomb was that of the Reverend
Thomas Allen, the first minister of Pittsfield, deceased in 1811, the
father of President William Allen of Bowdoin.

Hawthorne caught the eight o'clock stage the following morning.
He bought his ticket to Williamstown, but when the stage reached
North Adams, the stop before Williamstown, he dismounted, and regis-
tered at the Whig Tavern.

He arrived on Thursday. On Friday he walked out to find a place
to bathe. A stream flowed through the town from the mountains. It was
a wild highland rivulet, sometimes flowing through forest where the trees
were dark and erect, as when the Indians fished there, brawling and
tumbling and eddying over its rock-strewn current. It passed at the base
of cliffs hundreds of feet high, down which, by heavy rains or the melt-
ing snows, great pine trees had slid or tumbled headlong. The factories
were built along the stream. The girls looked out the windows to watch
the stages pass, their heads averted from the machinery. The boardinghouses for the mill girls were built beside the mills, long buildings, two
or three stories high. Some of them had bean vines growing around the
door. He walked along the stream, through a stretch of wilderness, and
then to the site of one of the factories, the girls staring from the windows, the two or three boardinghouses at the edge of the woods. It
seemed strange to him that the wild stream had been tamed to the purposes of men, making cottons and woolens, sawing boards and marble
and giving employment to so many men and girls. In a secluded spot
he found a place to bathe. The stream was deep enough to cover him as
he lay at length. He kept a careful memorandum of how often he bathed
—sometimes every day, sometimes every other day, occasionally once
a week.[5]

The tavern was more than a meeting place. It was formerly the
Old Black Tavern, a three-story brick building with eight-foot piazzas
on each story. It was owned by Alpheus and Orrin Smith, who had
opened it in 1836.[6] Orrin Smith was a widower of forty, with a twelve-
year-old son and infant twins. He was a dry jester, a sharp, shrewd
Yankee, with a Yankee's license of honesty. Smith sometimes drank
more than enough, and had peccadillos with the fair sex. He was a tall,

thin, hard-featured, pipe-smoking man, with a sly expression of almost hidden, grave humor, as if there was some deviltry pretty constantly in his mind. His inn was the center of Whig life. The long, many-pillared piazza in front was crowded with loungers watching the stages come and go.

Saturday morning was cloudy. All the near landscape lay unsunned. There was sunshine in the distant tracts in the valleys and in specks on the mountaintops. Mount Graylock looked somber and angry with the heavy gray mist overhead. From the height Hawthorne could see, between the ridges of the hills, long, wide, hollow valleys, extending for miles and miles, with houses scattered along them. He met an occasional wayfarer, a doctor, and two decent, brown-visaged country women in a wagon. He had already learned that there were seven doctors in North Adams. He met an underwitted old man on the road, gray, bald-headed, wrinkled, decently dressed, wearing leather shoes, and carrying his coat over one arm and his umbrella on the other, who insisted on shaking hands with him. He said he was a friend of mankind. Hawthorne was a little reluctant to shake hands with him, for fear his hands were dirty. The old man was on his way to visit a widow in the neighborhood. He asked Hawthorne if he was married. He waved his umbrella and gesticulated strongly; to add to his natural foolishness, he had been drinking. His manner was full of quirks and quips and eccentricities. His wife had been dead seven years. His children owned a circus. When he found Hawthorne was not married, he recommended him a certain maid who owned three hundred acres of ground. He gave Hawthorne a message to his sons in case they should ever meet, and then went on his way, shouting to Hawthorne to remember his message, while Hawthorne shouted back a request to be remembered to the widow.

On Sunday morning Hawthorne went down to the barroom and out on the gallery. The morning was bright and cheerful. A few loungers were sitting on the porch. A disagreeable figure, barefooted, dressed in a pair of homespun pantaloons and a very dirty shirt, approached the stoop. He was of waning middle age. One of his feet had been maimed by an ax. His arm had been amputated two or three inches below the elbow. His beard was of a week's growth, grim and grizzly. A huge dog followed him. He had been a handsome man in his prime, though he was now so beastly that no living thing except his dog would touch him without an effort. He said, "Good morning, gentlemen."

No one answered. At last one of the loungers said, "I don't know who you speak to—not me, I'm sure." He meant that he did not claim to be a gentleman.

"Why, I thought you'd all speak at once," said the stranger, laughing.

He sat down on the lowest step of the stoop. One of the men remarked on his bare feet. The stranger spoke of losing his toes by the glancing aside of an ax. He told of the grim fortitude with which he bore the pain, and from that began to speak of the pain of losing his arm. He set his teeth and drew his breath as he said that the pain was dreadful. There was a strange expression of remembered agony when he spoke of the pain of cutting the muscles and the particular agony at one moment when the bone was being cut asunder. He had borne the pain like an Indian; one of the men on the porch had observed him.

Hawthorne asked him if he still felt the hand that had been amputated. He replied that he did, always. His name was Haynes. He began to talk to Hawthorne about phrenology. He spoke with sense and acuteness, and with something of elevation in his manner—a studied elevation, perhaps—and with courtesy; but his sense had something out of the way in it, something wild and ruined and desperate. In his deep degradation there was something of the gentleman and man of intellect, an acuteness and trained judgment bespeaking a mind strong and cultivated. "My study is man," he said. And looking steadily at Hawthorne, "I do not know your name," he said, "but there is something of the hawk eye about you too."

Haynes had formerly been a lawyer. Drinking had reduced him to his present estate. He looked at the stump of his arm. "That hand could make a pen go fast," he said. When he lost his arm, people advised him to depend on public support. He said that if he lost the other arm he could still support himself and a barkeep. "The pain of the mind is a thousand times greater than the pain of the body," he said.

There was a dead horse near his house. He said he could not bear the smell of it. The stage agent remarked, "I should think you could not smell carrion in that house." Haynes dropped his head, with a little snort, as if his feelings were hurt; but immediately said that he took it in good part. He was a soapmaker. The offals used in that business gave an evil smell to his domicile. Squire Drury, a lawyer, said to him

FIRST CHURCH AND THE TOWN PUMP

THE CHILDREN OF JOHN AND CHARLOTTE STORY FORRESTER
(Portrait by Frothingham)

"I do but hold out my hand, and like some bright bird in the summer air, with her blue silk frock fluttering upwards from her white pantalets, she comes bounding across the street."—Hawthorne, of five-year-old Annie Marion Forrester.

SOPHIA AMELIA PEABODY   REVEREND CHARLES UPHAM

Reverend Charles Upham, minister of the First Church, authority on witchcraft, a brilliant biographer, and Hawthorne's political enemy.

Illustration from *The American Magazine,* during Hawthorne's editorship.

kindly, "You and I would have died long ago if we had not had the courage to live."

The others drifted away from the stoop. Hawthorne and Haynes continued to talk. The dog grew impatient to be gone. He thrust himself between Haynes's legs, rolled over on his back, seized his ragged trousers or playfully took his maimed bare foot in his mouth. At last Haynes said he must go and dress and shave—his beard had been a week growing and it might take a week to get rid of it. He rose from the stoop and went on his way, forlorn and miserable in the light of the cheerful summer Sunday morning, yet keeping his spirits up, preserving himself a man among men, asking nothing from them.[7]

III

The only concrete evidence that Hawthorne considered his tasks official is a notation in his notebooks that one morning he was occupied with an affair of stealing. A woman of forty was accused of having stolen a needle case and other trifles from a factory girl at a boarding-house. She came to the tavern to take passage on the stage. She was detained, and Squire Putnam, the justice of the peace, examined her. He had her searched by Laura, the chamber maid, and Eliza Chaseboro, the waitress. She protested. Her protests were taken as an indication of guilt, and she was searched regardless of them. The search was done with much fun and some sympathy. Eliza and Laura searched her from head to foot, inside and out, and found nothing that they sought. The woman gave up a pair of pantalettes, which she pretended she had taken by mistake.

She was left in the parlor of the inn. Hawthorne went in to question her. She was yellow, thin and battered, but with a country-ladylike aspect and manners. She began to talk to Hawthorne at once about the whole affair, speaking with great fluency and self-possession. She had the bitterness of a wronged person, and a sparkling eye.

Hawthorne went to his room. It was so near the back that he could hear the girls talking under his window. Eliza was telling another girl what had happened. She thought the poor woman's reluctance to be searched came from the poorness of her wardrobe and the contents of her hatbox. As they parted, Eliza said, "What do you think I heard somebody say about you? That it was enough to make anybody's eyes

start square out of their head, to look at such red cheeks as yours."
The other girl turned off the compliment with a laugh, and took her
leave.

Two pages of the careful notebook that Hawthorne kept of his
journey had been torn out and are lost. Since so much of the remainder
is closely detailed observation of the countryside, and the people, it is
possible that they contained references to the essential reason for his
trip. On the Tuesday following his arrival at North Adams he began
exploring Hudson's Brook. It wound through the town of North Adams,
falling swiftly, and providing power for the mills along its banks. Beyond the last factory it curved into the woods, and into a chasm, fifty
or sixty feet deep, cut into the marble. The cave was irregular, with
jutting buttresses, moss grown, with impending crags and tall trees
over it, their roots concealed from an observer in the depths, so they
seemed suspended in the open air. The marble had once arched over
the chasm. The roof had fallen, and fragments of marble were strewn
over the floor. The stream flowed crookedly through it. Boulders and
driftwood made obstructions so steep they made it hard to explore, and
occasional deep pools increased the difficulty. The deepest pool was in
the most uneven part of the cave. The bottom of the pool was covered
with soft stuff that made wading through it difficult; Hawthorne took
off his trousers and waded up to his middle in trying to explore it. He
reached the most interesting part of the cavern. The marks of the water
were cut into the marble walls of the cave. While Hawthorne was there
he heard voices. A small stone tumbled down the chasm. Looking up
from the depth he saw two or three men on the crags overhead. The
stone must have landed pretty close—"not liking to be to them the most
curious part of the spectacle," Hawthorne waded back and put on his
clothes.

He went repeatedly to Hudson's Cave. July passed. He had formed
no close acquaintances, but was still sitting in the tavern, listening to
the talk of the villagers. In the evening he sat on the stoop, silent and
observant from under the brim of his hat. One acquaintance was Dr.
Bob Robinson, stout, tall, round paunched, red faced, brutal looking,
who got drunk daily. He sat on the stoop, looking surly and speaking
to nobody; then got up and walked homeward, with a slight unevenness
of track, attended by a fine Newfoundland dog.

On August 10 Hawthorne attended the funeral of a child. There was an assemblage of people in a plain, homely apartment, most of the men in their ordinary clothes and one or two in their shirt sleeves. The coffin was placed in the midst of the mourners, covered with a velvet pall. A storm came up. The lightning flashed through the gloomy room, and the thunder rumbled among the surrounding hills. A Baptist minister prayed and read a passage of Scripture, alluding to the thunder as God's voice.

A few days later—August 25—there was another funeral, this one of a boy about ten years old. His coffin was laid in a wagon among some straw. As the funeral passed, a few men formed a brief procession in front of the coffin. Orrin Smith and Hawthorne joined them. They walked down the main street of North Adams to the old burying ground on a round hill, planted with cypresses. The grave was dug on the steep slope of the hill. The gravedigger was waiting there with two or three other men, leaning against the trees.

The procession approached the grave. The mother and father stood weeping at the upper end of the grave, the mother weeping with stifled violence. Orrin helped lift the coffin from the wagon and lowered it into the grave. Some earth had fallen into it, and the coffin was lifted again and the superflous earth removed with a hoe. Then it was lowered for the last time. The mother peeped forth to see why the coffin was raised up again. Orrin strewed some straw upon it—"the clods on the coffin-lid have an ugly sound." The Baptist minister whispered to the father. He removed his hat. The spectators did the same. He thanked them, "in the name of the mourners, for this last act of kindness to them."

"After the funeral I took a walk on the Williamstown road, towards the West. There had been a heavy shower in the afternoon, and clouds were scattered all over the sky—around Graylock and everywhere else. Those over the hills in the west, were the most splendid in purple and gold that I have ever seen—and there being a haze, it added inconceivably to their majesty and dusky significance."

The village viewed from the top of a hill, at sunset, had a peculiarly happy and peaceful look. It lay on a level surrounded by hills, and seemed as if it lay in the hollow of a large hand. He could see Union Village, the mill town, extending up a gorge of a hill. The rush of the streams came up the hill somewhat like the sound of a city. Sometimes he could hear the notes of a horn or bugle, sounding afar among the passes of the mountains, announcing the coming of the stagecoach from Bennington, or Troy, or Greenfield, or Pittsfield.[8]

He had found an intermediate place where the business of life did not intrude, where the passing moment lingered and became truly the present.[9] Hawthorne's thoughts on death were clear and somber. He had written of death in two of his finest stories, *The Haunted Mind* and *The Wives of the Dead*. In the depths of every heart, he thought, there is a tomb and a dungeon, though the lights, the music, and the revelry above may cause us to forget their existence and the buried ones, as prisoners, whom they hide. But sometimes, and oftenest at midnight, these dark receptacles are flung wide open. In an hour like this, when the mind has a passive sensibility but no active strength, when the imagination is a mirror, imparting vividness to all ideas, without the power of selecting or controlling them, "then pray that your griefs may slumber and the brotherhood of remorse not break the chain."

The heart never breaks at its first grave;[10] but the thought of the dead lying in their cold shrouds and narrow coffins, through the drear winter of death, was so powerful that the haunted mind could not be persuaded that they did not shiver as night settled on the town, the hills, and the burying ground where the white tombstone loomed between the cypresses. It might be that at the moment after death the soul rejoiced like a sleeper awakening from a troubled dream. It might be that our lives were like an hour of wakefulness at night, when yesterday has vanished among the shadows of the past and tomorrow has not yet emerged from the future. In such an hour of silent wakefulness, as in life itself, "you emerge from a mystery, pass through a vicissitude that you can but imperfectly control, and are borne onward to another mystery. Now comes the peal of a distant clock, with fainter and fainter strokes as you plunge deeper into the wilderness of sleep. It is the knell of a temporary death. Your spirit has departed and strays, like a free citizen, among the people of a shadowy world, beholding strange sights, yet without wonder or dismay. So calm, perhaps, will be the final change; so undisturbed, as if among familiar things, the entrance of the soul to its Eternal Home!"[11]

The grief of the living that recalled the dead, the first shaken and shadowy hours of the grief-stricken, when life seemed a nightmare from which one would awaken, when the mind was sustained by unacknowledged hopes—as the mother whose child was buried that afternoon had looked up when the coffin was lifted from the grave—such were the moments when the dead and the living seemed to intermingle, and memories and phantasms to pass without question into the everyday world. In *The Wives of the Dead*, Hawthorne had written his most poignant story, and the truest in our literature of the first phantasmagoric hours after the death of a beloved.

In *The Wives of the Dead* two young women learn at almost the same moment of the death of their husbands, who were brothers. The mourners have gone to their happier homes and left the two women alone. Sleep does not steal upon the sisters at the same time. Each dreams that she receives word that her husband is alive, and the report of his death false. Each tries to awaken the other, and refrains from doing so because each feels the other will awaken to thoughts of death and woe. *The Wives of the Dead* seems a tribute to his mother. It could be read as a simple story of the false report of the death of the two husbands, ending joyfully with the news of their safety. Yet depths within depths lay in its transparent clarity—it is also a story of the dreams and hopes of the wives of the dead in their anguish, a reaffirmation that the news of death is always false and a new statement of the promise of eternal life.[12]

IV

He loafed in the bar of the North Adams House, or the Whig Tavern, to use its new name, and listened to the talk. The Democratic Tavern was across the street. Talk about the liquor laws, machinery, soapmaking, dentists, religion, road building, the circus that came to town, the danger of transporting wild animals over the narrow roads, the newcomers to the tavern. The shaded road curved gently down the hill before the hotel to the stream at its base. The Whig Tavern was the stagecoach office, and stages arrived and departed as they had years ago from the Manning Stage Line office in Salem.

Lawyer Haynes was there, and Orin Wetherell, a millwright, and Otis Hodge, a blacksmith. Hodge was a man of about fifty—"a corpulent figure, big in the belly and enormous in the backsides." He wore a straw hat, a shirt open at the throat, a pair of torn cloth pantaloons, a costume not much different from that of Haynes. But his air of independence was such that no one could doubt that he was a man of importance in the community. He had a round jolly face, always mirthful and humorous and shrewd. Despite his corpulence, a pound of weight could not be spared from his abundance, any more than from the leanest man; he walked briskly and without a symptom of labor or pain in his motion. When he talked he straddled a chair, facing the back, his arms and his chin resting thereon. He was good-natured, good hearted, fond of a joke, and his conversation had a strong, unlettered sense, imbued with humor "as everybody's is in New England."

Hodge was a millowner. After supper a stranger, dressed in gray homespun, drove up to the inn in a wagon and sought out Hodge and began to inquire about a new kind of mill machinery. The stranger had an air of large wisdom and the tone of one accustomed to be heard with deference. He became acquainted with the millwrights and talked with them at length about the merits and peculiarities of the new invention. He was hospitable, and invited those with whom he did business to eat and drink with him. His superior air jarred on Lawyer Haynes. The conversation turned upon the nature of soap and the disagreeable smell associated with it. The stranger said, "There need not be any disagreeable smell in making soap."

"Now we are to receive a lesson," said Haynes, and the stranger gave a discourse on how he made soap without odor, draining away the offal of the hog, as not producing any soap anyway, and preserving the skin of the intestines for sausages.

Another character interested Hawthorne. He was a country dentist, twenty-four years old, a licensed Baptist preacher, six feet two inches in height, holding himself stiffly upright, so as to open his chest and counteract a consumptive tendency. He gave Hawthorne an account of his love affairs. It was curious that he seemed to find as much food for his conceit in having been jilted once or twice as in his conquests.

Another character was a boy named Joe. He was about four years old, barefooted, wearing a thin short jacket and full-breeched trousers. The men teased him, put a quid of tobacco in his mouth, under the pretense of giving him a fig, or set him down in a niche in the door, telling him to remain there a day and a half. When Joe became enraged he uttered a peculiar sharp, spiteful cry and struck at his tormentors with a stick. He was always in trouble, and yet would not keep away from the tavern. Hawthorne speculated about his future career, imagining him growing into a tavern-haunter, a country roué, spending a wild and brutal youth, ten years of the prime of his life in the state prison, and his old age in the poorhouse.[13] Hawthorne was mistaken, however. Joe grew to a respectable manhood, prospered, and went west.[14]

The waitress, Eliza Chaseboro, seemed to Hawthorne the strangest waitress that ever was. She listened in on all the conversation at the dinner table, making comments on it, and playing little tricks on the customers she knew, all of which was favorably received because she was a pretty girl. She was always simpering, moping and moving, as if trickeries and girlish follies were effervescing in her brain. When a stranger entered the dining room she said, "Now see how nicely I'll behave!" And so she did, but still making fun aside. She rewarded her favorite customers with great pieces of pie—"What can I do for you? Won't you bespeak two pieces of pie?" When a peddler came by with silk neckerchiefs, bandannas, suspenders, and combs, and tried to trade with the girls of the house, Eliza vowed that she bought more of peddlers than any other girl in the house.

These characters are of interest for several reasons. They became figures in Hawthorne's famous story, *Ethan Brand*. Many years later, Professor Bliss Perry, carrying Hawthorne's notebooks, retraced his steps in North Adams. He found the descriptions extraordinarily accurate. The old citizens could identify the characters from a line or two of Hawthorne's descriptions.

In the company of an acquaintance named Mr. Leach, Hawthorne set out over the Green Mountain road to Shelburne Falls. On this trip he met the old Dutchman with the diorama, in an incident he used, almost without change, in *Ethan Brand*. "We left our horse in the shed; and entering the little unpainted barroom, we heard a voice, in a strange, outlandish accent, explaining a diorama. It was an old man, with a full, gray-bearded countenance; and Mr. Leach exclaimed, 'Ah here's the old Dutchman again!' And he answered 'Yes, Captain, here's the old Dutchman'—though by the way he is a German, and travels the country with this diorama, in a wagon, and had recently been at South Adams, and was now returning from Saratoga Springs.

"We looked through the glass orifice of his machine, while he exhibited a succession of the very worst scratchings and daubings that can be imagined—worn out, too, and full of cracks and wrinkles, besmeared with tobacco smoke, and every otherwise dilapidated. There were none in a later fashion than thirty years since, except some figures that had been cut from tailors show bills. There were views of cities and edifices in Europe, and ruins—and of Napoleon's battles and Nelson's sea-fights; in the midst of which could be seen a gigantic, brown, hairy hand—the Hand of Destiny—pointing at the principal points of the conflict, while the old Dutchman explained. He gave considerable dramatic effect to his description, but his accent and intonation cannot be written. He seemed to take an interest and pride in his exhibition; yet when the utter and ludicrous miserability thereof made us laugh, he joined in the joke very readily. When the last picture had been exhibited, he caused a country boor, who stood gaping beside the machine, to put his head within it, and thrust his tongue out. The head becoming gigantic, a singular effect was produced . . . chill and bleak on the mountaintop, and a fire was burning in the barroom. The old Dutchman bestowed on everybody the title of Captain—perhaps because such a title has a great chance of suiting an American." [15]

Leach was an interesting companion. He was observant, noting a blacksmith in the tavern, and correctly guessing his profession because his right hand was larger than the other. Leach deduced—accurately— that another man was a tailor because his coat did not have a single wrinkle in it. With Leach, Hawthorne visited the limekiln that provides the setting for *Ethan Brand*:

"Remote from houses, far up on the hillside, we found a limekiln burning near the roadside; and approaching it, a watcher started from the ground, where he had been lying at his length. There are several of these limekilns in this vicinity; they are built circular with stones, like a round tower, eighteen or twenty feet high; having a hillock heaped around a considerable of their circumference, so that the marble may be brought and thrown in by cart loads at the top. At the bottom there is a doorway large enough to admit a man in a stooping posture. . . .

"In the one we saw last night, a hardwood fire was burning merrily beneath the superincumbent marble—the kiln being heaped full; and shortly after we came, the man (a dark, black-bearded figure in shirt-sleeves) opened the iron door, through the chinks in which the fire was gleaming, and thrust in huge logs of wood, and stirred the immense coals with a long pole; and showed us the glowing lime-stone—the lower layer of it. The glow of the fire was powerful, at the distance of several yards from the open door. He talked very sociably with us—being doubtless glad to have two visitors to vary his solitary night-watch; for it would not do for him to get asleep; since the fire should be refreshed as often as every twenty minutes.

"We ascended the hillock to the top of the kiln; and the marble was red-hot and burning with a bluish lambent flame, quivering up, sometimes, nearly a yard high, and resembling the flame of anthracite coal—only, the marble being in larger fragments, the flame was higher. The kiln was perhaps six or eight feet across. Four hundred bushels of marble were then in a state of combustion. The expense of converting this quantity into lime is about fifty dollars; and it sells for 24 cents per bushel at the kiln. We talked with the man about whether he would run across the top of the intensely burning kiln for a thousand dollars, barefooted; and he said he would for ten;—he said that the lime had been burning 48 hours, and would be finished in 36 more, and cooled sufficiently to handle in 12 more. He liked the business of watching it better by night than day; because the days were often hot; but such a mild and beautiful night as the last was just right. Here a poet might make verses, with moonlight in them—and a gleam of the fierce firelight flickering through them. It is a shame to use this brilliant, white, almost transparent marble in this way. A man said of it, the other day, that into some pieces of it, when polished, one could see a considerable distance; and instanced a certain gravestone.

"Mr. Leach told me how a girl, to whom he was once paying attention, with some idea of marrying her, made a confession of having forfeited her chastity. He had heard rumors of her having been indiscreet, with reference to a man who was formerly attentive to her—but had no idea of anything more than a merely pardonable indiscretion, in having trusted herself in long and solitary walks with this man. He began to talk with her on this subject, intending gently to reprehend her; but she became greatly agitated, and fell aweeping bitterly—her thoughts flying immediately to her guilt, and probably thinking that he was aware or suspicious of the full extent of it. She told so much, or betrayed so much, that he besought her to say no more. 'That was the only time, Mr. Leach,' sobbed she, 'that I ever strayed from the path of virtue.' Much might be made of such a scene—the lover's astoundment, at discovering so much more than he expected. Mr. Leach spoke to me as if one deviation from chastity might not be an altogether insuperable

objection to making a girl his wife!" [16] Hawthorne meant that Leach
spoke to him, of all people. He was the last man on earth to consider
that an insuperable objection.

V

In *Ethan Brand*, which he wrote many years later, Hawthorne
used these incidents and these characters almost without change. *Ethan
Brand* is the story of a mountain dweller, a limestone burner, who, in
his solitary watches in the night, begins to brood over the unpardonable
sin. What is the sin that lies outside the scope of Heaven's else-infinite
mercy? From brooding upon it, he became a stranger to his own people.
The doctor (bearing an uncanny resemblance to Dr. Bob Robinson)
and the blacksmith, a dead ringer for Otis Hodge, and the lawyer, an
exact copy of Lawyer Haynes, told him he was mad, and invited him to
join them in their drinks at the bar and forget the unpardonable sin.
They said he sat there at night until the devil came out of the flames
of the limekiln to share the dreadful task of imagining some mode of
guilt which could neither be atoned for nor forgiven. The two, so the
story ran, discussed and argued over the matter, considering and re-
jecting each possible sin, until at daybreak the fiend vanished.

In Hawthorne's story, Ethan Brand leaves his native hills and
becomes a learned and famous man. Certain experiments he conducts on
living people are darkly hinted at; he had apparently destroyed their
souls with his psychological experiments. And he had encountered somewhere in his travels the dark and sinister Jew of Nuremberg, the Wandering Jew in another guise, who seems to have engaged in similar experiments of his own. Then, exhausted and embittered, Ethan Brand
returns to the hills and the limekiln, famed as the man who had at last
found the unpardonable sin.

Passages from Hawthorne's notebook could be used in this story
intact. The setting is the limekiln he visited with Leach. The minor characters, a kind of chorus, are the barroom companions—unchanged, only
a little older, again inviting Ethan Brand to forget the unpardonable
sin and have a drink with them, and stumbling back to their grog when
he damns them for a group of filthy drunkards. The meeting with the
old Dutchman and his diorama is used almost word for word. Only the
Jew of Nuremberg is substituted for the old Dutchman, and contributes

one of the most hair-raising passages in Hawthorne's writing when he turns to Ethan Brand and remarks, "I find it a heavy burden in my show box, this unpardonable sin." And the few passages in the story that are not in the diary are Ethan Brand's revelation that after searching throughout the world he had found the unpardonable sin in his own heart. The idea that possessed his life had cultivated his powers to the highest point of which they were susceptible, but his heart had withered—had contracted—had hardened—had perished. He had lost his hold on the magnetic chain of humanity. "He was no longer a brother-man, opening the darkness or the dungeons of our common nature by the key of holy sympathy, which gave him a right to share in all its secrets; he was now a cold observer, looking on mankind as the subject of his experiment, and, at length, converting men and women to be his puppets, and pulling the wires that moved them to such degrees of crime as were demanded for his study . . . Thus Ethan Brand became a fiend . . ."

Hawthorne's story was not fiction at all. It was a literal description of a place, with imaginative meanings and interpretations cementing the blocks of reality together. To diffuse thoughts and imagination through the opaque substance of today—that was his own characterization of what he desired to do. *Ethan Brand* is the clearest indication in his writing of the process. It is as if a photographer should take a series of scenes, and by artfully altering some of the details, create an illusion of a picture at once recognizably true to the place and yet filled with a character and a significance that the place never had. In so far as the effect represented Hawthorne's purpose, he had accomplished it.

The only difficulty is that *Ethan Brand* is not a convincing story. It is startling, even shocking; yet it never holds the interest as the presentation of a dramatic situation, with alternative actions possible for the actors. It is presented only as a chapter from a discarded novel —a form probably chosen to heighten the suggestiveness of the descriptions of Brand's search for the unpardonable sin. The descriptions of the limekiln and the mountains are wonderful, and it is true that they became vivid in the story (as they do not in the diary) by the infusion of an imaginative drama playing around them. Yet the story is static. Its issue has been decided before the curtain rises. The fact that the characters were authentic representations of living people does not make them real—it seems rather that they posture somewhat uncomfortably at being brought on the stage, as if a producer should insist that only a genuine Danish prince could play Hamlet. The moral problem in the story, and its possible autobiographical significance have, I think, obscured another aspect of Ethan Brand. It is a kind of Berkshire landscape, mountain scenery, clouds and thunderstorms, brightness and gloom intermingled, faithfully reproducing the mood of his notebook.

Hawthorne was writing in his journal as if determined to answer his own harsh criticism of his stories, and to bring out into the sunlight the flowers that had blossomed in too retired a shade. He was trying to bring into his writing the average life of the people around him, and to make their doings and their characters the substance of his work.

He had brought a copy of *Twice-told Tales* to Pittsfield. He gave it to Orrin Smith's young niece.[17] His stories were not so remote from this hard-pressed life as he conceived them to be. Lemuel Pomeroy's troubled life in Pittsfield was wonderfully close to the tragic end of Major Molineaux, save that, in Pomeroy's case, it was well-nigh impossible not to present him in a sympathetic light. William Allen at Bowdoin (who resigned in the fall of 1838) might have been one of the characters in *Ethan Brand*. The niece of Orrin Smith might well have read *The Village Uncle* with a sense of wonder, as if she had glanced into a mirror and beheld there a beautiful face she scarcely dared believe her own.

Still, between the lyric quality of his finest work, the flawless cadenced sentences, the magical atmosphere, in which objects and people seemed bathed in a wonderous golden light—the still light of wine in a glass—[18] and these splintery scenes on the porch of the tavern, there was a great distance, a greater difference, that not even his own swift phrases could bridge. Hawthorne wrote doggedly, like a man serving a sentence: a walk in the hills, the features of a stranger, the jokes of a chambermaid. The intensity of feeling in his early writing was entirely absent from these vivid photographic scenes. Even in his walks in the rain through Salem the glimpses on the way, the pools of light on the street corners, the stagecoach lurching off the pavement, had a meaningfulness that made them forever memorable. They seemed part of some larger drama, of some great event, in whose outcome the reader was involved, though he might not understand its full magnitude or know why and how he had become an actor in it. There was no such significance attached to these walks in the hills or these days of waiting and listening in the barroom or on the stoop. The scenes were still beautifully clear and detailed, and the hand of the master was everywhere evident in them, but they had the queer pain of resolute effort, as if Hawthorne were forcing himself to go through with something against his own inclinations. Not forcing himself exactly, either, not in the sense of overcoming a revulsion or conquering a fear or weakness, but rather with the sad firmness that comes from devotion and sympathy, as if he felt he should love the hills and the people, and did not. Page after page of clear observation—cabins in the mountains, rough, rude, and dilapidated—sheep galloping and scrambling after him on the hillside, baaing with all their might with innumerable voices, as if they sought the greatest imaginable favor from him—the warm mornings, after rain, when the mist burst forth from the forests on the ascent of the mountains like smoke, the smoke of a volcano, then soared up and became a cloud in heaven. No one else could write so vividly of the scenes in life that are free to everyone. All this that he pictured was plain and everyday, no admission was charged and no questions were asked; there was not a room that the poorest citizen might not enter, and behold the same sights and listen to the same talk. At their best his notations were splendid landscapes and superb genre painting. All of them combined to a vision of a New England summer so real and down to earth, so unsparing in its recognition of hardship and dullness and yet so generous and quick in its perception of its beauty and its warmth, that no other work on New England equaled it.

Our philosophers have not taught us what is best, and our poets have not sung what is beautifullest, in the kind of life that we must lead; and so we still read the old English wisdom, and pluck upon the ancient strings.[19] So he wrote in the wisdom of his later years. He had set himself to do what no one else had done: to take the literal daily life of an American village and build from it alone the structure of a fiction, a story to relate and draw together its separate inconsequences; to find the meaning which bubbled up from it, rather than those which the wisdom of another land told him should be there. The naturalness of Fessenden's early poems had made so profound an impression on him because they came from the ordinary farmer's life; and his admiration for Fessenden was that he had the courage to break with a language they did not use, and write for them in their own tongue. His quarrel with his own works was that no part of the daily round of any group in his country was native to his own experience—neither the life of the sailors, though he should have known them best, nor the fishermen, the farmers, nor the workmen in the factories beside the rivers. The terms they used did not come naturally to his lips; he could not talk as they did, or write in his stories words they would instinctively use. In the long run this was an advantage. It forced him to search for the common units of experience, and to develop a style that partook of the life of his time without being actually of it, delicate as a cobweb spun in the branches of a tree. But he had not then recognized that his intellectual homelessness was a distinction and an asset, of growing value as the shadows lengthened on the Republic; and that his very aloneness made him not a survivor from an older order but a hesitant spokesman for the new.

VI

When Hawthorne left Salem, Sophia wrote to her sister that she had never known anyone for whom she had so full and at the same time so perfectly quiet an admiration. As he turned to leave his face seemed to her like the sun shining through a silver mist—a wonderful face. Hawthorne may have objected to such descriptions of Don Fernando, and found them a pleasant mannerism when applied to himself—though as a matter of fact they seemed somewhat more affected when applied to any New Englander than to the smoldering Latins. Personally, Hawthorne considered himself to have somewhat forbidding features—beetle browed, heavy, dark,—and he thought of himself as a gloomy figure as he strode along with his head down and a burden of somber thoughts oppressing him. Still, there may have been something in Sophia's description—about this time the faint and filmy romantic portraits, like the famous Osgood portrait of him, were becoming fashionable, the purpose of which seemed to be to make all literary men look like Shelley. In his portraits, Hawthorne looked startled, shy, beardless, and gentle. In his photographs he looked mean. In his portraits he seemed a poet, at least and certainly not more; in his photographs he seemed a square-jawed son and grandson of sea captains and privateers.

One afternoon, after her siesta, Sophia walked to the Hawthornes' to return a book. A walk that distance, alone, was almost an adventure for her. It took hours of determination and preparation. She always dressed carefully, and even extravagantly; she never knew how poor the family was, and made purchases they could not afford. She threaded her way over the streets of Salem where she rarely walked, nervous and uncertain, and gradually gaining confidence at the discovery that the walk had not weakened her. When she came to the Hawthornes' house, she saw an old woman wearing a hood, stooping over the flower bed, planting seeds. She lifted her smiling face, which must have been very pretty in her youth, and said, "How do you do, Miss Peabody?" But Sophia had never seen her before in her life. She asked Sophia to come in, but Sophia was flustered, and gave her the book and her thanks for it.

In Hawthorne's absence, the Peabody and Hawthorne sisters continued to discuss him as before. On September 17, a week before his return, Elizabeth Peabody wrote to Elizabeth Hawthorne:

My dear E.——— I am afraid I shall not be able to go and spend an evening with you while the girls are gone. Tomorrow, you know, is the eclipse. I wish you would come here in the afternoon. The graveyard is an open place to see it from, and I should be very glad of your company. Yesterday I heard of Nathaniel. A gentleman was shut up with him on a rainy day in a tavern in Berkshire, and was *perfectly charmed* with his luck.

In haste, yours,

E.P.P.

In this period Sophia believed, or pretended to believe, that Hawthorne's interest in the Peabody household was his interest in Elizabeth. To make it more difficult, Elizabeth seems to have believed it also. Sophia made an illustration for a new edition of *The Gentle Boy*. Her drawing was of the Puritan finding the boy asleep under the tree on which his father had been hanged. It was a frail, haunting, shadowy drawing, characteristic of her work. Her art was distinctive, personal, with a faint resemblance to Oriental prints; a century later it would have been fashionable. But New England painters were then working on colossal pictures like Washington Allston's "Belshazzar's Feast," which he had been painting for twenty years, and was unable to finish; and in comparison Sophia's work was quaint and wraithlike; a little more pallor and it would not have existed at all, but would have vanished from sight, leaving only a little whispering line here and there to prove there had once been a picture on the paper.

She grew weaker. Elizabeth grew stronger. What was it Elizabeth had thought when she first saw them together?—"What if he should fall in love with her?" When Hawthorne married Sophia he rescued her from harder captors than the wicked ogre of the fairy tales—drugs, headaches, years in bed, and more dangerous than any, the nervous, brittle, affected aestheticism of the New England intellectuals of the time.

When did Elizabeth become aware that Hawthorne's interest was in Sophia? "I am so sorry," Sophia wrote to Elizabeth, sometime in the winter after Hawthorne's return. She wrote of his visits and of their talks together—"I am so sorry," she wrote, though it still seemed that Elizabeth was uncomprehending. On one occasion when Hawthorne was in Salem he stopped at the Peabodys' to escort Mary to Miss Burley's. Sophia wanted to go with them. He refused to take her. "I am going," he said, "but you must not go. It is too cold. You certainly must not go." She said she was going, and that she was sorry she was not wanted. He laughed, and said she was not. She persisted. He said she would be made sick. She put on an incalculable quantity of clothes. Her father remonstrated with her. She quietly implored for permission. When at last she was ready, Hawthorne said he was glad she was going.

They walked quite fast, for she seemed to be walking on air. It was a splendid moonlight. They entered the parlor together. Sophia wrote to Elizabeth, who was living in Boston, that Miss Burley looked delighted. "When we came out it was much more moderate, and we got home very comfortably. Mr. H. said he thought of coming for me to walk on Friday, but he was afraid the walking was not good enough. I told him we were all disappointed at his vanishing that night, and he laughed greatly. He said he should not be able to come this evening to meet Very, because he had something to read, for he was engaged Monday and Tuesday evening and could not read then. I am so sorry. —Yours affectionately, Sophia." [20]

At about this time Hawthorne was appointed to a post in the Boston Custom House. The story persisted that Elizabeth Peabody, through her influence with George Bancroft, had got him the position, which forced him to move to Boston. He was appointed on January 17, 1839.[21]

Bancroft wrote to Levi Woodbury, secretary of the treasury, of the appointment, mentioning that Hawthorne was the biographer of Jonathan Cilley. Woodbury of course must have known that. He had probably known Hawthorne, or known of him, since around 1825, through Franklin Pierce.

Bancroft's mention of Cilley served another purpose. Woodbury was being attacked by Henry Wise and Seargent Prentiss, who had been re-elected to Congress. The Collector of Customs at New York had stolen $1,374,119 from the customs, resigned, and gone abroad. This particular grafter had not been Woodbury's appointment; he was an appointee of Andrew Jackson, and the New York Custom House had been an historic source of corruption. Woodbury nevertheless had inherited him. He himself reported the discovery of the loss to Congress, and outlined recommendations to recover the funds by retrenchment and prevent such thefts in the future.

The Whigs seized upon the case with such vigor that they made it the greatest single embarrassment of Van Buren's administration. Sergeant Prentiss in a bitter speech on December 26 outlined similar cases of corruption in three small communities, and said, "Would time permit, I could give you a hundred. . . . I could go on for a thousand and one nights; and even as in those Eastern stories, so in the chronicles of the office holders, the tale would ever be of heaps of gold, massive ingots, uncounted riches. Why, sir, Aladdin's lamp was nothing to it. . . . Some wish for $50,000, some for $100,000, some for a million; and behold, it lies in glittering heaps before them." Congress began to debate setting up a Committee of Inquiry, and it was at this time that Hawthorne's appointment was made.[22]

He moved to Boston, where he lived in close connection, apparently, with the Haleys, his second cousins through their relationship with John Forrester.[23] Hawthorne was now thirty-five years and six months old. He was a tall, reticent, vigilant, smooth-shaven man, with narrow features already slightly lined, a square determined chin, firm mouth, and gray eyes as observant as those of any writer of his time. He was five feet ten and a half inches tall, and weighed 150 pounds.[24] His hair was brown, and started far back on his forehead. He gave the appearance of being a man whose outstanding characteristic was a hard-won courage and independence—resolutely and even fiercely independent, as if he had been driven to the limit of his endurance and it would be hazardous to try to drive him further. He seemed a hard man to get to know, and a dangerous man to meddle with; a very slight change and his thin feature could be made to seem cold and hard. They were saved from that by the expression in his eyes, thoughtful, attentive, grave, questioning, but without harshness.

His duties at the beginning of his term in the Custom House are not known. The records were destroyed by fire in 1894.[25] There were three or four measurers on duty. Their function was to tally the cargoes as they were unloaded. There was a small office where the measurers awaited their calls to duty, with a coal fire in the salamander stove, desks, chairs, and the morning newspapers, the sailing schedules of the packets on the walls. Hawthorne walked to the Post Office after breakfast, thence to the Custom House, and, if there were no calls for him, sat down at the measurers' fire and read the *Morning Post.* At about nine-thirty he walked to the Athenaeum and read the current magazines until noon. He stopped again at the Custom House to see if a ship was ready, and after walking the length of Washington Street ate dinner, and returned to the Custom House about two. At six o'clock he sallied forth, ate oysters for his supper, bought the evening papers, and returned to his room between seven and eight o'clock, read a book, and went to bed at ten.[26]

When a ship came in he made his way out to the wharf and tallied the cargo while the stevedores, wheelers, and shovelers unloaded it. The Long Wharf where he worked was devoted to the ponderous, evil-smelling, inelegant necessities of life—salt, salt fish, oil, iron, molasses. Huge piles of cotton bales, twenty or thirty feet high, as high as a house, were stored upon it, barrels of molasses, casks of linseed oil, bars of iron. Trucks and carts moved across it, hauling cargoes to and from the vessels. Near the head of the wharf there was an old sloop which had been converted into a store for the sale of the woodenware made in Hingham. There were schooners at the wharf—the *Betsey, Emma-Jane, Sarah, Alice,* and long flatboats, taking up salt to carry it up the Merrimack canal to Concord, New Hampshire. One day the brig *Tiberius* arrived from an English port. It carried seventy factory girls to work in the factories. Some of them were pale and delicate looking, others rugged and coarse. There was a considerable display of legs as they landed. Hacks and omnibuses were waiting to take them to the Worcester

Railroad, and they shouted their good-byes and waved their handker-
chiefs as long as they were in sight.

A shipload of salt came in on the *Alfred Tyler*. At every sixth tub,
the old sailor, keeping tally for the *Alfred Tyler*'s captain, called out
to Hawthorne, "Tally, sir." Betweentimes, they talked. The old man
had served seven years in the British Navy and nine years in the American Navy. He was quiet, observant, brown haired, without a streak of
gray in it; he seemed fifty years old, and was seventy. He wore a
checked shirt and sailcloth trousers. Hawthorne asked him if he had
ever been in the Red Sea. He had—in 1803, in the American sloop of
war that carried General Eaton. Their talk was interrupted by his call
—"Tally, sir"—as the loads passed to the wharf. He said he hoped he
would die at sea, becase it would be so little trouble to bury him. The
stevedores called to ask him for a piece of spun-yarn, or a handspike,
or a hammer, or some nails, or for some of the ship's molasses, to
sweeten water.

The *Thomas Lowder*, a little, black, dirty vessel, arrived from St.
John, New Brunswick, with a load of coal. The Irish stevedores shoveled
the coal into Custom House tubs, to be craned out of the hold, and
others wheeled it away in wheelbarrows, to be loaded into wagons. The
first day Hawthorne walked the wharf, suffering from the intense cold.
The second day he sat in the tiny cabin, peering into the hold through
the interstices of the bulkhead. The cook of the vessel, a grimy, un-
shaven, middle-aged man, trimmed the fire in the cookstove and washed
his dishes in dirty water. From time to time a stevedore would poke his
head into the cabin and call "Cook!" The cook would fill a pipe, put a
live coal on it, and stick it into the Irishman's mouth. A boy rode the
horse that lifted the tubs from the hold.[27]

The bitter zero atmosphere came down the companionway and
threw its chill over him. He was pretty comfortable, though he found
when he reached home that he had staggered through the thronged
streets with coal streaks on his face. The custom house office was a
roughly genial place, with a stove, a few chairs, a newspaper, and a
table of the signals, wharves, and agents of the packets plying to and
from Boston. Hawthorne's cousin Eben Hawthorne worked in the Custom House. He was the son of the old selectman, Colonel John Hawthorne. He had left Salem in his youth, gone to sea, and lived in Mexico
and the West. He was nervous; his hands shook, and he darted across

the streets, cautioning Hawthorne, as if they were both in danger of being run over. He was a friend of the Reverend Charles Wentworth Upham in Salem, and told Hawthorne stories of John Hawthorne, the witchcraft judge who was their common ancestor. He was an old bachelor, truly forlorn, and the pride of ancestry was his great hobby. He kept old books and papers in his desk at the custom house, and told Hawthorne of all the oddities, eccentrics, recluses, bastards, queer men and women, in the Hawthorne ancestry. How much of this was true, and how much the gossip and speculation of an amateur antiquarian, Hawthorne did not say. Eben said that Philip English, the great merchant of Salem, in witchcraft days, had no legitimate male heirs. He had some bastards, but all his legitimate children were girls. One of these girls married a son of Judge John Hawthorne—"and thus all the legitimate blood of English is in our family." Eben said that English hated Judge John Hawthorne all his life for persecuting him, but when he lay on his deathbed he consented to forgive the Judge. "But if I get well," he said, "I'll be damned if I'll forgive him!" From matters of birth, pedigree, and family pride, Eben turned to politics. He boasted of having been the first Jackson man in Salem. He said that nobody should possess wealth longer than his own life, and that it should then return to the people. It was the most arrant democracy and radicalism Hawthorne had ever happened to hear.[28]

Another Custom House figure was William Pike. He was a shortish man, very stoutly built, with a short neck, a wrinkled forehead, a face dark and sallow, ugly, but with a pleasant, kindly, strong and thoughtful expression, stiff black hair starting bushy and almost erect from his forehead—a heavy but very intelligent countenance. He was a Methodist, and occasionally preached—he gave religious instruction to a class in the state prison. He was from Salem, a power in Salem Democratic party politics, and an authority on Salem folklore. He was a strong, stubborn, kindly nature. In his political hostilities he said he could never feel ill will against a person after he had personally met him.[29] He had formerly been a carpenter. A strong and lifelong friendship developed between Hawthorne and Pike. In his old age, after Hawthorne's death, Pike wrote his recollections of Hawthorne. They were doubtless of much interest, for Pike knew the side of Hawthorne that is most obscure—his official and political life. But Pike died soon after completing the book, and the manuscript was lost.[30]

Hawthorne left the Custom House, when the day's work was done, and sat before the fire in his room. Strife and wrangling, the east winds and the rain, combined to make his evenings solitary. Six or seven hours of cheerful solitude! Sometime in these hours alone the knowledge of his love for the strange and quiet girl of Salem grew upon him. He had fallen in love not only with her, but with his vision of her, some tender and poignant glimpse of her spirit that had moved him more than he had known he could be moved.

He could see visions more vividly by the dusky glow of firelight than by either daylight or lamplight, and at the twilit hour, before he lit his lamp, he invited Sophia to be with him in spirit. He had never, till now, had a friend who could give him repose. They had all disturbed him, and whether for pleasure or pain, it was still disturbance. But peace overflowed from her heart into his. He felt that there is a Now, and that Now must always be calm and happy, and that sorrow and evil are but evil phantoms that flit across it. Why had he not felt before that there was a present so powerful and so good? There was always in Hawthorne's thought some deep connection between love and reality; love was reality, and in its absence the spirit drifted, phantom-like, searching for meaning where there was none. Not in torment, like that of Ethan Brand, but in a world of half-perceptions, forever deceived by illusions, forever attributing significance to inconsequences; so he had lived, he felt, until she had given him reality. She was wonderful. Sorrow and evil now flitted, phantom-like, across the calm and happy surface of reality, not, as before, when it had seemed that his own half-unreal being had moved ghost-like through the rigid and clamorous evils of the world. So much had she given him. We are but shadows, he mused, we are not endowed with real life, and all that seems most real about us is but the thinnest substance of a dream—till the heart be touched. That touch creates us—then we begin to be—thereby we are beings of reality and inheritors of eternity.[31]

On March 3, 1839, Hawthorne received his first check, $204.17.*

---

* There may be some mistake here. Hawthorne's salary was always listed at $1,200 a year, until a bundle of Custom House records that escaped the fire was discovered. The difference between $1,200 and $1,500 a year was considerable at that time, when a man could live on $300 a year. Also, Hawthorne's first check is dated March 3, but March 3, 1839, fell on a Sunday. The answer is probably to be found in the confused state of the customs service finances, especially since a Congressional inquiry was pending.

He had not been in Salem for some time, doubtless because he had no money. He spent the weekend there, and as he started back to Boston on Monday morning he passed the Peabody house. Sophia was at the window. She seemed pale, and not so quiet as usual.

He did not reveal himself to her. If she saw him, she gave no sign of it. Two days passed. He reproached himself that he had not shown himself to her. Then they would have smiled, and their reminiscences would have been sunny instead of shadowy. He was afraid that perhaps she was not quite well that morning. He wrote to her on Wednesday afternoon, telling her to grow better and better—physically, for he protested against any spiritual improvement until he was able to keep pace with her. He wanted her to be strong and full of life, with a glow in her cheeks, to sleep soundly every night and get up every morning with a feeling as if she were newly created. Perhaps he was asking her to work a miracle within herself, yet not a greater one than he believed might be wrought by inward faith and outward aid.

He wanted to leave her as free as she left him, not even to tell her that he expected a letter from her, because she might reproach herself if she had not written it. She wondered if she wrote too often. He could not believe she was serious in asking the question. Her letters were no small portion of her spiritual food and helped keep his soul alive, when otherwise it might languish unto death. He kept them for the treasure of his still and secret hours, such hours as pious people spend in prayer. The communion that his spirit then held with hers had something of religion in it.[32]

They had agreed to keep their meetings secret. To throw off suspicion, and for protection, he would write only every other Saturday. They would spend the weekends together, but they would not meet on the Monday mornings when he returned to Boston. There could be no variations in this, hard as it was for her to bear. She could consider it a decree of fate. If she would but believe this she would be quiet. Otherwise, he said, she would flutter her wings and often, of necessity, flutter them in vain. He never gave the reason for the finality of his decision, except to tell her that he never caused her the slightest disappointment without pain and remorse on his part.[33]

The spring air was so delicious that it seemed as if the dismal old Custom House was situated in Paradise. He sat in the afternoons with his window open, to temper the glow of a huge coal fire. In the evenings he sat at his fireside from teatime until after eight o'clock, musing and dreaming about a thousand things, with every one of which some nearer or remoter thought of her was intermingled. He began his letter to her late, lest some idler should call and break the trend of his thoughts. It was well that he did so. He wished it were possible to convey them directly to her heart. Perhaps, when they were endowed with their spiritual bodies, they might send thoughts and feelings any distance, in no time at all, and transform them warm and fresh into the consciousness of those they loved. And what a bliss it would be if he could be conscious of some purer faculty, some more delicate sentiment, some lovelier fantasy, than could possibly have its birth in his own nature, and therefore be aware that his Dove was thinking through his mind and feeling through his heart! But, after all, perhaps it was not wise to intermix fantastic ideas with the reality of their affection.

"Let us content ourselves to be earthly creatures . . ."

He had never written so beautifully. His letters were poetry, Elizabethan, like the poetry in the last of Shakespeare's plays, the quiet and tender speeches with their dusky cello notes:

> *Let us content ourselves to be earthly creatures,*
> *And hold communion of spirit in such modes as*
> *   are ordained to us*
> *By letters (dipping our pens as deep as may be*
> *   into our hearts)*
> *By heartfelt words, when they can be audible*
> *By glances—through which medium spirits do*
> *   really seem to talk in their own language*
> *And by holy kisses, which I do think*
> *Have something of the supernatural in them.*
> And now goodnight, my beautiful Dove . . .[34]

He was up before dawn, and on the deck of the schooner in East Cambridge at sunrise. The earning of the longshoremen depended on their hours of work, and since they could not begin until the measurer arrived, he was always at his post before them. All day he walked the deck of the schooner, or sat waiting, while her cargo of coal was unloaded. The black-faced demons in the vessel's hold looked like forgemen.

He grew as black as a chimney sweeper. Late in the afternoon he purified himself of his stains and hurried to the Custom House to get Sophia's letter. He was very tired, sunburned, and sea flushed. He *knew* it would be there.[35] Sometimes her letters were left on his desk. Sometimes they were delivered to him at work, with the knowing smiles of his fellow measurers. He would never read them until he had washed the grime of the day's work away. Sometimes he took them, walked away where he could not be seen, and kissed them. In April, they became engaged.[36] Her letters to him have been lost. When he set out for England, after their marriage, he burned them, regretfully, noting in his diary that the world has no more such.[37] It was in all probability some simple matter that led him to destroy them—some innocent disclosure of the peril she was in, and of which she was only half conscious, or not conscious at all, but which, after a lapse of time, and their changed situations in the world, became transparent in her letters to him. He sent his letters to her by messenger if he could. Mary Peabody usually carried them. Once Elizabeth Peabody frightened Sophia with a rumor that a smallpox epidemic was raging in Boston. It was unture, and as Hawthorne tried to reassure Sophia, he wrote meaningfully: "Trust me, dearest, there is no need of heart quake on my account. You have been in greater danger than your husband." [38]

Sometimes, as he started to write to her, young John Forrester and Cousin Haley came into his room and argued politics until eleven. Haley grew so angry that he would not speak to Hawthorne for three days. Hawthorne was greatly pleased.[39] Alone, he was conscious of a peacefulness and contented repose such as he had never enjoyed before. Sophia could not have felt such quiet unless he had felt it too, nor could he unless she had. If either of their spirits had been troubled before, they were then in such close communion that both must have felt the same grief and turmoil. Her lost letters must have perfectly complemented his own. One day he was at the Custom House measuring twenty chaldrons of coal, and occasionally brawling with the French crew, when her letter was delivered to him. He turned his head away, so nobody saw him, pressed it to his lips and broke the seal.[40] It seemed to him the dearest letter she had ever written. But he thought so of each successive one.

He took her letter with him when he went to East Cambridge to measure coal. But the vessel was stuck in the mud. He came home, locked his door, and threw himself on the bed, with her letter in his hand, read it over, slowly and peacefully, and then, folding it up, rested his heart upon it and fell fast asleep.

Sophia dreamed that he had written to her saying something about "the continuance or not of our acquaintance." She was greatly distressed, and wrote to him. He replied to set her mind at rest, chiding her gently at thinking, even in a dream, that he would use such a phrase as "continuance or not of our acquaintance." [41] He could not remember his own dreams. He suspected that she mingled with them, flitting away before he was awake, leaving him doubtfully conscious of her visits.

One Tuesday in May he got a free day and hurried unexpectedly to Salem. He walked along the narrow street to the Peabody house, past the graveyard, and entered without knocking. George Peabody was ill upstairs. Sophia, too, was usually in her room. Hawthorne sat down in the parlor. He believed, he did not know why, that she would soon come downstairs and find him waiting there. He thought she would know instinctively that he was there. For half an hour he sat in the silent parlor. No one stirred. At last he knocked. Sophia had gone to Boston. Elizabeth was in Salem. Sophia was visiting Caroline Sturgis. It seemed really monstrous to Hawthorne that here, in her own home—or what was her own home—she should no longer be. He wrote to her, and interrupted his letter to stroll down to the Neck—"a beautiful, beautiful, beautiful sunshine, and air and sea." Then he hurried to Boston to find her.

Caroline Sturgis was the daughter of William Sturgis, who, with his partner, John Bryant, carried on more than half of all the trade between China and the United States. Captain Sturgis had shipped out on the *Caroline* as a boy before the mast, and returned, in five years, as her captain. William Sturgis had five daughters. His only son died at sixteen. His oldest daughter, Ellen, had recently married Dr. Robert Hooper. His second daughter married Samuel Hooper. His fourth daughter married Robert Shaw, one of the children at Brook Farm. His youngest daughter, Susan, married Dr. Henry Bigelow, the famous surgeon. [42] Ellen, who greatly admired Hawthorne, had three children; the youngest, Miriam, called Clover, became Mrs. Henry Adams. [43]

Hawthorne apparently did not know of the esteem in which he was held by the Sturgis family. Nor, at that time, did Sophia. When Hawthorne reached Boston he called at the Sturgis house. (Or the Hooper's, for Caroline may have been staying at her sister's.) "Oh, it was terrible to find you gone," he said when he saw Sophia. It was apparently evening—he made an appointment to meet her the next morning at the Athenaeum Gallery.

At eight o'clock she walked to the gallery. The morning was raw and cold, with a piercing east wind. He walked with her to the Sturgises', afraid that the wind would make her ill for a week. He went on to work, and returned in the evening. Caroline was busy with the children, and did not come down for half an hour. When she appeared, however, she was very agreeable, and so was Hawthorne—Caroline, Sophia remarked, admired him greatly. As he left, Hawthorne told Sophia he would be at the gallery the following morning, if possible.

She again braved the morning air and reached the gallery at eight o'clock. The day was cloudy. The gallery was empty, except for William Russell.[44] Russell was a teacher and writer, the founder of the *American Journal of Education*. He had once been an associate of Bronson Alcott. He had a school in Roxbury, where Elizabeth Peabody taught; he had been a friend of Elizabeth's for many years. He was living with the Alcotts at 6 Beach Street, where Alcott had started another school. It was on the verge of another scandal, as Alcott enrolled a Negro child with his white students. Russell was Scotch, a University of Glasgow graduate, with thin, ascetic features.[45]

An hour passed. The sun emerged from the clouds. Hawthorne appeared. He explained that he thought she would not come because the morning was so cold. They waited in the gallery for another hour. Hawthorne had begun to take an interest in painting. He went to Washington Allston's studio, and afterward stopped by to visit Elizabeth Peabody. Allston asked her what Sophia was painting; Elizabeth said she had several things agoing. Elizabeth had begun to talk of Hawthorne in the literary circles of Boston she frequented. She praised him to the Emersons, when she visited there; and learned that Emerson had a good opinion of him, though he had not read his works. She talked of him with George Bancroft, who said that he was the most efficient and best of the Custom House officers.[46] When Sophia repeated this to Hawthorne, he blushed deeply, and said, "What fame." [47]

The gallery began to grow crowded. They left. Hawthorne insisted on calling a cab for her. Whether these cold morning meetings were in the nature of an examination of him, or of her, or both, or whether they were made necessary because they could not meet in Salem, it is impossible now to say. Only a few people knew that they met, and still fewer knew they were in love. It was Elizabeth Peabody who was now talking everywhere of Hawthorne, and in whose company Hawthorne appeared when he appeared in society at all. Their secrecy could hardly have been greater if they had both been married and were both guilty of infidelity. Hawthorne was behaving exactly as he had with his writing. The ability to move back and forth between Salem and Boston made it possible for their relationship to seem casual in both towns, and their meetings no more frequent than would ordinarily be the case between two people with their interests and in their stations in life. Now, it should be pointed out that Hawthorne did not create this situation, any more than he had consciously planned the situation that developed because he had published his works anonymously. But finding it before him, he insisted that she should keep it. Why? The world might misjudge them, he told her. But, again, why should the world misjudge them?

Spring advanced into summer, and the footsteps of May could be traced across the islands in the harbor. "While I love you dearly," he wrote, "and while I am so conscious of the deep union of our spirits, still I have an awe of you that I never felt for anybody else. Awe is not the word, either, because it might imply something stern in you; whereas —but you must make it out for yourself. I do wish I could put this into words—not so much for your satisfaction (because I believe you will understand) as for my own. I suppose I should have pretty much the same feeling if an angel were to come from Heaven and be my dearest friend—only the angel could not have the tenderest of human natures too, the sense of which is mingled with this sentiment. Perhaps it is because, in meeting you, I really meet a spirit, whereas the obstructions of earth have prevented such a meeting in every other case. But I leave the mystery here. Some time or other it may be made plainer to me. But methinks it converts my love into religion. And then it is singular, too, that this awe (or whatever it be) does not prevent me from feeling that it is I who have charge of you. And will not you rebel? Oh, no; because I possess the power to guide only so far as I love you. My love gives me the right, and your love consents to it."

"Since writing the above, I have been asleep; and I dreamed that I had been sleeping a whole year in the open air, and that while I slept, the grass grew around me. It seemed, in my dream, that the bedclothes were spread beneath me; and when I awoke (in my dream) I snatched them up, and the earth under them looked black, as if it had been burnt —a square place, exactly the size of the bedclothes. Yet there were grass and herbage scattered over this burnt space, looking as fresh and bright and dewy as if the summer rain and the summer sun had been cherishing them all the time. Interpret this for me; but do not draw any sombre omens from it. . . ."[48]

He was kept busy at East Cambridge for several days, and did not stop at the Custom House. A letter from her was delivered to him there. She had been ill. He wrote in distress because he could not take care of her. He asked her to let their love be powerful enough to make her well; he would have faith in its efficacy, not expecting that it would work an immediate miracle but that it would make her so well at heart that she could not possibly be ill in body. He besought her to be careful of herself, remembering how much earthly happiness depended on her health, to be tranquil, and not to write to him—"unless your heart be unquiet and you think that you can quiet it by writing. May God bless you!" [49]

VII

The engagement, again at Hawthorne's insistence, was kept secret. It was doubtless the nature of his work that forced him to insist upon it. He had a position of considerable responsibility, serving as head of the department in the absence of Colonel Joseph Hall.[50] Hall was a man of forty-five, the father of six children, self-educated except for a few months at Andover, who became a colonel in the War of 1812. Hawthorne assigned the measurers to the incoming ships, and over his desk, at such times, the actual government tally of the imports of Boston Harbor passed. Yet it was not the technical side of the job that was hazardous, but the fearful political campaign of 1840. The Democrats carried the governorship of Massachusetts by one vote.

The campaign of the Whigs was directed against the Custom House. That venerable edifice, where the Revolution had started, if the Boston Massacre be taken as its starting point, seemed likely to be the starting place of another one. It was considered a source not only of political corruption but of revolution. In Boston the campaign was savage. Bancroft had appointed Orestes Brownson to a Custom House job. Brownson was thirty-seven, a six-foot farmer, vigorous and independent, self-educated. He became a Presbyterian at nineteen, a Universalist minister at twenty-three, a Communist at twenty-six, and an organizer of the Workingmen's party shortly afterward; then a Unitarian, after which he established a church of his own, the Society for Christian Union and Progress, after which he became a Catholic. In his paper Brownson attacked organized Christianity, the inheritance of wealth, and the penal code. His articles created a sensation. They were considered incitements to class war, a program for subduing the American people by physical force. Horace Greeley, Henry Wise, and Daniel Webster denounced Brownson; the Whigs maintained that the program revealed the true nature of the Democratic plans. The conservative Democrats complained about Brownson to Levi Woodbury, who wrote to Bancroft, "Everybody is loud in their denunciations of him. Why is he kept there? Why?"

Hawthorne's old friend Epes Sargent was on the staff of the Boston *Atlas*. The *Atlas* gave a clear statement of the intensity of feeling about the campaign: "It has been boastingly uttered that the blood of Whigs would soon flow down our streets; and a distinguished leader of the party, and an officer in the Boston Custom House, has recently stated that the Whigs should soon have a chance to experience the physical force of the loco-focos; that he would bring one hundred men in this city who would flog any thousand Whigs . . . and that while this battle was going on he would go up to Beacon Street and set fire to the Whig houses." [51]

In August, 1839, Hawthorne was in Salem; Sophia was well, and their meeting was blissful. He dreamed of her all night when he returned to Boston, and awakened at four o'clock in the morning rested and soothed at the memory of love. A toothache that had been bothering him began to subside. While he was working on a salt vessel in the harbor her letter was delivered to him. He read it amid all sorts of bustle and gabble of the Irishmen working around him.[52] He enjoyed working on the salt vessels. Salt was white and pure—there was something holy about salt. Butterflies—very broad-winged and magnificent —frequently came on board the salt ships. What did they have to do there, where there were no flowers, nor any green thing—nothing but brick storehouses, stone piers, black ships, toilsome men? He could not account for these "wandering gems of the air" unless they were the lovely fantasies of the mind.[53]

Hawthorne did not like his own appearance, even when his features were unswollen; it bothered him to look into a mirror and find his dark face and beetle brow staring at him. Mrs. Hooper invited him and Mary Peabody to dinner. As he started to go there he was ordered to East Cambridge to tally a cargo—a rush job. He got to East Cambridge and found that the ship was stuck in the mud. By the time he returned it was too late for dinner. He stopped at his room and wrote to Sophia. The swelling in his jaw went away, "leaving my visage in its former admirable proportions." [54] He had begun to dream of where they would live— a cottage somewhere beyond the sway of the east wind, yet within the limits of New England, where they could always be together, and have a place to be in—"what could we desire more? . . . and you should draw and paint and sculpture and make music and poetry too and your husband would admire and criticize." [55]

He settled his straw hat more firmly on his head and made his way to the end of Long Wharf. On these hot midsummer days he had the best job in Boston. A delightful breeze always blew on the wharf, fluttering and palpitating, sometimes shyly kissing his brow, then dying away, and then rushing upon him with livelier sport. "Late in the afternoon there was a sunny shower, which came down so like a benediction that it seemed ungrateful to take shelter in the cabin or to put up an umbrella. Then there was a rainbow, or a large segment of one, so exceedingly brilliant and of such long endurance that I almost fancied it was stained into the sky, and would continue there permanently. And there were clouds floating all about—great clouds and small, of all glorious and lovely hues (save that imperial crimson which was revealed to our united gaze)—so glorious, indeed, and so lovely, that had a fantasy of heaven's being broken into fleecy fragments and dispersed through space, with its blest inhabitants dwelling blissfully upon those scattered islands. . . . And the sea was very beautiful, too. Would it not be a pleasant life to—but I will not sketch out any more fantasies tonight." [56]

The days passed, until late fall, almost without incident. He had a difficult letter to write on behalf of an office seeker. He read Harriet Martineau's *Deerbrook*. Once he was called away from his regular

duties to quell a rebellion of coal shovelers on another ship. Once he
went to a party in Boston where Sophia also appeared. He was enchanted to see her unexpectedly enter the room. "You looked like a
vision, beautifullest wife, with the width of the room between us. Did
you get home safe and sound and with a quiet and happy heart?" [57]

On October 22 George Hillard called upon him. Hillard looked so
much like Abraham Lincoln that a photograph of one could almost be
substituted for the other. He was, however, a very Bostonian Lincoln,
learned, scholarly, witty, agreeable, ironic, a conservative to the end,
a faithful Whig long after the party had disappeared, editor of the
poetry of Edmund Spenser, biographer of Captain John Smith. He was
a companion of Longfellow, and carried messages between Longfellow
and Frances Appleton (who were soon to be married) at a time when
Longfellow was unwelcome at the Appleton home on Beacon Street.
Hillard's wife was the former Susan Tracy Howe, daughter of a famous
western Massachusetts judge. Hillard's biography of Captain John
Smith was an excellent piece of work. He wanted to soften the growing
antagonism between Massachusetts and Virginia; one way to do it was
to make New England studies of Virginia heroes.* It might also help
remind New Englanders that the history of the country did not begin
and end with them. Hillard was a close friend of Richard Cleveland,
Sophia's friend in Cuba, of Charles Sumner, and of Edward Crowninshield, old Ben Crowninshield's son. He was a lifelong admirer of Jeremiah Mason, whose memoirs he wrote. Justice Joseph Story, between
sessions of the Supreme Court, was teaching law at Harvard. Hillard
and Sumner were Story's most brilliant students. He virtually adopted
them.

Hillard was not robust. His slender, stooping form, his peculiar
walk, his open brow and pale, schoolboy face evoked in his friends a
sense of concern—they felt that his life should be different and more

---

* It seems to have been the result of a considered policy of New
England leaders of thought, and resulted in the deliberate suppression of
the enormous wealth of Federalist—and hence anti-Jefferson—literature.
The New Englanders themselves set aside much of their accumulated learning in the hope of improving their relations with the South in the period
before the Civil War. The penetrating, if hostile, characterizations of
Thomas Jefferson and his philosophy were set aside, a voluntary censor-
ship that was doubly tragic because it did not result in improved relations
with the South.

benignant, that he should have more health, more leisure, more means, in order that his gifts and accomplishment should be fulfilled. His conversation was delightful, and it required a scholar to tell which of the apt phrases that he made, with a quaint smile lighting up his face, were original with him and which were transplanted from a wide range of English literature. His office at Number 4 Court Street—*Farewell to Number 4*, he wrote after twenty years—was a literary court of appeals— the odor of books, the office dust, sunshine through the filmy panes, flies droning and humming, scratching pens, rustling papers, and the visitors —William Wetmore Story, Joseph Story's only son, Story himself, Longfellow, Whittier, Bancroft, Holmes, Tom Appleton, Ticknor, Samuel Gridley Howe, Webster, Prescott, James Russell Lowell, Emerson, Rufus Choate, Cornelius Felton, Josiah Quincy, Motley, William Lloyd Garrison, Adams, Lorings and Curtises—a large section of literary New England. It was fashionable to say of Hillard that he was very kind, and very charming, but he was not in his right place in life; and the authors of monumental works tended to regard him with an affectionate, patronizing air. There was always the comment that he should have done more than write his quiet unassuming memoirs of Story and Jeremiah Mason, of Richard Cleveland and John Brown and Fletcher Webster, and his biographies of Captain John Smith and— later—of General McClellan. It may be, however, that he was too far in advance of his time; and those curious allusive works, with their seasoned humor and their pemmican nutriment, would survive the coming times that destroyed so many.[58]

Hillard and Sumner had just opened their law office. Hillard did not have a single case in ten years. Then he had only one a year for sixteen years. He was a perpetual scholar; at Harvard he had lived in the home of the president, Josiah Quincy. He had completed his edition of Spenser's poems, which was to appear the next year. He asked Hawthorne to become a lodger at his house at 54 Pinckney Street. Hawthorne wrote to Sophia asking if she approved. She did; and so he moved into what were probably the finest quarters he had ever had, with a bureau on which he wrote between the two windows, and two lamps before him as he wrote, showing the polished shadings of the mahogany panels. A coal fire burned in the grate, a haircloth armchair stood before the fire, and a beautiful rug covered the floor. He wanted to call people in from the street to admire it. Sophia once visited there and sat in that chair, but did not like it. He had a mattress, which he liked better than a feather bed. Mrs. Hillard took excellent care of them, feeding them with eggs and baked apples and other delectable dainties.[59]

His love and his admiration constantly grew. She feared her own words, but he told her "your unreserve, your out-gushing frankness, is one of the loveliest results of your purity and innocence and holiness." [60] The tragedy of Sophia's brother George brought them more closely together. Sophia had not been told how critically ill George Peabody was until his collapse in the middle of November made it clear that there was no hope for him. Hawthorne could not come to Salem: he was suddenly called to an unexpected and indispensable engagement with General McNeil. General McNeil was one of the few officers to emerge from the War of 1812, in Hawthorne's opinion, with an unblemished reputation—another was Colonel Miller, who led the charge at Lundy's Lane, and in whose regiment Joseph Cilley had served. General McNeil married Franklin Pierce's sister—his half sister, more exactly, the only child of General Pierce's first marriage—and was thus a connecting link between Hawthorne and Pierce and Woodbury.[61] Hawthorne wrote to ask whether she wanted him to come the following Saturday and remain through Monday, or to wait until Thanksgiving and stay the remainder of the week.

The days were cold now, the air eager and nipping.[62] He comforted her: if her tears fell, it was best to let them flow, and then her grief would melt quietly forth. He wrote with a tenderness he had never expressed before, alternating his words of hope with light and gentle descriptions of his own quiet life, his letters like caresses. "You are yourself one of the angels who minister to your departing brother," he wrote.[63] How his thought had deepened since he visualized the grim afterworld by Parson Bradley's fireside! He caught the five-o'clock train Saturday evening, and reached her home by seven o'clock. He remained in Salem over the weekend, caught the two o'clock cars to Boston, and ate a supper of oysters on his way to his room. It seemed to him the only thing worth living for, that he had ever done, or been instrumental in, that God had made him the means of saving her from the heaviest anguish of her brother's loss.[64]

He wrote her with gentle humor about his own difficulties with work and the weather. His own eyes had an inflammation, too; they certainly smarted in an unwonted manner when he heard from her. He armored himself against the cold with a fur cap and two shirts. He disliked flannels, so he put one shirt on over another. The result pleased him, and he told her that as winter deepened he intended adding shirts, so that by midwinter she would not be able to get her arms around him; and then as the spring advanced he would discard them, one by one. . . . A busy social life threatened him. Sophia urged him to attend Emerson's lectures, and to hear Father Taylor preach. "Most absolute little Sophia, didst thou expressly command me to go to Father Taylor's church this very Sabbath? Now, it would not be an auspicious day for me . . . I have a cold, though, indeed, I fear I have partly conjured it up to serve my naughty purpose. Some sunshiny day, when I am wide awake and warm and genial, I will go and throw myself open to his blessed influence; but now there is only one thing that I feel anywise inclined to do, and that is to go to sleep . . . Our souls are in happiest unison, but we must not disquiet ourselves if every tone be not re-echoed from one to the other. . . . But I forewarn you, dearest, that I am a most unmalleable man; you are not to suppose, because my spirit answers to every touch of yours, that therefore every breeze, or even every whirlwind, can upturn me from my depths. Well, I have said my say in this matter. And now, here are the same snowflakes in the air that were descending when I began. Would that there were an art of making sunshine! Do you know any such art? Truly you do." [65]

As for Emerson: "Dearest, I have never had the good luck to profit much, or indeed any, by attending lectures; so that I think the ticket had better be bestowed on somebody who can listen to Mr. Emerson more worthily." [66] He rejoiced that work or other engagements prevented him attending dinner at George Bancroft's with Margaret Fuller. A strange error came into Hawthorne's biography as a result of his letters on these subjects. He always wrote to Sophia as his wife, and of himself as her husband. He carried on a long campaign to persuade her to sign her letters Sophia Hawthorne. She refused; then wrote a tiny and frightened signature at the bottom of the page. On April 22 he was invited to a party at General McNeil's. He wrote, "Why will not people let your poor persecuted husband alone?" It was a time of considerable trouble in the Custom House, not to mention the entire customs service. Colonel Hall was often ill, and when he was away, either at home indisposed, or in Maine on government business, Hawthorne took his place. The other measurers were often tied up with other work, or remained home because of illness. Hawthorne himself considered taking another post in the government, in Washington, but refused it because it would have taken him away for twelve or fourteen months out of the remaining twenty he planned to stay in the service. When his letters were published after his death, Mrs. Hawthorne changed the word "husband" to "me," making the sentence read: "Why will not people let poor persecuted me alone?"—a phrase that made his English biographers glance at him with a queer sidelong expression. Actually, it probably meant exactly what it said, and if persecuted was too strong a word in comparison with old Judge Hawthorne's treatment of the witches, it was not an exaggeration of the torment of an honest man in the customs service in the midst of its fearful scandals, and on the edge of an election that was to remove the Administration from office.

Hawthorne worked through the rainy spring, surrounded by brawling slang whangers. On the days of fine winter weather, when the posts and timbers of the wharves were half immersed in the water, and covered with the ice that the successive rising and falling of the tide left upon them, he warmed himself by the stove in the dirty little cabin of a schooner, among biscuit barrels, pots and kettles, sea chests and lumber.

Colonel Hall returned from Washington and gave him a present— a quire or two of superfine, gilt-edged paper, which he brought from Congress, and three sticks of red sealing wax. The gift might have been a testimonial to the letters he was writing.[67] Sophia's letters to him were the only ray of light that broke upon the dungeon where he worked. He folded them to his breast, and ever and anon they sent a thrill through him, for they were steeped with her love and it seemed as if her head was leaning against his breast. He longed to get home, to read them again and again. How happy were Adam and Eve! There was no third person to come between them, and all the infinity around them only served to press their hearts closer together. Would she sail away with him to discover some summer island? Did she not think that God had reserved one for them, since the beginning of the world? What a foolish husband he was! They had found such an Eden, such an island sacred to them, wherever, whether in Mrs. Quincy's boudoir or anywhere else, they had been clasped in each other's arms.[68]

VIII

The Peabody family moved to Boston, and settled in their famous house at 13 West Street. It was located just off Tremont Street, across the Common from the State House, five minutes' walk from Hawthorne's lodgings on Pinckney Street and about equidistant from his rooms and his working headquarters at the Long Wharf. It was a three-story brick town house, with a shop on the ground floor, where the Peabodys opened a bookstore. It was an excellent one, specializing in foreign books.

He wrote, and Elizabeth Peabody published, a brief history for children. It grew out of their talk in Salem on the occasion of Cilley's death, when Elizabeth had told him and his sister that she, too, would have Hawthorne help govern this great people, but by going to the fountains of greatness and power, the unsoiled souls, the children, and weaving for them his golden web.[69] He took her at her word. And the result, though the book was not widely popular, seemed in a queer way to justify her insight, if not for the children for whom it was written, for himself.

No one ever wrote history so happily. The terror of Cilley's death, the rigorous observation of contemporary life in western Massachusetts, the routine of the Custom House, the bitterness of contemporary politics—all these heavy clouds over his imagination seemed dissipated by the simple genial task of telling the story of his country's history to readers whose years alone censored a preoccupation with them. The mind could not linger over the violence of history or give away to forebodings in striving to make it intelligible to them; indeed, the acceptance of the task was in itself a movement of resistance to despair. "I sometimes apprehend that our institutions may perish before we realize the most precious of the possibilities they contain"[70]—so Hawthorne felt in the years before the Civil War, and in writing for children he had checked the drift of his own mind toward an acceptance of his own dark premonitions. The premonitions remained, for they were bred by the times, they were as real as the children of his imagination; and the conquest of them meant not preventing the tragedy they foreshadowed but minimizing its terrors. It might be that a generation lived in peace because their parents had refused to surrender to the inevitability of civil war; and that the war, when it came, did not completely destroy the country because those who fought it were the children of those who had tried to prevent its occurring.

He had chosen an awkward form for his stories. In *Grandfather's Chair* Hawthorne visualized an old patriot telling his grandchildren one episode after another of the royal governors who had occupied the chair in which he spent his declining years. That chair was made of oak, dark with age, rubbed and polished till it shone as bright as mahogany. The old grandfather telling his stories might have been modeled on Grandfather Manning, and the children who listened to him on Hawthorne, Ebie, and Louisa. The brief episodes are wonderful. They are but glimpses of history, a single scene, richly colored—the village of Salem on the edge of the forest, the few wretched hovels of the settlers, wigwams and cloth tents, pine trees, patches of garden ground and cornfield, clam diggers on the beach, and Lady Arabella staring through the lattice window of Mr. Endicott's house; Captain Phipps's Indian divers, plunging over the side of the boat at Porto de la Plata, and groping among the seaweed and sunken cannon for the treasure, two million dollars' worth, at the bottom of the sea; or an Indian boy reading John Eliot's translation of the Bible, casting his eyes over the mysterious page, and reading so skillfully that it sounded like wild music, as if the forest leaves were singing and the roar of distant streams pouring through the young Indian's voice.[71]

The biographies in *Famous Old People* were brief studies of Benjamin West, Sir Isaac Newton, Benjamin Franklin, Samuel Johnson and Queen Christina, an artist, a scientist, a Yankee, a philosopher, and a warrior queen. What was Hawthorne's purpose in choosing them? except that each symbolized some aspect of life intelligible to children, or embodied a virtue he desired to re-emphasize to them? Benjamin West, seven years old in 1745, studying a child's face in a cradle, slumbering peacefully with its waxen hands under its chin, and inspired thereby to try to capture its image with pen and ink, was a poignant example of an American artist, untaught and untrained, lacking even the essentials of his art. . . .

It seemed to be more difficult for Hawthorne to see Sophia than when they had lived in separate towns. The Peabody family settled at West Street and she again set out upon her round of visits, so like those of the period before she went to Cuba, to visit the Emersons at Concord, or to Malden, or to one of her relatives, where he could not or did not care to follow her. Or she was surrounded by the literary people who flocked to the Peabody bookstore. In August, before *Grandfather's Chair* was published, he went to Salem. He went to the Hurley Burley, he walked in the rain, he sat and talked for two hours with Elizabeth and Louisa, and he wrote to Sophia. He gave his letter to her father to deliver, and her father did not deliver it.

They were again in that tangle of cross-purposes and intrigue where nothing seemed ever to work right. They made appointments which were not understood, or they met, but there was some third party present. He wrote her at last, after another letter that Mary was to deliver had gone astray, that she was to send her letters to him by the post office—it was the best way. It seemed that once, at least, their romance came periously close to disaster; he wrote to her in distress of their parting without a word at the door of the Hooper's, and his concern at the mute, reproachful expression on her face as she turned to him before she went inside.[72]

His work had grown harrowing. The Democrats were being driven out of office. Sophia was frequently silent, withdrawn, and pale; distance had grown between her and the friends of a lifetime. Mary Foote could no longer understand her.[73] Her companions were now Elizabeth's friends, and she had never been as easily intimate with them as with less headstrong and intellectual folk. There is a clear development in Hawthorne's letters to her. He was at first grave and earnest, and, after their engagement, playful and at times, perhaps, breezier than Sophia liked him to be; this phase quickly ended, and gave way to a kind of frightened and impetuous outpouring of his heart, a revelation of his weaknesses and self-condemnation, almost as though he feared he had lost her.

Before the election Hawthorne again went to Salem. In the midst of the campaign, with full fury of the storm beating directly on the Custom House, and almost against himself, he had written *Grandfather's Chair*. The book was finished. When he gave the manuscript to Sophia to read it seemed to him the dullest of all books he could offer, and he wondered how many pages she could read without falling asleep. He hoped she could find something laudable in it, because he wanted her to tell him that he had done well. And as he sat in the old chamber under the eaves his heart suddenly overflowed with a knowledge of how much she meant to him and how sad was the thought of life without her.

It was ten-thirty in the morning, Friday, October 4, the bright fall morning of Salem, the air brisk and the sea gleaming. The old room in which he worked was unchanged from the days he had lived there, small, darkish, with its single window and its small desk and chair, the pine table, the washstand, the chest of drawers, the closet, the worn-out shoebrush. Here he had written them all—the tragic story of Alice Doane, and the vision of the brother and sister hurrying through the icy streets of Salem, the blue firmament glowing with an inherent brightness, the great stars burning in their sphere, the clouds burdened with radiance, and the trees hung with diamonds and the houses overlaid with silver. Here he had aroused himself from his work to find that the sky was light and the Manning stagecoach was rumbling through the street on the first morning run to Boston. And just as he had awakened then from the world of his fantasies to the daylight, so it seemed to him that she had called him from a world of shadows to reality. Thousands upon thousands of visions had appeared to him in that room—the plain pine boards of the meetinghouse, where the mother of the gentle boy, in sackcloth, her hair streaked with ashes, had mounted the pulpit with her firm, unwavering steps; and the stream in the woods where the pirate, dark and menacing, had cast his line while Ellen and her lovers watched. Here he had seen the anguish of Major Molineaux, and heard the laughter of the mob swelling in the narrow street, and imagined the scene of tension when the gray champion appeared from nowhere and dispersed the troops ready to fire. Here he had written all night, until his visions were a bright reality and the voices of his family like faint sounds in a dream. The gray dawns had found him wide awake and feverish, the victim of his own enchantment. Or, working all day, he had gone forth at nightfall, down through the center of town, where the old captains were trudging through the rain to the insurance company's office and the lights from the shop windows reflected on the shiny surface of the pavement. And here his mind had made its long voyages to the past, illuminating, like a searchlight focusing on one object after another in the gloom, a house, a scene, a moment of anguish, the wives of the dead. The visions faded, one into another; the days passed imperceptibly into years. He was now thirty-six years old; fifteen years had gone by since he began with his first intense energy and wild courage to throw a ghostly glimmer over the plain reality of his home town, and visualized a murder on the lonely road to Boston, entangled obscurely with a forgotten scene in a cabin, the wind blowing his dead father's hair, and the children crying in the dusky light.

What visions now replaced it! Newton studying the nature of light, and finding the goal of science in the ceaseless search for new revelations of the infinite wisdom and goodness of the Creator; Samuel Johnson standing in the market place, an old man, doing penance for having disobeyed his father as a child; and the children clambering over grandfather's chair to hear their stories retold. The moments when the heart gives back the warmth stored within it are never studied, they come unexpectedly, prompted by a sight, the smell of clover, a gift of tulips—something that suddenly calls to mind a recollection of childhood, the memory of love, a moment of happiness, or that transforms a dull forgotten pain, in a moment of self-realization, into its place with what caused it and in so doing ends it forever. It was not that in the depths of every heart there is a tomb and a dungeon, as he had written in *The Haunted Mind*, but rather that in the depths of his heart there lay the undiscovered element in his life, what it was that he had never found, either in his long studies of the past or in the clear surface observation of his travels.

He took his pen and began to write to Sophia. "Here I sit in my old accustomed chamber, where I used to sit in days gone by. Here I have written many tales—many that have been burned to ashes, many that doubtless deserved the same fate. This claims to be called a haunted chamber, for thousands upon thousands of visions have appeared to me in it; and some few of them have become visible to the world. If ever I should have a biographer, he ought to make great mention of this chamber in my memoirs, because so much of my lonely youth was wasted here, and here my mind and character were formed; and here I have been glad and hopeful, and here I have been despondent. And here I sat a long, long time, waiting patiently for the world to know me, and sometimes wondering why it did not know me sooner, or whether it would ever know me at all—at least, till I were in my grave. And sometimes it seemed as if I were already in the grave, with only life enough to be chilled and benumbed. But oftener I was happy—at least as happy as I then knew how to be, or was aware of the possibility of being. By and by, the world found me out in my lonely chamber, and called me forth—not, indeed, with a loud roar of acclamation, but, rather with a still, small voice,—and forth I went, but found nothing in the world that I thought preferable to my old solitude till now. And now I begin to understand why I was imprisoned so many years in this lonely chamber, and why I could never break through the viewless bolts and bars; for if I had sooner made my escape into the world, I should have grown hard and rough, and been covered with earthly dust, and my heart might have become callous by rude encounters with the multitude. But living in solitude till the fullness of time was come, I still kept the dew of my youth and the freshness of my heart. I used to think I could imagine all passions, all feelings, and states of the heart and mind; but how little did I know! Indeed we are but shadows; we are not endowed with real life, and all that seems most real about us is but the thinnest substance of a dream—till the heart be touched. That touch creates us—then we begin to be—thereby we are beings of reality and inheritors of eternity.

"Sometimes during my solitary life in our old Salem house, it seemed to me as if I had only life enough to know that I was not alive, for I had no wife then to keep my heart warm. But, at length, you were revealed to me, in the shadow of a seclusion as deep as my own. I drew nearer and nearer to you, and opened my heart to you, and you came to me, and will remain forever, keeping my heart warm and renewing my life with your own. You only have taught me that I have a heart— you only have thrown a light, deep downward and upward, into my soul. You only have revealed me to myself, for without your aid my best knowledge of myself would have been merely to know my own shadow— to watch it flickering on the wall, and mistake its fantasies for my own real actions. Do you comprehend what you have done for me?" [74]

IX

On April 12, 1841, Hawthorne left Boston by sleigh. He was chill and feverish; the buildings on either side seemed to press too close; the snowfall looked inexpressibly dreary coming down through an atmosphere of city smoke, and alighting on the sidewalk only to be marked by somebody's boots or overshoes. The sleigh left the pavement and the muffled hooftramps beat upon a desolate extent of country road. He revived somewhat as they rode fleetly and merrily along, by stone fences half buried in the wavelike drifts, through patches of woodland,

and passed scattered dwellings, whence puffed the smoke of country fires.[75]

Nine miles out of town they came to a dark farmhouse set back from the road. Even in the wild snowstorm it was the most beautiful place that Hawthorne had ever seen. An elm and a sycamore grew beside the house, and the grounds beside it were terraced down to a small brook, now frozen and its ice covered with the drifting snow. Below the house lay great wide pastures, level as a parade ground, across which the snow drifted. Beyond them there was a faint growth of trees edging the Charles River. On the opposite side of the house the pastures ended in a pine forest.

On one side of the entrance hall there was a low-ceilinged living room, and a dining room adjoining it, with a large, brick fireplace between them. A wood fire of stanch oak logs was burning, and the fitful gusts of the wintry snowstorm roared in the chimney. At the back of the house, opening from the dining room, was the large kitchen, with an old-fashioned open hearth. Across the hall were three adjoining bedrooms. The table in the dining room was covered with white linen; the house was immaculate.[76]

This was Brook Farm. It had not then the reputation it later acquired. There were fifteen people making this ordinary dwelling their home. Hawthorne knew some of them; the others he was meeting for the firt time. George Ripley and his wife Sophia Ripley he had undoubtedly met before; they were familiar figures in the groups that used the Peabody bookstore for their headquarters. Mrs. Ripley was the former Sophia Channing Dana, a tall woman, ardent and impulsive, gifted, brilliant, with a slight, graceful figure. She was a friend of Mary Foote in Salem.[77] She was nearsighted, but did not wear glasses. The farm was owned by her husband—not precisely owned, either, for the title was not transferred until the fall, though no one, apparently, knew it.[78] George Ripley was slender, pale, clean shaven, with curly brown hair and black eyes behind his gold-rimmed spectacles. He had left his pulpit at the Unitarian church at Purchase and Pearl Streets the year before, after fourteen years of service, and bought or taken possession of this farm on some informal arrangement, to establish a community that would build a better life.[79]

Brook Farm then had none of the glamour that was attached to it as an experiment in communal living by the enlightened spirits of New

England. It was just a farm on which a group of people, none of whom knew anything about farming, were going to try to make a living. Ripley had conceived his plan for it the previous summer. When Hawthorne resigned his job at the Custom House in January, Ripley persuaded him to join in the venture. Of Hawthorne's reasons for so doing, more later. For the time being he was becoming acquainted with his companions. The first to attract his attention was the vivacious Mrs. Almira Barlow, a widow with three boys. They lived in the rooms downstairs, across the hall from the living room. Before her marriage Mrs. Barlow had been Miss Penniman of Brookline, a famous beauty, and beautiful she was still, with her dark abundant hair, fine, perfectly developed figure, and a free, careless, generous way of expressing herself.[80] She dressed simply and carelessly, and in quiet moods seemed rather indolent; but when really in earnest she grew all alive to her finger tips. She was an admirable figure of a woman, on the verge of her richest maturity, blooming with such health and vigor that a man might have fallen in love with her for their sake alone.

The twilight fell sadly and silently out of the sky, its gray or sable flakes intermingling themselves in the fast descending snow. The storm seemed to Hawthorne a symbol of the cold, desolate, distrustful phantoms that invariably haunt the mind, on the eve of adventurous enterprises, to warn us back within the boundaries of ordinary life. His cold was getting worse.[81]

He studied his new companions. George Leach and his wife were a pair of uncompromising rebels. They were those grim doctrinaries who in every society apply its theories to the limit, and who always seem to have a moral advantage over its temperate members. They were real revolutionists—abolitionists, and station agents on the underground railway. They would eat no meat. They ate at a separate table. They disapproved of vaccination. They refused to permit their nephew, who lived with them, to be vaccinated. He contracted smallpox, and communicated it to thirty members of Brook Farm—this somewhat later, when it had grown, and after Hawthorne had left the community. When they left in turn they started a hotel which was a station of the underground. Enough—they were the real thing, and doubtless their very presence cast a chill over the radicals and the visionaries and the quiet Socialists who dreamed of a better life without violence in it and without violence in achieving it.[82]

Then there was George Bradford. He was thirty-four, quiet, absent
minded, and so overly conscientious that his excessive scruples were a
New England joke for a generation. When he applied for the position of
librarian at Harvard he dumfounded the president by carefully explaining his many disqualifications for the post. When he attended Harvard
Divinity School the weighty Andrews Norton, the terror of Unitarians,
told him: "Your discourse, Mr. Bradford, is marked by the absence of
every qualification which a good sermon ought to have." Bradford probably agreed with him. He was a peculiarly lovable character, with a
gentle and kindly humor, his wit tempered with an occasional slight
melancholy, and his sweetness and refinement visible in his features. He
had been a preacher, very briefly, and then became a teacher, with
mostly girls in his classes; but he always believed that the quality of
his work was falling off, and so he spent his entire life abandoning one
undertaking and starting over again. This conviction of his was completely erroneous, but it was inescapable. His discourse was marked by
a similar inability to stick to one subject. Mrs. Ripley said he would
not be happy in heaven unless he could see a way out. Georgianna
Kirby, a lively young English girl who lived at the farm, said he was
born at thirty-four and never got any older. Bradford made seven trips
abroad to prevent his teaching falling into mere routine, of which there
was no danger anyway, but his real interest was vegetable gardening,
and after he left Brook Farm he started a garden and peddled its
produce from back door to back door. He was always popular with
women, whether as a teacher or a gardener, and they seem to have regarded him with the affectionate good nature reserved for someone they
completely understood. He was an expert botanist, much admired by
Emerson for his ability to prune trees. He could not stay at Brook
Farm any more than at his schools, and one morning he came downstairs wearing a long overcoat and carrying an umbrella, with his belongings wrapped in a blue silk handkerchief, and announced that he
was going away. But before he left he had a confession to make, and
calling aside two young women he admired he told them gravely that
there were moments when he would not have lifted a finger to save
Charles Dana's life, so angry was he that Dana had lured them into
his German class when Bradford had wanted to teach them himself.[83]

Dana was his opposite, tall, handsome, firm, expressive, strong,
forceful, self-confident, with a powerful bass voice that rumbled out

his hearty jokes or was lifted in the refrain of "If you get there before I do" as he helped the young women with their housework. He got things done; he organized them efficiently; and he was the embodiment of masculine well-being at whose arrival the George Bradfords of the world desire to go somewhere else. He helped with the laundry, carried water, made pancakes, folded clothes, and in the barn on Sunday evening prepared food for the market—though all the young men of Brook Farm helped with the evening tasks, from "a desire to free the young women for participation in some further scheme of entertainment." Dana was then only twenty-two. He had shown none of the qualities, except the vitality and energy, that were to make him the famous founder and editor of the New York *Sun*. He was hardheaded, cool, ambitious, "a good hater with an early start," but he was also kindly and considerate, with pleasant manners and a natural dignity, hard working and determined; no one did more to make Brook Farm a success. Dana was born in Hinsdale, New Hampshire, left an orphan at an early age, and worked in an uncle's store in Buffalo, New York, until the store failed in the panic of 1837. He taught himself Latin in his spare time, and organized a club of literary men to criticize each other's works. He entered Harvard in 1839, but his eyesight failed after he sat up all night reading *Oliver Twist* by candlelight—and he left after a year and joined Brook Farm.[84]

Dana had not yet come to live at the farm, but he had taken part in the preliminary discussions and Hawthorne no doubt knew him. Around the fire on the day of Hawthorne's arrival there were others, Warren Burton, and Mrs. Minot Pratt and her three children. Minot Pratt was a painter, foreman of the *Christian Register*'s composing room. He had thrown his lot in with the community, and was leaving his job, but he did not come to the farm until summer, his family preceding him there. He was thirty-six. He was honest and courageous, a large man with a fine physique, with strong features, modest and dignified. He was an expert botanist, and wrote a book on the *Flora of Concord, Massachusetts*. Hawthorne admired Mr. and Mrs. Minot Pratt; they seemed to him good, sensible, matured people, and models of what a New England couple should be.[85]

Then there was Warren Burton, a Unitarian minister-at-large, and John Sullivan Dwight, a gentle soul who pioneered in musical criticism and introduced Beethoven to Boston, a short, slight, dignified man who was what was known in that day as a quiddle—i.e., one who is fussy over trifles. There were Samuel and Mary Robbins, David Mack and Lemuel Capen, and Ripley's sister, Marianna Ripley, a teacher. David Mack's wife was another friend of Mrs. Caleb Foote in Salem, who soon began to hear alarming things about the colony. They sat about the fire, Hawthorne reflected, a group that might lawfully dream of earthly happiness for themselves and mankind. They might give utterance to their wildest visions without dread of laughter or scorn. They had actually taken the final step. They had left the rusty iron framework of society. They had broken through the hindrances that keep most people on the weary treadmill of the established system. They had stepped down from the pulpit, or flung aside the pen, or closed the ledger—they had, each of them, given up what they had attained for the sake of showing mankind the example of a life governed by other than the cruel and false principles on which human society has all along been based.[86]

They propose nothing less than to create a better life. A better life! In twenty-five years, Ripley hoped and believed, the adventure they were then undertaking would have demonstrated that the curse of labor could be lifted from the world.[87] They proposed nothing less than to ease the laboring man of his burden of toil; nothing less would satisfy them or justify the sacrifice they were making. They proposed to profit by mutual aid. They would not gain wealth by wresting it from an enemy or filching it craftily from someone less shrewd then themselves —if, indeed, there were any such in New England. Nor would they win it by selfish competition with a neighbor. They proposed to offer up the earnest toil of their bodies, as a prayer no less than an effort for the advancement of their race.[88]

Hawthorne had saved at least $1,500 in his three years of toil in the Custom House.[89] He invested it in Brook Farm without a moment's regret. The greatest obstacle to being heroic, he thought, is the doubt whether one may not be going to prove oneself a fool. The truest heroism is to resist the doubt; the profoundest wisdom is to know when it ought to be resisted, and when to be obeyed. Now, the hope of establishing a better life on earth by such means was not a part of Hawthorne's habits of thought, any more than was Bridge's project for damming the Kennebec. But it was a part of the talk of the circles that Sophia lived in, and it was characteristic of him that, if he listened and approved, he would act, though the project threatened to delay their marriage and made his previous three years of grievous toil come to nothing. Never mind—the outlandish and impractical dreams of the visionaries were what he liked about them. "Whatever else I might repent of, therefore, let it be reckoned neither among my sins nor follies that I once had faith and force enough to form generous hopes of the world's destiny—yes!—and to do what in me lay for their accomplishment." [90]

It seemed at the moment that he could do very little. Now, Brook Farm almost succeeded. It came within a few hundred dollars of making a profit each year. Ripley had made a bad selection of land to begin with, for the soil was gravelly and much of it was overgrown, and could be cleared only at a ruinous cost. The Brook Farmers did not have enough experience in farming; and too many of them lacked the physical strength to do the work when skilled farmers guided them. Yet, with almost every mistake that could be made, they had a deficit of only a few hundred dollars the first year, and showed a profit the second year. If Ripley could actually have planned for twenty-five years, the farm by 1866 would have been a powerful demonstration of co-operative and creative effort—as powerful as the example of Derby's voyages to China were to an earlier generation. Even as it was, the steady increase in the value of the land, because of both its improvements and the increasing value of real estate, made the farm profitable beyond the yearly record of its cash transactions; and in fifty years, as Roxbury became part of Boston, the 170 acres of the farm could have been sold for enough to start fifty such projects. But Brook Farm was not actually planned on a 25-year program. It always operated from year to year. It had almost no capital except what Hawthorne put up. It had only two wealthy supporters, and they were not very wealthy. Their help amounted to little more than taking the mortgages on the property —no risk.[91]

Brook Farm was not a socialist or a communal experiment. It was an agricultural college. What happened was that Ripley and his sister organized schools, whose assets—which were apparently entirely on paper—were transferred to Brook Farm for their shares in the association. There were 24 shares of stock, at $500 a share. Ripley, his wife and sister, owned eight; Minot Pratt and his wife, five; Charles Dana, three; Hawthorne, two; Sarah Sterns, two; and Charles Whitmore, one. Three shares were owned by William Allen, a farmer. There should have been, then, $12,000 to begin with; there was actually $4,500, of which $1,000 was Hawthorne's investment. Ripley pledged his library at $400 for part of his subscrpition. The shares were to draw 5 per cent interest, and a member could supposedly withdraw with a year's notice, receiving his entire investment back, plus interest at 5 per cent.[92]

Brook Farm was to be a school. Boys were to be boarded at five dollars a week, and girls at four dollars a week. There were three divisions, primary, elementary, and a preparatory school of six years for the older children. It was accredited by Harvard. There were to be both boarders and workers in the colony. A day's labor was exchanged for a day's board. The women did the housework and taught and prepared food for market; the men ran the farm, and as the shops were built, worked at making sashes and blinds and other small manufactured objects.

In the summer of 1840 Ripley was visting his friend Theodore Parker at Roxbury when he conceived the plan of Brook Farm. The land he selected was a farm near Parker's West Roxbury church, 170 acres in the original purchase, with 22 acres added later. The association bought it for $10,500, but immediately mortgaged it for $11,000. One mortgage was taken by Daniel Wilder and Josiah Quincy, the president of Harvard. They were commissioners of the sinking fund of the Western Railroad Coporation. The second mortgage was taken by George Russell, Elizabeth Peabody's friend and associate, and by Henry Sturgis and Francis Shaw. A third mortgage of $500 was taken by Lucy Cabot. These last were people of property who were personal friends of some of the members, or who, like Shaw, were conservative on most issues but were resolutely and quietly opposed to slavery.[93] Brook Farm was started on nothing. When it is considered that fifteen people were there in April, and that the number grew steadily through the summer, that the farm eventually provided a livelihood for 150 people and had 4,000 visitors a year,[94] the achievement of beginning without capital becomes extremely impressive. It was not the plan or the work that made the farm fail, nor the legendary dreaminess of the Brook Farmers, of which too much has been made. Such mishaps as the smallpox epidemic were more important; the farm was sabotaged from the start.

It was the custom, at Brook Farm, to pay no attention to newcomers.[95] No one spoke to them when they arrived. Ripley must have had a strong conspiratorial streak in his otherwise amiable make-up, to enlist new boarders and workers and bring them in without notifying those already there; but the practice added to the unreality of the community. Strangers were constantly arriving, remaining a few days without identifying themselves, or being identified, and vanishing. There appeared to be a great many ministers among them, though one could not be sure.

For two days after Hawthorne's arrival the farm was snowbound. No work could be started. It did not matter to him, for he was in bed. He awakened the morning after his arrival with a raging furnace in his head. The doctor was called. He was, however, a homeopathic physician, who prescribed medicine in such tiny doses that in two weeks Hawthorne took about enough to be hid on the point of a needle. He was fed a watery gruel, and his ordinarily robust frame wasted away to its skeleton.[96] He wrote to Sophia that he had a cold. He must have had pneumonia. When he again stirred about the farm, it had a nightmarish appearance that, for him, it always had. Four black-garbed visitors were now added to the company, though they left without his learning who they were. He seems to have stepped out tentatively, uneasily, testing the ground under his feet as though it were thin ice, with the peculiar sense of dismay that accompanies the first illness of middle age, when the disorders that once vanished overnight hang on so stubbornly that it seems doubtful they will ever leave.

And added to the sense of unreality, which convalescence left him with, there was the unreal world of Brook Farm itself. It was not deliberately queer. On the contrary, the members were distinguished by their spirited efforts to be normal and ordinary farmers, but they always did something wrong, or dressed strangely without knowing that they did, or looked sad when there was nothing to be melancholy about, or happy when there was no cause for mirth, so that the comparison of the farm to an asylum is almost inescapable. The most natural comments seemed absurd and the most outlandish behavior excited no attention beyond, perhaps, a benign smile from the doctor. Reality was somehow shaken in Brook Farm, the shadows angular and misshapen, the farmers not really farmers, the preachers not really preachers, the doctors not really doctors. Yet Hawthorne's illness was real enough. The doctor who attended him, prescribing an infinitesimal dose of medicine, was like a character in *Alice in Wonderland*, prescribing a potion to

make one grow large or small. The beautiful Mrs. Barlow, who prepared
the gruel on which he grew thinner and thinner, appeared more and
more vivacious, high-spirited, and blooming with good health, as he felt
himself to be wasting away. The men of Brook Farm wore long coats
and heavy boots with two-inch soles, and seem to have resembled Russian peasants in a period when they were greatly oppressed by the
Czar. There was something Russian in the beards and melancholy, the
constant printing of pamphlets and magazines, the lying about on
the floor after supper, and the haunting music of the choir fading away
over the fields of West Roxbury as it might have drifted over the
steppes. The women wore short skirts and let their hair flow free; they
wore broad hats, or twined wreaths from wild vines and berries in each
other's hair. And what women! They were those calm, placid emanci-
pated women of New England, with their untroubled freedom of thought
and expression and desire, before whose simple boldness the boldest of
her radicals seemed timid. Nobody who lived at Brook Farm ever quite
lived it down, though there was never any scandal attached to it; it
was not so much that there were stories of sexual freedom as it was that
there wasn't. The talk was liberated; the women could talk freely, as
they did among themselves, and the freedom seemed to result in the
livelier motions of their bodies, their readier laughter, and their amused
glances which, if nothing else, called attention to their eyes. They no
longer had to behave as they were expected to behave; they could laugh
at Miss Margaret Fuller's lectures if they wanted to. Most of the
women had never done a bit of work in their lives, and they now scrubbed
floors and washed in the laundry, wearing plain print dresses which
somehow revealed that they possessed far handsomer figures than they
had had when they were teaching music or Greek. The women who
were accustomed to housework wanted none of it at the farm. They
said: "I like to see *ladies* work—it is time they did—we have done
enough of it." So the ladies washed and scrubbed the floor." [97]

When Hawthorne had recovered his strength he was given a pitch-
fork and led out through the dawn to the manure heap behind the barn.
The Brook Farmers arose at six-thirty, dined at twelve-thirty, and went
to bed by nine in these spring days of the hardest work on the farm. The
land had evidently not been fertilized for some time, for there were three
hundred and twenty wagonloads of manure piled up and waiting to be
spread—of all farmwork the hardest. The days passed. His hands grew

calloused, his back ached, and he came home at night covered with the stench of manure, too exhausted to write letters or even to think. He threw himself upon his bed and listened to the sound of the brook beside the house. An unutterable weariness came over him at the thought, more tiring than the work he had done, that the experiment had already failed. He had planned to build a house somewhere on the farm where he could live with Sophia. Now he knew that he could never do it. Perhaps he sensed that he could not even get his money back from Ripley. Mercifully, he could not brood upon these matters; he slept. Then he awakened and thought again of his wife with him in a house of their own beside this little stream.

He rarely wrote to her. He lived through the days doggedly, waiting until that first Sunday when he was to see her again. His head swam with exhaustion; by May 3 there remained three hundred loads of manure to be carted and spread over the fields.[98] His companions were as tired as he was. George Bradford hardened his hands with work on the farm; and even Dwight, the music critic, though he was indolent by nature and worked when he wanted to, put in his day labor. He said that it was good for him: he would never have lived to old age if it had not been for his years there. Dana was a good worker. Minot Pratt appeared, and learned to plow. His knowledge of botany and his love of flowers delayed him: he would stop in his work and transplant the wild roses to form a hedge along the road. John Allen (Mrs. Leach's brother), a farmer from Vermont, arrived and added skilled labor to their fumbling efforts. The fields took shape. The market garden was planted. The farmers liked to be assigned to work in the pasture near the river, one of the loveliest spots on the farm, from which it spread away in a broad expanse of sunny upland, dim groves, and dimmer woods.[99]

Hawthorne's body hardened; he prided himself on how much work he could do. He milked cows and planted peas, and went with William Allen to sell pigs at the stockyard at Brighton.[100] The farm brightened in the spring days; the grounds grew lovely. The house faced east, separated from the brook by two terraced embankments, with shrubs and flower beds and mulberries and spruce trees growing on them. The two downstairs rooms of the farmhouse were united to make one large dining room, with windows at each end, and with the big fireplace in the middle. Six long pine tables were ranged across the room, with

benches on either side; they were white, with white linen and white table-
ware. A cheerful buzz of conversation filled the air. The young girls of
the colony hurried through the supper dishes; the tables were cleared
away, and the young people danced. Amelia Russell taught them. She
was petite and engaging, and another of the candid women of the farm
whose lives there make its story piquant. The girls called her Miss
Muslin.

Most of the life was lived outdoors. Four of the boys bought a
boat, and equipped it with sails, a carpet and a compass, and sailed
beyond the Dedham Bridge, with Georgianna Kirby, Mary Gannett,
Abby Morton and Caddy Stoddard as passengers. There was just a
ripple on the surface of the water, just enough life in the clouds, and
just enough richness in the banks, with the pale-green elders near the
shore and the dark tall pines behind them. On the summer evenings the
music lovers of the colony walked nine miles to Boston to the concerts,
and back to the farm under the stars. When the piano arrived they had
another source of inspiration. When Sophia's cousin Christopher
Cranch visited the farm all the youngsters flocked around him. Cousin
Christopher was tall and slim, with a broad forehead and dark curly
hair, aged twenty-eight, a Unitarian minister, a poet, and a ventrilo-
quist. The children loved him because he could imitate locomotives and
the sounds of the barnyard. He played the piano, the flute, the guitar
and the violin, and had a fine baritone voice. He had made a manuscript
copy of Shubert's "Serenade," and sang it to the Brook Farmers, who
were thus among the first Americans to hear it. There was good music
at the farm, and good teachers, probably as good as there were in the
country. It would have been hard to find people better equipped than
John Dwight to teach Haydn and Mozart, or better able than Ripley
to discuss Kant and Spinoza, or more inspiring teachers than Mrs.
Ripley and George Bradford to translate Dante. The students after
the primary grades were free. They studied when they wanted to, only
being required to be indoors before the doors were locked by ten. They
worked an hour or two a day, the boys hoeing, the girls wiping dishes.

George Bancroft sent his sons to the Brook Farm School. There
were two boys from Manila, Lucas and José Corrales.—[101] "Lucas with
his heavy features and almost mulatto complexion; and José, slighter,
with a rather feminine face—not a gay, girlish one, but grave, reserved,
eying you sometimes with an earnest, but secret expression, and causing

you to question what sort of a person he is." [102] Hawthorne apparently did not know that one of the boys had leprosy. James Fuller, Margaret Fuller's younger brother, and Horace Sumner, Charles Sumner's brother, were students, and Deborah Gannett, the daughter of Reverend Gannett (assistant to Channing). It was Gannett who praised Hawthorne's works at a lecture in Salem—whereat, said Hawthorne, the audience hissed. Georgianna Kirby, a 22-year-old English girl lived at the farm with her fourteen-year-old brother. She had been befriended by Reverend Gannett after some unfortunate experience in England; she lived in his household before coming to the farm, where she exchanged eight hours of labor a day for her board and her tuition in the school.

Hawthorne took little part in the activities. He did no teaching. It was characteristic of him that he made friends with Tom Orange, a farmer who lived near by, and who watched the doings of the Brook Farmers with grave Yankee wisdom. The vegetarians of the farm disapproved of Orange because he did so much slaughtering. Orange was a character in his own right, stocky and solid, and a man of consequence in West Roxbury. In the exhilaration of their release from society's conventions, the Brook Farmers tended to look disdainfully at the world's people they had left behind.[103] But Hawthorne never stopped working, and he talked with Orange in the same spirit that he had studied the riverbank at Augusta or talked over the new arrivals in Salem with the tollgatherer on the bridge over the North River.

He wrote very rarely to Sophia. Sometimes he did not know where she was, as she set out on another round of those strange unhappy visits. The truth was that she was sick for two months, and did not want him to know it. He grew terribly tried, more tired than he had ever been, unable to read, scarcely able to write, scarcely able even to think, and sustained only by a faint glimmering dream that within a few days —this coming Tuesday—he would see her again. The farm grew very beautiful. He worked under a clear blue sky, on a hillside, and sometimes it seemed that he was working in the sky itself. The long rolling fields of the farm delighted him, and the little stream that flowed beside the house, though it had been made to flow in straight lines and round square corners in order to save land for tilling. He dreamed that when he and Sophia lived there they could lie in their room and listen to the sound of the brook bubbling over the stones. Then he knew, though he

dared not yet admit it to himself, that they would never live there. The
grass blushed green, and the slopes and hollows. The potatoes had not
come up, but he looked beneath the stone walls for violets to send to her,
that they might have the blissful fate of being treasured for a time in
her bosom. The work grew heavier. He could not write at all. He felt
that he could not live if he did not have the idea of her constantly before
him, and the sense of being in constant spiritual communion with her.

On June 1 he was still at work on the manure pile. That abominable
gold mine! Thank God, they anticipated getting rid of its treasures in
two or three days. "Of all hateful places, that is the worst; and I shall
never comfort myself for having spent so many days of blessed sunshine there. It is my opinion that a man's soul may be buried and perish
under a dung heap or in a furrow of the field, just as well as under a
pile of money." [104]

George Ripley knew, before many months were out, that the path
he had chosen led along a dangerous and probably impassable way.
In his farmer's blouse, wearing a wide straw hat and high boots, he
cleaned stables, milked cows, and carried vegetables. This clergyman
was as cool a gambler as Horatio Bridge had been; he met each reverse,
and they were many, without a change of expression. His first plan had
been to raise $50,000 to start Brook Farm. He launched it with $4,500.
A firm, devoted man, zealous without appearing to be so, persuasive,
eloquent, a hearty eater, never despondent, he was a prophet who was
also at ease with common men. He loved to walk, he enjoyed his sleep, he
dreaded taking cold, he relished New England cooking, and though he
had an encyclopedic mind, of enormous retentive power, and a mastery
of languages, his favorite reading was books on physiology and his
favorite activity was projecting, with his genius for clear, concise statement, visions of the ideal Christian society. The true followers of Jesus,
he said, are a band of brothers; they compose one family; they attach
no importance whatever to the petty distinctions of birth, rank, wealth,
and station. Feeling that they are in the pursuit of truth, in the love of
holiness, and in the hope of immortal life, they regard the common
differences of the world, by which men are separated from each other,
as lighter than the dust in the balance.

He was moderate in his statement of his views, but unyielding.
As a Christian, he said, he would aid in the overthrow of every form of
slavery. "I would free the mind from bondage and the body from chains;

I would not feel that my duty was accomplished while there was one human being, within the sphere of my influence, held in unrequited labor at the expense of another, destitute of the means of education, or doomed to penury, degradation, and vice by the misfortune of his birth."

Ripley did not like to have his statements of his beliefs construed as attacks on those who held others; he believed in the omnipotence of kindness, of moral intrepidity, of divine charity. "The defense of humanity is sometimes considered an attack on society; a sense of the evil of prevalent systems a reflection on the character of the men who sustain them."

His talk was enchanting even in an age of great talkers; and with his black eyes flashing behind his gold-rimmed spectacles, his pale, clean-shaven features animated, he made an impression far more lasting than his contemporary fame indicated. For fourteen years he had preached to a small congregation at Purchase Street, near the wharves. A Unitarian society had been especially gathered for him there soon after his graduation from Harvard. The men of his age went on to new successes, to editorships, authorships, wealthy marriages, or into politics and education, and still he remained in the same pulpit of the same small church, preaching with controlled ardor to a modest and undemanding congregation that had never really shared his ideas. The time came when he could no longer preach, though now his congregation did not want him to leave, and he delivered his wonderful farewell sermon: "The true followers of Jesus are a band of brothers. They look upon each other with mutual respect and honor; they have no struggle for pre-eminence; they have no desire for the chief seats in the synagogue, nor greetings in the market and the street; and the poor widow, who leaves the daily toil by which a suffering family is kept from want, to gather with the faithful in the house of worship, is welcomed with as warm a sympathy, and regarded with as sincere affection, and treated with just as much respect, as they who are arrayed in costly robes and who come from the length of office or the abodes of luxury, to look up to the common Father, in whose sight a pure heart and clean hands are alone of value. These ideals I have perhaps insisted on more strongly than others, for they have been near my heart; they are a part of my life; they seem to me to be the very essence of the religion which I was taught. The great fact of equality before God is not one to let the heart

remain cold; it is not a mere speculative abstraction; it is something
more than a watchword for a political party to gain power with, and
then do nothing to carry it into practical operation; it is a deep, solemn,
vital truth, written by the Almighty in the laws of our being, announced
with terrible distinctness to the oppressor by his beloved Son, and
pleaded for by all that is just and noble in the promptings of our nature . . . I cannot behold the degradation, the ignorance, the poverty,
the vice, the ruin of the soul, which is everywhere displayed in the very
bosom of the Christian society in our city, while men idly look on, without a shudder. I cannot witness the glaring inequalities of condition,
the hollow pretension of pride, the scornful apathy with which many
urge the prostitution of man, the burning zeal with which they run the
race of selfish competition, with no thought for the elevation of their
brethren, without the sad conviction that the spirit of Christ has well-
nigh disappeared from our churches, and that a fearful doom awaits
us. 'Inasmuch as ye have not done it unto one of the least of these, ye
have not done it unto me.' "

Ripley was not a Communist. He believed that the evils arising
from trade and money grew out of the defects of the social system, not
from an intrinsic vice in the things themselves. He feared that the aboli-
tion of private property would so destroy the independence of the individual as to interfere with the great object of all social reform—the
development of humanity. "The great problem," he said, "is to guarantee individualism against the masses on the one hand, and the masses
against the individual on the other." [105]

By summer it was plain that the farm could not continue as it had.
On August 22 Hawthorne wrote to Sophia that it was extremely doubtful that Ripley could locate his community on the farm. He could not
bring the owner to terms. "I am becoming more and more convinced that
we must not lean upon this Community. Whatever is done must be done
by my own undivided strength. I shall not remain here through the
winter . . . unless there will be a house ready for me in the spring."

In September the association was formed. The community had not
owned the land until this time. It appeared, indeed, that the association
was formed as much to protect what the Brook Farmers had already
invested, in both money and labor, as to organize a company that would
proceed from there on. Hawthorne was a member, with Dana, of the
finance committee. His actual connection with the farm was nearly

over, though he lent it another $400.[106] What probably happened is that no one, except Ripley himself, had known how little the farm had to go on, and that when the revelation was made Hawthorne's faith in the enterprise ended once and for all.

The association then bought the land which the farmers had been toiling upon all summer. They mortgaged it for enough to pay the previous owners. All these transactions bore the unmistakable stamp of a hasty receivership to avoid the scandal of immediate failure crushing Ripley and, perhaps even more, Sophia Ripley. The farm would not be a success, but the farmers would not, at least, be the laughingstock they were threatened with being.

The men of good will of Boston visited and rested there, Reverend Channing, Emerson, and George Russell, and Judge Story's gifted son, William Wetmore Story, Francis Shaw and others, bringing a screen of sociability and ease to hide Ripley's catastrophic failure. The farm's social life became hearty, even gay; and poor Ripley must have suffered more at the kindness of his friends than he would have if his noble dream had been crushed at once by his enemies. One fall day there was a picnic party in the woods, in honor of Frank Dana's sixth birthday, and Hawthorne jotted down in his notebook a glimpse of the scene that seemed to sum up Brook Farm. "I strolled into the woods, after dinner," he wrote, "with Mr. Bradford; and in a lonesome glade we met the apparition of an Indian chief, dressed in appropriate costume of blanket, feathers and paint, and armed with a musket." Almost at the same instant Deborah Gannett—always called Ora—bright, vivacious, dark haired, rich complexioned, and fifteen years old, dressed as a fortune-teller, came from among the trees and proposed to tell his future. He agreed, and while Ora was telling his fortune Ellen Slade, also fifteen, blonde, fair, quiet and composed, and dressed as the goddess Diana, let fly with an arrow and hit him on the hand. They were both very pretty —at least, pretty enough to make fifteen years enchanting. "Accompanied by these denizens of the wild wood, we went onward, and came to a company of fantastic figures, arranged in a ring for a dance or game. There was a Swiss girl, an Indian squaw, a Negro of the Jim Crow order, one or two foresters; and several people in Christian attire; besides children of all ages. Then followed childish games, in which the grown people took part with mirth enough—while I, whose nature it is to be a mere spectator of both sport and serious business, lay under the trees and looked on. Meanwhile, Mr. Emerson, and Miss Fuller, who had arrived an hour or two before, came forth into the little glade where we were assembled. Here followed much talk.

"The ceremonies of the day concluded with a cold collation of cakes and fruit. All was pleasant enough: 'an excellent piece of work; would't were done!' It has left a fantastic impression on my memory, this intermingling of wild and fabulous characters with real and homely ones, in the secluded nook in the woods. I remember them with the sunlight breaking through overshadowing branches, and they appearing and disappearing confusedly—perhaps starting out of the earth; as if the every day laws of nature were suspended for this particular occasion. There are the children, too, laughing and sporting about, as if they were at home among such strange shapes—and anon bursting into loud uproar of lamentation when the rude gambols of the merry makers chanced to overturn them. And apart, with a shrewd Yankee observation of the scene, study our friend Orange, a thickset, sturdy figure, in his blue frock, enjoying the fun well enough, yet rather laughing with a perception of its nonsensicalness, than at all entering into the spirit of the thing." [107]

Ripley's reaction to his increased trouble was characteristic: he enlarged the scope of the farm. It had now become something of a sensation in Boston. Another kind of visitor began to appear, Robert Owen, from his communal communities, and Albert Brisbane, with his plans for remodeling society according to the schemes of the French philosopher, Fourier, and Horace Greeley. But what was Mike Walsh doing among the visitors?[108] Mike Walsh was a revolutionary gangster. He was an Irish-born New Yorker, twenty-five years old in 1841, the son of the owner of a mahogany yard in New York City. Mike Walsh became a printer, drifted to New Orleans, worked as a Washington correspondent and returned to New York, where he announced that he was the leader of the subterranean Democrats, ignored by the political leaders. He organized the Spartan Association of young laborers. He introduced gang warfare into New York politics: the Spartans raided ward meetings and forcibly removed their enemies. Walsh founded a newspaper, the *Subterranean*, to arouse the working class against the capitalists and politicians who exploited them. His underground warriors elected him to Congress, where he delighted in cruel jokes on the members. He sent out false invitations inviting new members to nonexistent receptions at the White House, and gathered with his cronies to laugh when they arrived. He interrupted speeches with loud asides—when a new congressman, who had been an innkeeper, made his first speech, Walsh shouted, "John, a pitcher of ice water to No. 122!" at the oratorical pauses in the address. He went abroad, reputedly to get Russian contracts for a Brooklyn shipbuilding firm, on the eve of the Crimean War.[109]

Brook Farm went on its way to new disasters. Sir John Caldwell, the Secretary-General of Canada, visited the farm one Sunday, dined with the farmers, and died of apoplexy the next day. His valet, John Cheever, joined the community. Ripley transformed the association to a Fourierist Phalanx, but as the main building, costing $7,000 was completed, it caught fire, and was totally destroyed. There was no insurance, and Brook Farm was ended. The memory of it was bitter in New England. Mary Foote could not see why people like Sophia Ripley should be made to scrub floors, or wash anybody's clothes but her husband's; nor could she see why so many good people, who were needed in Boston, should be taken out of its life and cooped together in a farm they were not trained to run.[110]

During the Civil War, Brook Farm became a military encampment. Then it was clear that it was a most strategic spot. It commanded an approach to Boston. The fields were a parade ground. The buildings filled all the requirements of a military post. A month after the firing on Fort Sumter, a thousand men were hastily mobilized on its acres at the outskirts of the city. When the Civil War was over Major George Gordon returned to the post. Hawthorne in his most exuberant fancy had never imagined what the fate of the farm was to be, and as Major Gordon revisited it in memory and thought over the fate of the men who had trained there, it seemed to him that reality had forever and forever exorcised the fitful playday of the dreamers who had created Brook Farm, that the blood of the heroes had consecrated it, and that it had been redeemed by the solemn tread of soldiers across its green sod.[111]

X

Hawthorne had not told his mother of his plans for his marriage.[112] Perhaps he had doubted that it would ever take place. And then in all his writing of his mother there was the old dull pain that Longfellow found in all of Hawthorne's work, the old dull unlocalized ache so distinctive that it might almost be given his name, as diseases are named for the physicians who have made the deepest study of them.[113] He loved her, but there had been, since his boyhood, a sort of coldness between them, natural between two persons of such strong emotions as themselves. He could not think of her life with its quiet uncomplaining sorrow without thinking—let the interval between youth and age be filled with what happiness it might![114]

Sophia had vanished again. Spiritualist séances had been started at the bookstore on West Street, and he wrote her almost desperately asking that she not let herself be mesmerized. "Where art thou? My heart searches for thee. . . . It seems as if all evil things had more power over thee when I am away. Then thou art exposed to noxious winds, and to pestilence, and to death-like weariness; and, moreover, nobody knows how to take care of thee but thy husband. Everybody else thinks it of importance that thou shouldst paint and sculpture; but it would be no trouble to me, if thou shouldst never touch clay or canvas again. It is not what thou dost, but what thou art, that I concern myself about. And if thy mightiest works are to be wrought only by the anguish of thy head, and weariness of thy frame, and sinking of thy heart, then do I never desire to see another and this should be the feeling of all thy friends. Especially it ought to be thine, for thy husband's sake. . . ."

As he wrote it, the thought came to him that the words applied even more forcibly to him. In two weeks time he was leaving Brook Farm, and "I do think that a greater weight will then be removed from me, than when Christian's burden fell off at the foot of the cross." Even his Custom House experience was not such a thralldom and weariness; his mind and heart were freer. Labor was the curse of the world, and nobody could meddle with it without becoming proportionately brutified. Did she think that it was a praiseworthy matter that he had spent five months providing food for cows and horses? "Dearest, it is not so." [115]

Their future grew still darker. He could not get his savings from the association. He went to Salem. Homecoming must have been wonderfully relaxing after the strain and chaos of the farm, especially homecoming to such a home as his, where life went on as it always had, where Elizabeth still rambled on her long walks, going as far as Marblehead and picking violets and columbines, and where even Beelzebub, the cat, the same cat they had had when he went to Boston to edit the

American Magazine, missed him. There Louisa filled him with all the news—Mrs. Cleveland admired Charles Osgood's portrait of Hawthorne; Miss Susan Giddings told her they frequently heard of Hawthorne at Brook Farm from Mr. Farley. Mrs. Jared Sparks (Mary Silsbee) was boarding at Nahant for her health. Healy Barstow was seen walking around town in a velvet coat, looking very much like a play-actor. Why did Hawthorne work so hard? His mother was quite vehement about it. Ebe said she could not understand it; she thought he was to work only three hours a day for his board. Louisa could not bear to think of the hot sun beating upon his head. She said, "What is the use of burning out your brains in the sun, when you can do anything better with them?" [116]

Hawthorne was ruined. The work at the Custom House had gone for nothing, the work and the money invested in Brook Farm had vanished, he had no livelihood with which to support a wife, nor a home to take her to. He was again in his old chamber under the eaves, with the unsalable remnant of *Grandfather's Chair* as he had once had the fragment of *Seven Tales of My Native Land* and the copies of *Fanshawe.* In two weeks at Salem he left the house only once in the daylight. He stopped at the *Gazette* office to see Caleb Foote, but the editor was not in.[117] He stopped at the Athenaeum, and turned over a good many dusty books, and that was all. He had not a friend in the town where he had lived all his life.

His engagement to Sophia Peabody was not yet officially known to her friends. When she announced it, Mary Foote read Sophia's letter over and over, and thought back upon the three long years of secrecy that had separated them. She spent a wakeful night, and in the morning wrote Sophia a few words of affectionate sympathy: *Now that you have explained,* she said, I have nothing to forgive. Sophia had sometimes seemed strange, and she had missed her full and free expressions of sympathy, but "I congratulate you from my heart on the life which you entered three years ago." As for Hawthorne, it had always been a peculiar pleasure to Mary and Caleb Foote that they sympathized in their enthusiasm for everything that Hawthorne had written. And Sophia knew how much it had added to Mary Foote's happiness to find how Caleb immediately adopted her friends as his own. "So, you may well feel this to be an expression of our united sympathy and interest." [118] A mysterious letter! Perhaps too much should not be made of

it. Caleb was in trouble. The *Gazette* could not support his growing
family. He went to Washington, to try to pull political wires and secure
the postmastership; he was appointed, and scrupulously separated his
political and his editorial work, but a shadow fell upon the reputation
of the *Gazette* and never left it. The whole family fell sick with the
fever, and another of their children was lost that year: it would have
been difficult for Mary to have written a happier letter, even if she had
had a mind to do so. And then those three years of secrecy! How much
they explained of the strangeness of the life of both Sophia and Hawthorne!

He should have loved Salem, for the people had had a pretty generous faith in him ever since they had known him at all. But he was an
ungrateful blockhead, and he thought that all sinners should be sent on
a pilgrimage of the city, and made to spend a length of time there pro-
portionate to the enormity of their offenses. He did nothing. He walked
to the library, read, and in the evening, as he had done for so many
years, he walked to the hills or along the beach.

How immediately and irrevocably, if Sophia did not keep him out
of the abyss, he would relapse into the way of life in which he had
spent his youth. If it were not for her, the present world would see no
more of him forever. The sunshine would never fall on him, no more
than on a ghost. Once in a while people might discern his figure gliding
stealthily through the dim evening—that would be all. He would be
only a shadow of the night; it was Sophia who gave him reality and
made all things real for him.[119]

Now that his savings were gone, a curious lightheartedness seemed
to replace the forebodings, either for himself or for her, that had
oppressed him. The plans for their marriage went forward as before,
though they now had nothing to marry on, and, indeed, lived after
they were wed, on nothing, eating preserved fruits and bread and milk
for their Christmas dinner, or preparing a bowl of boiled potatoes for
breakfast.[120] There seemed to be no longer any fear on Hawthorne's
part but that he was a citizen of reality, and, as the spring advanced,
a happy one. He nerved himself to tell his mother and his sisters of his
plans. To his surprise his mother, looking better and more cheerful than
he had seen her in some time, inquired kindly about Sophia's health and
well-being. His sisters, too, began to sympathize as they ought, and all
was well.[121]

The marriage was set for July 9. Elizabeth Hoar came forward with a proposal that they live in Concord.[122] Hawthorne went there, and perhaps Sophia too, to examine the house in question. He returned with a confused impression of a dwelling of great age, old trees, long grass in the yard, dusky windowpanes, an old orchard, and a battlefield adjacent thereto. The house had heretofore been occupied exclusively by clergymen. It was awful to reflect how many sermons had been written in the Old Manse, and Hawthorne's misgivings were deepened when he saw the little study in the rear of the house, where he was to work. Its walls were blackened with the smoke of unnumbered years, and made still blacker by the grim prints of Puritan ministers that hung around. These worthies looked to him strangely like bad angels, or at least like men who had wrestled so continually and so sternly with the devil that somewhat of his sooty fierceness had been imparted to their own visages. Here Emerson, whose ancestor had built the house, wrote *Nature*.[123] Here Mary Foote's mother, Mary Wilder White, visited when she returned from Guadeloupe. She sat at the window in the west parlor after the family had gone to bed and stared at the river that had overflowed its banks and presented a little sea to her view. A balm of Gilead tree grew opposite the window. Her brother Henry had carved her name, and the name of Sarah Ripley, and his name, on its trunk, in the last hour he spent in Concord. In the garret, among the thousands of sermons, the unpublished dissertations on the Book of Job, the old musty volumes in Latin, were the letters Mary White had written.[124] By hundreds—no, by thousands—of invisible links the old house was connected with Hawthorne's life, and with his wife's life, but he did not know it. Did anyone? Perhaps; Emerson had been digging through the garret a few years before.

Hawthorne decided to take the house. Workmen came in, to repaper the walls, and a gardener, to lay out a vegetable garden beside the driveway leading to the front door. That gardener knew more of the old house than Hawthorne could ever learn. For thirty years he had tended its gardens. He was a Negro named James Garrison. A Concord villager came along from time to time to help him, a silent and observant unsociable individual named Thoreau.[125] All of this seems to have been done without Hawthorne's supervision. Affairs were now taken out of his hands. Did he know that Judge Hoar was a lifelong friend of Caleb Foote's father-in-law, Judge Daniel White? Probably not.

Late in May he met Emerson at the Boston Athenaeum. He and
Emerson were not friendly. He had with Emerson the natural reserve
of a man with the friends of his wife's family. Moreover, Emerson had
insulted him—or at least Elizabeth Peabody reported that he had, and
Hawthorne had not yet learned how quickly, and with what unerring
aim, Elizabeth could intervene to break a budding friendship of which
she did not approve, or which she feared. Emerson, according to Elizabeth, had said of Hawthorne's work that it had no insides—"he and
Bronson Alcott together would not make a man." [126]

This is not the time to write of Emerson, except to say that Hawthorne was, in a sense, Emerson's mistake; he never understood him; he
always misjudged him; and he perhaps considered Hawthorne at that
time as a politician, none too scrupulous, with literary interests, with
talents he indolently did not develop, and admissible only because of his
marriage into the family of the gifted Peabody girls. Any kindness he
showed him would have been for them. As for Hawthorne, he was for
many people a kind of alchemical instrument, used in detecting the
baser alloys in substances supposedly pure gold. It was not a role he
chose for himself, or one that he wanted; but such was his fate, and he
went through life leaving behind him deflated reputations and unmasked
villainies or, as in Emerson's case, a mere revelation of blindness and
human vanity where deeper perception might have been expected. The
fate pursued his biographers, and the present one is not unaware of the
hazard. Hawthorne was wounded by Emerson's comment. So he said,
rather stiffly, that there had perhaps been times when he would have
asked Emerson for the master word that would solve the riddle of the
universe, but now that he was happy there was no question to be put,
and he admired Emerson as a poet "of deep beauty and austere tenderness"—a fine characterization—and sought nothing from him as a philosopher. [127]

But Emerson at this meeting in the Boston Athenaeum had no more
philosophic message to deliver than that the garden at the Old Manse
was taking shape. It was, as it turned out, news of considerable wisdom,
and of far deeper import than could have been suspected—Sophia and
Hawthorne virtually lived on the produce from the garden, and at times
had nothing else to live on. Hawthorne sent Emerson's word on to
Sophia, and then left New England on another and still more mysterious
trip. With his former superior officer at the Custom House, Colonel

SAMUEL GRISWOLD GOODRICH

Hawthorne's publisher. "My mind is pretty much made up about this Goodrich. He is a good-natured man enough, but rather an unscrupulous one in money matters and not particularly trustworthy in anything."—Hawthorne *(New York Public Library)*

COLONEL JAMES WATSON WEBB
(New York Public Library)

REPRESENTATIVE HENRY WISE
(New York Public Library)

Hall, he went to Albany. They seem to have gone to New York and up the river to the capital of New York State. It was a trip for both business and pleasure, but Hawthorne said nothing of what its business was. At Albany, Hall left him, and went on into the interior, while Hawthorne visited with John Louis O'Sullivan.[128]

The June days passed slowly. Sophia, said Hawthorne, began to tremble and shrink back. She was afraid that she had acted too rashly in this matter, and wanted to wait another month or two before giving up her parents and sisters for such a questionable stranger as himself. "Ah, but it is too late! Nothing can part us now, for God himself hath ordained that we shall be one. So nothing remains, but to reconcile yourself to your destiny. Year by year we shall grow closer to each other; and a thousand years hence we shall be only in the honeymoon of our marriage. But I cannot write to you. The time for that species of communion is past."

A few days before the wedding Mary Peabody persuaded Sophia, or tried to persuade her, that it should be postponed another week. At this Hawthorne lost his temper; briefly, however, for he recovered it before he reached the end of the indignant letter he wrote to Sophia on the subject. They were married on July 9, 1842, at the Peabody home on West Street. The minister was a Unitarian, the Reverend James Freeman Clarke. "We made a Christian end," Hawthorne wrote to his sister, "and came straight to Paradise, where we abide at present writing. We are as happy as people can be, without making themselves ridiculous, and might be even happier; but as a matter of taste, we prefer to stop short at this point." [129]

The glimmering shadows lay half asleep between the door of the house and the road, on the summer afternoon when they first entered the Old Manse as their home. Between the two tall gateposts of rough-hewn stone they could see the gray front of the old parsonage at the end of an avenue of black ash trees. The wheels tracks leading to the door were almost overgrown with grass. A few cows and an old white horse were grazing by the roadside.

The song of the cricket was an audible stillness. Inside the silent house the grim portraits of the clergymen had been removed. Now there was no decoration except a purple vase of fresh flowers, against the cheerful, golden-tinted wallpaper. The shadow of a willow tree that swept against the eaves attempered the cheery western sunshine. Multitudes of bees buried themselves in the yellow blossoms of the summer squashes in the garden and hummingbirds supped airy food from the blossoms of the bean vines. Around the house the light of the calm and golden sunset grew lovely beyond expression, the more lovely for the quietude that so well accorded with the hour, when even the breeze hushed itself to rest. Each tree and rock, and every blade of grass, was distinctly imaged on the smooth surface of the Concord. The minutest things of earth and the broad aspect of the firmament were pictured equally without effort and with the same felicity of success. The sky glowed downward on the river at the base of the hill; the rich clouds floated through the unruffled bosom of the stream like heavenly thoughts through a peaceful heart.

The boundaries of Paradise reached from the riverbank to the summit of a wooded hill, about a mile distant. It contained a house, a garden, an old battlefield, an Indian campsite, the river, and an orchard. Throughout the summer there were cherries and currants; and then came autumn, with its immense burden of apples. In the stillest afternoon, if he listened, the thump of a great apple was audible, falling without a breath of wind, from the mere necessity of perfect ripeness. And, besides, there were peach trees, and pear trees that flung down bushels upon bushels of heavy pears. For an hour or two each morning Hawthorne worked in the garden. But he visited and revisited it a dozen times a day, standing in deep contemplation over his vegetable progeny —squash, beans, Indian corn, and early Dutch cabbage—with a love that nobody could share or conceive of. The summer squashes, with their beautiful and varied forms, seemed to him patterns that a sculptor would do well to copy, an endless diversity of urns and vases, shallow or deep, scalloped or plain. He listened with deep satisfaction to the hum of the bees, though when they had laden themselves with sweets they flew back to some unknown hive, which would give back nothing in requital of what his garden had contributed.

Or he walked down to the bank of the Concord, the river of peace and quietness, the most unexcitable and sluggish river that ever loitered imperceptibly toward the sea. It was three weeks before he could tell which way its current flowed. It slumbered between broad prairies, kissing the long meadow grass, bathing the overhanging boughs of elder bushes and willows, or the roots of elms and ash trees and clumps of maple. Flags and rushes, and yellow water lily and white pond lily, grew along its plashy shore. He found some heavy fragments of timbers, all green with half a century's growth of water moss, the remains of an old bridge that had once crossed the Concord here.

Between the battlefield and the northern side of the house there was a pasture, a hundred yards across, where, in some unknown age, before the white man came, there had been an Indian village. He found a splinter of stone, half hidden beneath the sod, and picking it up beheld an Indian relic. Spears and arrowheads and chisels and implements of war and labor and the chase were the yield of this pasture, and he found an exquisite sense of pleasure in picking up for himself an arrowhead that some warrior had dropped centuries before and that had never been handled since. His imagination pictured the Indian village and its encircling forest, the painted chiefs and warriors, the squaws at their household toil, the children sporting among the wigwams, the little wind-rocked papoose swinging from the branches of a tree.

How early in the summer the prophecy of autumn came! Earlier in some weeks than in others; sometimes even in the first weeks in July. There was no other feeling caused by this faint, doubtful, yet real perception of the year's decay, so blessedly sweet and sad in the same breath. In August the grass was still verdant on the hills and in the valleys. The foliage on the trees was as dense as ever, and as green; the flowers gleamed forth in richer abundance along the margin of the river, and by the stone walls, and deep among the woods. The days were as fervid as they had been a month before, and yet in every breath of wind and in every beam of sunshine he could hear the whispered farewell of summer. There was a coolness amid all the heat, a mildness in the blazing noon.

Hawthorne had come to the Old Manse dreaming of work to be done—profound treatises of morality, his layman's view of religion, histories, bright with picture, and gleaming over a depth of philosophic thought, at least a novel. He did not write them. The mornings grew colder, and at sunrise the leaves fell from the branches of the oak trees without a breath of wind, quietly descending by their own weight. All summer long they murmured like the noise of waters. His books were unopened. His neighbors who had prepared this perfect place to work in perhaps thought him indolent. To him, as to his sisters—to all who in childhood have felt Death lodge beside them and heard her whisper in the wind—there could never be enough reproach in the word "hermit" or enough appeal in the word "ambition" to break the spell of the blessed present. "Thank Heaven for breath," he wrote, "yes, for mere breath!" He reclined on the still unwithered grass and whispered to himself, "O perfect day! O beautiful world! O beneficent God!" It was to him the promise of a blessed eternity: "for our Creator would never have made such lovely days and have given us the deep hearts to enjoy them, above and beyond all thought, unless we were meant to be immortal. This sunshine is the golden pledge thereof." [130]

CHAPTER SIX

I

$\mathscr{O}$ur philosophers have not taught us what is best, Hawthorne concluded, on the eve of the Civil War, and our poets have not sung what is beautifullest, in the kind of life that we must lead. . . . The kind of life that we must lead! If the kind of life that was lived in Concord was not best, it was probably as good as any in the United States. Sky-blue river and river-blue sky, woodlots, old roads, deserted farms, oaks on the riverbank, pastures, yellow meadows, red bushes, iron-gray houses, granite rocks, wild orchards—"when I bought my farm," Emerson said, "I did not know what a bargain I had in the bluebirds, bobolinks and thrushes which were not charged in the bill." [1]

The kind of life that Hawthorne and Sophia lived in those early days of their marriage was simple almost beyond belief. For one thing, hard times were now a reality—they were in one of those periods when, as Emerson said, the lean kine begin to cast significant glances at the fat. The Hawthornes had breakfast at nine, dinner at three, and a late supper, an arrangement that economically enabled them to dispense with tea. After breakfast Sophia commanded him to take his pen in hand and write, and banished him upstairs to his study over the parlor. A rainy day—a rainy day, he began in his notebook—what is there to write about at all? Happiness has no succession of events; because it is part of eternity; and we have been living in eternity, ever since we came to this old Manse. [2]

He turned and turned around in the ten-foot square room. Inspiration vanished. In this room Emerson had written *Nature*. And before Emerson, thousands upon thousands of sermons had been written there. And now his own stories. But he could not write them! The portraits of the old clergymen had been taken from the walls, replaced by a golden-tinted wallpaper. Their removal might have symbolized the grim old Puritanism that had been vanquished by Channing—who, by the way, died this summer in Stockbridge.[3] And the sunnier and more hopeful view of the life that replaced it, the joy in nature, the love of music and painting, the faith in social progress and the dream of the coming human fraternity might have been symbolized by the lives of the two people who had taken over the Old Manse and made it their home. There were now no decorations in the room except a purple vase, a wedding gift of Margaret Fuller's, which Sophia kept always filled with flowers.

All would have been well, except that Hawthorne could not write. He stared out the window at the drenched landscape. All day long, and for a week together, the rain was drip—drip—dripping, and splash— splash—splashing from the eaves, and bubbling and foaming into the tubs beneath the spouts. He had set them out eagerly when the rain began since the Old Manse was out of water. He thought there could not be a more somber aspect of external nature than as then seen from the windows of his study. The study had three windows, set with little old-fashioned panes of glass, each with a crack across it. The two on the western side looked between the willow branches down into the orchard, with glimpses of the river through the trees.

The third window faced north. It commanded a broader view of the river. It was at this window that the Reverend William Emerson stood and watched the Battle of Concord—the "outbreak of a long and fateful struggle between two nations." There was a subject! On April 19—a date of curious significance in Hawthorne's life—in the year 1775 there had been fired the shots heard around the world.[4]

Emerson had recently found his grandfather's diary in the garret of the Old Manse. Appearing with the publication of a history of Concord, it clarified the events at the beginning of the Revolution, which had been obscured for sixty years. The objective of the British had been that little bridge over the Concord at the foot of the pasture—the rude bridge that arched the flood—though the slow-moving Concord, even in spring, could hardly be called in flood. A river needs a drop of at least an eighth of an inch a mile in order to flow at all, and the Concord had no steeper fall than that. People said that the only bridge that was ever washed away there was one which floated upstream in a windstorm.

Still it was a strategic river, fifty miles long, a hundred to three hundred feet across, and from two to fifteen feet deep. In the dim Revolutionary days sixty years before, it had been more strategic. Everything happened on that fateful day: alarms at daybreak, as the British troops reached Lexington; the hurried mobilization of the minutemen; the terrific moment when a hundred and fifty militia men, stationed on the northern slope of the burying ground, beheld eight hundred British troops approaching on the road from Lexington. The Americans, who had been hiding the military supplies stored in Concord, were amateurish, frightened, outnumbered, with the conflicting impulses of having been discovered in wrongdoing and a passionate determination to endure no more. They retreated beyond the common, and then, as the British scattered through the town, destroying whatever supplies they could find, they passed the Old Manse, crossed the bridge, and concealed themselves on a ridge on the opposite side.

The Battle of Concord appears to have been a classic military maneuver—really flawless, from the British point of view, although the Americans nevertheless had every right to consider it a victory. (When Hawthorne went to England he learned that the British also viewed the Battle of New Orleans as a British victory, somehow twisting it wrong-end foremost.) It seems impossible to imagine a better disposition of troops than the British made, or one which so completely enclosed the town and yet gave the invaders complete freedom of movement. Three companies crossed the bridge, passed the American position, and moved on to destroy the stores at Colonel Barrett's house. One company guarded the bridge. Two companies fell back toward the hill north of the Old Manse, covering the approaches to the bridge. The remaining British troops destroyed the supplies that they found in the town. The Americans, minutemen and militiamen, began to assemble at the bridge from all over the neighborhood, on the side of the Concord opposite the Old Manse. Numbering nearly three hundred, they formed at the bridge, the British on one side, the Americans on the other. Fighting began when the British removed some planks from the bridge. Two Americans were killed, and the British lost three killed and eight wounded. The British withdrew toward town. The Americans abandoned all attempts to keep order in their pursuit. Each man chose his own mode and time of attack.

It was now between ten and eleven o'clock. Three companies of British light infantry returned from searching Colonel Barrett's house. With the advantage of hindsight, it is apparent that the British could have destroyed the American force at the bridge. They had a force equal to the Americans on both sides. Their orders, however, were to destroy the stores, not to precipitate a general battle.

The northern window of the study looked out upon the entire battlefield. From his study the clergyman could have followed the movements of the Americans as they approached the bridge, and watched the British retreat, down the narrow road before the house, into the center of Concord. At this point the Americans displayed almost as great skill as the English. Directly opposite the front door of the parsonage they abandoned their pursuit and struck off to the east, circling behind the high peak of Jones' Hill, by-passing the town completely and cutting through the Great Meadows to a fork in the road at the opposite end of town. Here they waited to intercept the British as they returned on the Lexington Road. Thenceforth the advantage was entirely with them. The road was lined with Americans, firing from every house, barn, wall or covert, with accurate aim. After they had waylaid the enemy from one position they fell back from the road, ran forward, and came up again to repeat the maneuver.[5]

There was superb material for a novel in the events of that day. But no writer ever took the ingredients of a story so perfectly laid before him and wove them into a work of durable fiction. Inspiration never springs from what is calculated—never, at least, in Hawthorne's case, whose stories were of those momentary glimpses into the human heart when all artifice fails. Yet as he stood at the window of his study the happenings of that day made a powerful impression on his imagination, and why he played with the idea of it, and rejected it, gives an indication of how solidly constructed a subject had to be in his own mind before he would take it. Two thoughts were ever present in his mind. This had been a clergyman's study; and this window looked out upon a battlefield. "There needed but a gentle wind to sweep the battle smoke around this quiet house."

Hawthorne did not quite believe in the events of that day as history and legend related them. James Russell Lowell told him that a boy was chopping wood in the yard when the battle began, and went into battle with an ax in his hand, killing a wounded soldier with it. Strange, thought Hawthorne, that the boy should have been so diligently at work when the whole countryside had been startled out of its business by the arrival of the British.[6]

He paced about the room, turning from one window to the other, looking at the two pleasant little pictures of Lake Como on the walls and the sweet and lovely head of one of Raphael's Madonnas. What is there to write about at all? Happiness has no succession of events, he reflected, because it is part of eternity; and we have been living in eternity ever since we came to this Old Manse. "Our spirits must have flitted away, unconsciously, in the deep and quiet rapture of some long embrace; and we can only perceive that we have cast off one mortal part, by the more real and earnest life of our spirits . . ." "Would that my wife would permit me to record the ethereal dainties, that kind Heaven provided for us, on the first day of our arrival! Never, surely was such food heard of on earth—at least, not by me." [7]

II

"Two days after our arrival at the Old Manse," Sophia wrote to Mary Foote, "George Hillard and Henry Cleveland appeared for fifteen minutes, on their way to Niagara Falls. . . . We forgave them for their appearance here, because they were gone as soon as they had come, and we felt very hospitable. We wandered down to our sweet, sleepy river, and it was so silent all around us, and so solitary, that we seemed the only persons living. We sat beneath our stately trees, and felt as if we were the rightful inheritors of the old abbey, which had descended to us from a long line. The tree tops waved a majestic welcome, and rustled their thousand leaves like brooks over our heads." [8]

Thereafter, a busy social season. By August 5 their callers included George Prescott, who each day brought three quarts of milk, Emerson, Ellery Channing, Thoreau, Elizabeth Hoar, and a stranger identified only as a visitor in a gig. The butcher called two or three times a week. A farmer called to see about buying the hay in the pastures. There were also, Hawthorne noted, a colt, some cows, a few hens, and a timid black dog that stood at the end of the avenue, watching wistfully, but trotted away, his tail between his legs, when Hawthorne whistled to him. There appeared also a short, sturdy, stalwart, middle-aged man whose importance in Concord Hawthorne did not know. He had come to see about the cistern. The Old Manse was without a water supply. Before the rains came Hawthorne had to set out with a bucket in each hand, carrying water for Sophia's bath. The new cistern was installed just before the rain fell. The water poured into it like a cataract, but it seemed bewitched, for it still remained almost empty.

The days passed. He went fishing, but caught only a turtle and an eel. On August 6 he went fishing again. Some boys had taken the best places to fish, so he did not. On the 7th, Sunday, he walked to the hill opposite the Old Manse, and studied the town. On August 8 he began to write about the old house in his notebook. On the 9th he analyzed the orchard, and the next day, his garden. He bathed in the river once or twice a day, worked in his garden, where he had fifty hills of corn, went to his study each morning, to read, sleep or write, walked in the afternoon with Sophia, and read in the evening. "My life at this time," he wrote, "is more like that of a boy, externally, than it has been since I really was a boy. It is usually supposed that the cares of life come with matrimony; but I seem to have cast off all care, and live on with as much easy trust in Providence, as Adam could possibly have felt, before he learned that there was a world beyond his Paradise. My chief anxiety consists in watching the prosperity of my vegetables." [9]

III

Our philosophers have not taught us what is best, Hawthorne concluded. . . . Was that quite true? The best American philosopher lived on Lexington Street, half a mile away. "When I bought my farm," Emerson said, "I did not know what a bargain I had." He bought his farm in 1835, for $3,500. He got a plain, square wooden dwelling, a small mansion, set in a grove of pine trees, with tall chestnut trees in the yard. There was a yellow barn at the back, and a half-acre garden, full of roses and hollyhocks, and pastures sloping toward the Concord River, and a little brook. A long hall divided the lower floor of the house, making two large square rooms on each side. Emerson's study had a wall of books, a large mahogany table, a morocco writing pad, and a large fireplace. There were doors on both sides of the fireplace opening into the parlor, which was on the southern quarter of the house, a large bright room, light walls, a crimson rug on the floor, and a large mirror reflecting the cheerful firelight and the animated people before it.

"When I bought my farm I did not know what a bargain I had," Emerson said. "As little did I guess what sublime mornings and sunsets I was buying, what reaches of landscapes, and what fields and lanes for a tramp. Neither did I fully consider what an indescribable luxury is our Indian River, which runs parallel to our village street, and to which every house on that long street has a back door which leads down through the garden to the river bank; where a skiff or a dory gives you, all summer, access to enchantments new every day, and, all winter, miles of ice for the skaters. Still less did I know what good and true neighbors I was buying; men of thought and virtue, some of them now known the country through for their learning, or subtlety, or active and patriotic powers, but whom I had the pleasure of knowing long before the country did; and other men, not known widely, but known at home, farmers, not doctors of laws, but doctors of land, skilled in turning a swamp or a sand bank into a fruitful field, and where witch grass and nettle grew causing a forest of appletrees or miles of corn and rye to thrive. I did not know what groups of interesting schoolboys and fair schoolgirls were to greet me in the highway, and to take hold of one's heart at the school exhibitions." [10]

More than his friendship for the Peabodys, and his hope of getting to know Hawthorne, brought Emerson to the Old Manse. His ancestors had built it; those old folios that Hawthorne studied in the garret were their work. Emerson was thirty-nine and was at the height of his powers —"the most potent intellectual force on the continent." His recent lectures on the Philosophy of Modern History in Boston seemed to Horace Mann to be to human nature what Newton's *Principia* was to mathematics. Dr. Walter Channing, who attended the first lecture with Mann, said it made his head ache.[11]

Emerson had come through periods of darkness so obscure that Hawthorne's years of seclusion were sunlit in comparison—the death of his father in his childhood, the poverty of his mother, and the taunts of his schoolmates, who used to ask him and his brothers, since they had only one greatcoat among them, "Whose turn is it to wear the coat today?" Under the influence of his vigorous, erratic aunt, Mary Moody Emerson, an intellectual tyrant so powerful that only genius could escape her, Emerson entered college at fourteen and at fifteen taught school. (His brother William entered Harvard at thirteen and graduated at seventeen.) Frail and shy, Emerson was the least promising member of the brilliant family, ill of tuberculosis at twenty-three, when he sailed to Florida, too shy to prosper as a teacher and too quiet and with too many scruples to remain in his pulpit. "He does not make his best impression at a funeral," people said of him, and they told the story of the Revolutionary veteran who summoned Emerson to his deathbed, but rose in his wrath, when he showed some hesitation in handling his spiritual weapons, and said, "Young man, if you don't know your business you had better go home."

Emerson recovered, married at twenty-six, and within two years his nineteen-year-old wife died. His brother Edward, the admired, learned, eloquent, striving boy, suffered some mental derangement, went to the asylum, recovered, and lived thereafter in voluntary exile in Puerto Rico. Charles Emerson, the most brilliant member of the family, died at twenty-eight, on the eve of his marriage. Now Emerson had traveled abroad, married again, to Lidian Jackson—"mine Asia," he called her—and settled again in the town by the river to which he was linked by so many ties of blood and intellect.

Few days passed when he did not call at the Old Manse. Hawthorne troubled and puzzled him. "The painful solitude of man," he thought. And he thought Hawthorne a greater man than any of his words betrayed. In his company he felt sure of Hawthorne. He felt that Hawthorne needed sympathy and intellectual companionship, and because he lived near at hand, Emerson thought he could afford to wait. It was easy for Emerson to talk to him—"Only he said so little that I talked too much. . . ." [12]

Another tie made the Old Manse pleasant to him. The wife of its owner was Mrs. Sarah Bradford Ripley. The daughter of the warden of the state prison at Charleston, she had befriended Emerson since childhood. She, too, had in her childhood come under the domineering influence of Mary Moody Emerson. It was told of Mrs. Ripley, as a sign of her indifference to trifles, that she had once carried across Boston a broom that Miss Emerson had put in her hand to be carried to a new lodging. She carried it across Boston Common, from Summer Street to Hancock Street, without hesitation or remark. She was now almost fifty years old. She had rented the house to the Hawthornes while she lived with her husband at Waltham. She was, Emerson thought, the most amiable and tenderest of women, wholly sincere, thoughtful for others, absolutely without appetite for luxury or display or praise or influence—"A bright foreigner," Emerson called her, "she signalizes herself among the figures of this masquerade." Many years later Elizabeth Hoar wrote her biography. Sarah Ripley was the type of woman

Hawthorne had never known, uniting "the loveliest domestic character and untiring devotion to an extraordinary weight and variety of household duties with a lifelong enthusiasm for learning." She was absolutely without pedantry. She was a great teacher, with none of the excessive enthusiasms of the new generation that Elizabeth Peabody exemplified.

Nobody ever summed up more concisely than Mrs. Ripley the change in New England thought in her lifetime. In her young days, she said, the Unitarians had come out from the dry bones of cant and formalism, with a message to the understanding. "The goodness of God and man's comfortable position in this bright and convenient world were their constant theme. . . . But times are changed. The priest can no longer stand in the portico, calling out to those who are passing by, blinded by superstition or hoodwinked by authority. The understanding has had its day; the soul is hungering for food, and he that ministers at the altar must enter into the holy of holies himself, and bring it forth from thence. When the poor bees were buzzing yesterday with terror and dismay to find their foundations suddenly undermined with sulphur smoke, the doubt occurred whether superior beings might not regard the earthquakes and volcanoes which lay waste the face of our insignificant planet with as much indifference as we do the smoking of a bee-hive; whether the waste of individual life and happiness might not be as unimportant in the economy of the great whole. But the soul answers, no. It declares that its interests are eternal; that its intuitions come directly from the center of all life.—I am reading Timeus the Locrian, concerning the soul of the world and of nature, the work of an old Pythagorean philosopher supposed to have been contemporary with Socrates. I am refreshed by the utterances of these primitive worshippers of truth. They relieve me from the doubt whether the eyes of the soul, turned by Christian culture in one direction, may not see universal truths where it would have dreamed of no such thing if it had lived eighteen centuries ago. I return with deepened convictions to the simpler and sublimer teachings of Him to whom the Spirit was given without measure." [13]

If the kind of life that these women had lived was not best, it had nevertheless a quality the present age seemed to lack—a quiet harmony, a wise ardor, a brilliance achieved without striving for it—though its value lay in their characters rather than in the happenings, often tragic, that marked their way. Hawthorne never pictured women of this nature in his stories. The learned people of his fiction never—or rarely—used their learning in the way that, according to Emerson, Sarah Ripley used hers—"nobody ever heard of her learning until a necessity came for its use, and then nothing could be more simple than her solution of the problem proposed to her." The learned people of Hawthorne's stories were, like Ethan Brand, full of sinister knowledge which gave them control of the lives of the innocent. This problem had absorbed him since the time he had created the character of the wizard in *Alice Doane's Appeal*. It now became the dominant theme in the half dozen stories he wrote in the early days of his married life.

Our philosophers have not taught us what is best. . . . Was that quite true? It sometimes seemed that the philosophers had taught, but we had not learned. Hawthorne was bruised and battered by Brook Farm, for example, but Emerson had said, in refusing to join it, "This scheme was all arithmetic and comfort . . . a rage in our poverty to live rich and gentlemanlike, an anchor to leeward against a change of weather; a prudent forecast on the great questions of Pauperism and Poverty. . . . I do not wish to remove from my present prison to a prison a little larger. I wish to break all prisons. I have not yet conquered my own house. It irks and repeats. Shall I raise the siege of this hencoop and march baffled away to a pretended siege of Babylon? . . ." [14]

In the fall of 1842, Margaret Fuller visited the Emersons. She was then thirty-two, an aggressive and high-spirited woman, an incessant talker, with a long nose and a trick of constantly blinking her eyes— "She makes me laugh all the time," Emerson said; but Hawthorne, who had met her during her Conversations at the Peabody Book Store, said, "Would that Margaret Fuller would hold her tongue!" She was the first daughter of Timothy Fuller, "a maniacal Latinist," a Cambridge lawyer and politician, a Unitarian and a Jeffersonian, a shrewd, energetic, capable man with a lack of endearing personal qualities. He worked out a program for Margaret's education. She was taught Latin and English grammar simultaneously. She began reading Latin at six. She read Virgil, Horace, and Ovid at seven. At eight she discussed Shakespeare, Cervantes, and Molière. At thirteen she formed a passionate attachment for an Englishwoman she saw at church, and at fourteen was sent away to school. She rose at five, walked an hour, practiced the piano an hour, read French until eight, then studied philosophy until nine-thirty, after which she studied Greek until noon. She then went home, practiced on the piano until dinner at two, and read Italian for two hours. At six she walked or went for a drive and at eleven she retired, writing in her journal before going to bed. At sixteen she seemed eighteen or twenty, precocious physically as well as mentally, and her brother said she possessed the unpleasantness of forty Fullers.

She started a scandal in school by spreading stories about one girl after another, and when they recoiled upon her she collapsed. She had charge of the education of the younger children in her family—there were ten Fuller children—and after two years fell ill of brain fever. Recovering, she taught languages at Bronson Alcott's school, read German to Dr. Channing, and taught school in Providence before she started, on November 6, 1829, her Conversations in the Peabody home. Twenty or thirty women attended—Mrs. George Bancroft, Mrs. Barlow (of Brook Farm), Mrs. Emerson, Elizabeth Hoar, Mrs. Theodore Parker, Elizabeth, Mary and Sophia Peabody, Mrs. Josiah Quincy, Mrs. Ripley, Maria White (James Russell Lowell's fiancée), as well as Channings, Gardiners, Jacksons, Lees, Lorings, Putnams, Russells, Shaws, Sturgises, Tuckermans, Wards, and Whitings. She talked on Mistakes, Faith, Creeds, Woman, Demonology, Influence, Catholicism, The Ideal. The Conversations cost twenty dollars a season, and she gave them each year until 1844. She was the active editor of the *Dial*, which started in July, 1840. It had a circulation of one hundred. Emerson boosted its circulation to two hundred and fifty when he took it over. Theodore Parker said the *Dial* needed a beard and started the *Massachusetts Quarterly Review*. But the *Review*, people said, was a beard without a dial.[15]

Observing the solitude of the Hawthornes, perhaps, Margaret Fuller conceived of a way to end it. Her sister Ellen had married Ellery Channing. Young Channing, "that gnome," Hawthorne called him, had gone west and cleared land and built a log cabin with his own hands and lived in it a year, with great hardships. The project that Margaret Fuller had was that the Hawthornes should take Channing and his wife into the Old Manse as boarders.

The difficulty was that Hawthorne seemed quite content with his solitude. He had, however, made a mistake; he had proposed taking George Bradford of Brook Farm as a boarder. On her first visit to the Old Manse, August 14, Margaret broke into a particularly pleasant season of his life. He had been fishing and had caught a lot of fish. He worked in his garden, and picked cardinal flowers, pond lilies, pickerel flowers, and white arrowheads to bring home to Sophia. The novelist was in an abstracted mood when he walked home with Margaret Fuller through the moonlight. There was probably no opportunity for her to bring up the proposal them. She wrote in her journal that they watched the moon struggling with clouds. Hawthorne told her that he never wanted to leave this earth; it was beautiful enough.

It was the next day that George and Susan Hillard arrived at the Old Manse. Hawthorne found it a pleasant sensation when the coach rumbled up the avenue and wheeled round at the door, "for then I felt that I was regarded as a man with a wife and a household—a man having a tangible existence and locality in the world—when friends came to avail themselves of our hospitality. It was a sort of acknowledgment and reception of us into the corps of married people—a sanction by no means essential to our peace and well-being, but yet agreeable enough to receive. So my wife and I welcomed them cordially at the door, and ushered then into our parlor, and soon into the supper room—and afterwards, in due season, to bed. Then came my dear little wife to her husband, which is more than can be said of every wife in the world." At this point portions of Hawthorne's diary have been blotted out.[16]

They had breakfast of flapjacks and whortleberries, which they had picked on a neighboring hill, and the fish that Hawthorne had caught in the river—a splendid breakfast. At about nine o'clock Hawthorne and Hillard set out for a walk. It seems quite plain that Hawthorne wanted to talk with Hillard privately of his financial problem at Brook Farm. His savings, $1,400, were still invested in the Farm. He was still a trustee. The original agreement of the associates provided that any shareholder could withdraw his investment, with a year's notice, and presumably Hawthorne, as a trustee and member of the finance committee, was liable for the claims upon the farm. The problem was certainly one of the greatest delicacy. The first step was that Hawthorne should free himself of the trusteeship, again, it seems, without creating a great deal of comment, for the founders of Brook Farm, if he himself now had reservations about them, were the friends of his wife's family.

Hawthorne usually walked to Emerson's house around Jones' Hill, avoiding the town. In fact, he followed the path the Americans had taken when they intercepted the British retreat. On this Sunday morning, however, he presumably walked through Concord, for when he and Hillard arrived at Emerson's house, the philosopher drew them inside. He wanted to wait, before setting out with them, until the townspeople had gone to church. Hawthorne made no comment on this "scruple of external conscience." When an interval had passed, the three of them set out for Walden Pond.

They turned aside to visit Edmund Hosmer. Emerson had written an article about him in the current *Dial*, and had a high opinion of Hosmer's homely and self-acquired wisdom. They found Hosmer walking in his fields. He was the man who had sold Hawthorne his cistern. He was a short, stalwart and sturdy man, forty-two years old, somewhat uncouth and ugly to look at, but with a force of shrewd expression, and manners of natural courtesy. He had not much diffidence of expression. He spoke of the state of the nation, agriculture, and business in general —thoughts that had come to him at the plow, with the flavor and smell of the fresh earth about them. Yet Hawthorne fancied that Hosmer was not so natural as he had been before Emerson put him into print. He was now an oracle, and spoke as if truth and wisdom were uttering themselves in his voice—indeed, Hawthorne thought, Emerson had risked doing him much mischief.

Hawthorne, Emerson, and Hillard walked on to the pond. They turned left at the first road above Emerson's house, crossed Mill Brook, ascended the hill, picking enormous blackberries on the way, passed the Poor Farm, and so came to the graveled shores of the pond.

It was apparently Hawthorne's first visit there. It was beautiful and refreshing to his soul, after such long and exclusive familiarity with the tawny and sluggish Concord. Walden lay embosomed in among the wooded hills, not very extensive—half a mile long and a mile and a half in circumference—but large enough for waves to dance upon its surface. It looked like a piece of blue firmament, earth encircled. The shore had a narrow, pebbly strand, worth a day's journey to look at, for the sake of the contrast between it and the weedy, slimy, oozy margin of the river. The hills around were from forty to one hundred feet in height, covered with oak and pine. The water, cool at all seasons, was transparent to a depth of twenty-five feet; the bottom was pure-white sand.

Emerson went on his way. Hillard and Hawthorne remained at Walden Pond. They swam in its cold water. It may be that in these talks, for the first time, the story of what happened at Brook Farm came into the open. The farm was still operating. Ripley's plans had grown more audacious. He now intended to convert it into a Fourierist Phalanx. Apart from his involved investment, Hawthorne had no sympathy with the utopian schemes of Fourier—one of the most horrible notions he had ever heard of was Fourier's declaration that, after the ideal society was achieved, man's mastery of nature would be so complete that he could, if he wished, turn the briny water of the ocean into lemonade. Converting the farm into a phalanx would not only change its original character but becloud the motives of its original founders. Workshops were now being built on the farm. Visitors were swarming there by the hundreds. It had grown feverish, notorious, and dangerous. And then the bitterness of Hawthorne's own experience still rankled deeply—he had invested his money and his labor in good faith, shoveled manure for months, dug in the fields and worked in the pastures, carted pigs to market, milked the cows, and exhausted himself for what was no longer even an ideal he could believe in. "It does really seem as if not only my corporeal person, but my moral sense, had received a cleansing from that bath," he wrote. "A good deal of mud and river-slime had accumulated on my soul; but these bright waters washed it all away."

They walked home, dined, and separated to their several siestas. Sophia presided at dinner with all imaginable grace and ladylikeness. Hawthorne maintained an air of dignified hospitality at the other end of the table. In the afternoon they walked. Because a shower had dampened the grass, Sophia remained at home. When Hawthorne and the Hillards returned, they found her entertaining Mr. and Mrs. Storer and Elizabeth Hoar.

The Old Manse was haunted. Houses of any antiquity in New England, said Hawthorne, were so invariably possessed with spirits that the matter seemed hardly worth alluding to. The Hawthornes' ghost used to heave deep sighs in a particular corner of the parlor. Sometimes he rustled paper, as if turning over a sermon in the long upper entry. Then there was a ghostly serving maid, who used to be heard in the kitchen at deepest midnight, grinding coffee, cooking, ironing—although, Hawthorne said, no trace of anything accomplished could be detected the next morning. Hawthorne thought the ghost probably took one look at their improvements—the bright paint and paper, the carpet, cheerful pictures and flowers—uttered a groan, and vanished forever.

Now, however, after the guests had left, and the Hawthornes and Hillards were sitting in the parlor, the ghost appeared again. Hawthorne was stretched out on the sofa. The other three heard a rustling of a silken robe passing from corner to corner of the room, right among them. All three of them heard it distinctly. Susan Hillard was greatly startled. Hawthorne neither heard the rustle nor believed in it.

The next day, after the Hillards had left, Hawthorne went to one of the outhouses in which Dr. Ripley's library was stored and began to examine the doctor's library. He found the venerable doctor's broad-brimmed beaver hat, his silk hat, his study slippers, his iron tobacco box, all mixed up with manuscript sermons, old bundles of musty accounts, and numerous letters in feminine handwriting. He wanted to read those, but Sophia thought he should not.[17]

It is perhaps unfortunate that he did not. Mary Foote's mother had written some letters, years before, from Guadeloupe, which were found, many years later, in the Old Manse. Mary White (then Mary Wilder) had lived most of her life in Concord. Her stepfather, Dr. Isaac Hurd, owned all the land on the north side of Main Street, from the mill brook to the house of Samuel Hoar. He also owned two taverns and much land in the north part of Concord. There was a wonderful subject for Hawthorne in that packet of letters—the engagement of a seventeen-year-old New England girl to a French refugee, their trip to Guadeloupe to regain his plantations, the death of her husband and brother as they arrived at the island, and Mary's hairbreadth escapes during the Negro revolutions. She wrote of them with such precision and clarity that her letters were valuable military history—and she wrote, moreover, with a style Hawthorne could have admired, contributing (in collaboration with Mary Moody Emerson) under pseudonyms as obscure as his own, to the *Anthology*.[18]

Hawthorne never found her letters, or, if he did, never mentioned them. He found volumes of the *Christian Examiner* and the *Liberal Preacher*, modern sermons, the controversial works of Unitarian ministers "and all such trash." There was a dissertation on the Book of Job in twenty volumes, and little books, bound in black, dating back two hundred years or more, and very solemn, with the appearance Hawthorne would attribute to books of magic. There were Latin folios, books demolishing papistry, sermons, pamphlets, trash. He found no

treasure in them. All was dead and dead alike, the old and the new
equally frigid. Only the almanacs and newspapers brought the past
vividly before him, bits of magic looking glass among the books, with
the visages of a vanished century in them. The clergymen had produced
nothing half so real as the newspaper scribblers had thrown off in a
moment, without the slightest idea of permanence. The thought was dis-
heartening, and he turned away from the old books in sadness.

And went outdoors. Margaret Fuller had left a book at the house
on her visit Saturday. He set out to the Emersons' to return it to her.
Hawthorne did not walk through town. He circled around the hill,
again following, it seems, the same path the Americans had taken to
intercept the British retreat. And presently he wandered into a tract so
overgrown with bushes and underbrush that he could scarcely force his
way through. It incensed and depressed him at the same time. He floun-
dered around in the brush, with the briers brushing against his face and
intertwining themselves around his legs. It tormented him to death to
be annoyed by an innumerable host of petty impediments—he was ready
to lie down in rage and despair, rather than go a step farther.

Suddenly he came out of the brambles and into an open space
among the woods—a very lovely spot, with the tall old trees standing
around, as quiet as if nobody had intruded there throughout the whole
summer. A company of crows were holding their Sabbath in the tops
of some of the trees. They apparently felt themselves insulted or injured
by his presence, for with one consent they began to caw—caw—caw—
and, launching themselves sullenly into the air, took flight to some se-
curer solitude. He felt like someone who had inadvertently disturbed an
assembly of worshipers. There was no other sound except the song of
the crickets.

And as he stood there he realized that the summer was over. Alas
for the summer! The grass was still verdant on the hills and in the
valleys; the foliage of the trees was as dense as ever, and as green; the
days, too, were as fervid as they had been a month ago—and yet, in
every breath of wind, and in every beam of sunshine, there was an au-
tumal influence, a sort of coolness amid all the heat, and a mildness in
the brightness of the sunshine. A breeze could not stir, without thrilling
him with the breath of autumn.

He went on to the Emersons'. He left the book there. Emerson was
not at home, nor was Margaret Fuller. Hawthorne again left the road

and circled behind the hills, to the path that led to Sleepy Hollow. On one verge of the hollow, skirting it, was a terraced pathway, broad enough for a wheel track, overshadowed with oaks, stretching their long, knotted, rude, and rough arms between earth and sky. The hollow was perhaps four or five hundred feet in diameter, a shallow space scooped out in the woods, pretty nearly circular, the sunshine penetrating evenly along the pathway. There Hawthorne met Margaret Fuller, reclining near the path.

She said that she had been there all afternoon, reading or meditating. Nobody had broken her solitude. She was telling Hawthorne that no inhabitants of Concord ever visited Sleepy Hollow, when a whole group of people came by. Most of them took a path that led some distance away. An old man came near them, smiled, remarked on the beauty of the afternoon, and went on his way.

Hawthorne and Margaret talked about autumn—about the pleasure of getting lost in the woods—about the crows, whose voices Margaret had heard—about the experiences of early childhood, whose influences remain on the character after the recollection of them has passed away—about the sight of mountains from a distance, and the view from their summits—and other matters of high and low philosophy. Footsteps sounded on the path above them. A voice called out to Margaret. Emerson stepped out of the shadows.

He appeared to have had a pleasant time. He said there were Muses in the woods today, and whispers to be heard in the breezes. He invited Hawthorne to dinner. And he gave him and Sophia an invitation from Mrs. Ripley at Waltham to attend a party at her house, on the evening after the Phi Beta Kappa celebration—Hawthorne was elected a member of Phi Beta Kappa by the chapter at Bowdoin on September 8, 1842. If Sophia wished to go, Hawthorne said, she shall go, and spend the night, away from her poor desolate husband.

It was now nearly six o'clock, and they separated. The incident made a powerful impression on Hawthorne. He used it almost intact in *The Blithedale Romance*, making it a climax of the novel. He was somehow glad to be free of these people. At home, alone with Sophia, the moonlight seemed to him the most beautiful moonlight that ever hallowed this earthly world. When he went down to bathe in the river, which was as calm as death, it seemed like plunging down into the sky.

"But I had rather be on earth than even in the seventh Heaven, just now. . . ." [19]

IV

There never was such a tragedy as Margaret Fuller's story, in Hawthorne's opinion—the sadder and sterner because so much of the ridiculous was mixed up with it, and she could bear anything better than being ridiculous. She had not the charm of womanhood. But she was a person anxious to try all things and fill up her experiences in all directions; she had a strong and coarse nature, which she had done her utmost to refine, with infinite pains. But of course it could only be superficially changed. The solution of the riddle, he thought, lies in this direction.

She had stuck herself full of borrowed qualities, but which had no roots in her. She had set to work on her strong, heavy, unpliable, and in many respects, defective and evil nature, and adorned it with a mosaic of admirable qualities, such as she chose to possess, putting in here a splendid talent and there a moral excellence, and polishing each separate piece, and the whole together, till it seemed to shine afar and dazzle all who saw it. "It was such an awful joke that she should have resolved in all sincerity to make herself the greatest, wisest, best woman of the age. But she was not working on an inanimate substance, like marble or clay; there was something within her that she could not possibly carve out, to re-create or refine it; and, by and by, this rude old potency bestirred itself, and undid all her labor in the twinkling of an eye."

After all, this was later. They were now on friendly, if cautious, terms. Margaret now suggested to Sophia her plan to have Ellery and Ellen Channing board at the Old Manse. Sophia was not entirely opposed to it. Hawthorne, however, replied at once, by letter—"my conclusion is that the comfort of both parties would be put in great jeopardy." He meant no offense to her sister and Ellery—but Adam and Eve would probably have been unwilling to receive two angels as boarders into their paradise. The host and hostess could no longer live their natural life, and all four would be involved in an unnatural relation, "which the system of boarding out essentially and inevitably is."

It would make too much work for Sophia. All four were, moreover, sensitive people, and he advised Ellery and Ellen, if they did board, to board with the rudest family in Concord, where their feelings would not be suspectible to damage. He had indeed, he admitted reluctantly, thought of taking George Bradford into his household as a boarder. It was a hard thing to make clear. . . . It is not what Mr. Bradford is, but what he is not. . . . His negative qualities seem to take away his personality, and leave his excellent characteristics to be fully and freely enjoyed. I doubt, said Hawthorne pontifically, whether he be not precisely the rarest man in the world.[20]

Margaret Fuller certainly won on this exchange. Neither George Bradford nor Ellery and Ellen Channing boarded at the Old Manse. The autumn days passed. Emerson called again, bringing Mr. Frost, the parson—a good sort of humdrum parson enough, Hawthorne thought, though he found that his respect for clerical people as such, and his faith in the utility of their office, decreased daily. "We certainly do need a new revelation—a new system—for there seems to be no life in the old one."

Then Thoreau—whose name Hawthorne misspelled Thorow—dined with them. "He is a singular character—a young man with much of wild original nature still remaining in him; and so far as he is sophisticated, it is in a way and method of his own. He is ugly as sin, longnosed, queer-mouthed, and with uncouth and somewhat rustic, although courteous manners, corresponding very well with such an exterior. But his ugliness is of honest and agreeable fashion, and becomes him much better than beauty. He was educated, I believe, at Cambridge, and formerly kept school in this town; but for two or three years back, he has repudiated all regular modes of getting a living, and seems inclined to lead a sort of Indian life among civilized men—an Indian life, I mean, as respects the absence of any systematic effort for a livelihood. He has been for sometime an intimate of Mrs. Emerson's family; and, in requital, he labors in the garden and performs such other offices as may suit him—being entertained by Mr. Emerson for the sake of what true manhood there is in him. Mr. Thorow is a keen and delicate observer of nature—a genuine observer, which I suspect, is almost as rare—a character as even an original poet; and Nature, in return for his love, seems to adopt him as her special child, and shows him secrets which few others are allowed to witness. He is familiar with beast, fish, fowl, and reptile, and has strange stories to tell of adventures, and friendly passages with these lower brethren of mortality. Herb and flower, likewise, wherever they grow, whether in garden, or wild wood, are his familiar friends. He is also on intimate terms with the clouds, and can tell portent of storms."

Hawthorne liked Thoreau's writings: he had read only one article, on Natural History, in the *Dial*. Principally he admired Thoreau's skill with a boat. They rowed up the Concord. Thoreau managed the boat perfectly. He said that he had unknowingly hit upon the Indian method of paddling—when some Indians visited Concord, they told him so. Now, being in want of money, he would sell his boat for seven dollars. He called it the *Musketaquid*, the Indian name for the Concord. He had once taken it down the Concord to its junction with the Merrimack and thence to Newburyport, about eighty miles.

Hawthorne was gathering the windfallen apples in his orchard with Sophia and his sister Louisa when Thoreau arrived with the boat. He gave Hawthorne a lesson with the oars. Hawthorne found that he could row with two oars, but that he could not paddle. Thoreau told him that it was only necessary to will the boat to go in a certain direction and it would immediately take that course. It seemed to Hawthorne, on the contrary, to be bewitched and to take any direction except the right one. Also, it made him self-conscious that Sophia was watching him, and could not feel very proud of her husband's proficiency.

Now he had a boat, and in a few moments could leave the Old Manse and disappear on the quiet river. The Concord began at Egg Rock, when the Sudbury joined the Assabeth around a grassy island. On the Concord the wind was blowing against him, the black river dimpled over with little eddies and whirlpools, the billows beating against the bow of the boat with a sound like the flapping of a bird's wing, but when he turned into the Sudbury he floated quietly along a tranquil stream, sheltered from the breeze by the woods and a lofty hill. How he delighted in those sudden transitions from turmoil to calm! There was a kind of music in his life, in his observation, and he wrote of turning into the Sudbury with the same start of quiet pleasure he had felt when, forcing his way through the brambles, he had come upon the quiet glade and frightened the assembly of crows. His boat lingered gently on the current. The Sudbury flowed narrowly for a mile, past Mine Hill, the scene of an old copper mine, a high hill with pines on its summit. Then it widened into Fairhaven Bay, almost a small lake, seventy acres in extent, in the shape of a figure 8, with Mount Misery on the right bank and farmhouses along the shore.

On the cliffs on the southeastern side of Fairhaven Hill Thoreau used to sit and study the river. Winding paths led through the tangled berrybushes and great clumps of juniper on the bank, and the river flowed past a grove of tall pine trees, around Nine Mile Corner, and into a swamp, past the French farm, the Wood farm, the Hosmer farm, the Hurd farm, the Willard farm.

For a mile above the junction the Assabeth seemed to Hawthorne the loveliest stream on earth. On the left was a grove of old hemlocks, and beyond them the river seemed shut in like a lake, with graceful black willows, vines tangled in the trees, growing to the water's edge. He rowed past Watermelon Cove, Black Willow, Gibraltar, Birds Nest Island, Spencer Brook, Butterick Cove, Honeysuckle Island. Or, fishing at dawn, he rowed past beds of pond lilies on the low banks of the river, beds of them unfolding as the sunrise stole gradually from flower to flower. There were cardinal flowers illuminating the dark nooks among the shrubbery, and showers of broken sunshine coming through the trees, kingfishers and ducks breaking the surface of the water. At sunset the river turned to gold. At night he camped with Ellery Channing on the bank of the Assabeth, a fire of pine cones and dry branches, smoke ascending through the pines, the reflection of the fire glowing on the water.[21]

He was writing in his notebook, a few days after he had refused to have Ellery and Ellen as boarders, when Margaret Fuller and Sam Ward appeared unexpectedly. Samuel Gray Ward was the heir of a New York banking fortune. He had gone to Bancroft's Round Hill School, to Columbia, and had been Longfellow's classmate at Tübingen. His sister was Julia Ward, who was soon—in 1843—to marry Samuel Gridley Howe, Hawthorne's old editor and benefactor. Sam Ward was a cheerful host, fashionable and shrewd, presently to become famous as the King of the Lobby in Washington.[22] He thought there was no more charming drawing room in Boston than the quaint old parlor of the Old Manse.

They walked down the orchard to the riverbank. Hawthorne and Ward stretched out on the grass, while Margaret and Sophia sat on the rocks. Margaret was very brilliant. She talked to Hawthorne, Ward talked to Sophia—he seemed to consider her an enchanted mortal, in an

earthly Elysium. He asked her what they did. "Nothing to describe,"
she said, "yet very much in reality. We do not intend to accomplish
anything that can be told of, these lovely summer days."

Ward said, "I was idle two months after my marriage, but have
not had ten days of leisure since." He thought they should begin work
now, as their two months had passed. He said their honeymoon never
would end, which she could have assured him of.

Margaret at last asked Sophia to take him into the house and show
him the furniture. "He was delighted with our gallery," Sophia wrote,
"thought the furniture beautiful and also the views from the windows
of our chamber. In short, he was entirely pleased and I imagine he
thought my husband was a kingly man, far surpassing all he had anticipated, for who can prefigure him?" [23]

V

Emerson said to Hawthorne, about this time, "I shall never see you
in this hazardous way; we must take a long walk together. Will you go
to Harvard and visit the Shakers?" [24]

Hawthorne agreed, and on September 27 they set out. It was a fine
day. They walked through West Concord and to Stow, roughly following the Assabeth, and circled northward to Harvard Village, twenty
miles in the opposite direction from Boston and civilization. They had
barely started out when Hawthorne observed some fringed gentians
growing by the roadside. He wanted to turn back and take them to his
wife. It was the first time he had slept away from her. [25]

Both Emerson and Hawthorne were in excellent spirits. They
agreed that in order to have an eventful journey a traveler had to have
a dash of humor or extravagance in his make-up. They were both sober
men, easily pleased, kept on the outside of the land. They did not even
creep into a farmhouse on the pretext of wanting a glass of milk. If they
had no money, and asked for food or a night's lodging at a farm, it
would be so easy to break into some mesh of domestic history. They
might, for example, see the first blush mantle on the cheek of a young
girl when the mail stage came or did not come. And so on. Then they
talked of the old rural nobility that had vanished. Both Hawthorne and
Emerson were in Emerson's words, "old collectors who had never before

had opportunity to show each other their cabinets, so they could have filled with matter much longer days."

They reached Stow at noon. Even the barrooms were dull. A few years before a traveler could share the jokes and politics of the teamsters and farmers on the road. But the temperance societies had emptied the taverns. Hawthorne tried to smoke a cigar; but Emerson observed that he was soon out on the piazza.

In the late afternoon, before they had covered their twenty miles, a wagon passed them on the road. A friendly, fatherly gentleman, who knew Emerson's name and his father's name and history, picked them up, gave them a ride into town, installed them at the tavern, and introduced them to the notables in the town.

At six-thirty the next morning they set out for the Shaker Village, three and a half miles away. Emerson had caught cold. He had a disgraceful barking cough. Hawthorne was "inclined to play Jove more than Mercurius." The Shaker sisters prepared their breakfast. Two of the brethren gave them an honest account of their faith and practice. They were neither stupid nor worldly, like others Emerson had seen of their faith. And their settlement was of great value as a model farm, in the absence of the old rural nobility Emerson and Hawthorne had talked of the day before.

The society was interesting, too, as an experiment in socialism, "which so falls in with the temper of the times." Brook Farm, Fourier, the Chartist uprisings in England, Alcott's Fruitland, Robert Owens' experiments—there were some twenty-eight utopian colonies then operating. And then the religious revival sweeping New England gave an additional interest to the Shakers. William Miller, the Pittsfield-born revivalist who predicted the end of the world within the next year— sometime between March 21, 1843, and March 21, 1844—had gathered an enormous following. All pulpits except the Roman Catholic and the Episcopalian welcomed him; the more devout of his fifty thousand followers sewed long white robes and selected hilltops, on which they meant to await the last day. . . . Yet plainly enough, the visit of Emerson and Hawthorne to the Shaker Village was dull. The day was warm as July. They left early, walked through Littleton, thence to Acton, and sauntered leisurely homeward, finishing their nineteen miles before four in the afternoon.[26]

Emerson went south in the winter, and their developing friendship

was interrupted. In the spring it revived again, when Sophia left Concord, for two or three weeks, to assist her sister Mary in preparations
for her marriage to Horace Mann.

Mary Peabody was then thirty-six. She had changed a great deal
from the days she had spent with Sophia in Cuba. She had grown thin
and pale, and a settled weariness seemed to have come over her in the
years of toil for her family. The most sensible and levelheaded of the
Peabody girls, she had neither Elizabeth's enterprise nor Sophia's sensitivity. Elizabeth rustled from one project to another, teaching, lectur-
ing, writing; Sophia painted, visited, dreamed, talked, and wrote her
ethereal letters to her friends; but Mary seems only to have worked.
In some respects she seems the most intelligent and resourceful of the
three sisters, and it sometimes seems that she was Hawthorne's favorite
in the early day of his friendship for them. She was somewhat like him in
her quiet commonsensical observations that deflated the extravagances
of her sisters. He seemed always to be going out of his way to meet
her. On one occasion he had been invited to dine with her at the Hoopers'
when a mix-up of orders from the Custom House sent him on a fruitless
errand to Cambridge. The Hoopers were Mary's friends more than
Sophia's—"I do not know your husband personally," Mrs. Hooper
wrote to Sophia . . . Perhaps we shall meet very little hereafter, as indeed we have hardly been intimate heretofore; but I shall remember
you with interest. . . ."

And now Mary was to be married. . . . Sophia wrote to her: "I
do not know whether you were ever aware of the peculiar love I have felt
from childhood for my precious sister, who is now so blest. . . . Her still
and perfect disinterestedness, her noiseless self-devotion, her transparent truthfullness and all-comprehensive benevolence through life! No
words can ever express what a spear in my side it has been to see her
year after year toiling for all but herself, and growing thin and pale
with too much effort. Not that her heroic heart uttered a word of com-
plaint or depreciation. But so much the more did I feel for her. I saw
her lose her enchanting gayety, and become grave and sad, and yet
could do nothing to restore her spirits. I was hardly aware, until it was
removed, how weighty had been the burden of her unfullfilled life upon
my heart. At her engagement, all my wings were unfolded, and my body
was light as air." [27]

Her husband was then forty-seven. Mary was marrying a man with no faults except a belief in phrenology. Horace Mann never swore, never smoked, was never intoxicated; a man of lively affections and joyous nature, modest, elastic, and buoyant. Born in Franklin, Massachusetts, on May 4, 1796, the son of a farmer, his childhood was not happy. He believed in the rugged nursing of Toil, "but she nursed me too much." There were no play days, only play hours, very little schooling, and that extremely severe. His religious experiences have already been referred to. One of his brothers drowned at the age of twelve. At the funeral the minister spoke of dying unconverted. Horace heard his mother groan. A crisis took place in his experience. He revolted against the idea of so cruel a creator. He expected the foul fiend to appear from behind every hedge and carry him off. Sometimes he could see fiends and other horrid shapes distinctly. It required all his will, at such moments, to keep from screaming aloud.

He studied to divert himself. He earned money for his schoolbooks by braiding straw. In six months from the time he began to study Latin he prepared himself for college, and enrolled in the sophomore class at Brown University in 1816. He became a tutor in Latin and Greek there. He also became friendly with the family of the president, Asa Messer, whose daughter Charlotte, still a child, fell in love with him and wept when he graduated. Mann studied at the famous law school at Litchfield, Connecticut—"the best whist player, best scholar and best lawyer in the school"—and practiced for fourteen years, winning four out of every five of his cases. Then in a series of rapid steps—representative, state senator, president of the Senate—he had a successful political career, and gave it up to organize the Massachusetts Board of Education. Meanwhile he married, in 1830, Charlotte Messer, who died two years later. He lost his savings at about this time, and in 1833, aged thirty-seven, moved to Boston to begin a new career.

Horace Mann said, "The common school is the greatest discovery ever made by man." The work of organizing them was an almost unbelievable record of disappointments. At Great Barrington, he recorded that it was like trying to batten down Gibraltar with one's fist. In the Berkshires they explained there was no attendance at his meeting because the weather was fair, at Northhampton, because it was stormy. At Dedham, meager, spiritless, discouraging; at Salem, everything was badly arranged; one speaker did not appear, and the other said very little. At Wellfleet—a miserable, contemptible, deplorable, convention. At Eastham, Orleans, Brewster, and Devens, the schools and schoolhouses were very miserable. At Pittsfield, when the time came to open the convention, not a soul was present except himself. His office in Boston was set afire—"a gang of incendiaries infest the city," he noted soberly, after someone set another fire in his lodging house, over his room. Yet his work progressed. The legislature granted $6,000 for three years to the normal schools. There were atrocious attacks on the Board of Education in this period, and they increased when Samuel May (Bronson Alcott's brother-in-law) principal of the Normal School at Lexington, began making abolitionist speeches, to Mann's great distress. It interfered with lessons. Public interest and donations were affected, and, said Mann, we want good teachers in our common schools, regardless of the great question of abolition, which he also favored. It was not that he opposed abolition—but when would people grasp the great idea of effecting political reform by reforming the sources whence all evil proceeded?

Horace and Mary Mann in Europe were sober, unsparing observers, completely unimpressed by the sights that were expected to move all visitors profoundly. A man of the deepest humility, Mann was nevertheless an unconscious aristocrat, and he walked through the palaces, not precisely slumming but with the air of a teacher who has returned and found that his children have been wasting their time. What on earth possessed the builder of Eaton Hall at Liverpool, to invest $75,000 in a marble floor? He looked upon this exactly as he would have looked upon someone who had been found squandering money that should have been used for a schoolhouse.

In Liverpool, on their trip to Eaton Hall, they rode through avenues miles in length, skirted with hedge and all varieties of forest trees. It was in May; herds of cattle and deer were grazing on the grounds and there were swans on the quiet lakes. The weather was already early summer. Groups of women were at work in the fields, gathering in the new-mown hay, weeding the walks, carrying away on their backs the limbs of a tree that had been felled. Around the house there were grounds covering fifty-two acres—an area the size of Boston Common. There were hothouses, beds of ripening pineapples, peach trees, strawberries, cherries, and Egyptian lotus growing in vast vats, and sheds for mushrooms and potatoes. There seemed to be every variety of plant and flower and fruit that could be found anywhere on the globe. . . . The communication hall of the palace was 740 feet long. Mann was depressed by its richness. The statues, the pictures, the coats of mail, the magnificent tables, the splendid piano in the library, the young ladies' garden, all made him wonder—could there not also have been cultivated a sympathy for others' hearts? For hearts that were formed by nature in as fine a mold as their own, and, in the sight of God, at as high a price?

Horace Mann probably saw the inside of more prisons and asylums than anyone else except Dorothea Dix. There was not much variety in his view of Europe; he went from the palaces to the jails, and from the schools to the hospitals. What gave him his skeptical view of the achievements of the old country was probably that in the matters on which he was informed, none of the old countries—neither England, nor Germany, nor France—had anything to teach Massachusetts. He disapproved of the school bill, for it was designed to strengthen the Established Church, and of Westminster Abbey because there were so few real great men—Ben Jonson, Milton, Dryden, Pope, Addison, Watt, Wilberforce, Lord Mansfield—among the sham great in their chapels and niches. Smithfield Market, the Old Clothes Market, the Jews Quarter, and Grub Street, Billingsgate, Greenwich Hospital, with its seventeen or eighteen hundred mutilated sailors, survivors of every naval battle that England had fought for fifty years—all left him shaking his head at the degradation of its life. Even the English countryside displeased him. The fields were monotonously green. The trees were small. The English left too much land for grazing, and not enough for tillage. He wanted a bit of Cape Cod, for variety.

They visited the Lunatic Asylum at Hanwell, the Union Workhouse at Grays Inn Lane, the Pentenville Prison, where no prisoner ever saw the face of a fellow prisoner, so they could never be recognized after release. Prisons interested Mary because of the possibility of applying Unitarian teachings in them. If a prisoner believed that his sin made him the subject of eternal punishment, and that his relief from it could be gained only by his belief that another had taken upon himself the punishment due to the sinner, then, she reasoned, he will not be likely to have sufficient vitality of faith to resist subsequent temptation. But if he is made to realize that in every human soul there is a recuperative power which he can at will exercise for his own reformation, that his Creator is ready to accept his sorrowful repentance at any moment when it is sincere, and that he, as well as the best educated and most favored of fortune, has before him a future life of endless progress— a season of imprisonment might be made indeed a golden hour for him.[28]

VI

Sophia and Hawthorne in Concord were in a newer world. What accounted for the American desire to start new communities and found ideal societies? It was because the original settlement of New England was an attempt to found one, Hawthorne thought. Indeed, the whole United States was one.

While Sophia was in Boston for the marriage of Mary and Horace Mann, he sat in the parlor of the Old Manse talking of Brook Farm with Emerson. Brook Farm was involved in another disaster. It had come under the influence of Albert Brisbane, and was now a Fourierist Phalanx, a center of Fourierist propaganda, and was divided into three departments: agriculture, domestic industry, and mechanic arts. The Secretary-General of Canada visited it, dined there, and died of apoplexy the next day (October 22, 1843). Hawthorne had come out of Brook Farm with so hard a sense of political realities that only the old English conservatives pleased him. Reformers and radicals and liberals had nothing to say to a Brook Farmer.[29] It was perhaps embarrassing to him that at about this time his sister-in-law, Elizabeth Peabody, should write in the *Dial* of Brook Farm as *A Glimpse of Christ's Ideal Society*. "Minds incapable of refinement will not be attracted into this association," she said. "Whoever is satisfied with society as it is, whose sense of justice is not wounded by its common action, institutions, spirit of commerce, has no business with this community; neither has anyone who is willing to have other men, (needing more time for intellectual cultivation than himself) give their best hours and strength and bodily labor, to secure himself immunity therefrom. . . . Whoever is willing to receive from his fellowmen that for which he gives no equivalent will stay away from its precincts forever." [30]

Hawthorne had decided to take a vow of silence during Sophia's absence. He could not keep it, and was glad he could not—this talk with Emerson was the best he had ever had with him. They talked of

SEARGENT S. PRENTISS
(New York Public Library)

GEORGE BANCROFT
(New York Public Library)

THE PEABODY HOUSE ON CHARTER STREET
(Essex Institute)

HAWTHORNE AT THE TIME HE WENT TO
BROOK FARM
(Essex Institute)

MARGARET FULLER
(New York Public Library)

BOSTON CUSTOM HOUSE

Margaret Fuller—it was a great joy to Emerson to find that he had underrated his friend. . . . She was far more excellent than he had thought, he said, and he had never known any example of such steady progress to stage of thought and character. Unless Hawthorne misunderstood him, he said she was the greatest women of ancient or modern times, and the one figure in the world worth considering. Hawthorne may, however, have merely written this in his notebook for Sophia to read—she always wanted him to quote to her exactly what Emerson had said. Then they talked of Ellery Channing's poetry, which Emerson and Sam Ward were editing; then of Thoreau, who was leaving Emerson's household to serve as a tutor in the house of William Emerson on Staten Island. It appeared that Emerson had been put to some inconvenience in having Thoreau in his household. Then of Brook Farm. They talked of the singular moral aspect it presented. They agreed that it was very desirable that its history should be written, and its progress and development observed.

Emerson left, and Hawthorne went out to chop wood. A piece of wood flew up and struck him in the left eye. In the morning it was grievously discolored. At the angle of the eye and on the upper part of his nose there was a great spot of almost-black purple, and a broad streak beneath one eye, while green, yellow, and orange overspread the circumjacent country. People would think they had fought a pitched battle, and that Sophia had fled. Though it seemed, from his battered aspect, that he should have been the one to flee.

He entered the house in her absence with a desolate feeling, an inward unquietness, yet not without an intermingled sense of pleasure that the separation was temporary and scarcely real. The old pleasure in solitude had left him. He split wood and sawed more briskly than he ever had before; he tried to sleep, but sleep would not come; he wrote in his journal and wrote letters to his wife. His mind was vagrant and refused to work to any purpose. He drowsed in the evening, by lamplight, playing tunes on the music box that Henry Thoreau left in their keeping. At night he was afraid the ghost of the Old Manse would visit him in his wife's absence, but apparently, he observed dryly, he had come to see Sophia. He translated a little German, read *Candide*, and fell asleep over the articles in the *Dial*. Molly Brian, the maid, cooked him wonderful meals, to which he sat down in solitary splendor. Oh, those solitary meals! They were the most dismal part of his experience.

The silent dining room with its queer old high-backed chairs affected him with a kind of madness. He imagined that an entire company of diners was embodied in himself, that they all ate in silence, all rose from the table together and went into the study, where they all read an article on Oregon in the *Democratic Review*, all read a story in German by Tieck, and all, at five o'clock, with one accord, went out to split wood. Snowflakes drifted through the gray day. The dreary day was followed by a dreary evening— Ah, dearest, these dreary evenings! The lamplight did not brighten his spirits. He went to bed at ten, and waked at three-thirty, lay awake till dawn, slept until after six, and rose at seven, worked, or tried to work, until eleven, walked to the post office— usually to find no letter there—read at the library for an hour, and trudged home to another solitary meal. For two or three days he kept his vow of silence—"Come home soon," he wrote, "or thy husband will have forgotten the use of speech." And on the day of her return he wrote in his journal until ten minutes past six—she was due to arrive before ten minutes past seven—"Tonight—tonight—yes, within an hour —this Eden, which is no Eden to a solitary Adam, will regain its Eve.[31]

In the winter mornings Sophia awakened before dawn. She sewed, until Molly brought her fresh-drawn water. The sky brightened while she sewed by lamplight. Before breakfast Hawthorne went out to skate on the meadow. The lower field behind the house had flooded, and as the water froze it formed a mirror that reflected the first rays of the sun. Sophia watched him from the window. Wrapped in his cloak, stately and grave, Hawthorne moved over the ice like a self-impelled Greek statue. The morning was still cloudy and gloomy, the sky overcast, a storm threatening. The rising sun was still hidden behind the hill. The whole firmament suddenly glowed, rose colored, east, west, north and south, and the meadow sea was also a rose. In the tinted sunlight the distant figure of her husband moved over the field of mirrors. Sophia ran upstairs to the study and watched through the window that opened onto the river and the leafless trees beyond it. The light enchanted her. She was an artist, and perhaps never so much so as in these first months of their marriage when Hawthorne had forbidden her to paint; and now she saw this strange and eerie scene as vividly as if it were already on canvas before her. There was a genuine distinction in the subjects she chose, even though she rarely got beyond the point of describing them in letters to her friends—they were always unusual, not so much because of their subject matter as because they were subjects, for her, when some difference, the light, or a different grouping of figures, transformed the ordinary and everyday into a scene of dreamlike wonder. It would have been a marvelous picture had she painted it, fresh as a child's drawing—a frozen sea in a meadow, a rosy sky, a man skating alone over the glistening surface—a study in tremulous pink and threatening shadows, prismatic ice, opaline snow, gems above as clouds, oxygen everywhere. In 1842 the fashion in painting was such that her pictures—the sort of thing she responded to visually and described most vividly to her friends—would have seemed freakish and deliberately intended to shock; but a century later they could have taken their place on any gallery wall. Sophia saw such pictures everywhere—Louisa Morrell walking alone at twilight in the garden of her Cuban plantation; or Anna Shaw lying on the lawn at the Old Manse, her golden curls spread out on the shaded green grass; or Thoreau, Emerson, and her husband skating over the Concord, Thoreau figuring dithyrambic dances and making Bacchic leaps on the ice, Hawthorne wrapped in his cloak, stately and grave, and Emerson bending far forward, half lying on the air.

For the world's eye I care nothing, she wrote to her mother, but in the profound shelter of this home I would put on daily a velvet robe, and pearls in my hair, to gratify my husband's taste. Her record of their eventless life was its quiet scenes—Hawthorne reading *The Tempest* aloud to her at night, while she sewed. He told her about his life in Raymond, and gave her some of the wine Horatio Bridge had sent him. He read *Two Gentlemen of Verona*. She did not like it. Then he read *Love's Labour's Lost*. In the winter they read all of Shakespeare. That magician upstairs is very potent! Sophia wrote to Mary Foote in Salem.

Shakespeare is pre-eminent; Spenser is music. We dare to dislike Milton when he goes to Heaven. We do not recognize God in his picture of Him. There is something so penetrating and clear in Mr. Hawthorne's intellect, that now I am acquainted with it, merely thinking of him as I read winnows the chaff from the wheat at once. . . . From reading his books you can have some idea of what it is to dwell with Mr. Hawthorne. But only a shadow of him is found in his books. The half is not told there. Your true friend,

Sophia A. Hawthorne.

P. S. Mr. Hawthorne sends his love to your husband.[32]

In January, John Louis O'Sullivan spent three days at the Old Manse.[33] He had now taken over the *Democratic Review* and was its sole editor. The magazine, however, was almost without funds, and O'Sullivan, from paying five dollars a page when he launched it, could now pay only twenty dollars for an article. There was an interesting story behind the financing of the *Democratic Review*. O'Sullivan's father, after an obscure early career as a consul and a special agent at Tangier, Mogador, and the Canary Islands, entered the Navy, commanded the *Canton* off the coast of Peru, and then purchased a brig, the *Dick*, which was seized by the authorities in Buenos Aires on suspicion of piracy. This was in 1822, when John Louis O'Sullivan was nine years old. In 1836, when O'Sullivan was practicing law at 63 Cedar Street in New York, Congress awarded his mother damages of $19,968.08 for the false arrest of her husband fourteen years before. Part of this money launched the *Democratic Review*. O'Sullivan withdrew from the paper in 1840, soon after his marriage. The following year he was elected to the legislature, and took control of the paper again. He was an enthusiastic, visionary man, filled with schemes he could never quite realize, an author with an oratorical and vaporous style, useful in expressing the nebulous dreams he had of the future greatness of America. He coined the phrase "manifest destiny." He believed that within a relatively short time two hundred and fifty million people would live in the United States—thought-provoking statements to the ten million citizens of that day. He had had a most singular life. Born on a British warship off Gibraltar in November, 1813 (there was a plague in the harbor, and his mother was given refuge on the vessel), there seems never to have been any question aroused by the fact that the United States and Britain were then at war. His father, a special agent to the United States consul at Tangier, was accused by the consul of shaking down two Jewish merchants for $250, yet soon thereafter was appointed consul at Mogador. During Madison's administration, the President was astonished one night when O'Sullivan's mother,

dressed in man's clothing, appeared at the White House with her four
children and, telling a strange story of her wanderings from New
Orleans to Cincinnati after the death of her husband, begged for relief.[34]

Thoreau met O'Sullivan at the Concord Athenaeum and went to the
Hawthornes' to have tea with him. "He expressed a great deal of interest in your poems," Thoreau wrote to Emerson, "and wished me to
give him a list of them, which I did—he saying he did not know but he
should notice them. He is a rather puny-looking man, and did not strike
me. We had nothing to say to one another, and therefore said a great
deal. He, however, made a point of asking me to write for his review,
which I shall be glad to do. He is at any rate one of the not-bad, but
does not by any means take you by storm—no, nor by calm either,
which is the best way." [35]

Hawthorne had made the mistake of referring to the Old Manse
as Eden and to himself and Sophia as Adam and Eve. It may have been
his repeated mention of it that caused him at last to take his vow of
silence in Sophia's absence. For there could be only one result, among
the sophisticated intellectuals of Boston and Concord; if there was to
be an Eden, there must also be a Paradise lost. The Hillards and the
Sam Wards of the world were too quick and too witty not to take him
at his word, and his own curious humor probably inclined him in their
direction. Whatever sense of self-esteem he had was being subjected to a
fierce assault in these days. If he spoke patronizingly—or merely cas-
ually, but in a way that could be construed as patronizing—of one of
his neighbors, it developed that his neighbor was a celebrity, whose
intelligence Emerson—*Emerson*—respected. If he regarded his own
works highly, there was always the remembrance that Emerson's *Nature*
had been written in this very room. He wrote satirically of Margaret
Fuller, and, as if he had sowed the ground with dragon seed, legions of
her admirers appeared. Moreover, she herself suddenly began to write
much better and talk more effectively. Thoreau could row a boat, and
he could not; Ellery Channing could build a log cabin; Emerson could
be sociable; even his garden was a petty matter compared to those of
his neighbors—Emerson's neighbor, Mr. Bull, developed the Concord
grape. The answers came back the next day or so. He spoke, immediately the world presented him some chastening evidence of his ignorance
or incompetence. Even when he walked through the woods he became

entangled with briers, lost his way, and was ready to fall to the ground and weep with vexation—this in a community where Thoreau was a woodsman. His wife loved company, crowds, parties, a social life—he was almost sensationally silent in company. He was a modest man—a fact which never seemed to have occurred to his neighbors, who treated him as if they thought he had too high an opinion of himself.

Sophia's letters to her mother (in the midst of fulsome descriptions of her happiness and her husband's excellences) alluded to their lack of visitors. Or she wrote: "For dinner we did not succeed in warming the potatoes effectually, but they were edible, and we had meat, cheese and apples. This is Christmas Day. . . . I intended to make a fine bowl of chocolate for my husband's dinner, but he proposed to celebrate Christmas by having no cooking at all. We dined on preserved fruits and bread and milk.[36] One result was that, while Hawthorne was filling his notebook with descriptions of their idyllic life, Reverend Upham (who visited in Concord) was telling in Salem such harrowing stories of their poverty as to make it seem that they were in need of food. Hawthorne learned of this on a visit to Salem in December, while Sophia visited her family in Boston. He also heard that Upham was to resign his pastorship—another evidence of how good his sources of information were, since Upham did not resign until a year later.[37]

The Hawthornes were poor. In their years at the Old Manse, Hawthorne published only sixteen stories. At most he could have received only a few hundred dollars for them. He received very little. O'Sullivan paid him a hundred dollars of his debt seven years later. Brook Farm owed Hawthorne well over a thousand dollars, and it was apparently his belief that he could collect that led him to relax so confidently in his early days in Concord. Before the end of their first year in the Old Manse the problem was acute. He could not pay his household bills. Emerson told him to "whistle for it . . . everybody was in debt . . . all worse than he was."

The winter of 1844 was the coldest in a hundred years. Sophia thought it was a miracle that they survived two weeks in January in the house. She was carrying her first child, and her letters to her mother were filled with a kind of grave and quiet charm. She said their thoughts hung in icicles. Her powers of endurance were frozen solid. She wrote letters in the hope of some unoccupied carrier pigeon straying her way. Wind rushed through the upstairs hall, through a broken windowpane. The cook went to Boston, and Hawthorne did the house-work. He arose early, built fires in the kitchen and breakfast room, put on water for tea, baked potatoes and cooked rice, and sat by the stove reading, until Sophia appeared. "It was a magnificient comedy to watch him, so ready and willing to do these things to save me an effort, and at the same time so superior to it all, and heroical in aspect." After breakfast she sat beside him and sewed while he wrote at his desk. Louisa Hawthorne had sent her some exquisite silk flannel for little shirts, but it was not quite enough. Mrs. Emerson told Sophia she could find it at Jacobs on Tremont Street, for a dollar a yard, and Sophia asked her mother to buy some. When Hawthorne stopped work, they walked to the village. At night Hawthorne read Macaulay aloud. On the first of February the temperature increased thirty degrees, which said Sophia, thawed their minds. And so the winter passed.[38]

On February 25, 1844, Horace Mann, the first child of Horace and Mary Mann, was born. On March 3, 1844, Una Hawthorne was born. Her name was a graceful tribute to Sophia's mother, who was an authority on Spenser and who seems to have grown mellower and wiser in these years. John O'Sullivan was Una's godfather. Hillard did not quite approve, he wrote to Hawthorne, of naming the child after Spenser's heroine. It was too imaginative. If the little girl could pass her life playing upon a green lawn, with a snow-white lamb with a blue ribbon around its neck . . .[39] The child was beautiful. Hawthorne confessed his inability to see the excellences that others pointed out, yet there was no doubt that Una was almost as remarkable, in her own way, as his sister Elizabeth had been as a child, with the same strangely marked individuality and subtlety of character. As she grew older she became headstrong, imaginative, with something almost frightening to Hawthorne in the boldness with which she stepped into everything and shrank from nothing. She seemed not childlike to him, except in an elusive, elfin, occasional way; sometimes she seemed hard, unreasonable, and comprehending beyond her years, and then she was tender, angelic, appreciative of the delicacy she had seemed entirely to lack. Hawthorne liked to study her face with a sideways glance, to catch a fineness of expression that played across it and let him believe he could see her real soul. For then she was beautiful, with her beauty the most flitting, transitory, most uncertain and unaccountable affair that ever had a real existence, beaming out when nobody expected to find it and mysteriously passing away when he thought himself sure of it.[40]

"I thank you for your kind and warm congratulations on the advent of our little Una," Hawthorne wrote to Hillard—"a name which I wish you were entirely pleased with; as I think you will be by and by. Perhaps the first impression may not be altogether agreeable; for the name has never before been warmed with human life, and therefore may not seem appropriate to real flesh and blood. But for us, our child has already given it a natural warmth; and when she has worn it through her lifetime, and perhaps transmitted it to descendants of her own, the beautiful name will have become naturalized on earth—whereby we shall have done a good deed in bringing it out of the realm of Faery. I do not agree with you that poetry ought not to be brought into common life. . . .

"I find it a very sober and serious kind of happiness that springs from the birth of a child. It ought not to come too early in a man's life —not till he has fully enjoyed his youth—for methinks the spirit can never be thoroughly gay and careless again, after this great event. We gain infinitely by the exchange; but we do give up something, nevertheless. As for myself, who have been a trifler preposterously long, I find it necessary to come out of my cloud region, and allow myself to be woven into the sombre texture of humanity. There is no escaping it any longer. I have business on earth now, and must look about me for the means of doing it." [41]

For Sophia there were now abstracted days, as, during the summer, she took Una to Boston and watched her on the Common, astonished at her beauty, and pleased with the parade of admirers, Caroline Sturgis and Anna Shaw, William Wetmore Story and Senator Atherton of New Hampshire, who called and left their presents.[42] Hawthorne went to Salem, and returned to Concord without her. His financial problems were now acute, and yet it seems he could not bring himself to sue Ripley for the money he had invested in Brook Farm. He began seeing the former Brook Farmers again—George Curtis, who settled in Concord, and Frank Farley, who had left the farm to go to an insane asylum, and George Bradford, who was now peddling vegetables from door to door.[43]

He also began to renew his political friendships. O'Sullivan wrote to Bancroft about the Salem postmastership for him. This was the post that Caleb Foote had held, until holding it compromised the reputation of the *Gazette* and a change of administration removed him from office. Then, O'Sullivan suggested, there might be a consulate at Marseilles, Genoa, or Gibraltar, or a diplomatic post in China.[44] While O'Sullivan was writing in this fashion to Hawthorne and Bancroft, he was also writing to Henry Wise, under the pretext of asking Wise's help, to tell him that Hawthorne was seeking the post office at Salem, and reminding Wise that Hawthorne had written Cilley's biography.[45] This should have been enough to block Hawthorne's chances. In addition, the postmaster at Salem was a good Democrat —B. F. Browne— whose removal for Hawthorne's sake would have created even greater ill will in Salem than was already directed against Hawthorne—it would have shattered the small group of Democrats who supported him. Either way, then, O'Sullivan's suggestion could only have made trouble.

Bridge was still on the *Cyane*, cruising off the coast of Africa. He returned in November, and gave Hawthorne his manuscript journal, asking him to edit it. Bridge was in low spirits. Hawthorne insisted that he keep a journal, giving him some invaluable advice when he set out: "I would advise you not to stick too accurately to the bare fact, either in your description or your narrative; else your hand will be cramped, and the result will be a want of freedom that will deprive you of a higher truth than that which you strive to attain. Allow your fancy pretty free license, and omit no heightening touches because they did not chance to happen before your eyes. If they did not happen, they at least ought, which is all that concerns you. This is the secret of all entertaining travellers. If you meet any distinguished characters, give personal sketches of them. Begin to write always before the impression of novelty has worn off your mind, else you will be apt to think that the peculiarities which at first attracted you are not worth recording; yet those slight peculiarities are the very things that make the most vivid impression upon the reader. Think nothing too trifling to write down, so it be in the smallest degree characteristic. You will be surprised to find on re-perusing your journal what an importance and graphic power these little particulars assume."

Bridge complained that life had lost its charm, his enthusiasm was dead, and there was nothing worth living for. Sophia advised him to fall in love. Hawthorne agreed that Bridge should: "You would find all the fresh coloring restored to the faded pictures of life; it would renew your youth; you would be a boy again, with the deeper feelings and purposes of a man. Try it, try it,—first, however, taking care that the object is in every way unexceptionable, for this will be your last chance in life. If you fail you will never make another attempt." [46]

Hawthorne's advice on both accounts was excellent. He edited Bridge's *Journal of an African Cruiser* in the winter, and the book was a success, its sale reaching five thousand copies, two thousand in the first edition, and five hundred in England. Bridge had insisted upon Hawthorne's taking all the royalties, which, however, Hawthorne refused to do. In any event, the returns from this would not be realized until the middle of 1845, or thereabout, and Hawthorne's situation was now nearly desperate. It became almost customary for Sophia to visit at West Street in Boston while he visited in Salem. Yet the Peabodys' income depended on their bookshop, and his family in Salem was no more prosperous than it had been before.

VII

Thirty years or more had passed since Hawthorne's mother had retired to her room. The seclusion he attributed to himself had always been hers in reality. Winter and summer brought no change in her life, nor did good or bad fortune. She lived as prosperously, or as meagerly, now, as she had when the stagecoaches were flourishing. Her old age was no different from her early years. Hawthorne was now married, and had left the home, but she perhaps saw him as frequently as when he lived there.

She grew old without having been young, and retired without having had a life to retire from. When Hawthorne graduated from college she had already been living in seclusion for twelve years. In one of his first stories—*Wakefield*—he imagined a man on an impulse leaving his family, taking up his residence in a house near by, and studying the grief in the household he had left, year after year, until his life—or both his lives—passed away. Wakefield was irresolute compared to his mother. She had done as much without leaving her house. Voices drifted up the stairwell to her room—the angry discussions of the war, perhaps, politics, ships, storms, relatives, the land in Maine, until her unvaried life seemed the only permanence in a world of fleeting change. Her children grew older, and became men and women—the bushes grew into saplings and the saplings became trees—and still she remained by the wayside of life, until no exit appeared possible through the entangling depths of her obscurity.

And now the end of the world was at hand. The date for its destruction, as foretold by William Miller, came between March 21, 1843, and March 21, 1844, and on March 14, 1844, he reluctantly proclaimed it as near at hand. He had a million converts. Sincere, simple, troubled at the result of his prophecy, Miller was finally driven by his supporters to set an exact date. He gave it as October 22. The days passed. There were suicides, many of them, and the asylums were crowded with people who had been driven mad by fear of the awful day.[47] The faithful gathered in their assemblies. The levity with which doubters greeted word of this somber event had something forced about it. Hawthorne considered it significant that Miller's prophecy came just as plans like those of Brook Farm, for the earthly perfection of mankind, were flourishing. In his view, the debts that publishers owed him were enough to justify the general holocaust. And it seemed, perhaps, the only method of getting mankind out of the various perplexities into which they had fallen—yet he rather wished the world might endure until some great moral had been evolved. Disappearing now, what purpose would have been accomplished? The sphinx did not slay herself until her riddle had been guessed; will it not be so with the world? We cannot tell what mighty truths may have been embodied in act through the existence of the globe and its inhabitants. Perhaps it may be revealed to us after the fall of the curtain over our catastrophe. Or perhaps the whole drama, in which we have been involuntary actors, may have been performed for the instruction of another set of spectators.[48]

At the end of November, the followers of Father Miller dispersed. For Hawthorne's mother, however, the impending catastrophe brought no change in her life. She lived as she had during the war, and during the peace, and as, it seemed now, she would always live.

However strange her life was, when viewed as a whole, she never did anything strange, or acted queerly. There are few incidents recorded of her life, but in them she seems not only intelligent but exemplary. It was wonderful that her seclusion did not leave her embittered, or ignorant. In the fateful decisions of Hawthorne's life—his education, or his marriage—she seems to have been aware of what was going on long before he credited her with any knowledge or understanding. And there is no mistaking his deference to her opinion, or the concern with which he presented his arguments to her. She was aware at a very early age that her children were unusually gifted. It was a Hawthorne family trait, however, to pay little attention to their gifts, and to regard really exceptional intellectual achievements matter-of-factly, or even somewhat censoriously. The Peabodys, on the other hand, hailed each evidence of childish originality as proof of budding genius; or, it sometimes seems, hailed genius even if the evidence was lacking. Sophia's letters from Cuba were full of tribute to the remarkable quality of the Morrell children, and Elizabeth Peabody, of course, had written, in her *Record of a School*, the talks of Bronson Alcott and his students wherein the words of the children were almost reverently treasured.

There had never been such care given the Hawthornes in their childhood. Uncle Robert gloomed over their shortcomings, Aunt Mary scolded them, Grandmother Manning considered them impertinent— the whole family neglected them, and then punished them. This was not quite so severe as the treatment of children a generation or so before, in which it was soberly affirmed that children were vipers. Yet it was closer to that Puritanical view than to the heady enthusiasm of the Peabodys.

"All through our childhood," said Elizabeth Hawthorne, "we were indulged in all convenient ways, and were under very little control except that of circumstances . . . We were the victims of no educational pendantry. We always had plenty of books, and our minds and sensibilities were not unduly stimulated. If he had been educated for a genius it would have injured him excessively. He developed himself. I think mental superiority in parents is seldom beneficial to children. Shrewdness and good nature are all that is requisite. The Maker of a child will train it better than human wisdom could do." [49]

It was perhaps true of Elizabeth and Maria Louisa that they were indulged in all convenient ways; it does not seem to have been true of Hawthorne. And perhaps there came a time when, in looking back over his own early years (and especially in comparison with the view of the training of childhood that the Peabodys now advanced), it seemed to him that the Spartan severity that his mother's family had exercised in training him and his sisters had been only accidentally beneficial. Go to the untrammeled souls, Elizabeth Peabody had said, and weave for them a golden web. She must have known that Hawthorne could not do so, and could not in fact write for children from any point of view, with-

out opening the Pandora's Box of the memories of his childhood. There
are lines of inquiry, innocent on the surface, or even innocent in purpose, which lead somewhere along their path to an encounter half
foreseen, and half dreaded because it involves a final conflict with someone we love, or the shattering of a cherished illusion. So there are those
inquiries, accepted without thought at the moment they are made, which
sink like depth charges into the consciousness, to erupt, years later, with
greater destructive force because of their apparent simplicity.

It was inevitable, from the time Hawthorne began to associate with
such shrewd and subtle teachers of children as Elizabeth and Mary Peabody, that presently his own childhood would be brought into review.
And once this was done, it was plain that there would follow a questioning of his mother's action, or her inaction, and with it the alternatives
of bitterness or understanding as he looked back across the melancholy
picture of his life and hers. He loved her ; but there had been, since boyhood, "a sort of coldness of intercourse between us, such as is apt to
come between persons of strong feeling, if they are not managed
rightly." It would have taken very little to transform this reserve into a
sense of deeper estrangement. He was too levelheaded to entertain for
long a sense of having been defrauded. Yet surely the elaborate care and
attention which he now saw given to children of far less native ability
than, for example, his sisters, must have set in motion thoughts peculiarly poignant, revived at each recollection of the lonely woman who
lived by herself in a house filled with her children and her brothers and
sisters ; and at each recollection of the quiet, wasted evenings in the old
house on Herbert Street, where the bright and vivid sisters of his boyhood seemed to have changed all at once into the grave spinsters they
had become.

For his mother, however, the world must have appeared far
stranger. Her quiet son and her strong-minded daughters, eager children when her seclusion began, had grown into men and women between
sunrise and sunset. Unchanging days, solitary meals, quiet mornings
when the children were at school, quieter afternoons, without visits, or
walks, or shopping, a quiet evening when the children, themselves quiet
and relaxed, walked or read, and the silent house grew quieter still. Her
son glided out of the house like a ghost, a shadow of the night, as he said
of himself, and disappeared into the darkness. The last stage of her
brother's stage line had passed the last street lamp, and lurched off the

pavement into the dark and rutted road. Now even the stagecoaches
had vanished, and the voices drifting up the stair well spoke of things
she had never seen, of people she had not heard of, and of a kind of life
she did not know. Hawthorne could not bear to think about her life.
It would be a mockery if this were all, he thought; it would be a fiend,
and not God, who had created us. In his young manhood, when he was
a son and brother only, it seemed to him that the world had been made
for man's trial and testing. But when he had children of his own he
wanted its reformation and he wanted its life to be blessed, if only for
their sakes; and then, perhaps, he understood her.⁵⁰

VIII

Our philosophers have not taught us what is best, he said, on the
eve of the Civil War, and our philosophers have not sung what is beautifullest, in the kind of life that we must lead. . . . The kind of life he now
led was dark and troublesome. He moved between Concord and Salem
and Boston. In the early winter of 1844 Sophia and Una visited at the
house on Herbert Street. "For the first time since my husband can remember," Sophia wrote, "he dined with his mother! This is only one of
the miracles which the baby is to perform. Her grandmother held her on
her lap till one of us should finish dining, and then ate her own meal.
She thinks Una is a beauty, and, I believe, is not at all disappointed in
her. Her grandmother also says that she has the most perfect form she
ever saw in a baby. She waked this morning like another dawn, and
smiled beautifully, and was borne off to the penetralia of the house to
see Madam Hawthorne and aunt Elizabeth. My husband's muse is urging him now, and he is writing again. He never looked so excellently
beautiful. Una is to be dressed as sumptuously as possible today, to
visit her grandaunt Ruth Manning. Louisa wants her to overcome with
all kinds of beauty, outward and inward. I feel just made. All are quite
well here, and enjoy the baby vastly." ⁵¹

Even had Hawthorne been financially secure the period of transition
would have been difficult. His work was not going well. He had come to a
time when the quiet stories he had written before were no longer enough
to contain the sweep of experience he had known: the observations he
packed into them constantly broke their fragile symmetry. The change
in his fortunes, his new position as the husband of a brilliant and reason-

ably well-known little artist, also carried with it a responsibility for a different kind of work than that which had sufficed him in the past. And now we reach a point of great difficulty and complexity in terms of Hawthorne's creative life. He had written so steadily, in the previous years, that there was no real need for a greater productivity to establish his reputation; but of all his stories, only eighteen had been collected and appeared under his own name. He was known to the public as the author of *Twice-Told Tales* and *Grandfather's Chair*. He had outgrown this form of literature before the world knew that he had written it. There was upon him, therefore, an implicit responsibility to write something compatible with his greater standing and his developing abilities; but the something that he was called upon to write was not a simple continuation and enlargement of what he had previously done, and it was this, apparently, that he was expected to do.

It was not only that most of his work was still unknown, nor even that, in a sense, the best of it was, that makes his story so extraordinary; the strangeness of his career at this time is that the work to which his name was given was all of one sort. His early novel, his brilliant contributions to the *New England Magazine* in 1834 and 1835, his miscellaneous journalism, the popular histories he had written with his sister, the exact descriptions of his notebooks, the passion and the poetry of his love letters—little of this was reflected in the writing by which he was known to the public. Such stories as he had published under his own name had, indeed, a pale lunar glow; it was part of their mysterious beauty that they were but reflections of the intense experience poured into the writing he had done in secret. The radiance that filled his work, the light, Holmes said, that never fell on land or sea, had its source in them. He had chosen only the most concentrated of them for *Twice-Told Tales*, the most refined, and those with the least general appeal. They introduced him to the public as a writer of extraordinary genius within a very narrow range, and with a certain monotony of mood and repetitiousness of subject, as if he returned again and again to the same problem dissatisfied with each attempt to solve it. He had followed this work with the children's stories of *Grandfather's Chair*. Excellent as they were in their way, they nevertheless continued in the same path as the stories in his first book. They were weaker than those stories. A sort of surface sentimentality concealed their actual firmness, and made Hawthorne's range seem even narrower than his first book had promised. He was now definitely characterized as a writer of pale and ghostly subjects, gentle, good, moral, enlightened, didactic, ethereal, a little pansyish, and entirely lacking in the rigor of thought that marked the theologians or the passionate appeals of the abolitionists. Only his essays on Fessenden and Cilley were inconsistent with this literary character he had assumed; and in both cases they were memorials to his friends.

He was as hard as nails. But he now wrote only in the vein that he had begun to exploit, almost as if attempting to live up to the public figure that his own books had made of him. It seems to me that he never wrote so badly as in these years. *The Hall of Fantasy, The New Adam and Eve, Egotism, The Birthmark, The Celestial Railroad, The Procession of Life, Fire Worship, The Intelligence Office, The Christmas Banquet, Rappaccini's Daughter*, all of which were written and published in these years, have the weaknesses of his first stories, the strained allegories, the creaking stage machinery, the wearisome exhaustion of the same idea; but they lack the grace and delicacy of *The Haunted Mind* or *The Village Uncle* or the terrific power of *The Hollow of the Three Hills* or *Alice Doane's Appeal*. Where the note is one of horror, as in *Egotism*, the imagery is strained and ugly in comparison with the simple honesty of *Young Goodman Brown*. Where there is humor, as in *Earth's Holocaust*, in which all the unessentials of life are heaped together in one vast bonfire, the satire grows so heavy that the proper end of the story might be to throw it in with the rest. There is none of the comedy of *My Kinsman, Major Molineaux*, for example, or the genuine, if somewhat overworked humor of *Mr. Higginbottom's Catastrophe*. Hawthorne had cut himself off from history in these stories. They are exceptional in all his work in that they have no historical foundation. He had previously written stories which were contemporary incidents laid in times past, or, to a greater extent than has been recognized, were simply vivid dramatizations of historical events and sharp characterizations of historical figures. He now substituted for this a romantic background of old castles and madmen's laboratories; and replaced Sir William Pepperell or Governor Hutchinson with stories of sinister doctors working tragic experiments on human beings. It is because the thought in these stories is so powerful that their limitation as fiction becomes clear. In his early years he had taken the frail scaffolding of an incident and covered it with images of great beauty; he now erected

an iron framework and did not cover it at all, or covered it only here
and there with passages of highly polished prose, like fragments of
stained glass lodged among the girders.

IX

The three years we have spent here will always be to me a blessed
memory, Sophia wrote to her mother, because here all my dreams became realities. "I have got gradually weaned from it, however, by the
perplexities that have vexed my husband the last year, and made the
place painful to him. If such an involved state of things had come upon
him through any fault or oversight on his own part there would have
been a solid though grim satisfaction in meeting it. But it was only
through too great a trust in the honor and truth of others. There is
owing to him, from Mr. Ripley and others, more than thrice money
enough to pay all his debts; and he was confident that when he came
to a pinch like this, it would not be withheld from him. It is wholly
new for him to be in debt, and he cannot 'whistle for it,' as Mr. Emerson advised him to do, telling him that everybody was in debt, and that
they were all worse than he was. His soul is too fresh from Heaven to
take the world's point of view about anything. I regret this difficulty
only for him; for in high prosperity I should never have experienced the
fine temper of his honor, perhaps. But, the darker the shadow behind
him, the more dazzlingly is his figure drawn to my sight. I must esteem
myself happiest of women, whether I wear tow or velvet, or live in a
logcabin or in a palace . . ." [52]

Except for Bridge, Hawthorne had no contact with his old Bowdoin schoolmates in these years. The disasters that had befallen them
seemed to have ended with Cilley's death, unless, indeed, his own hardships indicated that he was now enduring the fate they had suffered.
In his *Christmas Banquet*, in which he imagined the most miserable people in the world assembling at dinner, he placed among them "a man
of nice conscience, who bore a bloodstain on his heart—the death of a
fellow creature—which, for his more exquisite torture, had chanced with
such a peculiarity of circumstances, that he could not absolutely determine whether his own will entered into the deed or not. Therefore, his
whole life was spent in the agony of an inward trial for murder, with a
continual sifting of the details of his terrible calamity, until his mind

had no longer any thought, nor his soul any emotion, disconnected with it." [53] The death of Cilley was still an issue in politics. The turmoil around Brook Farm was still a leading topic of discussion among New England intellectuals. Against the background of these experiences, and the vexations of his life in Concord, the character of his writing at this time seems even more remarkable. "Hawthorne left himself out of his work," says Professor Woodbury, "so far as a man can"—a fortunate circumstance, in his opinion, for he considered much of Hawthorne's work in these years weak and awkward, sentimental in its idyllic phases, and grotesque and puerile in its symbolism.[54]

Hawthorne published sixteen stories in these years, and they probably appeared in about the sequence in which they were written. They are of three general types—allegories attacking the Unitarians, like *The Celestial Railroad;* nature essays, like *Buds and Bird Voices,* and satirical essays, catalogues of imaginative creations, like *A Virtuoso's Collection,* in which Cinderella's glass slipper, King Arthur's sword, Ulysses' bow, Daniel Boone's rifle, Robinson Crusoe's parrot, Minerva's owl, Shelley's skylark, Bryant's waterfowl, Joseph's coat of many colors, Queen Mab's chariot, Christian's burden of sin, and so on, are gathered in a vast museum.

The Hall of Fantasy (February, 1843) is a comparable museum, this one containing the dreams and dreamers and visionaries of mankind—the inventions that never worked, the utopian societies that failed, castles in the air, machines for distilling heat from moonshine, making granite out of morning mist, and sunshine out of ladies' smiles, dyes out of sunsets, and fifty different kinds of perpetual motion. Here also is Father Miller, picturing the end of the world, while the multitude protest—parents wanted their children to grow up, lovers wanted their love consummated, reformers wanted time to test their theories, an inventor time to perfect his invention, a miser a chance to add to his fortune, and a little boy wanted the earth's destruction postponed until after Christmas.

The New Adam and Eve (February, 1843) carries the thought a step further, after the devastation, and imagines a newly created couple wandering among the deserted ruins of Boston, puzzling over the relics of a vanished world. They enter a department store, glancing at the silks, corsets, dresses, without knowing what to make of them; and thence to a church, a court of justice, the State House, a prison, a mansion on Beacon Street, a bookstore, a jeweler's shop, Bunker Hill, and the library at Harvard University.

Egotism, or the Bosom Serpent (March, 1843) is the story of a man afflicted with a snake perpetually gnawing his bosom, at first hiding away his dreadful affliction, and then forcing it upon the attention of everyone—nay, insisting that every man had a snake in his bosom, the miser a copperhead, a statesman a boa constrictor, a quarreling couple a house adder, and so on, "the type of each man's fatal error, or hoarded sin, or unquiet conscience." It was not to be tolerated that he should "break through the tacit compact by which the world has done its best to secure repose without relinquishing evil" and he was placed in an asylum. Released, he haunted his gloomy mansion, aware that his diseased self-contemplation engendered and nourished the serpent that could not abide with him if he could for one instant forget himself.

The Birthmark (March, 1843) repeats the same theme. A scientist marries a lovely woman, flawlessly beautiful except for a tiny birthmark, in the shape of a hand, on her cheek, a symbol of the imperfection that nature lays upon all her creatures. The birthmark comes to be an obsession with him, and at all seasons which should have been happiest his gaze returns to it, until his wife begs him to try the experiment he wants to make, preferring to risk death rather than live as she has, and dies as he triumphantly removes the one flaw in her beauty.

The Procession of Life (April, 1843) is an essay on the divisions of mankind, not by class, or color, or creed, but, first by all, those who suffer from the same diseases, then by intellect, then by those who suffer under similar afflictions, then the brotherhood of crime, then the truly good, the genuine benefactors of the race.

The Celestial Railroad (April, 1843) is Hawthorne's revision of *Pilgrim's Progress*, or, more exactly, his notion of *Pilgrim's Progress* as it would be rewritten in terms of Unitarian doctrine. Instead of Christian's toilsome progress toward the Heavenly City, a railroad rushes him speedily there, though the engineer appears to be the very individual with whom Christian struggled so mightily; the noxious vapors of hell have been piped for gaslights; a bridge (somewhat shaky) built over the Slough of Despond; a tunnel dug through Hill Difficulty; the materials used to fill the Valley of Humiliation.

X

Hawthorne's purpose in all this was to attack the vague diffuse optimism into which New England thought, under the guidance of the Unitarians, was drifting. Yet his own imagination led him astray and blunted the force of his satire. There was a kind of swampy luxuriancy in his writing; ideas followed one another too rapidly for a single compelling idea to emerge. Moreover, local allusions and personal comments broke in awkwardly. He introduced all his colleagues into *The Hall of Fantasy*, Lowell, Emerson, Jones Very, Longfellow, Washington Irving, Cooper, Washington Allston, Epes Sargent, O'Sullivan, Bronson Alcott, Orestes Brownson, and removed them when he included the story in *Mosses from an Old Manse*. "Hawthorne was attacking Transcendentalism," says Edward Mather; "he was condemning a theory of life and of behavior which was held sacred not only by his wife's family but by those, almost without exception, with whom he was in daily or weekly social intercourse. . . . It is difficult for the reader of today, picking up either *The Celestial Railroad* or *The Old Manse*, to realize 'the snub direct' which in those two works Hawthorne gave to the very men who, though not professing to admire him as a writer, were so interested in him that they importuned him with their attentions." [55] With one exception, these stories were published in his first two years at Concord. In 1845 he tried frantically to find an official post to provide a living for his wife and Una. The effort involved returning to the friends of his college days. He saw no more of Bancroft and Ripley; his hopes were now placed again in Pierce and Bridge, who gave him tangible reason to expect a position. It must have been clear to him by this time that Sophia and Elizabeth Peabody's friends were not people he could work with, and it may have been that Sophia herself, through her long letters to her mother, was responsible for revealing to the other side the intricate negotiations that securing a government job then entailed.

Sophia had never met Franklin Pierce. One day in May she was sitting at the window in the parlor of the Old Manse when she saw two men approaching up the avenue of black ash trees. She recognized Bridge, who, when he saw her, took off his hat and waved it in the air in a sort of playful triumph. She raised the sash, and Bridge introduced "Mr. Pierce." "I saw at a glance," she wrote her mother, "that he was a person of delicacy and refinement." Hawthorne was in the shed, chopping wood. Bridge caught a glimpse of him and began a sort of waltz toward him. "Mr. Pierce followed; and when they reappeared, Mr. Pierce's arm was encircling my husband's old blue frock. How his friends do love him! Mr. Bridge was perfectly wild with spirits. He danced and gesticulated and opened his round eyes like an owl." [56] Hawthorne borrowed a hundred dollars from Bridge, which met their current expenses, and took Sophia for a brief vacation, in midsummer, into central Massachusetts.[57]

The night of July 9, 1845, was their third wedding anniversary. Between nine and ten o'clock Ellery Channing knocked at the door of the Old Manse, and asked to borrow Hawthorne's boat. Ellery Channing was a slight, blue-eyed, bearded young man, with a ruddy, weatherbeaten face and the air of a retired philosophical woodchuck.[58] Martha Hunt, a nineteen-year-old teacher in one of the primary schools, had been missing all day, and her bonnet and shoes had been found on the bank of the Concord near Barrett's farm. Channing took the oars and Hawthorne the paddle. They rowed swiftly downstream in the darkness, past Honeysuckle Island and Butterick's Cove and under the Stone Bridge. About a quarter of a mile below the bridge they saw lights on the left bank of the river, and the dim figures of a number of people waiting for them. There was an oak tree on the shore there, a river landmark; the girl's belongings had been found beneath it. George Curtis lived in the house in plain sight on the hill above the oak tree.

General Butterick and a young man in a blue frock got into the boat with Hawthorne and Channing. The two men had long poles with hooks at the end. Ellery had a hay rake. Hawthorne steered the boat. There were waterweeds on the verge of the river; but after a few steps the bank went off very abruptly and the water speedily became fifteen or twenty feet deep. It was one of the deepest spots in the river.

Hawthorne rowed the boat past the spot where the bonnet had been found. Holding a lantern over the river, it was black as midnight, smooth, impenetrable, and keeping its secrets from the eye as perfectly as midocean would. The missing girl was well thought of. She was a girl of education and refinement, melancholy, accustomed to taking long walks in the woods, a member of a large family, affectionate, but uncultivated and incapable of responding to her demands. She was thought to be depressed and miserable for want of sympathy. There were sixty pupils in her classes.

Once or twice the pole or the rake caught in branches of water-weeds, which in the starlight looked like garments. Once Ellery and the General struck some substance at the bottom, which they at first mistook for the body, but it was probably a sod that had rolled in from the bank.

The young fellow in the blue frock sat next to Hawthorne, plying his long pole. They had drifted a little distance below the group of men on the bank when he gave a sudden start. "What's this?" he cried. Hawthorne felt in a moment what it was. He supposed the same electric shock went through everybody in the boat. "Yes; I've got her!" cried the young man, and heaving up his pole with difficulty, there was an appearance of light garments on the surface of the water.

He made a strong effort, and brought so much of the body above the surface that there could be no doubt of it. He drew her toward the boat, grasped her arm or hand, and Hawthorne steered the boat to the bank. In the starlight, dimly, he could see the dead girl, her limbs swaying in the water, close to the boat's side. His voice trembled when he spoke. On the bank the men, holding their lanterns aloft, stepped into the water. "Ah, poor child," said an elderly man. They carried her ashore and laid her under the oak tree, examining her by the light of their lanterns.

Hawthorne had never seen or imagined a spectacle of such perfect horror. As soon as she was taken from the water, blood began to stream from her nose. Something seemed to have injured her eye; perhaps it was the pole when it first struck her body. The complexion was dark red, the hands white and rigid. Her arms had stiffened in the act of strangling and were bent before her, with the hands clenched. One of the men put his foot upon her arm, for the purpose of reducing it by her side, but in a moment it rose again. A middle-aged man, David Butterick, fainted, and was found lying in the grass, insensible. It required much rubbing of hands and limbs to restore him.

One of the girl's brothers, twelve or fourteen years old, stood by, answering questions about his sister. He seemed not much moved, externally, but Hawthorne thought he was stunned and bewildered by the scene—his sister lying there, under the oak, at midnight, on the verge of the black river, with strangers clustering over her, holding their lanterns over her face.

Two rails were secured, boards and broken oars laid across them, and the body, wrapped in a quilt, laid upon this rude bier. All of them took turns in carrying the body or steadying it across the half mile of pasture to her father's house. The burden grew very heavy before they reached the door. The thought came to Hawthorne that if she could have foreseen how her maiden corpse would have looked—it would surely have saved her from the deed. Now he thought how strange and fearful it would have seemed if it could have been foretold, a day before, that he would help carry a dead body up that hill! When they reached the house the girl's grandfather appeared, holding a light, and after the body was laid on a table, he disappeared. Mrs. Minot Pratt, Hawthorne's old friend from Brook Farm, was in the room, to assist in laying out the body. She seemed at a loss how to proceed. Another woman, a woman of skill, appeared, and was in despair about the job, so rigid was the corpse. Hawthorne was told that on stripping the corpse they found a strong cord wound around the waist and drawn tight.[59]

XI

There was no inquest. The death of the girl was another of the experiences of Concord that made a powerful impression on Hawthorne's imagination—he used it almost without change in *The Blithedale Romance*, as he also used the singular meeting with Emerson and Margaret Fuller in Sleepy Hollow. There were now only a few months remaining of their life in the Old Manse. On October 1, Reverend Ripley and Mrs. Ripley were returning, and Hawthorne had nowhere to take his family.

Bridge again came to his rescue. He was then stationed at the Portsmouth Navy Yard and had spacious bachelor quarters. He invited the Hawthornes, Senator and Mrs. Pierce, Senator and Mrs. Atherton, of New Hampshire, and Congressman Fairfield, of Maine, to spend two weeks with him there.[60] Atherton was particularly detested by the abolitionists. He was the author of the gag rule, which from 1838 to December 3, 1844, provided that all bills or petitions relating to slavery should be laid on the table without being debated, printed, or referred. Fairfield was a relative, probably an uncle, of a brilliant young Bowdoin graduate, John Fairfield Hartley. At that time Bowdoin students believed that if there was one of their members destined to become world famous it was John Fairfield Hartley. He entered the Treasury in 1838 as a clerk, and served for forty years, for many years assistant secretary, regardless of the changes of administration, not widely known, but recognized among the officials as the best revenue lawyer in the country.[61]

Hawthorne was growing portly. He now weighed a hundred and seventy pounds, more than he had ever weighed before. The life in the Navy Yard pleased him—the free and social mode of life among the officers and their families, meeting at evening on the doorsteps, or stopping in familiarly. Bridge had been uneasy about the stiffness of his gathering, and therefore persuaded his sisters and some of his friends from Washington to help entertain them. They succeeded admirably. The Commandant of the Yard, Captain Storer, seemed to Hawthorne a man without brilliancy, of plain aspect and simple manners, but just, upright, kindly, and with an excellent practical intellect. His next in rank was Commander Pearson, "an officer-like, middle-aged man, with such cultivation as a sensible man picks up about the world, and with what little literary tincture he imbibes from a bluish wife."

Then there were "the rough-hewn first lieutenants, with no ideas beyond the service; the Doctor, priding himself on his cultivation and refinement, pretending to elegance, sensitive, touchy; the sailing-master, an old salt, tossed about by fifty years of stormy surges, and at last swept into this quiet nook, where he tells yarns of his cruises and duels, repeats his own epitaph, drinks a remarkable quantity of grog, and complains of dyspepsia; the old fat major of marines, with a brown wig, not pretending to imitate natural hair, but only to cover his baldness and grayness with something that he imagines to be unsightly— he smells potently of snuff, but has left off wine and strong drink for the last twenty-seven years—a Southerner, all astray among our New England manners, but reconciling himself to them, like a long practiced man of the world, only somewhat tremulous at the idea of a New England winter. The lieutenant of marines, a tall, red-headed man, between thirty and forty, stiff in his motions, from the effects of a palsy contracted in Florida—a man of thought, both as to his profession and other matters, particularly matters spiritual; a convert, within a few years past, to papistry—a seer of ghosts—a dry joker, yet sad and earnest in his nature—a scientific soldier, criticizing Jackson's military talent, fond of discussion, with much more intellect than he finds employment for—withal, somewhat simple."

Hawthorne made a few trips away from the yard. He visited the Reverend Dr. Burroughs, the rector of St. John's Episcopal Church in Portsmouth, "a most genial old clergyman . . . with nothing Calvinistic about him; a man of cheerful gossip; no enemy to a quiet glass of wine." Two or three miles from the Navy Yard, on Kittery Point, stood the residence of Sir William Pepperell, the subject of a biographical article Hawthorne had published in *The Token* twelve years before. He examined the house with great interest, and described it carefully in his notebook. "In the vicinity of the Navy Yard, an engineer officer, stationed for a year or two past on a secluded point of the coast, making a map, minutely finished on a very extensive scale, and has the aspect of a fine liver; his companion, a civil engineer, with much more appearance of intellectual activity. Their map is spread out in a room that looks forth upon the sea and islands, and has all the advantages of sea air—very desirable for summer, but gloomy as a winter residence."

Bridge had pleasant recollections of this visit—boating, fishing, driving, and an entire absence of formality. He thought it principally memorable because it succeeded in its main object—that of influencing men of prominence—Atherton and Fairfield—to exert themselves in Hawthorne's behalf. He believed that the gathering was principally responsible for Hawthorne's appointment, the next year, to his post in the Custom House at Salem. He was probably right. There were at least three separate groups of people working to get Hawthorne an appointment. O'Sullivan continued to work through Bancroft, though his effort had the queer air of his previous effort to have Hawthorne appointed postmaster. He persuaded Bancroft to offer Hawthorne a clerkship at the Charlestown Navy Yard, at $900 a year. This offer was made when Hawthorne returned from Portsmouth. He refused it.[62] As Hawthorne's position grew more desperate another champion, and a powerful one, came to his side. This was Charles Sumner. He had made his entrance into public life that summer, with a Fourth of July oration on peace, and his first political speech that fall at a meeting to oppose the admission of Texas as a slave state. At the Whig convention in September he urged the Whig party to adopt a consistent antislavery policy. His support of Hawthorne doubtless came by way of his friendship with Hillard, though it may be that the indirect influence went beyond Hillard to Judge Story, who was the teacher and adviser of both Hillard and Sumner. "You will think I never appear," Sumner wrote to Mrs. Bancroft, "except as a beggar. Very well. I never beg for myself. But I do beg most earnestly for another; for a friend of mine, and of your husband's, for a man of letters, of gentleness." [63]

He had heard that day (January 9, 1846) of the poverty of the Hawthornes. They had been evicted from the Old Manse. The Ripleys had not notified them that they were returning. The first word they had of it was when carpenters appeared. They made a tremendous racket among the outbuildings. They strewed the grass with pine shavings and chips of chestnut joists. They cleared away the woodbine and removed the mosses from the Old Manse. At the end of September Hawthorne in desperation asked Bridge to lend him a hundred and fifty dollars, saying they were to be turned out of the house the following week. Bridge lent him a hundred dollars.[64] The Hawthornes planned first to live in the kitchen of the Manning house in Salem. Louisa Hawthorne insisted they should have the parlor. Hawthorne went to Salem and Sophia took Una to her parents' home in Boston.[65] And Hawthorne again sat in the old chamber "where I wasted so many years of my life" and tried to write. Bridge's book went into its second edition. His publishers urged Hawthorne to write a History of Witchcraft. He began instead collecting his previously published stories into *Mosses from an Old Manse*, and writing the long autobiographical article that, giving the book its title, compensates, by the grace of its prose and the serenity of its mood, for the horror stories that make up so much of the rest of the book.

"When will you come back?" Sophia wrote to him from Boston. "Mr. Hillard said you promised to go there again. You can always come here. . . . I bless God," she wrote, "for such a destiny as mine; you satisfy one beyond all things." [66] Yet Hawthorne must have had a melancholy picture of his life work at that time. He could no longer write imaginative literature for the magazines. It required a constant freshness of mind, else the deterioration of the article was quickly apparent. Hack work was preferable—translations, schoolbooks, newspaper scribbling. With the Democratic triumph in November, he knew he could get a government job; the task was to get one that was suitable.[67]

"He lived on almost nothing," Sumner wrote to Mrs. Bancroft;

"but even that nothing has gone. . . . He is an ornament of the country, nor is there a person of any party who would not hear with delight that the author of such Goldsmithian prose as he writes, had received honor and office from his country. Some of his savings were lent to Mr. Ripley at Brook Farm; but he is not able to repay them, and poor Hawthorne (that sweet, gentle, true nature) has not the wherewithal to live." [68] On September 6, 1845, Hawthorne asked Hillard to bring suit against Ripley and Dana for damages of $800. The action was begun at Cambridge, but postponed until March 9, 1846. The trial was then held at Concord, and the court awarded Hawthorne damages of $560.12, plus costs of $25.28—a total of $585.40.[69]

By that time the worst of his troubles, in a financial sense, were over. In terms of his work they were not. It seems to have been agreed that he was to receive the post of either surveyor or naval officer at the Salem Custom House. Pierce wrote to Robert Walker, the Secretary of the Treasury, asking Hawthorne's appointment as surveyor, and telling him that Senator Atherton would confer with him on the subject. Ex-Congressman John Fairfield who urged his appointment, as did Colonel Charles Green, editor of the Boston *Post*, George Bancroft, the officials of the Democratic party in Essex County, and Horace Connolly, Hawthorne's distant kinsman, his aunt Susie Ingersoll's adopted child.[70]

The Salem Democrats had already arranged to have Richard Lindsley appointed surveyor and George Mullett naval officer.[71] George Mullett had previously been appointed surveyor, but his nomination was rejected by the Senate. Many of the conflicts around the office had their source in the party confusion resulting from the Harrison-Tyler election. After Harrison's death, Tyler nominated two Democrats in succession, both rejected, and then nominated Nehemiah Brown: "one of that peculiar class of politicians styled Tyler Democrats." Polk retained Brown in office until Hawthorne's appointment. This circumstance proved to be important. The Whigs were not supporters of the man Hawthorne displaced. They had no interest in supporting Brown in office. Reverend Upham on one occasion told Hawthorne, in the presence of David Roberts, that he need never fear removal under a Whig administration, inasmuch as he had not displaced a Whig when he took office.[72]

On the Democratic side the situation was almost as complex. Lindsley was asked, according to Mullett, to withdraw as a candidate for the surveyorship, to make room for Hawthorne. Mullett, who was his friend, was asked to persuade Lindsley to withdraw. He was reluctant to do so, since he had circulated the original petitions asking Lindsley's appointment. Moreover, he and Lindsley were close friends. He offered to withdraw as naval officer, and give that post to Hawthorne. This the politicians refused to permit. He then went to Lindsley with this proposal: that they should both withdraw, and serve as inspectors under Hawthorne. Lindsley was reluctant, but at length agreed, and, according to Mullett, they wrote to Washington urging Hawthorne's appointment.[73] There is, of course, no record of this transaction in the files of the Treasury; it was a party, not an official, agreement. Mullett wrote his recollections many years later, for Hawthorne's daughter, and though it seems unlikely that the proceedings were exactly as he described them, they were probably substantially true. There were unquestionably bitter feelings aroused that local men, working in the Custom House and steady party supporters, had been passed over for a newcomer, a lukewarm politician, a writer, the wandering son of an old family, and a man who had written in a far from flattering spirit of Salem.

XII

The Custom House stood at the head of Derby's Wharf. A portico of half a dozen pillars ornamented its front, supporting a balcony, beneath which a flight of wide granite steps descended toward the street. Over the entrance hovered a wooden eagle, carved by Abraham True, with outspread wings, a shield before his heart. "With the customary infirmity of temper that characterizes this unhappy fowl," Hawthorne wrote, "she appears, by the fierceness of her beak and eye, and the general truculency of her attitude, to threaten mischief to the inoffensive community." For three and a half hours each forenoon the flag of the Republic, with the thirteen stripes turned vertically instead of horizontally, indicating a civil, and not a military post, floated or drooped from the loftiest point on the roof.[74]

Hawthorne's duties began on Thursday, April 9, 1846, a quiet day, with but two arrivals in the port, the *Retrieve* and the *E. H. Herrick*, and one sailing, the brig *Richmond*.[75] There had been a change, as great as the difference in his own life, in the port of Salem. That old wharf which stretched beyond the Custom House out into the bay, now dilapidated, with the tides sometimes overflowing it, had been, in his childhood, one of the busiest spots in one of the busiest ports on earth. Now there were only decayed wooden warehouses on it, and at the base and in the rear of the buildings the track of many languid years could be seen in a border of unthrifty grass. Halfway down the wharf, where once the priceless cargoes of silks and tea and coffee and rum had been unloaded, there might now be a bark or a brig, discharging hides, or a Nova Scotia schooner, pitching out her cargo of firewood.

On the left hand as you entered the Custom House there was a large office, fifteen feet square, with a high ceiling, with two windows overlooking Derby's Wharf and a third, across a narrow lane, a portion of Derby Street. The room was cobwebbed, dingy with old paint, and its floor strewn with gray sand. There was a stove, an old pine desk, a three-legged stool, two or three battered wooden chairs, a *Digest of the Revenue Laws*, a score or two of volumes of the Acts of Congress, and a tin speaking tube leading through the ceiling. This was the main office where the work of the Custom House was transacted.[76] Hawthorne pretended it was his office when he described where he worked, probably to simplify matters—it was the sort of office he loafed in during his years in the Boston Custom House—though in fact he had a private office, beyond that occupied by the naval officer. The main room he described was where the men under him—Richard Lindsley, George Mullett, Stephen Harraden, Nathan Millett, Abel Lawrence, Daniel Bray, Hardy Phippen, and Joseph Noble—awaited their calls to duty when the ships entered. He had the same relation to them that Colonel Hall had to him and his fellow inspectors in Boston.

Pacing from corner to corner, or lounging on the long-legged stool, with his elbow on the desk, and his eyes wandering up and down the columns of the morning newspapers—so he recollected his days in the office. The morning papers! It had been many years since his days in Boston when he read them thoroughly. The *Gazette* had suddenly become interesting again. On the day he took office it carried an account of one of those remarkable incidents which had characterized it forty years before—a sailor in New Orleans picked up a sixteen-year-old girl, took her to a haunt of vice, stopped at a bar to get a drink, and discovered that she was his sister. A policeman found them weeping in the streets, he threatening to kill himself and her. The *Gazette* made a feature of such incidents, without identifying the people. Usually they were supposed to have occurred in France. Then there was news of Lucy Larcom, the eighteen-year-old factory girl who worked in the Lawrence Mills at Lowell, whose literary gifts had recently been discovered, and who was now considered one of the best women writers in the country. She was leaving the next day for Illinois, where she attended school for three years.

Friday morning the *Rattler* came in from Brazil, with a cargo of castor nuts, rubber, anisette, and balsam copaiba, and the *Romp* arrived from Cayenne with a cargo of molasses. This was almost as it had been in the old days. Captain James Deering of the *Rattler* and Captain William Leander of the *Romp* carried their ships' papers, in a tarnished tin box, into the Custom House, which stirred with activity—the owners of the *Rattler*, Bertram and Shepard, appeared, and John Shotwell and James Pond, the owners of the *Romp;* and the smart young merchants' clerks, "the germ of the wrinkle-browed, grizzle-bearded, care-worn merchant." Captain Leander reported that the *Romp* had sighted a mysterious burning ship that was then much in the news, unidentified, supposed to be cotton-laden.—The *Retrieve* and the *Conquest* cleared for Nova Scotia, the *Columbia* for Philadelphia, the *Herrick* for New York, and the *Invincible* for the Indies.

Hawthorne professed to have had nothing to do, in his years at the Custom House, except pace the floor. Not so at all. In his first week of duty the *Juliet* arrived from Philadelphia, with a cargo of coal for his uncle-by-marriage, John Dike; the *Alabama*, from New York, with flour and grain; and there arrived also the *Cherokee*, the *Mary Ann*, the *Tarquin*, the *Julia Ann*, the *Richard*, the *James*, the *Charles*, the *Hebe*, the *Solomon Francis*, the *Paragon*, the *Mount Hope*, the *Star*, the *Zaine*, the *Elivia*, the *Lewis*, the *Robert Pulsford*, the *Rebecca*, the *Laurel*, and the *Rainbow* (not a Salem vessel) after an 80-day voyage from Canton.[77]

Why, then, did Hawthorne profess to have done nothing in these years? If it was a joke, a pose he had adopted and willfully maintained, it had become a stupid one. The port was not dead (save in comparison with its greatest days); the Custom House was not dull; his fellow workers were not somnolent; he was not an idle dreamer and part-time scribbler miscast as a customs official. He was a hard-eyed, hard-working, honest and conscientious customs official who had written a great many stories and published a few of them under his own name—*Mosses from an Old Manse* had just appeared. [There is a photograph of him taken about this time, an extraordinary picture, completely unlike the idealized portraits that had been painted of him—high forehead, lined cheeks, face turned slightly toward the left, teeth clenched, an appearance of defiance, firmness, and above all, that of a dangerous man to meddle with.[78]]

And then the fury of politics was so great that the pose he adopted would have been a physical impossibility. The whole customs service was a mess, from which the corruption spread to infect the entire political life of the country. Salem was certainly no better than the other ports. In Hawthorne's first week in office the papers carried news of the death of Edward Palfrey, who had held the post from 1838 to 1841.[79] Palfrey was for many years editor of the Salem *Advertiser*. He was appointed surveyor by Tyler, and served for some time during a recess of the Senate, which then refused to confirm his appointment. He afterward worked in the Boston Custom House.[80] The confusion over his appointment was characteristic of the entire service.

The Deputy Collector in Salem, for the forty-six years before 1829, was William Oliver. For thirty-six years he had the care of all the money received and paid out. In the December quarter of 1807 (before the embargo), the duties secured in Salem amounted to $513,000. In 1808 they amounted to $504,326.82. Most of this was in gold. Oliver weighed the bag of gold at the bank in Salem and weighed it again in Boston; and kept his hand on the bag until he delivered it in Boston. His memory was so exact that he could remember the exact tonnage of vessels without referring to the books. From duties of millions of dollars a year in the great days of the port, the revenues collected now came to about $153,000 a year.

For many years the Administration had been Democratic—forty years—and the Democrats consequently had responsibility for the situation at Salem as elsewhere. Yet the Democrats had never actually controlled the Custom House. William Oliver was brought into the service as a boy of fourteen by Major Joseph Hiller (Richard Jeffery Cleveland's father-in-law), who had been appointed by Washington. The boy who replaced Oliver was in the office with him for forty years.[81] In addition to these aged functionaries, whose terms of service reached back to the early days of the Republic, the Custom House at Salem was exceptional because the Collector of the Port, who had most of the appointments in his power, was an aged hero, General James Miller, whose exploits at the Battle of Lundy's Lane, in the War of 1812, protected him from removal from office regardless of scandal, administrative changes, or the incompetence or dishonesty of his subordinates.

General Miller was now feeble. It was only with the assistance of a servant, and by leaning his hand heavily on the iron balustrade, that he could slowly and painfully ascend the Custom House steps, and, with a toilsome progress across the floor, attain his customary chair beside the fireplace. There he used to sit, gazing with a somewhat dim serenity of aspect at the figures that came and went, amid the rustle of papers, the administering of oaths, the discussion of business, the casual talk of the office. His countenance in repose was mild and kindly. When no longer called upon to speak or listen, either of which operations cost him an evident effort, his face would subside into its former not uncheerful quietude.[82]

Miller's exploit had been almost incredible. He was in command of the 21st U.S. Infantry which, on July 25, 1814, charged the hill at Lundy's Lane and captured the British battery there—"the most obstinately contested battle, perhaps, ever fought on the American continent"—and won a victory so impressive that it compensated in a large measure for the bitter record of defeat in the war. The circumstances of the battle were peculiar. A large British force, newly reinforced after its defeat at Chippewa, crossed the Niagara River at Queenstown and marched to attack an American supply base. An American force of only 1,200 men under Winfield Scott was at once dispatched to make a demonstration against Queenstown after the British had crossed. At seven o'clock in the evening this small American force unexpectedly met the entire British Army at the head of Lundy's Lane.

The Americans charged. The British, apparently thrown off balance by this midget assault, mounted a battery on the crest of a hill, commanding the slope that the attack must climb, and fought defensively. The main body of the American troops rushed to the scene. One brigade, in which Joseph Cilley (Jonathan Cilley's brother) was a lieutenant, ran three miles to join the fighting. What was most remarkable was that the small American force, as darkness settled on the field, did not merely attempt to hold its ground. The night was clear, moonlit, and calm. About ten o'clock General (then Colonel) Miller, was ordered to charge the hill. He said, "I'll try, sir." This was the phrase that seemed to Hawthorne to breathe the soul and spirit of New England hardihood, comprehending all perils and encountering all. It seemed such an easy phrase to speak, but no one, on the verge of such a task of danger and glory, had ever spoken it. Moreover, Miller seemed to Hawthorne a gentle man, one to whose innate kindness he could confidently appeal, with a stubborn and ponderous endurance, and an integrity as unmalleable and unmanageable as a ton of iron ore.

And so his regiment charged the battery. Lieutenant Cilley's company led the charge. There were fewer than three hundred men left in the regiment. Two regiments ordered to its support quailed and turned back. There was an old rail fence, overgrown with shrubbery, some thirty feet from the cannon on the crest of the hill. The men reached the fence, rested across it, took good aim, fired and rushed, and then fought hand to hand at the guns. There were seven brass cannon on the crest and not a British soldier left to fire them; and there were only 126 left of the three hundred Americans. Every commissioned and noncommissioned officer on the field was killed or wounded, from Winfield Scott to Joseph Cilley, who lost an eye and suffered a fractured thigh bone. The British charged twice at close quarters in an attempt to recapture the crest. They charged three times with the whole line. As dawn broke they drew back to await reinforcements, while the handful of American survivors, suffering from hunger and thirst, collected arms and ammunition from the bodies scattered on the hillside. With full troops the British assaulted again and were driven back, then retiring from the field, with casualties of 878 to 743 American losses.[83]

The veneration in which Miller was held prevented either Whigs or Democrats from interfering much with the affairs of the Salem Custom House. His son Ephraim, the deputy collector, did most of the actual work, and so with this structure—the aged hero as a figurehead, his son in actual charge, the old-timers, whose experience reached far back, solidly entrenched in office—there was little opportunity to effect any lasting changes in it. It drowsed along, guilty, perhaps, of minor graft, year after year, rather than of such stupendous thefts as those from the New York Custom House. Yet meanwhile the port was perishing. Year by year the cargoes that had come there were diverted to Boston and New York, where they increased, imperceptibly and needlessly, the vast commerce of those ports.

Each morning, then, Hawthorne appeared at his office (dressed in his new broadcloth suit of black, with a vest of satin, tailored by Earle's in Boston) and dispatched his eight inspectors to the incoming ships. He lived first at Herbert Street, while Sophia, who was expecting another child to be born in June, remained in Boston.[84] He walked along the streets he had so often trod as a boy, climbed the steps, greeted the Naval Officer, John Howard, whose favorite topics of conversation were Shakespeare and Napoleon. He entered his office and read his morning papers. A certain permanent Custom House official, Zachariah Burchmore, kept the office functioning among so many antiquarians and newcomers—he was prompt, acute, clear minded, bred from boyhood in the Custom House, with perfect integrity, "a kind forebearance toward our stupidity," the mainspring that kept the wheels in motion. He gave Hawthorne a new idea of what talent was; he was ideally fitted for the place he held.

There was also a certain permanent inspector, of whom Hawthorne's sketch is a satirical masterpiece. The only person in the list of employees who fits the description seems to be William Lee—"his sire, a Revolutionary colonel, and formerly collector of the port, had created an office for him, and appointed him to fill it, at a period of the early ages which few living men can now remember. This Inspector, when I first knew him, was a man of fourscore years or thereabouts, and certainly one of the most wonderful specimens of wintergreen that you would be likely to discover in a lifetime's search. With his florid cheek, his compact figure, smartly arrayed in a bright-buttoned blue coat, his brisk and vigorous step, and his hale and hearty aspect, altogether he seemed—not young indeed, but a kind of new contrivance of Mother Nature in the shape of man, whom age and infirmity had no business to touch. His voice and laugh, which perpetually re-echoed through the Custom House, had nothing of the tremulous quaver and cackle of an old man's utterance; they came strutting out of his lungs, like the crow of a cock, or the blast of a clarion. Looking at him merely as an animal—and there was very little else to look at—he was a most satisfactory object, from the thorough healthfulness and wholesomeness of his system, and his capacity, at that extreme age, to enjoy all, or nearly all, the delights which he had ever aimed at, or conceived of. The careless security of his life in the Custom House, or a regular income, with but slight and infrequent apprehensions of removal, had no doubt contributed to make time pass lightly over him. The original and more potent cause, however, lay in the rare perfection of his animal nature, the moderate proportion of intellect, and the very trifling admixture of moral and spiritual ingredients; these latter qualities, indeed, being in barely enough measure to keep the old gentleman from walking on all fours."

As Hawthorne came to work he found this patriarch sitting with his companions in old-fashioned chairs tipped on their hind legs back against the wall. Often they were asleep. Occasionally they might be heard talking together, in voices between a speech and a snore. The old patriarch seemed to Hawthorne to have no soul, no heart, no mind, but he had one vast advantage over his four-footed brethren: his ability to recollect the good dinners it had been no small part of the happiness of his life to eat. "There were flavors on his palate that had lingered there not less than sixty years or seventy years. . . . I have heard him smack his lips over dinners, every guest at which, except himself, had long been food for worms. . . . A tenderloin of beef, a hindquarter of fowl, a sparerib of pork, a particular chicken, or a remarkably praiseworthy turkey, which had perhaps adorned his board in the days of the elder Adams, would be remembered; while all the subsequent experience of our race, and all the events that heightened or darkened his individual career, had gone over him with as little permanent effect as a passing breeze. The chief tragic event of the old man's life, so far as I could judge, was his mishap with a certain goose which lived and died some twenty or forty years ago; a goose of most promising figure, but which, at table, proved so inveterately tough that the carving knife would make no impression on its carcass, and it could only be divided with an axe and handsaw."

Thus his companions. Old men, old ships, an old port, little to do —how distant the dreams of Brook Farm seemed in this company! And how distant the idle summers in Concord! Yet he felt more at home here, closer to reality, more at ease, and his name, stenciled on pepper bags and baskets of annatto, and cigar boxes, reached into circles where it never penetrated on a title page. Even the earthy old inspector was desirable, as a change of diet, to a man who had known Bronson Alcottt. The collector's junior clerk, aged nineteen, graver in his manners than the old inspector, wrote poetry, and occasionally spoke of books to Hawthorne, "as matters with which he might possibly be conversant." Otherwise his life was all official. He found that he liked it. Captain

Burchmore, one of the inspectors, was an old shipmaster. Scarcely a day passed that he did not stir Hawthorne to laughter and admiration by his marvelous gifts as a storyteller. If Hawthorne could have preserved the picturesque force of his style, and the humorous coloring that nature taught him to throw over his descriptions, the result, he honestly believed, would have been something new in literature . . . "A better book than I shall ever write was there; leaf after leaf presenting itself to me, just as it was written out by the reality of the flitting hour. . . . These perceptions have come too late. At the instant, I was only conscious that what would have been a pleasure once was now a hopeless toil. There was no occasion to make moan about this state of affairs. I had ceased to be a writer of tolerably poor tales and essays, and had become a tolerably good Surveyor of the Customs. That was all."

The old gentlemen were afraid of him. It pained and at the same time amused him to behold the terrors that attended his advent: "to see a furrowed cheek, weather-beaten by half a century of storm, turn ashy pale at the glance of so harmless an individual as myself; to detect, as one or another addressed me, the tremor of a voice, which, in long-past days, had been wont to bellow through a speaking trumpet hoarsely enough to frighten Boreas himself to silence." Most of them were Whigs and they knew Hawthorne was a Democrat. They also knew that, according to the prescribed code in such matters, it would have been nothing short of duty, in a politician, to bring every one of those white heads under the ax of the guillotine. Hawthorne knew it too, but could never quite find it in his heart to act upon the knowledge. "Much and deservedly to my own discredit, therefore, and considerably to the detriment of my official conscience, they continued, during my incumbency, to creep about the wharves, and loiter up and down the Custom House steps. They spent a good deal of time, also, asleep in their accustomed corners, with their chairs tilted back against the wall; awakening, however, once or twice in a forenoon, to bore one another with the several thousandth repetition of old sea stories and mouldy jokes, that had grown to be passwords and countersigns among them.

"The discovery was soon made, I imagine, that the new Surveyor had no great harm in him. So, with lightsome hearts, and the happy consciousness of being usefully employed—in their own behalf at least, if not for our beloved country—these good old gentlemen went through the various formalities of office. Sagaciously, under their spectacles, did they peep into the holds of vessels! Mighty was their fuss about little matters, and marvelous, sometimes, the obtuseness that allowed greater ones to slip between their fingers! Whenever such a mischance occurred —when a wagonload of valuable merchandise had been smuggled ashore, at noonday, perhaps, and directly beneath their unsuspicious noses— nothing could exceed the vigilance and alacrity with which they proceeded to lock, and double-lock, and secure with tape and sealing-wax, all the avenues of the delinquent vessel."

Unless people were more than commonly disagreeable, it was Hawthorne's habit—a foolish habit, he said—to contract a fondness for them. And as he had a paternal and protective attitude toward the inspectors, he soon grew to like them all. "It was pleasant, in the summer forenoons—when the fervent heat, that almost liquified the rest of the human family, merely communicated a genial warmth to their half-torpid systems—it was pleasant to hear them chattering in the back entry, a row of them all tipped against the wall, as usual; while the frozen witticisms of past generations were thawed out, and came bubbling with laughter from their lips." [85]

Political turmoil was too great for so pleasant an atmosphere to survive. A war party was forming. The *Gazette* reprinted the New York *Express*'s bold pronouncement, that Polk was contemptible, a forty-nine man to some, and a fifty-four forty to others. This cryptic denunciation referred to Polk's wavering on the Oregon question. At that time Oregon Territory was held, under the Oregon Convention, in joint occupancy by the British and Americans, open to the citizens and subjects of both powers, its final disposition to be determined by the will of the majority of permanent settlers. This measure seems in retrospect to have been wiser than it was then considered, and certainly wiser than the disposition of most boundary disputes on the continent. The House had already passed its notice to terminate the Oregon Convention, following the platform of the Democratic party, which claimed all of Oregon, and the measures now went to the Senate.

The House adjourned to attend the debate in the Senate chamber. The ladies crowded on the floor of the Senate chamber in violation of the rules (who so lawless, when they make up their minds to be so?), and there followed a scene so terrific, as Senator Crittenden rebuked Senator Allen from Ohio, that veteran Washington correspondents wrote there had been nothing like this for years and years, since

Webster's terrible denunciation of Charles J. Ingersoll. The treaty was abrogated in a tempest and whirlwind of passion, such raving and storming, beating of desks, stamping of feet, clapping of hands, as was never seen this side of a lunatic asylum.—Meanwhile, the Mexican border dispute was growing critical. John Slidell's mission to Mexico had failed, and the American Army, arriving at Point Isobel, found the customhouse and several other buildings burned by the Mexican commander of the port. General Zachary Taylor pursued, and at the Little Colorado met, a force of a hundred and fifty Mexicans who informed him that their orders were to fire if the stream were crossed. Taylor brought up his artillery, crossed the stream, and the Mexicans retreated.[86]

There seemed to be something in Salem that acted as a narcotic on Hawthorne, rendering more conspicuous, whenever he remained there, his own drowsy lack of progress and the brilliant careers of his friends, and muffling such tempestuous news in a wrapping of domestic interests. On June 22, 1846, his son Julian was born. Sometime in this period Una, who was not strong, contracted scarlet fever. The family had established itself temporarily in a house on Chestnut Street, one of the loveliest residential streets in America. Sophia and the children remained in Boston, however, in a house on Carver Street, until the fall, and Hawthorne commuted each day to work. They then moved into the house on Chestnut Street, which, however, was so small that there was no place for Hawthorne to work in it, except in the nursery.[87]

The procession of his friends who had passed him by continued steadily onward. When John Quincy Adams was stricken at his desk in Congress, Horace Mann was, somewhat to his own surprise, elected to his place.[88] When the Mexican War began, Franklin Pierce (who had declined Polk's offer of the attorney generalship) was appointed colonel of the 9th Regiment, and in March, 1847, commissioned a brigadier general in the Army. Hawthorne went to Boston to see him on the eve of his departure for Vera Cruz. Pierce's command included regiments from the extreme North, the South, and the West; he was extremely busy, since the transports were waiting to receive the troops. He looked so fit to be a soldier that there could be no doubt of his good fortune in the field. Pierce was perhaps too much of a family man to be either a politician or a soldier. He had given up his career in Washington because of his wife's frail health. His son, Frank Robert, had died in 1844, at the age of four, leaving only one child to them, a boy of seven. Hawthorne said farewell to Pierce in the midst of a company of his officers and the friends he was to leave behind. Was there something mildly ironic in Hawthorne's observing "the severest point of the crisis was over, for he had already bidden his family farewell"? [89] Pierce went on to Mexico and to moderate renown. True, a story circulated that he had evaded action by pretending injury before the Battle of Contreras. He had actually displayed the greatest courage. He won no such glory as the officers of the regular Army, but that was hardly to be expected —he was not a soldier by profession, and one of his first speeches in Congress had been a forthright attack on West Point.

Hawthorne went back to Salem, back to the Custom House, back to his office. Captain Burchmore told him a story about an immense turtle he saw on a voyage to Batavia, twenty feet long, with a head bigger than any dog's you will ever see, and prickles on his back a foot long, and when he told of it in Batavia, an old pilot exclaimed, "What —have you seen Bellysore Tom?"—for that monstrous turtle had been in that same latitude for twelve years, and was often mistaken for a rock, and was well known to the pilots, who often threw him a piece of meat. Old Lee agreed, saying he had often heard of Bellysore Tom. But Hawthorne was growing tired of Burchmore's traveler's tales, and old Lee was a notorious liar.[90] The country went off to war; the Oregon question was arbitrated; his friends went on to greater successes— Longfellow wrote *Evangeline* after Hawthorne had suggested the story to him—and he went faithfully each day to his office. The sound of his footsteps pacing the floor, from the front entrance to the side door of the Custom House, disturbed the slumbers of the inspectors and the weighers and gaugers, who used to say that the surveyor was walking the quarter-deck.[91]

The coming of children into the Hawthorne family created continuing changes—Una was forbidden, at length, to enter what Sophia called Mrs. Hawthorne's mysterious chamber, because it was too cold, and there was no rug on the floor, and she was afraid the child would catch cold. So the brief venture of Hawthorne's mother into the world ended. Elizabeth Hawthorne then entertained Una in her rooms, but Una at length revealed that each day her aunt had been giving her candy, and the result was a family quarrel whose outcome seems to have been that Elizabeth did not see Hawthorne for about two years. Then she stopped in one evening, when Sophia had gone to Boston, and asked him to go for a walk with her.[92]

XIII

Hawthorne began making little notes of the children's sayings. The first of these was when Una was only a little over a year old. They were walking in Boston Common and passed an organ-grinder's monkey, and Una, shocked by the monkey's horrible ugliness, began to cry. She called a weathercock "a wind-turn." A lightning rod she called "a lightning catch." "Mama, I see part of your smile," she said to Sophia, who characteristically brought her hand to her mouth, palm outward, when she smiled. And she spoke to an imaginary child, "The syrup of my bosom." The Hawthorne children excelled at this sort of grave childish remark. Or, perhaps, Hawthorne merely excelled at recording the sayings that most children make, but which are unheard or forgotten. He jotted down sayings of adults as well. His friend Pike described the old mate of a vessel: "He looked as if he had been standing up thirty years against a northeast storm." And Hawthorne also recorded a bit of dialogue he perhaps intended to use: "Corwin is going to Lynn; Oliver proposes to walk thither with him." "No," says Corwin, "I don't want you. You take great long steps; or, if you take short ones, 'tis all hypocrisy. And besides, you keep humming all the time."

Yet there was a difference between these casual notations and the exact observations he now made of the children. Between March 19, 1848, and September 5, 1849, he devoted eight days to almost microscopic examination of how they spent their days, how they dressed, where they played, what they said. Most remarkably, he kept an exact timetable of their days. He had certain reservations about the training the children were receiving, especially Julian. He thought Julian was being softened by it, and that the hard blows of reality, when he grew older, would affect him too greatly. He wanted Julian to be tempered and hardened without losing his affectionateness, and this was what he feared was not being done. There was no solitary wandering in Julian's childhood, no playing with country cousins, or the equivalent, and if he was spared many hazards he was also, perhaps, in danger of growing up in an environment too unreal to endure. "Are you a good little boy?" he asked Julian.

"Yes," Julian said.

"What are you good for?"

"Because I love all people."

Hawthorne almost groaned as he wrote this down. "His mother will be in raptures at this response—a heavenly infant, powerless to do anything, but diffusing the richness of his pure love throughout the moral atmosphere, to make all mankind happier and better!!!!!" [93] His own view of life, never very rosy, was growing harder. *Mosses from an Old Manse* had barely been published when its publishers, Wiley and Putnam, failed. (Putnam was a relative of Sophia's.) His mother's health, never strong, was now failing rapidly, and his sister Louisa also was often ill.[94] He was not a popular public official. The politicians did not approve of him, for he took no part in political warfare, and his own refusal to do so seemed to imply some feeling of superiority to the daily concerns of their world. The merchants—Pingree, Phillips, Shepard, Upton, Kimball, Bertram, Hunt—did not like him. They considered him arrogant. And then the old malignancy that seemed to live in Salem occasionally revealed itself.

There were scores of purposeless enemies, men ready to drive him from the Custom House, if the opportunity presented itself, just as, thirty years before, the boys he went to school with had pulled him down from the platform when he started to declaim. Forty years later, many years after his death, there were still a score of "these strange malignants" walking the streets of Salem. They blocked every attempt to erect a memorial to him. It was not until after the death of the last of them that local research on his life was possible.[95]

The stories that he hoped to write, as he jotted them down in his notebook, took on a different cast. "A story of the effect of revenge," he wrote, "in diabolizing him who indulges in it." And he thought of the Committee of Vigilance that had been set up to discover Captain White's murderer as a good machinery for a sketch or a story.[96]

This was in November, 1847, a short time after the election. In Salem 1,674 votes were cast for Zachary Taylor, 537 for Van Buren, and 379 for Cass.[97] The Whigs were in power. Hawthorne had expected to be turned out of office. As the election passed, however, he discovered that while a man "leans on the mighty arm of the Republic, his own proper strength departs from him. He loses, in an extent proportion to the weakness or force of his original nature, the capability of self-support." The election of Taylor was a conservative victory. It was a defeat for the Jacksonian radicals who followed Van Buren. In view of these considerations, and bearing in mind his lukewarm partisanship and his original selection for the post as recognition of his literary achievements, he felt, with mingled regret and shame, that his prospects of retaining office were better than those of his Democratic brethren.

He could not concentrate. His intellect seemed to be dwindling away, exhaling without his being conscious of it, like ether out of a vial, so that at every glance he found a smaller and less volatile residuum. The wretched numbness did not end with the three and a half hours he spent in the office. It went with him on his seashore walks and on his rambles in the country.[98] The sensation was vaguely familiar to him. He had experienced something like it when he worked in the Boston Custom House—a sense of things being out of place, of not being quite sure of reality and illusion, of being unable to ascertain whether objects had solid substance or were merely gaseous and vapory. In those days the illusions had been fanciful. He went on errands to ships that were not in port, and vigorously denied reports of epidemics that did not exist. He heard of the death of the Reverend Dr. Harris, a famous old Unitarian clergyman, and the next day beheld, or thought he beheld, the old gentleman at his accustomed post in the Boston Athenaeum, reading the Boston *Post*.[99]

He could not now regard these queer happenings as if they did not exist. An apparition haunted the front yard of the house of Mall Street. (In October, 1847, he moved his family into a large and comfortable house there, paying $200 a year rental.) The front parlor was quite near the street. He had often, while sitting in the parlor, in the daytime, had a perception that somebody was passing the windows—but, on looking toward them, nobody was there. In the past he had ridiculed Sophia's ghosts. Now he again and again had the certainty that someone was passing the window, and raised his head to find that the front dooryard was deserted. The appearance was never observable when looking directly at the window, but only by a sidelong or indirect glance. At last he spoke of it to Sophia. She was equally aware of the specter. She said that it always seemed to be entering the yard from the street, never going out. This was his own impression.

He sat often in the living room, without light, except from the coal fire and the moon. Moonlight produced a very beautiful effect in the room, falling so white on the carpet and showing its figures so distinctly; making all the room so visible, and yet so different from a morning or noontide visibility. There were all the familiar things— every chair, the tables, the couch, the bookcase, all the things he was accustomed to in the daytime, but now it seemed as if he were remembering them through a lapse of years, rather than seeing them with the immediate eye. A child's shoe—the doll, sitting in her little wicker carriage—all objects, which have been used or played with during the day, though still as familiar as ever, are invested with something like strangeness and remoteness. The coal fire threw an unobtrusive tinge through the room. Its faint ruddiness tempered the colder spirituality of the moonbeams. In such a light, it seemed to him, the ghosts of persons very dear might glide noiselessly in and sit quietly down, without fear. It would be a matter of course to look around and find some familiar form in one of the chairs. Outside, the moonlight made a delicate tracery with the branches of the trees. In the mirror on the wall he could see, deep within it, the glow of the burning coal fire. He went to bed. Then he arose and reopened the sitting-room door, again and again, to peep back at the warm, cheerful solemn repose, the white light, the faint ruddiness, the dreamlike dimness.

His mother came to live with them. She caused them no trouble. The ghost, his vague, torpid imagination, the monotony of his work, the uncertainty of his future, his restlessness, all combined to make him study his own household as if trying to hold fast to a tangible reality in a world of artifice and calculation. All day long, and for days at a time, he studied the children at play. There was in this quiet observation none of Longfellow's evening delight with the children's hour, or the sentiment of the barefoot-boy recollections of childhood, or the rapturous admiration of Elizabeth Peabody at the innocent wisdom of children. He pretended to read or write, while they played around him. Julian was dressed in a little knit jacket, bordered and girdled with purple and scarlet—a check gown underneath—knit garters on his short legs—one leather shoe and one of cloth embroidered. His curled hair looked like a prim, formal, old-fashioned wig. Una was dressed in a dark, shaded, thin-woolen morning gown, his favorite dress on her, for it showed her praiseworthy little legs. Her auburn curls fell over her shoulders with extreme grace.

Nine-thirty on a Sunday morning in March. Julian climbed into the chair beside him, two or three times every minute. Una came in. She put him so far behind in his work that he was tempted to give it up. Sophia came in. She took one child in each hand and walked with them across the room, glancing at him through the sunshine that fell on the carpet.

Why did he not rise, give up his work, and walk with them outdoors through the perfect morning? The moment passed. Una and Julian walked together, the little boy aping a manly stride. Una proposed playing Puss in the Corner. There was a quick tattoo of feet on the floor. Julian uttered a complaining cry about something or other. Una ran and kissed him. She said to her father, "Papa—*this* morning I am not going to be naughty at all."

They began playing with rubber balls. Julian tried to throw his in the air. He usually succeeded in dropping it over his head. It rolled away and he reached for it, asking, "Where ball?"

Sophia brought them a large picture book and sat on the floor, with a child on each side, displaying the pictures. "Oh, what a dirty mouth!" she said to Julian. "What do little lambs do?" He imitated a lamb's bleat. She got a wet napkin to wash his face and hands. Una took the picture book, which was too unwieldy for her to handle. Julian cried to have it in his own hand. Sophia returned, took the book, and said, "Oh, if Papa could only write down this little face!" He had just written in his notebook his inability to describe Una's delicate features, their grace, spirit, and sensibility.

Una was going for a walk with Dora. She put on a purple, fur-lined coat, with a diamond buckle in front, a white satin bonnet, and white-striped purple stockings. She had a cold. Wonderful it was in those days that they gave children what was called an "air-bath," holding them up, for a few moments after their bath, in the open air. Julian wanted to go with them. He trudged about the room, repeating, "Go!—go!" He ran across the room with a swagger that made Hawthorne laugh. Julian heard him, and as if aware of the ludicrousness of his walk, came to his elbow and looked up into his face. Una promised to be a good girl, not to run away, to mind Dora, and not to step in the mud. As they left, Julian escaped to the hall and ran up the stairs. Dora caught him and brought him back. He was scolded again. Then he stood quiet at his chair by the window, watching Dora and Una walk away.

His mother proposed to read to him. They sat down together. He put his head under her arm. She showed him pictures of hands, with fingers extended and folded. He imitated these positions with his own chubby hands. She exclaimed, "Why, Julian, I did not put on your napkin," and started up, putting the book on the table. He immediately took it and began turning the leaves by himself. When the napkin was tied around his neck, he cried out, "Ap-ple, ap-ple!" She got him one, and scraped it with a spoon, while he sat on her knee, opening his mouth wide enough to swallow the great globe itself. Then he laid his head on her bosom and repeated, at her dictation, "Love mama." He sat on the floor, requesting permission to turn the pages of the picture book himself. "Oh, Julian," said Sophia, in unutterable wonder and admiration.

He climbed into Hawthorne's chair, nearly fell, was frightened— until, seeing that Hawthorne was likewise startled, pretended to stumble again, and then laughed in his face. His mother brought him his milk. He drank three cupfuls, and asked for more. He was undressed, and made ready for bed, running away from Sophia, in the felicity of utter nakedness, when she tried to put on his nightgown.

Two hours had passed. In another hour Una and Dora returned from their walk. Sophia was lying down. Louisa Hawthorne was in her room upstairs. Una had insisted on going to Dr. Flint's church, where they sat in the gallery and heard two or three hymns. Then they went to Mr. Lee's, where Una made herself at home, playing with Josephine's playthings, and she insisted on being carried in Dora's arms from the Franklin Building to the house—a long way. Nevertheless, Dora said, she had been a nice little girl. They vanished into the kitchen. He could hear the sound of her voice, airy as sunshine. Then she went upstairs to Louisa, and he was alone.

At ten minutes past one, Sophia brought Julian in, his face like a great red apple, but as yet hardly awake. She dressed him for a walk with Dora. "Alk, oh!" he said, to signify that he understood. "Oh, you little splendor— Oh, you little splendor of the world!" cried Sophia, overwhelmed with admiration. She put on his black beaver hat, with a noble ostrich feather and paste buckle. "Oh, enchanting!—was ever anything so beautiful!" Next his India-rubber overshoes and gaiters, then his mittens, then a plaid silk cravat tied around his neck. He set forth, holding Dora by the hand.

Enter Una. "Where is little Julian?"

"He has gone out for a walk."

"No; but I mean, where is the place of little Julian, that you have been writing about him?"

He pointed to the page, at which she looked with all possible satisfaction, and stood watching the pen as it hurried forward.

"I'll put the ink nearer to you," she said. "Papa, are you going to write all this?" she added turning over the book. "Papa, why do you write downstairs?—you never wrote downstairs before."

He told her that he was writing about herself. "That's nice writing," she said.

A few minutes after seven, Hawthorne went out for his evening walk. The night was cloudy. He rounded Buffum's Corner, over the same ground he had so often walked in the past, coming to the edge of the neighborhood of the Hawthorne house on Union Street and the Manning house on Herbert Street, and then returned home in half an hour. Julian was in bed. He called for rice and water, asked to see the stars, and so finally took his departure. Una was then four, Julian three months less than two. The days and years melted away so rapidly that Hawthorne hardly knew whether they were little children at their parents' knees or already a maiden and a youth—a woman and a man. Watching them grow, he thought, this present life has hardly substance enough to be the image of eternity. The future too soon becomes the present, which, before we can grasp it, looks back upon the past. It must, he thought, be only the image of an image, and our next existence may be only one remove from reality. "We dwell in the shadow cast by Time which is itself the shadow cast by Eternity."

It was one of Una's characteristics never to shut a door. Julian, on the other hand, *always* shut the door, whatever hurry he was in. He gave up cheerfully whatever object he had in mind. "Well," he said benignly, after being remonstrated or reasoned with, and turned joyfully to something else. If his house of blocks fell down, he built it up patiently, only smiling at each new catastrophe. Una would have blazed up in a passion and tossed her building materials across the room. When her beauty was really visible "it is rare and precious as the visit of an angel; it is a transfiguration—a grace, delicacy, an ethereal fineness, which, at once, in my secret soul, makes me give up all the severe opinions I may have formed of her." She had a way of looking so steadily into Hawthorne's features as to make him feel abashed, and Sophia would beg her not to look so directly into her soul. She could not bear to be laughed at. Her natural bent was toward the passionate and the tragic. Her mother taught her to walk gracefully by balancing a book on her head. Mother and daughter walked slowly about the study, balancing books on their heads. At four Una could write, figure, and talk with a spontaneity which seems remarkable, but which Hawthorne called a half-unconscious rhapsody, rhythmical, flowing along like a river dim and vague. "Oh, how my leg aches, hearing reading," she said, and then learning this was a joke—her understanding tired— she repeated it constantly, and said, after she had grown tired sewing a towel for her father, "Oh, my leg is so tired of sewing." The two children were continually impersonating someone or other—Dora the maid, a mother, a baby, a peddler, a marketman. They played incessant little dramas, with plots too vague to be stated—Una was the daughter, and the dolly her little baby, while Julian was the grandmother. He sat wrapped in a red shawl, doing nothing, his fat rosy face breaking constantly into smiles, while Una busied herself around him, frowning frequently at her venerable parent.[100]

XIV

While these domestic scenes were unfolding, the Democrats and Whigs of Salem were preparing for action. When Taylor was elected there was a general reshuffling among the officeholders. Benjamin Browne, the postmaster, resigned in favor of his chief clerk, a Whig, who was appointed by Polk to the office. General Miller resigned as collector of the port in favor of his son, who also was appointed by Polk before leaving the Presidency. Ephraim Miller also was a Whig. The new postmaster, however, was at odds with the regular Whig party machinery in Salem, and Miller also was at odds with the Whigs. The Democrats had thus stolen a march on their opponents, who could not change the postmaster without creating a conflict in their own ranks, or remove Miller without removing one Whig to make room for another.

They retaliated by demanding the appointment of one of their own number to the post of deputy collector, which Ephraim Miller had held before his father's resignation. They drew up a petition in favor of Captain Allen Putnam, signed by an impressive number, and presented it to Miller. After a long delay, he refused to act upon it. The Whigs were divided among themselves in their choice of a candidate for naval officer. The only offices in the Custom House that were appointed by the government were the collector, the naval officer, and the surveyor. The others were appointed by the collector. President Taylor had said, before the election, that he would make no removals except for dishonesty and unfaithfulness. Miller took the position that he should wait for the action of the government, and make no changes until the practice of President Taylor and the Secretary of the Treasury, in regard to removals from office, had become clear. The Whigs claimed that the Democrats considered Hawthorne, because of his literary reputation, safe from removal. Hence they professed to see a group of sinister politicians sheltering themselves behind a man of undoubted integrity, just as, in another sense, they had once hidden behind the military reputation of General Miller.[101]

In ignorance of this feeling, Hawthorne relaxed as the weeks passed and no action was taken on his appointment. The life of the Custom House went on about as before. Ships arrived and cleared in almost the same number as in the past. There was no news in this quiet port. Louis Napoleon, the new President of France, the epidemic of Asiatic cholera sweeping the country, the battles of the Mexican War, refought in Congress, Daniel King, the new congressman, who had defeated Robert Rantoul, and the continual revelations of the amount of gold in California filled the newspapers.

The summer was hot. The temperature at Nantucket was the highest ever recorded. The epidemic swept north up the Mississippi and raged along the routes of the gold seekers. There were 166 deaths in New Orleans in January, in forty-eight hours; 20,000 people left the city. The disease was prevalent on the river boats; there were nine deaths on the Cincinnati steamer *North River*. There was cholera at Fort Lawson, Texas, and at Baylor there were forty deaths in one hour, and forty more in one night. By June there were 500 deaths in one week in St. Louis, and thirty-eight cases in New York, with twenty-four deaths.

There was news of riots in California, where brandy sold for $7,000 a barrel, and where the supply of gold seemed inexhaustible. One 250-pound nugget, worth $75,000, had been discovered, and kept secret by the government for fear that the news would not be believed. The various parties of Massachusetts men setting out seemed to be doing well. They invested $600 apiece, organizing their companies with $15,000 capital—205 ships were in California or bound there, and reports came back of $100,000 gathered soon after arrival. Indians attacked a wagon train and killed sixty-eight of seventy-two emigrants. But the Ophir Company from Boston was beyond Fort Kearny, with no sickness, and the animals were in fine order. The Sagamore Company at Lynn was a few miles behind, all well. There were thousands of wagons—for two hundred and fifty miles there was a continuous stream of wagons, always in sight.

Cholera spread. There were now fifty-one cases in Buffalo, twenty-six in Richmond, thirty-nine in New York. In St. Louis, of 949 deaths, 733 were from cholera—2,004 in five weeks. In Nashville there were 700 cases. There were two cases discovered in Boston. Such was the news when, on Friday, June 8, word came over the telegraph that Hawthorne had been removed from office, and Captain Allen Putnam appointed his successor.[102]

Hawthorne immediately wrote to Hillard. He said that he had not been able to do any more on his salary than pay his debts and support his family. "If you could do anything in the way of procuring me some stated literary employment, in connection with a newspaper, or as corrector of the press to some printing establishment, it could not come at a better time. Perhaps Epes Sargent, who is a friend of mine, would know of something. I shall not stand upon my dignity; that must take care of itself. Perhaps there may be some subordinate office connected with the Boston Athenaeum. Do not think anything too humble to be mentioned to me. . . . I wrote to Longfellow, the other day, and told him that I would dine with him on his next invitation; and that you would come too. I should like soon to meet you and him.

"The intelligence has just reached me, and Sophia has not yet heard of it. She will bear it like a woman—that is to say, better than a man." [103]

He felt like a man who, while contemplating suicide, has the good hap to be murdered. Sophia wrote to her parents, told them not to worry, and said she had never seen her husband so happy. His elation, however, was brief. He had not then realized that his enemies not only wanted his job—they meant to humiliate and disgrace him as well. It was strange to him to observe the bloodthirstiness that developed in the hour of his enemies' triumph, and to be conscious that he was its object. He had not been much of a Democrat before; he now became one. The

Democrats had been in office for so long that they had grown used to it, and did not gloat over their victories. It seemed to him that there were few uglier traits than the tendency of men he now learned at first hand—to grow cruel, merely because they had the power of inflicting harm.[104] A fierce and bitter spirit of malice and revenge swept the party of his enemies. It dismayed him. From whence did it spring? Who was organizing the movement that removed him?

He should have resigned the moment Taylor was elected. Failing that, he should have resigned at the inauguration of the Whigs. He had been deceived by the simplest of all self-delusions—a vague feeling that his literary work, which he always professed to regard so lightly, protected him from the fate of his colleagues. He had believed it, not without misgivings; he had taken the bait, encouraged by his wife's faith in his genius, his friends' praise—though neither Bridge nor Pierce could be called literary critics—and his own calm confidence. He had believed Reverend Upham when he said that Hawthorne would not be removed in the event of a Whig victory. His belief was the final revelation of his literary self-esteem. When he carried the news home to Sophia, she said, "Now you can write your book." [105]

Allen Putnam, the new surveyor, called on him in his office.[106] Hawthorne received him pleasantly, though his situation was galling. The moment a man's head drops off, he reflected, is seldom, or never, precisely the most agreeable of his life. He had never longed so deeply for seclusion, and now found himself very much in the public eye, careening about like Irving's Headless Horseman, ghostly and grim, and longing to be buried, as a politically dead man ought.[107]

Monday morning the papers were full of his case. "The lightning has struck at last," said the *Register*, a Whig paper, "and in so unexpected a quarter as to create great consternation among the *ins*, who felt themselves so safe. The election telegraph announced on Friday that Captain Allen Putnam had been appointed Surveyor of the Port of Salem, in place of Nath. Hawthorne, esq., the present incumbent. Captain Putnam is a highly respectable shipmaster, every way qualified for the office, and will discharge its duties with great honor to himself and advantage to the public interest. He will undoubtedly prove a very efficient and popular officer . . ." The next issue added the afterthought that he would be "far more competent than a mere literary man can be."

Hidden away in the text of this story were sentences less biting.

Hawthorne, it said, was not obnoxious, or to be classed with those who had made themselves so offensive as public officers. "Certainly he is not to be classed with the crew who have ruled the Custom House so long, and with whom he has been forced to hold companionship so uncongenial, probably, with his refined tastes, and brilliant literary turn of mind. . . . Personally, we have none but the kindest feelings toward Mr. Hawthorne, and the warmest wishes for his prosperity, and we should be sorry to rank him with his temporary associates, the clique of plotters . . ." The *Register* said that the Custom House had been for twenty years a house of refuge for locofoco politicians. "Here were the headquarters of the political managers who continued to keep the party *conveniently small*." [108]

Hillard wrote to Hawthorne that he should make an effort to be reinstated. Hawthorne replied that the thought of doing so made him sick at heart. He made a brief answer to the charges which, Hillard said, had been brought against him. He had written a few reviews, and two theatrical criticisms, for the Salem *Advertiser*—no political articles. He had written no political articles at all, except his essay on Cilley. He had never marched in a torchlight parade or made a political speech. His party work consisted of having listened to part of a political speech by Robert Rantoul and to part of another by Caleb Cushing.[109] Hillard, who was, of course, a leading Whig, apparently wanted Hawthorne to give more details.

Then Hawthorne sent in another letter a few days later (June 18, 1849). He was answering some vague charges in the Boston *Atlas*. He recounted the history of his predecessors in office, to make it clear that he had not replaced a Whig when he became surveyor. For witnesses he quoted the man he had replaced, and Reverend Upham, who had told him he need never fear removal under a Whig administration. He had never been a delegate to any convention. His name had been given as a member of the town committee of the Democratic party, but he had never been notified of his selection, never attended a meeting, never acted officially.[110] The Whig inspectors under him were charged with having received less money—about $100 a year—than the Democrats. Actually, in the first year of Hawthorne's term, the four Democratic inspectors had received $636 (Lindsley); $633 (Mullett); $597 (Harraden) and $591 (Nathan Millett). The four Whigs had received from

$513 to $462.[111] Hawthorne replied that he had acted under the direction of Colonel Miller, a Whig.[112]

During these days of confusion, Sophia's father wrote from Boston some sensible advice and some valuable information. At the close of the session of the legislature he was in the State House, and fell in with Mr. Upham. Dr. Peabody asked if he thought Hawthorne would be turned out. Upham was quite cozy about it, and said he thought nothing would be done. There was a sort of mystification in his manner.

Now, Dr. Peabody suggested, the papers denouncing Hawthorne to the Treasury should be secured, or copied; the names of the signers taken, and suits for damages started. A false statement depriving a man of his livelihood is, he said, a libel and an actionable offense. There would be plenty of Whigs who would support him, and "it will be nuts to politicians on his side to make capital out of it. I should like to have Mr. Upham asked what sort of a prayer he makes nowadays, and what sort of a prayer he made after he put his name to that document. I should like to ask him if he ever heard of the Ninth Commandment. Tell Mr. Hawthorne to be busy, but not to fire till he gets his battery well manned and charged, and then he will make a Buena Vista conquest." [113]

Horace Mann wrote, offering to help Hawthorne be reinstated. Samuel Hooper was active in his behalf, as was Mr. Howes. The letters then poured in on the Secretary of the Treasury, William Meredith. Rufus Choate; George Ticknor, the Spanish scholar, a Whig; Horace Mann; John O'Sullivan; Benjamin Barstow, Zachariah Burchmore, Jr., William Pike, B. F. Browne—these last five prominent Salem Democrats —and the editor of the Salem *Advertiser,* all testified in Hawthorne's behalf. Even the Whig editor of the *Register* informed the Treasury Department by letter that Hawthorne's sudden removal seemed extraordinary in Salem. Avery Holbrook, a prominent Salem Whig, accused the Treasury directly of acting secretly in Hawthorne's case and of willfully identifying him with the radicals in office when he had been, in fact, out of sympathy with them.

All this created a reaction in Hawthorne's favor. For a time it appeared that President Taylor was going to reinstate him, or that a compromise would be worked out, giving Allen Putnam the deputy collector's post and restoring Hawthorne to the surveyorship. The original letter asking Hawthorne's removal has never been located in the Treasury files. Hawthorne seems to have contemplated a libel suit against Upham, but desired instead to do his best "to kill and scalp him in the public prints; and I think I shall succeed."

On July 3 the Whig ward committees met. There were some thirty-two men present—Nathaniel Silsbee, Jr., the Mayor of Salem, Upham, Wheatland, Perkins, Allen, Horace Connolly—a distinguished list. They passed a number of resolutions. They urged Ephraim Miller's removal as collector, approved Hawthorne's removal, and asked that old General James Miller, now decrepit, be reappointed. They appointed a committee to name a candidate for deputy collector. They appointed Upham, Thomas Trask, and Henry Russell to write a memorial to the government explaining their views. Russell declined to serve and Silsbee was appointed in his place.

Three days later they met again. This time there were more than thirty-six present—Caleb Foote was among the newcomers, though Horace Connolly did not attend this meeting. William Oliver was nominated for deputy collector.[114] With General Miller restored as collector, and the aged veteran Oliver as deputy, the Custom House would be almost as it had been in the long years before Hawthorne took office— a revelation of the insincerity of the Whig attack on the Custom House as a refuge for Democratic radicals.

Upham was then called upon to read his report. He was the most satisfactory villain that ever was, Hawthorne said, for at every point he was consummate. He was then forty-seven. Hawthorne made good his threat, when he drew the character of Judge Pyncheon in *The House of the Seven Gables*—the man of eminent respectability. The church acknowledged it; the state acknowledged it. It was denied by nobody. He had a smile on his face akin to the shine on his shoes, a portly figure, a dark, square countenance, a shaggy depth of eyebrows, a look of exceeding good humor and benevolence, although, perhaps, he seemed somewhat unctuous rather than spiritual, and when crossed, or caught off his guard, he might seem cold, hard, immitigable, relentless, stern— until reminded of his position in the world, whereupon the sultry, dog-day heat of his benevolence again revealed itself. No one would venture a word against his sincerity as a Christian, respectability as a man, or courage and fidelity as the often-tried representative of his political party. True, there were hints of ancestral traits—greediness hid beneath a broad benignity of smile shining like a noonday sun along the streets—of deep purposes, and a relentless, crafty, bold, impervious consciencelessness in following them, trampling on the weak, and, when necessary, beating down the strong. The purity of his character; the faithfulness of his public service; his devotion to his party; his remarkable zeal as president of a Bible society; his integrity as treasurer of a widows' and orphans' fund; his prayers at morning and evening, and grace at meals; his efforts in the temperance cause; the snowy whiteness of his linen; the polish of his boots; the handsomeness of his gold-headed cane; the cut of his coat; the scrupulousness with which he paid public notice, in the street, by a bow, a lifting of the hat, a nod, or a motion of the hand, to all and sundry of his acquaintances, rich and poor; the smile of glad benevolence wherewith he made it a point to gladden the whole world—all these, however, made such hidden malignancy seem unthinkable.[115]

"Honorable William M. Meredith, Secretary of the Treasury of the United States," Upham began. "We, the undersigned, in the name of the supporters of the present national administration, in the city of Salem, Massachusetts, beg leave to submit the following representation . . ."

For perhaps an hour his speech went on. It must have been curious to Caleb Foote to listen to the medley of bitter charges of partisanship, political corruption, dishonesty, fraud, iniquity, mingled with expressions of profound admiration, respect, honor, exoneration, exculpation, sympathy, and apology. Hawthorne was charged with flagrant extortions and corruptions, with robbing the Whig inspectors, oppressing them systematically, and outraging their feelings. The aspersions were cruel, unfounded, and false. They were followed by tribute to Hawthorne's "true manliness of character." His supporters were called personal or literary friends, living in distant places, who were attempting to bring reproach on the Whigs of Salem, and to interfere in the party affairs. Hawthorne was pictured as the dupe and abused instrument of others, ignorant of business, inexperienced in politics, and with slight interest in his office. "What!" said Charles Sumner, "that smooth, smiling, oily, man of God!" Sophia wrote to her mother, who was vacationing in the mountains, to remain there—it was too hot for her to return just then.

When it appeared that the government had decided to reinstate Hawthorne, Upham hurried to Washington to confer with the Treasury officials. It appears that the original charges that had been made, and which had resulted in Hawthorne's sudden dismissal, had been so easily proved false that Upham was forced to amplify them. His assistants were Nathaniel Silsbee, Jr., the Mayor of Salem, and N. B. Mansfield. They had the assistance of Daniel King of Danvers, the newly elected congressman. When the storm broke, and it became clear that their charges could not be sustained, they amended them, the letter containing the original charges meanwhile disappearing. They also now professed to be acting in Hawthorne's own interest. Salem authorities, ordinarily charitable in writing of their townsmen, or guarded in making any reflections on their motives, have no reticence in this case. They say flatly that the men who led the attack had neither Hawthorne's welfare nor the public good in mind—"Their motives were clearly indicated by personal and political motives." [116]

If Hawthorne was, or had been, a confidential Treasury agent, the conduct of the department in Washington becomes a good deal clearer. It otherwise seems either extremely timid. It had removed an honest and faithful public servant without cause, other than a few vague charges by a handful of local politicians, without investigation and without giving him an opportunity to be heard. Or it had acted so arbitrarily and thoughtlessly as to give rise to doubt as to whether the Treasury officials were intellectually competent to handle the financial affairs of the Republic. The talk of spoils belonging to the victor is not an adequate explanation in this case. There were bigger spoils. Hawthorne was neither important enough, as an official, to make his removal political news nor, in the midst of a scandal, to make it a matter of political housecleaning. It is noteworthy that Hawthorne was at first elated at his sudden dismissal, and that he did not, in the entire controversy, express any condemnation of the men in Washington who had listened so readily to Upham. The Treasury was not merely the incoming secretary; it had its permanent officials, of whom the brilliant young Bowdoin graduate, John Hartley, was now outstanding. Hawthorne had no quarrel with them. All his feelings was directed against the local men who had denounced him. Yet he took no action against them, beyond denying their charges. The result was that the charges, those which reached the public prints, were muffled and confused, and whispered accusations replaced them. These were undoubtedly too venomous, and too well informed with local gossip, not to be painful.

Early in July Hawthorne heard that new charges were to be

brought against him. He wrote to Horace Mann and asked him to secure a copy of them from the Treasury. He had contemplated demanding them publicly, in the newspapers, in order to answer them. He did not because it would prolong the controversy and, he added significantly, make his reinstatement more difficult. He could hardly have meant at this time his reinstatement at his previous post. These new charges proved to be ugly. Hawthorne was accused of suspending two inspectors for refusing to pay party subscriptions. It was said that he delegated the task of dismissing them to a subordinate, and (presumably after the payments had been made) reinstated them.

This was false, but difficult to explain. The order to dismiss the temporary inspectors came from the Treasury Department in Washington. There were only two such in the Salem Custom House. They were Lindsley and Nathan Millett, both men of large families, and no resources, Democrats, and irreproachable as officers. To comply with the spirit of the Treasury order without ruining both men, Hawthorne suspended them during an inactive season of the year, in such a fashion that they might return to duty as soon as business justified it. Hawthorne took his order to Ephraim Miller and Zachariah Burchmore. Burchmore thought the inspectors should remain where they were until further notice from the Treasury. The responsibility lay with the collector's department, not with his office, so he made no objection. There his knowledge of the matter ended. He kept his copy of the order.

Meanwhile, however, one of the staff had heard of the order from Washington, and of Hawthorne's compliance with it. He went to Lindsley and Millett and told them of it. He did this without Hawthorne's knowledge or authority. Hawthorne believed, from his experience in Boston, that there probably was a movement on foot to squeeze an assessment out of the two inspectors on the threat of dismissal. One of them, he believed, turned traitor and, under the threats and promises of Upham and his friends, brought his evidence to bear directly on Hawthorne.

Meanwhile Burchmore was turned out of office. He was willing to tell his side of the story. But the other man involved was still in the Custom House at a salary of $1,500 a year. He was a poor man, in debt, and wished to remain in office only long enough to get a few hundred dollars, to enable him to get to California and get a new start in life. He would, if necessary, come forward with his story, but he preferred to wait until he was removed. Hawthorne had no object to obtain worth purchasing at the sacrifice he must make. Consequently, he remained silent, and the stories grew. By August he meant to remove to the country, and "bid farewell forever to this abominable city." [117]

XV

He had begun to write *The Scarlet Letter*. The book had been growing in his mind during his years in the Custom House, but he had been unable to work on it. He now set himself to write with an intensity he had not experienced since he had written *Seven Tales of My Native Land*, more than a score of years before. The book shaped itself readily and easily in its first chapters. He was driven by stronger external motives, and a more passionate impulse within, than he had felt for many years. He wrote steadily, until his visions were a bright reality, and the play of his children, and the illness of his mother, seemed like faint happenings in a dream. His characters became more real than life to him. He was inspired: he had the sense of certainty that comes with inspiration, the clear images, the vivid scenes that follow one another inexhaustibly, the pure flow of language. He wanted to diffuse thought and imagination through the opaque substance of today, and thus to make it a bright transparency; to spiritualize the burden that began to weigh so heavily; to seek, resolutely, the true and indestructible value that lay hidden in petty and wearisome incidents. . . . And so, though he called it folly to do as he did, in turning back to a vanished age, he nevertheless fulfilled his purpose while denying that he did so.[118] The prison, which the founders of the utopian colony found it necessary to build, the pillory, where Hester stood with her child, the scarlet letter on her breast, the terrible moment in which, standing before the multitude, she recognized her husband in the crowd—all these had an intensity and clarity his work had never before possessed.

The story had, in addition, a directness unparalleled in his writing and, in view of his position at the moment, a courage unparalleled in American literature. It seems doubtful that all the tracts of the feminists accomplished so much to improve the position of women in American society as the single powerful scene of Hester Prynne walking from the jail to the scaffold, and enduring the gaze of a thousand unrelenting eyes, all fastened upon her, and concentrated at her bosom.

There are no shadings, of humor or grace, or romance, to soften the impact of these first scenes. *The Scarlet Letter* began without hesitation or reticence, smashing with terrific power against the most jealously guarded belief in the social code of the Puritans. The truth was all he cared for, his daughter wrote softly, many years later; and the book is his affirmation of its power.

It is this that makes its moral so confused. It was not guilt that Hawthorne was picturing, not the consequence of sin, but hypocrisy, the vast organized social deceit of mankind, the fury of its cherished falsehoods. The first scenes in the book end the discussion. There was no crime on Hester's part, and no sin of her and her unknown lover, to equal the leaden infliction it was her doom to endure. Hawthorne's genius was never so telling as in his choice of where to begin this somber and thrilling narrative. Not with Hester's leaving her unloved husband, or her meeting the young clergyman, or the months preceding the birth of her child, or the birth of little Pearl—none of the links to common experience to render her less a symbol. The prison door opened and the guilty woman stepped forth. Thereafter the scenes mounted in a series of imaginative triumphs, each more vivid and beautiful than the last, like fragments from the last movements of some unknown symphony whose opening movements have been lost. The trumpets and brasses sound and fade away, echoing some theme unheard before and yet dimly recognizable; the scene is all color and pageantry, the slow march to the gallows, the luxuriant sunlit setting, the slow, Oriental procession of magistrates and ministers, like figures from some Eastern opera rather than a New England village; the fiery implacable trumpet notes symbolizing the relentless power of the state, all but drowning out a poignant line of exquisite beauty that wavers like the sound of music blown about by the wind. The crowds had expected the prisoner to be cringing and beaten; her beauty shone out and made a halo of the misfortune and ignominy in which she was enveloped. The child in her arms bore the taint of deepest sin in the most sacred quality of human life, working with such effect that the world was only darker for her beauty and more lost for the infant she had borne. Standing on the gallows, almost at the point of screaming aloud, or of casting herself on the ground, or of going mad, she suddenly begins to dream of her childhood in England, her eyes glazing—and the green fields and her childish sports and quarrels relieve her spirit from the cruel weight and hardness of reality.

Hawthorne's mother was very ill. She was stricken on the 26th of July.[119] When the fight over the Custom House was coming to a climax —his old friend Burchmore had just been removed—Hawthorne was called to her room. She was semiconscious, and spoke and moved with difficulty. She put her clasped hands to her head. The curtains were drawn. The room was in semidarkness. The old coldness between them, the long years of seclusion, now took their toll: he was constrained, benumbed, with a dull feeling of regret and remembrance, and yet with no sense of overpowering emotion struggling within him.[120] Dr. Pierson was attending her. Pierson was the best of Salem physicians, a simple, kindly man, famous for his charity, beloved in the city, where a large part of the population owed him their lives, as well as a great deal of money. He was an old friend of the Peabody family, and had taken Wellington Peabody into his office and taught him medicine, at a time when Wellington was in disgrace.[121]—Hawthorne could not comprehend the reality of his mother's illness. The next day he remained away from her room. Sophia remained with her, holding her in her arms while she sat up for breath.

He tried to keep stubbornly at work while Sophia cared for his mother, sitting in the chamber where she lay, constantly weaker. A pleasant breeze blew across the yard from the North River. The children played under the elm tree and the pear tree and the plum trees that overshadowed the grassy plot beside the old gray house. Their voices rose like the song of birds. The doors and windows were all open.

Una was describing her grandmother's sickness to Julian. "Oh, you don't know how sick she is, Julian; she is as sick as I was, when I had the scarlet fever in Boston."

She had been to see her grandmother and had spent some time in the chamber, fanning the flies from the grandmother's face. Julian was riding his hobby horse. "It would be very painful for little Julian to see," she said, "for she is very sick indeed; and sometimes she almost cries, but she is very patient with her sickness."

"Why, Una," said Julian, "if I were to see her I would stroak her, and she would be very quiet."

Julian then assumed the character of his mother, and Una became Julian. He talked pathetically about how he would feel if Julian were to faint away and go to God. They both suddenly assumed other characters. Una became a lady. Julian became a coachman. All day long Hawthorne watched them play. Once he saw Julian dancing and Una drumming on an empty pail. "I'm a monkey," Julian said.

Una explained, "I'm the music man."

Julian lay on the couch in the character of his grandmother. Una became Mrs. Dike. "Now stretch out your hands to be held. Will you have some of this jelly?" Julian started up to take some of the imaginary jelly. "No; Grandmamma lies still." Julian smacked his lips. "You must not move your lips so hard. Do you think Una had better come up?"

"No!"

"You feel so, don't you?"

Una became her grandmother, and Julian became Sophia, taking care of her. She groaned and spoke with difficulty; roused herself, called for wine, and lay down again. Una's actions recalled to Hawthorne, with frightful distinctness the scene of the day before. Julian became his grandmother again. "You're dying now," said Una, "so you must lie still."

"I shall walk, if I'm dying," said Julian. He tramped about the room. Julian then became Dr. Pierson. Una talked with him about the patient. "I think we'd better have Dr. Cummings," she said.

"We can't have any more talking; I must go!" said Julian. He then became Dr. Cummings. Outdoors, the children played with a tame, black-crested hen that wandered into the yard. They picked her up, stroked her feathers, fought over her, pulling her both ways, until Hawthorne thought they would pull her apart, and gave up in disgust when the fowl committed an unpardonable sin on Una's apron. She came to Hawthorne, looking ashamed, her little nose expressive of much disgust. Then Una went for a walk with Dora.

Hawthorne returned to his mother's chamber. It was about five o'clock. The room was dark, a line of sunlight coming through the crevices in the curtain. His sister Louisa and his aunt Priscilla were with his mother. Louisa pointed to a chair by the bed. Hawthorne did not sit down. He knelt at the bedside and took his mother's hand. She murmured a few indistinct words, to take care of his sisters. Priscilla left the room. Hawthorne felt the tears gather in his eyes. He tried to restrain them. Suddenly he began to sob. For a long time he knelt beside her, holding her hand. The darkest hour of his dark life swept over him, wild and despairing thoughts, until it seemed he saw the whole of human existence at once, standing in the dusty midst of it, the mockery of a close so dark and wretched, a fate beyond wrong. He grew calm again. God would not have made the close so dark and wretched if there were nothing beyond. It would have been a fiend, and not God, who created us and measured out our existence.

Then he stood at the window. Through a crevice in the curtain he saw Una at play, my little Una of the golden locks, looking so beautiful and full of life that she seemed life itself. The shouts, laughter, and cries of the two children came up to the room. At one moment Una's voice rose clear and distinct. "Yes, she is going to die." The words pained him. Una's usual way of speaking of death was to say "going to God." He wished she had spoken so. It would have been hopeful and comforting, spoken in her bright young voice. It occurred to him— apparently for the first time—that she was repeating or enforcing the words of some older person who had just spoken.[122] A curious calm determination replaced the pain of his thought of his mother. It was as if a burden of doubt had dropped from him, in the midst of grief, or as if his grief, nowise lessened, had grown quiet, not slumbering, but as a fierce and wild horse grows tame. Sophia was frightened for him. She thought he was near a brain fever—a breakdown.—In the morning his mother still lived, but had grown weaker. She no longer suffered, but faded as a day fades, and died in the afternoon of July 31, 1849.

"I am weary, weary, weary," Sophia said, "heart and head." Elizabeth and Louisa were desolate, and while all their hearts were aching with sorrow and care, one of Mrs. Hawthorne's kin was like some marble-souled fiend. Sophia hoped wearily God would forgive her. She felt now—what had so changed their view of Hawthorne's mother?— that they had lost an angel of excellence. The funeral was at four o'clock on Thursday, August 2.[123] When it was over Sophia went to Boston to rest, and to search for a new place to live, leaving Hawthorne with the children. He bathed and dressed them, listening to them play, and wrote down their words in his notebook. They transformed themselves into Mr. and Mrs. Horace Mann, and visited themselves. They found a spider—"Oh what a monstrous father-long-legs!" said Julian.

"No, it is not a father-long-legs, but a monstrous spider, with a little body and long legs, just like a man."

"Why has he so long legs?"

"God made them so, Julian," said Una wisely.

Una then transformed herself into her mother. She got into a little box, which was understood to be a boat, and with a parasol in one hand and a stick in the other, rowed away to find a house. She returned in a marvelous short time, and announced that the house would do.

Mr. Manning called. The Uncle Robert of Hawthorne's childhood was now a gray-haired old gentleman of whom Hawthorne spoke with respect. Julian persisted in calling him Miss Manning.[124] Horace Mann sent Hawthorne an invitation to come and see him about being reinstated in his post at the Custom House. Hawthorne no longer had any desire to regain it. "I mean, as soon as it is possible—that is to say as soon as I can find a cheap, pleasant, and healthy residence—to remove into the country, and bid farewell forever to this abominable city; for, now that my mother is gone, I no longer have anything to keep me here."

He wrote a long, detailed account of the entire controversy, and sent it to his brother-in-law, to keep "in case of accidents." Meanwhile, Sophia found a house in the country. Her friend Caroline Sturgis had married William Aspinwall Tappan, of Lenox. Across the road from their home, a mile and a half from the village, was a cozy little red house by the lake, bright with pictures, with an orchard adjoining and a spruce grove near by. There was a garden in front, and a barnyard on one side. This house the Hawthornes could have. Caroline wanted them to live there, rent-free. Hawthorne refused to do so—some stated sum was necessary as rent, he believed, or there was too great a danger of misunderstanding on both sides.[125]

The Tappans were angels—at any rate, Caroline Tappan was. Assurance of a place to live, at that time, must have been invaluable to Hawthorne, sufficiently reassuring so that he did not need to take it. Eleven years had passed since he had visited the Berkshires. In the meantime they had grown fashionable. The farmhouses of the little village south of Pittsfield had become estates where Bostonians spent their summers. Sam Ward's place was beyond the Bullard and Tappan estates; Anna Shaw had bought the old Hotchkiss place; Oliver Wendell Holmes visited his ancestral farm on the road to Lenox each year for seven blessed summers; and Herman Melville bought the old Arrowhead Inn, south of Pittsfield (once a farm owned by his kinspeople), where, he said, he spent a good deal of time patting the trees on the back. The Berkshires were still a Whig stronghold. Lenox was evenly divided—fifty-two Democrats and fifty-six Whigs. Its literary colony was of a different order from that of Concord—wealthy, sophisticated, good-natured, without a Transcendentalist or a Brook Farmer within miles. Catharine Sedgwick had brought Harriet Martineau and Fanny Kemble, to Lenox and she persuaded William Ellery Channing to come to the Berkshires in the last year of his life.

The hillsides sloped away down to the small valley, filled with rich thick woods, in the center of which the jewellike lake lay gleaming. Beyond the valley the hills rose one above another to the horizon. In the mornings troops of clouds and wandering shadows of rain and all-prevailing sunbeams chased each other over the wooded slopes and down into the dark hollow where the lake slept. There was a quiet, hidden beauty in the life of the country. It was strangely like the life that Sophia had lived in Cuba—visits, outdoor parties, horseback rides before breakfast. Said Fanny Kemble, the English actress, who bought a farm there—"We laugh, we sing, we talk, we play, we discuss, we dance, we ride, drive, walk, run, scramble and saunter and amuse ourselves extremely; and enjoy every day delightful intercourse with the Sedgwicks."

The Sedgwicks dominated the country as the Derbys had once dominated Salem. Catharine Sedgwick was still famed as the author of *Hope Leslie* and *Redwood*, a woman of fifty, well formed, with regular features, a pleasing smile and a soft voice, and gentle captivating manners. She lived in a wing of the Sedgwick house, and her school was on another part of the grounds. It was a famous girls' academy. When the school was in session the village brightened with the young faces of her students on the porch and lawn, "and now and then, moving among them, with something of an air of mystery, the form of one who was a fine specimen of the New England gentlewoman." They overflowed their rooms and took over the village hotel which, said Fanny Kemble, was never so graced as when it had its blossoming time, with bright young faces shining about in every direction.[126] Fall was the time to visit the Berkshires. The Hawthornes were not yet able to move, however. They did not have enough money. Both Louisa and Elizabeth Hawthorne were dependent upon them, at least in part. The winter in Lenox promised to be even colder than the winter in Salem, and they were occupied with the struggle for bread. So they decided to remain until spring in the town where—there was no longer any question about it—Hawthorne was afraid of an "accident" befalling him.

XVI

John O'Sullivan sent them $100 of his debt from the *Democratic Review*. Hawthorne could also draw in advance on his writing—another hundred dollars. With this he expected to get through the winter. The continuity of his inspiration had been broken, yet he wrote intensely, nine hours a day, intending to make *The Scarlet Letter* one of a series of stories in a new book.[127]

O'Sullivan was in difficulties. One of his sisters had married a Cuban planter, and O'Sullivan had become the leading advocate for the annexation of the island. He had succeeded in interesting President Polk in his schemes, had several interviews with him, and Polk presented his plan to his Cabinet for discussion. The result was that Polk decided to offer Spain $100,000,000 for the island. When this offer was tentatively made and rejected, almost as an insult, O'Sullivan entered into correspondence with James Buchanan, Polk's secretary of state. The defeat of the Democrats did not lessen his zeal. O'Sullivan was intimately connected with Narciso Lopez. When Lopez made his second attempt to seize Cuba with a force of Cuban patriots and American soldiers of fortune, O'Sullivan was his American adviser—one of them, at any rate, and one of the most prominent. He operated in New Orleans, where Lopez, through his friendship with Pierre Soulé, had his headquarters.[128] Soulé was a French revolutionist, exiled from France, elected to the Senate from Louisiana, and entrusted by Polk with negotiations for the purchase of Cuba.[129] O'Sullivan was arrested in New Orleans for his part in outfitting the *Creole*.

The Scarlet Letter had ceased to be a short story and had become a novel. It must have been clear to Hawthorne after he had written the first few chapters that he was creating a book which was unique—a work so individual that it had no predecessors and could have no followers, perfectly formed and complete in itself. He was writing one of the world's greatest works of fiction. Whether he knew that it was also unique among the great novels of the world is doubtful. He had a sense of its quality, but no real knowledge of its power. It possessed him; he could not free himself of it; and his uneasiness is testified to in his plans to hedge it about with a long introduction and to frame it with other stories to temper its dark finality. What was its moral? What did it say? The moral that he found in Dimmesdale's tragic life—"Be true! Be true! Be true! Show freely to the world, if not your worst, yet some trait whereby the worst may be inferred!"—seemed the saddest thought in the whole sad story of fear and revenge. True to what? To his weakness? to his sin? to his inability to confess and to let Hester bear the burden of guilt alone? Yet this was what he had done; this was his worst which he was unable to show freely to the world. Professor Woodberry observed that the moral of the novel was not the Puritan faith of New England. "In the scheme of Puritan thought," he wrote, "the atonement of Christ is the perpetual miracle whereby salvation comes, not only hereafter, but in the holier life led here by grace. There is no Christ in this book. Absolution, so far as it is hinted at, lies in the direction of public confession, the efficacy of which is directly stated, but lamely nevertheless; it restores truth, but does not heal the past. Leave the dead past bury its dead, says Hawthorne, and go on to what may remain; but life once ruined is ruined beyond recall. So Hester, desirous of serving in her place the larger truth she has come to know, is stayed, says Hawthorne, because she recognized the impossibility that any mission of divine and mysterious truth should be confided to a woman stained with sin, bowed down with shame, or even burdened with a life-long sorrow. That was never the Christian gospel nor the Puritan faith." [130]

Nor does it seem a broad enough statement of Hawthorne's achievement. The first novel in American fiction to take its rank with the masterpieces of world literature was the story of a doctor, a clergyman, and the woman they loved. If the doctor represents science, it is a representation of science crippled and barren, that is, one which is divorced from any moral purpose, and is, indeed, relentlessly at war with the figure which, more than any other, embodies the moral force of the community. The fulfillment that Hester could not find with her husband she found with Dimmesdale, after she had fled from him. The child was the child of her union with him, as plain a moral as was the fact that the marriage to science was barren. That science which had no place within it for what was Dimmesdale's whole life—and that religious faith so constrained that it had no comprehension of the material world that was the sphere of science—were but half-worlds; each to the other the dark side of the moon. The preacher has his greater fervor from his inability to incorporate into his own scheme of life the truth of nature that Hester and her child represent. The doctor has his greater brilliance in the rocket release of his knowledge from the moral teachings that the minister imperfectly yet actually expresses, and in his freedom —since Hester and the child are not his—from the family cares of the world around him. Surely this moral of the novel is in Hester's counsel to those who come to her, that, at some brighter period, when the world should have grown ripe for it, in Heaven's own time, a new truth would be revealed, in order to establish the whole relation between man and woman on a surer ground of mutual happiness. What Hawthorne believed its nature would be could hardly be stated more clearly.

Without inferring any biographical accuracy in the portrait, it seems unquestionable that the figure of Reverend Dimmesdale was modeled on Reverend Channing. Hawthorne had created a kind of early Channing among the most rigorous of the first Puritan Fathers. The selflessness, the eloquence, the frailty, the tenderness, the hesitant and yet powerful checking of the forthright, black-and-white morality of the Puritans, the shyness and scrupulousness that grew more marked as the popular love and admiration for him grew—these are true to the facts of Channing's life as they are to Hawthorne's portrait of Dimmesdale. "While thus suffering under bodily disease, and gnawed and tortured by some black trouble of the soul, and given over to the machinations of his deadliest enemy, Reverend Dimmesdale achieved a brilliant popularity in his sacred office. He won it, indeed, by his sorrows." [131] So Hawthorne described Dimmesdale. And thus Dr. Furness wrote of Channing: "He was of those that mourn. . . . In his early years there is much that awakens in the reader a melancholy that amounts to pain. His ill-health, his profound sensibility, the dimness of his views . . . in regard to the Orothodox doctrines of the day, give us the impression of a very sad and struggling soul, a saint walking in darkness." [132]

Hawthorne said of Dimmesdale: "He was a person of very striking aspect, with a white, lofty and impending brow, large, brown, melancholy eyes, and a mouth which, unless when he forcibly compressed it, was apt to be tremulous, expressing both nervous sensibility and a vast power of self-restraint. . . . His form grew emaciated; his voice, though still rich and sweet, had a certain and melancholy prophecy of decay in it; he was often observed, on any slight alarm or other sudden accident, to put his hand over his heart, with a first a flush and then a paleness, indicative of pain." [133]

And this is a description of Channing at the Federal Street Church in Boston: "With a somewhat rapid and elastic step, a person small in stature, thin and pale, and carefully enveloped, ascends the pulpit-stair. . . . For a moment he deliberately and benignantly surveys the large congregation, as if drinking in the influence of so many human beings. . . . In the hollow eye, the sunken cheeks, and the deep lines around the mouth, the chronic debility of many years has left an ineffaceable impress. But on the polished brow, with its rounded temples, shadowed by one falling lock, and on the beaming countenance, there hovers a serenity which seems to brighten the whole head with a halo." When he spoke: "There are no expletives, no fulminations, no fanatical out-pourings. . . . Sin and degradation are made to appear unspeakably mournful when measured by the majestic innate powers, the celestial destiny, appointed to the most debased; every spirit becomes venerable to us, as heir of God and co-heir of Christ, as the once lost but now found, the prodigal yet dearly loved child of the Heavenly Father." [134]

And thus Hawthorne wrote of Dimmesdale: "His intellectual gifts, his moral perceptions, his power of experiencing and communicating emotion, were kept in a state of preternatural activity by the prick and anguish of his daily life. His fame, though still on its upward slope, already overshadowed the soberer reputations of his fellow clergymen, eminent as some of them were. There were scholars among them, who had spent more years in acquiring abstruse lore, connected with the divine profession, than Mr. Dimmesdale had lived; and who might well, therefore, be more profoundly versed in such solid and valuable attainments than their youthful brother. There were men, too, of a sturdier texture of mind than his, and endowed with a far greater share of shrewd, hard, iron or granite understanding; which duly mingled with a fair proportion of doctrinal ingredient, constitutes a highly respectable, efficacious, and unamiable variety of the clerical species. There were others, again, true saintly fathers, whose faculties had been elaborated by weary toil among their books, and by patient thought, and etherealized, moreover, by spiritual communications with the better world, into which their purity of life had almost introduced these holy personages, with their garments of mortality still clinging to them. All that they lacked was the gift that descended upon the chosen disciples at Pentecost, in tongues of flame—symbolizing, it would seem, not the power of speech in foreign and unknown languages, but that of addressing the whole human brotherhood in the heart's native language." [135]

Midway in his composition of the novel Hawthorne began to suffer from a painful earache which delayed him and rendered work difficult.[136] He rarely left the house, perhaps once a week. He worked in an upstairs room, crouching over a stove. The children played in the parlor. The Hawthornes' possessions, never rich, had become shabby, the carpets ragged and the parlor littered with the children's playthings. Sophia had decided to try to paint again—there had always been a market for her paintings. She thought she would work three hours a day in Hawthorne's study, there being no other place where she could have privacy. She was forty years old, her husband forty-five. In this situation the novel went on. Hawthorne's weight, in the Custom House, had reached 178 pounds. He was now thin, nervous, his emotions close to the surface. It was as if he dreaded and feared this book, which struck so close to home and attacked so many of the convictions of his family and the family of his wife. For many years the goodness of God and man's bright and comfortable situation in the universe had been the theme of the preaching of Channing's followers, and he was now casting a light which revealed the illusions that had grown up in its wake, and which revealed, simultaneously, the rigidity and intolerance of the Puritanism they opposed. He could hardly bring himself to read the last chapters of the book to Sophia. He was under so great an emotional strain that his voice trembled and broke. As for the effect of the book on her, he said that it broke her heart.[137]

He walked to the post office on January 17, 1850, when the story was nearly finished. A cold west wind was blowing. The streets of Salem have an icy glaze on these midwinter days, wind-swept and deserted. There was a letter from Hillard. He carried it to the vestibule of the post office and opened it. Hillard had collected a sum of money from Hawthorne's admirers and sent it to him. The amount is not known; it was considerable. "It is only paying," Hillard explained, "in a very imperfect measure, the debt we owe you for what you have done for American literature. . . . Let no shadow of despondency, my dear friend, steal over you. Your friends do not and will not forget you."

The tears came to his eyes. He walked out into the street and turned down Mall Street, bending against the wind that blew toward him, glad of the wind that gave his eyes an excuse for being red and bleared. The money would smooth his path for a long time to come. It was bitter for him to have to take it. Ill success in life was a matter of shame to him; the fault of failure is attributed to the man who fails. So he thought of other men, and he could not shun its point or edge in taking it home to his own heart. So there was something very bitter— and much that was very sweet—mingled with the tears that came to his eyes.[138]

He finished the book on February 7, 1850. He intended to add other stories to it—a book called *Old Time Legends*. He was now worried about his health, yet would not confess it to Sophia—he never owned up to not feeling perfectly well to her, for she sermonized him too much on the subject. He thought that if he could get out in the country he would be all right. An hour or two of daily labor in a garden, a daily ramble in the country, a walk on the seashore, were all he needed.[139]

He was huddled over the stove one day when a visitor appeared. He was James Fields, a burly, pleasant individual, with a finely shaped head, born in Portsmouth, who was, like the Hawthornes, the son of a sea captain. He had a brief wait in Salem before catching his train to Boston, and called on Hawthorne. Fields had become a partner, in 1845, in William Ticknor's publishing house. Ticknor and Fields had bought the property of Wiley and Putnam when that firm went bankrupt, and thus had become Hawthorne's publisher. Fields had begun the practice of publishing books at the firm's risk and expense, supporting their authors and advancing their reputations, precisely as they did with the celebrated English authors on their list. He was probably shocked and alarmed at Hawthorne's appearance and his evident poverty. Much of his later recollection of this meeting has the doubtful details of a genial after-dinner speaker's story, but its concluding passage is undoubtedly true. Hawthorne refused to turn over what he had been writing to Fields, or even discuss it. There was a chest of drawers in the room, and Fields thought it likely Hawthorne had a story hidden away in it. He said so. Hawthorne seemed surprised, but shook his head.

Fields looked at his watch. He had just time to catch his train to Boston. He said good-bye, telling Hawthorne not to come out into the cold entry. He said that he would be back in Salem in a few days and would come back and see him again. As he was hurrying down the stairs, Hawthorne called to him. He stepped out into the entry with a roll of manuscript in his hand. "How in Heaven's name did you know this was there?" he asked. "It is either very good or very bad, I don't know which." [140]

Fields read the manuscript on the train. He urged that the story be elaborated and made into a single volume. Whether he was responsible for the novel itself taking the shape it now has seems doubtful; there is the evidence of Sophia's letters, and Hawthorne's own feeling about the book, to indicate that it had originally been conceived as a work and more important than any he had undertaken before. Yet Fields unquestionably insisted on bringing it out as a book in itself, not as one story in a book of stories. It was published in haste—perhaps in desperate haste. The long introductory essay, *The Custom House*, valuable as it is for its information on the customs service, and remarkable as it is as a demonstration of Hawthorne's versatility, with its humor, its sharp caricatures, and its bland account of stupendous, matter-of-fact, taken-for-granted incompetence and graft, is inappropriate as an introduction to *The Scarlet Letter*. It was rushed into print, so hurriedly that there was no time to correct the passages in which Hawthorne referred to the nonexistent other stories in the volume. Hawthorne wanted to make the book less shocking. He wanted to dilute its subject matter with other topics. The fierce attack on Salem in *The Custom House* is in effect a lightning rod to protect the novel itself.

The book was published early in April. It created a sensation. The first edition of four thousand copies was sold out in ten days. A second printing was sold out before it was ready for delivery. It sold steadily for months, fifty years later it was still selling steadily, and had sold probably four hundred thousand copies. [141] Mary Foote had never known a book that drew forth such a variety—so much?—of criticism. It seemed to her a wonderfully beautiful book, full of genius and thrilling power. Yet she thought it a very painful book. This old friend of Sophia's girlhood seemed stunned by its relentless honesty. Writing the reviews for her husband's newspaper, wearing out her eyes on *Lord Willoughby's Diary*, *Lady Fanshawe's Memoirs*, and *A Week on the Concord and Merrimack Rivers*—there were as many specks as words on a page of printing these days—she did not know what to say of

The Scarlet Letter. It seemed to her a good moral that there is no repentance without truth; the sinner must be sincere not only with himself, but with others, to gain any peace, or make any progress. She was not sure, however, and others differed. She thought there was not an appreciation of the *highest* moral power in it. "I must say," she wrote, "it is a very painful book," as if no one knew, or few people knew, quite how painful it was.[142]

Sophia had fled with the children to Lenox. The house on the Tappan estate was not ready for occupancy. Hawthorne was ill. He was harassed in spirit, and had a cold which seemed dangerous; the cold, brain work, and disquiet gave him a nervous fever. His eyes glowed like two immense spheres of troubled light. His face was wan and shadowy.[143] He was in hiding. He read nothing. He did not go near the village of Lenox. He knew no more of what was going on in the world than if he had emigrated to the moon. For a month or more he never saw a newspaper. When he picked one up it seemed queer and unreal—it was an antislavery paper. For several days he lay in an upstairs room in the cottage. William Tappan brought two men and plowed up the field beside the house, a real favor. He said he was glad to find that Hawthorne had a cold—it proved he was mortal.

In June Hawthorne recovered and walked to the village. The air had the magic brightness of summer to a convalescent, the colors abnormally bright, the fields brilliant green, the sky unearthly blue. He wanted a drink—some plain brandy and water, or a little rum and molasses.[144] His feet rested uneasily on the solid earth. He spent long hours lying under the pines beside the lake. Beyond the porch of the cottage, on the summer mornings, the mist filled the whole length and breadth of the valley. It hid everything except a few treetops which here and there emerged, glorified by the early sunshine. Four or five miles off to the southward rose the summit of Monument Mountain, and seemed to be floating on a cloud. The dome of Taconic looked blue and indistinct, and hardly so substantial as the vapory sea that almost rolled over it. When the mist rose the lake became visible, reflecting a perfect image of its own wooded banks and the summits of the more distant hills.[145]

Meanwhile the book he had written went on its way. He could never return to Salem. The moral problem that Mary Foote could not solve, and that Professor Woodberry found unreal, was met by its unnumbered readers, who found its truth in the simple injustice of Hester's fate. He had done more than he set out to do. He had taken the grim old legend and given it universal meaning; he had taken the world's symbol of shame and degradation and transformed and ennobled it in the greatest work of art his country had produced.

"He has *done it*," said Oliver Wendell Holmes, "and it will never be harsh country again. . . . A light falls upon the place not of land or sea! How much he did for Salem! Oh, the purple light, the soft haze, that now rests upon our glaring New England! He has *done* it, and it will never be harsh country again."[146]

NOTES

CHAPTER ONE

I

1. The information on Hawthorne's birthplace is found in *Haunts of Hawthorne in Salem, Massachusetts,* by John Dennis Hammond Gauss, privately printed, Salem, the Naumkeag Trust Company; in the Essex Institute Historical Collections, Salem, Vol. III, No. 3, March, 1871; and in information supplied by Miss Florence M. Osborne, librarian of the Essex Institute. The location of Newports Restaurant, and the character of the neighborhood, is taken from *The Trial of John Francis Knapp,* an anonymous pamphlet on the White murder, published July 20, 1830, in the possession of the New York Public Library. The location of the Manning blacksmith shop is given in *Early Modes of Travel,* by Robert Rantoul, Essex Institute Historical Collections.
2. *An Account of Salem Common,* B. F. Browne, Essex Institute Historical Collections, February, 1862.
3. Contemporary advertisements, Salem *Gazette.*
4. *An Account of Salem Common;* also, *Poem,* by Reverend Charles T. Brooks, in *An Account of the Commemoration, by the Essex Institute, of the Fifth Half Century of the Landing of Governor John Endicott,* Essex Institute, 1789.
5. *Simon Forrester of Salem and His Descendants,* Henry Wycoff Belknap, Essex Institute Historical Collections, Vol. LXXI, January, 1935; also, *A Half Century in Salem,* Marianne Silsbee (Boston: Houghton Mifflin, 1887).
6. *The History of Salem, Massachusetts,* by Sidney Perley. Salem, 1924.
7. *Simon Forrester.*
8. *History of Salem.*
9. *A Study of Hawthorne,* by George Lathrop. Boston: J. R. Osgood, 1876.
10. *Nathaniel Hawthorne, A Modest Man,* by Edward Mather, New York: Thomas Y. Crowell, 1940. Throughout this volume I have used the term "legislature" to designate the Massachusetts General Court.
11. *Hawthorne and His Wife,* Julian Hawthorne. Boston: Houghton Mifflin, 1896.
12. Hawthorne to R. H. Stoddard, *National Review,* 1853, quoted in *Haw-*

444 Nathaniel Hawthorne

thorne and His Wife . . . "I was born in the town of Salem, Massachusetts, in a house built by my grandfather, who was a maritime personage. The old household was in another part of town, and had descended in the family ever since the settlement of the country; but this old man of the sea exchanged it for a lot of land situated near the wharves, and convenient to his business, where he built a house (which is still standing) and laid out a garden, where I rolled on a grass-plot under an apple tree, and picked abundant currants." There is no other reference to the house as having been *built* by Captain Daniel Hawthorne. *Diary and Letters* of Benjamin Pickman, 1740-1819, edited by George F. Dow, is the authority for the statement that Captain Joseph Hardy conveyed to his son-in-law, Benjamin Pickman, in 1685, a lot of land on what is now Union Street, Salem. Previous to the transfer, however, Pickman had built a house on the lot where he lived. In 1772 it was owned by Daniel Hawthorne of Salem, mariner—Florence M. Osborne, the Essex Institute. The tone of Hawthorne's reference to his grandfather and other comments by him strongly suggest that his mind was poisoned about his father's family. See especially the notes of Elizabeth Hawthorne, quoted in *Hawthorne and His Wife,* on Hawthorne and Simon Forrester; also Hawthorne's reference to Forrester in *Peter Goldethwaite's Treasure.*

13. A son of Colonel William Hawthorne, born Aug. 11, 1639, was also named Nathaniel, as was a son of Colonel John Hawthorne, born Nov. 25, 1678, who settled in England. The sixth child of Joseph Hawthorne, baptized Aug. 31, 1729, Captain Daniel Hawthorne's older brother, also was named Nathaniel.

14. *Maritime History of Massachusetts,* by S. E. Morison.

15. *Annals of Salem,* by Joseph B. Felt. Salem: W. and B. S. Ives, 1827.

16. *Simon Forrester.* I have converted pounds into dollars, calculating the pound at five dollars in view of the greater purchasing power of the dollar at the time, as giving a fairer impression of the extent of Forrester's fortune.

17. Portraits in the Essex Institute by an unknown artist, probably painted in Hamburg about 1780; also, Marianne Silsbee.

18. *Annals of Salem.* There are also several instances of capture outside Salem Harbor in the contemporary newspaper accounts of the days preceding the battle of the *Chesapeake* and the *Shannon,* in the War of 1812; and in the Salem *Gazette,* May 21, 1813.

19. *Simon Forrester.*

II

20. Perley: Hawthorne, letter to Stoddard; *The Driver Family,* Harriet Ruth Cooke (Cambridge: John Wilson and Son, 1889); *Hawthorne and His Wife.* The list of Captain Nathaniel Hawthorne's commands has not previously been compiled. It has been pieced together for this volume

from the daily record of Arrivals and Departures in the Ship News of the Salem *Gazette,* from 1795 to 1808, by Mrs. Robert Cantwell.

21. *Simon Forrester.* See also *Ship Registers of the District of Salem and Beverly,* by A. Frank Hitchings and Stephen Willard Phillips, Essex Institute Historical Collections, April, 1903, through October, 1906. Since the index is incomplete, it is necessary to go over each entry to trace the ramifications of ownership, though not in the case of Forrester.

22. Memorial letters by Timothy Williams of Salem, quoted in Belknap.

23. *Annals of Salem.* Mr. Belknap's study of Simon Forrester, based to some extent on the Reverend Mr. Bentley's partisan diary, does not mention the education of his sons, which, in part at least, refute the charges of intemperance and irregularity that Bentley directed against Forrester.

24. *John Pickering,* by Sarah Orne Pickering. Boston: Privately Printed, 1887.

25. *The Flowering of New England,* by Van Wyck Brooks. New York: Dutton, 1938.

26. Morison.

27. *Ship Registers;* see also *Gideon Tucker's Memorandum of Prices of Houses, Vessels and Goods Sold in Salem,* 1821-1826, Essex Institute Historical Collections, Vol. LXIV, April, 1928; and the Salem *Gazette. Biographical Notes,* by Nathaniel Silsbee, Essex Institute Historical Collections, Vol. XXXV, January, 1899, is an invaluable source book on the cost and profits of the voyages.

28. *Ship Registers.*

29. Captain Nathaniel Hawthorne's logbook, unpublished, owned by the East India Marine Society, preserved in the Essex Institute.

30. Dictionary American Biography, entry on Jacob Crowninshield.

31. Captain Hawthorne's logbook is spare, unadorned, brief and factual. It has none of the literary finish of some of the logs of the Salem captains, many of which were consciously written to be preserved, and were decorated with drawings of much artistic merit; nor has it the fresh, unlettered candor or the frequent poignancy of John Crowninshield's diary. Yet its simple repetitions probably give a truer picture of the monotony of the long voyages than would a more literary effort; and here and there throughout the volume there are memorable phrases and passages. See especially his account of the sailors taken ashore at Ascension Island, the first sight of the North Star, and his weariness with the long struggle with the "hardhearted" east wind.

32. The date of Captain Daniel Hawthorne's death is given in Perley; and the time of the arrival of the *America* in Salem in the Ship News of the Salem *Gazette.*

III

33. *The Manning Families of New England and Descendants,* by William H. Manning. Salem, 1902.
34. Manning.
35. Manning: also Felt, and *History of the Essex Lodges of Freemasons,* by B. F. Browne, Essex Institute Historical Collections. Much of the material on the Manning family in this section of the book is taken from the files of the *Gazette,* and has not previously been printed in the biographies of Hawthorne. It is a singular fact that there was another family headed by a Richard Manning living in Salem prior to the arrival of the Richard Manning who was Hawthorne's grandfather, according to B. F. Browne—*An Account of Salem Common,* Essex Institute Historical Collections, Vol. IV. No. 1. February, 1862. This Richard Manning was known as Squire Manning. He was a former shipmaster who had become a moneylender. Two bachelor brothers and three maiden sisters of this family lived together in condition of outward poverty on Essex Street. Jacob, an infirm man, made shoes; the three sisters kept a variety shop. They accumulated great wealth, working steadily and spending almost nothing. "Their long accumulated earnings enriched two sons of a deceased sister, Mary, who . . . married John Hodge . . ." This was apparently the origin of the fortune of the Hodges family, Benjamin Hodges (1754-1806), a shipmaster for Derby, master of the famous *Grand Turk,* being president of the Salem bank organized in 1803, founder of the East India Marine Society; an honorable and worthy man.
36. Manning; also *Nathaniel Hawthorne,* by George Woodbury. Boston: Houghton Mifflin, 1902; also, *Raymond, Maine, Scrapbook,* compiled by Cyrus S. Wittam, of the Portland *Daily Press,* in the Maine Historical Society, Portland, Me.; also *Eastern Daily Argus,* April 19, 1913, Bridgton News, Nov. 27, 1936; Raymond, Maine, *Maine Recorder.*
37. Salem *Gazette:* April 4, 1803; May 15, 1804; Oct. 9, 1804; Nov. 27, 1804; March 11, 1806; April 15, 1806. See especially the issues of Nov. 3, 1807; July 13, 1804, July 4, 1804; March 2, 1802; June 29, 1802, et req.—Dec. 30, 1808; May 4, 1813; the issues containing the eyewitness accounts of the battle of the *Chesapeake* and *Shannon* in Salem Harbor, and the editorials on the death of Hamilton.
38. *An Account of Salem Common.* B. F. Browne.
39. April 4, 1803. Salem *Gazette.*
40. Salem *Gazette,* in an editorial reprinted from the Providence *Gazette,* July 6. 1804.

IV

41. Captain Nathaniel Hawthorne's logbook, and Ship News, Salem *Gazette*.
42. *Memories of Hawthorne*, by Rose Lathrop Hawthorne. Boston: Houghton Mifflin, 1897.
43. Nathaniel Hawthorne, letter to Stoddard.
44. Salem *Gazette*, Jan. 1, 1802; Jan. 1, 1803; Jan. 1, 1804. Also Felt, *Annals of Salem*.
45. Robert Rantoul. Also, the Bridgton (Me.) *News*, Nov. 27, 1936; Felt, *Annals of Salem*, for the Manning orchards, and the Issue of the Essex Institute Historical Collections, Vol. XV, July-October, 1878, *An Account of the Commemoration of the Fifth Half Century of the Landing of Governor John Endicott in Salem, Massachusetts*, page 136. The most complete account of the family is in three papers by Manning Hawthorne: *Maria Louisa Hawthorne*, Essex Institute Historical Collections, Vol. LXXV, April, 1939; *Hawthorne's Early Years*, and *Hawthorne Prepares for College, New England Quarterly*, 1938.
46. Salem *Gazette*, May 15, 1805. The name of Richard Manning, Jr., does not appear on the list for 1806.
47. The story of the Gardiner lawsuit is told in Phillips, *Political Fights and Local Squabbles in Salem*, although he does not mention that Colonel John Hawthorne (Hawthorne's uncle; the title was honorary) was involved. The vote of the town meeting is in the *Gazette*, March 11, 1806, which also gives the findings of John Pickering and the Federalist committee on the town expenses and the costs of the Gardiner lawsuit. The feeling of the Federalists about John Hawthorne's action in debarring Gardinier from voting is expressed in a letter to the editor, Isaac Cushing, in the *Gazette*, July 10, 1804: "May it not fairly and candidly be asked, whether John Hawthorne, esq. did not preside, as one of the selectmen of Salem, in town meeting for the choice of representatives, when he was himself a candidate for the seat? . . . He exercised the authority he was vested with in debarring, in favor of his own election, a citizen from voting, whom a decision of the Supreme Court had declared entitled to vote—and which same tribunal had decreed a fine on Col. Hawthorne for refusing the same citizen's vote on a former occasion . . ."

V

48. The clearest exposition of Federalist thought at the time is perhaps in *Memoirs of Jeremiah Mason*, by George Hillard (Cambridge: Privately printed, 1873); with incidental revelations in *Life and Letters of Joseph Story*, by William Wetmore Story. Boston: Charles C. Little and James Brown, 1851.

49. The account of the Fourth of July celebration, 1804, is taken almost without change from the Salem *Gazette*.
50. Ship News, Salem *Gazette*.
51. Captain Hawthorne's logbook.
52. Salem *Gazette*, Ship News, Oct. 16, 1804: "Arrived, Ship *Mary and Eliza*, Captain Nathaniel Hawthorne in 113 days from Batavia. Left there: *Betsy*, Ranks; the *Levant*, Silsbee, Boston; *Liberty*, Vickey; the *William Smith* of Baltimore;—the *Argo* of Salem, sailed for Calcutta, June 11; the *Canton* of Philadelphia, left Angus Roads, 20 June . . . the *Print* of Salem and the *America* of Philadelphia, sailed for home June 15—the *Martha Washington* of Gloucester left Batavia—June 17. *Union* (Hodges) for Calcutta, and *Mandarin*, Becket, for Sumatra, sailed 19th June—Parted with the *Martha Washington*, *Calder*, off Java Head —spoke, June 22, Java Head 8 leagues distant, the *Union*, Johnson, Newport, 147 days out, for Batavia—Sept. 30, schooner *Morning Star*, from Phil. for West Indies—5 days out; Oct. 9, Ship *Imperial*, Peterborn, of Baltimore, for Liverpool, 5 days out.

"Captain Hawthorne who left Batavia about the 15th June last reports that all the crop of coffee was exhausted, and no more was to be had for the season. 6 or 7 American ships had been obliged to leave the port for Bengal and other places without procuring any. No less than 45 neutral ships, principally American, had loaded there from Sept. to June."

Later arrivals from the East Indies confirmed Captain Hawthorne's account.
53. *Simon Forrester*.
54. Ship News, Salem *Gazette*. A diligent search of subsequent issues failed to unearth any further mention of Captain Hawthorne until the voyage of the *Nabby*.
55. Salem *Gazette*, Feb. 14, 1806; May 4, 1806.
56. Salem *Gazette*, Feb. 7, 1809.
57. *Life of Daniel Webster*, by Claude Fuess; and *Maritime History of Massachusetts*. See also, *Life and Letters of Joseph Story*, and the *Memoirs of Jeremiah Mason*.
58. Salem *Gazette*, Oct. 14, 1807.
59. *Maritime History of Massachusetts*.
60. *Hawthorne and His Wife*.

CHAPTER TWO

I

1. *Hawthorne and His Wife.*
2. *American Notebooks,* edited by Randall Stewart. Hawthorne's recollections of the Fosters were not included in the early editions of his notebooks, edited by his widow and his son. The Vital Records of Salem are the source of information on the fate of Mary Ann Foster.
3. *Old Modes of Travel,* by Robert Rantoul. The schedules are given in contemporary advertisements in the *Gazette.* See also, *New England and Her Institutions,* by One of Her Sons (Jacob Abbott). The American Popular Library. Boston: John Allen, 1835. Jacob Abbot was a Bowdoin schoolmate of Hawthorne's.
4. *Our Old Home,* by Nathaniel Hawthorne.
5. *The Manning Families.*
6. *Our Old Home.*
7. *Hawthorne and His Wife.*
8. *A Half Century in Salem.*
9. Manning Hawthorne, review of Edward Mather's *Hawthorne, a Modest Man,* in the *New England Quarterly,* June, 1941.
10. *Maria Louisa Hawthorne.*
11. The material on the Storys is found in *Life and Letters of Joseph Story,* and in *Dr. Elisha Story of Marblehead and Some of His Descendants,* by Frank Gardner, M.D., Essex Institute, 1915.
12. Elizabeth Hawthorne's recollections, quoted in *Hawthorne and His Wife.*
13. Manning Hawthorne.
14. The *Connecticut Courant,* quoted in the Salem *Gazette.*
15. There are vivid accounts of the resentment in New England during the war in Caleb Foote's autobiography, printed in *Mary and Caleb Foote,* in Samuel Goodrich's *Personal Recollections,* and in *History of the Hartford Convention,* by Theodore Dwight, Boston: Russell Odiorne and Co., 1833.
16. Salem *Gazette,* June, 1813; also the Encyclopedia Americana's account of the engagement, for Lawrence's traditional outcry, and for the disaffection of the crew. There are different interpretations of the difficulties connected with Lawrence's funeral. George Crowninshield sailed to Halifax under a flag of truce, and returned with the bodies of Lawrence and Ludlow. Morison, in his *Maritime History* stresses the hostility of the town, the refusal of some of the churches to permit the service to be held in them, and the close vote by which the East India Society voted to attend. Such citizens as Caleb Foote and Marianne Silsbee, anxious to defend the reputation of the city, emphasized the

patriotic response of the majority of the citizens. The truth seems to be that Salem was frightened rather than hostile. The best description of the success of the British war of nerves is to be found in Caleb Foote's autobiography. He emphasizes the constant raids, which kept the people apprehensive, the night alarms, the British tactics of harrying along the coast, spreading confusion and disorder, rather than actually invading.

17. Salem *Gazette* obituary, April 20, 1813: "In Newbury yesterday afternoon, Mr. Richard Manning, aged 59, a very respectable citizen of this town. He left his family, in perfect health, on Saturday, on a journey to the eastward, had proceeded as far as Newbury, and on the following morning was arrested by the hand of death—being found in his bed in a fit of apoplexy. His funeral will be this day at 5 o'clock from his late dwelling in Herbert Street, which his relatives and friends are desired to attend.

"In this town, Mrs. Rachel Hawthorne, widow of Capt. Daniel Hawthorne, aged 79."

The brief notice of Hawthorne's grandmother's death involved no disrespect. The obituary of Richard Manning, is, however, of the sort reserved only for very distinguished citizens. It is curious that none of Hawthorne's biographers pointed out the coincidence of the death of his two grandparents on the same day, with the obvious emotional effect of such an event on an imaginative child.

II

18. *Maria Louisa Hawthorne.*
19. *Simon Forrester.*
20. *Annals of Salem.*
21. *The Flowering of New England.*
22. *Political Fights and Local Squabbles in Salem.*
23. *Maria Louisa Hawthorne.*
24. Manuscript note by Manning Hawthorne, in the Essex Institute. The date of Richard Manning's death is incorrectly given on his tombstone.
25. *History of the Essex Lodge of Freemasons.*
26. I have been unable to learn from Dartmouth College whether or not Nathaniel Peabody was a graduate. It should be said that not holding a college degree was not, at that time, a reflection on the professional ability or standing of a physician, and might be the reverse. Many physicians received their college degrees after years of successful practice. It was customary for an able physician to take a student in with him and train him individually.
27. *Personal Recollections of Nathaniel Hawthorne,* by Horatio Bridge. New York: Harper and Brothers, 1893.

28. Hawthorne's autobiographical letter to Stoddard, quoted in *Hawthorne and His Wife*. The tragedy of the Tarbox family is related in *Early Years*, and in the *Raymond Scrapbook*.
29. *New England and Her Institutions* contains a vivid picture of the land clearing.
30. *Hawthorne's First Diary*, by S. T. Pickard. The story of this book is of great interest. It is based on a number of anonymous communications which were sent to the Portland (Me.) *Transcript*. The sender explained that he had come into the possession of a book in Hawthorne's handwriting, a diary covering his years in Raymond, in the front of which was an inscription stating that it was a gift from his uncle, Richard Manning. The diary seemed genuine, though the sender had not sent the book, but had merely copied passages from it. Upon checking its details with inhabitants of Raymond, the editor of the *Transcript* decided that the work was authentic, and made an effort to locate its finder, who had mailed the passages from Alexandria, Va., leaving no address.

After an extended search, the sender was identified as William Symmes, a mulatto, who had lived in Raymond as a boy, and had known Hawthorne. He explained by letter that he had received the diary from Francis Redoux. Redoux was a Portland dancing teacher, a Frenchman, a veteran of the Napoleonic Wars, who married Richard Manning's widow (see Chap. V) and lived in the Manning house in Raymond after Richard Manning's death. While moving some furniture for Redoux, the book came to light, and Redoux gave it to Symmes.

The editor of the *Transcript*, in trying to locate Symmes, asked for the assistance of the United States Secret Service in Washington. His request seemed to cause them some embarrassment, and he eventually discovered that Symmes was an employee of the department. By the time he learned this, however, Symmes had left, and was reportedly living in Florida. Meanwhile, another long section of the diary was sent to the *Transcript* office, supposedly transcribed from the same source. After another search for Symmes, the trail led to the boarding-house where he had lived, and the newspaper was able to learn no more than that he was believed to be dead.

A very careful check of the manuscript was then made. It was published. Julian Hawthorne decided that the diary was a forgery. George Parsons Lathrop, Hawthorne's son-in-law, however, accepted it as genuine. On internal evidence, it seemed, in part at least, Hawthorne's work, and revealed so much familiarity with Raymond and with family history that, if not written by Hawthorne, it must have been written by someone very close to him. It was then discovered that one entry was false, since it referred to an event which had taken place after the diary was supposedly written. The book was withdrawn from publication. Yet the single false entry need not have discredited the entire diary. It is equally possible, since the diary was sent to the newspaper office a few pages at a time, that most of it was genuine, and that the false entry or entries were calculated to cast suspicion, not only upon the nature of Hawthorne's life in Raymond, but upon all his notebooks. The diary gives a pleasant and matter-of-fact picture of life in Raymond. At the time it was published, none of the biographies of Hawthorne included the story of the Manning land purchases in Maine, or the story of the Raymond land grant.

31. *Raymond Scrapbook.*
32. Hawthorne: autobiographical letter.
33. *Blithedale Romance,* by Nathaniel Hawthorne.
34. "Sketches from Memory: Our Evening Party among the Mountains," by Nathaniel Hawthorne, *New England Magazine,* November, 1835. Reprinted in *Mosses from an Old Manse.*
35. The material on the Reverend Caleb Bradley and the town of Stroudwater has been made available to me by Dr. Allston Frost Hunt, of Westbrook, Me., whose father was the Reverend Mr. Bradley's physician.
36. Dr. Hunt.
37. Portrait, the New York Public Library.
38. Salem *Gazette.*
39. Mr. Clifford Shipton, custodian of the archives, Harvard.
40. Dr. Hunt.
41. Much of the material on the town of Stroudwater is taken from an unpublished manuscript by Dr. Hunt, called *Andrew Hawes Told Me.* Andrew Hawes was the village storekeeper, who lived to a great age. Mr. Charles Maxfield, of Westbrook, knew the Reverend Mr. Bradley in his childhood, and has given me an enlightening picture of him, his family, and his standing in the community.
42. *The American Magazine of Useful and Entertaining Knowledge,* May, 1836. *The Duston Family* is reprinted in *Hawthorne as Editor,* by Arlin Turner. Baton Rouge: University of Louisiana Press, 1941.

III

43. Manning Hawthorne, *Hawthorne's Early Years.*
44. *The Essex Antiquarian,* Vol. 4. March, 1900. Information supplied through the courtesy of Miss Florence Osborne.
45. *A Half Century in Salem.*
46. *Hawthorne and His Wife.*
47. *Annals of Salem,* also Manning Hawthorne, and the anniversary issue of the Historical Collections of the Essex Institute. Robert Manning's book, *Fruit Trees,* and his specialized studies on pear trees, I have not read. *Fruit Trees* was published in 1838, and, like Fessenden's out-of-

print works, may be enlightening in view of the subsequent decline of New England orchards.

48. *Maria Louisa Hawthorne.*
49. *Our Old Home.*
50. *Maria Louisa Hawthorne.*
51. *Hawthorne and His Wife.*
52. *Maria Louisa Hawthorne.*
53. *A Half Century in Salem.*
54. Manning Hawthorne.
55. "Hawthorne's Spectator," edited by Elizabeth L. Chandler, *New England Quarterly,* April, 1931. The *Spectator* is in the possession of the Essex Institute.
56. *Some Localities about Salem;* also Poem, by Charles Brooks, anniversary issue, Essex Institute Historical Collections.
57. *Maria Louisa Hawthorne.*

IV

58. Manning Hawthorne.
59. *Some Localities about Salem.*
60. Marianne Silsbee, *A Half Century in Salem.*
61. There is a brief biography of Dr. Benjamin Lynde Oliver in the Essex Institute Historical Collections, Vol. LXVIII, January, 1936. The files of the *Gazette* revealed an occasional item of interest, as did *John Pickering,* by Sarah Orne Pickering, privately printed, Boston, 1887.
62. *Young Longfellow,* by Laurence Thompson; also, *Sergeant Prentiss,* by Dallas Dickey, Louisiana State University Press.
63. *Simon Forrester;* also, Salem *Gazette.*
64. *Some Localities about Salem.*
65. *An Account of Salem Common.*
66. *The Dolliver Romance,* by Nathaniel Hawthorne.
67. *Essex Institutes,* Vol. LXVIII, January, 1932; also the Anniversary Issue of the Historical Collections.
68. *Nathaniel Hawthorne, a Modest Man,* by Edward Mather. New York: Thomas Y. Crowell.
69. The growing schedule of the Manning stage line is given in the advertisements in the *Gazette.*
70. *Hawthorne and His Wife.*
71. *Nathaniel Hawthorne,* by George Woodberry. Boston: Houghton Mifflin, 1902.
72. Manning Hawthorne.
73. *Nathaniel Hawthorne,* by George Woodbury.
74. Elizabeth Hawthorne's recollections, in *Hawthorne and His Wife.*
75. *Our Old Home.*

76. There had been but three public executions since the Revolution, all for murder, and Clark's was the first for the crime of arson. There were reports that a mob would storm the jail and free him. Hawthorne's curious sophistication in such events is indicated by his mentioning to his mother the authorship of newspaper articles on Clark's execution, such things usually being confidential in those days. There is an account of Clark's trial in a pamphlet volume printed in 1821, now in the New York Public Library.
77. *Nathaniel Hawthorne, a Modest Man.*
78. *Hawthorne Prepares for College.*
79. Woodberry.

V

80. Manning Hawthorne.
81. *Old Modes of Travel.*
82. Manning Hawthorne.
83. *Personal Recollections of Nathaniel Hawthorne.*
84. *Franklin Pierce,* by Nathaniel Hawthorne.
85. "Jonathan Cilley," by Nathaniel Hawthorne, *Democratic Review,* September, 1838.
86. *Memoirs of Jeremiah Mason.* See also, Beveridge's *John Marshall,* Fuess's *Daniel Webster.* There is additional material on Mason in *Bench and Bar in New Hampshire.*
87. *Personal Recollections of Nathaniel Hawthorne.*
88. *American Notebooks.*

VI

89. Manning Hawthorne; also *Personal Recollections.*
90. *New England and Her Institutions.* Jacob Abbott, the author, was a recent graduate of Bowdoin. He includes in his book a letter from a Bowdoin freshman who might well have been his brother John Abbott, Hawthorne's classmate.
91. Robert Manning, letter to Mrs. Hawthorne, quoted by Manning Hawthorne.
92. *Memoirs of Jeremiah Mason;* also, *Franklin Pierce.*
93. Hawthorne's letters, quoted by Manning Hawthorne.
94. *Personal Recollections.*
95. *New England and Her Institutions.*
96. Hatch, *History of Bowdoin College.*
97. *The Cleveland and Cleveland Families.*
98. Horatio Bridge; also *Young Longfellow.*
99. Mr. Kenneth Boyer, librarian, Bowdoin College.
100. Jacob Abbott.

101. Manning Hawthorne.
102. Horatio Bridge. I am indebted to Mr. Clifford Shipton, custodian of the archives at Harvard, for providing figures on the comparable costs at Harvard, and for correcting my first estimates of the expenses of a college year in 1821-1825.
103. Manning Hawthorne. It is extremely difficult to gauge the purchasing power of the dollar at the time. A college graduate, beginning as a lawyer or minister, could expect to earn about $500 a year. Board and room was $2.50 to $3.50 a week. Massachusetts Hall at Bowdoin cost $11,000. Webster argued the Dartmouth College Case for $500. Four years at college cost between $500 and $1,000—a carpenter's earnings, at shipbuilding, for a very long period. The following partial list of wholesale prices in Salem as of Oct. 21, 1818, may help clarify the picture of what a college education cost in terms of the cost of commodities: Hams cost 16 ¢ a pound; butter, 15 ¢; cheese, 12 ¢; chocolate, 22 ¢; coffee, 32 ¢; fish, 6 ¢; flour, $10.25 a barrel; molasses, 54 ¢ a gallon; soap, 13 ¢ a pound; brandy, $1.75 a gallon; sugar, 14 ¢ a pound; sherry, 70 ¢ a gallon. In view of these prices, the cost of a college education seemed disproportionately high, and the cost of the disciplinary fines even more so.
104. Autobiographical letter to Stoddard; also, Bridge.
105. *History of Bowdoin.*
106. *New England and Her Institutions.*
107. *Young Longfellow.*
108. *Personal Recollections.*
109. *New England and Her Institutions.*
110. *The Cleveland and Cleveland Families;* also, *History of Bowdoin* and *Memories of Jeremiah Mason.*
111. *Personal Recollections.*
112. Salem *Gazette,* 1818; also, *History of Augusta, Maine.*
113. *Personal Recollections;* also, Hawthorne's dedication of *The Snow Image,* to Bridge.
114. *History of Bowdoin.*
115. *Personal Recollections.* I have taken the liberty of using a few details from Hawthorne's story of college, *Fanshawe,* when they seem plainly applicable to the scenery around Bowdoin.
116. *History of August, Maine,* by James W. North.
117. Rev. William Ellery Channing.
118. *Personal Recollections.*
119. *History of Bowdoin College.*
120. *Personal Recollections.*
121. *Hawthorne's Pot-8-0 Club,* by Harriet Tapley.
122. *Jonathan Cilley,* by Nathaniel Hawthorne.
123. *History of Bowdoin,* Hatch.
124. *Personal Recollections of Nathaniel Hawthorne.*

125. Material from the Bowdoin College Library.
126. *Everyman's Encyclopedia.*
127. Bridge, *Personal Recollections.*
128. Dictionary of American Biography.
129. Hawthorne: *Sketches from Memory.*
130. Dictionary of American Biography; also, *William Pitt Fessenden,* by Francis Fessenden. There is a vivid description of Fessenden and Lincoln in Carl Sandburg's *Abraham Lincoln, the War Years.*
131. Fanshawe.
132. *Hawthorne and His Wife.*
133. Manning Hawthorne.
134. *Raymond Scrapbook.*
135. Material supplied by Mr. Kenneth Boyer, librarian, Bowdoin College.
136. *History of Bowdoin,* Hatch.
137. Hawthorne, letter to Elizabeth, quoted in *Hawthorne and His Wife.*

VII

138. Autobiographical letter to Stoddard, in *Hawthorne and His Wife;* also, Henry James, *Hawthorne.*
139. *Life of Horace Mann,* by Mary Tyler Peabody Mann. Boston: Walker, Fuller and Co., 1865.
140. *Channing,* by C. T. Brooks. Boston: Roberts Brothers, 1880.
141. *Italian Notebooks.*
142. "Thomas Green Fessenden," by Nathaniel Hawthorne. *The American Monthly Magazine,* January, 1838.
143. *Hawthorne and His Wife.*
144. Lathrop, *A Study of Hawthorne.*
145. *A Memoir of Ralph Waldo Emerson,* by James Eliot Cabot. The memories of Jeremiah Mason at Yale, Webster at Dartmouth, Channing and Story at Harvard, Hawthorne's recollections of Franklin Pierce at Bowdoin, Thompson's, *Young Longfellow,* and contemporary accounts such as Jacob Abbott's, are sources for a picture of college life which seems, when considered as a whole, so unpleasant that one wonders why it did not evoke more public discussion and criticism.
146. *Dictionary of American Biography;* also, Jesse Appleton, *The Immensity of God,* in the New York Public Library.
147. Librarian, Bowdoin College.
148. *Personal Recollections.*
149. *Young Longfellow.*
150. *Ship Registers;* also Ship News, Salem *Gazette.*
151. *Hawthorne and His Wife.*
152. Manning Hawthorne.
153. *The Manning Families.*

154. *Personal Recollections.*
155. *Love Letters.*
156. *Life of Franklin Pierce,* by Nathaniel Hawthorne. It is interesting to note that another biography of Pierce, by Bartlett, was published during the campaign of 1852. It is in many respects superior to Hawthorne's cool and detached study—by no means so well written or so carefully polished, but containing a good deal of information that Hawthorne either did not have or considered unnecessary. Hawthorne did not mention such enlightening incidents as Pierce's quarrel with Allen, or his early speeches in Congress, including his opposition to West Point as it was then organized, or the many instances of almost intermittent purpose, as if Pierce almost willfully abandoned his struggles at the very point of victory. They serve to make him a more human and likable character, and far more understandable as a politician.
157. *Life of Franklin Pierce.*
158. *Personal Recollections.*
159. *Franklin Pierce.*
160. *Pierce;* also, *Fanshawe.*
161. *American Notebooks;* Hawthorne's entry on Williams College.
162. *Personal Recollections.*
163. *Young Longfellow;* also, *Personal Recollections.*

VIII

164. Elizabeth Hawthorne, in *Hawthorne and His Wife;* also, *The Devil in Manuscript* and *Alice Doane's Appeal.*

IX

165. I have taken minor liberties with *Alice Doane's Appeal,* as with other of Hawthorne's stories whose outlines are essential to his biography, not, certainly, with the feeling that they are thereby improved, but in order to abbreviate them and bring them within the scope of the narrative. In *Alice Doane's Appeal* I have placed the events in chronological order, and tried to restore it as it was, according to Hawthorne's own description, before he added the scenes in which he read the story aloud to two Salem girls.

CHAPTER THREE

I

1. *Memories of Hawthorne,* by Rose Hawthorne Lathrop. Boston: Houghton Mifflin, 1897.
2. *Hawthorne and His Wife.*

3. *Personal Recollections.*
4. *Hawthorne and His Wife.*
5. The archives of the Salem Athenaeum are stored in the Essex Institute.
6. Elizabeth Hawthorne, in *Hawthorne and His Wife.*
7. *American Notebooks* (Mrs. Hawthorne's edition); also, *Some Localities about Salem.*
8. *Alice Doane's Appeal.*
9. Map of Salem Harbor: Maine Historical Society.
10. *Footsteps on the Seashore.*
11. *The Haunted Mind.*
12. Introduction to *The Scarlet Letter.*
13. *Footsteps on the Seashore.*
14. *American Notebooks* (Julian Hawthorne edition).
15. *Hawthorne and His Wife.*
16. Manning Hawthorne, review of *A Modest Man;* also *Maria Louisa Hawthorne,* and *Address before the Essex Bar Association,* by William D. Northand (Salem, 1885).
17. *Night Sketches Beneath an Umbrella.*
18. *The Toll-Gatherer's Day.*
19. *Books Read by Nathaniel Hawthorne.*
20. *Old News.*

II

21. *Hawthorne and His Wife;* also *Hawthorne, a Modest Man.*
22. Elizabeth Hawthorne's recollections, in *Hawthorne and His Wife.*
23. Introduction to *Fanshawe* (Old Manse edition), by H. E. Scudder.
24. *Ship Registers.*
25. *Memoirs of Jeremiah Mason.*

III

26. *Love Letters.*
27. *Brook Farm,* by Lindsay Swift.
28. A number of Hawthorne's stories and sketches, not included in his own collections of his works, and not claimed by him, have been tentatively identified (by Donald Clifford Gallup; see Bibliography). The *New England Quarterly* has reprinted the following list of stories in the *Gazette*: "The Battle Omen" (Tuesday, Nov. 2, 1830); "The Hollow of the Three Hills" (Friday, Nov. 12, 1830; "Sir William Phipps" (Tuesday, Nov. 23, 1830); "An Old Woman's Tale" (Dec. 21, 1830); "Dr. Bullivant" (Jan. 11, 1831). Except for "The Battle Omen," these stories are all generally attributed to Hawthorne, though he reprinted only "The Hollow of the Three Hills." It is interesting to note that they were all published at the time of the executions for the White murder, in the period between the executions of the two Knapp brothers.

29. *Memories of Hawthorne.*
30. *Love Letters.*
31. Elizabeth Peabody's recollections, in *Hawthorne and His Wife.*
32. *Hawthorne and His Friends,* by B. F. Sanborn.
33. *Recollections of a Lifetime,* by Samuel Griswold Goodrich.

IV

34. *Caleb and Mary Wilder Foote.*
35. *Recollections of a Lifetime.* Also, *Hawthorne and His Wife,* and Woodberry's *Nathaniel Hawthorne.*
36. Introduction to *Twice-Told Tales.*
37. Woodberry, *Nathaniel Hawthorne.*
38. Dictionary of American Biography.
39. Woodberry, *Nathaniel Hawthorne.*

V

40. *Some Localities about Salem.* Also, *Ship Registers.*
41. *English Notebooks.*
42. *American Notebooks* (Mrs. Hawthorne's edition); also, *Love Letters,* and *Memories of Hawthorne.*
43. This partial list of the careers of Hawthorne's schoolmate has been pieced together from *Personal Recollections,* the *History of Bowdoin College,* the Encyclopedia *Americana,* the Dictionary of American Biography, and scattered reference volumes used in preparing this biography.
44. *Hawthorne and His Wife.*
45. *History of Augusta, Maine.*
46. *American Notebooks.*
47. *Memoirs and Services of Three Generations of the Cilley Family.* Also, Hawthorne's *Jonathan Cilley.*
48. *Young Longfellow.*
49. "Nathaniel Hawthorne and the Museum of the East India Marine Society," Charles E. Goodspeed, *American Neptune,* Vol. V, October, 1945.
50. "Hawthorne in the Boston Custom House," Edwin T. Jepson, *Bookman* (Hawthorne anniversary issue), 1904.
51. *Life of Franklin Pierce;* Dictionary of American Biography; the Pittsfield *Sun,* May 23, 1851.
52. *The Trial of Joseph Francis Knapp;* also, *Salem and the Indies,* by James Duncan Phillips. Boston: Houghton Mifflin, 1947.
53. *Some Localities about Salem.*
54. *Ship Registers;* also, *Reminiscences of Salem,* by Mrs. Harriet S. Terry. Essex Institute Historical Collections, January, 1948.
55. *Trial of Joseph Knapp;* also, *Ship Registers* and *Annals of Salem.*
56. *Trial of Joseph Knapp.*

57. *Life and Literature Fifty Years Ago*, by Horace William Shaler Cleveland.
58. *Danield Webster; Caleb and Mary Wilder Foote; Annals of Salem; Trial of John Francis Knapp.*

VI

59. *Sketches from Memory*, by Nathaniel Hawthorne.

VII

60. *Nathaniel Hawthorne*, Woodberry.
61. *The Age of Jackson*, Arthur Schlesinger.
62. *Seargent Prentiss* and *Caleb and Mary Wilder Foote.*
63. *Hawthorne, Critic of Society*, by Lawrence Hall.

VIII

64. There is a brief account of Upham's life, in the memoir of his son, in the Essex Institute Historical Collections, June, 1920.
65. *Caleb and Mary Wilder Foote.*
66. *George Ripley.*
67. *Caleb and Mary Wilder Foote.*
68. Hawthorne's letter to his aunt, in *Hawthorne and His Wife.* For a good example of Upham's ability, see his *Life of Sir Harry Vane* in Jared Sparks, *Library of American Biography.*
69. *Daniel Webster.*
70. *Maria Louisa Hawthorne.*
71. *The Age of Jackson;* also, *Memoirs of Jeremiah Mason.*
72. *Maria Louisa Hawthorne.*
73. *History of Canterbury, New Hampshire.*
74. Encyclopedia *Americana.*
75. *Maria Louisa Hawthorne.*
76. Elizabeth Hawthorne's recollections, in *Hawthorne and His Wife.* I have accepted *The Village Uncle* as autobiographical, following her comment, since I have found in other passages that her observations about her brother, made in her old age, prove on research to have a deeper significance than would seem possible.
77. *The Village Uncle.*
78. *The House of the Seven Gables.*
79. *The Village Uncle.*
80. Elizabeth Hawthorne's recollections.
81. *American Notebooks* (Mrs. Hawthorne's editions.).

CHAPTER FOUR

I

1. *Hawthorne as Editor,* by Arlin Turner.
2. *Thomas Green Fessenden,* by Nathaniel Hawthorne.
3. Dictionary of American Biography.
4. *Thomas Green Fessenden.*
5. Dictionary of American Biography.
6. *Hawthorne as Editor.*
7. *Hawthorne as Editor;* also the files of *The American Magazine of Useful and Entertaining Knowledge.*
8. *Thomas Green Fessenden.*
9. *Hawthorne as Editor.*

II

10. *Thomas Green Fessenden.*

III

11. The material in this section is taken from the files of the *American Magazine,* and from Turner's *Hawthorne as Editor.* In view of Hawthorne's life-long interest in Dr. Harris—see *The Ghost of Dr. Harris* and *The American Notebook*—his quotations from Leonard Withington are of interest, for Withington was the author of a satirical portrait of Harris.
12. *Old Modes of Travel.*

IV

13. *Hawthorne and His Wife.*
14. *Hawthorne as Editor.*
15. *The American Magazine of Useful and Entertaining Knowledge.*
16. *Hawthorne as Editor.*
17. *Hawthorne and His Wife.*
18. *Thomas Green Fessenden.*
19. *Hawthorne as Editor.*
20. Woodberry, *Nathaniel Hawthorne.*

V

21. *Hawthorne and His Wife.*
22. *Hawthorne and His Wife.*
23. *American Notebooks.*
24. *History of Augusta, Maine.*

25. *Personal Recollections;* also *Hawthorne and His Wife.*
26. *History of Augusta.*
27. *Personal Recollections;* also *Hawthorne and His Wife.*
28. Salem *Gazette. The Age of Jackson* and Fuess's *Daniel Webster* contain good account of the crisis.
29. *History of Augusta.*
30. Goodrich, *Recollections of a Lifetime.*
31. *Hawthorne and His Wife.*
32. *History of Augusta.*
33. *Hawthorne and His Wife.*
34. *History of Augusta.*
35. Salem *Gazette.*
36. *Hawthorne and His Wife.*
37. Introduction, *Twice-Told Tales.*
38. *Memoirs of Jeremiah Mason.*
39. *Personal Recollections.*

The story of the Wilkes Exploring Expedition is briefly told in the biography of Charles Wilkes, included in *Sea Dogs of the Sixties,* by Jim Dan Hill. The Wilkes expedition seems to have been a success up to the very time Wilkes's 19-volume account of it appeared. Charles Wilkes was a methodical, conscientious officer, former superintendent of charts and instruments in the Navy Department at Washington, who more than anything else needed a writer of Hawthorne's ability to rescue his exploits from his own accounts of them. He led his little squadron into an early paradise in the South Sea Island, like those which Melville wrote about in *Typee,* where the native girls swam for miles to meet the ships, and climbed aboard, plaiting their dark wet hair, anointing their bodies with fragrant oil which they carried in little shells, and then reclined on the boats as they gave themselves to the sailors. The superintendent of charts and instruments had no equipment for recording such a phenomenon. The record of the expedition that Hawthorne did not write was written by the chaplain, Stewart, whose works were used by Melville when he came to write his South Sea romances.

It is interesting to speculate on what Hawthorne would have made of the cruise. The Wilkes expedition sailed to the Fijis, to the Northwest Coast of North America, to the Antarctic, and Australia. Wilkes was court-martialed for having given the commander of the British a chart of the Antarctic he had explored. The charge was more or less a technicality; the two commanders exchanged information to facilitate their work. But Wilkes's orders specifically stated in one minor clause that none of the findings of the expedition were to be revealed until the squadron returned. Wilkes was cleared. He was the officer who, during the Civil War, seized the Confederate commissioners, Mason and

Slidell, from the British steamer *Trent,* very nearly bringing Great Britain into the war on the side of the Confederacy.

The loss of Hawthorne's opportunity to make the voyage rankled all his life. See his comments, in the *English Notebooks,* on his talks with Captain Walter Gibson, an adventurer who had lived in the East Indies and been imprisoned by the Dutch. When he came to know Melville he could listen by the hour to Melville's tales of the islands.

Soon after the failure of the *American Magazine* Hawthorne was in Salem. He wrote to his sister Louisa that the blockheads on the *Gazette,* in their eagerness to praise him, had actually praised his successor, Alden Bradford. I looked up this issue of the *Gazette,* and found it, in view of Hawthorne's relations with Foote, very interesting. The article in question is a favorable notice of the most recent issue of the *American Magazine.* It consists in part of a long quotation on education, unsigned, the sense of which is that the specialized knowledge of the self-taught individual, the farmer or mechanic, is equal in his own field to the specialized learning of the college graduate. Its thought is bold and the prose is truly remarkable. But what probably interested Hawthorne more in this issue of the *Gazette* was that it also included the personnel of the exploring expedition which was announced for the first time, with Hawthorne's name conspicuously absent.

To make the disappointment greater, the *Gazette* repeated that it had learned that in addition to the official list a Salem youth was to be included. This was Horatio Hale, who was to be the expedition's philologist. Hale was a protégé of John Pickering's. *The Life of John Pickering* contains a number of interesting letters on Hale's appointment. Hale sailed on the *Peacock* from Hampton Roads in August, 1838. On April 15, 1839, he wrote to Pickering from Valparaiso that "we have been far less fortunate than we anticipated." His health was so bad he doubted that he would be able to continue the cruise. On November 28, 1840, he wrote again to Pickering, from Honolulu, on the eve of setting out for the Northwest Coast. Restrictions "against transmitting to the United States any account of the proceedings of the squadron" prevented his going into detail. Hale's report was finished in 1844. It could not be printed immediately because the narrative of the voyage was to appear first, and Hale left the details of its printing in competent hands and went to Europe.

40. *Daniel Webster.*
41. *History of Augusta.*
42. *American Notebooks,* Nathaniel Hawthorne.
43. *Hawthorne and His Wife.*

VI

44. *American Notebooks.*
45. Encyclopedia *Americana.*
46. "The Sister Years," by Nathaniel Hawthorne, published in the Salem *Gazette,* Jan. 1, 1838, reprinted in the later editions of *Twice-Told Tales.* Each New Year's Day the Salem *Gazette* published a review of the past year and a forecast of the next, as a supplement, which the newsboys sold to the subscribers, the newsboys receiving all the money taken in.
47. Hawthorne, *American Notebooks.*

VII

48. *Hawthorne,* by Moncure D. Conway.
49. *Jonathan Cilley,* by Nathaniel Hawthorne.
50. *Maine Sources in the House of the Seven Gables,* by Thomas Morgan Griffiths. Waterville, Me., 1945.
51. *American Notebooks.*
52. I am indebted to Lieutenant Charles Mixer, librarian of the United States Naval Academy at Annapolis, and Louis H. Bolander, associate librarian, for the service records of Captain Percival and Commander Downes and Captain Scott. There is an excellent brief sketch of Percival in the Dictionary of American Biography.
53. *American Notebooks.*
54. Dictionary of American Biography.
55. *American Notebooks.*

VIII

56. *History of Augusta.*

IX

57. *Thomas Green Fessenden.*
58. Directory of the Twenty-fifth Congress. I am indebted to Mrs. Clare Boothe Luce, then congresswoman from Connecticut, for securing for me the directory, as well as photostatic copies of the Report of the Committee of Inquiry on the Graves-Cilley Duel.
59. *Seargent Prentiss,* by Dallas Dickey. Louisiana State University Press.
60. *Memoirs and Services of the Cilley Family.*
61. Carl Sandburg, *Abraham Lincoln, the War Years.*
62. Dictionary of American Biography.
63. *The Age of Jackson.*
64. *Memoirs and Services of the Cilley Family.*

65. Report of the Committee of Inquiry on the Late Duel.
I have condensed the report somewhat, without making any changes of sense or, I believe, of emphasis. It is difficult to exaggerate the quality of writing and thought in this document. I know of no official document so dramatically written. The present account is taken almost entirely from it, with minor additions from *Memoirs and Services of the Cilley Family*.
The author of the report is not identified in it. Mr. Robert C. Gooch, chief of the General References and Bibliography Division of the Library of Congress, and Dr. C. Percy Powell of the Division of Manuscripts, have tried to determine which member of the Committee of Inquiry might be the author. Mr. Gooch's analysis is as follows:
"The Select Committee of the House of Representatives, appointed to investigate the causes which led to the death of the Hon. Jonathan Cilley consisted of seven members: Isaac Toucey of Connecticut, Democrat, chairman; William W. Potter of Pennsylvania, Democrat; George Grennell, Jr., of Massachusetts, probably a Whig; Franklin H. Elmore of South Carolina, a States Rights Democrat; Seaton Grantland of Georgia, probably a Whig; and James Rariden of Indiana, Whig. . . . Concerning the authorship of the report which this committee submitted on April 21, 1838, we may eliminate Messrs. Grennell and Rariden, since they submitted a minority report, and Mr. Elmore, who formulated his views in a third report. Nor is Mr. Potter likely to have been much concerned in drafting the report, since he was absent from the last six meetings of the committee between April 14 and April 21. We have found no evidence which would bear upon the respective shares of the remaining three members. . . . The original papers of the committee in the Papers of the House of Representatives . . . include no drafts of the report itself. Isaac Toucey . . . was active both in the Committee of which he was chairman, and in defending its report on the floor of the House, and it seems a reasonable assumption that his was the major share, at least, in its composition."
66. *Personal Recollections*.
67. *Report of the Cilley-Graves Duel*.
68. Research by Miss Shirley Larson, New York Public Library.
69. *Report of the Cilley-Graves Duel*.
70. Research by Miss Ella Gilchrist, librarian, Thomaston, Me.
71. *Jonathan Cilley*, by Nathaniel Hawthorne.
72. *Report of the Cilley-Graves Duel*.
73. *Memoirs and Services*.
74. *Report of the Cilley-Graves Duel*.

X

75. *American Notebooks* (Randall Stewart edition).
76. Elizabeth Peabody, in *Hawthorne and His Wife*.
77. *Memoirs and Services of the Cilley Family*.
78. *American Notebooks* (Randall Stewart edition).
79. Charles Sumner, in *Young Longfellow*.
80. *Memories of Hawthorne*.
81. *Nathaniel Hawthorne, A Modest Man*.
82. *Hawthorne and His Wife;* also *A Memoir of Ralph Waldo Emerson* and *The Flowering of New England*.
83. *A Modest Man*.
84. *Hawthorne and His Wife*.
85. *Hawthorne and His Wife*.

XI

86. *Memories of Hawthorne*.
87. *The Peabody Family;* also, Dictionary of American Biography.
88. *Some Localities about Salem*.
89. Elizabeth Peabody, in *Hawthorne and His Wife*.
90. *Hawthorne and His Wife*.
91. Sophia Peabody's diary, in *Hawthorne and His Wife*. The excerpts are undated. The account of her movements is admittedly speculative, there seeming to be no way to get at the time in Elizabeth Peabody's recollections of her sister.
92. Elizabeth Peabody, in *Hawthorne and His Wife;* also, Henry Tuckerman, *Book of the Arts*. New York: Putman, 1867.
93. Dictionary of American Biography.
94. *The Harvard Medical School*, by Thomas Harrington. New York: Lewis Publishing Co., 1905; also, the *New England Register*, Vol. 49.
95. Mrs. Peabody's letters to Sophia, in *Hawthorne and His Wife*.
96. Letters from Cuba to Mary White, in the Rosary Hills Home; also, letter to Mrs. Mary White Foote, from Concord, in *Memories of Hawthorne*.
97. Diary, in *Hawthorne and His Wife*.
98. Proceedings of the Massachusetts Historical Society, XIX.
99. Sophia Peabody diary, undated, in *Hawthorne and His Wife*.
100. Elizabeth Peabody's recollections, in *Hawthorne and His Wife*.
101. Sophia Peabody to Mary White, letter to the Rosary Hills House.
102. Dictionary of American Biography.

XII

103. Sophia Peabody kept her diary in the form of letters to her family, making an entry each day, usually a page or more, and sending the collected days every fortnight or so, occasionally making little drawings and decorations on the margins of the pages. Her family in Salem bound the letters in book form, and they were read by her friends and passed from hand to hand. They were originally two volumes of the Cuban diary. Julian Hawthorne, when he wrote *Hawthorne and His Wife,* referred to them and drew on them briefly, but expressed the belief that they should be published as a separate book. He quoted from only the first volume, which describes the voyage.

In trying to straighten out the chronological record of Sophia Peabody's life, I ran across letters from her written in Salem bearing dates which, if Elizabeth Peabody's account was correct, could not have been written by her, for she was then supposedly in Cuba. I was unable to locate either of her Cuban diaries, to settle the point, until Mr. Van Wyck Brooks, through the kindness of Mr. Theodore Maynard, learned that there were a number of Mrs. Hawthorne's letters in the Rosary Hill Home at Hawthorne, N. Y. Mr. Maynard was writing a biography of Rose Hawthorne, Hawthorne's youngest daughter, the founder of the Home.

Rosary Hills Home is a hospital for cancer incurables. Rose Hawthorne married George Lathrop, one-time editor of the *Atlantic Monthly.* Their only child died at the age of five years. After she joined the Catholic Church, Mrs. Lathrop established, in the lower East Side of New York, the first of her hospitals, taking into her tenement apartment people who were dying of cancer, and caring for them. She became Sister Mary Alphonsa, and a special order was created for her, and a number of hospitals have been built, under the care of members of the order. The patients are those for whom medical science can offer no hope of recovery, and it is a condition for admission that they have no means of support. The hospital at Hawthorne stands on a high hill above the village, a group of new buildings, immaculate, and set back above rolling landscaped groups, the atmosphere about them cheerful and quiet and peaceful, except for the poignant thought that must impress every visitor that the patients upon entering know that they have no hope of leaving, and that their very presence there is an admission that their cases are considered hopeless.

The custodian of Sophia Hawthorne's letters and diaries is Sister Mary Josefa, who generously permitted me to read them, and to whom I am indebted for many acts of kindness as I worked over them on the long summer afternoons in the hospital. Only the second volume of Sophia Peabody's Cuban diary is at Rosary Hills, but fortunately Sophia wrote a series of letters to Mary White covering the same period, and these came into the possession of Rose Hawthorne. There are also a number of letters from Sophia, after her marriage, to Elizabeth Peabody, and another diary written while she was in England. The letters, especially the early ones, are delightful. After Hawthorne became famous, and Mrs. Hawthorne was conscious of his position, she wrote more guardedly, and there is a stiffness and social awareness that make her later letters seem affected to other generations; but her early writing is spontaneous and fresh, her comments keen, and her brief characterizations very acute. Her letters challenge comparison with those of Mary Wilder White from Guadeloupe a generation before her, though her interests were predominantly artistic and social, while Mary Wilder White's were military—of necessity—and religious.

104. I am indebted to Señores Reinaldo Fernandez Rebull, consul general for Cuba at New York, and Rafael P. Gonzalez Muñoz, undersecretary of state of Cuba, for directing my inquiries as to the region where Sophia Peabody lived to Señor Tomas de Justiz, of the Academia de la Historia de Cuba.

Señor Tomas de Justiz made his research into the region the subject of a paper addressed to the academy. It is so beautifully phrased that it can be summarized only with difficulty. He says that the questions excite a true curiosity because they refer to an epoch filled, like thick-piney woods, with legends and traditions, to a region of which few maps remain, and to an ancient hidalgo society of great kindness and charm, of which only limited documents are now in existence. Details in Sophia Peabody's letters, inadvertent to those who have not dedicated themselves to study of the subject, permitted, however, perfectly clear and concise conclusions. The principal interest of Señor Tomas de Justiz's paper is in its identification of the families that Sophia and Mary Peabody visited. "The members of the Morrel family, well known in Cuba, distinguished and of Spanish origin, were obliged to leave Santo Domingo (in the revolution of Toussaint L'Ouverture) establishing themselves in the region that today bears their name; where they built a hacienda and probably a mill or factory, some two leagues northeast of Salvador. The coffee plantation, Recompensa, was much more to the north, some sixteen kilometers from Morrell, southwest of San Luis, and six leagues from the mouth of the San Luis River. . . . The family of Don Juan de Zayas was one of the richest and most cultured. . . . Their ancient hacienda was located between the Bacunagua and Los Palacios Rivers, in a section remembered not only for its past of riches but also for its cultured and distinguished population, the great center Francia, so called because the French who had escaped from Haiti lived there a number of years. . . . History preserves some names, and among these appears Señor Manuel de Zayas, a companion of Narciso Lopez, perhaps a harbor pilot, who disappeared after the disaster to that general, to reappear, second in command to Carlos Manuel de Cespedes, later taken prisoner and shot in August of 1875."

XIII

105. Cuban diary, Saturday, Aug. 2, 1834.
106. Letter from Horace William Shaler Cleveland, quoted by Sophia Peabody.
107. Rose Lathrop says, in *Memories of Hawthorne*, that the story Hawthorne wrote for Sophia was probably *Edward Randolph's Portrait*. In view of the Cuban diaries, there seems to be no question of it.
108. *Edward Randolph's Portrait*.

XIV

109. Cuban diary, Aug. 24, 1834, *et seq.*
110. Señor Tomas de Justiz.

XV

111. *Memories of Hawthorne.*
112. *Hawthorne and His Wife.*
113. *Memories of Hawthorne.*
114. *A Half Century in Salem.*
115. *Memories of Hawthorne.*
116. *A Half Century in Salem.*
117. *Caleb and Mary Wilder Foote.*
118. *Caleb and Mary Wilder Foote.*
119. *Memories of Hawthorne.*
120. *A Half Century in Salem.*
121. *Life of Alexander Wilson,* by William B. O. Peabody. Boston: Hilliard, Gray and Company, 1839.

CHAPTER FIVE

I

1. *History of Pittsfield, Massachusetts,* by J. E. A. Smith. Research by Miss Ruth Wittan, Berkshire Athenaeum.
2. *Memories of Hawthorne.* The letters of Sophia Peabody on the eve of Hawthorne's departure for western Massachusetts are undated and are not complete. Part are printed in *Hawthorne and His Wife*, part in *Memories of Hawthorne*, part in Mrs. Hawthorne's edition of the *American Notebooks*. Some study is required to join them together. The explosion of the powder magazine in Pittsfield had occurred a few days before.

3. *American Notebooks.*
4. *History of Pittsfield.*

II

5. *American Notebooks.*
6. *History of Berkshire County.*
7. *American Notebooks.*

III

8. *American Notebooks.*
9. *The Haunted Mind.*
10. *The Dolliver Romance.*
11. *The Haunted Mind.*
12. *The Wives of the Dead.*

IV

13. *American Notebooks.*
14. *The Amateur Spirit; Hawthorne in North Adams,* by Bliss Perry.
15. *American Notebooks.*
16. *American Notebooks.*

V

17. *Hawthorne in North Adams.*
18. Oliver Wendell Holmes in *Memories of Hawthorne.*
19. *Our Old Home.*

VI

20. *Memories of Hawthorne.*
21. "Hawthorne in the Boston Custom House."
22. *Seargent Prentiss,* by Dallas Dickey.
23. Hawthorne to Sophia, April 18, 1839.
24. *Hawthorne and His Wife.*
25. *Hawthorne in the Boston Custom House.*
26. Hawthorne to Sophia, March 11, 1840.
27. *Memories of Hawthorne.*
28. *American Notebooks.*
29. *Memories of Hawthorne.*
30. *Documentary History of the Salem Custom House,* by Davis Little. The story is told by Little, quoting Augustus Smith, that during the Civil War, before Hawthorne's death, Pike met with Pierce, Hawthorne, Burchmore, Dr. George Loring, Daniel Lord, Samuel Fuller, Nicholas Bovey, Lewis Jocelyn, Ed. Peabody, and other Democrats in Pike's farmhouse. A lad named Tommy Watson was present when Hawthorne and Pierce rode up from the depot. He was not wanted at

the reception, so Pike sent him on a rush order to the corner for matches. When he returned, the reception was over. Pike said, "Now, Tommy, I will pay you." "No matter now, Mr. Pike," said Tommy. "It will be just as well in the morning." "Yes," said Pike, "but I may be dead in the morning." "Oh, well, never mind," said Tommy. "It would not be much loss." When the laughter subsided, Pierce turned to Pike and said, "That is pretty serious joking, 'Squire." Pike finished his memoirs in 1876, but his health failed while he was copying them for the printer, and the manuscript was lost, reportedly burned.

31. *Hawthorne and His Wife.*
32. Hawthorne to Sophia Peabody, March 6, 1839.
33. Hawthorne to Sophia Peabody, March 7, 1839.
34. Hawthorne to Sophia Peabody, April 2, 1839.
35. Hawthorne to Sophia Peabody, April 4, 1839, 9:30 P.M.
36. Sophia to Mary Foote, April 22, 1842.
37. *American Notebooks.*
38. *Love Letters,* Jan. 24, 1840.
39. Hawthorne to Sophia Peabody, April 18, 1839.
40. Hawthorne to Sophia Peabody, April 30, 1839.
41. Hawthorne to Sophia Peabody, May 3, 1839.
42. *Edward Sturgis and His Descendants,* Roger F. Sturgis.
43. *Memories of Hawthorne*: Ellen Hooper to Sophia Hawthorne.
44. *Memories of Hawthorne*: Sophia Peabody to Elizabeth Peabody, May 19, 1839.
45. *Pedlar's Progress; The Life of Bronson Alcott,* Odell Shepard.
46. Elizabeth to Sophie Peabody: June 23, 1839, in *Memories of Hawthorne.*
47. Sophia to Elizabeth: June 29, 1839, in *Memories of Hawthorne.*
48. Hawthorne to Sophia: May 26, 1839, in *Hawthorne and His Wife.*
49. *Love Letters,* Oct. 10, 1839.

VII

50. David B. Hall, *The Halls of New England.* Albany: Munsell, 1883.
51. *George Bancroft.*
52. Hawthorne to Sophia, Aug. 8, 1839.
53. *Memories of Hawthorne*: Sept. 9, 1839; also Sept. 23, 1839.
54. Hawthorne to Sophia, Aug. 9, 1839.
55. Hawthorne to Sophia, Oct. 11, 1839.
56. Hawthorne to Sophia, Aug. 21 and Aug. 25, 1839.
57. Hawthorne to Sophia, Oct. 3, 1839.
58. *Memoir of George Hillard,* by Palfrey; also, *Young Longfellow,* William Wetmore Story, and Dictionary of American Biography.
59. *Love Letters,* Nov. 17, 1839.
60. *Love Letters,* April 6, 1839.

61. *Franklin Pierce.*
62. *Love Letters,* Nov. 21, 1839.
63. *Love Letters,* Nov. 19 and 20, 1839.
64. *Love Letters,* Nov. 25, 1839.
65. *Love Letters,* March 15, 1840.
66. *Love Letters,* Dec. 1, 1839.
67. *Love Letters,* April 3, 1840.
68. *Love Letters,* April 21, 1840.

VIII

69. Elizabeth Peabody to Elizabeth Hawthorne, in *Hawthorne and His Wife.* Undated, but apparently written, from internal evidence, on March 1, 1838.
70. *Our Old Home.*
71. *Grandfather's Chair, a History for Youth,* by Nathaniel Hawthorne. Boston: E. P. Peabody, 1841.
   There were originally three small books, *Grandfather's Chair,* Nov. 1840. *Famous Old People,* Dec. 30, 1840; and *Liberty Tree,* Feb. 27, 1841. A fourth, *Biographical Stories for Children,* included additional stories, and was published in 1842 by Tappan and Dennett in Boston. Part One—*Grandfather's Chair*—includes the stories of The Lady Arabella, The Red Cross, Roger Williams, The Pine Tree Shillings, The Quakers, The Indian Bible, Governor Broadstreet, and Captain Phipps and the Sunken Treasure of Porto de la Plata. Part Two —*Famous Old People*—told of Master Ezekial Cheever and the Old Fashioned School, Cotton Mather and the Small Pox, Governor Shirley and the Siege of Louisberg; The Acadian Exiles, The Siege of Quebec, Thomas Hutchinson and the History of Massachusetts. Part Three— The Liberty Tree—tells of the Stamp Act, the Hutchinson Mob, the Boston Massacre, the Battle of Lexington, the Siege of Boston, the Tory's Farewell, Grandfather's Dream. Part Four—*Biographical Stories for Children*—included Benjamin West, Sir Isaac Newton, Samuel Johnson, Oliver Cromwell, Benjamin Franklin, and Queen Christina of Sweden.
72. *Love Letters,* May 19, 1840.
73. Mary White to Sophia Peabody, April 23, 1842, in *Caleb and Mary Wilder Foote.*
74. Hawthorne to Sophia, in *Hawthorne and His Wife.*

IX

75. *The Blithedale Romance.* Hawthorne was at pains in his introduction to the novel to state that the characters were not modeled on the Brook Farmers, but he did not deny that he had pictured himself in Cover-

dale, and it is true in fact, as in the novel, that he arrived at the farm during a snowstorm.

76. *Brook Farm,* by Lindsay Swift.
77. *Caleb and Mary Wilder Foote.*
78. *Brook Farm.*
79. *George Ripley,* by O. B. Frothingham.
80. *Brook Farm.*
81. *The Blithedale Romance.*
82. *Brook Farm.*
83. *Brook Farm:* see also, *The Flowering of New England.*
84. Dictionary of American Biography; also *Brook Farm* and *George Ripley.*
85. *American Notebooks.*
86. *The Blithedale Romance.*
87. *Brook Farm.*
88. *The Blithedale Romance.*
89. *George Ripley.* See also, *Hawthorne's Suit against Ripley and Dana.*
90. *The Blithedale Romance.*
91. *Brook Farm.*
92. *George Ripley.*
93. *Brook Farm.*
94. *George Ripley.*
95. *Brook Farm.*
96. *The Blithedale Romance.*
97. Mary Wilder Foote, March 2, 1842.
98. *Love Letters.*
99. *Brook Farm.*
100. *American Notebooks.*
101. *Brook Farm.*
102. *American Notebooks.*
103. *Brook Farm.*
104. *Love Letters.*
105. *George Ripley.*
106. *Brook Farm;* also, *Hawthorne's Suit against Dana and Ripley.*
107. *American Notebooks.*
108. *George Ripley.*
109. Dictionary of American Biography; also, *Memories of Many Men and Some Women,* by Maunsell B. Field. Being Personal Recollections of Emperors, Kings, Queens, Princes, Presidents, Statesmen, Authors, and Artists at Home and Abroad. During the Last Thirty Years (New York: Harpers, 1874). Field's book is not altogether reliable, but it is valuable for its cynical view of events too often treated with greater solemnity than they deserve; and in its bland parody of the ponderous memoirs and autobiographies of the time is highly amusing reading. Many of the members of royalty Field glimpsed as they passed by in a

crowd; many of the statesmen were newly elected officials who exercised great ingenuity to avoid giving him a job. Field was secretary of the Legation in Paris. He was a friend of George N. Saunders, who was an agent of the Colt Firearms Company, selling revolvers to Napoleon III. Field's recollection of Hawthorne was that when Hawthorne saw him coming he jumped over a fence and ran away.

110. Mary Wilder Foote.
111. *From Brook Farm to Cedar Mountain,* by Major George Gordon. Boston: James R. Osgood, 1883.

X

112. *Hawthorne and His Wife.*
113. Randall Stewart's notes in the *American Notebooks.*
114. *American Notebooks,* July 29, 1849.
115. *Love Letters,* June 12 and Aug. 18, 1841.
116. *Hawthorne and His Wife;* Louisa Hawthorne to Nathaniel, May 10, June 11, and Aug. 3, 1841.
117. *Love Letters,* Sept. 3, 1841; Jan. 27, 1841.
118. Mary Wilder Foote to Sophia Peabody: April 23, 1842.
119. *Love Letters,* Sept. 3, 1841.
120. *Memories of Hawthorne.* Sophia Hawthorne to her mother, undated extracts from a diary kept at Concord.
121. *Hawthorne and His Wife.*
122. *Memories of Hawthorne.*
123. *Mosses from an Old Manse.*
124. *Mary Wilder White.*
125. *Hawthorne and His Friends.*
126. *Hawthorne, a Modest Man.*
127. *Mosses from an Old Manse.*
128. *Love Letters.*
129. *Hawthorne and His Wife.*
130. *Mosses from an Old Manse.*

CHAPTER SIX

I

1. *A Memoir of Ralph Waldo Emerson.*
2. *American Notebooks.*
3. *Channing.*
4. *Mosses from an Old Manse.*
5. *Concord: Historic, Literary and Picturesque.*
6. *Mosses from an Old Manse.*
7. *American Notebooks.*

II

8. *Memories of Hawthorne.*
9. *American Notebooks.*

III

10. *A Memoir of Ralph Waldo Emerson.*
11. *Horace Mann.*
12. *A Memoir of Ralph Waldo Emerson.*
13. *Sarah Ripley*, by Elizabeth Hoar.
14. *A Memoir of Ralph Waldo Emerson.*
15. *Hawthorne, a Modest Man;* and *Margaret Fuller, Whetstone of Genius*, by Mason Wade.
16. *American Notebooks.*
17. *American Notebooks;* also, *Concord: Historic, Literary and Picturesque;* and *Brook Farm.*
18. *Mary Wilder White.*
19. *American Notebooks.*

IV

20. *Hawthorne and His Wife.*
21. *American Notebooks;* also *Mosses from an Old Manse* and *Concord.*
22. *Margaret Fuller.*
23. *Memories of Hawthorne.*

V

24. *A Memoir of Ralph Waldo Emerson.*
25. *American Notebooks.*
26. *A Memoir of Ralph Waldo Emerson.*
27. *Memories of Hawthorne.*
28. *Horace Mann.*

VI

29. *English Notebooks.*
30. *George Ripley.*
31. *American Notebooks.*
32. *Memories of Hawthorne.*
33. *Hawthorne and His Friends.*
34. *John Louis O'Sullivan and Manifest Destiny*, by Fletcher Pratt.
35. *Hawthorne and His Friends.*
36. *Memories of Hawthorne.*
37. *Hawthorne and His Wife.*
38. *Memories of Hawthorne.*
39. *Hawthorne and His Wife.*

40. *American Notebooks.*
41. Letter to George Hillard, March 24, 1844, included in the Old Manse edition of Hawthorne's collected works.
42. *Memories of Hawthorne.*
43. *American Notebooks.*
44. *Hawthorne and His Wife.*
45. *Hawthorne,* by Moncure Conway.
46. *Personal Recollections.*

VII

47. *Freedom's Ferment,* by Alice Felt Tyler.
48. *The Hall of Fantasy.*
49. *Memories of Hawthorne.*
50. *American Notebooks.*

VIII

51. *Hawthorne and His Wife.*

IX

52. *Memories of Hawthorne.*
53. *Mosses from an Old Manse.*
54. *Nathaniel Hawthorne.*

X

55. *Hawthorne, a Modest Man.*
56. *Memories of Hawthorne.*
57. *American Notebooks* (Randall Stewart edition).
58. *Hawthorne and His Friends.*
59. *American Notebooks.*

XI

60. *Personal Recollections.*
61. *Memories of Many Men and Some Women.*
62. *American Notebooks.*
63. *Hawthorne, a Modest Man.*
64. *American Notebooks.*
65. *Hawthorne and His Wife.*
66. *Memories of Hawthorne.*
67. Letter to Hillard: March 24, 1844.
68. *Hawthorne, a Modest Man.*
69. *Hawthorne's Suit against Ripley and Dana.*
70. *Hawthorne's Removal from the Salem Custom House.*
71. *Memories of Hawthorne.*
72. Hawthorne's letter to Horace Mann, in *Memories of Hawthorne.*
73. *Memories of Hawthorne*: George Mullett's letter to Rose Hawthorne.

XII

74. *The Custom House,* by Nathaniel Hawthorne.
75. Salem *Gazette.*
76. *The Custom House.*
77. Salem *Gazette.*
78. *Hawthorne's Removal from the Salem Custom House.*
79. Salem *Gazette.*
80. *Memories of Hawthorne.*
81. *Documentary History of the Salem Custom House.*
82. *The Custom House.*
83. Encyclopedia *Americana;* also, *Memoirs and Services of Three Generations of the Cilley Family.*
84. *Hawthorne and His Wife.*
85. *The Custom House.*
86. Salem *Gazette.*
87. *Hawthorne and His Wife.*
88. *Horace Mann.*
89. *Franklin Pierce.*
90. *American Notebooks.*
91. *The Custom House.*
92. *Hawthorne and His Wife;* also, *Memories of Hawthorne.*

XIII

93. *American Notebooks.*
94. *Hawthorne and His Wife.*
95. *Memories of Hawthorne.*
96. *American Notebooks.*
97. *Hawthorne's Removal from the Salem Custom House.*
98. *The Custom House.*
99. "The Ghost of Dr. Harris," by Nathaniel Hawthorne, *Nineteenth Century,* January, 1900.
100. *American Notebooks.*

XIV

101. *Hawthorne's Removal from the Salem Custom House;* also, *Memories of Hawthorne.*
102. Salem *Gazette;* also Essex *Register.*
103. Letter to Hillard, Old Manse edition of Hawthorne's works.
104. *The Custom House.*
105. *Hawthorne and His Wife.*
106. Essex *Register,* June 18, 1849.
107. *The Custom House.*

108. Essex *Register*.
109. Letter to Hillard, June 12, 1849, in Collected Works.
110. Letter to Hillard, June 18, 1849, in *Hawthorne's Removal from the Salem Custom House*.
111. *Memorial of the Whig Ward Committees of Salem to the Secretary of the Treasury*, by Charles W. Upham, in *Hawthorne's Removal from the Salem Custom House*.
112. Hawthorne to Horace Mann, in *Memories of Hawthorne*.
113. *Memories of Hawthorne*.
114. *Hawthorne's Removal from the Salem Custom House*.
115. *The House of the Seven Gables*.
116. *Hawthorne's Removal from the Salem Custom House*.
117. Hawthorne to Horace Mann, in *Memories of Hawthorne*. The men are not identified by name in this letter. Their identities are made plain in *Hawthorne's Removal from the Salem Custom House*.

XV

118. *The Custom House*.
119. Sophia Hawthorne to her mother, in *Hawthorne and His Wife*.
120. *American Notebooks*.
121. *Caleb and Mary Wilder Foote;* also, *The Peabody Family*. Wellington Peabody worked in Whipple's bookstore, which specialized in charts for mariners, under Dr. Pierson. About 1834 Wellington became resident physician at the private infirmary of Dr. McFarland in New Orleans. He reportedly died of yellow fever on September 29, 1837. Neither Mary Louise Marshall, Librarian of the Tulane University School of Medicine, nor George King Logan, of the New Orleans Public Library, who examined the archives at my request, have been able to find any record of his work in McFarland's hospital, or of his death.
122. *American Notebooks*.
123. *Hawthorne and His Wife*.
124. *American Notebooks*.
125. *Memories of Hawthorne*.
126. *Lenox and the Berkshire Highlands*.

XVI

127. *Hawthorne and His Wife*.
128. *John Louis O'Sullivan and Manifest Destiny*.
129. Encyclopedia *Americana*.
130. *Nathaniel Hawthorne*.
131. *The Scarlet Letter*.

132. *Channing.*
133. *The Scarlet Letter.*
134. *Channing.*
135. *The Scarlet Letter.*
136. *Hawthorne and His Wife.*
137. *Personal Recollections.* Hawthorne made this remark half jokingly. It could hardly have been made any other way. He wrote to Bridge that when he read the last chapters to Sophia his voice heaved and swelled "as if I were tossed up an down on an ocean as it subsides after a storm." He said of its effect on Sophia: "It broke her heart and sent her to bed with a grievous headache, which I look upon as a triumphant success."
138. Hawthorne to Hillard, in the Old Manse edition.
139. *Personal Recollections.*
140. *Hawthorne, a Modest Man.*
141. *Golden Multitudes,* by Frank Luther Mott. New York: Macmillan, 1947.
142. *Caleb and Mary Wilder Foote.*
143. *Hawthorne and His Wife.*
144. Hawthorne to Zachariah Burchmore, in *Hawthorne, Rebellious Puritan,* by Lloyd Morris. New York: Harcourt Brace, 1927.
145. *Tanglewood Tales.*
146. *Memories of Hawthorne.*

BIBLIOGRAPHY

The Collected Works of Nathaniel Hawthorne, Old Manse Edition, Twenty-two Volumes, with introductory and bibliographical notes by H. E. Scudder, and an introduction by Rose Hawthorne Lathrop. Houghton Mifflin, 1900.

The Essex Institute Historical Collections, 1861-1947. Salem, Mass. The Essex Institute. Edited by Harriet Sylvester Tapley.

The Salem *Gazette*. 1796-1849.

Abbott, Jacob. *New England and Her Institutions, by One of Her Sons.* Boston: John Allen, 1835.

Adams, Mrs. Henry. *The Letters of Mrs. Henry Adams,* edited by Ward Thoron. Boston: Little, Brown, 1936.

Appleton, Jesse. *The Works of Rev. Jesse Appleton.* Andover: Gould and Newman, 1837.

Arvin, Newton. *Hawthorne.* Boston: Little, Brown, 1929.

————. *The Heart of Hawthorne's Journals.* Boston: Little, Brown.

Bartlett, David. *The Life of General Franklin Pierce.* Buffalo: G. H. Derby & Co., 1852.

Bartlett, George B. *Concord, Historic, Literary and Picturesque.* Boston, 1885.

Batchelor, Rev. Dr. George. *The Salem of Hawthorne's Time.* Essex Institute Historical Collections, January, 1948.

Bell, Charles H. *The Bench and Bar of New Hampshire.* Boston: Houghton Mifflin, 1894.

Belknap, Henry Wycoff. *Simon Forrester of Salem and Some of His Descendants.* Essex Institute Historical Collections, January, 1935.

Beveridge, Albert J. *Life of John Marshall.* Boston: Houghton Mifflin, 1919.

Bridge, Horatio. *Personal Recollections of Nathaniel Hawthorne.* New York: Harpers, 1893.

Brooks, Charles T. *William Ellery Channing.* Boston: Roberts.Brothers, 1880.

Brooks, Henry M. *Some Localities About Salem.* Essex Institute Historical Collections, 1894.

Brooks, Van Wyck. *The Flowering of New England.* New York: Dutton, 1938.

Browne, B. F. *An Account of Salem Common.* Essex Institute Historical Collections, February, 1862.

Burton, Katharine. *Sorrow Built a Bridge, A Daughter of Hawthorne.* New York: Longmans, Green, 1937.

Cabot, James Elliot. *A Memoir of Ralph Waldo Emerson.* Boston: Houghton Mifflin, 1887.

Chandler, Elizabeth L., "Hawthorne's Spectator," *New England Quarterly.* April, 1931.

Channing, William E. *The Works of William E. Channing.* Boston: Crosby, Nichols and Company, 1853.

Cilley. *Memoirs and Services of Three Generations of the Cilley Family.* *Courier Gazette,* Rockland, Me.

Cleveland, Edmund Jones and Horace Elliot, *Genealogy of the Cleveland and Cleaveland and Families.* Hartford, 1879.

Cleveland, Horace William Shaler, *Life and Literature Fifty Years Ago.* Boston: Cupples and Hurd.

Conway, Moncure D. *Hawthorne.* London: Walter Scott, 1895.

Cooke, Harriet Ruth. *The Driver Family.* Cambridge: John Wilson and Son, 1889.

Crawford, Mary Caroline. *Famous Families of Massachusetts.* Boston: Little, Brown, 1930.

Crowninshield, John. *Journal of Captain John Crowninshield When Master of the Ship Belisarius at Calcutta.* 1797-1798. Essex Institute Historical Collections, October, 1945, through July, 1946.

Currier, John. *History of Newbury, Massachusetts.* Boston: Donnell and Upham, 1902.

Derby, Perley, and Dr. Frank Gardner. *Elisha Story of Boston and Some of his Descendants.* Essex Institute, 1915.

Dickey, Dallas C. *Sergeant Prentiss: Whig Orator of the Old South.* Baton Rouge: Louisiana State University Press, 1945.

Dwight, Theodore. *History of the Hartford Convention.* Boston: Russell, Odiorne & Co., 1833.

Emmons, Nathanael. *The Works of Nathanael Emmons.* Boston: Crocker and Brewster, 1842.

Felt, Joseph B. *Annals of Salem.* Salem: W. and S. B. Ives, 1827.

Fessenden, Francis. *Life and Public Services of William Pitt Fessenden.* Boston: Houghton Mifflin, 1907.

Field, Maunsell B. *Memories of Many Men and Some Women.* New York: Harpers, 1874.

Frothingham, O. B. *George Ripley.* Boston: Houghton Mifflin, 1882.

Fuess, Claude M. *Life of Daniel Webster.* Boston, Little, Brown, 1930.

Gallup, Donald Clifford. "On Hawthorne's Authorship of the The Battle Omen," *New England Quarterly,* 1936.

Gauss, John Dennis Hammond. *Haunts of Hawthorne in Salem, Massachusetts.* Privately printed: The Naumkeag Trust Company, Salem.

Gerber, John C. "Form and Content in *The Scarlet Letter.*" *New England Quarterly,* November, 1944.

Goodrich, Samuel Griswold. *Recollection of a Lifetime, or Men and Things I Have Seen.* New York: Miller, Orton and Mulligan, 1856.

Gordon, Major George. *From Brook Farm to Cedar Mountain.* Boston: James R. Osgood and Co., 1883.

Gorman, Herbert. *Hawthorne.* New York: Doran, 1927.

Griffith, Thomas Morgan. *Maine Sources in the House of the Seven Gables.* Waterville, Me., 1945.

Hall, Lawrence Sargeant. *Hawthorne, Critic of Society.* New Haven: Yale University Press, 1944.

Hampton, William J. *Our Presidents and Their Mothers.* Cornhill Publishing Co.

Hatch, Louis C. *The History of Bowdoin College.* Portland, Me.: Loring, Short and Hormon, 1927.

Haven, Samuel. *Proceedings of the Massachusetts Historical Society, XIX,* 1881-1882.

Hawthorne, Hildegarde. *Hawthorne, Romantic Rebel.* New York: Century, 1933.

Hawthorne, Julian. *Hawthorne and His Wife.* Boston: Houghton Mifflin, 1896.

Hawthorne, Manning. *Maria Louisa Hawthorne.* Essex Institute Historical Collections, April, 1939. "Nathaniel Hawthorne Prepares for College," *New England Quarterly,* March, 1938. "Nathaniel Hawthorne at Bowdoin College," *New England Quarterly,* Vol. 13, 1940. "Hawthorne and 'The Man of God.' " *The Colophon,* No. 2, Vol. II.

Hill, Jim Dan. *Sea Dogs of the Sixties.* University of Minnesota Press, 1935.

Hoar, Elizabeth. *Mrs. Samuel Ripley.* In *Worthy Women of Our First Century,* edited by Mrs. O. J. Whiter and Miss Agnes Irwin. Philadelphia: J. B. Lippincott, 1877.

James, Henry. *Hawthorne.* New York: Harpers, 1879.

Knapp. *Trial of John Francis Knapp for the Murder of Joseph White.* Anonymous pamphlet, July 20, 1870.

Lathrop, George. *A Study of Hawthorne.* Boston: James R. Osgood and Co., 1876.

Lathrop, Rose Hawthorne. *Memories of Hawthorne.* Boston: Houghton Mifflin, 1887.

Leavitt, William. *History of the Essex Lodge of Freemasons.* Essex Institute Historical Collections, February, 1861.

Little, David Mason. *Documentary History of the Salem Custom House.* Essex Institute Historical Collections, January through July, 1931.

Lyford, James Otis. *History of Canterbury, New Hampshire* (2 vols.). Concord: Rumford Press, 1912.

Mallory, R. de Witt. *Lenox and the Berkshire Highlands.* New York: Putnams, 1902.

Mann, Mary Tyler Peabody. *Horace Mann.* Boston: Walher, Fuller and Co., 1865.

Manning, William H., *The Manning Families of New England and Descendants*. Salem: 1902.

Mason, Jeremiah. *Memoirs of Jeremiah Mason*, edited by George Hillard. Cambridge: Privately printed, 1873.

Mather, Edward (E. A. Mather Jackson). *Nathaniel Hawthorne, A Modest Man*. New York: Crowell, 1940.

Metzdorf, Robert F. "Hawthorne's Suit against Ripley and Dana," *American Literature*. Durham, N. C., 1940.

Morison, Samuel Eliot. *Maritime History of Massachusetts*. Boston: Houghton Mifflin and Co., 1930. "Nathaniel Hawthorne and Elizabeth Hawthorne, Editors." *The Colophon*, September, 1939.

North, James W. *History of Augusta, Maine*. Augusta: Clapp and North, 1870.

Nye, Russell, *George Bancroft, Brahmin Rebel*, New York: Knopf, 1945.

Palfrey, Francis W. *George Hillard*. Boston: Massachusetts Historical Society, XIX, 1881-1882.

Peabody, Salim. *The Peabody Family*. Salem: 1912.

Perley, Sidney. *The History of Salem, Massachusetts*. Salem: 1924.

Perry, Bliss. *The Amateur Spirit: Hawthorne in North Adams*. Boston: Houghton Mifflin, 1904.

Phillips, James Duncan. *Salem in the Seventeenth Century*. Boston: Houghton Mifflin, 1933.

————. *Salem in the Eighteenth Century*. Boston: Houghton Mifflin, 1937.

————. *Salem and the Indies*. Boston: Houghton Mifflin, 1947.

Phillips, Stephen Willard. *Political Fights and Local Squabbles in Salem*. Essex Institute Historical Collections, January, 1946.

Phillips, Stephen Willard (with A. Frank Hitchings). *Ship Registers of the District of Salem and Beverly*. Salem: The Essex Institute, 1906.

Pickard, Samuel T. *Hawthorne's First Diary, with an Account of Its Discovery and Loss*. Boston: Houghton Mifflin, 1897.

Pickering, Sarah Orne. *John Pickering*. Boston: Privately printed, 1887.

Pratt, Julius W. *John O'Sullivan and Manifest Destiny*. New York History, XIV, No. 3, July, 1933.

Rantoul, Robert. *Early Modes of Travel*. Essex Institute Historical Collections.

Russell, Phillips. *Emerson, the Wisest American*. New York: Brentano, 1929.

Sanborn, F. B. *Hawthorne and His Friends*. Cedar Rapids, Iowa; Torch Press, 1908.

Sandburg, Carl. *Abraham Lincoln, the War Years*. New York: Harcourt, Brace, 1939.

Sargeant, Epes. *Songs of the Sea and Other Poems*. Boston: J. Munroe and Company, 1847.

Schlesinger, Arthur, *The Age of Jackson*. Boston: Little, Brown, 1945.

Shepard, Odell. *Pedlar's Progress, the Life of Bronson Alcott*. Boston: Little, Brown, 1938.

Silsbee, Marianne. *A Half Century in Salem.* Boston: Houghton Mifflin, 1887.

Silsbee, Nathaniel. *Biographical Notes.* Essex Institute Historical Collections, January, 1899.

Smith, J. E. A. *History of Pittsfield, Massachusetts.* Boston: Lee and Shephard, 1869-76.

Stackpole, Everett S. *History of New Hampshire.* New York: American Historical Society.

Stewart, Randall (editor). *The American Notebooks of Nathaniel Hawthorne.* New Haven: Yale University Press, 1932.

————. *The English Notebooks of Nathaniel Hawthorne.* New York: Modern Language Association, 1941.

————. "Recollections of Hawthorne by His Sister Elizabeth." *American Literature,* Vol. 16, No. 14, January, 1945.

Story, William Wetmore. *Life and Letters of Joseph Story.* Boston: Charles C. Little and James Brown, 1851.

————. *George Hillard.* Massachusetts Historical Society, XIX, 1881-1882.

————. "Hawthorne and Politics." *New England Quarterly,* 1932.

Sturgis, Roger. *Edward Sturgis of Yarmouth, Massachusetts, and His Decendants.* Boston: Stanhope Press, 1914.

Swift, Lindsay. *Brook Farm.* New York: Macmillan, 1900.

Tapley, Harriet Sylvester. *Books Read by Nathaniel Hawthorne.* Essex Institute Historical Collections, January, 1932.

————. "Letters to Sophia." *The Huntington Library Quarterly,* August, 1944.

————. *Hawthorne's Pot-8-0 Club at Bowdoin College.* Essex Institute Historical Collections, January, 1931.

Thayer, S. Proctor. *History of Berkshire County.* New York: Beers, 1885.

Thompson, Lawrence. *Young Longfellow.* New York: Macmillan, 1938.

Tileson, Mary Wilder. *Caleb and Mary Wilder Foote, Reminiscences and Letters.* Boston: Houghton Mifflin, 1918.

————. *Mary Wilder White,* by Elizabeth Amelia Dwight, edited by Mary Wilder Tileson. Boston: Everett Press, 1903.

Turner, Arlin. *Hawthorne as Editor.* Baton Rouge: Louisiana State University Press, 1941.

————. "Hawthorne as Self-Critic." *South Atlantic Quarterly,* 1938.

————. "Hawthorne and Martha's Vineyard." *New England Quarterly,* June, 1938.

————. "Hawthorne's Literary Borrowings." *The Modern Language Association of America,* June, 1936.

————. "Hawthorne and Reform." *New England Quarterly,* 1942.

————. "Autobiographical Elements in Hawthorne's *The Blithedale Romance.*" University of Texas *Studies in English,* 1935.

————. *Hawthorne's Methods of Using His Source Materials.* Baton Rouge: Louisiana State University Press, 1940.

Toucey, Isaac. *Report of the Committee of Inquiry on the Late Duel of the Honorable Jonathan Cilley and the Honorable William Graves.*

Tyler, Alice Felt. *Freedom's Ferment, Phases of American Social History to 1860.* Minneapolis: University of Minnesota Press, 1944.

Wilson, James Grant (editor). *Presidents of the United States.* New York: Appleton.

Wittam, Cyrus S. *Raymond, Maine, Scrapbook.* Portland: Maine Historical Society.

Woodberry, George. *Nathaniel Hawthorne.* Boston: Houghton Mifflin, 1902.

INDEX